Essentials, 4e

New! This edition is plugged in to the world of contemporary business. In other words, it features expanded coverage of and detailed attention to technology and E-business. All of the following discussions have been added to the text of *Business 4e*:

1. *The Global Economy in the Twenty-First Century / Building Your Business Skills: Analyzing the Price of Doing E-Business*
4. *Success and Failure in Small Business: Emergence of E-Commerce*
7. *Focus on the Customer-Service Link: E-Commerce: The "Virtual Presence" of the Customer*
8. *Learning to Motivate: Student Advantage*
9. *New Challenges in the Changing Workplace: Managing Knowledge Workers*
11. *Determining Prices: Pricing for E-Business Objectives / Pricing Strategies and Tactics: Fixed Versus Dynamic Pricing for E-Business / The Importance of Promotion: Advertising Media / Internet Advertising / Data Mining and Data Warehousing / Wholesaling: The Advent of the E-Intermediary / The Boom in Electronic Retailing / Physical Distribution and E-Customer Satisfaction*
12. *The Expanding Scope of Information Systems / Electronic Business and Communications Technologies / New Options for Organizational Design: The Networked Enterprise / Systems for Knowledge Workers and Office Applications*
14. *The Changing Money and Banking System: The Impact of Electronic Technologies*
15. *The "Old" Economy Versus the "New": What's a "Blue Chip" Now?*

New! With this edition we introduce a brand-new video library. Each chapter now concludes with an engaging video exercise that puts concepts into real business contexts. Each exercise asks students to analyze a real-world situation and to perform specific activities through discussion questions and follow-up material. All of the following cases were developed specifically for *Business 4e*.

1. *Factors to Consider: Lands' End*
2. *Entering the Global Marketplace: Lands' End and Yahoo!*
3. *Catering to Serious Users: Patagonia*
4. *Doing Business Privately: Amy's Ice Creams*
5. *The Management Picture: Quick Takes Video (I)*
6. *The Management Picture: Quick Takes Video (II)*
7. *Channeling Resources: Regal Marine*
8. *Learning to Motivate: Student Advantage*
9. *Channeling Human Resources: Showtime*
10. *Niche Noshing: Terra Chips*
11. *Promoting White Moustaches: The "Got Milk?" Campaign*
12. *Space Age IT at Boeing*
13. *Accounting for a Few Billion Sold: McDonald's*
14. *The World's Lenders: The World Bank and the IMF*
15. *Information Pays Off: Anatomy of a Stock Trade*

Ebert/Griffin

FOURTH EDITION

Business Essentials

Ronald J. Ebert
University of Missouri–Columbia

Ricky W. Griffin
Texas A&M University

Upper Saddle River, New Jersey 07458

Acquisitions Editor: David Parker
Editor-in-Chief: Jeff Shelstad
Editorial Assistant: Ashley Keim
Senior Developmental Editor: Ronald Librach
Media Project Manager: Anthony Palmiotto
Executive Marketing Manager: Debbie Clare
Managing Editor (Production): Judy Leale
Production Editor: Marcela Maslanczuk
Permissions Coordinator: Suzanne Grappi
Associate Director, Manufacturing: Vincent Scelta
Production Manager: Arnold Vila
Design Manager: Pat Smythe
Art Director: Kevin Kall
Interior Design: Pat McDermond
Cover Design: Kevin Kall
Cover Illustration/Photo: Superstock, Inc.
Illustrator (Interior): Electragraphics
Associate Director, Multimedia Production: Karen Goldsmith
Manager, Print Production: Christy Mahon
Composition: Carlisle Communications
Full-Service Project Management: Ann Imhof, Carlisle Communications
Printer/Binder: Courier Kendallville

Credits and acknowledgments borrowed from other sources and reproduced, with permission, in this textbook begin on page 435.

Pearson Education LTD.
Pearson Education Australia PTY, Limited
Pearson Education Singapore, Pte. Ltd
Pearson Education North Asia Ltd
Pearson Education, Canada, Ltd
Pearson Educación de Mexico, S.A. de C.V.
Pearson Education—Japan
Pearson Education Malaysia, Pte. Ltd

10 9 8 7 6 5 4 3 2 1
ISBN 0-13-067544-X

To Mary

The love of my life
— (R.J.E.)

For Glenda

My own personal
Florence Nightingale
— (R.W.G.)

Overview

Contents

PART VI

Understanding Financial Issues **362**

CHAPTER 14 Understanding Money and Banking **362**

CHAPTER 15 Understanding Securities and Investments **386**

From the Authors **Ron Ebert and Ricky Griffin**

As we sat down to prepare the final touches to this revision, we both kept seeing TV appearances of prominent leaders who were encouraging U.S. citizens to carry on with every-day activities—at leisure and at work—in response to the recent turmoil and state of our nation. Are we up to the challenge of finding the "calm within the storm"? History tells us so! Along with millions of individuals, the world's best-known businesses find themselves reel-ing amidst the dramatic events that are re-shaping the ways we live, work, and prepare for the future. Amidst all these changes, businesses continue to fuel our economy, and their signifi-cant role in our society and throughout the world has never been more evident. The foremost business dilemma is how to provide some sort of stability— for employees, owners, suppliers, and consumers—while steering through new uncharted paths. The answer lies in businesses maintaining an adaptive organizational culture, one that expects change as a way of life and builds processes for change into its business strategy. More than ever before, leading busi-nesses have learned how to anticipate new developments and how to respond quickly and creatively.

Therefore, for our introductory business students, there is great value to be gained from understanding how business, government, and citizens, together, influence the ways that business is conducted in different societies. Students need to gain a fundamental working knowledge about every aspect of business and the environment in which business prospers. And make no mistake about it: We have prosperity despite occasional, sometimes even violent, disruptions. Through it all, businesses continue to adapt; the rules of the game are constantly changing throughout the business environment and across the range of business practices. Even aside from the recent violence and tragedies, there are new forces at work. Nowadays, companies come together on short notice for collaborative projects and then, just as quickly, return to their original shapes as separate (and often competing) entities. Employees and companies share new ideas about work—about where it takes place, about how it gets done, about who determines roles and activities in the workplace. With communications technologies having shattered the barriers of physical distance, tight-knit teams with members positioned around the world share information just as effectively as groups huddled together in the same room.

In nearly every aspect of business today, from relationships with customers and suppliers to employees and stockholders, there are new ways of doing things, and a lot of them are surpassing traditional business practices, with surprising speed and often with better competitive results. Along with new ways come a host of unique legal and ethical issues to challenge the creativity and judgment of people who do business. For all of these reasons we, as authors and teachers, felt a certain urgency when it became obvious that, in revising ***Business Essentials*** for its fourth edition, we had to capture the flavor and convey the excitement of the new economy in all of its rapidly evolving practices.

Ron Ebert
Ricky Griffin

One way a textbook, or any successful product, succeeds in the long term is by close reevaluation on a regular basis and attention to market feedback. Based upon our market observations and your suggestions, we've streamlined *Business Essentials* to 15 chapters, organized into 6 parts, plus 2 appendixes. This streamlined organization should make the material even more manageable for both semester and quarter courses. The strengths that have made it the market best-seller continue:

- Cutting edge
- Current
- Succinct
- Price sensitive

What's new ...

New! IT'S A WIRED WORLD

In each chapter, boxes titled **"It's a Wired World"** offer brief real-world examples of steps established businesses are taking to keep pace with both new and old competitors in the e-business environment.

> **IT'S A WIRED WORLD**
> **"These Two Companies Are a Natural Fit"**
>
> Even a high-tech giant can't be an expert in every new development in the digital world. Consider, for example, America Online <www.aol.com> (including its CompuServ service <www.compuserve.com>—America's largest online Internet service provider) with 22 million subscribers. AOL's customers have Internet access through traditional phone lines. But AOL is thinking about ways to give them even faster Internet service by means of high-speed cable lines. Traditional phone lines are slower than cables in connecting to the Net. They're also slower in downloading information and slower in reading graphics files.
>
> AOL already knows that if it's going to stay competitive in the home Internet market, it will need to offer customers faster Internet capability, but they haven't yet exploited their cable technology in the Internet market.
>
> Now consider the situation at Time Warner Inc. <www.timewarner.com/corp>—a cable service provider that also happens to be the world's top media and entertainment company. Time Warner Inc. wants to harness the power of the Internet, which it sees as the future avenue for distributing its entertainment products. Unfortunately, Time Warner can't deliver magazines like *Time, People,* and *Sports Illustrated* without Internet technology. Nor can Time Warner deliver movies and music for downloading. Time Warner's problem, then, was how to get digital when it wasn't skilled at the technology. Ultimately, doing things internally turned out to be too corporate merger valued at $166 billion—the largest ever. The new firm, AOL Time Warner Inc., gains the advantages of each partner's technological expertise and resources. AOL, of course, has Internet expertise. It also has 22 million customers who can purchase and download Time Warner's entertainment products from the Internet. Meanwhile, Time Warner brings not only 13 million cable TV subscribers to the merger but also expertise in the high-speed cable lines that AOL needs for faster Internet services. This large base of cable-ready households will be a big boost for AOL because only 6 percent of Web users currently have the high-speed (cable-modem) access that can be up to 100 times faster than modems on traditional phone lines (which are

> **WEB Connection**
>
> 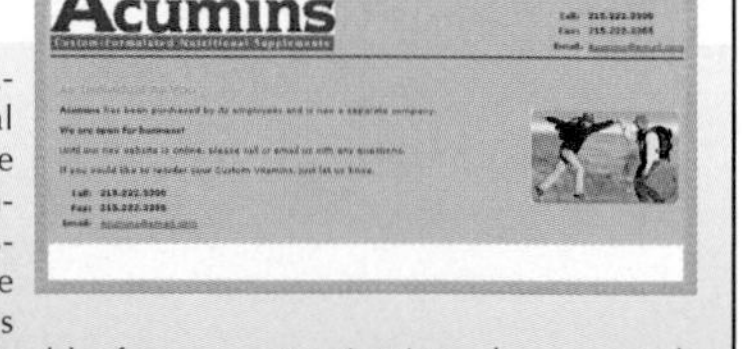
>
>
> Because "a one-size-fits-all vitamin can't supply you with optimal nutrition," Acumins will customize the precise blend of vitamins, minerals, and herbs that each customer wants. To find out how the process works—and how the Net is essential to businesses in the world of mass-customization—log on to the Acumins Web site. Go to **www.prenhall.com/ebert** for questions.
>
> www.acumins.com

New! WEB Connection

Each chapter contains a new feature called **"WEB Connection"** that relates the Internet to the chapter's topics. The WEB Connection includes a real company's URL, screen shot, description of the company's mission, and an Action Challenge posted on the companion Web site for the book.

New! Exercising Your Ethics.

To bring ethics to the forefront, we've introduced a new end-of-chapter feature, **"Exercising Your Ethics,"** to motivate students to resolve an ethical situation. Each dilemma includes a description of the situation and then concludes with student questions that focus on how to approach and resolve an ethical challenge.

EXERCISING YOUR ETHICS

Supplying the Right Answers

THE SITUATION
Networked systems facilitate the sharing of information among companies and often include sensitive customer data. This exercise challenges you to think about ethical considerations that arise in developing information technologies and using them in a networked system.

THE DILEMMA
Home Sweet Home-e (HSH-e) was an e-business start-up that sold virtually everything imaginable in home furnishings—from linens and towels to cleaning supplies and furniture. Using computers at home, HSH-e members could shop in virtual storefronts, chat online with other home shoppers, talk live with virtual store clerks, and pay electronically in a one-stop Web site. In reality, HSH-e was a *virtual store*: a network of numer-

New! Video Cases and Exercises.

The fourth edition of *Business Essentials* includes a brand new video library.

Each chapter now concludes with an engaging video exercise that puts chapter concepts into a dramatic real-business context. Each video exercise asks students to analyze an interesting real company and includes discussion questions and assignment material.

VIDEO EXERCISE

Space Age IT at Boeing

Learning Objectives

The purpose of this video exercise is to help you:

1. Understand why businesses must manage information
2. Understand the role of information systems within an organization
3. Recognize the ways in which information systems contribute to efficiency and productivity

BACKGROUND INFORMATION
The world's leading manufacturer of commercial communications satellites, Boeing Satellite Systems <www.boeing.com/satellite> is a wholly owned subsidiary of The Boeing Co. <www.boeing.com> with customers in 14 countries. It has sent more than 180 spacecraft into orbit and employees more than 8,000 people, each of whom works with a personal computer or laptop. The company's information system (IS) integrates data from all departments, including sales, finance, engineering, manufacturing, legal, human resources, and so on.

THE VIDEO
Vice President and Chief Information Officer (CIO) K. S. Radhakrishnan discusses not only the role of information systems in the organization, but also some tighter thanks to e-commerce and new applications of IT.

QUESTIONS FOR DISCUSSION
1. What role does information systems play in the Boeing Satellite Systems division?
2. What do you think are some of the advantages of automatic data entry and integration? List as many as you can think of.
3. What are some ways in which IT affects productivity and efficiency? List as many as you can.

FOLLOW-UP ASSIGNMENT
The only competitor with Boeing's the aircraft division is Airbus <www.airbus.com>. Log on to the career opportunities section of the Airbus Website and try to locate open positions in information management, information systems, or information technology. What are the requirements for these jobs? The responsibilities? What specific tasks will employees need to perform in these positions?

FOR FURTHER EXPLORATION
Visit The Boeing Co. home page at <www.boeing.com> and use the Internet to explore a divisions other than Boeing Satellite Systems. What appear to be the information needs of this division? What IT applications might be useful to its managers? Its employees? Do you think that this division's IS might need to connect with that of any other Boeing divisions? Which ones, and why?

Business

Ebert/Griffin

Hallmark Strengths!

Fully Updated!

New! Two Part Case Vignettes.

To engage students in real-life business situations, each chapter opens with a compelling vignette describing how an individual or organization has responded to an opportunity or challenge.

Part V

CHAPTER 12

Managing Information Systems and Electronic

After Reading This Chapter, You Should Be Able To:

1. Explain why businesses must manage *information* and show how computer systems and communication technologies have revolutionized *information management.*
2. Identify and briefly describe three elements of *data communication networks*—the Internet, the World Wide Web, and intranets.
3. Describe five *new options for organizational design* that have emerged from the rapid growth of information technologies.
4. Discuss different information-system *application programs* that are available for users at various organizational levels.
5. Briefly describe the content and role of a *database* and the purpose of *database software* for information systems.

"Life, The Universe, and Everything"

Why does a boss want information on such varied topics as the anatomy of dragonflies, juvenile crime, and Japanese irises instead of just standard reports on department budgets and sales figures? And if gathering these eclectic tidbits is high on the agenda, how does a firm use its "knowledge workers" to build a networked information system for getting it? Consider the information system at Highsmith, Inc.

opportunities for companies. He bench... employees are focused only on internal operations, they won't see the bigger picture, so he encourages a more eclectic approach of information gathering from a broad range of sources. New cultural trends and political forces eventually change the way a society thinks and lives, and Highsmith doesn't want to get caught short when they do: He wants to foresee changes that can reshape the social environment, and he wants to be prepared in advance rather than forced to react after the fact. Clues might emerge from unexpected and seemingly unrelated sources ranging from

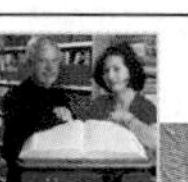

Continued from page 307

Researching with a Purpose

On Duncan Highsmith's organizational chart, the library is listed on the same level as the firm's other important functions, including marketing, human resources, and accounting. As part of the information system, it adds the power of the Internet to human judgment. It also directs information toward the people who can use it and get results with it, and it's readily available and affordable.

The strength of the system is its knowledge-management tool: Lisa Guedea Carreño. Although Guedea Carreño relies on the Internet, she also realizes that as an information source it isn't necessarily all that it's cracked up to be. It's full of hype and promises, and it's unfamiliar territory to new users. Web-search services—Internet search directories

Some Web services report information only for sites that pay to be listed and ignore others. Even among those that report on a huge number of companies, some may give preferential treatment—that is, more favorable reports—to business partners.

To help internal Highsmith users, Guedea Carreño has thus devised her own rules of thumb for navigating the Net efficiently, sorting through Web sites to discard the bad and retain the useful. Through experience, she's compiled a checklist and some questions. Here's a sample:

- *Quality control.* A quick rule is watch for typos. If it's typed sloppily, the site's content is also probably of questionable quality.
- *Timeliness.* Is the information current? Does the site tell you when it was updated? If not, chances are it's old information (and thus not information at all).

The story continues . . .

The story is then revisited at the end of the chapter, where it concludes with more information and follow-up questions tailored to help students analyze the case, either on their own or in class as a group activity. All vignettes have all been fully updated to keep current.

End-of Chapter Activities

Fully Updated!

EXPLORING THE WEB

On the Cutting Edge with Experts

Most firms rely on expert assistance to get started on network development and buy the technology they need for their Internet systems. Cisco Systems Inc. is the worldwide leader in Internet networking, providing most of the systems that make the Internet work. By looking at Cisco's products, including hardware, software, and services, we can get an idea about both the needs of Internet users and some of the leading-edge solutions that are available. To learn about Cisco, its products, and its customers, visit its Web site at:

<www.cisco.com/>

Exploring the Web Exercises.

In these exercises, students are directed to the Internet and given hands-on activities designed to enhance their understanding of important chapter topics.

Building Your Business Skills.

These popular end-of-chapter exercises consist of activities that allow students to apply their knowledge and critical thinking skills to an extended problem drawn from a wide range of realistic business experiences. Each of these exercises has been specifically designed to satisfy the general criteria laid out in the Secretary of Labor's Commission of Achieving Necessary Skills (SCANS) requirements.

BUILDING YOUR BUSINESS SKILLS

The Art and Science of Point-and-Click Research

This exercise enhances the following SCANS workplace competencies: demonstrating basic skills, demonstrating thinking skills, exhibiting interpersonal skills, working with information, applying system knowledge, and using technology.

GOAL

To introduce students to World Wide Web search sites.

BACKGROUND

In a recent survey of nearly 2,000 Web users, two-thirds stated that they used the Web to obtain work-related information. With an estimated 320 million

CRAFTING YOUR BUSINESS PLAN

Getting Wired into Better Information

THE PURPOSE OF THE ASSIGNMENT

1. To familiarize students with issues involving information systems that a sample firm faces in developing its business plan, in the framework of *Business PlanPro (BPP)* (Version 4.0).
2. To demonstrate how communications technologies, the Internet, and database considerations can be integrated as components in the *BPP* planning environment.

FOLLOW-UP ASSIGNMENT

After reading Chapter 12 in the textbook, open the BPP software and look around for information about plans for computer and communications technologies as they apply to a sample firm: Travel Agency *(Adventure Travel International). Begin first by looking at ATI's* Plan Outline, 1.0 Executive Summary, *to get acquainted with the firm. Then respond to the following questions:*

1. How have the Internet and related communications technologies changed the travel agency industry? [Sites to see in *BPP* (for this question): In the Plan Outline screen, click in turn on each of the following: **3.2 Competitive Comparison** and

Crafting Your Business Plan Exercises.

These chapter-ending exercises have been streamlined to make it easier for students to grasp and complete quickly. Students examine sample plans from a variety of businesses using the Windows-based *Business Plan Pro* 4.0 software. Students and instructors can also take the exercises further if they choose because this powerful educational version also allows students to begin creating their own professional business plans with step-by-step instructions. Version 4.0 allows planners to publish plans to a protected Internet site, where students can access all or part of posted plans. The educational version of the best-selling *Business PlanPro* Software can be packaged with the text for a nominal additional cost of $10.00.

Business

Contemporary Themes Integrated

Greater Attention on Business-to-Business Relationships.

Although many students and observers of business are familiar with business-to-consumer transactions, they are less aware of the enormous world of business-to-business commerce. To give students more awareness, we have presented examples that reveal the economic significance of B2B relationships throughout the fourth edition. *Here are a few examples...*

- *In Chapter 1* the box entitled **"Electronic B2B in Auto Industry"** provides a great illustration on B2B transactions and relationships among companies.
- *In Chapter 4* in the section entitled **"Importance to Big Business,"** we describe how small businesses buy from and sell to big businesses, a good example of B2B transactions.
- *In Chapter 7* the section entitled **"Supply Chain Management"** describes Dell computer's supply chain and how Dell links its activities to those of its suppliers and shippers.

Successes and Failures with E-business.

The enormous number of online startups, as well as the entry into e-commerce of traditional brick-and-mortar firms, continue to have a profound impact on consumers and the worldwide economy. Each chapter includes ***"It's a Wired World"*** boxes that show examples of a success or failure on some firm's e-business experience. Plus, throughout the book we discuss requirements the e-business model imposes on employees, workplace behavior, marketing, organizational design, suppliers, and customers. *Here are a few examples...*

- *In Chapter 9,* see **"Companies Put Web to Work as Recruiter"**: It shows how several organizations (e.g., DVCi Technologies, U.S. Army, Andersen Consulting) use the Internet for recruiting.
- *In Chapter 10,* the box entitled **"Better Health Through Cyberspace Demographics"** shows how Network Health Systems uses online data gathering and data warehousing to help other businesses better manage the health care risks for their employees.
- *In Chapter 15,* the box entitled **"Opening the Portals to Cross-Border Trading"** reveals how European stock markets (e.g., Frankfurt, Germany) are using e-technology that allows cross-border stock trading that was not previously feasible.

Supply Chain Management.

Supply chains have become a prominent business resource for improving customer service and for increasing the added value as materials move from initial sources to final destinations. ***Chapter 7, "Managing Operations and Improving Quality,"*** addresses supply chain strategy and explains how supply chain management gets better results for chain members and end consumers.

Growth of International Business.

Many businesspeople and observers of the business world see globalization of the economy as the great challenge for this new century. To keep students aware of this challenge, we have based many of the examples, vignettes, and assignments in this book on the experiences of global companies. ***Chapter 2, "Understanding the Global Context of Business,"*** provides full coverage of this important topic.

Ebert/Griffin

Throughout the Text

Here are a few examples...

- *In Chapter 5,* the section entitled "**Setting Strategic Goals**" describes strategic goal setting by Volkswagen's CEO for global performance in European and U.S. markets.
- *In Chapter 10,* the section entitled "**The International Marketing Mix**" discusses international variations for product, pricing, promotion, and distribution decisions.
- *In Chapter 14,* the section entitled "**The International Payments Process**" illustrates the steps in the international flow of funds with an example of payments and transactions for business exchanges between a Greek firm and a U.S. firm.

Significance of Entrepreneurship and Small Business.

We recognize that many students will not go to work for large corporations; we have provided balanced coverage of both small and large companies throughout the text. ***Chapter 4, "Understanding Entrepreneurship and Small Business,"*** is comprehensive. In addition, examples throughout the book deal with small businesses and entrepreneurial actions, and many chapters contain sections that apply specific practices and issues to the special concerns of small business.

Here are a few examples...

- *In Chapter 1,* the section entitled "**Entrepreneurs**" discusses James Kimsey and the start-up of AOL, followed by its evolution into a large firm.
- *In Chapter 3,* the opening vignette for the chapter presents the evolution of Patagonia from its beginnings as a small business.
- *In Chapter 10,* the section "**Small Business and the Marketing Mix**" discusses small-business variations for decisions on products, pricing, promotion, and distribution.

Need to Manage Information and Communication Technology.

In our information-based society, the people and organizations who learn how to obtain and use information will succeed. The explosive growth of information systems stems from fast-paced emergence of communications technologies that provide instant and wireless linkages among people and organizations. We cover this important topic in detail in ***Chapter 12, "Managing Information Systems and Electronic Commerce."***

Role of Ethics and Social Responsibility.

Because business ethics and social responsibility have been generating much discussion in recent years, we devote a full chapter to this topic, ***Chapter 3, "Conducting Business Ethically and Responsibly."*** We also treat issues of business ethics and social responsibility in our examples and cases. For further insights we have included at the end of each chapter a new feature called ***"Exercising Your Ethics,"*** which challenges students to resolve an ethical dilemma relating directly to the topics discussed in the chapter.

Companion Web Site for Students and Faculty!

www.prenhall.com/ebert

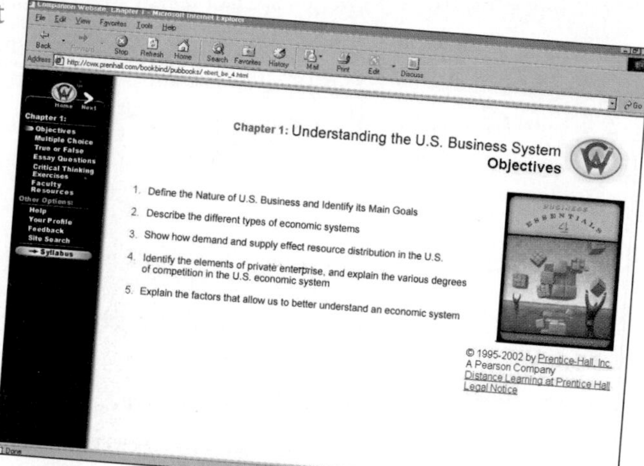

The Companion Web site is a fully customizable environment that ties students and faculty to text-specific resources. This powerful Prentice Hall Web site offers chapter-specific current events, Internet exercises, and downloadable supplements. The site also includes an online study guide containing true/false, multiple-choice, and essay questions.

Interested in an online stock market game to liven up your course?

Visit our Companion Web site for a link to **fantasystockmarket.com** to introduce your students to the challenging world of personal investing. Available on the instructor's side of the site is a concisely written stock market game integration guide to ease your use of this real-world learning tool.

Special Features:

- **Individual homepages for students and faculty.** These pages provide easy, one-click navigation to our vast, dynamic database of online teaching and learning resources. Faculty and students can organize the online resources for all of their classes on this single, customizable homepage.
- **A powerful new point-and-click syllabus creation tool** that faculty can use for each course and section they teach. Additionally, faculty can annotate and link each resource on the Companion Web site to their syllabi. **Faculty can even upload their own personal resources to our site** and have these resources available to their students via their personalized syllabus.
- **Faculty can post messages set to appear automatically on every student homepage for any length of time.**

Online Course Resources

The continuous evolution of online course materials at Prentice Hall has taken us from providing a course management shell to offering robust material that could be incorporated into that shell. Now we are raising the bar again by offering a **prebuilt** online course that can be used as is or tailored to your specific needs.

This **Special Online Course for *Business Essentials,* 4e** provides a wealth of material to enhance the student experience and is available in the Blackboard, CourseCompass, and WebCT platform.

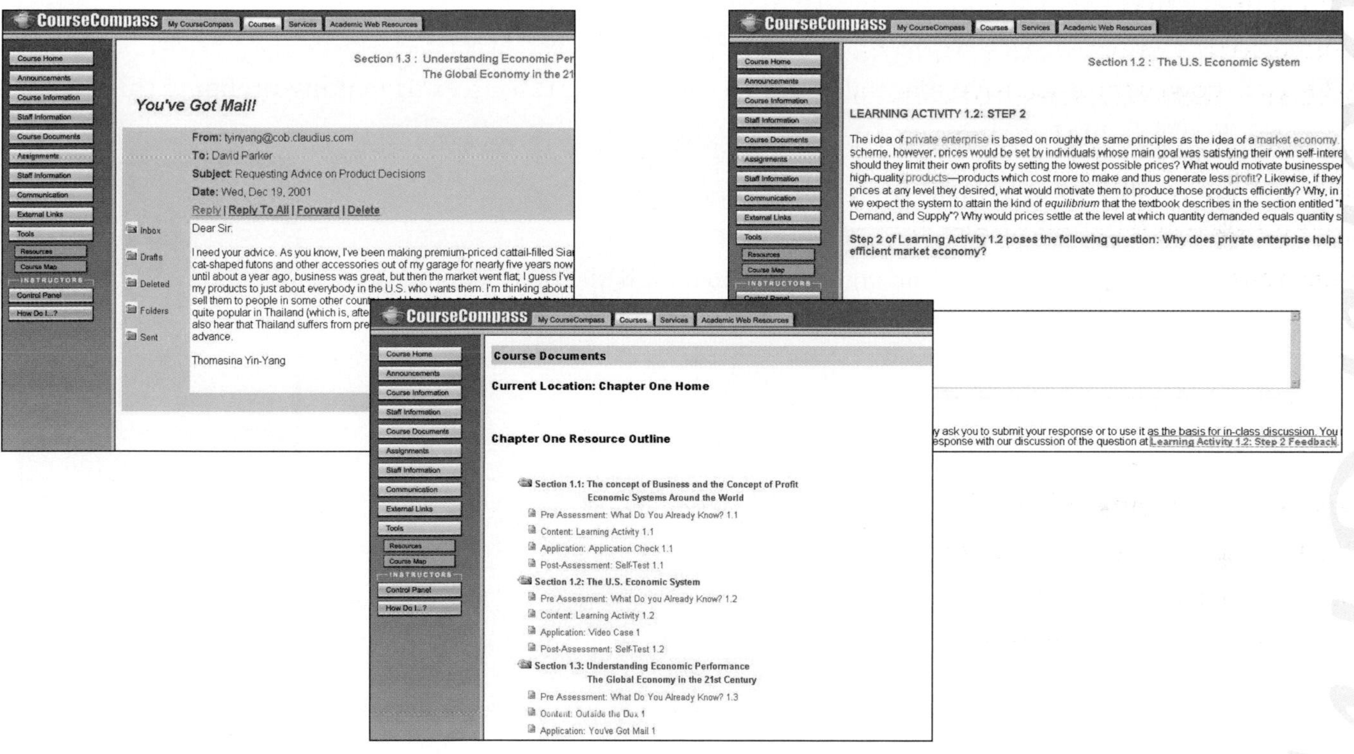

It includes the following:

- Each chapter is divided into **Lessons,** which explain important chapter concepts and expand definition of key terms.
- Each lesson begins with a **prereadiness assessment quiz.**
- **Learning Activities** follow and take the information presented in the chapter and use it to give students an experiential understanding of the concepts.
- In each lesson, students will complete an **application** — either a **"You Have Mail"** or an **"Out of the Box"** exercise. The **"You Have Mail"** exercises ask students to use what they have just learned to answer a question posed by a fictional supervisor, coworker or client. The **"Out of the Box"** exercises allow students to defend opinions and invent creative solutions to practical problems.
- Lastly, students will complete a **post-assessment** quiz to examine proficiency.

Business

An Unparalleled

Supplements Package

Ebert/Griffin

The instructional resource package accompanying this text is specially designed to simplify the task of teaching and learning. Several new and exciting items have been added.

All New! Instructor's Resource Manual

This all-new, comprehensive manual contains time-saving resources to making prepping this course a snap. Each chapter contains:

- brief chapter outline and chapter summaries
- changes to the new edition
- detailed lecture outlines and notes customized for both PowerPoint users and acetate users
- sample syllabi
- pop quizzes for every chapter
- answers to all end-of-chapter questions, problems, and assignments
- a detailed *Video Guide* with answers to video exercise questions
- suggested classroom exercises and classroom projects, and supplemental cases
- useful Web sites

All New! Test Item File

This new **two-volume *Test Item File*** contains **approximately 4,000 questions,** all of which have been carefully checked for accuracy and quality. This comprehensive set consists of multiple-choice, true/false, and essay questions. Each test question is ranked by level of difficulty (easy, moderate, or difficult) and contains section and learning objective references to allow the instructor a quick and easy way to balance the level of exams or quizzes. In addition, we have a special section that contains test questions for all boxed features and vignettes in each chapter. The *Test Item File* reinforces students' understanding of key terms and concepts and requires them to apply their critical-thinking and analytical skills. In addition, this test item features two pre-created sample tests for every part plus a mid-term and final exam for immediate use or distribution — an arrangement that provides both maximum flexibility and ease of use.

All New! Prentice Hall's *Computerized Test Manager* 4.2—ESATEST 2000 (Windows Version)

Our user-friendly software allows you to generate error-free tests quickly and easily by previewing questions individually on the screen and then selecting randomly by query or by number. The *Computerized Test Manager* allows you to generate random tests with our extensive bank of questions. You can also edit our questions/answers and even add some of your own. You can create an exam, administer it traditionally or online, and analyze your success with the simple click of the mouse. The newest version of our *Computerized Test Manager*, ***ESATEST 2000,*** has been improved to provide users with a vast array of new options.

All New! Telephone Test Preparation

For those instructors who prefer not to use the *Computerized Test Item File*, Prentice Hall provides a special 800 call-in service for ease of use. All you need to do is call the **800 Testing Help Desk** to have a customized test created. The test can then be delivered by e-mail, U.S. mail, or overnight carrier.

All New! Color Acetate Transparency Program

A set of color transparency acetates, available to instructors on request, highlights text concepts and supplies additional facts and information to help bring concepts alive in the classroom and enhance the classroom experience. All are keyed to the *Instructor's Resource Manual.*

All New! Videos

A set of 15 specially selected videos (one for each chapter) is available to adopters.

1. Factors to Consider: Lands' End
2. Entering the Global Marketplace: Lands' End and Yahoo!
3. Catering to Serious Users: Patagonia
4. Doing Business Privately: Amy's Ice Creams
5. The Management Picture: Quick Takes Video I
6. The Management Picture: Quick Takes Video II
7. Channeling Resources: Regal Marine
8. Learning to Motivate: Student Advantage
9. Channeling Human Resources: Showtime
10. Niche Noshing: Terra Chips
11. Promoting White Moustaches: The "Got Milk?" Campaign
12. Space Age IT at Boeing
13. Accounting for a Few Billion Sold: McDonald's
14. The World's Lenders: The World Bank and the IMF
15. Information Pays Off: Anatomy of a Stock Trade

All New! PowerPoint Presentation

Enhance your classroom presentations with this well-developed PowerPoint presentation set. **More than 500 text-specific PowerPoints** highlight fundamental concepts by integrating key graphs, figures, and illustrations from the text. PowerPoint slides come **complete with lecture notes**, which are available in the *Instructor's Resource Manual* or on the *Instructor's Resource CD*. Free to adopters, PowerPoints are available on CD or can be downloaded from the Instructor's Resource Web site at **www.prenhall.com/ebert**.

New Version! Business PlanPro Software and Exercises

Business PlanPro 4.0 (BPP) software provides students with a step-by-step approach to creating a comprehensive business plan. Preformatted report templates, charts, and tables do the mechanics so students can focus on the thinking. *Business PlanPro* software can be packaged with the textbook for a nominal fee of $10.

All New! Mastering Business Essentials CD

Mastering Business Essentials is the first fully integrated CD-ROM that uses video-enhanced interactive exercises that are truly cross-functional. The CD revolves around the e-business CanGo, an online entertainment company that is faced with real-world, on-the-job predicaments. The twelve interactive episodes are presented on the last page and inside back cover linking the appropriate chapters with the matching episodes.

The format for each episode includes:

(1) unique video scenarios that set up each episode
(2) informative and stimulating interactive exercises with follow-up video clips
(3) additional case and discussion questions.

The **Mastering Business Essentials CD** can be shrink-wrapped with this text for FREE!

The following topics are covered:

The Goal of the Firm and Social Responsibility	Leadership
The Economic Way of Thinking	Marketing Concepts/Strategy
Ethical Issues	Understanding Consumer Behavior
Concepts of Strategic Management	Strategy and Operations
Working in Groups and Teams	Managerial Accounting and Cost Behavior
Work Motivation	Raising Capital

All New! E-Business and E-Commerce Supplement

In the new world of business, you'll run into e-commerce no matter what direction you turn. Take your students behind the scenes to explore the dynamic world of e-business with this new value-pack supplement. This unique print supplement provides an overview of the basic concepts of e-business and e-commerce, an introduction to popular search sites, a wide range of business-related sites and addresses, and an up-to-the minute look at online job searches and career sites. The Web component of this supplement provides updated coverage of the latest trends, challenges, and hot concepts in e-commerce, plus additional interactive exercises. Go to **www.prenhall.com/ebiz.** This great supplement can be value-packaged with the text for FREE!

All New! Financial Times Offer

FINANCIAL TIMES
World business newspaper.

We are pleased to announce our new partnership with the *Financial Times* to offer a 15-week print subscription for $10 with our this text. The Prentice Hall textbook + subscription package will contain a 16-page, full-color *Financial Times* Student Guide, shrink-wrapped with the textbook. Bound inside the Student Guide will be a postcard that entitles the student to claim a prepaid 15-week subscription. The student mails in the reply card and the subscription should begin in 5 to 7 business days.

Study Guide

A Student Study Guide reinforces key concepts and tests student comprehension. For each chapter the following items are included: learning objectives, questions (true/false, multiple-choice, short-answer, essay, and critical-thinking), instructional games matching terms and definitions, word scramble, and a brain teaser to reinforce study skills and provide core study tips.

Beginning Your Career Search, 2nd edition

This concise book by James S. O'Rourke IV offers some straightforward, practical advice on how to write a résumé, where and how to find company information, how to conduct oneself during an interview, marketing yourself online, and tips on the interview process. Included in the book are copies of sample introductory, cover, follow-up, and thank-you letters. This book can be value-packed with the text at no additional cost.

Acknowledgments

Although two names appear on the cover of the book, we could never have completed the fourth edition without the assistance of many fine individuals. Everyone who worked on the book was committed to making it the best that it could be. Quality and closeness to the customer are things that we read a lot about today. Both we and the people who worked with us took these concepts to heart in this book and made quality our watchword by listening to our users and trying to provide what they want.

First, we would like to thank all the professionals who took time from their busy schedules to review materials for *Business Essentials:*

Roanne Angiello
Bergen Community College

Michael Baldigo
Sonoma State University

Ed Belvins
Devry Institute of Technology

Mary Jo Boehms
Jackson State Community College

Harvey Bronstein
Oakland Community

Gary Christiansen
North Iowa Area Community College

Michael Cicero
Highline Community College

Karen Collins
Lehigh University

Pat Ellebracht
Northeast Missouri State University

John Gubbay
Moraine Valley Community College

Dr. Shiv Gupta
University of Findlay

Karen W. Harris
Montgomery College

Edward M. Henn
Broward Community College

Robert W. James
Devry University

James H. Kennedy
Angelina College

Betty Ann Kirk
Tallahassee Community College

Sofia B. Klopp
Palm Beach Community College

Kenneth J. Lacho
University of New Orleans

Keith Leibham
Columbia Gorge Community College

Robert Markus
Babson College

John F. Mastriani
El Paso Community College

William E. Matthews
William Paterson University

Bronna McNeeley
Midwestern State University

Thomas J. Morrisey
Buffalo State College

William Morrison
San Jose State

David William Murphy
Madisonville Community College

Scott Norwood
San Jose State University

Joseph R. Novak
Blinn College

Glenn Perser
Houston Community College System

Constantine Petrides
Borough of Manhattan Community College

Roy R. Pipitone
Eric Community College

William D. Raffield
University of St. Thomas

Richard Randall
Nassau Community College

Betsy Ray
Indiana Business College

Richard Reed
Washington State University

Christopher Rogers
Miami-Dade Community College

Phyllis Schafer
Brookdale Community College

Lewis Schlossinger
Community College of Aurora

Robert N. Stern
Cornell University

Arlene Strawn
Tallahassee Community College

Jane A. Treptow
Broward Community College

Janna P. Vice
Eastern Kentucky University

Patricia R. Ward
Upper Iowa University

Phillip A Weatherford
Embry-Riddle Aeronautical University

Jerry E. Wheat
Indiana University Southeast

Lynne Spellman White
Trinity Christian College

JoAnn Wiggins
Walla Walla College

Pamela J. Winslow
Berkeley College of Business

A number of other professionals also made substantive contributions to the text, ranging from draft material on specialized topics to suggested resource materials to proposals for cases and examples. In particular, we are greatly indebted to Elisa Adams for her inventive and timely contributions as a professional writer and researcher. The supplements package for *Business Essentials,* fourth edition, also benefited from the able contributions of several individuals at Prentice Hall. We would like to thank those people for developing the finest set of instructional and learning materials for this field.

Meanwhile, a superb team of professionals at Prentice Hall made this book a pleasure to write. Authors often get the credit when a book is successful, but the success of this book must be shared with an outstanding group of people in New Jersey. Our development editor, Ron Librach, has been a true product champion and has improved both the book and the package in more ways than we can list. Managing editor Judy Leale, and Marcy Maslanczuk, the production editor, also made many truly outstanding contributions to the project.

We also want to acknowledge the contributions of the entire team at Prentice Hall Business Publishing, including acquisitions editor David Parker; Jeff Shelstad, editor in chief; Debbie Clare, executive marketing manager; Annie Todd, director of marketing; Steve Deitmer, director of development; Arnold Vila, production manager; Melinda Alexander, photo researcher; and Kevin Kall who designed this edition of *Business Essentials.*

Our colleagues at the University of Missouri-Columbia and Texas A&M University also deserve recognition. Each of us has the good fortune to be a part of a community of scholars who enrich our lives and challenge our ideas. Without their intellectual stimulation and support, our work would suffer greatly. Phyllis Washburn, Dr. Griffin's staff assistant, deserves special mention of the myriad contributions she has made to this project as well.

Finally, our families. We take pride in the accomplishments of our wives, Mary and Glenda and draw strength from the knowledge that they are there for us to lean on. And we take joy from our children, Matt, Kristen, Ashley, and Dustin. Sometimes in the late hours when we're ready for sleep but have to get one or two more pages written, looking at your pictures keeps us going. Thanks to all of you for making us what we are.

Ronald J. Ebert
Ricky W. Griffin

About the Authors

Ronald J. Ebert is Emeritus Professor at the University of Missouri-Columbia where he teaches in the Management Department and serves as advisor to students and student organizations. Dr. Ebert draws upon more than 30 years of teaching experience at such schools as Sinclair College, University of Washington, University of Missouri, Lucian Blaga University of Sibiu (Romania), and Consortium International University (Italy). His consulting alliances include such firms as Mobay Corporation, Kraft Foods, Oscar Mayer, Atlas Powder, and John Deere. He has designed and conducted management development programs for such diverse clients as the American Public Power Association, the United States Savings and Loan League, and the Central Missouri Manufacturing Training Consortium.

His experience as a practitioner has fostered an advocacy for integrating concepts with best business practices in business education. The five business books he has written include translations in Spanish, Chinese, and Romanian languages. Dr. Ebert has served as the Editor of the *Journal of Operations Management*. He is a Past-President and Fellow of the Decision Sciences Institute. He currently serves as Consultant and External Evaluator for *Quantitative Reasoning for Business Studies* an introduction-to-business project sponsored by the National Science Foundation.

Ricky W. Griffin is Professor of Management and holds the Blocker Chair in Business Administration in the Mays College & Graduate School of Business at Texas A&M University. He also currently serves as Executive Associate Dean. He previously served as Head of the Department of Management and as Director of the Center for Human Resource Management at Texas A&M. His research interests include workplace aggression and violence, executive skills and decision making, and workplace culture. Dr. Griffin's research has been published in such journals as *Academy of Management Review, Academy of Management Journal, Administrative Science Quarterly,* and *Journal of Management*. He has also served as Editor of *Journal of Management*. Dr. Griffin has consulted with such organizations as Texas Instruments, Tenneco, Amoco, Compaq Computer, and Continental Airlines.

Dr. Griffin has served the Academy of Management as Chair of the Organizational Behavior Division. He has also served as President of the Southwest Division of the Academy of Management and on the Board of Directors of the Southern Management Association. He is a Fellow of both the Academy of Management and the Sourthern Management Association. He is also the author of several successful textbooks, each of which is a market leader. In addition, they are widely used in dozens of countries and have been translated into numerous foreign languages, including Spanish, Polish, and Russian.

Business Essentials

CHAPTER 1

Understanding the U.S. Business System

After reading this chapter, you should be able to:

1. Define the nature of U.S. business and identify its main goals.
2. Describe different types of global *economic systems* according to the means by which they control the *factors of production* through *input and output markets.*
3. Show how *demand* and *supply* affect resource distribution in the United States.
4. Identify the elements of *private enterprise* and explain the various degrees of *competition* in the U.S. economic system.
5. Explain the factors that allow us to better understand and evaluate the performance of an economic system.
6. Discuss the current economic picture in the United States and summarize expert opinions about its future.

What's Hot on the Cyberspace Hit List

Electronic commerce is a major part of every industry and marketplace these days. So-called e-businesses such as Amazon.com, America Online, and eBay are all less than 10 years old but have already become household names and major players in the transformation of the United States into an information-based economy. Faced with this rapid and dynamic change, staid older businesses that want to remain vital and effective have found it necessary to refocus their own operations to encompass the Internet and electronic commerce. Some, such as IBM and Disney, have made successful transitions while others have faltered.

The music industry is an especially interesting arena for e-commerce competition—one in which both newcomers and established firms continue to struggle to find just the right approach to integrating the Internet into their operations. Giants like Universal Music Group <www.universalmusic.com>, Warner Music Group <www.timewarner.com/corp/about/music/index.html>, Sony Music <www.sonymusic.com>, BMG Entertainment <www.bmgentertainment.com>, and EMI <www.emi.com> have long dominated the recorded-music business. However, they are facing new and complex challenges as the Internet plays an increasingly significant role in their marketplace. New e-businesses pose both serious threats and significant opportunities for these media giants.

Consider the case of David Goldberg and Launch Media. When Goldberg, a music fanatic, was only 24 years old, he landed a plum job as director of new business development for Capitol Records. Goldberg

> *"Our role is to teach the industry to do things differently."*
>
> —Marc Achiller, CEO, Electra Artists

was interested in extending the Capitol library of popular music, which ranged from Frank Sinatra to the Beatles, into new arenas. He wanted to promote Capitol's music products on CD-ROM games and to focus heavily on new and emerging forms of electronic media for both promoting and delivering music to consumers.

But senior executives at Capitol weren't interested. They listened politely, but they adopted few of his ideas and gave him little encouragement in his efforts to push into new products and product lines. They apparently believed that the old tried-and-true method of recording music on disks and tapes, advertising and promoting new recordings in magazines and on the radio, and then distributing them through traditional retailing channels was never going to change.

Finally, Goldberg left Capitol in frustration and created Launch Media <www.launch.com>, which has quickly become one of the top five music-information sites on the Internet. NBC and Sony Music are two of the biggest investors in Goldberg's fledgling enterprise, and when the firm went public in April 1999, the value of his personal stake mushroomed to $12 million. Although the firm's stock price plummeted during the dot-com crash of 2001, it remains a viable operation that continues to attract investors.

Unlike some entrepreneurs in other industries and markets, Goldberg has never been interested in taking over the music business. What he wants to do is change it. And more and more industry experts are coming around to his point of view. "Our role," says one industry consultant who sees things Goldberg's way, "is to teach the industry to do things differently."

Some industry experts worried that Internet sites would render traditional recording companies obsolete—that consumers would simply download all the music they wanted directly from various Web sites controlled by artists or upstart Web outfits and that the recording companies would be squeezed out. But those in the know quickly realized that this isn't how things would work out. Instead, the Internet is emerging as a new catalyst for old and new music businesses alike. Web sites like launch.com are becoming platforms for more and more interaction among consumers, performers, and recording labels. Indeed, music-information sites on the Internet, such as MTV.com, MP3.com, tunes.com, UBL.com, and launch.com, are attracting millions of visitors each month—and generating millions of dollars in revenues.

The big companies still play a vital role in all this information-related activity. For example, they still control most of the recordings, handle much of the advertising and promotion, and provide the "human contact" that remains an essential part of all entertainment enterprises. Consumers, meanwhile, can visit Web sites in the comfort of their own homes and download trial music cuts to sample music that they might want to buy. Then they can easily purchase CDs—in addition to concert tickets, posters, shirts, and other paraphernalia—directly from the same sites. Granted, performers can leverage bigger cuts of the profits, but Goldberg and others like to point out the obvious advantages of keeping everybody happy.

The challenge of building and sustaining a new business to meet changing and newly emerging customer needs is as common to small firms like Launch Media as it is to billion-dollar corporations such as Warner Music Group and Sony Music. A changing marketplace creates a need for the kind of innovative responses that have long characterized business in the United States. Such responses require vision, careful attention to quality and customer service, substantial financial commitment, internal accounting controls, and well-defined marketing strategies designed to help businesses grow over time.

These and a host of other forces provide the main themes for stories of success and failure that are told repeatedly in the annals of enterprise in the United States. As you will see in this chapter, these forces are also the key factors in the U.S. market economy. You will see, too, that although the world's economic systems differ markedly, standards for evaluating success or failure are linked to a system's capacity to achieve certain basic goals.

Our opening story is continued on page 25

THE CONCEPT OF BUSINESS AND THE CONCEPT OF PROFIT

What do you think of when you hear the word *business*? Does your mind conjure up images of huge corporations such as General Motors and IBM? Are you reminded of smaller firms such as your local supermarket? Or do you think of even smaller one-person operations such as the dry cleaner around the corner? Each of these organizations is a **business**—an organization that provides goods or services to earn profits. Indeed, the prospect of earning **profits**—the difference between a business's revenues and its expenses—is what encourages people to open and expand businesses. After all, profits reward owners for taking the risks involved in investing their money and time.

business
An organization that provides goods or services to earn profits

profits
The difference between a business's revenues and its expenses

Today, businesses produce most of the goods and services we consume. They also employ most of the working people in the United States. Moreover, new forms of technology, service businesses, and international opportunities promise to keep production, consumption, and employment growing indefinitely. In turn, profits from businesses are paid to millions of owners and stockholders. Taxes on businesses help support governments at all levels. In many cases, businesses also support charitable causes and provide community leadership.

In this chapter, we begin our introduction to business by looking at its role in both the U.S. economy and U.S. society. There are a variety of economic systems around the world. Once you understand something about the systems of most developed countries, you will better appreciate the workings of the U.S. system. As we will see, the effects of economic forces on businesses and the effects of businesses on the economy are dynamic—and, indeed, sometimes volatile.

ECONOMIC SYSTEMS AROUND THE WORLD

A U.S. business operates differently from a business in, say, France or the People's Republic of China, and businesses in these countries vary from those in Japan or Brazil. A major factor in these differences is the economic system of a firm's home country, in which it conducts most of its business. An **economic system** is a nation's system for allocating its resources among its citizens, both individuals and organizations. In this section we show how economic systems differ according to the ownership or control of these resources, which are often called factors of production. We will also describe the basic economic systems that are used in different countries.[1]

economic system
A nation's system for allocating its resources among its citizens

"The point is to get so much money that money's not the point anymore."

Factors of Production

The key difference between economic systems is the way in which they manage the **factors of production**—the basic resources that a country's businesses use to produce goods and services.[2] Traditionally, economists have focused on four factors of production: labor, capital, entrepreneurs, and natural resources. Newer perspectives, however, tend to broaden the idea of "natural resources" to include all physical resources. In addition, information resources are now often included as well.[3]

factors of production
Resources used in the production of goods and services—labor, capital, entrepreneurs, physical resources, and information resources

labor (or human resources)
The physical and mental capabilities of people as they contribute to economic production

capital
The funds needed to create and operate a business enterprise

Labor The people who work for businesses provide labor. Sometimes called **human resources, labor** includes both the physical and mental contributions people make as they are engaged in economic production. America Online <www.aol.com>, for example, employs over 12,000 people. The operations of a firm like AOL require a widely skilled workforce, ranging from software engineers to marketing specialists to financial analysts.

Capital Obtaining and using material resources and labor requires **capital**—the funds needed to operate an enterprise. (In strict economic terms, *capital*, as a factor of production, usually refers only to financial resources; in reality, it may also include certain other resources as well.) Capital is needed to start a business and to keep it operating and growing. AOL requires millions of dollars (and millions more in equipment and other assets) to run its sprawling Internet operations. A major source of capital for most smaller businesses is personal investment by owners. Personal investment can be made by the individual entrepreneurs, by partners who start businesses together, or by investors who buy stock. Revenue from the sale of products is another important ongoing source of capital.

Entrepreneurs AOL was started by James Kimsey, who possessed the technical skills to understand how the Internet works, the conceptual skills to see its enormous future potential, and the risk-taking acumen to bet his own career and capital on its promise. Many economic systems need and encourage entrepreneurs like Kimsey, who start new businesses and who make the decisions that expand small businesses into larger ones. These people embrace the opportunities and accept the risks inherent in creating and operating businesses.

physical resources
Tangible things organizations use in the conduct of their business

Physical Resources **Physical resources** are the tangible things that organizations use to conduct their business. They include natural resources and raw materials, office and production facilities, parts and supplies, computers, and other equipment. AOL, for example, requires land, buildings, and computers. The CDs that the firm uses to distribute its software are provided by other manufacturers, and forest products are used for packaging.

information resources
Data and other information used by business

Information Resources While the production of tangible goods once dominated most economic systems, today **information resources** play a major role. Businesses themselves rely heavily on market forecasts, the specialized expertise and knowledge of people, and various forms of economic data for much of their work. Much of what they do results in either the creation of new information or the repackaging of existing information for new users and different audiences. AOL does not produce tangible products. Instead, it provides numerous online services for its millions of subscribers in exchange for monthly access fees. Essentially, AOL is in the information business.

planned economy
Economy that relies on a centralized government to control all or most factors of production and to make all or most production and allocation decisions

market economy
Economy in which individuals control production and allocation decisions through supply and demand

Types of Economic Systems

Different types of economic systems manage these factors of production in different ways. In some systems, ownership is private; in others, the factors of production are owned or controlled by the government. Economic systems also differ in the ways decisions are made about production and allocation. A **planned economy**, for example, relies on a centralized government to control all or most factors of production and to make all or most production and allocation decisions. In a **market economy**, individuals—producers and consumers—control production and allocation decisions through supply and demand. We will describe each of these economic types and then discuss the reality of the *mixed market economy*.

Planned Economies The two most basic forms of planned economies are *communism* (discussed here) and *socialism* (discussed as a mixed market economy). As originally proposed by nineteenth-century German economist Karl Marx, communism is a system in which the government owns and operates all sources of production. Marx envisioned a society in which individuals would ultimately contribute according to their abilities and receive economic benefits according to their needs. He also expected government ownership of production factors to be only temporary: Once society had matured, government would "wither away" and the workers would gain direct ownership.[4]

Many Eastern European countries and the former Soviet Union embraced communist systems until the latter years of the twentieth century. In the early 1990s, one country after another renounced communism as both an economic and a political system. Today, Cuba, North Korea, Vietnam, and the People's Republic of China are among the few nations with avowedly communist systems. Even in these countries, however, planned economic systems are making room for features of the free enterprise system from the lowest to the highest levels.

Market Economies A **market** is a mechanism for exchange between the buyers and sellers of a particular good or service (like *capital*, the term *market* can have multiple meanings). To understand how a market economy works, consider what happens when a customer goes to a fruit market to buy apples. While one vendor is selling apples for $1 per pound, another is charging $1.50. Both vendors are free to charge what they want, and customers are free to buy what they choose. If both vendors' apples are of the same quality, the customer will buy the cheaper ones. If the $1.50 apples are fresher, though, the customer may buy them instead. In short, both buyers and sellers enjoy freedom of choice.

market
Mechanism for exchange between buyers and sellers of a particular good or service

The "Wired World" box in this chapter discusses a much more complicated and technologically sophisticated market that has been created to bring buyers and sellers together using the Internet. This market is an outgrowth of a trend in information technology called "business to business," or "B2B." While most early commercial Internet applications were directed toward consumers, B2B is a more recent development that some experts think might handle trillions of dollars of annual business activity in just a few years.

Input and Output Markets Figure 1.1 provides a useful and more complete model for better understanding how the factors of production work in a pure market economy. According to this view, businesses and households interact in two different market relationships.[5] In the **input market**, firms buy resources from households, which then supply those resources. In the **output market**, firms supply goods and services in response to demand on the part of households. (We provide a more detailed discussion of supply and demand later in this chapter.)

input market
Market in which firms buy resources from supplier households

output market
Market in which firms supply goods and services in response to demand on the part of households

As you can see in Figure 1.1, the activities of these two markets create a circular flow. Ford Motor Co., for example, relies on various kinds of inputs. It buys labor directly from households, which may also supply capital from accumulated savings in the form of purchases of Ford stock. Consumer buying patterns provide information when Ford must decide which models to produce and which to discontinue. In turn, Ford uses these inputs in various ways and becomes a supplier to households when it designs and produces various models of automobiles, trucks, and sports utility vehicles and offers them for sale to consumers.

Individuals, meanwhile, are free to work for Ford or an alternative employer and to invest in Ford stock or in alternative forms of saving or consumption. Similarly, Ford can create whatever vehicles it chooses and price them at whatever value it chooses. But consumers are then free to buy their next car from Ford or Toyota or BMW. This process contrasts markedly with that of a planned economy, in which individuals may be told where they can and cannot work, companies are told what they

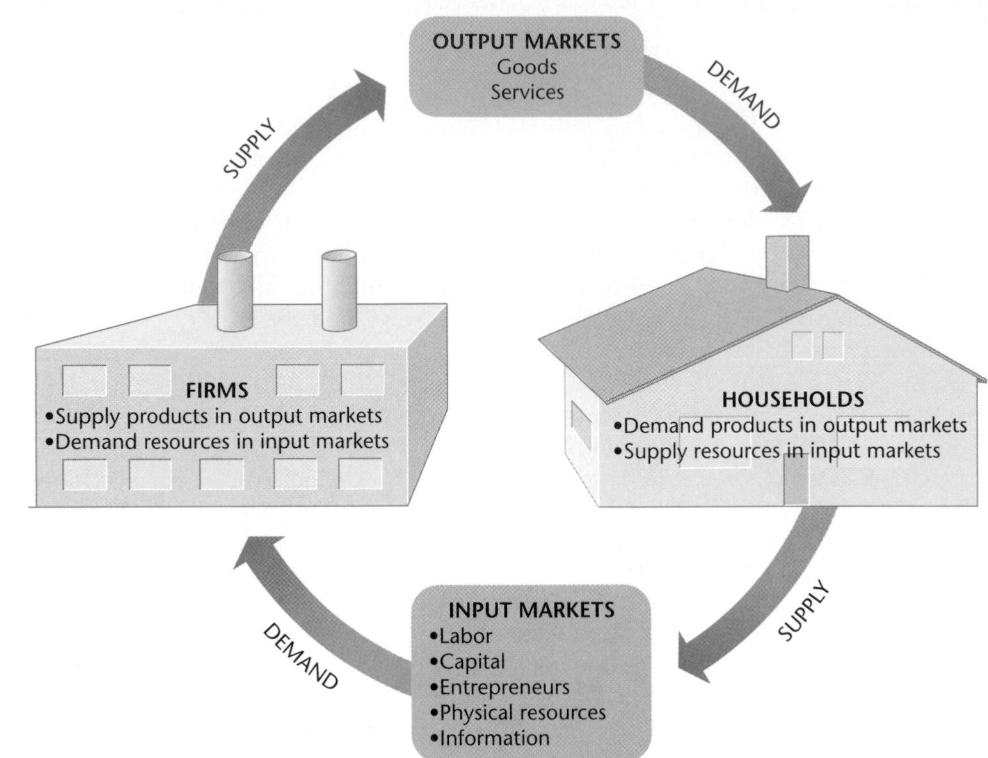

Figure 1.1
Circular Flow in a Market Economy

can and cannot manufacture, and consumers may have little or no choice as to what they purchase or how much they pay. The political basis of market processes is called **capitalism**, which provides for the private ownership of the factors of production and encourages entrepreneurship by offering profits as an incentive. The economic basis of market processes is the operation of demand and supply, which we discuss in the next section.

capitalism
Market economy that provides for private ownership of production and encourages entrepreneurship by offering profits as an incentive

Mixed Market Economies In their pure theoretical forms, planned and market economies are often seen as two extremes or opposites. In reality, however, most coun-

According to the model of circular flow in a market economy, this German Wal-Mart <www.walmartstores.com> *shopper plays a role in the output market: she demands goods that are supplied by a firm in the retailing business. Think of the German farmers from whom Wal-Mart buys the produce shown here as households that supply the input market with labor, time, skills, and investment in land.*

IT'S A WIRED WORLD

Electronic B2B in the Auto Industry

As we observed in the text, a market is a mechanism for exchange between the buyers and sellers of a particular good or service. In earlier times, markets were actual physical settings where buyers and sellers would gather to conduct transactions. While such market settings are still used for selling things such as fish, fruits and vegetables, and antiques and collectibles, many commercial markets today differ in a fundamental respect: Buyers and sellers do not actually meet at the same place, but rather arrange their exchanges via mail orders, telephones, fax machines, and so forth. The growth of the Internet is making it even easier for some buyers and sellers to transact business at great distances.

A good example of this trend is the recently announced partnership among some of the world's largest automobile manufacturers. It all started when various individual automakers began to create their own global purchasing Web sites. Ford Motor Co., for instance, planned a site it called AutoXchange. The company intended to post all of its global procurement needs on the site, while also requesting that its suppliers post availability and prices for parts and equipment.

When it became apparent that other automakers were planning to do the same thing, major suppliers to the auto industry realized that they might soon be facing an unwieldy array of separate Web sites for each car company—a situation that would potentially drive up rather than reduce their own costs. Thus, a coalition of the largest suppliers approached Ford and General Motors with a novel proposal: Why not team up and create a single site that could be used by both automakers and by their suppliers?

Ford and GM executives quickly saw the wisdom of this idea and then convinced DaimlerChrysler to join them. Now the Big Three plan to establish a single Web site to serve as a marketplace for all interested automobile manufacturers, suppliers, and dealers—essentially, a global virtual market including all firms in the industry. Almost immediately, France's Renault and Japan's Nissan, which is controlled by Renault, indicated a desire to join; Toyota also indicated strong interest. In addition, both Ford and GM indicated that they would encourage their foreign affiliates and strategic partners as well. The partners who are building the Web site intend to establish it as a self-contained organization that will eventually offer shares to the public.

Many experts believe that the impact of this global electronic market will be tremendous. It currently costs GM about $100 in ordering costs to buy parts or supplies the traditional way—with paper or over the telephone. However, the firm estimates that its ordering costs will drop to less than $10 under the new system. Clearly, the automakers will realize substantial cost savings. Suppliers, too, will benefit in various ways. Besides having more information about the immediate needs of different customers, they will be able to buy and sell among themselves.

tries rely on some form of **mixed market economy**—a system featuring characteristics of both planned and market economies. Many of the former Eastern bloc countries are now adopting market mechanisms through a process called **privatization**—the process of converting government enterprises into privately owned companies. In recent years this practice has spread to many other countries as well. For example, the postal system in many countries is government-owned and government-managed, regardless of whether the country has a planned or market economy. The Netherlands, however, recently began the process of privatizing its TNT Post Group N.V., already among the world's most efficient post office operations.[6] Similarly, Canada has recently privatized its air traffic control system. In each case, the new enterprise reduced its payroll, boosted efficiency and productivity, and quickly became profitable.[7]

In the partially planned system called **socialism**, the government owns and operates selected major industries. In such mixed market economies, the government may control banking, communication, transportation, and industries that produce such basic goods as oil and steel. Smaller businesses, such as clothing stores and restaurants, are privately owned. Many Western European countries, including England and

mixed market economy
Economic system featuring characteristics of both planned and market economies

privatization
Process of converting government enterprises into privately owned companies

socialism
Planned economic system in which the government owns and operates only selected major sources of production

France, allow free market operations in most economic areas but maintain government control in others, such as health care. Government planners in Japan give special centrally planned assistance to new industries that are expected to grow.

THE U.S. ECONOMIC SYSTEM

Understanding the complex nature of the U.S. economic system is essential to understanding the environment in which U.S. businesses operate. In this section, we describe the workings of the U.S. market economy in more detail. Specifically, we examine markets, the nature of demand and supply, private enterprise, and degrees of competition.

Markets, Demand, and Supply

A market economy consists of many different markets. We have already noted the general nature of input and output markets. But beyond these general distinctions, virtually every input used by business and every good or service created by business has its own market. In each of these markets, businesses decide what inputs to buy, what to make and in what quantities, and what prices to charge. Likewise, customers decide what to buy and how much they are willing to pay. Literally billions of such exchanges take place every day between businesses and individuals, between different businesses, and among individuals, businesses, and governments. Moreover, exchanges conducted under conditions in one place often have an impact on exchanges elsewhere.

In 2000 and early 2001, for example, several factors conspired to affect computer purchases. For one thing, many companies had increased their computer budgets in the late 1990s in anticipation of Y2K problems but were then able to cut those budgets after the new millennium arrived. For another, some companies began to reallocate their technology dollars, spending less on desktop computers and more on back-office equipment to run e-businesses. In addition, some firms simply started to slow down their upgrade cycles on the grounds that brand-new computers were not sufficiently superior to those they had purchased a few years earlier. Thus, rather than upgrade employee computers every two or three years, some firms started upgrading only every three or four years. As demand in the United States dropped, firms like Dell and IBM had to lower prices to keep sales from slumping too far, and lower prices meant lower profits per unit. At the same time, however, demand in other parts of the world, most notably China and India, was increasing, although not enough to fully offset domestic declines. Finally, projected lower profits induced investors to pay less for the stocks of some computer firms, causing those prices to fall as well.[8]

demand
The willingness and ability of buyers to purchase a good or service

supply
The willingness and ability of producers to offer a good or service for sale

law of demand
Principle that buyers will purchase (demand) more of a product as its price drops and less as its price increases

law of supply
Principle that producers will offer (supply) more of a product for sale as its price rises and less as its price drops

demand and supply schedule
Assessment of the relationships between different levels of demand and supply at different price levels

The Laws of Demand and Supply On all economic levels, decisions about what to buy and what to sell are determined primarily by the forces of demand and supply.[9] **Demand** is the willingness and ability of buyers to purchase a product (a good or a service). **Supply** is the willingness and ability of producers to offer a good or service for sale. Generally speaking, demand and supply follow basic laws:

- The **law of demand**: Buyers will purchase (*demand*) more of a product as its price drops and less of a product as its price increases.
- The **law of supply**: Producers will offer (*supply*) more of a product for sale as its price rises and less as its price drops.

The Demand and Supply Schedule To appreciate these laws in action, consider the market for pizza in your town. If everyone in town is willing to pay $25 for a pizza (a high price), the town's only pizzeria will produce a large supply. If everyone is willing to pay only $5 (a low price), however, the restaurant will make fewer pizzas. Through careful analysis we can determine how many pizzas will be sold at different prices. These results, called a **demand and supply schedule**, are obtained from marketing research and other systematic studies of the market. Properly applied, they help managers better understand the relationships among different levels of demand and supply at different price levels.

Demand and Supply Curves The demand and supply schedule, for example, can be used to construct demand and supply curves for pizza in your town. A **demand curve** shows how many products—in this case, pizzas—will be *demanded* (bought) at different prices. A **supply curve** shows how many pizzas will be *supplied* (baked) at different prices.

Figure 1.2 shows hypothetical demand and supply curves for pizzas. As you can see, demand increases as price decreases; supply increases as price increases. When the demand and supply curves are plotted on the same graph, the point at which they intersect is the **market price** or **equilibrium price**—the price at which the quantity of goods demanded and the quantity of goods supplied are equal. Note in Figure 1.2 that the equilibrium price for pizzas in our example is $10. At this point, the quantity of pizzas demanded and the quantity of pizzas supplied are the same: 1,000 pizzas per week.

Surpluses and Shortages What if the restaurant chooses to make some other number of pizzas? For example, what would happen if the owner tried to increase profits by making more pizzas to sell? Or what if the owner wanted to reduce overhead, cut back on store hours, and reduce the number of pizzas offered for sale? In either case, the result would be an inefficient use of resources and lower profits. For instance, if the restaurant supplies 1,200 pizzas and tries to sell them for $10 each, 200 pizzas will not be purchased. The demand schedule clearly shows that only 1,000 pizzas will be demanded at this price. The pizza maker will, thus, have a **surplus**—a situation in which the quantity supplied exceeds the quantity demanded. The restaurant will lose the money it spent making those extra 200 pizzas.

Conversely, if the pizzeria supplies only 800 pizzas, a **shortage** will result: The quantity demanded will be greater than the quantity supplied. The pizzeria will lose the extra money it could have made by producing 200 more pizzas. Even though consumers may pay more for pizzas because of the shortage, the restaurant will still earn lower profits than if it had made 1,000 pizzas. In addition, it will risk angering customers who cannot buy pizzas. To maximize profits, therefore, all businesses must constantly seek the right combination of price charged and quantity supplied. This right combination is found at the equilibrium point.

This simple example involves only one company, one product, and a few buyers. Obviously, the U.S. economy is far more complex. Thousands of companies sell hundreds of thousands of products to millions of buyers every day. In the end, however, the result is much the same: Companies try to supply the quantity and selection of goods that will earn them the largest profits.

demand curve
Graph showing how many units of a product will be demanded (bought) at different prices

supply curve
Graph showing how many units of a product will be supplied (offered for sale) at different prices

market price
(or **equilibrium price**)
Profit-maximizing price at which the quantity of goods demanded and the quantity of goods supplied are equal

surplus
Situation in which quantity supplied exceeds quantity demanded

shortage
Situation in which quantity demanded exceeds quantity supplied

Private Enterprise and Competition

Generally speaking, market economies reflect the operation of a **private enterprise** system—a system that allows individuals to pursue their own interests without government restriction. In both theory and the reality of contemporary practice, private enterprise requires the presence of four elements: *private property rights, freedom of choice, profits*, and *competition.*

- *Private property.* Ownership of the resources used to create wealth is in the hands of individuals.
- *Freedom of choice.* You enjoy the right to sell your labor to any employer you choose. You can also choose which products you want to buy, and producers can usually choose whom to hire and what to produce.
- *Profits.* The lure of profits (and freedom) inevitably leads some people to abandon the security of working for someone else and to assume the risks of entrepreneurship. Obviously, anticipated profits also play a large part in individuals' choices of the goods or services they will produce.

private enterprise
Economic system that allows individuals to pursue their own interests without undue governmental restriction

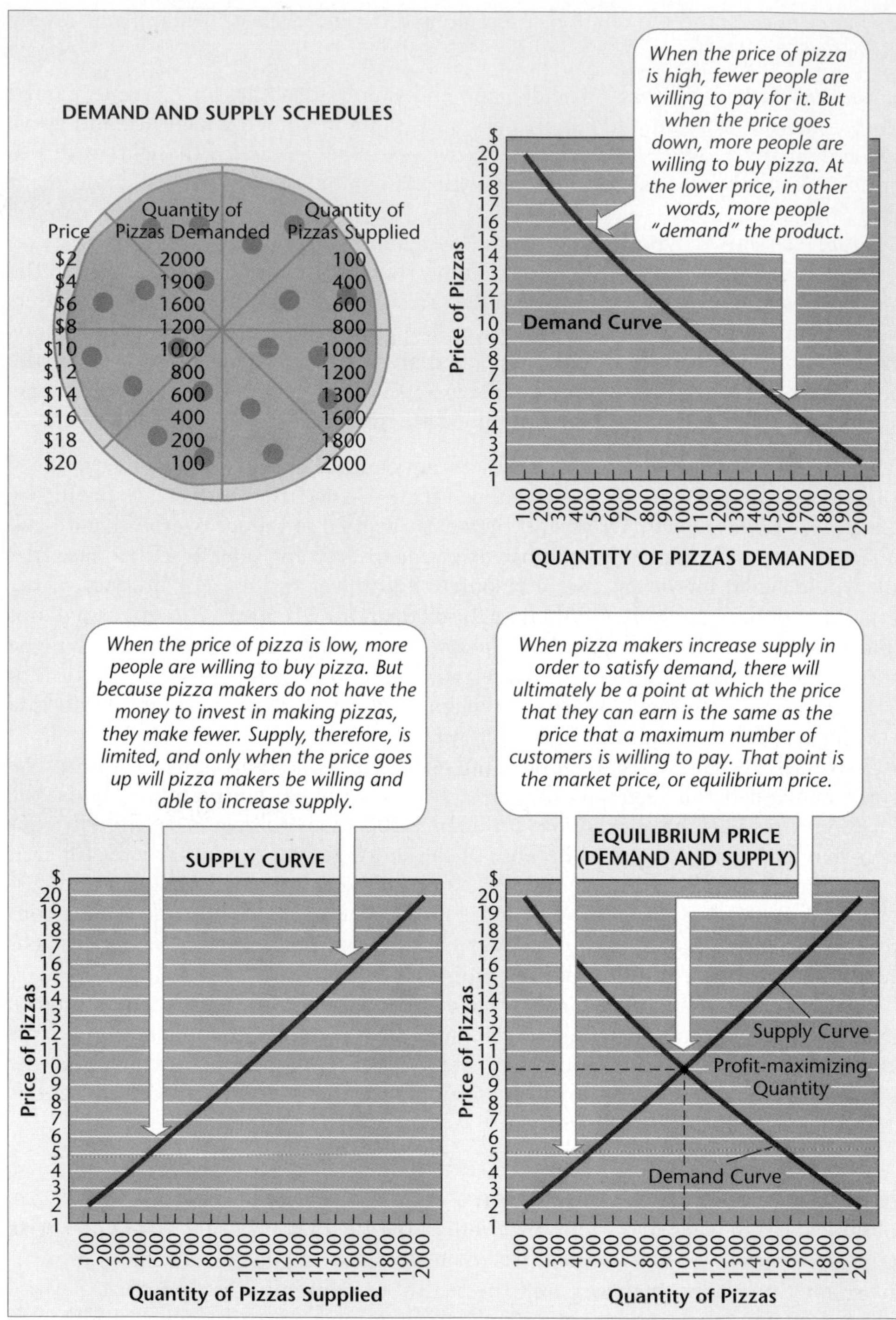

Figure 1.2
Demand and Supply

competition
Vying among businesses for the same resources or customers

- *Competition.* If profits motivate individuals to start businesses, competition motivates them to operate their businesses efficiently. **Competition** occurs when two or more businesses vie for the same resources or customers. To gain an advantage over its competitors, a business must produce its goods or services efficiently and must be able to sell them for prices that earn reasonable profits. To achieve these goals, a business must convince customers that its products are either better or less expensive than those of competitors. Competition, therefore, forces all businesses to make their products better or cheaper. A company that produces inferior, expensive products is sure to be forced out of business. We discuss competition much more fully in the next section.

Characteristic	Perfect Competition	Monopolistic Competition	Oligopoly	Monopoly
Example	Local farmer	Stationery store	Steel industry	Public utility
Number of competitors	Many	Many, but fewer than in pure competition	Few	None
Ease of entry into industry	Easy	Fairly easy	Difficult	Regulated by government
Similarity of goods or services offered by competing firms	Identical	Similar	Can be similar or different	No directly competing goods or services
Level of control over price by individual firms	None	Some	Some	Considerable

Table 1.1
Degrees of Competition

Degrees of Competition Not all industries are equally competitive. Economists have identified four basic degrees of competition within a private enterprise system: *perfect competition, monopolistic competition, oligopoly*, and *monopoly*. Table 1.1 summarizes the features of these four degrees of competition.

Perfect Competition For **perfect competition** to exist, two conditions must prevail:

perfect competition
Market or industry characterized by numerous small firms producing an identical product

1. All firms in a given industry must be small.
2. The number of firms in the industry must be large.

Under such conditions, no single firm is powerful enough to influence the price of its product or service in the marketplace. As a result, prices are determined by such market forces as supply and demand.

In addition, these conditions also reflect four important principles:

1. The products offered by each firm are so similar that buyers view them as identical to those offered by other firms.
2. Both buyers and sellers know the prices that others are paying and receiving in the marketplace.
3. Because each firm is small, it is easy for any single firm to enter or leave the market.
4. Going prices are set exclusively by supply and demand and accepted by both sellers and buyers.

Agriculture is a good example of perfect competition in the U.S. economy. For example, the wheat produced on one farm is essentially the same as that produced on another. Both producers and buyers are well aware of prevailing market prices. Moreover, it is relatively easy to start producing wheat and relatively easy to stop when doing so is no longer profitable.

Monopolistic Competition Fewer sellers are involved in **monopolistic competition** than in pure competition, but because there are still many buyers, sellers try to make their products at least appear to be different from those of competitors. Differentiating strategies include brand names (Tide and Cheer), design or styling (Polo and Tommy Hilfiger jeans), and advertising (Coke and Pepsi). For example, in an effort to attract health-conscious consumers, the Kraft Foods division of Philip Morris <www.kraftfoods.com/index.cgi> actively promotes such differentiated products as low-fat Cool Whip, low-calorie Jell-O, and sugar-free Kool-Aid.

monopolistic competition
Market or industry characterized by numerous buyers and relatively numerous sellers trying to differentiate their products from those of competitors

Monopolistically competitive businesses may be large or small, but still able to easily enter or leave the market. For example, many small clothing stores compete successfully with large apparel retailers such as Liz Claiborne <www.lizclaiborne.com> and The Limited <www.limited.com>, and bebe stores, inc. (with a small *b*) <www.bebe.com>

WEB Connection

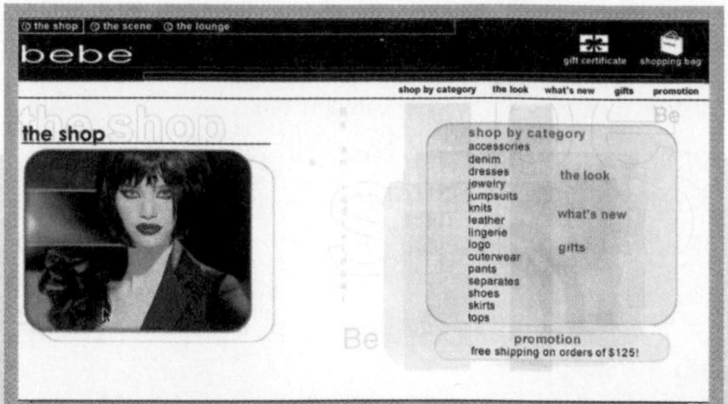

Like Gap Inc., bebe stores is a vertical retailer that manufactures and brands its own clothing. With over 100 stores nationwide (plus stores in Vancouver, Toronto, and London), bebe targets sexy, trendy clothing at mall prices to women in their 20s and 30s. To see how the company uses the Internet both to sell its products and to expand brand awareness, log on to its Web site.

www.bebe.com

is a good case in point. The relatively small clothing chain controls its own manufacturing facilities and can respond just as quickly as firms like Gap <www.gap.com/onlinestore.gap> to changes in fashion tastes. [10] Many single-store clothing businesses in college towns compete effectively by developing their own designs for T-shirts and caps and then copyrighting slogans and logos to prevent others from copying them. Product differentiation also gives sellers some control over the prices they charge. For instance, even though Sears shirts may have similar styling and other features, Ralph Lauren Polo shirts can be priced with little regard for the lower price of Sears shirts. But the large number of buyers relative to sellers applies potential limits to selling prices: Although Polo might be able to sell shirts for, say, $20 more than a comparable Sears shirt, it could not sell as many shirts if they were priced at $200 more.

oligopoly
Market or industry characterized by a handful of (generally large) sellers with the power to influence the prices of their products

Oligopoly When an industry has only a handful of sellers, an **oligopoly** exists. As a general rule, these sellers are quite large. The entry of new competitors is difficult because large capital investment is necessary. Consequently, oligopolistic industries (the automobile, rubber, airline, and steel industries) tend to stay that way. Thus, only two companies, both among the biggest in the world, manufacture large commercial aircraft: Boeing (a U.S. company) and Airbus (a European consortium). Furthermore, as the trend toward globalization continues, most experts believe that, as one forecaster puts it, "global oligopolies are as inevitable as the sunrise."[11]

"Global oligopolies are as inevitable as the sunrise."

—Business historian Louis Galambos

Individual oligopolists have more control over their own strategies than monopolistically competitive firms. At the same time, however, the actions of any one firm can significantly affect the sales of every other firm. For example, when one firm reduces prices or offers incentives to increase sales, the others usually protect their sales by doing the same. Likewise, when one firm raises prices, the others generally follow suit. Therefore, the prices of comparable products are usually quite similar. When a major airline announces a new program of fare discounts, the others mimic this strategy almost immediately. Just as quickly, when the fare discounts end for one airline, they usually end for all the others at the same time.

monopoly
Market or industry in which there is only one producer, which can therefore set the prices of its products

natural monopoly
Industry in which one company can most efficiently supply all needed goods or services

Monopoly A **monopoly** exists when an industry or market has only one producer. Obviously, a sole supplier enjoys complete control over the prices of its products. Its only constraint is the fall of consumer demand in response to increased prices. In the United States, laws such as the Sherman Antitrust Act (1890) and the Clayton Act (1914) forbid many monopolies and regulate the prices charged by so-called **natural monopolies** (industries in which one company can most efficiently supply all the needed goods or services).[12] Many local electric companies are natural monopolies because they can supply all the power needed in their local area. Duplicate facilities—such as two power plants and two sets of power lines—would be wasteful.

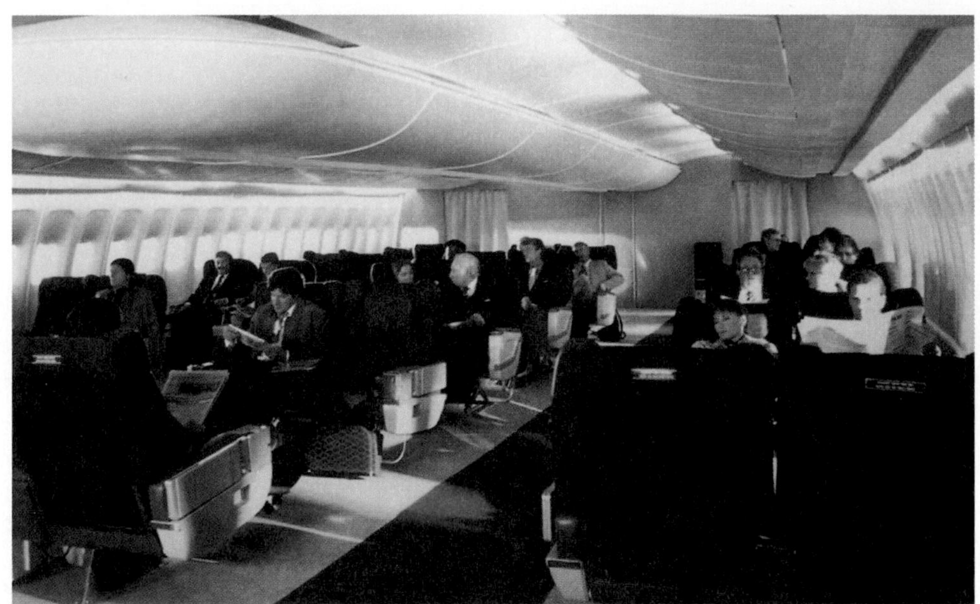

Founded in 1970 as a consortium that now includes four European companies, Airbus Industrie <www.airbus.com> is developing the world's largest airplane. It's code-named A3XX and would carry 555 passengers on overseas routes—137 more than the 747-400 built by Boeing <www.boeing.com>, Airbus's only true competitor in the oligopolistic commercial jet industry. Airbus calls Boeing's 747-400 "30-year-old technology" and is climbing steadily toward its goal of gaining 50 percent of the worldwide market for over-100-seat airplanes.

UNDERSTANDING ECONOMIC PERFORMANCE

In this section, we take a much closer look at the two key goals of the U.S. economic system: *economic growth* and *economic stability*. We begin by focusing on the tools with which we measure economic growth, including *aggregate output, standard of living, gross domestic product*, and *productivity*. We then discuss the main threats to economic *stability*—namely, *inflation* and *unemployment*. We conclude by discussing government attempts to manage the U.S. economy in the interest of meeting national economic goals.

Economic Growth

At one time, about half the population of this country was involved in producing the food that we needed. Today, less than 2.5 percent of the U.S. population works in agriculture. Agricultural efficiency has improved because we devised better ways of producing products and invented better technology for getting the job done. We can, therefore, say that agricultural production has *grown* because we have been able to increase total output in the agricultural sector.

Aggregate Output and Standard of Living We can apply the same concepts to a nation's economic system, but the computations are vastly more complex. A fundamental question, then, is how we know whether or not an economic system is growing. Experts call the pattern of short-term ups and downs (or, better, expansions and contractions) in an economy the **business cycle**. The main measure of *growth* in the business cycle is **aggregate output**: the total quantity of goods and services produced by an economic system during a given period.[13]

To put it simply, an increase in aggregate output is *growth* (or *economic growth*).[14] When output grows more quickly than the population, two things usually follow:

- *Output per capita*—the quantity of goods and services per person—goes up.
- The system provides relatively more of the goods and services that people want.[15]

When these two things occur, people living in an economic system benefit from a higher **standard of living**, which refers to the total quantity and quality of goods and services that they can purchase with the currency used in their economic system.

business cycle
Pattern of short-term expansions and contractions in an economy

aggregate output
Total quantity of goods and services produced by an economic system during a given period

standard of living
Total quantity and quality of goods and services that people can purchase with the currency used by their economic system

Table 1.2
U.S. GDP and GDP per Capita

GROSS DOMESTIC PRODUCT(GDP) ($ BILLION)	GDP: REAL GROWTH RATE (%)	GDP PER CAPITA: PURCHASING POWER PARITY
9,255.00	4.1	$33,900

Among other things, then, growth makes possible higher standards of living. Thus, in order to know how much your standard of living is improving, you need to know how much your nation's economic system is growing. Let's start to address this question by considering the data in Table 1.2.

gross domestic product (GDP)
The value of all goods and services produced in a year by a nation's economy through domestic factors of production

gross national product (GNP)
The value of all goods and services produced by an economic system in a year regardless of where the factors of production are located

Gross Domestic Product The first number in the table, **GDP,** or **gross domestic product**, refers to the total value of all goods and services produced within a given period by a national economy through domestic factors of production. Obviously, GDP is a measure of aggregate output: Generally speaking, if GDP is going up, aggregate output is going up; if aggregate output is going up, the nation is experiencing *economic growth*.

Sometimes economists also use the term **gross national product (GNP)**, which refers to the total value of all goods and services produced by a national economy within a given period regardless of where the factors of production are located. What, precisely, is the difference between GDP and GNP? Consider an American-owned automobile plant in Brazil. The profits earned by the factory are included in U.S. GNP—but not in GDP—because its output is not produced domestically (that is, in the United States). Conversely, those profits are included in Brazil's GDP—but not GNP—because they are produced domestically (that is, in Brazil). Calculations quickly become complex because of different factors of production. The labor, for example, will be mostly Brazilian but the capital mostly American. Thus, wages paid to Brazilian workers are part of Brazil's GNP even though profits are not.

Real Growth Rate GDP and GNP usually differ by less than 1 percent, but GDP is the preferred method of calculating national income and output. With that in mind, let's look at the middle column in Table 1.2. Here we find that the *real growth rate of U.S. GDP*—the growth rate of GDP *adjusted for inflation and changes in the value of the country's currency*—is 4.1 percent. How good is that rate? Remember: *Growth depends on output increasing at a faster rate than population.* The U.S. population is growing at a rate of 0.91 percent. The *real growth rate* of the U.S. economic system, therefore, seems quite healthy, and our standard of living should be improving.

GDP per Capita The number in the third column of Table 1.2 is in fact a reflection of standard of living: *GDP per capita* means GDP per person. We get this figure by dividing total GDP ($9.255 trillion) by total population, which happens to be about 275.5 million. In a given period (usually calculated on an annual basis), the United States produces goods and services equal in value to $33,900 for every person in the country.[16] Figure 1.3 shows both GDP and GDP per capita in the United States between 1900 and 1995. GDP per capita is a better measure than GDP itself of the economic well-being of the average person.

nominal GDP
GDP measured in current dollars or with all components valued at current prices

Real GDP "Real GDP" means that GDP has been adjusted. To understand why adjustments are necessary, assume that pizza is the only product in a hypothetical economy. In 2001, a pizza cost $10; the next year, a pizza cost $11. In both years, exactly 1,000 pizzas were produced. In 2001, the local "GDP" was $10,000 ($10 × 1,000); in 2002, the local "GDP" was $11,000 ($11 × 1,000). Has the economy grown? No: Because 1,000 pizzas were produced in both years, *aggregate output* remained the same. The point is to not be misled into believing that an economy is doing better than it is. If it is *not* adjusted, local GDP for 2002 is **nominal GDP**: GDP measured in current dollars or with all components valued at current prices.[17]

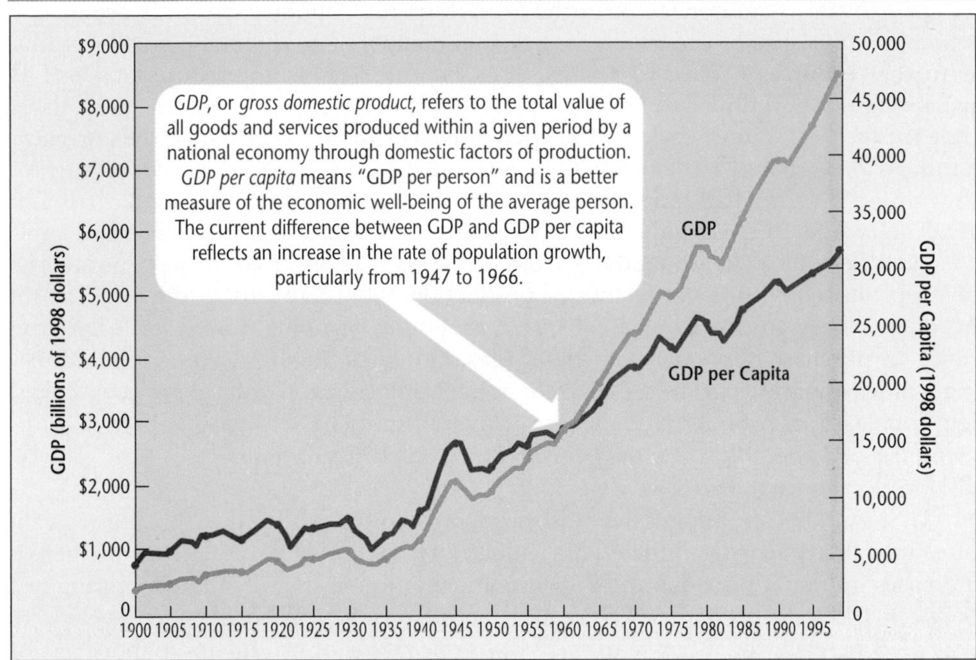
GDP, or gross domestic product, refers to the total value of all goods and services produced within a given period by a national economy through domestic factors of production.
GDP per capita means "GDP per person" and is a better measure of the economic well-being of the average person. The current difference between GDP and GDP per capita reflects an increase in the rate of population growth, particularly from 1947 to 1966.
GDP
GDP per Capita
GDP (billions of 1998 dollars)
GDP per Capita (1998 dollars)
$9,000
$8,000
$7,000
$6,000
$5,000
$4,000
$3,000
$2,000
$1,000
0
50,000
45,000
40,000
35,000
30,000
25,000
20,000
15,000
10,000
5,000
0
1900 1905 1910 1915 1920 1925 1930 1935 1940 1945 1950 1955 1960 1965 1970 1975 1980 1985 1990 1995

Figure 1.3
GDP and GDP per Capita

real GDP
GDP calculated to account for changes in currency values and price changes

purchasing power parity
Principle that exchange rates are set so that the prices of similar products in different countries are about the same

Purchasing Power Parity In our example, *current prices* would be 2001 prices. On the other hand, we calculate **real GDP** when we calculate GDP to account for *changes in currency values and price changes*. When we make this adjustment, we account for both GDP and **purchasing power parity**—the principle that exchange rates are set so that the prices of similar products in different countries are about the same. Purchasing power parity gives us a much better idea of *what people can actually buy with the financial resources allocated to them by their respective economic systems*. In other words, it gives us a better sense of standards of living across the globe.

Coca-Cola

The GDP of the African nation of Angola is $11.6 billion. Adjusted to calculate purchasing power parity, GDP per capita is $1,000. Angolans can buy a 12-ounce bottle of Coke for 8 new kwanza (the country's currency), or about 40 cents. Thus, although the country is extremely poor, Coke is not prohibitively expensive: working from about 8 A.M. to 7. P.M., street vendors like this one in the capital of Luanda can sell 5 cases and take home $8 per day. If he works 6 days a week, he makes more than enough to pay the rent. As for the Coca-Cola Co. <www.cocacola.com>, *sales in Angola have warranted the construction of a new $33 million bottling plant.*

productivity
Measure of economic growth that compares how much a system produces with the resources needed to produce it

Productivity A major factor in the growth of an economic system is **productivity**, which is a measure of economic growth that compares how much a system produces with the resources needed to produce it. Let's say, for instance, that it takes 1 U.S. worker and 1 U.S. dollar to make 10 soccer balls in an 8-hour workday. Let's also say that it takes 1.2 Saudi workers and the equivalent of $1.2 (in riyals, the currency of Saudi Arabia) to make 10 soccer balls in the same 8-hour workday. We can say, then, that the U.S. soccer-ball industry is more *productive* than the Saudi soccer-ball industry. The two factors of production in this extremely simple case are labor and capital.

Now let's look at productivity from a different perspective. If more products are being produced with fewer factors of production, what happens to the prices of these products? They go down. As a consumer, therefore, you would need less of your currency to purchase the same quantity of these products. In short, your standard of living—at least with regard to these products—has improved. If your entire economic system increases its productivity, then your overall standard of living improves. In fact, *standard of living improves only through increases in productivity.*[18] Real growth in GDP reflects growth in productivity.

U.S. workers are among the most productive in the world. Figure 1.4 gives us just one way of measuring improved productivity. It shows the relationship between increases in output per hour and hourly compensation in the U.S. manufacturing sector between 1993 and 1999. You can read the graph this way: While the increase in output was 33.3 percent, the increase in the cost of one factor of production (labor) was only 25.3 percent. In this respect, therefore, productivity improved.[19]

Productivity in the United States, then, is increasing, and as a result, so are GDP and GDP per capita. Ultimately, increases in these measures of growth mean an improvement in the standard of living. But, obviously, things don't always proceed so smoothly. Figure 1.4, for example, reveals periods in which productivity growth was considerably less than in others. What factors can inhibit the growth of an economic system? There are several such factors, but we'll focus on two of them: *balance of trade* and the *national debt.*

Balance of Trade Its *balance of trade* is the economic value of all the products that a country *exports* minus the economic value of *imported* products. The principle here is quite simple:

- A *positive* balance of trade results when a country exports (sells to other countries) more than it imports (buys from other countries).
- A *negative* balance of trade results when a country imports more than it exports.

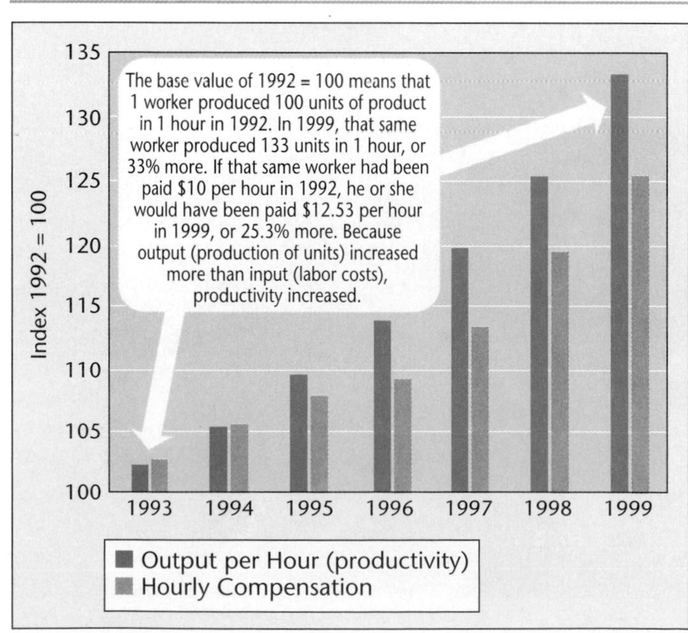

Figure 1.4
Productivity and Labor Compensation in U.S. Manufacturing

A negative balance of trade is commonly called a *trade deficit*. In 2000, the United States compiled a deficit (as it has every year since the mid-1970s), spending nearly $345 billion more on imports than it received for exports. The United States is thus a *debtor nation* rather than a *creditor nation*.

How does a trade deficit affect economic growth? The deficit exists because the amount of money spent on foreign products has not been paid in full. In effect, therefore, it is borrowed money, and borrowed money costs more money in the form of interest. The money that flows out of the country to pay off the deficit can't be used to invest in productive enterprises, either at home or overseas.

National Debt Its **national debt** is the amount of money that the government owes its creditors. As of this writing, the U.S. national debt was over $5.7 *trillion*. (You can find out the national debt on a given day by going to any one of several Internet sources, including the U.S. National Debt Clock at <www.brillig.com/debt_clock>.)

national debt
Total amount that a nation owes its creditors

How does the national debt affect economic growth? While taxes are the most obvious way the government raises money, it also sells *bonds*—securities through which it promises to pay buyers certain amounts of money by specified future dates. The government sells bonds to individuals, households, banks, insurance companies, industrial corporations, nonprofit organizations, and government agencies, both at home and overseas. These bonds are attractive investments because they are extremely safe: The U.S. government is not going to *default* on them (that is, fail to make payments when due). Even so, they must also offer a decent return on the buyer's investment, and they do this by paying interest at a competitive rate. By selling bonds, therefore, the U.S. government competes with every other potential borrower—individuals, households, businesses, and other organizations—for the available supply of loanable money. The more money the government borrows, the less money is available for the private borrowing and investment that increase productivity.[20]

Economic Stability

We have thus far learned a great deal about economic systems and the ways in which they allocate resources among their citizens. We know that households, for example, receive capital in return for labor. We know that when households enter consumer markets to purchase goods and services, their decisions (and those of the firms trying to sell them goods and services) are influenced by the laws of demand and supply. We know that the laws of demand and supply result in equilibrium prices when the quantity of goods demanded and the quantity of goods supplied are equal. We know that households enjoy higher standards of living when there is balanced growth in the quantity of goods demanded and the quantity of goods supplied. We know that we can measure growth and productivity in terms of gross domestic product and standard of living in terms of the purchasing power parity of a system's currency: Living standards are stable when purchasing power parity remains stable.

We may thus conclude that a chief goal of an economic system is **stability**: a condition in which the amount of money available in an economic system and the quantity of goods and services produced in it are growing at about the same rate. Now we can focus on certain factors that threaten stability—namely, *inflation* and *unemployment*.

stability
Condition in which the balance between the money available in an economy and the goods produced in it are growing at about the same rate

inflation
Occurrence of widespread price increases throughout an economic system

Inflation **Inflation** is the occurrence of widespread price increases throughout an economic system. How does it threaten stability? Inflation occurs when the amount of money injected into an economy outstrips the increase in actual output. When this happens, people will have more money to spend, but there will still be the same quantity of products available for them to buy. As they compete with one another to buy available products, prices go up. Before long, high prices will erase the increase in the amount of money injected into the economy. Purchasing power, therefore, declines.

Obviously, then, inflation can also hurt you as a consumer because your primary concern when deciding whether to purchase a product is price. In other words, you will probably decide to make a purchase if the value of the product justifies the price that

Table 1.3
When Did the Cost of a Hamburger Go Up?

YR1 INCOME	YR2 INCOME	YR2 % INCREASE OVER YR1 BASE	YR3 INCOME	YR3 % INCREASE OVER YR1 BASE
$5,000	$10,000	100	$17,500	250
YR1 HAMBURGER PRICE	**YR2 HAMBURGER PRICE**	**YR2 % INCREASE OVER YR1 BASE**	**YR3 HAMBURGER PRICE**	**YR3 % INCREASE OVER YR1 BASE**
$2	$4	100	$7.50	275

you'll have to pay. Now look at Table 1.3, which reduces a hypothetical purchase decision to three bare essentials:

1. Your household income over a three-year period
2. The price of a hamburger over a three-year period
3. The rates of increase for both over a three-year period

In which year did the cost of a hamburger go up? At first glance, you might say in both YR2 and YR3 (to $4 and to $7.50). In YR2, your income kept pace: Although a hamburger cost twice as much, you had twice as much money to spend. In effect, the price to you was the same. In YR3, however, your income increased by 250 percent while the price of a hamburger increased by 275 percent. In YR3, therefore, you got hit by inflation (how hard, of course, depends on your fondness for hamburgers!). This ratio—the comparison of your increased income to the increased price of a hamburger—is all that counts if you want to consider inflation when you're making a buying decision. Inflation, therefore, can be harmful to you as a consumer because *inflation decreases the purchasing power of your money.*

Measuring Inflation: The CPI What is a good way to measure inflation? Remember our definition of inflation as the occurrence of widespread price increases throughout an economic system. It stands to reason, therefore, that we can measure inflation by measuring price increases. To do this, we can turn to such price indexes as the **consumer price index (CPI)**: a measure of the prices of typical products purchased by consumers living in urban areas.[21]

consumer price index (CPI)
Measure of the prices of typical products purchased by consumers living in urban areas

Here's how the CPI works. First we need a *base period*—an arbitrarily selected time period against which other time periods are compared. The CPI base period is 1982 to 1984, which has been given an average value of 100. Table 1.4 gives CPI values computed for selected years. The CPI value for 1951, for instance, is 26. This means that one-dollar's worth of typical purchases in 1982-1984 would have cost 26 cents in 1951. Conversely, you would have needed $1.63 to purchase the same one-dollar's worth of typical goods in 1998. The difference registers the effect of inflation. In fact, that's what an *inflation rate* is—*the percentage change in a price index.*

Thus, we can calculate the *CPI rate of inflation* by using the data in Table 1.4. To find the inflation rate between 1997 and 1998, you need to know the *change* from one year to the next. To find this change, simply subtract the value of 1997 from the value of 1998:

$$163.0 - 160.5 = 2.5$$

Now apply the following formula:

$$\text{Inflation rate} = \frac{\text{Change in price index}}{\text{Initial price index}} \times 100$$

or

$$\frac{2.5}{160.5} \times 100 = 1.6\%$$

YEAR	CPI
1951	26.0
1961	29.9
1971	40.6
1981	90.9
1989	124.0
1990	130.7
1991	136.2
1992	140.3
1993	144.5
1994	148.2
1995	152.4
1996	156.9
1997	160.5
1998	163.0

Table 1.4
Selected CPI Values

Unemployment Finally, we need to consider the effect of unemployment on economic stability. **Unemployment** is the level of joblessness among people actively seeking work in an economic system. When unemployment is low, there is a shortage of labor available for businesses to hire. As they compete with one another for the available supply of labor, businesses raise the wages that they are willing to pay. Then because higher labor costs eat into profit margins, they raise the prices of their products. Thus, although consumers have more money to inject into the economy, this increase is soon erased by higher prices. Purchasing power declines.

unemployment
Level of joblessness among people actively seeking work

There are at least two related problems. If wage rates get too high, businesses will respond by hiring fewer workers and unemployment will go up. Businesses could, of course, raise prices to counter increased labor costs, but if they charge higher prices, they won't be able to sell as much of their products. Because of reduced sales, they will cut back on hiring and, once again, unemployment will go up. What if the government tries to correct this situation by injecting more money into the economic system—say, by cutting taxes or spending more money? Prices in general may go up because of increased consumer demand. Again, purchasing power declines and, indeed, inflation may set in.

Recessions and Depressions Finally, unemployment is sometimes a symptom of a systemwide disorder in the economy. During a downturn in the business cycle, people in numerous different sectors may lose their jobs at the same time. As a result, overall income and spending may drop. Feeling the pinch of reduced revenues, businesses may cut spending on the factors of production—including labor. Yet more people will be put out of work and unemployment will only increase further. Unemployment that results from this vicious cycle is called *cyclical unemployment*.[22]

In examining the relationship between unemployment and economic stability, we are, thus, reminded that when prices get high enough, consumer demand for goods and services goes down. We are also reminded that when demand for products goes down, producers cut back on hiring and, not surprisingly, eventually start producing less. Consequently, of course, aggregate output decreases. When we go through a period during which aggregate output declines, we have a *recession*. During a recession, producers need fewer employees—less labor—to produce products. Unemployment, therefore, goes up.

How do we know whether or not we're in a recession? Clearly we must measure aggregate output. Recall that this is the function of real GDP, which we find by making necessary adjustments to the total value of all goods and services produced within a given period by a national economy through domestic factors of production. A **recession**, therefore, is more precisely defined as a period during which aggregate output, as measured by real GDP, declines. A prolonged and deep recession is a **depression**.[23]

recession
Period during which aggregate output, as measured by real GDP, declines

depression
Particularly severe and long-lasting recession

fiscal policies
Government economic policies that determine how the government collects and spends its revenues

"A warning light is flashing on the dashboard of the economy. We can't just drive on and hope for the best."

—President George W. Bush, 2001

monetary policies
Government economic policies that determine the size of a nation's money supply

stabilization policy
Government policy, embracing both fiscal and monetary policies, whose goal is to smooth out fluctuations in output and unemployment and to stabilize prices

Managing the U.S. Economy

The government also acts to manage the U.S. economic system through two sets of policies: fiscal policies and monetary policies. It manages the collection and spending of its revenues through **fiscal policies**. Tax increases, for instance, can function as fiscal policy, not only to increase revenues but to manage the economy as well. Thus, in January 2001, President George W. Bush proposed a tax cut of $1.6 trillion. Said the president: "A warning light is flashing on the dashboard of the economy. We just can't drive on and hope for the best."[24] Bush was referring to evidence that the economy was slowing—or, more accurately, that its growth rate was decreasing—and was arguing that his tax cut would stimulate renewed economic growth. The administration was calling for government action to bring stability to the economic system.

Monetary policies focus on controlling the size of the nation's money supply. Working primarily through the Federal Reserve System (the nation's central bank), the government can influence the ability and willingness of banks throughout the country to lend money. It can also influence the supply of money by prompting interest rates to go up or down.

In the year preceding President Bush's call for a tax cut, the Federal Reserve Bank (the Fed) had raised interest rates six times. Why? Because it saw signs of an economy threatened by both inflation (rising prices) and recession (a slowing growth rate).[25] The power of the Fed to makes changes in the supply of money is the centerpiece of the U.S. government's monetary policy. The principle is fairly simple:

- Higher interest rates make money more expensive to borrow and thereby reduce spending by those who produce goods and services; when the Fed restricts the money supply, we say that it is practicing a *tight monetary policy*.
- Lower interest rates make money less expensive to borrow and thereby increase spending by those who produce goods and services; when the Fed loosens the money supply—and, thus, stimulates the economy—we say that it is practicing an *easy monetary policy.* Thus, the Fed cut interest rates several times in late 2001 to help the economy recover from the terrorist attacks in the United States on September 11.

In short, the Fed can influence the aggregate market for products by influencing the supply of money. Taken together, fiscal policy and monetary policy make up **stabilization policy**: government economic policy whose goal is to smooth out fluctuations in output and unemployment and to stabilize prices.[26]

THE GLOBAL ECONOMY IN THE TWENTY-FIRST CENTURY

As we move into the twenty-first century, it is useful to end our discussion of the U.S. business system with a brief look back and a more detailed look ahead. The decade of the 1990s saw a sustained period of expansion and growth that increased business profits, boosted individual wealth, and fueled optimism that growth might continue indefinitely. During the latter part of 2000 and early in 2001, however, economic growth began to stall. Business profits began to taper off, many stock portfolios declined in value, and optimism waned. But experts themselves disagreed as to whether the slowdown was only temporary or represented a major shift in the U.S. economy whose effect might be felt for years.[27]

Three Major Forces

So what does the future hold? First of all, most experts see three major forces driving the economy for the next decade:

- The information revolution will continue to enhance productivity across all sectors of the economy, but most notably in such information-dependent industries as finance, media, and wholesale and retail trade.[28]

- New technological breakthroughs in such areas as biotechnology will create entirely new industries.
- Increasing globalization will create much larger markets while also fostering tougher competition among global businesses; as a result, companies will need to focus even more on innovation and cost cutting.[29]

Figures 1.5 through 1.7 clearly illustrate the significance of these forces. Figure 1.5 highlights the increased use of the Internet per 1,000 people for the entire world and for North America, Western Europe, and the Asia Pacific region for 1995 and 2000. As you can see, it also provides an estimate for 2005. The trends are clear and unambiguous: More and more people are using the Internet, and although the United States still leads the way, Western Europe is catching up and the Asia Pacific region is growing rapidly as well.

Figure 1.6 (page 24) amplifies these trends by isolating information-technology spending as a proportion of gross domestic product for numerous countries. Again, while the United States continues to lead the way, other countries are clearly catching up.[30]

Finally, Figure 1.7 (page 25) underscores the fact that world exports are again booming. Exports grew rapidly from the late 1980s through 1997 but then flattened and subsequently declined for two years. This downward trend was primarily attributable to the currency crisis and resultant economic downturn in Asia. Between 1999 and 2000, however, exports again began increasing and are projected to continue to rise at least through 2002.[31] Taken together, then, these data clearly reinforce the significance of information, technology, and globalization as the economic forces to be reckoned with in the twenty-first century.

Projected Trends and Patterns

As a result of these forces, economists also predict certain trends and patterns in economic indicators and competitive dynamics for at least the rest of this decade. Projected trends and patterns include the following:

- Although some experts now foresee a potential recession, most forecasters predict that the economy will remain relatively strong; however, almost all predict that it is not likely to grow at the same levels as in the 1990s.
- Inflationary surges and large budget deficits will likely be avoided.
- Countries that encourage free trade, innovation, and open financial systems will bounce back first and will prosper in the long term.
- The most successful businesses will be those that are able most effectively to master new technologies and keep abreast of their competitors.[32]

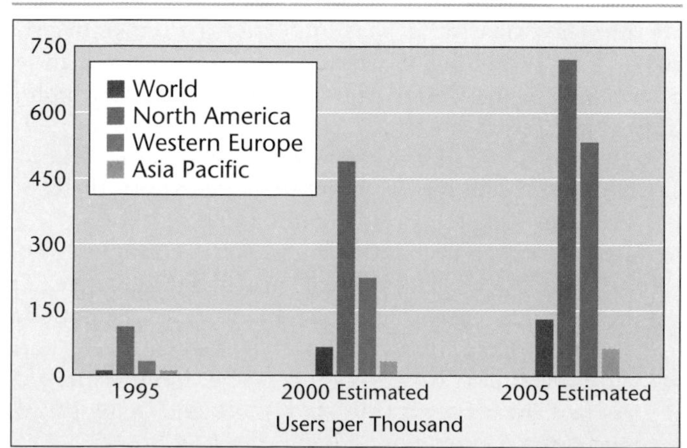

Figure 1.5
Internet Users per 1,000 People

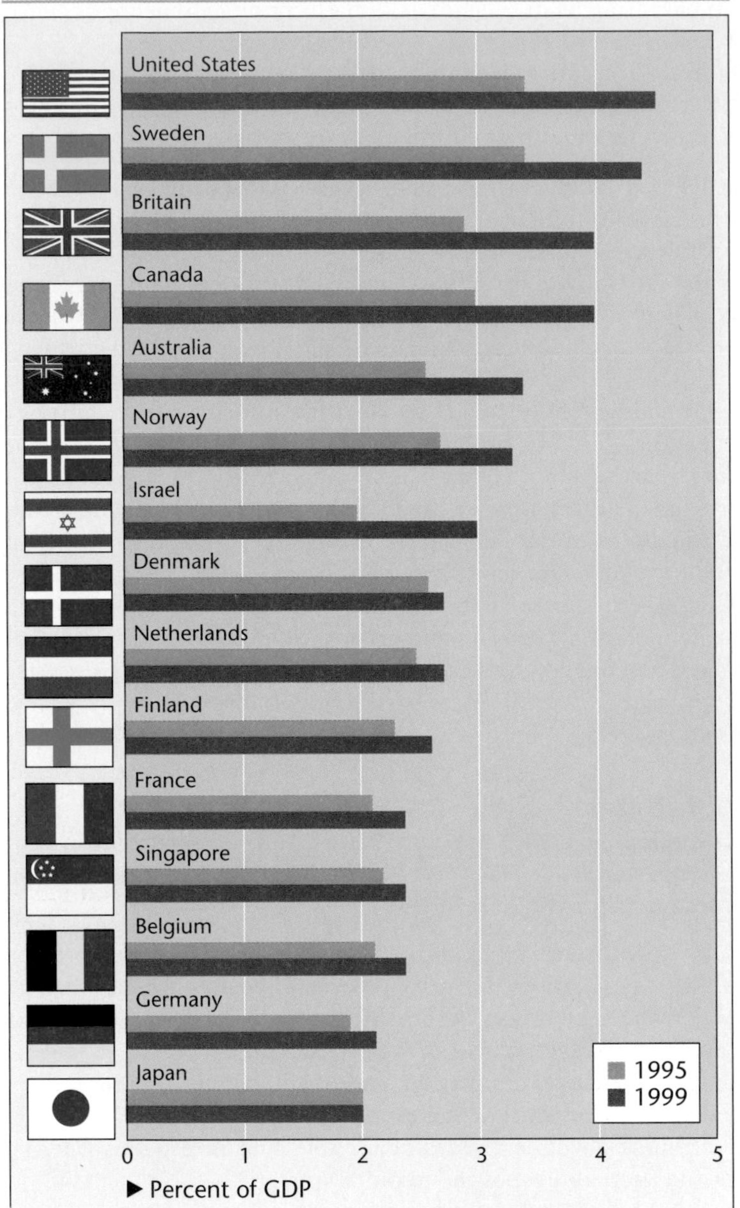

Figure 1.6
Information-Technology Spending

On the other hand, it is important to remember that the picture is not entirely rosy. The following statistics are sobering reminders that although domestic confidence in the United States is running at very high levels, some changes are still desirable:

- Because we import far more than we export, the U.S. trade deficit continues to grow, making the United States a debtor nation.
- Income inequality in the United States continues to be a problem. Although the medium household income is nearly $40,000 a year, the bottom fifth of U.S. households receives less than 4 percent of the national income. The top fifth, on the other hand, receives almost 50 percent of the national income.
- Consumer debt is steadily increasing. Nonbusiness bankruptcies increased over 60 percent between 1991 and 2000, and many people are not saving enough to ensure a comfortable retirement.
- About 44 million Americans lack health insurance.[33]

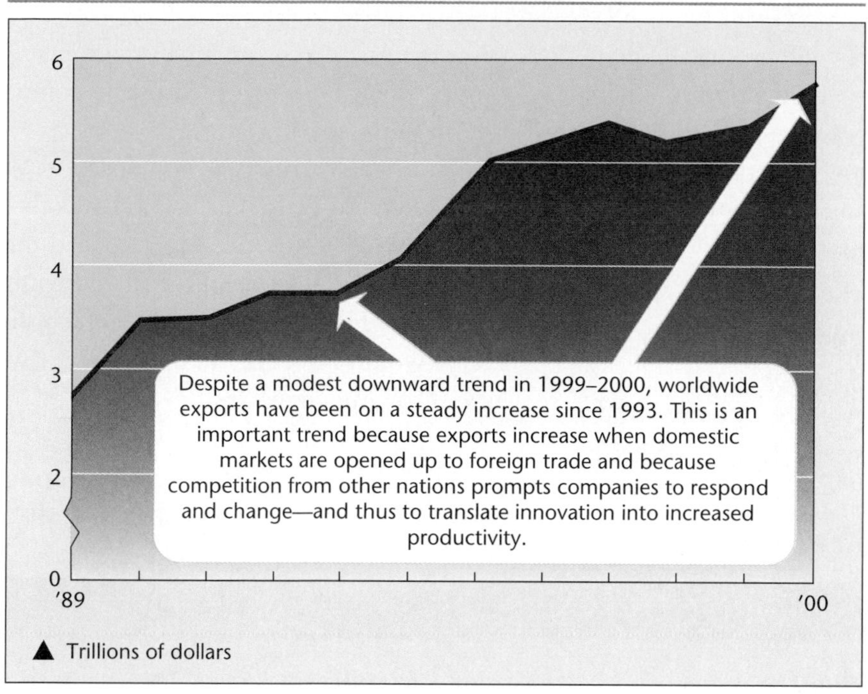

6
5
4
3
2
0
'89
'00
Trillions of dollars
Despite a modest downward trend in 1999–2000, worldwide exports have been on a steady increase since 1993. This is an important trend because exports increase when domestic markets are opened up to foreign trade and because competition from other nations prompts companies to respond and change—and thus to translate innovation into increased productivity.

Figure 1.7
The Export Resurgence

Still, all things considered, both the U.S. domestic economy and the global economy are in good shape in most respects. While leading indicators have stalled, the solid economic foundation built in the 1990s should serve as a platform for new growth and expansion in the near future. Businesses and entrepreneurs will continue to enjoy opportunities for growth and expansion for at least the next several years, and managers astute enough to navigate the competitive waters will probably arrive at greater prosperity.

But don't forget the old saying: If it were easy, everyone would do it. Thus, it's important for all managers—both current and future—to develop and maintain a comprehensive understanding of business so they can take more effective advantage of the opportunities and better address the challenges that they will face. This book will play a fundamental role in providing you with this understanding.

Continued from page 4

Sounding Out the Music Industry Oligopoly

The U.S. market for recorded music is an oligopoly controlled by five big firms:

- Universal/Polygram (24.5% market share)
- Warner Music (18.2% share)
- Sony Music (16.6% share)
- EMI Group PLC (12.9%)
- BMG Entertainment (12.2%)

As we noted at the outset of this chapter, there are also five major music-information sites on the Internet. What is less clear, however, is how the music business itself will change in response to the growth of the Internet.

One scenario calls for Web information sites to become a normal but separate part of the market—the recorded-music giants will continue to produce music and the information sites will simply be part of the marketing process. According to a different scenario, the big music companies will eventually disappear and be replaced by Internet sites that make it easier and cheaper to get music. A third scenario sees the big music companies moving into the information business, either by initiating their own operations or by buying existing companies.

Questions for Discussion

1. Why is the recorded music market currently an oligopoly?
2. Explain how recorded-music companies and Internet-information sites use the factors of production in different ways.
3. Discuss some ways in which pricing, demand, and supply affect both recorded-music companies and Internet-information sites.
4. Which of the three scenarios posed at the end of the vignette do you regard as most likely? Why?
5. Suppose each of the five big recorded-music companies were to buy one of the Internet-information businesses. Forecast the ways in which this turn of events would affect the industry. What would you expect to happen next?

SUMMARY OF LEARNING OBJECTIVES

1 Define the nature of U.S. *business* and identify its main goals. *Businesses* are organizations that produce or sell goods or services to make a profit. *Profits* are the difference between a business's revenues and expenses. The prospect of earning profits encourages individuals and organizations to open and to expand businesses. The benefits of business activities also extend to wages paid to workers and to taxes that support government functions.

2 Describe different types of global *economic systems* according to the means by which they control the *factors of production* through *input* and *output markets*. An *economic system* is a nation's system for allocating its resources among its citizens. Economic systems differ in terms of who owns or controls the five basic *factors of production*: labor, capital, entrepreneurs, physical resources, and information resources. In *planned economies*, the government controls all or most factors. In *market economies*, which are based on the principles of *capitalism*, individuals and businesses control the factors of production and exchange them through *input and output markets*. Most countries today have *mixed market economies* that are dominated by one of these systems but include elements of the other. The process of *privatization* is an important means by which many of the world's planned economies are moving toward mixed market systems.

3 Show how *demand* and *supply* affect resource distribution in the United States. The U.S. economy is strongly influenced by markets, demand, and supply. *Demand* is the willingness and ability of buyers to purchase a good or service. *Supply* is the willingness and ability of producers to offer goods or services for sale. Demand and supply work together to set a *market* or *equilibrium price*—the price at which the quantity of goods demanded and the quantity of goods supplied are equal.

4 Identify the elements of *private enterprise* and explain the various *degrees of competition* in the U.S. economic system. The U.S. economy is founded on the principles of *private enterprise: private property rights, freedom of choice, profits,* and *competition*. Degrees of competition vary because not all industries are equally competitive. Under conditions of *perfect competition*, numerous small firms compete in a market governed entirely by demand and supply. An *oligopoly* involves a handful of sellers only. A *monopoly* involves only one seller.

5 Explain the factors that allow us to better understand and evaluate the performance of an economic system. The basic goals of the U.S. economic system are *economic growth* and *economic stability*. Indicators of how well the economy is meeting these goals include aggregate output, standard of living, gross domestic product, and productivity. The basic threats to meeting goals of growth and stability include inflation and unemployment. The U.S. government uses *fiscal policies* to manage the effects of its spending and revenue collection and *monetary policies* to control the size of the nation's money supply.

6 Discuss the current economic picture in the United States and summarize expert opinions about its future. The United States is riding the crest of a long-term economic boom, although economic growth has substantially slowed in recent months. Unemployment and inflation remain low. Experts believe that these trends will continue for at least another few years. Important areas of the economy will include information technology, other forms of technological innovation, and globalization.

QUESTIONS AND EXERCISES

Questions for Review

1. What are the five factors of production? Is one factor more important than the others? If so, which one? Why?
2. What is GDP? Real GDP? What does each measure?
3. Explain the differences between the four degrees of competition and give an example of each. (Do not use the examples given in the text.)
4. Why is inflation both good and bad? How does the government try to control it?

Questions for Analysis

5. In recent years, many countries have moved from planned economies to market economies. Why do you think this has occurred? Can you envision a situation that would cause a resurgence of planned economies?
6. Identify a situation in which excess supply of a product led to decreased prices. Identify a situation in which a shortage led to increased prices. What eventually happened in each case? Why?
7. Explain how current economic indicators such as inflation and unemployment affect you personally. Explain how they will affect you as a manager.

Application Exercises

8. Choose a locally owned and operated business. Interview the owner to find out how the business uses the factors of production and identify its sources for acquiring them.
9. Visit a local shopping mall or shopping area. List each store that you see and determine what degree of competition it faces in the immediate environment. For example, if there is only one store in the mall that sells shoes, that store represents a monopoly. Note the businesses with direct competitors (two jewelry stores) and describe how they compete with one another.
10. Go to the library or log onto the Internet and research 10 different industries. Classify each according to degree of competition.

EXPLORING THE WEB

Knowing the Difference Between Right and Left

Yes, Virginia, there is a central planning support group. It even has a Web site. Review the Marxism Page at:

<www.anu.edu.au/polsci/marx/>

and then consider the following questions:

1. Note the use of the term *Marxism* throughout the contents of the home page. If you click to the Contemporary Marxist Material page, you'll note that the predominant term is *socialism*. What do you think accounts for this difference in usage or emphasis?
2. Read *The Communist Manifesto* and play devil's advocate: Select two of the criticisms that Karl Marx and Friederich Engels leveled at capitalism in 1848 and defend the position that they are at least as applicable now as the authors believed them to be 150 years ago.

Or visit the National Center for Policy Analysis at:

<www.ncpa.org/policy.html>

Scroll down to and click on the Privatization Issues page posted by the center, a lobbying organization that seeks to shift control of key economic resources from the public to the private sector. Although we tend to think of privatization as an issue facing former communist and socialist nations, you can explore this site to learn about different facets of the privatization issue here in the United States. Examine several sections of this site, and then consider the following questions:

1. What does the center mean by "Privatization Innovations"? Choose one of the examples given and summarize the center's argument for privatizing it.
2. Identify two "Privatization Deterrents" and explain the center's reasons for characterizing each as a barrier to privatization.
3. Identify five or six of the center's "Candidates for Privatization." Then choose one or two about which you disagree and explain why.

EXERCISING YOUR ETHICS

Prescribing a Dose of Competitive Medicine

THE PURPOSE OF THE ASSIGNMENT

Demand and supply are key elements of the U.S. economic system. So, too, is competition. This exercise will challenge you to better understand the ethical context of demand, supply, and competition.

THE SITUATION

Assume that you are a businessperson in a small community, where you own and manage one of two local pharmacies. The population and economic base are relatively stable. Each of the two local pharmacies controls about 50 percent of the market. Each is also reasonably profitable, generating solid if unspectacular revenues.

THE DILEMMA
You have just been approached by the owner of the other pharmacy. He has indicated an interest either in buying your pharmacy or in selling you his. He complains that neither of you can substantially increase your profits. If one pharmacy, he says, raises its prices, customers will simply start shopping at the other one. He tells you outright that if you sell out to him, he plans to raise his prices by 10 percent. He believes that the local market will have little choice but to support such an increase for two reasons: (1) The town is too small to attract any national competitors, such as Walgreen, and (2) local customers can't go elsewhere to shop because the nearest town with a pharmacy is over 40 miles away.

QUESTIONS FOR DISCUSSION
1. What are the roles of supply, demand, and competition in this scenario?
2. What are the underlying ethical issues?
3. What would you do if you were actually faced with this situation?

BUILDING YOUR BUSINESS SKILLS

Analyzing the Price of Doing E-Business

This exercise enhances the following SCANS workplace competencies: demonstrating basic skills, demonstrating thinking skills, exhibiting interpersonal skills, and working with information.

GOAL
To encourage students to understand how the competitive environment affects a product's price.

THE SITUATION
Assume that you own a local business that provides Internet access to individuals and businesses in your community. Yours is one of four such businesses in the local market. Each of the four firms charges the same price: $12 per month for unlimited dial-up service. Your business also provides users with e-mail service; two of your competitors also offer e-mail service. One of these same two, plus the fourth, also provides the individual user with a free, simple, personal Web page. One competitor just dropped its price to $10 per month, and the other two have announced their intentions to follow suit. Your break-even price is $7 per customer. You are concerned about getting into a price war that may destroy your business.

METHOD
Divide into groups of four or five people. The assignment of each group is to develop a general strategy for handling competitors' price changes. In your discussion, take the following factors into account:

1. How the demand for your product is affected by price changes
2. The number of competitors selling the same or a similar product
3. The methods you can use—other than price—to attract new customers and retain your current customers

ANALYSIS
Develop specific pricing strategies based on each of the following situations:

- Within a month after dropping the price to $10, one of your competitors raises the price back to $12.
- Two of your competitors drop their prices further—to $8 a month. As a result, your business falls off by 25 percent.
- One of your competitors that has provided customers with a free Web page has indicated that it will start charging an extra $2 a month for this optional service.
- Two of your competitors have announced they will charge individual users $8 a month but will charge a higher price (not yet announced) for businesses.
- All four providers (including you) are charging $8 a month. One goes out of business, and you know that another is in poor financial health.

FOLLOW-UP QUESTIONS
1. Discuss the role that various inducements other than price might play in affecting demand and supply in the market for Internet service.
2. Is it always in a company's best interest to feature the lowest prices?
3. Eventually, what form of competition is likely to characterize the market for Internet service?

CRAFTING YOUR BUSINESS PLAN

Making Scents of Competition

THE PURPOSE OF THE ASSIGNMENT
1. To acquaint you with the process of navigating the *Business PlanPro (BPP)* software package (Version 4.0).
2. To stimulate your thinking about how two chapter topics—forms of competition and factors of production—can be integrated as components in the *BPP* planning environment.

FOLLOW-UP ASSIGNMENT
After reading Chapter 1 in the textbook, open the BPP *software and look around for information about types of competition and factors of production as it applies to*

a sample firm: Flower Importer (Fantastic Florals, Inc.). Perform the following steps for this assignment:

1. Open the *BPP* program, examine the Welcome screen, and click on **Open a Sample Plan.** Examine the names of the sample companies that are listed on *BPP*.
2. From the **Open a Sample Business Plan** dialogue box, click on a sample company—Flower Importer (*Fantastic Florals, Inc.*); then click on **Open.**
3. The screen you are looking at—**Text: 1.0 Executive Summary**—contains various kinds of information about *Fantastic Florals, Inc.* Explore the information panels on the screen to see what an Executive Summary looks like in *BPP*.
4. Now go to the menu bar at the bottom of the screen and click on **Plan Outline.** Scroll down the outline to see the categories within the business plan. Then click on some of the lines that you think might contain information about two of the chapter topics—forms of competition and factors of production. For example, **3.2 Competitive Comparison,** may be one of the likely places to find information on forms of competition. As you explore, see how many of this company's factors of production (labor, capital, entrepreneurs, physical resources, information resources) you can find. Try to identify at least one example of each factor in *Fantastic Florals, Inc.*'s business plan.
5. After finishing with one sample company, you can get to any other company by going to the top of the screen and clicking on **File** (on the menu bar). Then beneath that, select **Open Sample Plan.** This will exit you from the current company file and take you to the **Open Sample Plan** dialogue box, where you can select another sample company.
6. When you are finished, you can close the program by going to the top of the screen and clicking on **File** (on the bar menu). Then beneath that, select **Exit.**

VIDEO EXERCISE

Factors to Consider: Lands' End

LEARNING OBJECTIVES

The purpose of this video exercise is to help you

1. Understand the concept of profit.
2. Understand the nature of supply and demand.
3. Identify factors of production.

BACKGROUND INFORMATION

Lands' End began in 1963 by selling sailing equipment by catalog. By the late 1970s, its focus had shifted to clothing. In 1980, the company established a toll-free phone service that operated 24 hours a day, and by 1984 the Lands' End catalog appeared monthly. Today, the publicly owned firm, which boasts sales of $1.3 billion (for fiscal 2000), is one of the largest apparel brands in the United States, with numerous specialty catalogs and a growing international reputation.

THE VIDEO

This segment introduces Lands' End, the well-known retail-clothing catalog company, and the internal and external business environments in which it operates. You will see how the company deals with supply and demand, what kind of competition it faces, and where it goes to satisfy its production needs. The video also shows the company's employees at work and explains how the firm has grown from its entrepreneurial origins.

QUESTIONS FOR DISCUSSION

1. How does Lands' End gauge demand for its products?
2. Where does Lands' End find labor resources?
3. Why would Lands' End's managers be concerned about making a profit?

FOLLOW-UP ASSIGNMENT

Consider a relatively small local business with which you are familiar—a favorite restaurant or independent bookstore. What do you think happens to the profits of this business? What would happen if the business suffered a loss in a given year?

FOR FURTHER EXPLORATION

Visit the Lands' End Web site <www.landsend.com> and locate the company's "Principles of Doing Business." Which of these relate to profit and loss? To demand and supply? To factors of production? What do you think is the purpose of publishing these principles on the company's Web site?

CHAPTER 2

Understanding the Global Context of Business

After reading this chapter, you should be able to:

1. Discuss the rise of international business, describe the major world marketplaces, and identify the United States' major trading partners.
2. Explain how different forms of *competitive advantage, import-export balances, exchange rates,* and *foreign competition* determine the ways in which countries and businesses respond to the international environment.
3. Discuss the factors involved in deciding to do business internationally and in selecting the appropriate *levels of international involvement* and *international organizational structure.*
4. Describe some of the ways in which *social, cultural, economic, legal,* and *political differences* among nations affect international business.

The New ETO (European Theater of Operations)

First they secured their domestic battlefields. Now they're moving into foreign territory ready to face stiff opposition from local forces. We're not talking about military conflicts. The battles we are referring to are the head-to-head confrontations awaiting U.S. Internet enterprises as they try to establish beachheads in new markets in other countries, especially Europe.

Companies such as Amazon.com, Yahoo! <www.yahoo.com>, eBay <www.ebay.com>, America Online <www.aol.com>, and E*Trade <www.etrade.com> have emerged as the key players among Internet enterprises. Although some of these firms have yet to earn a profit, each is well managed, financially solvent, and firmly entrenched in its chosen niche. As the economic shakeout in late 2000 and early 2001 eliminated weaker competitors, each was ready to extend its reach to foreign markets, starting with Europe.

At first, both emerging European Internet enterprises and industry observers thought that U.S. companies would have a tough go of it. They argued that locals had a better understanding of European consumers and local market conditions, which would put the U.S. companies at a significant disadvantage. U.S. companies, however, proved to be more globally savvy than many people had predicted. A stock market adjustment to tech stocks in early 2000 undermined the financing options of the European start-ups, giving the Americans just the opportunity they needed to move ahead.

Amazon.com has found it relatively easy to transport its entire operating system to European locations.

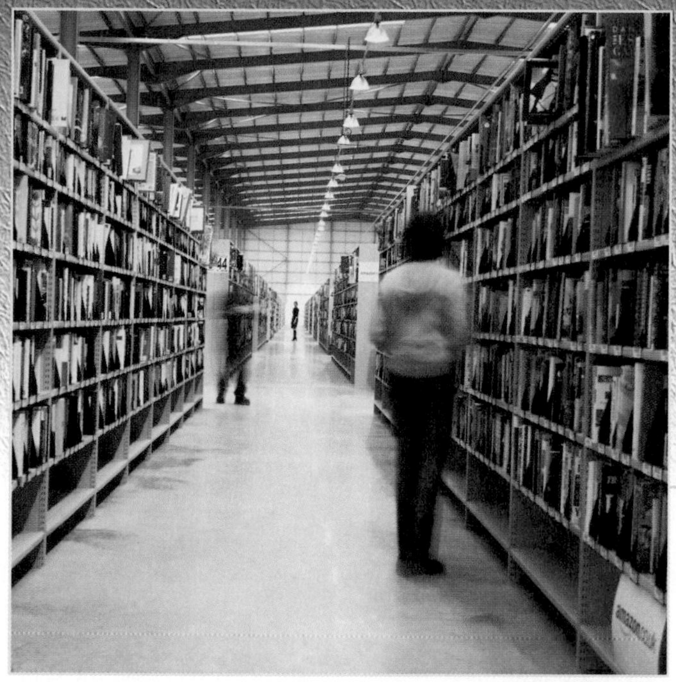

"We can adopt 80 percent of our American business model."

—Steve Frazier, director of Amazon.com's British operations

"We can adopt about 80 percent of our American business model," says the company's managing director in Britain. Although Amazon.com's British Web site features books and CDs by English writers and performers, the back office, distribution, and marketing functions are replicas of their U.S. counterparts. Amazon.com's European sales are five times larger than those of its nearest competitor, Bertelsmann's BOL Ltd <www.bol.de>.

Many other American companies are gaining in strength and market share. Yahoo! is Europe's leading Internet portal, with more than twice as many users as Deutsche Telekom's T-Online <www.t-online.de>, the leading European-based Internet service provider and portal. Internet auction giant eBay, Inc. is eight times larger than QXL <www.qxl.com>, its closest European rival. Americans are solidifying their European footholds. Although E*Trade originally entered the European market by franchising its early operations, it has since bought out its former partners and has also emerged as a major player in European financial markets.

Meanwhile, once prominent European Internet firms, including Boo.com, Freeserve <www.freeserve.com>, and last-minute.com, have gone under, put themselves up for sale, or been leap-frogged by U.S. rivals. In addition to financial problems facing would-be European competitors, American firms can point to a couple of key factors in their success. For one thing, they have taken a more systematic and focused approach to entering markets. Because more than 80 percent of European Internet commerce is located in Britain, Germany, and France, most U.S. companies have focused almost exclusively on these countries. This strategy has allowed them to concentrate their resources and generate strong market penetration where it matters most. In contrast, most European firms have tried to set up shop across the continent, spreading themselves too thin and rendering themselves vulnerable to domestic-market upheavals.

Our opening story continues on page 52

THE RISE OF INTERNATIONAL BUSINESS

The total volume of world trade today is immense—over $8 trillion in merchandise trade alone each year. Foreign investment in the United States and U.S. investment abroad have each passed the $1 trillion mark.[1] As more and more firms engage in international business, the world economy is fast becoming a vast and complex interdependent system—a process called **globalization**. Indeed, we often take for granted the diversity of goods and services available today as a result of international trade. Your television set, your shoes, and even your morning cup of coffee may be U.S. **imports**—products made or grown abroad and sold in the United States. At the same time, the success of many U.S. firms depends in large part on **exports**—products made or grown here and shipped for sale abroad.

globalization
Process by which the world economy is becoming a single interdependent system

import
Product made or grown abroad but sold domestically

export
Product made or grown domestically but shipped and sold abroad

The Contemporary Global Economy

International trade is becoming increasingly central to the fortunes of most nations of the world, as well as to their largest businesses. Whereas in the past many nations followed strict policies to protect domestic business, today more countries are aggressively encouraging international trade. They are continuing to open their borders to foreign business, offering incentives for their own domestic businesses to expand internationally, and making it easier for foreign firms to partner with local firms through various alliances. Similarly, as more and more industries and markets become global, firms that compete in them are also becoming global.

Several forces combined to spark and sustain globalization. For one thing, governments and businesses became more aware of the benefits of globalization to their countries and shareholders. Thus the **World Trade Organization (WTO)** <www.wto.org> came into being on January 1, 1995. The 140 member countries are required to open their markets to international trade, and the WTO is empowered to pursue three goals:

World Trade Organization (WTO)
Organization through which member nations negotiate trading agreements and resolve disputes about trade policies and practices

1. Promote trade by encouraging member nations to adopt fair trade policies and practices.
2. Reduce trade barriers by promoting multilateral negotiations among member nations.
3. Establish fair procedures for resolving disputes among member nations.

In addition, new technologies make international travel, communication, and commerce increasingly easier, faster, and cheaper than ever before. For example, a telephone call between New York and London once required operator assistance, took as long as half an hour to connect, and cost over $200 for a three-minute conversation. Now that same call can be direct-dialed and costs only a few dollars.

Likewise, transatlantic travel once required several days aboard a ship. Today, travelers can easily fly between most major cities in the United States and Europe in less than a day. Finally, there are competitive pressures: Sometimes, a firm simply must enter foreign markets to keep up with its competitors.

In this section, we examine some key factors that shaped—and are shaping—today's global business environment. First, we identify and describe the *major world marketplaces*. Then we discuss some important factors that determine the ways in which both nations and their businesses respond to the international environment: the roles of different forms of *competitive advantage, import-export balances*, and *exchange rates*.

The Major World Marketplaces

The contemporary world economy revolves around three major marketplaces: North America, Europe, and Asia. This is not to say that other regions are unimportant, nor is it to suggest that all countries in these three regions are equally important. However, these three geographic regions are home to most of the world's largest economies, biggest multinational corporations, most influential financial markets, and highest-income consumers.

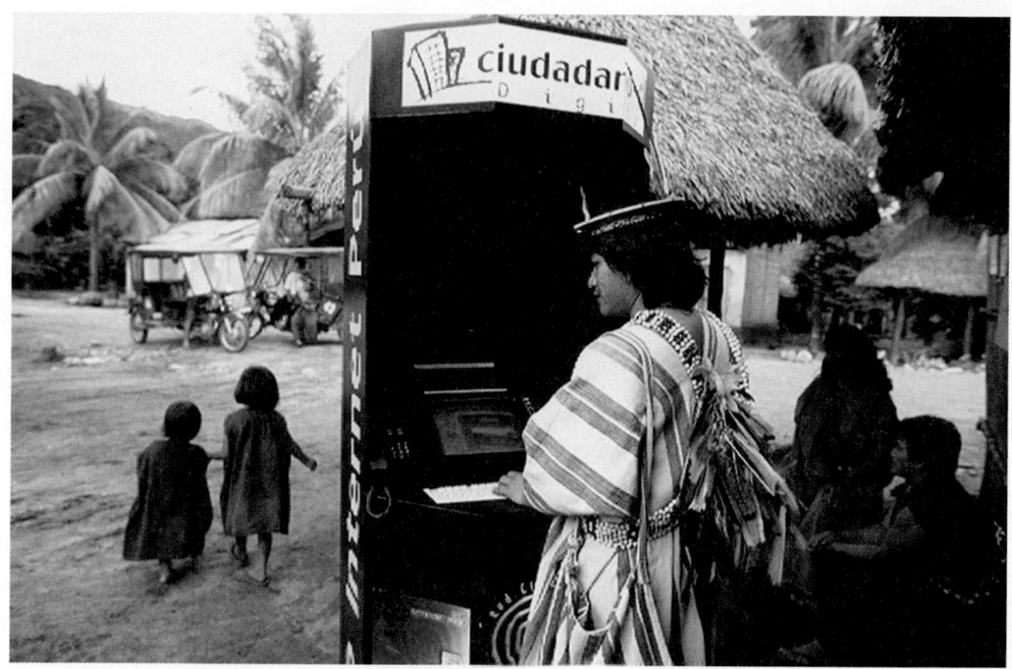

At booths run by Internet Perú <www.rcp.net.pe>, the nation's largest online service, native Ashaninkas line up to sell their traditional crafts over the Net. From fewer than 5 million users in 1998, Latin America will grow to 19 million by 2003. E-commerce sales should balloon from $167 million to $8 billion in the same period.

The World Bank, an agency of the United Nations <www.worldbank.org>, uses per capita income—the average income per person—as a measure to divide countries into one of three groups:[2]

- *High-income countries* are those with per capita income greater than $9,386. These include the United States, Canada, most of the countries in Europe, Australia, New Zealand, Japan, South Korea, Kuwait, the United Arab Emirates, Israel, Singapore, and Taiwan. Hong Kong, though technically no longer an independent nation, also falls into this category.
- *Middle-income countries* are those with per capita income of less than $9,386 but more than $765. Some of the countries in this group are the Czech Republic, Greece, Hungary, Poland, most of the countries comprising the former Soviet Bloc, Turkey, Mexico, Argentina, and Uruguay. Some of these nations, most notably Poland, Argentina, and Uruguay, are undergoing successful industrialization and economic development and are expected to move into the high-income category soon.
- *Low-income countries*, also called *developing countries*, are those with per capita income of less than $765. Some of these countries, such as China and India, have huge populations and are seen as potentially attractive markets for international business. Due to low literacy rates, weak infrastructures, unstable governments, and related problems, other countries in this group are less attractive to international business. For example, the East African nation of Somalia, plagued by drought, civil war, and starvation, plays virtually no role in the world economy.

North America The United States dominates the North American business region. It is the single largest marketplace and enjoys the most stable economy in the world. Canada also plays a major role in the international economy. Moreover, the United States and Canada are each other's largest trading partner. Many U.S. firms, such as General Motors <www.gmcanada.com> and Procter & Gamble <www.pg.com/canada>, have maintained successful Canadian operations for years, and many Canadian firms, such as Northern Telecom <www.nt.com> and Alcan Aluminum <www.alcan.com>, are also major international competitors.

Mexico has also become a major manufacturing center, especially along the U.S. border, where cheap labor and low transportation costs have encouraged many

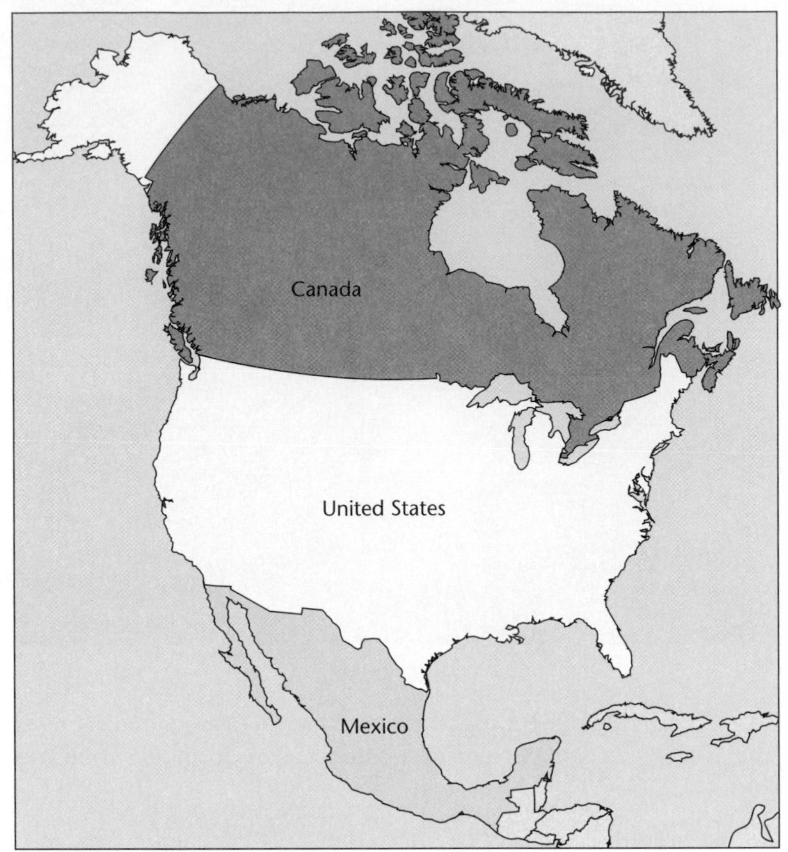

Figure 2.1
The North American Marketplace and the Nations of NAFTA

firms, from the United States and other countries, to build manufacturing plants. The auto industry has been especially active. For example, DaimlerChrysler <www.daimlerchrysler.com>, General Motors <www.gm.com>, Volkswagen <www.vw.com>, Nissan <www.nissandriven.com>, and Ford <www.ford.com> have large assembly plants in this region. Moreover, several of their major suppliers also built facilities in the area. From 1993 to 1999, exports of automobiles and automobile parts from Mexico increased from $7.2 billion to $20.4 billion, and the auto industry in Mexico now employs 380,000 workers. The automotive industry grew by 10 percent in 2001 and is expected to grow even more rapidly in 2002 and 2003.[3]

All three of these nations, shown in Figure 2.1, enjoyed the benefits of the North American Free Trade Agreement (NAFTA). According to this agreement, ratified in 1994, the three nations will systematically eliminate tariffs and other major trade barriers. NAFTA has also created several million new jobs in all three countries and substantially boosted mutual trade. Moreover, there is speculation that NAFTA will eventually expand to include other Latin American countries, with Chile seen as the most likely new member.

Europe Europe is often regarded as two regions—Western and Eastern Europe. Western Europe—dominated by Germany, the United Kingdom, France, and Italy—has long been a mature but fragmented marketplace. But the transformation of the European Union (EU) in 1992 into a unified marketplace increased the region's importance (see Figure 2.2). Major international firms such as Unilever <www.unilver.com>, Renault <www.renault.com>, Royal Dutch/Shell <www.shell.com>, Michelin <www.michelin.com>, Siemens <www.siemens.de>, and Nestlé <www.nestle.com> are all headquartered in Western Europe.

E-commerce and technology have also become increasingly important in this region.[4] There has been a surge in Internet start-ups in southeastern England, the Netherlands, and the Scandinavian countries, and Ireland is now the world's number-two exporter of

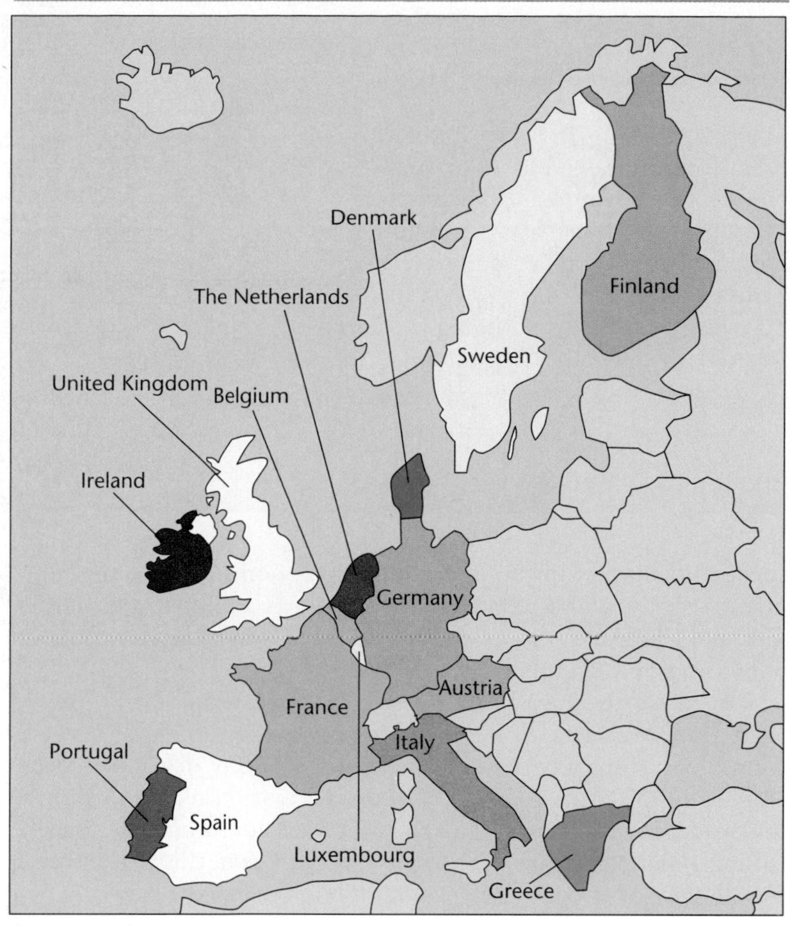

Figure 2.2
Europe and the Nations of the European Union

software (after the United States).[5] Strasbourg, France, is a major center for biotech start-ups. Barcelona, Spain, has many flourishing software and Internet companies, and the Frankfurt region of Germany is dotted with both software and biotech start-ups.[6]

Eastern Europe, which used to be primarily communist, has also gained in importance, both as a marketplace and as a producer. For example, such multinational corporations as Daewoo <www.daewoo.com>, Nestlé, General Motors, and ABB Asea Brown Boveri <www.abb.com> have set up operations in Poland. Similarly, Ford, General Motors, Suzuki <www.suzuki.com>, and Volkswagen have all built new factories in Hungary. On the other hand, governmental instability has hampered economic development in Russia, Bulgaria, Albania, Romania, and other countries in this region.

Pacific Asia Pacific Asia consists of Japan, China, Thailand, Malaysia, Singapore, Indonesia, South Korea, Taiwan, the Philippines, and Australia. Some experts still identify Hong Kong as a separate part of the region, although the former city-state is now actually part of China. Vietnam, too, is sometimes included in the region. Fueled by strong entries in the automobile, electronics, and banking industries, the economies of these countries grew rapidly in the 1970s and 1980s. Unfortunately, however, a currency crisis in the late 1990s slowed growth in virtually every country of the region.

The currency crisis aside, however, Pacific Asia is an important force in the world economy and a major source of competition for North American firms. Led by firms such as Toyota <www.toyota.com>, Toshiba <www.toshiba.com>, and Nippon Steel <www.nsc.co.jp/english>, Japan dominates the region. In addition, South Korea (with such firms as Samsung <www.samsung.com> and Hyundai <www.hyundai.com>), Taiwan (owner of Chinese Petroleum <www.cpc.com.tw/english> and manufacturing home of many foreign firms), and Hong Kong (a major financial center) are also

WEB Connection

Letsbuyit.com is an Internet retailer founded and headquartered in Sweden. It targets European customers with a retailing concept called "co-buying." To learn more about the idea of "the power of consumers joining in numbers"—and to find out more about the company's products and distribution process—visit its Web site.*

* You'll want the United Kingdom site if you're an English-speaking browser.

www.letsbuyit.com

successful players in the international economy. China, the most densely populated country in the world, continues to emerge as an important market in its own right. In fact, the Chinese economy is now the world's third-largest economy behind the United States and only slightly behind Japan.

As in North America and Western Europe, technology promises to play an increasingly important role in the future of this region. In Asia, however, the emergence of technology firms has been hampered by a poorly developed electronic infrastructure, slower adoption of computers and information technology, a higher percentage of lower-income consumers, and the aforementioned currency crisis. Thus, although the future looks promising, technology companies in this region are facing several obstacles as they work to keep pace with foreign competitors.[7]

Figure 2.3 is a map of the Association of Southeast Asian Nations (ASEAN) countries of Pacific Asia. ASEAN (pronounced *OZZIE-on*) was founded in 1967 as an organization for economic, political, social, and cultural cooperation. In 1995, Vietnam became the group's first communist member. Today, the ASEAN group has a population of over 400 million and a GNP of approximately $350 billion.

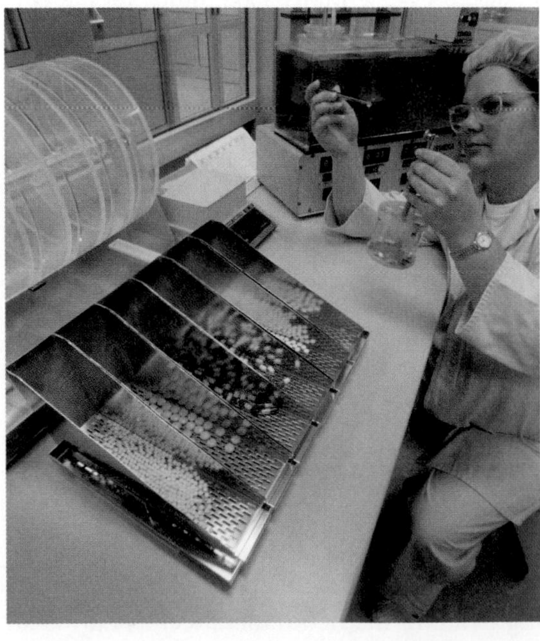

Egis is a Hungarian pharmaceutical company that has developed a number of new hypertension drugs. Because it hopes to sell these drugs in the United States and Europe, Hungarian membership in the European Union would be a plus for Egis, as well as for numerous start-ups and privatized companies in Eastern Europe.

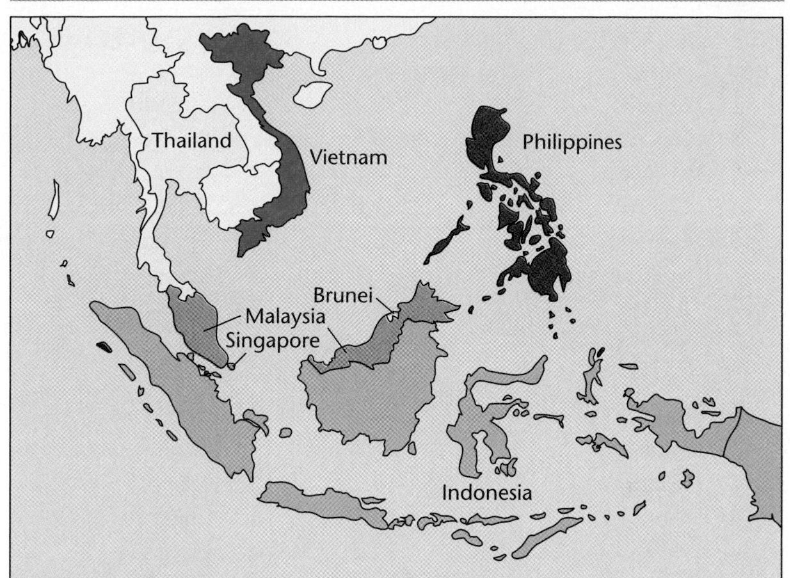

Figure 2.3
The Nations of ASEAN

Table 2.1 lists the major trading partners of the United States. As we noted earlier, these partners come from all over the world and include high-, middle-, and low-income countries. The left side of the table identifies the 25 countries from which the United States buys the most goods and services. China, for example, is our fourth-biggest supplier, Italy the tenth, and Brazil the sixteenth. The right side of the table identifies the 25 largest export markets for U.S. businesses. As you can see, the United Kingdom is our fourth-biggest export market, Singapore the tenth, and Italy the sixteenth. Note that many countries are on both lists (indeed, Canada is at the top of both), whereas others appear on only one list.

Forms of Competitive Advantage

Why are there such high levels of importing, exporting, and other forms of international business activity? Because no country can produce all the goods and services that its people need. Thus, countries tend to export products that they can produce better or less expensively than other countries, using the proceeds to import products that they cannot produce as effectively.

Of course, this principle does not fully explain why various nations export and import *what* they do. Such decisions hinge partly on the advantages a particular country may enjoy regarding its abilities to create and/or sell various products and resources.[8] Traditionally, economists focused on *absolute* and *comparative advantage* to explain international trade. But because this approach focuses narrowly on such factors as natural resources and labor costs, a perspective has emerged that focuses on a more complex view of *national competitive advantage.*

absolute advantage
The ability to produce something more efficiently than any other country can

Absolute Advantage An **absolute advantage** exists when a country can produce something cheaper and/or of higher quality than any other country. Saudi oil, Brazilian coffee beans, and Canadian timber approximate absolute advantage, but examples of true absolute advantage are rare. In reality, "absolute" advantages are always relative. For example, most experts say that the vineyards of France produce the finest wines in the world. But the burgeoning wine business in California attests to the fact that producers there can also produce very good wine—wines that are almost as good as French wines and that also come in more varieties and at lower prices.

comparative advantage
The ability to produce some products more efficiently than others

Comparative Advantage A country has a **comparative advantage** in goods that it can produce more efficiently or better than other goods. For example, if businesses

TOP 25 U.S. SUPPLIER COUNTRIES Rank/Country		1999 Imports ($ Bil.)	TOP 25 U.S. EXPORT MARKETS Rank/Country		1999 Imports ($ Bil.)
1	Canada	198.7	1	Canada	166.6
2	Japan	130.9	2	Mexico	86.9
3	Mexico	109.7	3	Japan	57.5
4	China	81.8	4	United Kingdom	38.4
5	Germany	55.2	5	Germany	26.8
6	United Kingdom	39.2	6	Korea	23.0
7	Taiwan	35.2	7	Netherlands	19.4
8	South Korea	31.2	8	Taiwan	19.1
9	France	25.7	9	France	18.9
10	Italy	22.4	10	Singapore	16.2
11	Malaysia	21.4	11	Belgium/Luxembourg	13.4
12	Singapore	18.2	12	Brazil	13.2
13	Thailand	14.3	13	China	13.1
14	Philippines	12.4	14	Hong Kong	12.7
15	Venezuela	11.3	15	Australia	11.8
16	Brazil	11.3	16	Italy	10.1
17	Ireland	11.0	17	Malaysia	9.1
18	Hong Kong	10.5	18	Switzerland	8.4
19	Israel	9.9	19	Saudi Arabia	7.9
20	Switzerland	9.5	20	Israel	7.7
21	Indonesia	9.5	21	Philippines	7.2
22	Belgium/Luxembourg	9.5	22	Ireland	6.4
23	India	9.1	23	Spain	6.1
24	Netherlands	8.5	24	Venezuela	5.4
25	Saudi Arabia	8.3	25	Thailand	5.0

Table 2.1
The Major Trading Partners of the United States

in a given country can make computers more efficiently than they can make automobiles, then that nation's firms have a comparative advantage in computer manufacturing. The United States has comparative advantages in the computer industry (because of technological sophistication) and in farming (because of fertile land and a temperate climate). South Korea has a comparative advantage in electronics manufacturing because of efficient operations and cheap labor. As a result, U.S. firms export computers and grain to South Korea and import VCRs and stereos from South Korea. The "Wired World" box in this chapter describes how comparative advantage played a key role in the historical development of Finland's Nokia Corp.

national competitive advantage
International competitive advantage stemming from a combination of factor conditions, demand conditions, related and supporting industries, and firm strategies, structures, and rivalries

National Competitive Advantage

In recent years, a theory of national competitive advantage has become a widely accepted model of why nations engage in international trade.[9] Basically, **national competitive advantage** derives from four conditions:

1. *Factor conditions* are the factors of production that we identified in Chapter 1.
2. *Demand conditions* reflect a large domestic consumer base that promotes strong demand for innovative products.
3. *Related and supporting industries* include strong local or regional suppliers and/or industrial customers.
4. *Strategies, structures, and rivalries* refer to firms and industries that stress cost reduction, product quality, higher productivity, and innovative new products.

IT'S A WIRED WORLD

Nokia Puts the Finishing Touches on a Telecommunications Giant

On the surface, one would assume that the major industrialized countries—the United States, Germany, and Japan—would be leading the way in information technology. But while this is generally true, a surprising upstart (Nokia Corp.) in a relatively remote part of the world (Finland) is at the forefront of today's emerging global communication network.

Ironically, conditions in Finland actually provide a unique catalyst for the Nokia success story. Many parts of the Finnish landscape are heavily forested, and vast regions of the country are sparsely populated. Creating, maintaining, and updating wired land-based communication networks is difficult and extremely expensive. But wireless digital systems are a relative bargain. As a result, conditions were perfect for an astute, forward-looking company like Nokia <www.nokiausa.com> to strike gold.

Nokia was formed in 1865 by Fredrik Idestam, a Finnish engineer. The company's early success is quite consistent with the theory of comparative advantage. Idestam's young company set up shop on the Nokia River in Finland to manufacture pulp and paper, using the area's lush forests as raw material. Nokia flourished in anonymity for about a century, focusing almost exclusively on its domestic market.

In the 1960s, however, management decided to expand regionally. In 1967, with the government's encouragement, Nokia took over two state-owned firms, Finnish Rubber Works and Finnish Cable Works. But it was in 1981 that a seminal event dramatically altered Nokia's destiny: Because it had done so well with the Rubber and Cable operations, the Finnish government offered to sell Nokia 51-percent ownership of the state-owned Finnish Telecommunications Co.

Because Nokia had already been developing competencies in digital technologies, the firm seized the opportunity and started pushing aggressively into a variety of telecommunications businesses. For example, Nokia created Europe's first digital telephone network in 1982. A series of other acquisitions and partnerships subsequently propelled Nokia into the number-one position in the global market for mobile telephones. Today, the firm commands a 27-percent market share in cellular telephones, comfortably ahead of second-place Motorola's 17 percent.

But Nokia hasn't been content to rest on its laurels. To the contrary, the company continues to expand into new and emerging markets. Foremost among these is technology for providing cellular phones with reliable and affordable Web content. Nokia was first out of the gate in this area and quickly established its own innovation, WAP (an acronym for *wireless application protocol*), as the likely standard that other firms will have little choice but to license for their own use. In 1999, for example, Nokia reached agreements with both Hewlett-Packard and IBM to install WAP software in their network servers. In 2000 it acquired secure-transaction software maker Network Alchemy.

Figure 2.4 shows why these four attributes are sometimes referred to as a national "diamond": The interaction of the elements of the diamond determines the environment in which a nation's firms compete.

When all of these attributes exist, a nation will be inclined to engage in international business. Japan, for instance, has an abundance of natural resources and strong domestic demand for automobiles. Its automobile producers have well-oiled supplier networks, and domestic firms have competed intensely with each other for decades. This set of circumstances explains why Japanese automobile companies like Toyota <www.toyota.com>, Honda <www.hondacorporate.com>, Nissan <www.nissandriven.com>, and Mazda <www.mazda.com> are generally successful in foreign markets.

Import-Export Balances

Although international trade involves many advantages, trading with other nations can pose problems if a country's imports and exports do not strike an acceptable balance. In deciding whether an overall balance exists, economists use two measures: *balance of trade* and *balance of payments*.

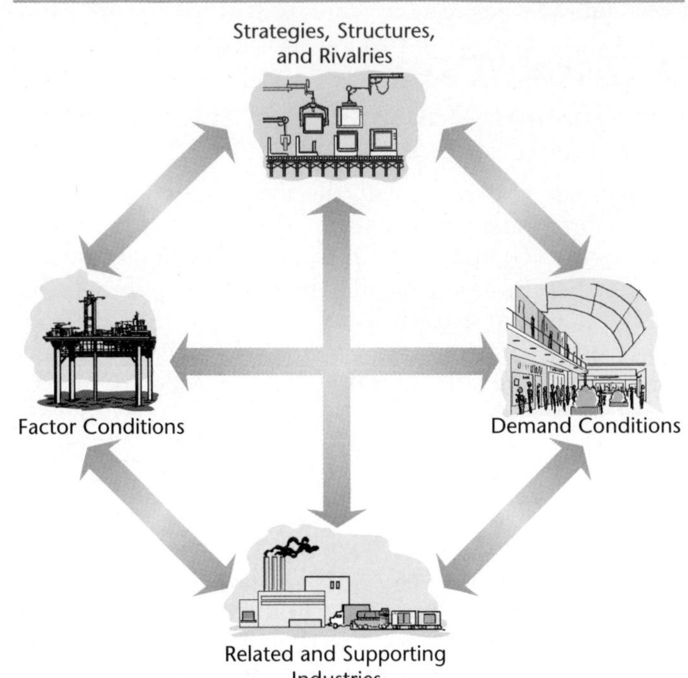

Figure 2.4
Attributes of National Advantage

balance of trade
Economic value of all products a country imports minus the economic value of all products it exports

Balance of Trade A nation's **balance of trade** is the total economic value of all products that it imports minus the total economic value of all products that it exports. Relatively small trade imbalances are common and are generally unimportant. Large imbalances, however, are another matter. In 1999, for example, the United States had a negative balance of *merchandise trade* of $347.1 billion and a positive balance of *service trade* of $79.6 billion. The result is an overall negative trade balance of $267.5 billion. This large negative balance continues to be a concern for U.S. business and political leaders.

trade deficit
Situation in which a country's imports exceed its exports, creating a negative balance of trade

trade surplus
Situation in which a country's exports exceed its imports, creating a positive balance of trade

Trade Deficits and Surpluses When a country's imports exceed its exports—that is, when it has a negative balance of trade—it suffers a **trade deficit.** In short, more money is flowing out of the country than flowing in. A positive balance of trade occurs when a country's exports exceed its imports and it enjoys a **trade surplus:** More money is flowing into the country than flowing out. Trade deficits and surpluses are influenced by an array of factors such as the absolute, comparative, or national competitive advantages enjoyed by the relevant trading partners, the general economic conditions prevailing in various countries, and the effect of trade agreements. For example, higher domestic costs, greater international competition, and continuing economic problems of some of its regional trading partners have slowed Japan's exports from the tremendous growth it enjoyed several years ago. But rising prosperity in both China and India has resulted in strong increases in both exports from and imports to those countries.

In general, the United States suffers from fairly large trade deficits with Japan ($73.4 billion), China ($68.7 billion), Germany ($28.4 billion), Canada ($32.1 billion), Mexico ($22.8 billion), and Taiwan ($16.1 billion). In any given year, the United States may also have smaller deficits with other countries. Our present trade deficit with Singapore is only $1.9 billion.

Conversely, the United States enjoys healthy trade surpluses with many countries. For example, the most current figures report a $10.9 billion trade surplus with the Netherlands, $6.5 billion with Australia, $3.8 billion with Belgium-Luxembourg, and $2.4 billion with Egypt. At the lower end of the spectrum, U.S. trade surpluses with Jordan and Haiti are $300 million each.[10]

Balance of Payments The **balance of payments** refers to the flow of money into or out of a country. The money that a nation pays for imports and receives for exports—its balance of trade—comprises much of its balance of payments. Other financial exchanges are also factors. For example, money spent by tourists, money spent on foreign-aid programs, and money spent and received in the buying and selling of currency on international money markets all affect the balance of payments.

balance of payments
Flow of all money into or out of a country

For many years, the United States enjoyed a positive balance of payments (more inflows than outflows). Recently, the balance has been negative. That trend, however, is gradually reversing itself, and many economists soon expect a positive balance of payments. Some U.S. industries have positive balances, whereas others have negative balances. U.S. firms such as Dow Chemical <www.dow.com> and Monsanto <www.pharmacia.com> are among the world leaders in chemical exports. The cigarette, truck, and industrial machinery industries also enjoy positive balances. Conversely, the metalworking-machinery, electrical-generation, airplane-parts, and auto industries suffer negative balances because the United States imports more than it exports.

Exchange Rates

The balance of imports and exports between two countries is affected by the rate of exchange between their currencies. An **exchange rate** is the rate at which the currency of one nation can be exchanged for that of another.[11] The actual exchange rate between U.S. dollars and French francs has recently been about 6.8 to 1. But let's simplify things by supposing an exchange rate between U.S. dollars and French francs is 5 to 1. This means that it costs 1 dollar to "buy" 5 francs; alternatively, it costs 5 francs to "buy" 1 dollar. This exchange rate means that 1 dollar or 5 francs have exactly the same purchasing power.

exchange rate
Rate at which the currency of one nation can be exchanged for the currency of another country

At the end of World War II, the major nations of the world agreed to establish fixed exchange rates. Under *fixed exchange rates*, the value of any country's currency relative to that of another country remains constant. Today, however, *floating exchange rates* are the norm, and the value of one country's currency relative to that of another varies with market conditions. For example, when many French citizens want to spend francs to buy U.S. dollars (or goods), the value of the dollar relative to the franc increases, or gets stronger; *demand* for the dollar is high. A currency is said to be strong when demand for it is high. It is also strong when there is high demand for the goods that are manufactured at the expense of that currency. Thus, the value of the dollar rises with the demand for U.S. goods. On a daily basis, exchange rates fluctuate by very small degrees. Significant variations usually occur over greater spans of time.

Fluctuation in exchange rates can have an important impact on the balance of trade. Suppose, for example, that you want to buy some French wines priced at 50 francs per bottle. At an exchange rate of 5 francs to the dollar, a bottle will cost you \$10 ($50 \div 5 = 10$). But what if the franc is weaker? At an exchange rate of 10 francs to the dollar, that same bottle of wine would cost you only \$5 ($50 \div 10 = 5$).

If the dollar were stronger in relation to the franc, the prices of all American-made products would rise in France and the prices of all French-made products would fall in the United States. As a result, the French would buy fewer American-made products, and Americans would be prompted to spend more on French-made products. The result could conceivably be a U.S. trade deficit with France.

Exchange Rates and Competition Companies conducting international operations must watch exchange-rate fluctuations closely because changes affect overseas demand for their products and can be a major factor in international competition. In general, when the value of a country's domestic currency rises—becomes stronger—companies based there find it harder to export products to foreign markets and easier for foreign companies to enter local markets. It also makes it more cost-efficient for domestic

Table 2.2
Canadian vs. U.S. Prices

Common Product	Niagara Falls, New York	Niagara Falls, Ontario
Saturday stay at Days Inn, with jacuzzi	$260	$165
Whopper with cheese at Burger King	$2.39	$2.18
	Seattle	**Vancouver, British Columbia**
Lauryn Hill CD	$17.99	$12.60
Nintendo 64 game system	$130	$119
Grande latte at Starbucks	$2.70	$2.29
Levi's 501 jeans at the Original Levi's Store	$50	$45

companies to move production operations to lower-cost sites in foreign countries. When the value of a country's currency declines—becomes weaker—just the opposite occurs. Thus, as the value of a country's currency falls, its balance of trade should improve because domestic companies should experience a boost in exports. There should also be a corresponding decrease in the incentives for foreign companies to ship products into the domestic market.

A good case in point is the recent decline of the Canadian dollar relative to the U.S. dollar. In the mid-1990s, the Canadian dollar was relatively strong compared to the U.S. dollar. As a result, Canadian consumers frequently shopped for bargains on U.S. soil. But a global currency crisis in 1997 brought with it longer-lasting effects in Canada than in the United States. For the last several years, the Canadian dollar has been somewhat weaker than the U.S. dollar. It is now cheaper, therefore, for U.S. consumers to do just what their Canadian counterparts used to do—drive across the border to shop. Table 2.2 illustrates the effects of this trend. For example, the same hamburger costing $2.39 in Niagara Falls, New York, sells for only $2.18 (in U.S. currency) just across the border in Ontario, Canada. Likewise, a cafe latte in Seattle costs $2.70 but only $2.29 (again, in U.S. currency) in Vancouver. As one Vancouver store owner puts it, "There has been an exact switch. Five years ago, we would go down to Seattle to get good deals. Now the Americans come here for shopping."[12]

> *"Five years ago, we would go down to Seattle to get good deals. Now the Americans come here."*
>
> —Store owner in Vancouver, Canada

The U.S. Economy and Foreign Trade Figures 2.5 and 2.6 highlight two series of events: (1) recent trends in U.S. exports and imports and (2) the trade deficit that has resulted. As Figure 2.5 shows, both imports into the United States from other countries and exports from the United States to other countries have increased steadily over the last 10 years—a trend that is projected to continue. In 1999, the United States exported $965,242 billion in goods and services.

In the same year, the United States imported $1,221,213 billion in goods and services. Because imports were greater than exports, the United States had a trade deficit of $255,971 billion (the difference between imports and exports). The trade deficits for the years between 1990 and 2000 are shown in Figure 2.6. The difference in exports and imports in this case is a *deficit* because more money flowed out of the country to pay for imports than flowed into the country from the sale of exports. Had exports been greater than imports, the difference would have been a *surplus*.

INTERNATIONAL BUSINESS MANAGEMENT

Wherever a firm is located, its success depends largely on how well it is managed. International business is so challenging because the basic management responsibilities—planning, organizing, directing, and controlling—are much more difficult to carry out when a business operates in several markets scattered around the globe.

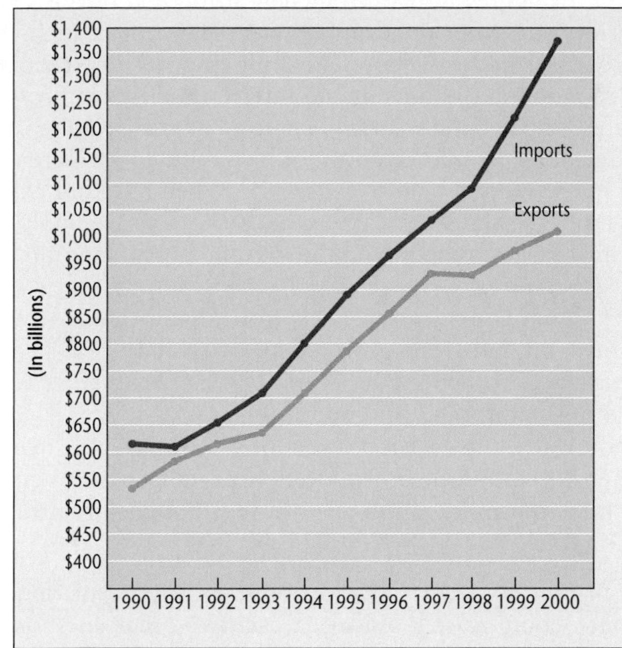

Figure 2.5
U.S. Imports and Exports

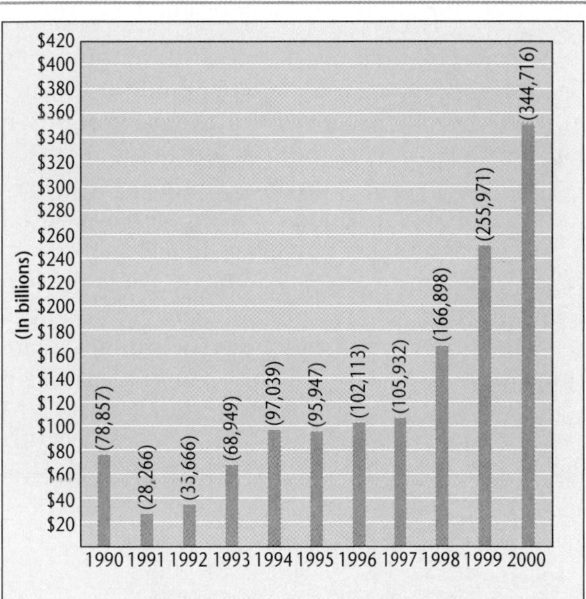

Figure 2.6
U.S. Trade Deficit

Managing means making decisions. In this section, we examine the three most basic decisions that a company's management must make when faced with the prospect of globalization. The first decision is whether to go international at all. Once that decision has been made, managers must decide on the company's level of international involvement and on the organizational structure that will best meet its global needs.

Going International

As the world economy becomes globalized, more and more firms are conducting international operations. Wal-Mart <www.walmart.com>, for example, was once the quintessential U.S. growth company; but as managers perceived both fewer opportunities for expansion inside the United States and stronger competition from domestic competitors, they decided that foreign expansion was the key to future growth.

By aggressively opening new stores and buying existing retail chains in other countries, Wal-Mart quadrupled its foreign sales to $14 billion between 1995 and 1999. Because this total represents only about 10 percent of the firm's total revenues, Wal-Mart managers have made international expansion and sales growth their primary goal for the future. Today the firm has stores in the United Kingdom, Mexico, Canada, Germany, Brazil, Argentina, China, and South Korea and has ambitious plans for continued international expansion.[13] When asked to explain why his firm set up shop in Germany, the Wal-Mart executive in charge simply noted that "Germany, being the third-largest economy in the world, is very important to us and one obviously that we can't ignore."

> *"Germany, being the third-largest economy in the world, is very important to us and one obviously that we can't ignore."*
>
> —Ron Tiarks, Wal-Mart executive in Germany

This route, however, is not appropriate for every company. Companies that buy and sell fresh produce and fish may find it more profitable to confine their activities to limited geographic areas: Storage and transport costs may be too high to make international operations worthwhile. As Figure 2.7 shows, several factors enter into the decision to go international. One overriding factor is the business climate in other nations. Even experienced firms have encountered cultural, legal, and economic roadblocks (these problems are discussed in more detail later in this chapter).

Gauging International Demand In considering international expansion, a company should also consider at least two other questions:

1. Is there a demand for this company's products abroad?
2. If so, must those products be adapted for international consumption?

Products that are successful in one country may be useless in another. Snowmobiles, for example, are popular for transportation and recreation in Canada and the northern United States and actually revolutionized reindeer herding in Lapland. However, there is no demand for snowmobiles in Central America. Although this is an extreme example, the point is basic to the decision to go international: Foreign demand for a company's product may be greater than, the same as, or weaker than domestic demand. Market research and/or the prior market entry of competitors may indicate whether there is an international demand for a firm's products.

One very large category of U.S. products that travels well is American popular culture. Many U.S. movies, for example, earn as much or more abroad than in their

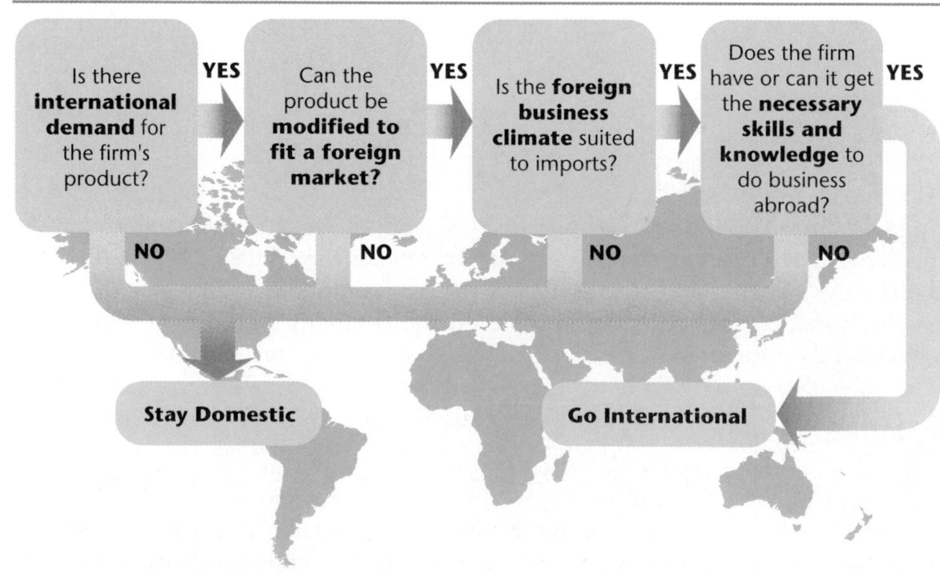

Figure 2.7
Going International

In Vietnam, the domestic film industry is short of funds and produces movies of such poor quality that audiences prefer American-made films. They don't even have to be recent. Four years after its initial release, a theater in the capital of Hanoi was showing the 1996 Tom Cruise hit Mission Impossible. Other imported films and TV shows come from South Korea, Japan, and China.

domestic release. While *Star Wars: Episode 1—The Phantom Menace* took in over $431 million in U.S. box office revenues, it garnered another $492 million at international box offices.[14] Billions of dollars are also involved in popular music, television shows, books, and even street fashions. Teenagers in Rome and Beirut sport American baseball caps as part of their popular street dress. Super Mario Brothers is advertised on billboards in Bangkok, Thailand, and Bart Simpson piñatas are sold at bazaars in Mexico City. Vintage Levi's from the 1950s and 1960s sell for as much as $3,000 in countries such as Finland and Australia.

Adapting to Customer Needs If there is international demand for its product, a firm must consider whether and how to adapt that product to meet the special demands and expectations of foreign customers. Movies, for example, have to be dubbed into foreign languages. Likewise, McDonald's restaurants sell wine in France, beer in Germany, and meatless sandwiches in India to accommodate local tastes and preferences. Ford products must have their steering wheels mounted on the right if they are to be sold in England and Japan. When Toyota launches upscale cars at home, it retains the Toyota nameplate; but those same cars are sold under the Lexus nameplate <www.lexus.com> in the United States because the firm has concluded that American consumers will not pay a premium price for a Toyota. Similarly, the firm even designed its new full-scale pick-up truck solely for the American market because Ford and General Motors sell so many big trucks in the United States; there is no domestic market in Japan for those same trucks.

Levels of Involvement

After a firm decides to go international, it must decide on the level of its international involvement. Several different levels of involvement are possible. At the most basic level, a firm may act as an *exporter* or *importer*, organize as an *international firm*, or operate as a *multinational firm*. Most of the world's largest industrial firms are multinationals.

Exporters and Importers An **exporter** is a firm that makes products in one country and then distributes and sells them in others. An **importer** buys products in foreign

exporter
Firm that distributes and sells products to one or more foreign countries

importer
Firm that buys products in foreign markets and then imports them for resale in its home country

"How can I sleep when people in other time zones are already up and making money?"

markets and then imports them for resale in its home country. Exporters and importers tend to conduct most of their business in their home nations. Both enterprises entail the lowest level of involvement in international operations and are excellent ways to learn the fine points of global business. Many large firms began international operations as exporters. IBM <www.ibm/planetwide/europe> and Coca-Cola <www.thecoca-cola-company.com/world>, among others, exported to Europe for several years before building manufacturing facilities there.

Exporting and importing have steadily increased over the last several decades. For example, exports from the United States totaled $344 billion in 1980, $708 billion in 1990, and exceeded $1.3 trillion in 2000. Conversely, imports into the United States have risen from $335 billion in 1980 to $1 trillion in 1990 to $1.4 trillion in 2000.[15] Although big business was responsible for much of this growth, many smaller firms have also become very successful exporters.[16] For example, San Antonio's Pace Foods <www.pacefoods.com>, a maker of Tex-Mex products, began actively exporting to Mexico after discovering that Mexican consumers enjoyed its picante sauce as much as U.S. consumers.

international firm
Firm that conducts a significant portion of its business in foreign countries

International Firms As firms gain experience and success as exporters and importers, they may move to the next level of involvement. An **international firm** conducts a significant portion of its business abroad. International firms also maintain manufacturing facilities overseas. Wal-Mart, for instance, is an international firm. Most of the retailer's stores are in the United States, but as we noted earlier, the company is rapidly expanding into various foreign markets.

Although an international firm may be large and influential in the global economy, it remains basically a domestic firm with international operations: Its central concern is its own domestic market. Wal-Mart, for example, still earns 90 percent of its revenues from U.S. sales. Product and manufacturing decisions typically reflect this concern. Burlington Industries <www.burlington.com>, Toys "R" Us <www.toysrus.com>, and BMW <www.bmw.com> are also international firms.

multinational firm
Firm that designs, produces, and markets products in many nations

Multinational Firms Most **multinational firms** do not ordinarily think of themselves as having domestic and international divisions. Instead, planning and decision making are geared to international markets. Headquarters locations are almost irrelevant. Exxon Mobil, Nestlé, IBM, and Ford are well-known multinationals.

The economic importance of multinationals cannot be underestimated. Consider the economic impact of the 500 largest multinational corporations. In 2000, these 500 firms generated $7.2 trillion in revenues and $444 billion in owner profits and

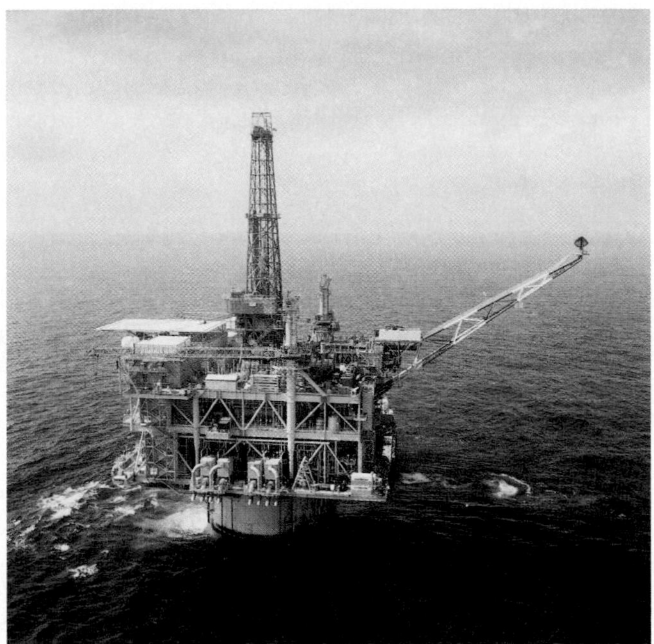

No global company enjoys greater profits than Exxon Mobil <www.exxon.mobil.com>. The multinational oil-and-gas business pumps 4.3 million barrels of oil from 27,000 wells located around the world. In one year, this platform in the Gulf of Mexico will produce at least $9 billion worth of oil. With operations in 200 countries, last year Exxon Mobil collected $210 billion in revenues, made $17.7 billion in profit, and got $47 billion bigger.

employed 24 million people. In addition, they bought supplies, materials, parts, equipment, and materials from literally thousands of other firms and paid billions of dollars in taxes. Moreover, their products affected the lives of hundreds of millions of consumers, competitors, investors, and even protestors.[17]

International Organizational Structures

Different levels of involvement in international business require different kinds of organizational structure. For example, a structure that would help coordinate an exporter's activities would be inadequate for the activities of a multinational firm. In this section, we consider the spectrum of international organizational strategies, including *independent agents, licensing arrangements, branch offices, strategic alliances*, and *foreign direct investment*.

Independent Agents An **independent agent** is a foreign individual or organization that agrees to represent an exporter's interests in foreign markets. Independent agents often act as sales representatives: They sell the exporter's products, collect payment, and make sure that customers are satisfied. Independent agents often represent several firms at once and usually do not specialize in a particular product or market. Levi Strauss <www.levi.com> uses agents to market clothing products in many small countries in Africa, Asia, and South America.

independent agent
Foreign individual or organization that agrees to represent an exporter's interests

Licensing Arrangements Companies seeking more substantial involvement in international business may opt for **licensing arrangements**. Firms give individuals or companies in a foreign country exclusive rights to manufacture or market their products in that market. In return, the exporter typically receives a fee plus ongoing payments called *royalties*. Royalties are usually calculated as a percentage of the license holder's sales.

licensing arrangement
Arrangement in which firms choose foreign individuals or organizations to manufacture or market their products in another country

Franchising is a special form of licensing that is also growing in popularity. McDonald's <www.macdonalds.com/corporate/franchise/outside> and Pizza Hut <www.pizzahut.com> franchise around the world. Similarly, Accor SA <www.accor.com/sf>, a French hotel chain, is franchising its Ibis, Sofitel, and Novotel hotels in the United States.

Branch Offices Instead of developing relationships with foreign companies or independent agents, a firm may send some of its own managers to overseas **branch offices**. A company has more direct control over branch managers than over agents or license holders. Branch offices also give a company a more visible public presence in foreign countries. Potential customers tend to feel more secure when a business has branch offices in their country.

branch office
Foreign office set up by an international or multinational firm

strategic alliance (or joint venture)
Arrangement in which a company finds a foreign partner to contribute approximately half of the resources needed to establish and operate a new business in the partner's country

Strategic Alliances In a **strategic alliance**, a company finds a partner in the country in which it would like to conduct business. Each party agrees to invest resources and capital into a new business or else to cooperate in some way for mutual benefit. This new business—the alliance—is then owned by the partners, who divide its profits. Such alliances are sometimes called *joint ventures*. The term *strategic alliance*, however, has arisen because of the increasingly important role that such partnerships play in the larger organizational strategies of many major companies.

The number of strategic alliances among major companies has increased significantly over the last decade and is likely to grow even more. In many countries, including Mexico, India, and China, laws make alliances virtually the only way to do international business within their borders. Mexico, for example, requires that all foreign firms investing there have local partners. Similarly, Disney's new theme park currently under construction near Hong Kong is a joint venture with local partners.

In addition to easing the way into new markets, alliances give firms greater control over their foreign activities than independent agents and licensing arrangements. At the same time, all partners in an alliance retain some say in its decisions. Perhaps most important, alliances allow firms to benefit from the knowledge and expertise of their foreign partners. Microsoft, for example, relies heavily on strategic alliances as it expands into new international markets. This approach has successfully enabled the firm to learn the intricacies of doing business in China and India, two of the hardest emerging markets to crack.

foreign direct investment (FDI)
Arrangement in which a firm buys or establishes tangible assets in another country

"There can be no doubt that foreign direct investment has joined international trade as a primary motor of globalization."

—Director-General Renato Ruggerio, World Trade Organization

Foreign Direct Investment The term **foreign direct investment (FDI)** means buying or establishing tangible assets in another country.[18] Dell Computer, for example, is building a new assembly plant in Europe. As we noted, Disney is building a new theme park in Hong Kong; Volkswagen is building a new factory in Brazil. Each of these activities represents foreign direct investment by a firm in another country. Likewise, Ford's purchase of Land Rover from BMW and Unilever's acquisition of both Ben & Jerry's and Slim-Fast also represent major examples of FDI.[19] FDI in the United States by foreign firms in 1999 totaled $294 billion. U.S. firms invested $980 billion in other countries.[20] "There can be no doubt," says the director-general of the World Trade Organization, "that foreign direct investment has joined international trade as a primary motor of globalization."[21]

BARRIERS TO INTERNATIONAL TRADE

Whether a business is truly multinational or sells to only a few foreign markets, several factors will affect its international operations. Its success in foreign markets is largely determined by the ways in which it responds to *social, economic*, and *political barriers* to international trade.

Social and Cultural Differences

Any firm planning to conduct business in another country must understand the social and cultural differences between the host country and the home country. Some differences, of course, are fairly obvious. Companies must, for example, take language factors into account when making adjustments in packaging, signs, and logos. Pepsi-Cola <www.pepsico.com> is exactly the same product whether it is sold in Seattle or Moscow—except for the lettering on the bottle. Less universal products, however, face a variety of conditions that require them to adjust their practices. In Thailand, for example, Kentucky Fried Chicken <www.kfc.com> has adjusted its menus, ingredients, and hours of operation to suit Thai culture. Similarly, when Bob's Big Boy <www.bobs.net> launched new restaurants in that same country, it had to add deep-fried shrimp to the menu.

A wide range of subtle value differences can also affect international operations. For example, many Europeans shop daily. To U.S. consumers accustomed to weekly supermarket trips, the European pattern may seem like a waste of time. For many Europeans, however, shopping not only involves buying food but is also an outlet for meeting friends and exchanging political views. Consider the implications of this cultural difference for U.S. firms selling food products in European markets. First, large American supermarkets are not the norm in many parts of Europe. Second, people who shop daily do not need large refrigerators and freezers.

Economic Differences

Although cultural differences are often subtle, economic differences can be fairly pronounced. In dealing with mixed economies like those of France and Sweden, firms must be aware of when, and to what extent, the government is involved in a given industry. The French government, for instance, is heavily involved in all aspects of airplane design and manufacturing. The impact of economic differences can be even greater in planned economies like China and Vietnam.[22]

Legal and Political Differences

Governments can affect international business activities in many ways. They can set conditions for doing business within their borders or even prohibit doing business altogether. They can control the flow of capital and use tax legislation to either discourage or encourage international activity in a given industry. In the extreme, they can even confiscate the property of foreign-owned companies. In this section, we discuss some of the more common legal and political issues in international business: *quotas, tariffs,* and *subsidies; local content laws*; and *business practice laws.*

Quotas, Tariffs, and Subsidies Even free market economies establish some system of quotas and/or tariffs. Both quotas and tariffs affect the prices and quantities

WEB Connection

When entrepreneur Ahmed Zayat bought the Egyptian national beer company in 1997, the quality of its flagship brand, Stella, was not very dependable. Moreover, drinking alcohol is considered a sin among Muslims. But Al Ahram has now introduced a line of nonalcoholic beers that it hopes to market throughout the Muslim world. To find out more about the company—and about business in the Middle East—contact the brewery's Web site.

www.alahrambeverages.com

of foreign-made products. A **quota** restricts the number of products of a certain type that can be imported into a country. By reducing supply, the quota raises the prices of those imports. For example, Belgian ice-cream makers can ship no more than 922,315 kilograms of ice cream to the United States each year. Similarly, Canada can ship no more than 14.7 billion board feet of softwood timber per year to the United States. Quotas are often determined by treaties. Moreover, better terms are often given to friendly trading partners, and quotas are typically adjusted to protect domestic producers.

quota
Restriction on the number of products of a certain type that can be imported into a country

embargo
Government order banning exportation and/or importation of a particular product or all products from a particular country

tariff
Tax levied on imported products

The ultimate form of quota is an **embargo**: a government order forbidding exportation and/or importation of a particular product—or even all the products—from a particular country. Many nations control bacteria and disease by banning certain agricultural products. The United States has embargoes against Cuba, Iraq, Libya, and Iran. Consequently, U.S. firms are forbidden from investing in these countries, and products from these countries cannot legally be sold on American markets.

A **tariff** is a tax on imported products. Tariffs directly affect prices by raising the price of imports. Consumers pay not only for the products but also for tariff fees. Tariffs take two forms. *Revenue tariffs* are imposed strictly to raise money for governments. Most tariffs, however, are *protectionist tariffs*, which are meant to discourage the import of particular products. For example, firms that import ironing-board covers into the United States pay a tariff of 7 percent of the price of the product. Firms that import women's athletic shoes pay a flat rate of 90 cents per pair plus 20 percent of the price of the shoes. Each of these figures is set through a complicated process designed to put foreign and domestic firms on reasonably even competitive ground.

subsidy
Government payment to help a domestic business compete with foreign firms

A **subsidy** is a government payment to help a domestic business compete with foreign firms. Subsidies are actually indirect tariffs: They lower prices of domestic goods rather than raise prices of foreign goods. Many European governments subsidize farmers to help them compete with U.S. grain imports.

Quotas and tariffs are imposed for a variety of reasons. The U.S. government aids domestic automakers by restricting the number of Japanese cars that can be imported into this country. National security concerns have prompted the United States to limit the extent to which certain forms of technology can be exported to other countries (for example, computer and nuclear technology to China). The recent relaxation of controls on the licensing of technology has contributed to the export boom that we described earlier in this chapter. The United States is not the only country that uses tariffs and quotas. Italy imposes high tariffs on imported electronic goods to protect domestic firms. A Sony Walkman costs almost $150 in Italy, and CD players are prohibitively expensive.

protectionism
Practice of protecting domestic business against foreign competition

The Protectionism Debate In the United States, **protectionism**—the practice of protecting domestic business at the expense of free market competition—has long been controversial. Supporters argue that tariffs and quotas protect domestic firms and jobs, therefore, sheltering new industries until they are able to compete internationally. They argue that the United States needs such measures to counter measures imposed by other nations. Other advocates justify protectionism in the name of national security. A nation, they argue, must be able to produce the goods needed for its survival in the event of war. Thus, the U.S. government requires the U.S. Air Force to buy all its planes from U.S. manufacturers.

Critics cite protectionism as a source of friction between nations. They also charge that it drives up prices by reducing competition. They maintain that although jobs in some industries would be lost as a result of free trade, jobs in other industries (for example, electronics and automobiles) would be created if all nations abandoned protectionist tactics.

Protectionism can sometimes take on almost comic proportions. Neither Europe nor the United States grows bananas; however, both European and U.S. firms buy and sell bananas in numerous foreign markets. A disagreement flared up when the European

Recently, the United States, responding to European insistence on importing bananas from its own former colonies (as opposed to those in which U.S. companies are heavily invested), imposed a 100-percent tariff on \$520 million worth of European exports, including Roquefort and foie gras. French farmers retaliated by attacking the domestic facilities of American multinationals.

Union (EU) imposed a quota on bananas imported from Latin America—a market dominated by two large U.S. firms, Chiquita <www.chiquita.com> and Dole <www.dole.com>—in order to help firms based in current and former European colonies in the Caribbean. To retaliate, the United States imposed a 100-percent tariff on certain luxury products imported from Europe, including Louis Vuitton handbags <www.vuitton.com>, Scottish cashmere sweaters, and Parma ham.[23]

Local Content Laws Many countries, including the United States, have **local content laws**—requirements that products sold in a particular country be at least partly made there. Typically, firms seeking to do business in a country must either invest there directly or take on a domestic partner. In this way, some of the profits from doing business in a foreign country stay there rather than flowing out to another nation. In some cases, the partnership arrangement is optional but wise. In Mexico, for instance, Radio Shack de Mexico is a joint venture owned by Tandy Corp. <www.radioshackunlimited.com> (49 percent) and Mexico's Grupo Gigante <www.gigante.com.mx> (51 percent). Both China and India currently require that a foreign firm wishing to establish a joint venture with a local firm must hold less than 50 percent ownership in the partnership, with the local partner having the controlling ownership stake.

local content law
Law requiring that products sold in a particular country be at least partly made there

Business Practice Laws Many businesses that enter new markets encounter a host of problems in complying with stringent and often changing regulations and other bureaucratic obstacles. Such practices fall under the heading of the host country's **business practice laws**. For example, as part of its entry strategy into Germany, Wal-Mart has had to buy existing retailers rather than open new ones. Why? Because the German government is not currently issuing new licenses to sell food products. Likewise, the firm had to discontinue its standard practice of promising to refund the price difference on any item sold for less elsewhere: In Germany, the practice is illegal. Finally, Wal-Mart must comply with local business-hour restrictions: Stores cannot open before 7 A.M., must close by 8 P.M. on weeknights and 4 P.M. on Saturday, and must remain closed on Sunday.

business practice law
Law or regulation governing business practices in given countries

cartel
Association of producers whose purpose is to control supply and prices

Sometimes, a legal—even an accepted—business practice in one country is illegal in another. In some South American countries, for example, it is sometimes legal to bribe business and government officials. The formation of **cartels**—associations of producers that control supply and prices—has given tremendous power to some nations, such as those belonging to the Organization of Petroleum Exporting Countries (OPEC). U.S. law forbids both bribery and cartels.

dumping
Practice of selling a product abroad for less than the cost of production

Finally, many (but not all) countries forbid **dumping**—selling a product abroad for less than the cost of production.[24] U.S. antidumping legislation is contained in the Trade Agreements Act of 1979. This statute sets tests for determining two conditions:

1. If products are being priced at "less than fair value."
2. If the result unfairly harms domestic industry.

In 1999, for example, the United States charged Japan and Brazil with illegally dumping steel at prices as much as 70 percent below normal value. The government then imposed a significant tariff on steel imported from those countries in order to protect local manufacturers.[25]

Continued from page 31

It's a Smallworld.com After All

As we saw in the opening segment of our story, the Internet represents a major but unpredictable venue for international business competition. Things can change virtually overnight. Many U.S. firms were given little chance of making significant headway in Europe, and now they are dominant players.

The Internet is making it easier than ever before to compete in foreign markets—as long as you know how. Smallworld.com is a New York firm specializing in online games. The company's most complex project to date was creating an engine to power online baseball games. Once this task had been accomplished, Smallworld set out to transfer its new technology to England, where it would create and market an online soccer game. In the early planning stages, however, the firm discovered that it had a deep talent pool of soccer-knowledgeable programmers in New York. Therefore, smallworld could proceed without any direct foreign investment.

Stories like this will be played out in many versions in the future. Although Asia is behind Europe in e-commerce, it will no doubt catch up very quickly. The same battles currently being fought in Europe will repeat themselves in Japan, China, Australia, India, and major markets throughout Southeast Asia. Firms in these nations already are building a base from which to hold off not only Americans but Europeans.

As the Japanese now compete quite successfully in many U.S. markets (such as automobiles) and dominate certain others (such as consumer electronics), e-commerce companies being launched in Asia today will be formidable competition, not only in their homelands but in Europe and the United States.

E-commerce firms from every corner of the globe will no doubt be waiting for just the right opportunities. As many European companies discovered, one misstep in the domestic market may allow firms from around the world to establish beachheads. Because so many of the traditional barriers to international expansion simply don't apply to e-commerce, no one can afford to get too comfortable.

Questions for Discussion

1. How might an e-businesses define the geographic boundaries of its markets differently from other firms?
2. How do the various forms of competitive advantage relate to e-businesses engaged in international commerce?
3. How do exchange rates affect e-commerce firms?
4. At what level of international involvement are such firms as Amazon.com, eBay, and Yahoo! currently operating?
5. What are some of the barriers to international trade that might be most relevant to e-commerce firms?

SUMMARY OF LEARNING OBJECTIVES

1 **Discuss the rise of international business, describe the major world marketplaces, and identify the United States' major trading partners.** More and more firms are engaged in international business. The term *globalization* refers to the process by which the world economy is fast becoming a single interdependent system. The three major marketplaces for international business are *North America* (the United States, Canada, and Mexico), *Western Europe* (which is dominated by Germany, the United Kingdom, France, and Italy), and the *Pacific Rim* (where the dominant country, Japan, is surrounded by such rapidly advancing nations as South Korea, Taiwan, Hong Kong, and China). The United States' major trading partners include Canada, Mexico, Japan, the United Kingdom, Taiwan, and Germany.

2 **Explain how different forms of *competitive advantage, import-export balances, exchange rates,* and *foreign competition* determine the ways in which countries and businesses respond to the international environment.** The different forms of competitive advantage are critical to international business. With an *absolute advantage*, a country engages in international trade because it can produce a product more efficiently than any other nation. *Comparative advantages* exist when they can produce some items more efficiently than they can produce other items. *National competitive advantage* stems from a combination of factor conditions, demand conditions, related and supporting industries, and firm strategies, structures, and rivalries. The *import-export balance*, including the *balance of trade* and the *balance of payments*, and *exchange rate differences* in national currencies affect the international economic environment and are important elements of international business.

3 **Discuss the factors involved in deciding to do business internationally and in selecting the appropriate *levels of international involvement* and *international organizational structure*.** In deciding whether to do business internationally, a firm must determine whether a market for its product exists abroad and, if so, whether it has the skills and knowledge to manage such a business. It must also assess the business climates of other nations to make sure that they are conducive to international operations.

A firm must also decide on its level of international involvement. It can choose to be an *exporter* or *importer*, to organize as an *international firm*, or to operate as a *multinational firm*. The choice will influence the organizational structure of its international operations, specifically, its use of *independent agents, licensing arrangements* (including *franchising*), *branch offices, strategic alliances*, and *direct investment*.

4 **Describe some of the ways in which *social, cultural, economic, legal,* and *political differences* among nations affect international business.** *Social* and *cultural differences* that can serve as barriers to trade include language, social values, and traditional buying patterns. Differences in economic systems may force businesses to establish close relationships with foreign governments before they are permitted to do business abroad. *Quotas, tariffs, subsidies*, and *local content laws* offer protection to local industries. Differences in *business practice laws* can make standard business practices in one nation illegal in another.

QUESTIONS AND EXERCISES

Questions for Review

1. How does the balance of trade differ from the balance of payments?
2. What are the three possible levels of involvement in international business? Give examples of each.
3. How does the economic system of a country affect the decisions of outside firms interested in doing business there?
4. What aspects of the culture in your state or region would be of particular interest to a foreign firm considering doing business there?

Questions for Analysis

5. Make a list of all the major items in your bedroom, including furnishings. Try to identify the country in which each item was made. Offer possible reasons why a given nation might have a comparative advantage in producing a given good.
6. Suppose that you are the manager of a small firm seeking to enter the international arena. What basic information would you need about the market that you are thinking of entering?
7. Do you support protectionist tariffs for the United States? If so, in what instances and for what reasons? If not, why not?
8. Do you think that a firm operating internationally is better advised to adopt a single standard of ethical conduct or to adapt to local conditions? Under what kinds of conditions might each approach be preferable?

Application Exercises

9. Interview the manager of a local firm that does at least some business internationally. Why did the

company decide to go international? Describe the level of the firm's international involvement and the organizational structure(s) it uses for international operations.

10. Select a product familiar to you. Using library reference works to gain some insight into the culture of India, identify the problems that might arise in trying to market this product to Indian consumers.

EXPLORING THE WEB

Tapping into the CIA

One of the best sources of information about foreign countries is the CIA's *World Factbook*. Visit its Web site and then consider the following questions.

<www.odci.gov/cia/publications/factbook/index.html>

1. Assume that you are a manager interested in learning more about the market potential for your firm's products in a certain foreign country. What information from this site might be most helpful?
2. How accurate and reliable would you expect this information to be? Why?
3. What additional information do you think you might need? How and where might you go to look for it?

EXERCISING YOUR ETHICS

Paying Heed to Foreign Practices

THE PURPOSE OF THE ASSIGNMENT

Managers conducting business in other countries must often contend with a wealth of differences in legal systems, customs, mores, and business practices. This exercise will help you better understand how these differences can affect the success of managers and companies trying to conduct business in foreign markets.

THE SITUATION

Assume you are an up-and-coming manager in a regional U.S. distribution company. Because of the nature of your industry, firms are only just now beginning to enter foreign markets. You have been assigned to head up your company's new operations in a certain Latin American country. Because at least two of your competitors are also trying to enter this same market, your boss has urged you to move as quickly as possible. You also sense that your success in this assignment will likely determine your future with the company.

You have just completed several meetings with local government officials and are quite pessimistic about your ability to get things moving quickly. You have learned, for example, that it will take 10 months to get a building permit for a facility that your firm wants to build. Moreover, after the building has been constructed, it will take another six months to get the utilities installed. Finally, the telephone company says that it may take up to two years to provide your facility with the telephone-line capabilities that you need for high-speed Internet access.

THE DILEMMA

Various officials, however, have indicated that time frames could be considerably shortened if you were willing to pay special "expediting" fees. You realize, of course, that these "fees" are nothing more than bribes, and you're well aware that the practice of paying such "fees" is both unethical and illegal in the United States. In this country, however, it's not illegal and not even considered unethical. Moreover, if you don't pay while one of your competitors does, you will be at a major competitive disadvantage. In any case, your boss is not likely to understand the long lead times necessary to get the operation running. Fortunately, you have access to a source of funds that would not be detectable to the home office.

QUESTIONS FOR DISCUSSION

1. What are the key ethical issues in this situation?
2. What do you think most managers would do in this situation?
3. What would you do?

BUILDING YOUR BUSINESS SKILLS

Putting Yourself in Your Place

This exercise enhances the following SCANS workplace competencies: demonstrating basic skills, demonstrating thinking skills, exhibiting interpersonal skills, and working with information.

GOAL

To encourage students to apply global business strategies to a small-business situation.

BACKGROUND

Some people might say that Yolanda Lang is a bit too confident. Others might say that she needs confidence—and more—to succeed in the business she's chosen. But one thing is certain: Lang is determined to grow INDE, her handbag design company, into a global enterprise. At only 28 years of age, she has time on her side—if she makes the right business moves now.

These days, Lang spends most of her time in Milan, Italy. Backed by $50,000 of her parents' personal savings, she is trying to compete with Gucci, Fendi, and other high-end handbag makers. Her target market is American women who are willing to spend $200 and more on a purse. Ironically, Lang was forced to set up shop in Italy because of the snobbishness of these same customers, who only buy high-end bags if they are European-made. "Strangely enough," she muses, "I need to be in Europe to sell America."

To succeed, she must first find ways to keep production costs down, which is a tough task for a woman working in a male-dominated business culture. Her fluent Italian is an important advantage, but she often turns down inappropriate dinner invitations. She also has to figure out how to get her 22-bag collection into stores worldwide. Although retailers are showing her bags in Italy and Japan, she's had little luck in the United States. "I intend to be a global company," says Lang. The question is how to succeed first as a small business.

METHOD

Step 1

Join together with three or four other students to discuss the steps that Lang has taken so far to break into the U.S. retail market. These steps include:

- Buying a mailing list of 5,000 shoppers from Neiman Marcus, a high-end department store, and selling directly to these customers.
- Linking with a manufacturer's representative to sell her line in major U.S. cities while she herself concentrates on Europe.

Step 2

Based on what you learned in this chapter, suggest other strategies that might help Lang grow her business. Working with group members, consider whether the following options would help or hurt Lang's business. Explain why a strategy would be likely to work or why it would be likely to fail.

- Lang could relocate to the United States and sell her goods abroad through an independent agent.
- Lang could relocate to the United States and set up a branch office in Italy.
- Lang could find a partner in Italy and form a strategic alliance that would allow her to build her business on both continents.

Step 3

Working alone, create a written marketing plan for INDE. What steps would you recommend Lang take to reach her goal of becoming a global company? Compare your written response with those of other group members.

FOLLOW-UP QUESTIONS

1. What are the most promising steps that Lang can take to grow her business? What are the least promising?
2. Lang thinks that her trouble breaking into the U.S. retail market stems from the fact that her company is unknown. How would this circumstance affect the strategies suggested in Steps 1 and 2?
3. When Lang deals with Italian manufacturers, she is a young, attractive woman in a man's world. Often, she must convince men that her purpose is business and nothing else. How should Lang handle personal invitations that get in the way of business? How can she say no while still maintaining business relationships? Why is it often difficult for American women to do business in male-dominated cultures?
4. The American consulate has given Lang little business help because her products are made in Italy. Do you think the consulate's treatment of an American businessperson is fair or unfair? Explain your answer.
5. Do you think Lang's relocation to Italy will pay off? Why or why not?
6. With Lang's goals of creating a global company, can INDE continue to be a one-person operation?

CRAFTING YOUR BUSINESS PLAN

Considering the World

THE PURPOSE OF THE ASSIGNMENT

1. To familiarize students with issues faced by a firm that has decided to go global.
2. To determine where, in the framework of the *BPP* business plan, global issues might appropriately be presented.

FOLLOW-UP ASSIGNMENT

After reading Chapter 2 in the textbook, open the BPP *software and examine the information dealing with the types of global business considerations that would be of concern to the sample firm of* Acme Consulting. *Then respond to the following items:*

1. What products does Acme plan to offer and in which international markets will they be competing?

[Sites to see in *BPP* (for this assignment): In the Plan Outline screen, click on **1.0 Executive Summary;** then click on **1.2 Mission** and then **4.0 Market Analysis Summary** and **4.1 Market Segmentation.** Next, while still in the Plan Outline screen, click on **2.0 Company Summary.** Finally, in the Plan Outline screen, click on **5.2 Strategic Alliances.**]

2. In Acme's business plan, see if you can find any discussion of the international organizational structures used by Acme's competitors. Do you think this information is adequate or inadequate? [Sites to see in *BPP* for this item: In the Plan Outline screen, click on **4.3.2 Distribution Service** and **4.3.4 Main Competitors.**]
3. What is the planned organization structure for Acme's international activities? Would you categorize Acme's relationship to its Paris partner as that of a branch office or that of a strategic alliance? [Sites to see in *BPP* for this item: In the Plan Outline screen, click on **6.1 Organization Structure** and then on **6.2 Management Team.**]
4. Chapter 2 states that going international requires "necessary skills and knowledge." Does Acme's business plan indicate that the company possesses the skills and knowledge to succeed internationally? [Sites to see in *BPP* for this item: In the Plan Outline screen, click on **6.0 Management Summary** and then on **6.2 Management Team.** Next, in the Plan Outline screen, click on **3.1 Service Description** and then click on **3.2 Competitive Comparison.**]

VIDEO EXERCISE

Entering the Global Marketplace: Lands' End and Yahoo!

LEARNING OBJECTIVES

The purpose of this video exercise is to help you

1. Understand the different reasons businesses undertake international expansion.
2. Identify the financial and marketing issues involved in selling products and services internationally.
3. Recognize the influence of culture on business decisions made by international firms.

BACKGROUND INFORMATION

- Yahoo! <www.yahoo.com> is an Internet search engine headquartered in Santa Clara, California. Its principal product is an ad-supported Internet directory that links users to millions of Web pages on demand. Yahoo! leads the field in volume of traffic (over 95 million pages viewed each day) and now has offices in Europe, Asia, and Canada, as well as a global network of 22 world properties.
- Lands' End <www.landsend.com> began in 1963 by selling sailing equipment through a catalog. Today the publicly owned firm is one of the largest apparel brands in the United States, with a regular monthly catalog, numerous specialty catalogs, and a growing international reputation. In 1991, Lands' End sent catalogs to customers in the United Kingdom for the first time, and in 1993, it opened a warehouse and phone center there. In the following year, Lands' End started operations in Japan, and in 1995, it launched its interactive retail Web site. Lands' End opened a phone center in Germany in 1996.

THE VIDEO

This video segment shows how two very different companies have approached the same goal—expansion into international business. You will see how each copes with cultural, financial, monetary, and marketing differences as well as differences in language and methods of payment. See whether you can identify the areas in which each firm chose to adapt to the needs and expectations of the international marketplace. Distinguish these areas from the areas in which each company maintained its original product or policy.

QUESTIONS FOR DISCUSSION

1. Compare the different reasons why Lands' End and Yahoo! decided to expand internationally.
2. How did Lands' End succeed in establishing itself in the United Kingdom and Japan?
3. How did Yahoo! succeed in France and China?
4. What international issues have provided the greatest challenges for each company?

FOLLOW-UP ASSIGNMENT

Obtain a mail-order catalog from any major U.S. clothing company and assess its product offerings and customer policies. Which of these, if any, do you think would need to be altered if the company wanted to sell overseas? How can the company customize these aspects of its business? Do you think it is likely that this company would be successful in international business? Why or why not?

FOR FURTHER EXPLORATION

Visit Yahoo!'s Web site <www.yahoo.com>. Explore some of the features and functions that appeal to you. Then, select one of the international sites listed at the bottom of the home page and compare it to the U.S. site. Identify the changes that have been made to suit the target country's language and customs. What elements of the site have not been changed? What do you think motivated the design and content choices that Yahoo! made in the overseas site?

CHAPTER 3

Conducting Business Ethically and Responsibly

After reading this chapter, you should be able to:

1. Explain how individuals develop their personal *codes of ethics* and why ethics are important in the workplace.
2. Distinguish *social responsibility* from *ethics*, identify *organizational stakeholders*, and trace the evolution of social responsibility in U.S. business.
3. Show how the concept of social responsibility applies both to environmental issues and to a firm's relationships with customers, employees, and investors.
4. Identify four general *approaches to social responsibility* and describe the four steps that a firm must take to implement a *social responsibility program.*
5. Explain how issues of social responsibility and ethics affect small business.

A Tale of Two Companies

As Charles Dickens once said, "It was the best of times, it was the worst of times." From an environmental perspective, the same might be said of the social performance of different companies. Businesses exist for one fundamental purpose—to earn profits for their owners. However, the manner in which they work to fulfill this purpose—and the lengths to which they are willing to go to earn even greater profits—can vary dramatically. Consider the quite different cases of Patagonia, Inc., a small privately held outdoor-apparel business, and IBP, Inc., a publicly held corporation and the world's largest processor of fresh beef.

Patagonia <www.patagonia.com> was founded in 1973 by a group of surfers in Ventura, California, led by Yvon Chouinard. Chouinard still runs the business today. The founders enjoyed spending part of their time hiking and mountain climbing, but they felt that the equipment available for such activities was often of poor quality, overpriced, or both. Their objective, then, was to become a provider of high-quality, reasonably priced outdoor equipment. They expressed this objective in the form of an unusual goal—to do the right thing. "Business[people] who focus on profits," says Chouinard, "wind up in the hole. For me, profit is what happens when you do everything else right."

At first, "doing the right thing" meant making the most useful, durable, and environmentally friendly products possible. For instance, mountain climbers had for years embedded steel chocks into rocks for

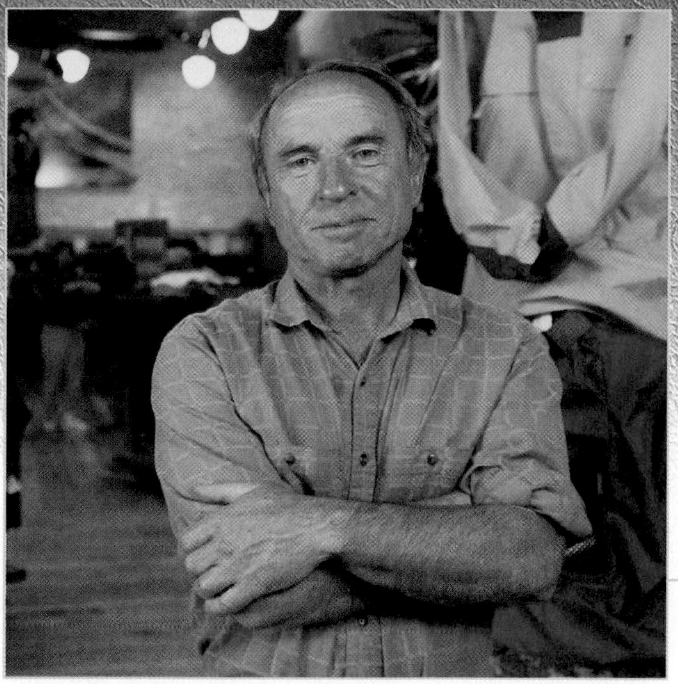

> *"Businesspeople who focus on profits wind up in the hole. For me, profit is what happens when you do everything else right."*
>
> —Yvon Chouinard, founder and CEO of Patagonia, Inc.

attaching ropes and creating hand- and footholds. But Patagonia began selling aluminum chocks because they were less damaging to the natural rock face. Once the firm started making outdoor adult clothing, it quickly added a line of children's clothing as well—not because there was a known market for such products but because they wanted to find a use for the scraps of leftover fabric. Patagonia also markets one line of shirts made of fibers from recycled plastic bottles and another line of shirts made from hemp, which is easy to grow organically.

As the firm grew, its environmental concerns also became more tangible. In 1996, Patagonia decided to use only organic cotton—cotton that satisfies two criteria: (1) It is grown without fertilizers and (2) it is grown without chemical insecticides. This decision created a problem, however, because most cotton grown and sold in the United States fails to meet one or the other of the two requirements for being organic. Thus, Patagonia started dealing directly with farmers, instructing them as to what the company wanted to buy and guaranteeing them competitive prices to reduce their risk. In a few cases, Patagonia even had to co-sign loans so that some farmers could buy new equipment and technology to meet the company's stringent requirements.

Perhaps Patagonia's boldest step took place when Chouinard mandated that 1 percent of Patagonia's revenues would be given to environmental groups each year. (Because the firm is private, its financial records are not disclosed. Estimates suggest that the firm generates about $180 million in revenues each year.) Chouinard himself is actively involved in efforts aimed at removing dams from rivers and returning the rivers to their natural state.

Needless to say, not every company has such a strong social orientation. Iowa Beef Packers <www.ibpinc.com> was founded by A. D. Anderson and Currier Holman. They felt that the meat-processing industry needed modernization and new technology and saw a significant business opportunity. Anderson and Holman began setting up meat-processing plants in rural areas, starting with Denison, Iowa, in 1960. They chose rural locations in part to be closer to cattle raisers and in part because they thought rural workers would be unlikely to unionize. The firm was eventually renamed IBP, Inc. and grew to include plants in small towns in Iowa, Texas, Idaho, Washington, Kansas, and

Illinois. It also established a pork-processing plant in China and sales offices in Canada, Japan, Korea, Mexico, Russia, Taiwan, and the United Kingdom, in addition to those in the United States. In 1999, it reported profits of $313 million from revenues of $14.1 billion.

The company grew rapidly by using highly automated and efficient plants and kept costs low by paying low wages and providing few worker benefits. But low wages and difficult working conditions led to sour labor relations, and workers did in fact unionize. In 1965, the workers struck IBP over low wages. Another major strike occurred in 1969, this one accompanied by vandalism, death threats, and 56 bombings.

Aside from its labor problems, IBP also has had difficulties in other areas. In the early 1970s, for example, Holman was found guilty of paying a mob-related broker $1 million to ensure that unions wouldn't interfere with the firm's New York City distribution plans. Later in the decade, IBP was investigated for anti-competitive practices, although the inquiry was subsequently dropped. In the 1980s, IBP was fined $2.6 million and penalized by OSHA for not reporting hand injuries caused by meat-cutting equipment. Another major strike over wages and working conditions crippled the firm in 1999. By early 2000, IBP was also under investigation by numerous state and federal investigators for alleged environmental misconduct.

Our opening story continues on page 81

ETHICS IN THE WORKPLACE

Just what is *ethical behavior*? **Ethics** are beliefs about what is right and wrong or good and bad. An individual's personal values and morals and the social context in which it occurs determine whether a particular behavior is seen as being ethical or unethical. In other words, **ethical behavior** is behavior that conforms to individual beliefs and social norms about what is right and good. **Unethical behavior** is behavior that individual beliefs and social norms define as wrong and bad. **Business ethics** is a term often used to refer to ethical or unethical behaviors by a manager or employee of an organization.

Because ethics are based on both individual beliefs and social concepts, they vary from person to person, from situation to situation, and from culture to culture. Social standards, for example, tend to be broad enough to support certain differences in beliefs. Without violating the general standards of the culture, therefore, individuals may develop personal codes of ethics that reflect a fairly wide range of attitudes and beliefs. Thus, what constitutes ethical and unethical behavior is determined partly by the individual and partly by culture.

ethics
Beliefs about what is right and wrong or good and bad in actions that affect others

ethical behavior
Behavior conforming to generally accepted social norms concerning beneficial and harmful actions

unethical behavior
Behavior that does not conform to generally accepted social norms concerning beneficial and harmful actions

business ethics
Ethical or unethical behaviors by a manager or employer of an organization

Assessing Ethical Behavior

By definition, what distinguishes ethical from unethical behavior is often subjective and subject to differences of opinion.[1] So how does one go about deciding whether or not a particular action or decision is ethical? Figure 3.1 presents a simplified three-step model for applying ethical judgments to situations that may arise during the course of business activities:

1. Gather the relevant factual information.
2. Analyze the facts to determine the most appropriate moral values.
3. Make an ethical judgment based on the rightness or wrongness of the proposed activity or policy.

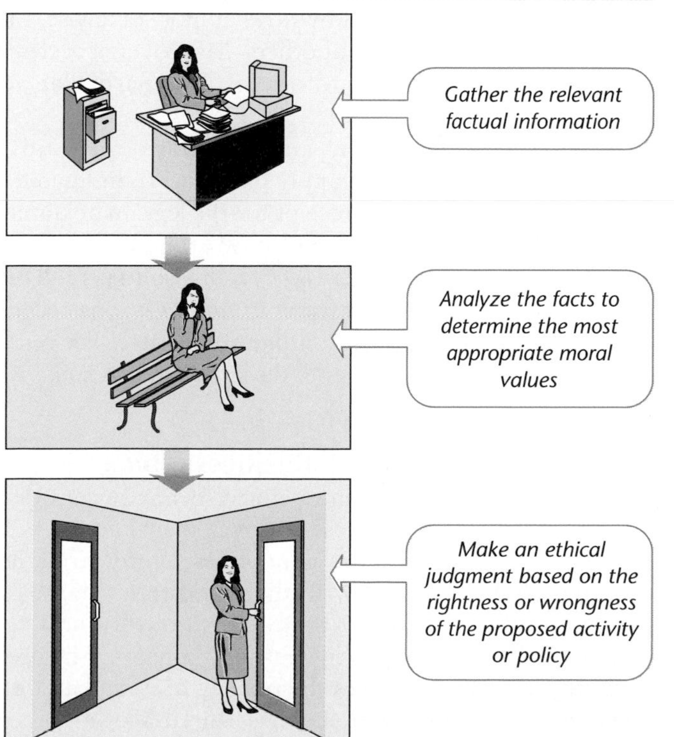
Gather the relevant factual information
Analyze the facts to determine the most appropriate moral values
Make an ethical judgment based on the rightness or wrongness of the proposed activity or policy

Figure 3.1
Steps in Making Ethical Judgments

Unfortunately, the process does not always work as smoothly as the scheme in Figure 3.1 suggests. What if the facts are not clear-cut? What if there are no agreed-upon moral values? Nevertheless, a judgment and a decision must be made. Experts point out that, otherwise, trust is impossible; and trust, they add, is indispensable to any business transaction.

In order to assess more fully the ethics of a particular behavior, we need a more complex perspective. To illustrate this perspective, let's consider a common dilemma faced by managers involving their expense accounts. Companies routinely provide managers with accounts to cover work-related expenses when they are traveling on company business or entertaining clients for business purposes. Common examples of such expenses include hotel bills, meals, and rental cars or taxis. Employees are expected to claim only those expenses that are accurate and work-related. For example, if a manager takes a client out to dinner while traveling on business and spends $100 for dinner, submitting a receipt for that dinner to be reimbursed for $100 is clearly accurate and appropriate. Suppose, however, that the manager then has a $100 dinner the next night in that same city with a good friend for purely social purposes. Submitting that receipt for full reimbursement would be unethical. A few managers, however, will rationalize that it is okay to submit a receipt for dinner with a friend. They will argue, perhaps, that they are underpaid and are just increasing the income due them.

Other principles that come into play in a case like this include various ethical norms. Consider four such norms and the issues that they entail:

- *Utility*: Does a particular act optimize what is best for those who are affected by it?
- *Rights*: Does it respect the rights of the individuals involved?
- *Justice*: Is it consistent with what we regard as fair?
- *Caring*: Is it consistent with people's responsibilities to each other?

Figure 3.2 is an expanded version of Figure 3.1 that incorporates the consideration of these ethical norms.

Now let's return to the case of the inflated expense account. While the utility norm would acknowledge that the manager benefits from padding an expense account, others, such as coworkers and owners, do not. Likewise, most experts would agree that it does not respect the rights of others. Moreover, it is clearly unfair and compromises the manager's responsibilities to others. This particular act, then, appears to be clearly unethical.

Figure 3.2, however, also provides mechanisms for considering unique circumstances—those that apply only in certain limited situations. Suppose, for example, the manager loses the receipt for the legitimate dinner but retains the receipt for the social dinner. Some people will now argue that it is okay to submit the illegitimate receipt because our manager is only doing so to get full reimbursement. Others, however, will continue to argue that submitting the wrong receipt is wrong under any circumstances. We won't pretend to arbitrate the case. For our purposes, we will simply make the following point: Changes in the situation can make issues more or less clear-cut.

Company Practices and Business Ethics

Organizations try to promote ethical behavior and discourage unethical behavior in numerous ways. As unethical and even illegal activities by both managers and employees plague more and more companies, many firms have taken additional steps to encourage ethical behavior in the workplace. Many, for example, establish codes of conduct and develop clear ethical positions on how the firm and its employees will conduct their business. An increasingly controversial area regarding business ethics and company practices involves the privacy of e-mail and other communications that take place inside an organization. The "Wired World" box in this chapter discusses these issues more fully.

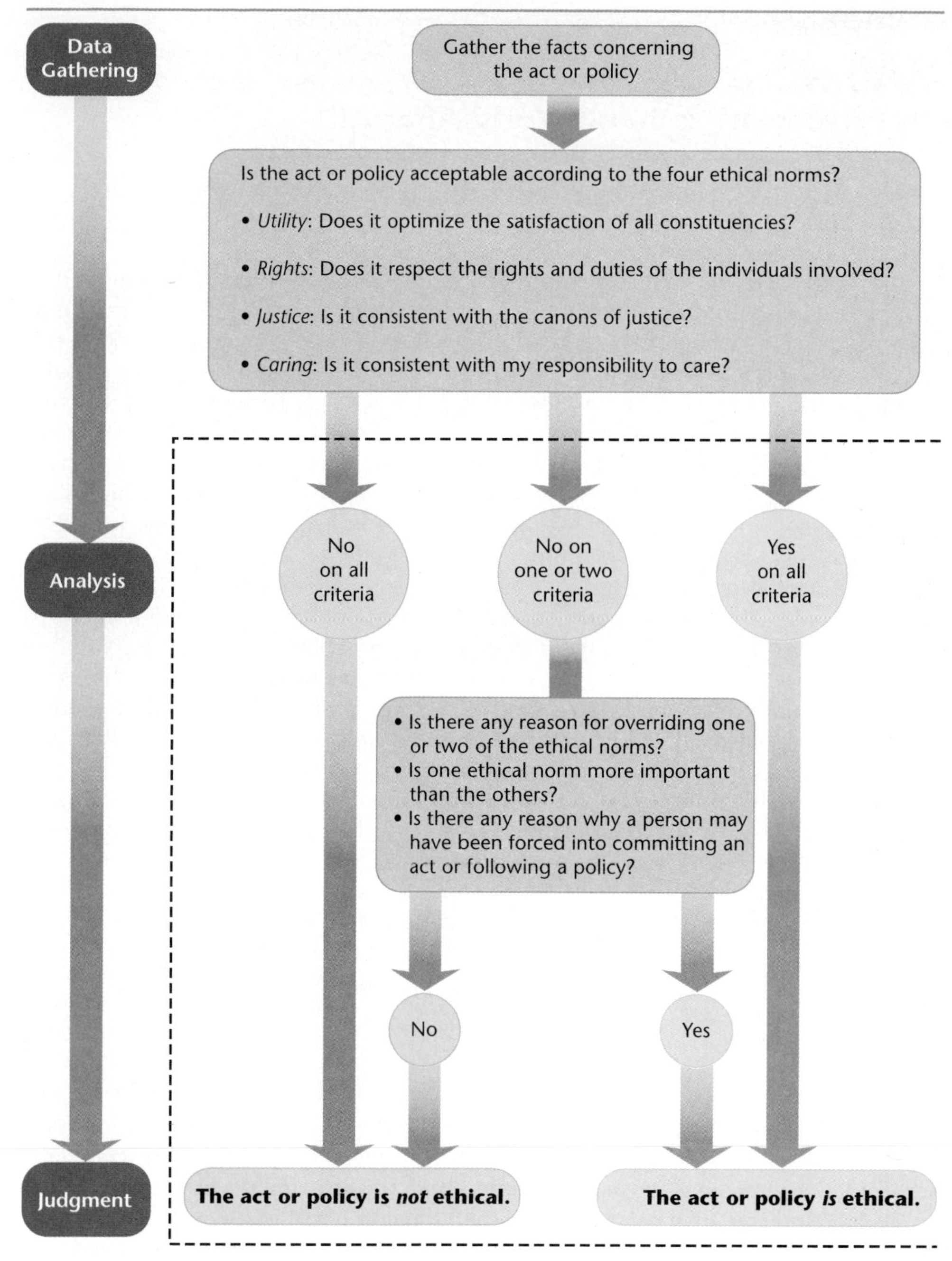
Data Gathering
Gather the facts concerning the act or policy
Is the act or policy acceptable according to the four ethical norms?
• Utility: Does it optimize the satisfaction of all constituencies?
• Rights: Does it respect the rights and duties of the individuals involved?
• Justice: Is it consistent with the canons of justice?
• Caring: Is it consistent with my responsibility to care?
Analysis
No on all criteria
No on one or two criteria
Yes on all criteria
• Is there any reason for overriding one or two of the ethical norms?
• Is one ethical norm more important than the others?
• Is there any reason why a person may have been forced into committing an act or following a policy?
No
Yes
Judgment
The act or policy is not ethical.
The act or policy is ethical.

Figure 3.2
Expanded Model of Ethical Judgment Making

Perhaps the single most effective step that a company can take is to demonstrate top management support. For instance, when United Technologies <www.utc.com>, a Connecticut-based industrial conglomerate, published its 21-page code of ethics, it also named a vice president for business practices.[2] In contrast, recall the story of IBP in our opening vignette. One of the firm's founders, Currier Holman, was found guilty of bribing a mobster to influence organized labor in New York City. Such actions by senior managers often set the tone in organizations (namely, that it's okay to do whatever is necessary in order to boost profits).

Case: The Tylenol Scare An excellent and now classic illustration of the power of ethical commitment involves Johnson & Johnson <www.jnj.com>. In 1982, capsules of the company's Tylenol pain reliever were found laced with cyanide. Managers at J&J quickly recalled all Tylenol bottles still on retailers' shelves and then went public with

IT'S A WIRED WORLD

When It Comes to Privacy, It's a Small World After All

As just about everyone today knows, e-mail has virtually become the standard method of communication in the business world. Most people enjoy its speed, ease, and casual nature. But e-mail also has its share of problems and pitfalls. One challenge, of course, is privacy. Many people assume the contents of their e-mail are private, but there may in fact be any number of people authorized to see it. Some experts have even likened e-mail to postcards sent through the U.S. mail: They pass through a lot of hands and before a lot of eyes, and, theoretically, many different people can read them.

The courts, for example, have held that e-mail messages sent and/or received during working hours and on company equipment are the property of the business. Compaq Computer has one full-time employee who does nothing but randomly scan e-mail messages that pass through the company's servers and monitor improper Internet usage among employees. Although less than half of all U.S. businesses have formal electronic communication policies, they do have the power of the law behind them when they do establish policies or procedures.

Aside from organizational scrutiny, people also face the threat of hackers breaking into and wreaking havoc with the company's computer network, including its e-mail system. Indeed, e-mail is one of the easiest routes for hackers to use to gain access to other parts of a firm's computer system. Once inside, they can read sensitive e-mail messages, destroy them, or send them to other people.

Finally, many users have good reason to regard themselves as the worst enemies to their own privacy. A surprisingly common error is inadvertently sending e-mail to the wrong address—even to a large group of people. More than one starry-eyed e-mailer has dispatched a love note to the wrong person. Even worse, a simple inadvertent click of the mouse can send a sensitive or inflammable message intended for a single recipient to everyone in the company.

But e-mail is actually only part of the privacy issue. Other concerns have arisen concerning general privacy over the Internet and cellular telephones. For consumers, Internet privacy is an especially important issue. Companies, for instance, have the capacity to monitor which Web sites individuals visit, how long they stay there, what they buy, and how frequently they return. They can use this information to make referrals to other companies that might then want to target new advertising to those individuals. Cellular and cordless telephones are not nearly as private as hard-wired phones—indeed, tapping into or eavesdropping on a cellular conversation is amazingly easy. Not surprisingly, then, concerns about the shrinking world in which we can enjoy privacy are beginning to take on an increasingly higher profile with each passing day.

candid information throughout the crisis. Its ethical choices proved to be a crucial factor in J&J's campaign to rescue its product: Both the firm and the brand bounced back much more quickly than most observers had thought possible.[3]

"My apologies to the consumers of Belgium."

—Former Coca-Cola CEO Douglas Ivester, when Belgian schoolchildren got sick from a bad batch of Coke

Case: The Coca-Cola Scare A more recent example involves the operations of Coca-Cola in Europe <www.thecoca-colacompany.com/world>. First, some Belgian schoolchildren suffered minor illnesses after drinking Coke made from a bad batch of carbon dioxide. Then Coke cans shipped from the company's plant in Dunkirk, France, contained some fungicide on the bottom. Neither problem was serious, but, together, the two events created a public relations problem. After Belgian officials ordered that Coke be removed from store shelves, Douglas Ivester, who was Coke CEO at the time, flew to Brussels and made a public statement: "My apologies to the consumers of Belgium." The CEO's action, while coming perhaps a bit late, served to help quell the furor.[4]

In addition to demonstrating an attitude of honesty and openness, as in the case of Coca-Cola, firms can also take specific and concrete steps to formalize their commitment to ethical business practices. Two of the most common approaches to formalizing commitment are *adopting written codes* and *instituting ethics programs*.

In 1999, some Belgian schoolchildren got sick after drinking Coke. The problem was a bad batch of carbon dioxide, and there was no health hazard. At first, Coke saw no reason to take action. But then the company got caught in the middle of Belgian political infighting over the incident, and Coke was removed from retail shelves for several days. Finally, former Coke CEO Douglas Ivester apologized to Belgian consumers in a series of full-page newspaper ads, adding contritely, "I should have spoken with you earlier."

Adopting Written Codes Many companies, including Johnson & Johnson, Texas Instruments <www.ti.com/corp/docs/company/ethics>, McDonald's <www.macspotlight.org/company/publications>, Starbucks <www.starbucks.com>, and Dell Computer <www.dell.com>, have adopted written codes of ethics that formally acknowledge their intent to do business in an ethical manner. The number of such companies has risen dramatically in the last three decades, and today virtually all major corporations have written codes of ethics.

Figure 3.3 illustrates the essential role that corporate ethics and values should play in corporate policy. You can use it to see how ethics statements might be structured most effectively. Basically, the figure suggests that although business strategies and practices can change frequently and business objectives occasionally, an organization's core principles and values should remain steadfast. Hewlett-Packard, for example, has

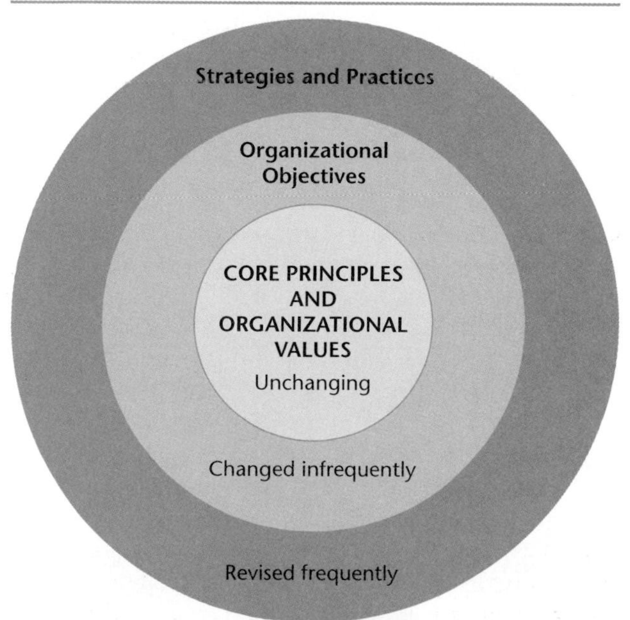

Figure 3.3
Core Principles and Organizational Values

had the same written code of ethics, called *The HP Way*, since 1957, and it has served the firm well for over 40 years. The essential elements of *The HP Way* are as follows:

- We have trust and respect for individuals.
- We focus on a high level of achievement and contribution.
- We conduct our business with uncompromising integrity.
- We achieve our common objectives through teamwork.
- We encourage flexibility and innovation.

Instituting Ethics Programs Instances such as the Tylenol case suggest that ethical responses can be learned through experience. But can business ethics be taught, either in the workplace or in schools? Not surprisingly, business schools have become important players in the debate about ethics education. Most analysts agree that even though business schools must address the issue of ethics in the workplace, companies must take the chief responsibility for educating employees. In fact, more and more firms are doing so.

For example, both ExxonMobil <www.exxonmobil.com/overview> and Boeing <www.boeing.com/companyoffices/aboutus/ethics> have major ethics programs. All managers must go through periodic ethics training to remind them of the importance of ethical decision making and to update them on the most current laws and regulations that might be particularly relevant to their firms. Others, such as Texas Instruments, have ethical "hot lines"—numbers that an employee can call, either to discuss the ethics of a particular problem or situation or to report unethical behavior or activities by others.

SOCIAL RESPONSIBILITY

social responsibility
The attempt of a business to balance its commitments to groups and individuals in its environment, including customers, other businesses, employees, and investors

organizational stakeholders
Those groups, individuals, and organizations that are directly affected by the practices of an organization and who therefore have a stake in its performance

Ethics affect individual behavior in the workplace. **Social responsibility**, however, refers to the way in which a business tries to balance its commitments to certain groups and individuals in its social environment.[5] These groups and individuals are often called **organizational stakeholders**: those groups, individuals, and organizations that are directly affected by the practices of an organization and, therefore, have a stake in its performance.[6] Major stakeholders are identified in Figure 3.4.

The Stakeholder Model of Responsibility

Many companies that strive to be responsible to their stakeholders concentrate first and foremost on five main groups: *customers*, *employees*, *investors*, *suppliers*, and the *local communities* where they do business. They may then select other stakeholders that are particularly relevant or important to the organization and try to address their needs and expectations as well.

Customers Businesses that are responsible to their customers strive to treat them fairly and honestly. They also seek to charge fair prices, honor warranties, meet delivery commitments, and stand behind the quality of the products they sell. L.L. Bean

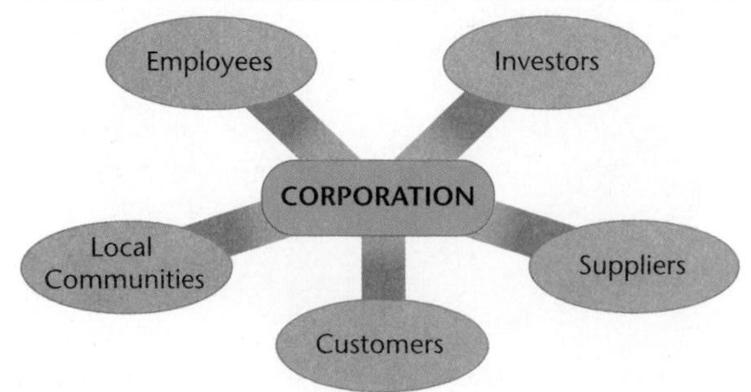

Figure 3.4
Major Corporate Stakeholders

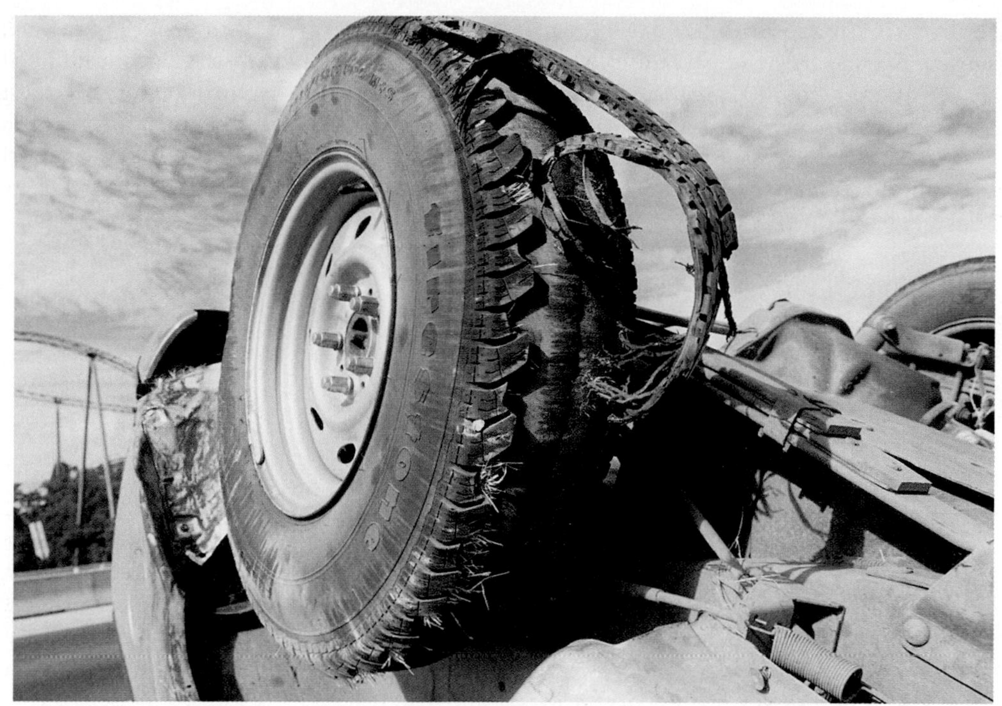

In August 2000, Bridgestone/Firestone Inc. <www.firestone.com> announced a consumer-protection recall of 6.5 million light-truck tires that blew or lost tread and that may have contributed to dozens of fatal accidents. The cost to the tire manufacturer was $350 million. The cost to Ford Motor Co. <www.ford.com>, which had installed—and issued warranties for—most of those 6.5 million tires on its sport-utility vehicles ran to $500 million. The next year, following further consumer-protection measures, Ford took an after-tax charge of $2.1 billion to replace another 13 million Firestone tires.

<www.llbean.com>, Land's End <www.landsend.com>, Dell Computer, and Johnson & Johnson are among companies with excellent reputations in this area.

Employees Businesses that are socially responsible in their dealings with employees treat workers fairly, make them a part of the team, and respect their dignity and basic human needs. Organizations such as MBNA <www.mbna.com/about careers>, Continental Airlines <www.continental.com>, 3M Corporation <www.3m.com>, Hoechst Celanese <www.hoechst.com>, and Southwest Airlines <www.southwest.com> have all established strong reputations in this area. In addition, many of the same firms also go to great lengths to find, hire, train, and promote qualified minorities.

Investors To maintain a socially responsible stance toward investors, managers should follow proper accounting procedures, provide appropriate information to shareholders about financial performance, and manage the organization to protect shareholder rights and investments. They should be accurate and candid in assessing

"The employees have to assume a share of the blame for allowing the pension fund to become so big and tempting."

future growth and profitability and avoid even the appearance of impropriety in such sensitive areas as insider trading, stock-price manipulation, and the withholding of financial data. In 2001, for example, Computer Associates, the world's fourth-largest software company, was accused of having overstated sales and revenues for years in order to bolster investor confidence in its financial health. The day after the first report of manipulation, the company's shares fell 8.7 percent, reducing its market value by nearly $2 billion.[7]

Suppliers Relations with suppliers should also be managed with care. For example, it might be easy for a large corporation to take advantage of suppliers by imposing unrealistic delivery schedules and reducing profit margins by constantly pushing for lower and lower prices. Many firms now recognize the importance of mutually beneficial partnership arrangements with suppliers. Thus, they keep them informed about future plans, negotiate delivery schedules and prices that are acceptable to both firms, and so forth. Ford <www.ford.com> and Wal-Mart <www.walmart.com> are among the firms acknowledged to have excellent relationships with their suppliers.

Local Communities Finally, most businesses try to be socially responsible to their local communities. They may contribute to local programs like Little League baseball, get actively involved in charitable programs like the United Way, and strive to simply be a good corporate citizen by minimizing their negative impact on the community. Target Stores <www.targetcorp.com>, for example, donate a percentage of sales to the local communities where they do business.

The stakeholder model can also provide some helpful insights on the conduct of managers in international business. In particular, to the extent that an organization acknowledges its commitments to its stakeholders, it should also recognize that it has multiple sets of stakeholders in each country where it does business. DaimlerChrysler <www.daimlerchrysler.com>, for example, has investors not only in Germany but also in the United States, Japan, and other countries where its shares are publicly traded. It also has suppliers, employees, and customers in multiple countries, and its actions affect many different communities in dozens of different countries.

The Evolution of Social Responsibility

Both U.S. society and U.S. business have changed dramatically in the last two centuries. Not surprisingly, so have views about social responsibility. Many scholars identify at least three different phases in the evolution of social responsibility.

The Entrepreneurial Era The first phase corresponds to the era in the late nineteenth century that was characterized by the entrepreneurial spirit and the *laissez-faire* philosophy. The enormous empires of men such as John D. Rockefeller, J. P. Morgan, and Cornelius Vanderbilt exercised tremendous economic power, but abuses of power inevitably led to public backlash. During this era of labor strife and predatory business practices, both individual citizens and the government first became concerned about unbridled business activity. This concern was translated into the nation's first laws regulating basic business practices.

The Great Depression The second major phase in the evolution of social responsibility occurred during the Great Depression. In the 1930s, many people blamed the failure of businesses and banks and the widespread loss of jobs on a general climate of business greed and lack of restraint. Out of the economic turmoil emerged new laws that described an expanded role for business in protecting and enhancing the general welfare of society.

The Era of Social Activism The third major phase began with the social unrest of the 1960s and 1970s, when business was often characterized as a negative social force. Some critics even charged that defense contractors had promoted the Vietnam War to spur profits. Eventually, increased activism prompted increased government regulation in a variety of areas: Health warnings were placed on cigarettes, and stricter environmental protection laws were enacted.

Contemporary Social Consciousness

Social consciousness and views toward social responsibility continue to evolve. Today's attitudes seem to be moving toward an enlightened view stressing the need for a greater social role for business. Some observers suggest that an increased awareness of the global economy and heightened campaigning on the part of environmentalists and other activists have combined to make many businesses more sensitive to their social responsibilities.

For example, retailers such as Sears <www.sears.com> and Target <www.targetcorp.com> have policies against selling handguns and other weapons. Likewise, national toy retailers KayBee and Toys "R" Us <www.toysrus.com> refuse to sell toy guns that look too realistic. Firms in numerous other industries have also integrated socially conscious thinking into their production plans and marketing efforts. The production of environmentally safe products has become a potential boom area, as many companies introduce products designed to be "environmentally friendly."

Electrolux, a Swedish appliance maker <www.electrolux.com>, has developed a line of water-efficient washing machines, a solar-powered lawn mower, and, for Brazil, the first refrigerators that are free of ozone-depleting refrigerants. Herman Miller, a Michigan-based office-furniture business <www.hermanmiller.com>, uses recycled materials and focuses on products that are simple in design, durable, and recyclable. Ford <www.ford.com> has set up an independent brand called Think to develop and market low-pollution, electric-powered vehicles.

AREAS OF SOCIAL RESPONSIBILITY

When defining its sense of social responsibility, a firm typically confronts four areas of concern: responsibilities toward the *environment*, its *customers*, its *employees*, and its *investors*.

Responsibility Toward the Environment

During the first several months of his administration, the harshest criticism directed at President George W. Bush was leveled at his environmental policies. For example, he openly championed proposals for oil exploration in protected areas of Alaska, and he has steadfastly rejected the proposals of the 1997 Kyoto Protocol dealing with global warming. "We know the surface temperature of the earth is rising," admits Bush, but he argues that his policies reflect a sound combination of free market expansion and exploration balanced against environmental protection and conservation.[8]

> *"We know the surface temperature of the earth is rising."*
>
> —President George W. Bush

Figure 3.5, however, tells a troubling story. The chart shows atmospheric carbon dioxide (CO_2) levels for the period between 1750 and 2000 and offers three possible scenarios for future levels under different sets of conditions. The three projections—lowest, middle, highest—were developed by the Intergovernmental Panel on Climate Change <www.ipcc.ch>, which calculated likely changes in the atmosphere during this century if no efforts were made to reduce so-called *greenhouse emissions*—waste industrial gases that trap heat in the atmosphere. The criteria for estimating changes are population, economic growth, energy supplies, and technologies: The less pressure exerted by these conditions, the less the increase in CO_2 levels. Energy supplies are measured in *exajoules*—roughly the annual energy consumption of the New York Metropolitan area.

Under the lowest, or best-case, scenario, the population would only grow to 6.4 billion people, economic growth would be no more than 1.2 to 2.0 percent a year, and energy supplies would require only 8,000 exajoules of conventional oil. However,

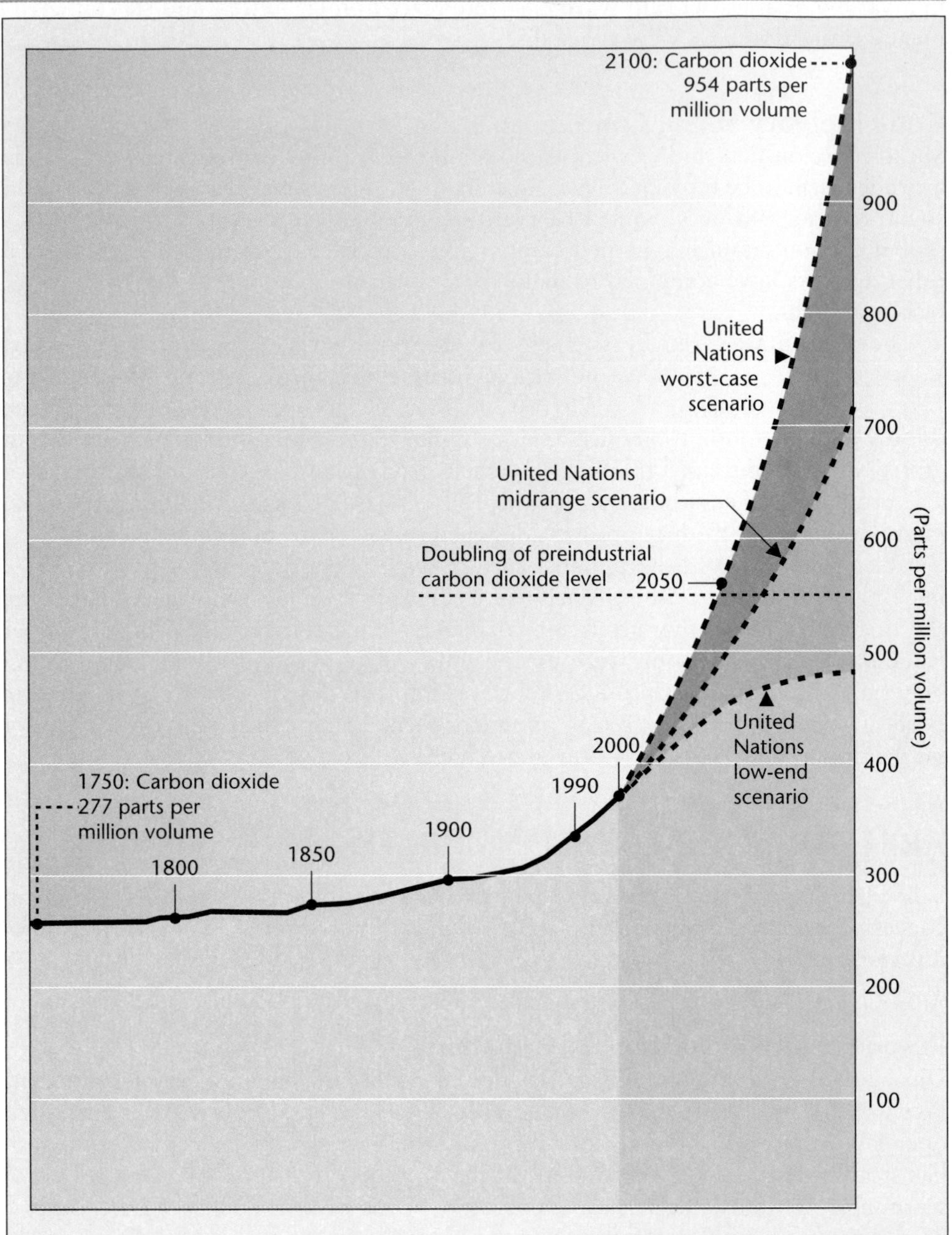

Figure 3.5

CO_2 Emissions, Past and Future

> *"We're conducting a global experiment. And we're all in the test tube."*
>
> —Researcher on greenhouse emissions

under the highest, or worst-case, scenario, the population would increase to 11.3 billion people, annual economic growth would be between 3.0 and 3.5 percent, and energy supplies would require as much as 18,400 exajoules of conventional oil.

The resulting changes in climate would be relatively mild; we would hardly experience any day-to-day changes in the weather. We would, however, increase the likelihood of having troublesome weather around the globe: droughts, hurricanes, winter sieges, and so forth. The charges leveled against greenhouse emissions are disputed, but as one researcher puts it, "The only way to prove them for sure is hang around 10, 20, or 30 more years, when the evidence would be overwhelming. But in the meantime, we're conducting a global experiment. And we're all in the test tube."[9]

Controlling *pollution*—the injection of harmful substances into the environment—is a significant challenge to contemporary business. Although noise pollution is now attracting increased concern, air, water, and land pollution remains the greatest problem in need of solutions from governments and businesses alike. In the following sections, we focus on the nature of the problems in these areas and on some of the current efforts to address them.[10]

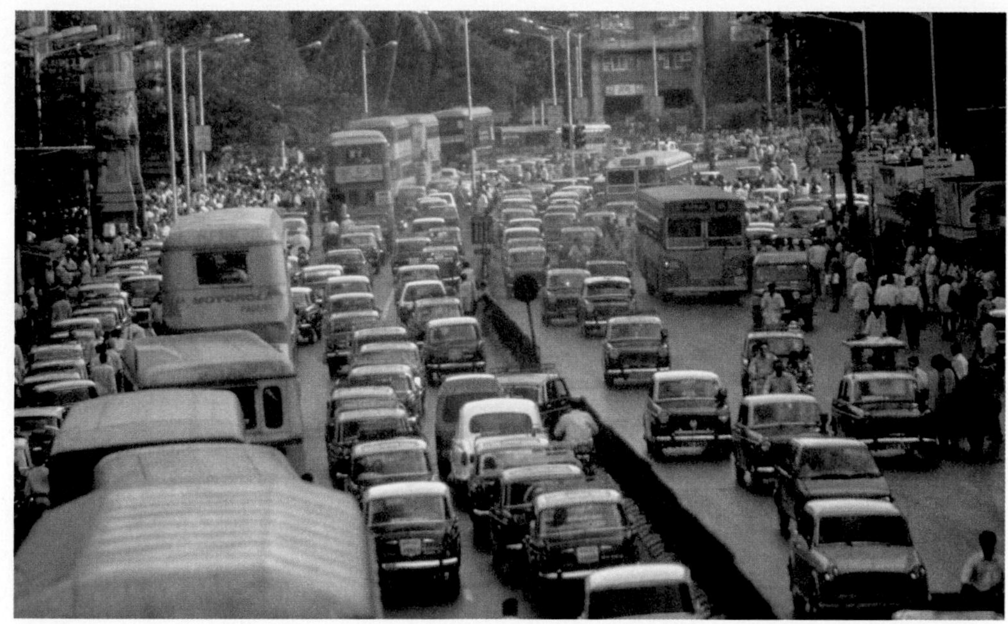

With India's population growing by 20 million people every year and city traffic doubling every five years, Indian cities are facing increasingly high levels of air pollution. As bad as urban air is in New Delhi, Bombay, and Calcutta, five countries actually produce more carbon gases than India. From the top down, they are the United States, the former Soviet Union, China, Japan, and Germany.

Air Pollution Air pollution results when several factors combine to lower air quality. Carbon monoxide emitted by automobiles contributes to air pollution, as do smoke and other chemicals from manufacturing plants. Air quality is usually worst in certain geographic locations, such as the Denver area and the Los Angeles basin, where pollutants tend to get trapped in the atmosphere. For this very reason, the air around Mexico City is generally considered to be the most polluted in the entire world.

Legislation has gone a long way toward controlling air pollution. Under new laws, many companies must now install special devices to limit the pollutants they expel into the air. But such efforts are costly. Air pollution is compounded by such problems as acid rain, which occurs when sulfur is pumped into the atmosphere, mixes with natural moisture, and falls to the ground as rain. Much of the damage to forests and streams in the eastern United States and Canada has been attributed to acid rain originating in sulfur from manufacturing and power plants in the midwestern United States.

Water Pollution Water becomes polluted primarily from chemical and waste dumping. For years, businesses and cities dumped waste into rivers, streams, and lakes with little regard for the consequences. Cleveland's Cuyahoga River was once so polluted that it literally burst into flames one hot summer day. After an oil spill in 1994, a Houston ship channel burned for days.

Thanks to new legislation and increased awareness, water quality in many areas of the United States is improving. The Cuyahoga River now boasts fish and is even used for recreation. Laws forbidding phosphates (an ingredient found in many detergents) in New York and Florida have helped to make Lake Erie and other major waters safe for fishing and swimming again. Both the Passaic River in New Jersey and the Hudson River in New York are much cleaner now than they were just a few years ago.

Land Pollution There are two key issues in land pollution. The first is how to restore the quality of land that has already been damaged. Land and water damaged by toxic waste, for example, must be cleaned up for the simple reason that people still need to use them. The second problem, of course, is the prevention of future contamination. New forms of solid-waste disposal constitute one response to these problems. Combustible wastes can be separated and used as fuels in industrial boilers, and decomposition can be accelerated by exposing waste matter to certain microorganisms.

WEB Connection

Founded by three young Californians who were into surfing and rock climbing, Patagonia started out in 1973 as a seller of high-quality outdoor wear. The company is also quite particular about the impact of its materials and processes on the environment and actively enforces environmentally friendly practices on the part of its suppliers. Visit its Web site to find out more about Patagonia's environmental policies.

www.patagonia.com

> *"Handling hazardous waste is an incredibly complicated area. It's very easy to inadvertently step over the line."*
>
> —Anne McNamara, general counsel for American Airlines

Toxic Waste Disposal An especially controversial problem in land pollution is toxic waste disposal. Toxic wastes are dangerous chemical or radioactive by-products of manufacturing processes. U.S. manufacturers produce between 40 and 60 *million* tons of such material each year. As a rule, toxic waste must be stored; it cannot be destroyed or processed into harmless material. Few people, however, want toxic waste storage sites in their backyards. American Airlines <www.im.aa.com> recently pled guilty—and became the first major airline to gain a criminal record—to a felony charge that it had mishandled some hazardous materials packed as cargo in passenger airplanes.[11] While fully acknowledging the firm's guilt, Anne McNamara, American's general counsel, argued that "This is an incredibly complicated area with many layers of regulation. It's very easy to inadvertently step over the line."

Recycling Recycling is another controversial area in land pollution. *Recycling*—the reconversion of waste materials into useful products—has become an issue not only for municipal and state governments but also for many companies engaged in high-waste activities. Certain products, such as aluminum beverage cans and glass, can be very efficiently recycled. Others, such as plastics, are more troublesome. For example, brightly colored plastics like detergent and juice bottles must be recycled separately from clear plastics like milk jugs. Most plastic bottle caps, meanwhile, contain a vinyl lining that can spoil a normal recycling batch. Amber plastic beer containers, currently being test-marketed by Philip Morris's Miller Brewing Co. <www.millerbrewing.com>, cannot be mixed for recycling with clear soda bottles.[12] Nevertheless, many local communities actively support various recycling programs including curbside pickup of aluminum, plastics, glass, and pulp paper. Unfortunately, consumer awareness and interest in this area—and, thus, the policy priorities of business—are more acute at some times than at others.

Responsibility Toward Customers

A company that does not act responsibly toward its customers will ultimately lose their trust—and thus their business. Moreover, the government controls or regulates many aspects of what businesses can and cannot do regarding consumers. The Federal Trade Commission (FTC) <www.ftc.gov> regulates advertising and pricing practices. The Food and Drug Administration (FDA) <www.fda.gov> enforces guidelines for labeling food products.

Unethical and irresponsible business practices toward customers can result in government-imposed penalties and expensive civil litigation. For example, Abbott

Laboratories <www.abbott.com> recently agreed to pay $100 million to settle accusations that the firm failed to meet federal quality standards when it made hundreds of different medical test kits. The FDA indicated that it was the largest fine the agency had ever levied.[13]

Social responsibility toward customers generally falls into two categories: providing quality products and pricing products fairly. Naturally, firms differ as much in their level of concern about their responsibility toward customers as in their approaches to environmental responsibility. Yet unlike environmental problems, many customer problems do not require expensive solutions. In fact, most problems can be avoided if companies simply adhere to regulated practices and heed laws regarding consumer rights.

Consumer Rights Much of the current interest in business responsibility toward customers can be traced to the rise of **consumerism**: social activism dedicated to protecting the rights of consumers in their dealings with businesses. The first formal declaration of consumer rights protection came in the early 1960s when President John F. Kennedy identified four basic consumer rights. These rights are now backed by numerous federal and state laws:

consumerism
Form of social activism dedicated to protecting the rights of consumers in their dealings with businesses

1. Consumers have a right to safe products.
2. Consumers have a right to be informed about all relevant aspects of a product.
3. Consumers have a right to be heard.
4. Consumers have a right to choose what they buy.

American Home Products <www.ahp.com> provides an instructive example of what can happen to a firm that violates one or more of these consumer rights. Throughout the early 1990s, the firm aggressively marketed a drug called Pondimin, its brand name for a diet pill containing fenfluramine. In 1996, doctors wrote 18 million prescriptions for Pondimin and other medications containing fenfluramine. In 1997, however, the FDA reported a linkage between the pills and heart-valve disease. A class-action lawsuit against the firm charged that the drug was unsafe and that users had not been provided with complete information about possible side effects. American Home Products eventually agreed to pay $3.75 billion to individuals who had used the drug.[14]

Unfair Pricing Interfering with competition can take the form of illegal pricing practices. **Collusion** occurs when two or more firms agree to collaborate on such wrongful acts as *price fixing*. A few years ago, for example, the FTC investigated pricing-related business practices at Toys "R" Us, the largest toy retailer in the country.

collusion
Illegal agreement between two or more companies to commit a wrongful act

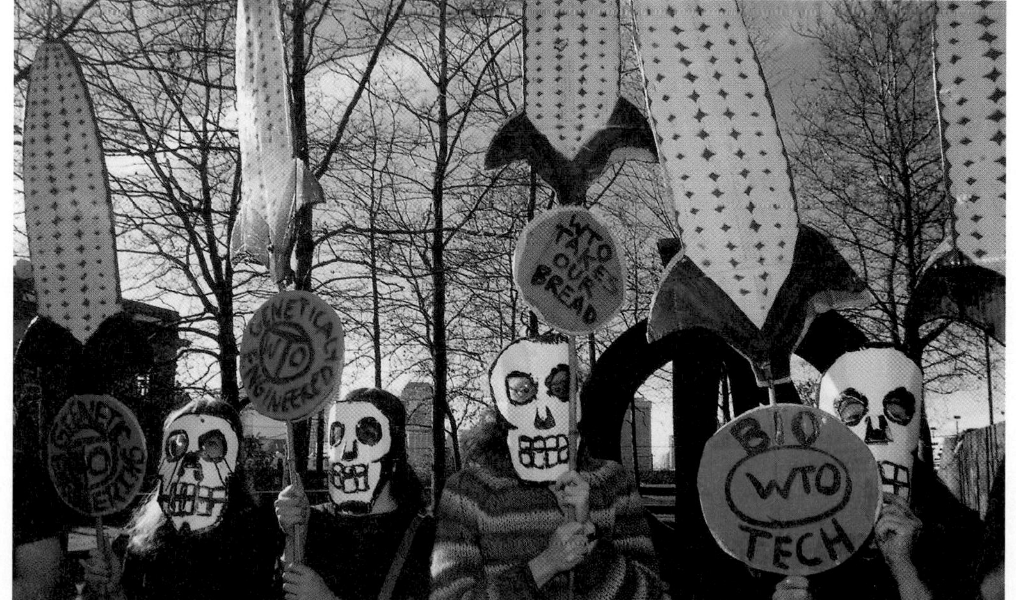

To consumer-rights advocates like these protestors, foods that have undergone genetic modification (GM) to make them resistant to herbicides and pests are "frankenfoods." Such crops, they charge, make people sick and cause damage to the environment. They also contend that the policies of the World Trade Organization (WTO) <www.wto.org>, which promotes international trade, encourage the production of frankenfoods as exportable commodities.

Investigators charged that Toys "R" Us routinely pressured major suppliers to limit quantities or delay shipments of hot-selling toys to warehouse clubs such as Sam's Club or Costco. This practice would have given Toys "R" Us a head start on selling the toys at higher prices than those charged by the warehouse clubs. Although Toys "R" Us denied the charges, the firm contended that it had the right to tell suppliers that it may choose to not stock toys that are sold to warehouse clubs.

More recently, the U.S. Justice Department <www.usdoj.gov> charged three international pharmaceutical firms with illegally controlling worldwide supplies and prices of vitamins. France's Rhone-Poulenc <www.aventis.com> cooperated with the investigation, helped break the case several months earlier than expected, and was not fined. Switzerland's F. Hoffmann-LaRoche <www.laroche-sa/fr> was fined $500 million and one of its senior executives was sentenced to four months in a U.S. prison. Germany's BASF <www.basf.com> was fined $225 million.[15]

Under some circumstances, firms can also come under attack for *price gouging*—responding to increased demand with overly steep (and often unwarranted) price increases. For example, when DaimlerChrysler launched its PT Cruiser in 2000, demand for the vehicles was so strong that some dealers sold them only to customers willing to pay thousands of dollars over sticker prices. A similar practice was adopted by some Ford dealers when the new Thunderbird was launched in 2001.

Ethics in Advertising In recent years, increased attention has been given to ethics in advertising and product information. Because of controversies surrounding the potential misinterpretation of words and phrases such as *light, reduced calorie, diet*, and *low fat*, food producers are now required to use a standardized format for listing ingredients on product packages. Similarly, controversy arose in 2001 when it was discovered that Sony had literally created a movie critic who happened to be particularly fond of movies released by Sony's Columbia Pictures <www.spe.sony.com> unit. The studio had been routinely using glowing quotes from a fictitious critic in advertising its newest theatrical releases. After *Newsweek* magazine reported what was going on, Sony hastily stopped the practice and apologized.

Another issue concerns advertising that some consumers consider morally objectionable. Benetton <www.benetton.com>, for example, aired a series of commercials featuring North Carolina inmates on death row. The ads, dubbed "We, on Death Row," prompted such an emotional outcry that several states either sued the company or threatened legal action, and Sears dropped the Benetton USA clothing line.[16] Other ads receiving criticism include Victoria's Secret <www.victoriassecret.com> models in skimpy underwear and campaigns by tobacco and alcohol companies that apparently target young people. For instance, although R. J. Reynolds <www.rjr.com> was forced to retire its longtime "spokesperson" Joe Camel, many beer commercials still feature animated frogs and lizards and other child-friendly characters.

Responsibility Toward Employees

In Chapter 9, we will see how a number of human resource management activities are essential to a smoothly functioning business. These activities—recruiting, hiring, training, promoting, and compensating—are also the basis for social responsibility toward employees.

Legal and Social Commitments Socially responsible behavior toward employees has both legal and social components. By law, businesses cannot practice numerous forms of illegal discrimination against people in any facet of the employment relationship. For example, a company cannot refuse to hire someone because of ethnicity or pay someone a lower salary than someone else on the basis of gender. Such actions must be taken for job-related purposes only. A company that provides its employees with equal opportunities for rewards and advancement without regard to race, sex, or

WEB Connection

Headquartered in the Netherlands, ESOMAR, the World Association of Opinion and Marketing Research Professionals, is composed of more than 4,000 members—ad and media agencies and public and government institutions—in over 100 countries. ESOMAR publishes ethical "Guidelines" on a variety of marketing-research–oriented activities, ranging from "Interviewing Children" to "Conducting Marketing and Opinion Research Using the Internet."

www.esomar.nl

other irrelevant factors is meeting both its legal and its social responsibilities. Firms that ignore these responsibilities run the risk of losing productive, highly motivated employees. They also leave themselves open to lawsuits.

In the opinion of many people, social responsibility toward employees goes beyond equal opportunity. According to popular opinion, an organization should strive to ensure that the workplace is physically and socially safe. It should also recognize its obligations to help protect the health of its employees by providing opportunities to balance work and life pressures and preferences. From this point of view, social responsibility toward workers would also include helping them maintain proper job skills and, when terminations or layoffs are necessary, treating them with respect and compassion.

Ethical Commitments: The Special Case of Whistle-Blowers Respecting employees as people also means respecting their behavior as ethically responsible individuals. Suppose, for instance, an employee discovers that a business has been engaging in practices that are illegal, unethical, or socially irresponsible. Ideally, this employee should be able to report the problem to higher-level management, confident that managers will stop the questionable practices.

Too often, however, individuals who try to act ethically on the job find themselves in trouble with their employers. If no one in the organization will take action, the employee might elect to drop the matter. Occasionally, however, the individual will inform a regulatory agency or perhaps the media. At this point, the person becomes what is popularly known as a **whistle-blower**—an employee who discovers and tries to put an end to a company's unethical, illegal, or socially irresponsible actions by publicizing them.[17] The Al Pacino–Russell Crowe movie *The Insider* featured the story of a tobacco-industry whistle-blower named Jeffrey Wigand.

whistle-blower
Employee who detects and tries to put an end to a company's unethical, illegal, or socially irresponsible actions by publicizing them

Unfortunately, whistle-blowers are sometimes demoted, and even fired, when they take their accusations public. Jeffrey Wigand was fired. "I went from making $300,000 a year," he reports, "plus stock options, plus, plus, plus—to making $30,000. Yes, there is a price I've paid."[18] Even if they retain their jobs, they may still be treated as outsiders and suffer resentment or hostility from coworkers. Many coworkers see whistle-blowers as people who simply can't be trusted.

> *"I went from making $300,000 a year plus stock options to making $30,000."*
>
> —Jeffrey Wigand, whistle-blower

The law does offer some recourse to employees who take action. The current whistle-blower law stems from the False Claims Act of 1863, which was designed to prevent contractors from selling defective supplies to the Union Army during the Civil War. With 1986 revisions to the law, the government can recover triple damages from fraudulent contractors. If the Justice Department does not intervene, a whistle-blower can proceed with a civil suit. In that case, the whistle-blower receives 25 to 30 percent of any money recovered.[19]

When Phillip Adams worked in the computer industry, he discovered a flaw in the chip-making process that, under certain circumstances, could lead to data being randomly deleted or altered. He reported the flaw to manufacturers but several years later found that one company, Toshiba <www.toshiba.com>, had ignored the problem and continued to make flawed chips for 12 years. He went on to report the problem and became actively involved in a class action lawsuit based heavily on his research. Toshiba eventually agreed to a $2.1 billion settlement. Adams's share was kept confidential, but he did receive a substantial reward for his efforts.[20] The prospect of large cash rewards has also generated a spate of false or questionable accusations.

Responsibility Toward Investors

Because shareholders are the owners of a company, it may sound odd to say that a firm can act irresponsibly toward its investors. Managers can abuse their responsibilities to investors in several ways. As a rule, irresponsible behavior toward shareholders means abuse of a firm's financial resources. In such cases, the ultimate losers are indeed the shareholder-owners who do not receive their due earnings or dividends. Companies can also act irresponsibly toward shareholder-owners by misrepresenting company resources.

Improper Financial Management Occasionally, organizations or their officers are guilty of blatant financial mismanagement—offenses that are unethical but not necessarily illegal. Some firms, for example, have been accused of paying excessive salaries to senior managers, of sending them on extravagant "retreats" to exotic and expensive resorts, and of providing frivolous "perks," including ready access to corporate jets, lavish expense accounts, and memberships at plush country clubs.

In such situations, creditors can often do little, and stockholders have few options. Trying to force a management changeover is a difficult process that can drive down stock prices—a penalty that shareholders are usually unwilling to impose on themselves.

check kiting
Illegal practice of writing checks against money that has not yet been credited at the bank on which the checks are drawn

Check Kiting Certain unethical practices are illegal. **Check kiting**, for instance, involves writing a check against money that has not yet arrived at the bank on which it is drawn. In a typical scheme, managers deposit customer checks totaling, say, $1 million into the company account. Knowing that the bank will not collect all of the total deposit for several days, they proceed to write checks against the total amount deposited, knowing that their account is so important to the bank that the checks will be covered until the full deposits have been collected.

Insider Trading When someone uses confidential information to gain from the purchase or sale of stocks, that person is practicing *insider trading*. Suppose, for example, that a small firm's stock is currently trading at $50 a share. If a larger firm is going to buy the smaller one, it might have to pay as much as $75 a share for a controlling interest. Individuals who are aware of the impending acquisition before it is publicly announced might, therefore, be able to gain by buying the stock at $50 in anticipation of selling it for $75 after the proposed acquisition is announced.[21]

Individuals in a position to take advantage of such a situation generally include managers of the two firms and key individuals at banking firms working on the financial arrangements. For example, a former junior analyst with Salomon Smith Barney <www.smithbarney.com> was charged with insider trading in conjunction with a proposed merger between Washington Gas Light and Consolidated Natural Gas. Another banker with the same firm and three associates were charged with insider trading that resulted in $1.8 million in illegal profits ahead of six pending mergers, including WorldCom's bid for MCI. A compliance officer at BT Securities <www.bt.com> pled guilty to charges that he passed insider information about BT clients to his brother and two other individuals, who reaped $275,000 in illegal profits.[22]

Misrepresentation of Finances Certain behavior regarding financial representation is also illegal. In maintaining and reporting its financial status, every corporation must conform to *generally accepted accounting principles* (*GAAP*) (see Chapter 13). Sometimes, however, managers project profits far in excess of what they actually expect to earn. When the truth comes out, investors are disappointed.

IMPLEMENTING SOCIAL RESPONSIBILITY PROGRAMS

Thus far, we have discussed social responsibility as if there were some agreement on how organizations should behave. In fact, there are dramatic differences of opinion concerning the role of social responsibility as a business goal. Some people oppose any business activity that threatens profits. Others argue that social responsibility must take precedence over profits.

Even businesspeople who agree on the importance of social responsibility will cite different reasons for their views. Some skeptics of business-sponsored social projects fear that if businesses become too active, they will gain too much control over the ways in which those projects are addressed by society as a whole. These critics point to the influence that many businesses have been able to exert on the government agencies that are supposed to regulate their industries. Other critics claim that business organizations lack the expertise needed to address social issues. They argue, for instance, that technical experts, not businesses, should decide how to clean up polluted rivers.

Proponents of socially responsible business believe that corporations are citizens and should, therefore, help to improve the lives of fellow citizens. Still others point to the vast resources controlled by businesses and note that they help to create many of the problems social programs are designed to alleviate.

Approaches to Social Responsibility

Given these differences of opinion, it is little wonder that corporations have adopted a variety of approaches to social responsibility. Not surprisingly, organizations themselves adopt a wide range of positions on social responsibility.[23] As Figure 3.6 illustrates, the four stances that an organization can take concerning its obligations to society fall along a continuum ranging from the lowest to the highest degree of socially responsible practices.

Obstructionist Stance The few organizations that take what might be called an **obstructionist stance** to social responsibility usually do as little as possible to solve social or environmental problems. When they cross the ethical or legal line that separates acceptable from unacceptable practices, their typical response is to deny or cover up their actions. For example, IBP, which we profiled at the outset of this chapter, may take this stance. Firms that adopt this position have little regard for ethical conduct and will generally go to great lengths to hide wrongdoing.

obstructionist stance
Approach to social responsibility that involves doing as little as possible and may involve attempts to deny or cover up violations

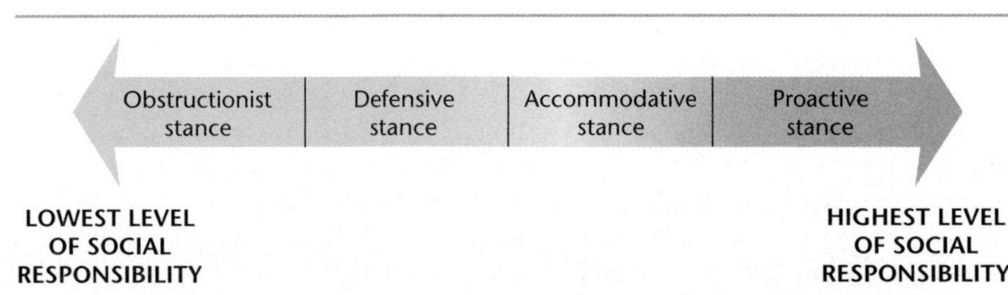

Figure 3.6
Spectrum of Approaches to Corporate Social Responsibility

Defensive Stance One step removed from the obstructionist stance is the **defensive stance**, whereby the organization will do everything that is required of it legally but nothing more. This approach is most consistent with arguments against corporate social responsibility. Managers who take a defensive stance insist that their job is to generate profits. Such a firm, for example, would install pollution-control equipment dictated by law but would not install higher-quality equipment even though it might further limit pollution.

Tobacco companies generally take this position in their marketing efforts. In the United States, they are legally required to include warnings to smokers on their products and to limit advertising to prescribed media. Domestically, they follow these rules to the letter of the law but use more aggressive marketing methods in countries that have no such rules. In many Asian and African countries, cigarettes are heavily promoted, contain higher levels of tar and nicotine than those sold in the United States, and carry few or no health warning labels. Firms that take this position are also unlikely to cover up wrongdoing, will generally admit to mistakes, and will take appropriate corrective actions.

defensive stance
Approach to social responsibility by which a company meets only minimum legal requirements in its commitments to groups and individuals in its social environment

accommodative stance
Approach to social responsibility by which a company, if specifically asked to do so, exceeds legal minimums in its commitments to groups and individuals in its social environment

proactive stance
Approach to social responsibility by which a company actively seeks opportunities to contribute to the well-being of groups and individuals in its social environment

Accommodative Stance A firm that adopts an **accommodative stance** meets its legal and ethical requirements but will also go further in certain cases. Such firms voluntarily agree to participate in social programs, but solicitors must convince them that given programs are worthy of their support. Both Shell and IBM, for example, will match contributions made by their employees to selected charitable causes. Many organizations respond to requests for donations to Little League, Girl Scouts, youth soccer programs, and so forth. The point, however, is that someone has to knock on the door and ask: Accommodative organizations do not necessarily or proactively seek avenues for contributing.

Proactive Stance The highest degree of social responsibility that a firm can exhibit is the **proactive stance**. Firms that adopt this approach take to heart the arguments in favor of social responsibility. They view themselves as citizens in a society and proactively seek opportunities to contribute. The most common—and direct—way to implement this stance is by setting up a foundation through which to provide direct financial support for various social programs. Table 3.1 lists the top 15 largest corporate foundations based on total giving to social programs.

Table 3.1
Top 15 Corporate Foundations

RANK	NAME/STATE	TOTAL GRANTS	AS OF FISCAL YEAR END DATA
1.	Ford Motor Company Fund (MI)	$97,789,429	12/31/99
2.	Bank of America Foundation, Inc. (NC)	90,999,532	12/31/99
3.	SBC Foundation (TX)	64,047,020	12/31/99
4.	Wal-Mart Foundation (AR)	62,617,641	01/31/00
5.	AT&T Foundation (NY)	39,626,024	12/31/99
6.	BP Amoco Foundation, Inc. (IL)	36,944,795	12/31/99
7.	GE Fund (CT)	36,126,991	12/31/99
8.	Verizon Foundation (NY)	35,332,818	12/31/99
9.	The Chase Manhattan Foundation (NY)	35,227,314	12/31/99
10.	Fannie Mae Foundation (DC)	33,926,500	12/31/99
11.	The UPS Foundation (GA)	32,838,108	12/31/99
12.	The Procter & Gamble Fund (OH)	32,269,866	06/30/99
13.	General Motors Foundation, Inc. (MI)	30,482,845	12/31/99
14.	Hoechst Marion Roussel Health Care Foundation for the Ill (MO)	28,650,012	12/31/99
15.	Lucent Technologies Foundation (NJ)	27,738,988	09/30/99

An excellent example of a different kind of proactive stance is the Ronald McDonald House <www.mcdonalds.com> program undertaken by McDonald's Corp. These houses, located close to major medical centers, can be used by families for minimal cost while sick children are receiving medical treatment nearby. Similarly, some firms, such as UPS <www.ups.com>, Home Depot <www.homedepot.com>, and US West <www.uswest.com>, employ individuals who hope to compete in the Olympics and support them in various ways. UPS, for instance, underwrites the training and travel costs of four employees competing for Olympic berths and allows them to maintain flexible work schedules.[24] These and related programs exceed the accommodative stance—they indicate a sincere commitment to improving the general social welfare and thus represent a proactive stance to social responsibility.

Remember, however, that these categories are not sharply distinct: They merely label stages along a continuum of approaches. Organizations do not always fit neatly into one category or another. The Ronald McDonald House program has been widely applauded, but McDonald's has also come under fire for allegedly misleading consumers about the nutritional value of its food products. Likewise, while UPS has sincere motives for helping Olympic athletes, the company will also benefit by featuring the athletes' photos on its envelopes and otherwise promoting its own benevolence. Even though IBP may take an obstructionist stance in some cases, many individual employees and managers at this firm have no doubt made substantial contributions to society in a number of different ways.

Managing Social Responsibility Programs

Making a company socially responsible in the full sense of the social response approach takes a carefully organized and managed program. In particular, managers must take steps to foster a companywide sense of social responsibility. Figure 3.7 summarizes those steps.[25]

1. *Social responsibility must start at the top*. Without the support of top management, no program can succeed. Thus, top management must embrace a strong stand on social responsibility and develop a policy statement outlining that commitment.
2. *A committee of top managers must develop a plan detailing the level of management support*. Some companies set aside percentages of profits for social programs. Levi Strauss, for example, earmarks 2.4 percent of pretax earnings for worthy projects. Managers must also set specific priorities. For instance, should the firm train the hard-core unemployed or support the arts?
3. *One executive must be put in charge of the firm's agenda*. Whether the role is created as a separate job or added to an existing one, the selected individual must

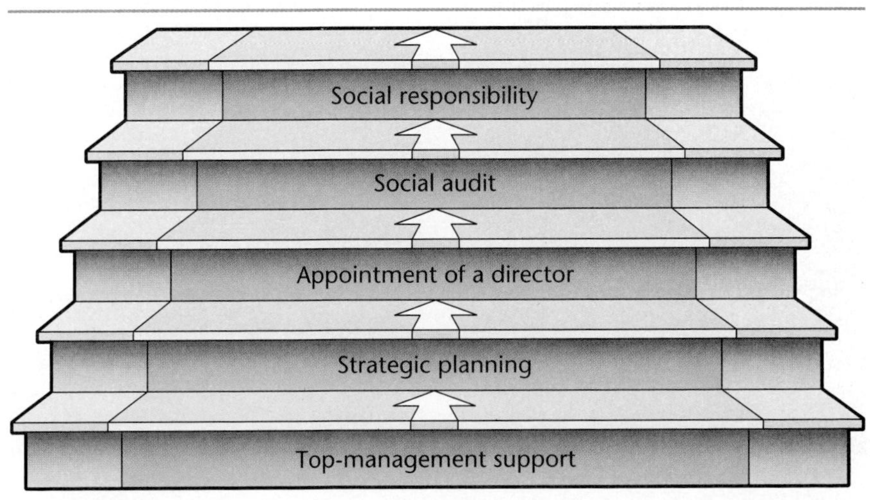

Figure 3.7
Establishing a Social Responsibility Program

monitor the program and ensure that its implementation is consistent with the firm's policy statement and strategic plan.

4. *The organization must conduct occasional **social audits**: systematic analyses of its success in using funds earmarked for its social responsibility goals.*[26] Consider the case of a company whose strategic plan calls for spending $100,000 to train 200 hard-core unemployed people and to place 180 of them in jobs. If at the end of a year the firm has spent $98,000, trained 210 people, and filled 175 jobs, a social audit will confirm the program's success. But if the program has cost $150,000, trained only 90 people, and placed only 10 of them, the audit will reveal the program's failure. Such failure should prompt a rethinking of the program's implementation and its priorities.

social audit
Systematic analysis of a firm's success in using funds earmarked for meeting its social responsibility goals

Social Responsibility and the Small Business

As the owner of a garden supply store, how would you respond to a building inspector's suggestion that a cash payment will speed your application for a building permit? As the manager of a liquor store, would you call the police, refuse to sell, or sell to a customer whose identification card looks forged? As the owner of a small laboratory, would you call the state board of health to make sure that it has licensed the company with whom you want to contract to dispose of medical waste? Who will really be harmed if a small firm pads its income statement to help it get a much-needed bank loan?

Many of the examples in this chapter illustrate big-business responses to ethical and social responsibility issues. Such examples, however, show quite clearly that small businesses must answer many of the same questions. Differences are primarily differences of scale.

At the same time, these are largely questions of *individual* ethics. What about questions of *social* responsibility? Can a small business, for example, afford a social agenda? Should it sponsor Little League baseball teams, make donations to the United Fund, and buy light bulbs from the Lion's Club? Do joining the chamber of commerce and supporting the Better Business Bureau cost too much? Clearly, ethics and social responsibility are decisions faced by all managers in all organizations, regardless of rank or size. One key to business success is to decide in advance how to respond to the issues that underlie all questions of ethical and social responsibility.

The owners of Hermitage Artists salvage boxes and shipping crates from supermarkets, which would otherwise compact them and dump them in landfills. From such raw materials Hermitage makes artifacts ranging from small wooden boxes and frames to religious statues and elaborate desks. This small business in Troy, NY, combines environmentalism and the spirit of so-called "tramp art" by making salable objects of art out of discarded materials and is a collaborative operation run by men who were once homeless.

Continued from page 60

Some Ethical Rants and Raves

Managers at Patagonia and IBP apparently have quite different approaches to the idea of social responsibility. Patagonia always puts its social agenda at the forefront of everything it does. In early 2000, for example, the firm set up a major new Internet operation to sell more efficiently to consumers. There's nothing particularly socially conscious about doing that, but one of the site's more interesting features is a section called "Rants & Raves." Here customers can post online reviews and comments about Patagonia products—both positive and negative. Even a firm as socially active as Patagonia is not always above criticism. Some people, for instance, criticize the company for donating money to such radical groups as Earth First.

IBP, meanwhile, has continued to face a raft of problems. On January 12, 2000, the U.S. Justice Department, acting on behalf of the Environmental Protection Agency <www.epa.gov>, filed a lawsuit accusing IBP of violating numerous federal air, water, and hazardous-waste laws at the company's flagship plant and former headquarters in Dakota City, Nebraska. The government charged that IBP emitted up to 1,800 pounds of hydrogen sulfide per day from the Dakota City plant without informing federal regulators (disclosure is required if total emissions exceed 100 pounds per day) and that IBP violated the federal Clean Water Act by dumping excessive ammonia into the Missouri River. The suit charged IBP with either failing to file or else filing incorrectly federal toxic air reports at several plants in Iowa, Nebraska, and Kansas.

In addition, various agencies in states where IBP operates have investigated numerous allegations about pollution. Idaho's State Division of Environmental Quality charged IBP with exceeding state wastewater guidelines by as much as 1,200 percent. While the Illinois state attorney general sought fines against IBP for violating the state's odor law, officials in Nebraska were still watching the federal investigation to see if there have been violations of state regulations.

In early 2001, IBP announced that it had agreed to be acquired by Tyson Foods <www.tyson.com> for $3.2 billion. Shortly after the agreement was announced, however, Tyson moved to call off the merger because of numerous accounting irregularities at IBP that had substantially overstated the firm's value. In June 2001, however, a settlement was reached and Tyson did buy IBP but for a somewhat lower price—only $2.7 billion. Perhaps new ownership will bring with it a new commitment to ethical and socially responsible business practices.

Questions for Discussion

1. Compare and contrast the concept of social responsibility at Patagonia and IBP.
2. Characterize each company's approach to its customers, employees, and other stakeholders.
3. Which approach to social responsibility is each firm taking?
4. At which firm would you rather work? Why? Which firm's stock would you prefer to own (assume that Patagonia is publicly traded)? Why?
5. Using the Internet, research recent developments in the cases against IBP.

SUMMARY OF LEARNING OBJECTIVES

1 **Explain how individuals develop their personal *codes of ethics* and why ethics are important in the workplace.** Individual *codes of ethics* are derived from social standards of right and wrong. *Ethical behavior* is behavior that conforms to generally accepted social norms concerning beneficial and harmful actions. Because ethics affect the behavior of individuals on behalf of the companies that employ them, many firms are adopting formal statements of ethics. Unethical behavior can result in loss of business, fines, and even imprisonment.

2 **Distinguish *social responsibility* from ethics and trace the evolution of social responsibility in U.S. business.** *Social responsibility* refers to an organization's response to social needs. One way to understand social responsibility is to view it in terms of *stakeholders*—those groups, individuals, and organizations that are directly affected by the practices of an organization and, therefore, have a stake in its performance. Until the second half of the nineteenth century, businesses often paid little attention to stakeholders. Since then, however, both public pressure and government regulation, especially as a result of the Great Depression of the 1930s and the social activism of the 1960s and 1970s, have forced businesses to consider the public welfare, at least to some degree. A trend toward increased social consciousness, including a heightened sense of environmental activism, has recently emerged.

3 **Show how the concept of social responsibility applies both to environmental issues and to a firm's relationships with customers, employees, and investors.** Social responsibility toward the environment requires firms to minimize pollution of air, water, and land. Social responsibility toward customers requires firms to provide products of acceptable quality, to price products fairly, and to respect consumers' rights. Social responsibility toward employees requires firms to respect workers both as resources and as people who are more productive when their needs are met. Social responsibility toward investors requires firms to manage their resources and to represent their financial status honestly.

4 **Identify four general *approaches to social responsibility* and describe the four steps a firm must take to implement a *social responsibility program*.** An *obstructionist stance* on social responsibility is taken by a firm that does as little as possible to address social or environmental problems and that may deny or attempt to cover up problems that may occur. The *defensive stance* emphasizes compliance with legal minimum requirements. Companies adopting the *accommodative stance* go beyond minimum activities, if asked. The *proactive stance* commits a company to actively seek to contribute to social projects. Implementing a social responsibility program entails four steps: (1) drafting a policy statement with the support of top management, (2) developing a detailed plan, (3) appointing a director to implement the plan, and (4) conducting *social audits* to monitor results.

5 **Explain how issues of social responsibility and ethics affect small businesses.** Managers and employees of small businesses face many of the same ethical questions as their counterparts at larger firms. Small businesses face the same issues of social responsibility and the same need to decide on an approach to social responsibility. The differences are primarily differences of scale.

QUESTIONS AND EXERCISES

Questions for Review

1. What basic factors should be considered in any ethical decision?
2. Who are an organization's stakeholders? Who are the major stakeholders with which most businesses must be concerned?
3. What are the major areas of social responsibility with which businesses should be concerned?
4. What are the four basic approaches to social responsibility?
5. In what ways do you think your personal code of ethics might clash with the operations of some companies? How might you try to resolve these differences?

Questions for Analysis

6. What kind of wrongdoing would most likely prompt you to be a whistle-blower? What kind of wrongdoing would be least likely? Why?
7. In your opinion, which area of social responsibility is most important? Why? Are there areas other than those noted in the chapter that you consider important?
8. Identify some specific ethical or social responsibility issues that might be faced by small-business managers and employees in each of the following areas: environment, customers, employees, and investors.

Application Exercises

9. Develop a list of the major stakeholders of your college or university. As a class, discuss the ways in which you think the school prioritizes these stakeholders. Do you agree or disagree with this prioritization?
10. Using newspapers, magazines, and other business references, identify and describe at least three companies that take a defensive stance to social responsibility, three that take an accommodative stance, and three that take a proactive stance.

EXERCISING YOUR ETHICS

Taking a Stance

THE SITUATION

A perpetual debate revolves around the roles and activities of business owners in contributing to the greater social good. Promoting the so-called *proactive stance*, some people argue that businesses should be socially responsible by seeking opportunities to benefit the society in which they are permitted to conduct their affairs. Others maintain that because businesses exist to make profits for owners they have no further obligation to society than that (the *defensive stance*).

THE DILEMMA

Pair up with one of your classmates. Using a coin toss, each of you should select or be assigned one side of this debate. You and your partner should then enter into a dialogue to formulate the three most convincing arguments possible to support each side. Then select the single strongest argument in support of each position. Each team of two partners should then present to the class its strongest arguments for and against social responsibility on the part of business.

QUESTIONS FOR DISCUSSION

1. Which side of the debate is easier to defend? Why?
2. What is your personal opinion about the appropriate stance that a business should take regarding social responsibility?
3. To what extent is the concept of social responsibility relevant to nonbusiness organizations such as universities, government units, health care organizations, and so forth?

EXPLORING THE WEB

Setting Your Sites on Ethics

Texas Instruments (TI) was a pioneer in the area of business ethics. TI was one of the very first corporations in the United States to create and publish a code of ethics for managers and employees. To learn more about ethics at TI, visit the company Web site and then answer the questions that follow:

<www.ti.com/corp/docs/ethics/home.htm>

1. Over all, how beneficial do you think this Web site would be for a Texas Instruments employee interested in corporate ethics?
2. Visit the area in the Web site and review the information dealing with ethics across the organization. How useful do you find this information to be?
3. Visit the area in the site about ethics in the global market. What are the strengths and weaknesses of this area?
4. One area of the Web site features an ethics quiz designed to help employees get a sense of the ethics of a particular action. How practical is this section?
5. If you were developing an ethics Web site for another company, would you pattern it after the TI site? Why or why not?
6. Why don't more companies have Web sites like this one?

BUILDING YOUR BUSINESS SKILLS

To Lie or Not to Lie: That Is the Question

This exercise enhances the following SCANS workplace competencies: demonstrating basic skills, demonstrating thinking skills, exhibiting interpersonal skills, and working with information.

GOAL

To encourage students to apply general concepts of business ethics to specific situations.

BACKGROUND

Workplace lying, it seems, has become business as usual. According to one survey, one-quarter of working American adults said that they had been asked to do something illegal or unethical on the job. Four in 10 did what they were told. Another survey of more than 2,000 secretaries showed that many employees face ethical dilemmas in their day-to-day work.

METHOD

STEP 1

- Working with four other students, discuss ways in which you would respond to the following ethical dilemmas. When there is a difference of opinion among group members, try to determine the specific factors that influence different responses.
- Would you lie about your supervisor's whereabouts to someone on the phone?
- Would you lie about who was responsible for a business decision that cost your company thousands of dollars to protect your own or your supervisor's job?
- Would you inflate sales and revenue data on official company accounting statements to increase stock value?
- Would you say that you witnessed a signature when you did not if you were acting in the role of a notary?
- Would you keep silent if you knew that the official minutes of a corporate meeting had been changed?
- Would you destroy or remove information that could hurt your company if it fell into the wrong hands?

STEP 2

Research the commitment to business ethics at Johnson & Johnson <www.jnj.com> and Texas Instruments <www.ti.com/corp/docs/ethics/ home.htm> by clicking on their respective Web sites. As a group, discuss ways in which these statements are likely to affect the specific behaviors mentioned in Step 1.

STEP 3

Working with group members, draft a corporate code of ethics that would discourage the specific behaviors mentioned in Step 1. Limit your code to a single typewritten page, but make it sufficiently broad to cover different ethical dilemmas.

FOLLOW-UP ASSIGNMENT

1. What personal, social, and cultural factors do you think contribute to lying in the workplace?
2. Do you agree or disagree with the following statement? "The term *business ethics* is an oxymoron." Support your answer with examples from your own work experience or that of a family member.
3. If you were your company's director of human resources, how would you make your code of ethics a "living document"?
4. If you were faced with any of the ethical dilemmas described in Step 1, how would you handle them? How far would you go to maintain your personal ethical standards?

CRAFTING YOUR BUSINESS PLAN

Going in the Ethical Direction

THE PURPOSE OF THE ASSIGNMENT

1. To familiarize students with some of the ethical and social responsibility considerations faced by sample firms in the *Business PlanPro (BPP)* (Version 4.0) planning environment.
2. To show where ethical and social responsibility considerations can be found in various sections of the *BPP* business plan.

FOLLOW-UP ASSIGNMENT

After reading Chapter 3 in the textbook, open the BPP *software and look around for information about the types of ethical considerations and social responsibility factors that would be of concern to the sample firm* of Southeast Health Service *(Southeast Health Plans, Inc.). Then respond to the following items:*

1. Do you think a company in Southeast's line of business should have a code of ethics? Call up Southeast's Business Plan Outline. [Click on **Plan Outline** on the Plan Manager screen.] In which sections of Southeast's business plan would you expect to find its code of ethics? Go into those sections from the Plan Manager screen and identify information about their code of ethics. What did you find?
2. The textbook states that a firm's social responsibility includes providing quality products for its customers. Explore Southeast's business plan and describe its position on providing quality products. [Sites to see in *BPP* for this item: In the Plan Outline screen, click on **1.0 Executive Summary.** Then click on and read each of **1.1 Objectives, 1.2 Mission**, and **1.3 Keys to Success.**]
3. Another dimension of social responsibility is pricing products fairly. Search through Southeast's plan to identify information about the fairness of pricing for services it offers. Does Southeast's planned gross margin reflect "fair pricing"? Why or why not? [Sites to see in *BPP* for this item: In the Plan Outline screen, click on **3.1 Competitive Comparison** and then on **3.3 Sourcing.** After returning to the Plan Outline screen, click on **5.1.1 Pricing Strategy** and then **1.0 Executive Summary.**]

VIDEO EXERCISE

Catering to Serious Users: Patagonia

LEARNING OBJECTIVES

The purpose of this video exercise is to help you

1. Recognize the ethical challenges facing businesses today.
2. Understand the ways in which firms can act responsibly.
3. Understand the relationship between ethics and quality.

BACKGROUND INFORMATION

Yvon Chouinard founded Patagonia over 20 years ago, making climbing gear by hand for his friends. Today, the company makes clothing for a wide variety of activities with a focus on function, durability, and innovation. Its rigorously field-tested products are available worldwide, and it has offices in North America, Europe, and Japan, with a headquarters in Ventura, California. In addition to its commitment to customers—"serious users who rely on the product in extreme conditions"—the firm is responsible to its employees by providing a family-friendly workplace, and to the environment by donating millions of dollars to environmentalist groups in the United States and abroad.

THE VIDEO

The video segment describes the founding of Patagonia and its commitment to high-quality products. It details the company's recent struggle to maintain financial stability while avoiding the runaway growth that its managers fear would have a damaging effect on the natural environment.

QUESTIONS FOR DISCUSSION

1. In what ways does Patagonia demonstrate its ethical commitment to employees?
2. What is the relationship between ethics and quality that Patagonia strives to maintain?
3. How would you reconcile Patagonia's highly developed sense of social responsibility with its decision to lay off 20 percent of its workforce?

FOLLOW-UP ASSIGNMENT

Choose a company in the service sector that claims to be socially responsible. In what ways are its stated ethical objectives confirmed or contradicted by its approach to employees, customers, investors, and the natural environment?

FOR FURTHER EXPLORATION

Visit the Patagonia Web site <www.patagonia.com> and explore the page "About Us." Of special interest are the "Selected Essays" in which various writers and employees, including founder Yvon Chouinard, talk about the company's history and philosophy. Read Chouinard's essay, "Patagonia: The Next 100 Years," and scan two or three of the other articles. Do these essays express a consistent viewpoint about the company's mission? Try to put the firm's philosophy in your own words. Do you think it is a sustainable business strategy? Why or why not?

Understanding Entrepreneurship and Small Business

After reading this chapter, you should be able to:

1. Define *small business,* discuss its importance to the U.S. economy, and explain which *types of small business* best lend themselves to success.
2. Explain *sole proprietorships* and *partnerships* and discuss the advantages and disadvantages of each.
3. Describe *corporations,* discuss their advantages and disadvantages, and identify different kinds of corporations.
4. Describe the basic issues involved in creating and managing a corporation and identify recent trends and issues in corporate ownership.
5. Describe the *start-up decisions* made by small businesses and identify sources of *financial aid* available to such enterprises.
6. Identify the advantages and disadvantages of *franchising.*

Planting the Seeds of a Netpreneurial Idea

Cliff Sharples, Lisa Aufranc, and Jamie O'Neill became close friends in graduate school, and the bonds grew even stronger when they all went to work for Trilogy Software in Austin, Texas, in 1995. Indeed, Cliff and Lisa were married as they were making the transition to their new jobs. But all three had known from their days together in school that they wanted to start their own business, and so, only 10 weeks after moving to Austin, they left Trilogy and set out to find a niche for a new business start-up.

Interestingly, they knew immediately *how* they wanted this business to work. They just didn't know *what* they wanted to sell. All three were firm believers that the Internet was on the verge of becoming a major venue for business, and they also had a very solid understanding of how firms market products. They wanted to combine their knowledge of marketing with the power of the Internet.

Initially they created a three-person partnership legally named the Asbury Group—a name derived from a popular gathering place on the campus of Northwestern University, where they had met. They used this legal framework to engage in some consulting activities while they figured out what business they really wanted to launch. Why did they elect to use the partnership arrangement at first? Basically, for two reasons: (1) It was easy to set up, and (2) they knew it would only be temporary.

Shortly thereafter, they settled on gardening supplies and equipment as the product base for their

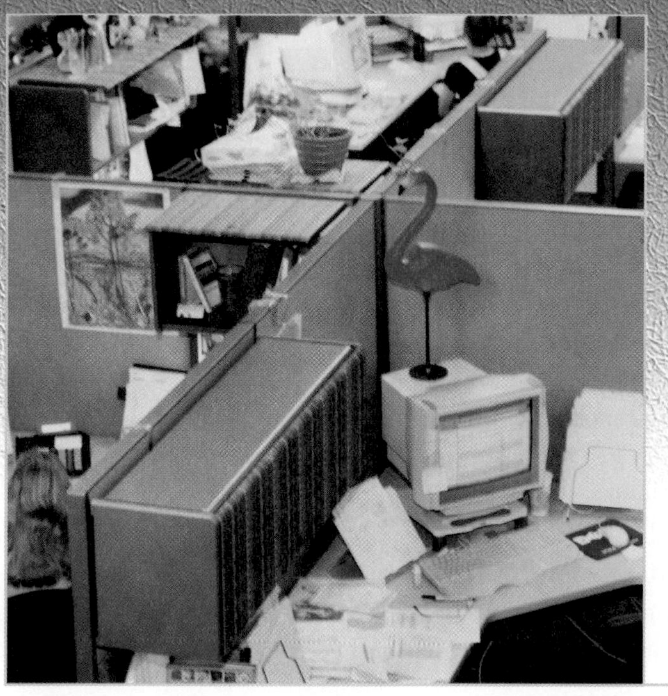

> *"We were not scrounging around in the dark looking for cool ideas. We knew e-commerce was going to be huge. And when we hit on gardening, it felt so right."*
>
> —Jamie O'Neill, Garden Escape chief operations officer

"real" business. "We were not scrounging around in the dark looking for cool ideas," says O'Neill. "We knew e-commerce was going to be huge. And when we hit on gardening, it felt so right." They named the company Garden Escape and paid $2,500 for the rights to the Web site name Garden.com.

They also divided up the management tasks to fit their own talents and interests. Specifically, Cliff Sharples was named president and CEO and assumed responsibilities for overall strategies. As chief operations officer, Jamie O'Neill took charge of the day-to-day management and administration of the company. Lisa Sharples became chief marketing and merchandising officer, handling product mix, promotional strategies, and so forth. Finally, the three founders brought in a fourth partner, Andy Martin, as chief technology officer.

After they settled on the general direction in which they wanted to go, they incorporated Asbury in order to take advantage of the legal benefits of corporate ownership. As part of the incorporation process, they also changed the name of the business to Garden Escape. During the early period of their start-up, they had plenty of capital with which to work. Indeed, so many investors wanted a piece of the new company that the founders actually turned down some of them.

Garden.com was officially launched on March 20, 1996, the first day of spring, when its Web site went live. In July of that same year, the firm opened a publishing office in Des Moines, Iowa, and announced the impending publication of an upscale magazine called *Garden Escape*. The idea was to publish a print magazine that would complement the Garden.com Web site. Garden.com also formed a strategic alliance with PRIMEDIA to distribute the magazine to key locations at airport and major metropolitan-area newsstands. The company hired Doug Jimerson, editor of *Better Homes and Gardens*, to run the magazine business. In early 1999, the corporation officially changed its name to Garden.com to match the URL of its centerpiece Web site.

In 1999, with all phases of their business up and running, their strategy fine-tuned, Garden.com established as a major Web site for garden-related products, and *Garden Escape* magazine off the ground, Cliff, Lisa, and Jamie decided that the time was ripe for an initial public offering (IPO) of stock to raise additional capital. In September 1999, 4.1 million shares of common stock were offered at a price of $12 a share. The IPO, therefore, generated almost $50 million in additional capital.

This cash infusion brought with it heady optimism and the means both to continue operations and to expand into new markets. By mid-2000, however, most of the new capital was gone. Because investors had begun to shun dot-com businesses that had yet to turn a profit, another stock offering was not feasible. Thus, as its cash began to dry up in the summer of 2000, Garden.com was simply unable to secure the additional funding that it needed to remain afloat. The firm may also have had flawed control systems that failed to alert senior managers to the impending cash shortage: Had they known earlier of the impending shortfall, they may have been able to cut costs more quickly and/or secure additional financing before the investment community began to pull out of the dot-com sector.

In November 2000, when it became apparent that new funds were not available for Garden.com, Cliff, Jamie, and Lisa began looking for another company that would assume partial or full ownership of Garden.com in exchange for the new financial investment necessary to keep the business in operation. When they were unsuccessful, they shut down operations and began selling off their remaining business assets.

Regardless of the specific reasons for Garden.com's initial success and eventual failure, both current and would-be entrepreneurs can learn some valuable lessons from its story. For one thing, a business can never have too much money. For another, while investors may tolerate periodic losses, they can quickly become impatient if losses mount too quickly and profits remain elusive. Furthermore, business owners and managers must never let their guard down—no matter how rosy things look, a cash shortage, especially when combined with shifts in the financial and investment sector, can spell trouble for any business.

Our opening story continues on page 108

WHAT IS A SMALL BUSINESS?

The term *small business* defies easy definition. Clearly, locally owned and operated restaurants, hair salons, and accounting firms are small businesses, and giant corporations such as Sony, Caterpillar, and Eastman Kodak are big businesses. Between these two extremes fall thousands of companies that cannot be easily categorized.

The U.S. Department of Commerce <www.osec.doc.gov> considers a business "small" if it has fewer than 500 employees; but the U.S. **Small Business Administration (SBA)** <www.sba.gov>, a government assistance agency for small businesses, regards some companies with 1,500 employees as small. The SBA bases its definition on two factors: (1) *number of employees* and (2) *total annual sales*. For example, manufacturers are defined as "small" according to the first criterion and grocery stores according to the second. Thus, although an independent grocery store with $13 million in sales may sound large, the SBA still sees it as a small business when its revenues are compared with those of truly large food retailers.

Small Business Administration (SBA)
Federal agency charged with assisting small businesses

Because it is sometimes difficult to define a small business in strictly numerical terms, we define a **small business** as one that is independently owned and managed and does not dominate its market. A small business, then, cannot be part of another business: Operators must be their own bosses, free to run their businesses as they please. In addition, to be considered small, a business must have relatively little influence in its market. For example, although Compaq Computer <www.compaq.com> and Dell Computer <www.dell.com> were both certainly small businesses when they were founded by entrepreneurs in 1984, they are now among the dominant companies in the personal computer market.

small business
Independently owned and managed business that does not dominate its market

The Importance of Small Business in the U.S. Economy

As Figure 4.1 shows, most U.S. businesses employ fewer than 100 people, and most U.S. workers are employed by small firms. For example, Figure 4.1(a) shows that 86.09 percent of all U.S. businesses employ 20 or fewer people; another 11 percent employ between 20 and 99 people. In contrast, only about one-tenth of 1 percent employ 1,000 or more workers. Figure 4.1(b) shows that 25.60 percent of all U.S. workers are employed by firms with fewer than 20 people; another 29.10 percent work in firms that employ between 20 and 99 people. The vast majority of these companies are owner operated.[1] Figure 4.1(b) also shows that 12.70 percent of U.S. workers are employed by firms with 1,000 or more total employees.

The contribution of small business can be measured in terms of its effects on key aspects of the U.S. economic system, including *job creation*, *innovation*, and *importance to big business*.

Job Creation Relative job growth among businesses of different sizes is not easy to determine. It is clear, however, that small business—especially in certain industries—is an important source of new (and often well-paid) jobs in this country. According to the SBA, seven of the 10 industries that added the most new jobs in 1998 were in sectors dominated by small businesses. Moreover, small businesses currently account for 38 percent of all jobs in high-technology sectors of the economy.[2]

In reality, of course, jobs are created by companies of all sizes, all of which hire workers and all of which lay them off. Although small firms often hire at a faster rate than large ones, they are also likely to eliminate jobs at a far higher rate. Small firms are also the first to hire in times of economic recovery, large firms the last. Conversely, however, big companies are also the last to lay off workers during economic downswings.

Innovation History has shown that major innovations are as likely to come from small businesses (or individuals) as from big businesses. For example, small firms and individuals invented the personal computer and the stainless-steel razor blade, the transistor radio and the photocopying machine, the jet engine and the self-developing

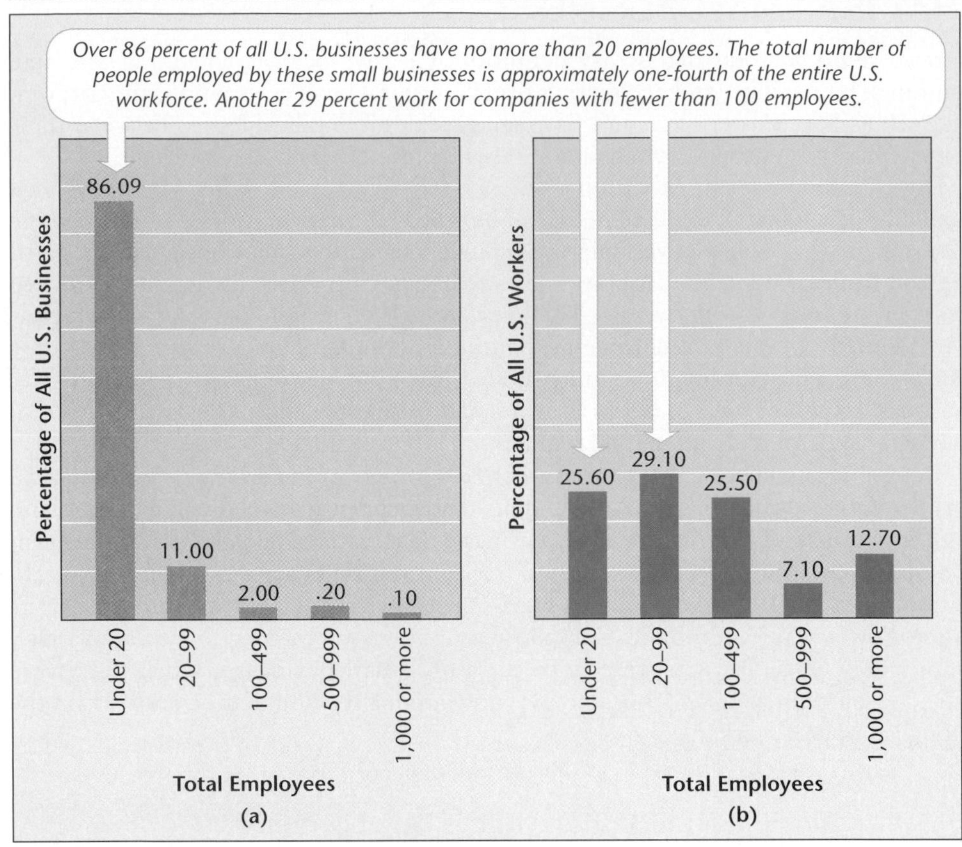

Figure 4.1

The Importance of Small Business in the United States

photograph. Today, says the SBA, small businesses supply 55 percent of all "innovations" introduced into the American marketplace.[3]

Importance to Big Business Most of the products made by big manufacturers are sold to consumers by small businesses. For example, the majority of dealerships selling Fords, Chevrolets, Toyotas, and Volvos are independently owned and operated. Moreover, small businesses provide big businesses with many of the services, supplies, and raw materials they need. Microsoft <www.microsoft.com>, for instance, relies heavily on small businesses in the course of its routine business operations, outsourcing much of its routine code-writing functions to hundreds of sole proprietorships and other small firms.

Popular Areas of Small-Business Enterprise

Not surprisingly, small businesses are more common in some industries than in others. The major small-business industry groups are *services, retailing, construction, financial and insurance, wholesaling, transportation*, and *manufacturing*. Obviously, each group differs in its requirements for employees, money, materials, and machines. Remember: The more resources an industry requires, the harder it is to start a business and the less likely that the industry is dominated by small firms. Remember, too, that *small* is a relative term: The criteria (number of employees and total annual sales) differ from industry to industry and are often meaningful only when compared with businesses that are truly large. Figure 4.2 shows the distribution of all U.S. businesses employing fewer than 20 people across industry groups.

Small-business services range from shoeshine parlors to car rental agencies, from marriage counseling to computer software, from accounting and management consulting to professional dog walking. Partly because they require few resources, service businesses are the fastest-growing segment of small-business enterprise. A retail busi-

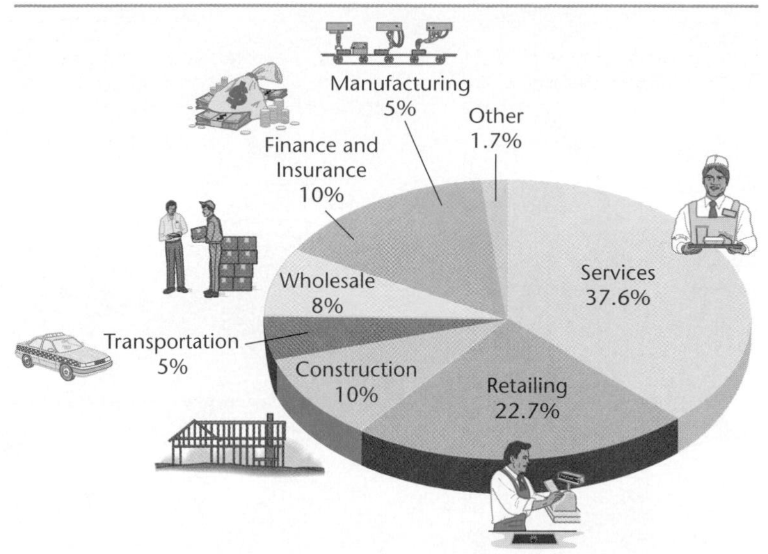

Figure 4.2
Small Business by Industry

ness sells directly to consumers products manufactured by other firms. Usually, people who start small businesses favor specialty shops—for example, big men's clothing or gourmet coffees—that let them focus limited resources on narrow market segments.

About 10 percent of businesses with fewer than 20 employees are involved in construction. Because many construction jobs are relatively small local projects, local construction firms are often ideally suited as contractors. Financial and insurance businesses also comprise about 10 percent of all firms with less than 20 employees. In most cases, these businesses are either affiliates of or sell products provided by larger national firms.

Small-business owners often do very well in wholesaling, too—about 8 percent of businesses with fewer than 20 employees are wholesalers. A wholesale business buys products from manufacturers or other producers and then sells them to retailers. Wholesalers usually buy goods in bulk and store them in quantities at locations that are convenient for retailers. For a given volume of business, therefore, they need fewer employees than manufacturers, retailers, or service providers.

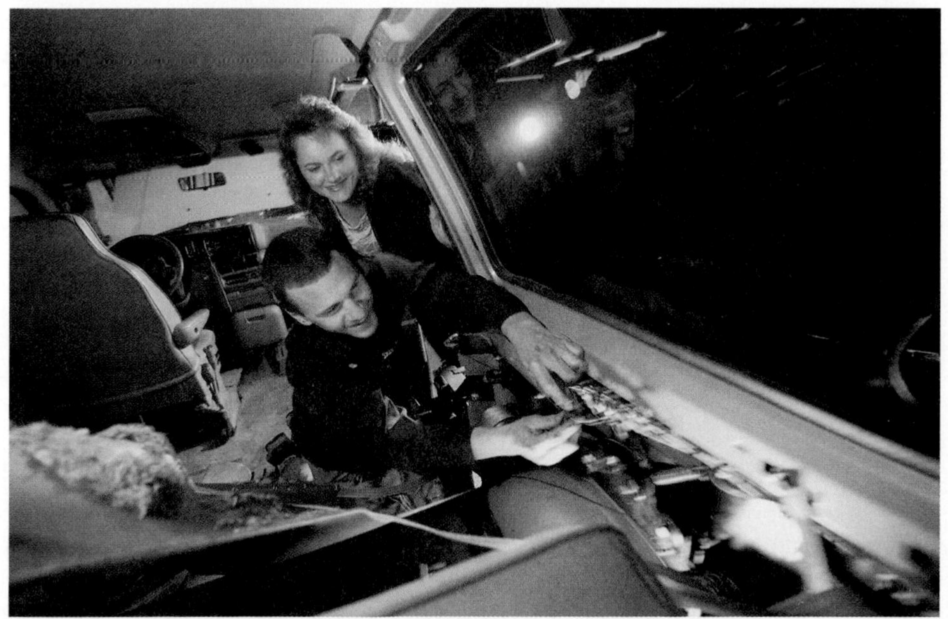

Peter and Christina Ruprecht operate a small business in the service sector. Located in Fairfield, New Jersey, Drive-Master Co., Inc. <www.drivemaster.net> *makes driving systems for the physically challenged and adapts vans so that they can be driven by disabled persons from wheelchairs. The company was started by Ruprecht's father, who lost the use of both legs to polio in 1952, and today, it distributes through 400 dealerships nationwide.*

Excelsior-Henderson Motorcycle Manufacturing Co. <www.excelsior-henderson.com> is proof that small businesses can be built in the manufacturing sector. Based in Belle Plaine, Minnesota, the company was founded by brothers Dave (left) and Dan Hanlon and Dave's wife Jennie in 1993. They started with money from 400 investors and then went public, raising nearly $100 million. Only then did they actually start constructing a factory, designing motorcycles, and hiring experts in manufacturing, sales, marketing, and engineering.

Some small firms—about 5 percent of all companies with fewer than 20 employees—do well in transportation and transportation-related businesses. Such firms include local taxi and limousine companies, charter airplane services, and tour operators. More than any other industry, manufacturing lends itself to big business. This is not to say that there are no small-business owners who do well in manufacturing—about 5 percent of businesses with fewer than 20 employees are involved in some aspect of manufacturing. Indeed, it is not uncommon for small manufacturers to outperform big business in such innovation-driven industries as chemistry, electronics, toys, and computer software.

TYPES OF BUSINESS ORGANIZATIONS

Whether they run small agricultural enterprises, large manufacturing concerns, or virtual e-commerce firms, all business owners must decide which form of legal organization best suits their goals: *sole proprietorship, partnership*, or *corporation*. Because this choice affects a host of managerial and financial issues, few decisions are more critical. In choosing a form of organization, entrepreneurs must consider their own preferences, their immediate and long-range needs, and the advantages and disadvantages of each form. Table 4.1 summarizes and compares the most important differences among the three major business forms.

Sole Proprietorships

sole proprietorship
Business owned and usually operated by one person who is responsible for all of its debts

The most basic legal form of business organization, the **sole proprietorship**, is owned and usually operated by one person.[4] Today, about 73 percent of all businesses in the United States are sole proprietorships; however, they account for only about 5 percent of the country's total business revenues.[5] Although a sole proprietorship is usually small, it may be as large as a steel mill or a department store.

Advantages of Sole Proprietorships Freedom is perhaps the most important benefit of sole proprietorships. Because they own their businesses completely, sole proprietors answer to no one but themselves. Furthermore, sole proprietorships are simple to form. Sometimes a proprietor can go into business simply by putting a sign on the door. The simplicity of legal setup procedures makes this form of organization appealing to self-starters and independent spirits, as do low start-up costs.

Business Form	Liability	Continuity	Management	Sources of Investment
Proprietorship	Personal, unlimited	Ends with death or decision of owner	Personal, unrestricted	Personal
General Partnership	Personal, unlimited	Ends with death or decision of any partner	Unrestricted or depends on partnership agreement	Personal by partner(s)
Corporation	Capital invested	As stated in charter, perpetual or for specified period of years	Under control of board of directors, which is selected by stockholders	Purchase of stock

Table 4.1

Comparative Summary: Three Forms of Business

Finally, a particularly appealing feature of sole proprietorships is the tax benefits extended to new businesses that are likely to suffer losses in their early stages. Tax laws permit sole proprietors to treat sales revenues and operating expenses as part of their personal finances. They can thus cut their taxes by deducting business losses from income earned elsewhere (from personal sources other than the business).

Disadvantages of Sole Proprietorships A major drawback of sole proprietorships, however, is **unlimited liability**: A sole proprietor is personally liable for all debts incurred by the business. If the business fails to generate enough cash, bills must be paid out of the proprietor's own pocket. Another disadvantage is lack of continuity: A sole proprietorship legally dissolves when the owner dies. Although the business can be reorganized if a successor is prepared to take over, executors or heirs must otherwise sell the assets of the business.[6]

unlimited liability
Legal principle holding owners responsible for paying off all debts of a business

Finally, a sole proprietorship depends on the resources of a single individual. In many cases, owners' managerial and financial limitations put limits on their organizations. Sole proprietors often find it hard to borrow money, not only to start up but also to expand. Many commercial bankers fear that they will not be able to recover loans when sole proprietors become disabled or insolvent.

Partnerships

The second form of legal organization is the partnership, which is frequently used by professionals.[7] The most common type of partnership, the **general partnership**, is simply a sole proprietorship multiplied by the number of partner-owners. There is no legal limit to the number of parties who may form a general partnership—the average number is slightly fewer than 10. Moreover, partners may invest equal or unequal sums of money and may earn profits that bear no relation to their investments. Thus, a partner with no financial investment in a two-person partnership could receive 50 percent or more of the profits if he or she has some other contribution to offer—say, a well-known name or special expertise.

general partnership
Business with two or more owners who share in both the operation of the firm and the financial responsibility for its debts

Advantages of Partnerships The most striking advantage of general partnerships is their ability to grow with the addition of new talent and money. Because lending institutions prefer to make loans to enterprises that are not dependent on single individuals, partnerships find it easier to borrow money than sole proprietorships. They can also invite new partners to join by investing in the company.

Like a sole proprietorship, a partnership can be organized by meeting only a few legal requirements. Even so, all partnerships must begin with an agreement of some kind. All but two states subscribe to the Revised Uniform Limited Partnership Act.

WEB Connection

Pentagram is a design firm with 17 full-time partners and 160 employees working out of offices in San Franciso, New York, London, and Austin, Texas. To find out how the company itself characterizes the working relationships between its "principals" and "design teams," log on to its Web site.

www.pentagram.com

This statute describes a written certificate that requires the filing of specific information about the business and its partners. Partners may also agree to bind themselves in ways not specified by the certificate. In any case, a partnership agreement should answer questions such as the following:

- Who invested what sums of money?
- Who will receive what share of the profits?
- Who does what and who reports to whom?
- How may the partnership be dissolved? In the event of dissolution, how will assets be distributed?
- How will surviving partners be protected from claims made by a deceased partner's heirs?

Although it helps to clarify matters for the partners themselves, the partnership agreement is strictly a private document—no laws require partners to file their agreements with any government agency. Nor are partnerships regarded as legal entities—in the eyes of the law, a partnership is just two or more people working together. Because partnerships have no independent legal standing, the Internal Revenue Service taxes partners as individuals.

Disadvantages of Partnerships For general partnerships, as for sole proprietorships, unlimited liability is the greatest drawback: By law, each partner may be liable for all debts incurred in the name of the partnership. If any partner incurs a business debt (with or without the knowledge of the other partners), all partners may still be held liable.

Partnerships also share with sole proprietorships the potential lack of continuity: When one partner dies or leaves it, the original partnership dissolves, even if one or more of the other partners want it to continue. The dissolving of a partnership need not cause a loss of sales revenues. Surviving partners may form a new partnership to retain the old firm's business. A related disadvantage is the difficulty of transferring ownership. No partner may sell out without the consent of the others. A partner who wants to retire or to transfer interest to a son or daughter must have the other partners' consent.

Corporations

There are about 4.6 million corporations in the United States. As you can see from Figure 4.3, although they account for about 20 percent of all U.S. businesses, they generate about 89 percent of all sales revenues.[8] Almost all larger businesses use this form, and corporations dominate the global business landscape. According to the most recent available data, ExxonMobil <www.exxonmobil.com>, the world's largest

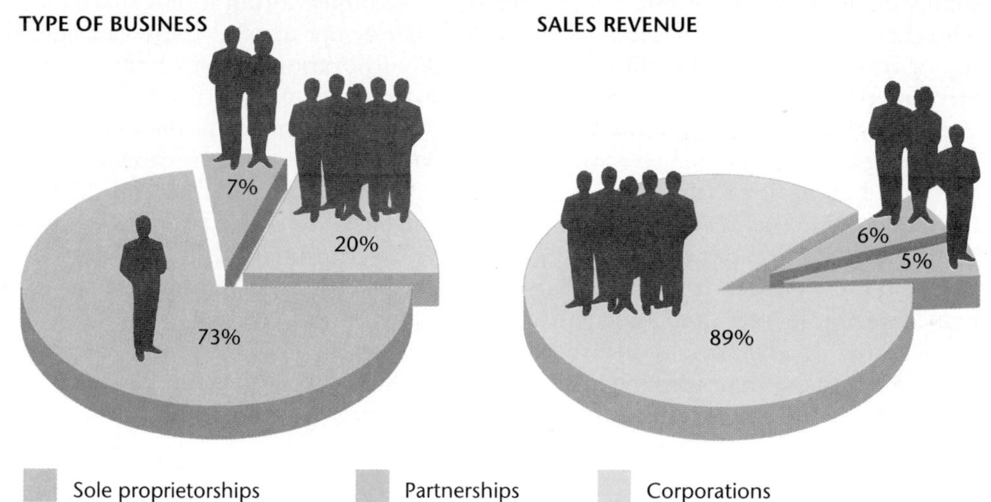

Figure 4.3
Proportions of U.S. Firms in Terms of Organization Type and Sales Revenue

petroleum and petrochemicals business, posted annual revenue of over $210 billion, with total profits of almost $18 billion. Even "smaller" large corporations post huge sales figures. Qualcomm <www.qualcomm.com>, a San Diego developer of digital wireless products that ranks 500th among U.S. corporations, posted a profit of $670 million on annual sales of $3.2 billion. Given the size and influence of this form of ownership, we will devote a great deal of attention to various aspects of corporations.[9]

The Corporate Entity When you think of corporations, you probably think of giant businesses such as General Motors and IBM. Indeed, the very word *corporation* inspires images of size and power. In reality, however, the tiny corner newsstand has as much right to incorporate as a giant automaker. Moreover, the incorporated newsstand and GM would share the characteristics of all **corporations**: legal status as separate entities, property rights and obligations, and indefinite life spans.[10]

corporation
Business that is legally considered an entity separate from its owners and is liable for its own debts; owners' liability extends to the limits of their investments

In 1819, the U.S. Supreme Court defined a corporation as "an artificial being, invisible, intangible, and existing only in contemplation of the law." By these words, the Court defined the corporation as a legal person. Thus, corporations may perform the following activities:

- Sue and be sued
- Buy, hold, and sell property
- Make and sell products to consumers
- Commit crimes and be tried and punished for them

Advantages of Incorporation The biggest advantage of regular corporations is **limited liability**: The liability of investors is limited to their personal investments in the corporation.[11] In the event of failure, the courts may seize and sell a corporation's assets but cannot touch the personal possessions of investors. For example, if you invest $1,000 in a corporation that goes bankrupt, you may lose your $1,000, but no more. In other words, $1,000 is the extent of your liability.

limited liability
Legal principle holding investors liable for a firm's debts only to the limits of their personal investments in it

Another corporate advantage is continuity. Because it has a legal life independent of its founders and owners, a corporation can, at least in theory, continue forever. Shares of stock may be sold or passed on from generation to generation. Moreover, most corporations also benefit from the continuity provided by professional management. Finally, corporations have advantages in raising money. By selling more stock, they can expand the number of investors and the amount of available funds. Continuity and the legal protections afforded to corporations tend to make lenders more willing to grant loans.

Disadvantages of Incorporation Although one of the corporation's chief attractions is ease of transferring ownership, this same feature can also complicate the lives of managers. For example, consider the case of a basic **tender offer**—an offer to buy

tender offer
Offer to buy shares made by a prospective buyer directly to a target corporation's shareholders, who then make individual decisions about whether to sell

shares made by a prospective buyer directly to the target corporation's shareholders, who then make individual decisions about whether or not to sell.[12] Now consider the recent travails of several California-based bank corporations. First of all, one bank, First Interstate, tried to gain control of one of its largest competitors, Bank of America <www.bankofamerica.com>, by buying Bank of America shares on the open market. First Interstate was unable to acquire enough Bank of America shares to gain control and ended up having to sell its shares at a big loss. In its weakened financial state, First Interstate then became a target itself and was purchased by a third bank corporation, Wells Fargo & Company <www.wellsfargo.com>. Unfortunately, the corporate marriage paid few dividends for Wells Fargo because the cost of integrating the two companies was far greater than anticipated.

Another disadvantage of incorporation is the start-up cost. Forming a corporation is more expensive than forming a sole proprietorship or a partnership. For one thing, corporations are heavily regulated, and incorporation entails meeting the complex legal requirements of the state in which the firm is chartered.

double taxation
Situation in which taxes may be payable both by a corporation on its profits and by shareholders on dividend incomes

closely held (or private) corporation
Corporation whose stock is held by only a few people and is not available for sale to the general public

publicly held (or public) corporation
Corporation whose stock is widely held and available for sale to the general public

S corporation
Hybrid of a closely held corporation and a partnership, organized and operated like a corporation but treated as a partnership for tax purposes

limited liability corporation, or LLC
Hybrid of a publicly held corporation and a partnership in which owners are taxed as partners but enjoy the benefits of limited liability

professional corporation
Form of ownership allowing professionals to take advantage of corporate benefits while granting them limited business liability and unlimited professional liability

Double Taxation The greatest potential drawback to corporate organization, however, is **double taxation**. First, a regular corporation must pay income taxes on company profits. In addition, stockholders must pay taxes on income returned by their investments in the corporation. Thus, the profits earned by corporations are essentially taxed twice—once at the corporate level and again at the ownership level. In contrast, because profits are treated as owners' personal income, sole proprietorships and partnerships are taxed only once.

Because of the various advantages and disadvantages of the corporation as a form of business ownership, various legal statutes have led to the creation of different kinds of corporations. These laws are generally intended to help specific kinds of businesses take advantage of the benefits of the corporate model without assuming all of the attending disadvantages. We discuss these various corporate forms next.

Types of Corporations Corporations may be broadly classified as either public or private. But within these broad categories, we can identify the specific types of corporations summarized in Table 4.2.[13]

- *Private and Public Corporations.* The most common form of corporation in the United States is the **closely held corporation**, often referred to simply as a **private corporation.** The stock of a closely held corporation is held by only a few people and is not available for sale to the general public. The controlling group of stockholders may be a family, a management group, or even the firm's employees.

  When shares are publicly issued, the firm becomes a **publicly held corporation**, frequently called a **public corporation.** The stock of a public corporation is widely held and available for sale to the general public.
- *S Corporations.* The **S corporation**, a relatively new form of business ownership, is a hybrid of a closely held corporation and a partnership. Such a firm is organized and operates like a corporation. For tax purposes, however, it is treated as a partnership. Several stringent legal conditions must be met for a firm to qualify as an S corporation.
- *Limited Liability Corporations.* Another relatively new hybrid form of ownership is the **limited liability corporation**, or **LLC**. The owners of such a business are taxed like partners, each paying personal taxes only. However, they also enjoy the benefits of limited liability accorded to corporations. LLCs have grown in popularity in recent years, partially because of IRS rulings that allow corporations, partnerships, and foreign investors to be partial owners.
- *Professional Corporations.* The **professional corporation** is also a relatively fast-growing form of ownership. These corporations are most likely comprised of doctors, lawyers, accountants, and similar groups of professionals. They are not immune from unlimited liability, however: Professional negligence by a member

Type	Distinguishing Features	Examples
Closely Held	Stock held by only a few people	Blue Cross/Blue Shield
	Subject to corporate taxation	MasterCard
		Primestar
Publicly Held	Stock widely held among many investors	Dell Computer
		Starbucks
	Subject to corporate taxation	Texas Instruments
Subchapter S	Organized much like a closely held corporation	Minglewood Associates
	Subject to additional regulation	Entech Pest Systems
	Subject to partnership taxation	Frontier Bank
Limited Liability	Organized much like a publicly held corporation	Pacific Northwest Associates
	Subject to additional regulation	Global Ground Support
	Subject to partnership taxation	Ritz Carlton
Professional	Organized like a partnership	Norman Hui, DDS & Associates
	Subject to partnership taxation	B & H Engineering
	Limited business liability	Anderson, McCoy & Orta
	Unlimited professional liability	
Multinational	Spans national boundaries	Toyota
	Subject to regulation in multiple countries	Nestlé
		General Electric

Table 4.2

Types of Corporations

of such a business is still accompanied by personal liability on the part of that individual.

- *Multinational or Transnational Corporations.* Yet another relatively new form of corporation is the **multinational** or **transnational corporation**. As the term implies, this form of corporation spans national boundaries. Stock in such an enterprise may be traded on the exchanges of several countries, and managers are likely to be from several different countries.

multinational or **transnational corporation**
Form of corporation spanning national boundaries

MANAGING A CORPORATION

Creating a corporation—regardless of its type—can be complicated. In addition, once the corporate entity has come into existence, it must be managed by people who understand the complex principles of **corporate governance**—the roles of shareholders, directors, and other managers in corporate decision making. In this section, we discuss the principles of *stock ownership* and *stockholders' rights* and describe the role of *boards of directors*. We then examine some of the most important trends in corporate ownership.

corporate governance
Roles of shareholders, directors, and other managers in corporate decision making

Corporate Governance

Corporate governance, which is specified for each firm by its bylaws, involves three distinct bodies. **Stockholders** (or **shareholders**) are the real owners of a corporation—investors who buy shares of ownership in the form of stock. The *board of directors* is a group of people elected by stockholders to oversee the management of the corporation. Corporate *officers* are top managers hired by the board to run the corporation on a day-to-day basis.[14]

stockholder (or **shareholder**)
Owner of shares of stock in a corporation

stock
Share of ownership in a corporation

Stock Ownership and Stockholders' Rights Corporations sell shares in the business, called **stock**, to investors who then become stockholders, or shareholders. Profits are distributed among stockholders in the form of dividends, and corporate managers serve at their discretion. Stockholders are the owners of a corporation. As noted earlier, in a closely held corporation, only a small number of people own the stock. In a publicly held corporation, on the other hand, large numbers of people own the stock.

preferred stock
Stock that offers its holders fixed dividends and priority claims over assets but no corporate voting rights

common stock
Stock that pays dividends and guarantees corporate voting rights but offers last claims over assets

board of directors
Governing body of a corporation that reports to its shareholders and delegates power to run its day-to-day operations while remaining responsible for sustaining its assets

chief executive officer (CEO)
Top manager hired by the board of directors to run a corporation

Corporate stock may be either preferred or common. **Preferred stock** offers holders fixed dividends, much like the interest paid on savings accounts. Preferred stockholders are so called because they have preference, or priority, over common stockholders when dividends are distributed and, if a business liquidates, when the value of assets is distributed.

Common stock usually pays dividends only if the corporation makes a profit, and holders of common stock have the last claims to any of the company's assets if it folds. Dividends on both common and preferred stock are paid on a per-share basis. Another difference involves voting rights. Preferred stockholders generally have no voting rights. Common stockholders always have voting rights, with each share of stock carrying one vote.

Boards of Directors By law, the governing body of a corporation is its **board of directors.** Boards communicate with stockholders and other potential investors through such channels as the annual report—a summary of the company's financial health. Directors also set policy on dividends, major spending, and executive salaries and benefits. They are legally responsible for corporate actions and are increasingly being held liable for them.

Officers Although board members oversee the corporation's operation, most of them do not participate in day-to-day management. Rather, they hire a team of managers to run the firm. As we have already seen, this team, called *officers*, is usually headed by the firm's **chief executive officer,** or **CEO,** who is responsible for the firm's overall performance. Other officers typically include a *president*, who is responsible for internal management, and *vice presidents*, who oversee various functional areas such as marketing and operations.

Figure 4.4 summarizes the rights and responsibilities of each group in the corporate governance hierarchy.

Special Issues in Corporate Ownership

In recent years, several special issues have arisen or grown in importance in corporate ownership. The most important of these trends are *joint ventures* and *strategic alliances*, *employee stock ownership plans*, and *institutional ownership*. Other important issues in contemporary corporate ownership involve *mergers, acquisitions, divestitures*, and *spin-offs*.

strategic alliance
Strategy in which two or more organizations collaborate on a project for mutual gain

joint venture
Strategic alliance in which the collaboration involves joint ownership of the new venture

employee stock ownership plan (ESOP)
Arrangement in which a corporation holds its own stock in trust for its employees, who gradually receive ownership of the stock and control its voting rights

Joint Ventures and Strategic Alliances Joint ventures and strategic alliances have become increasingly popular in business today. In a **strategic alliance,** two or more organizations collaborate on a project for mutual gain. When the partners share ownership stakes in what is essentially a new enterprise, it is called a **joint venture.** The number of strategic alliances has increased rapidly in recent years on both domestic and international fronts.[15]

Employee Stock Ownership Programs As the term suggests, the **employee stock ownership plan (ESOP)** allows employees to own a significant share of the corporation through what are essentially trusts established on behalf of the employees. Current estimates suggest that there are now almost 10,000 ESOPs in the United States. The growth rate in new ESOPs has slowed a bit in recent years, but they still are an important part of corporate ownership patterns in the United States.[16]

STOCKHOLDERS
As investors who purchase ownership shares in the corporation, stockholders are its owners. They elect . . .
BOARD OF DIRECTORS
. . . the board of directors, who set major policies and report to stockholders and other investors through annual reports and other summaries. They are legally responsible for corporate actions and hire . . .
OFFICERS
. . . corporate officers, who are responsible for the corporation's overall performance.

Figure 4.4
Corporate Governance Hierarchy

Institutional Ownership Most individual investors do not own enough stock to exert any influence on the management of big corporations. In recent years, however, more and more stock has been purchased by **institutional investors**. Because they control enormous resources, these investors—especially mutual and pension funds—can buy huge blocks of stock. For example, the national teachers' retirement system (TIAA-CREF) <www.tiaa-cref.org> has assets of over $255 billion and invests much of that amount in stocks. Institutional investors now own almost 40 percent of all the stock in the United States.

institutional investor
Large investor, such as a mutual fund or a pension fund, that purchases large blocks of corporate stock

Mergers, Acquisitions, Divestitures, and Spin-Offs In addition to the various special issues in corporate ownership described previously, another highly visible and important set of issues includes mergers, acquisitions, divestitures, and spin-offs. Whereas mergers and acquisitions involve the legal joining of two or more corporations, divestitures and spin-offs involve either the sale by one corporation of one or more of its business operations to another corporation or the creation of a new one.

merger
The union of two corporations to form a new corporation

acquisition
The purchase of one company by another

Mergers and Acquisitions (M&As) A **merger** occurs when two firms combine to create a new company. In an **acquisition**, one firm buys another outright. Even though many such events are publicly called mergers, in reality they are acquisitions. Why? Because one of the existing firms will almost always control more than half of the ownership of the newly combined firm. In general, when the two firms are of roughly the same or comparable size, the combination is usually called a merger even if one firm is assuming control over the other. When the acquiring firm is substantially larger than the acquired firm, it is more likely called an acquisition. Today M&As remain an important form of corporate strategy: They allow firms to increase product lines, expand operations, go international, and create new enterprises in conjunction with other organizations.

divestiture
Strategy whereby a firm sells one or more of its business units

spin-off
Strategy of setting up one or more corporate units as new, independent corporations

Divestitures and Spin-Offs Sometimes a corporation adopts the opposite strategy: It decides to take a part of its existing business operations and either sell it to another corporation or set it up as a new and independent corporation. Several reasons might motivate such a step. For example, a firm might decide that it needs to focus more specifically on its core businesses and thus sell off unrelated and/or underperforming businesses. Such a sale is called a **divestiture**.

In other cases a firm might decide to sell part of itself to raise capital. Such a sale is known as a **spin-off**. Sometimes, a firm spins off a part of itself not because it necessarily needs the capital but because it determines that one or more of its business units may actually be more valuable as a separate company. The Limited <www.limited.com>, for example, spun off three of its subsidiaries, Victoria's Secret, Bath & Body Works, and White Barn Candle Co., to create a new firm called Intimate Brands, Inc. <www.intimatebrands.com>, which it then offered through an IPO. The Limited retained an 84 percent ownership in Intimate Brands but also enjoyed an infusion of new capital through the spin-off.

ENTREPRENEURSHIP

In earlier sections, we discussed several popular forms of business and models for business ownership. We also described a couple of firms that started small and grew larger (sometimes much larger). In each of these cases, growth was spurred by the imagination and skill of the entrepreneurs who operated those companies. Although the concepts of *entrepreneurship* and *small business* are closely related, in this section we begin by discussing some important, though often subtle, differences between them. Then we describe some key characteristics of entrepreneurial personalities and activities.

The Distinction Between Entrepreneurship and Small Business

entrepreneur
Businessperson who accepts both the risks and the opportunities involved in creating and operating a new business venture

Many small-business owners like to think of themselves as **entrepreneurs**—people who assume the risk of business ownership with a primary goal of growth and expansion.[17] However, a person may be a small-business owner only, an entrepreneur only, or both. Consider a person who starts a small pizza parlor with no plans other than to earn enough money from the restaurant to lead a comfortable life. That person is clearly a small-business owner. With no plans to grow and expand, however, that person is not really an entrepreneur.

Conversely, an entrepreneur starts with one pizza parlor and fulfills the ambition of turning it into a national chain to rival Domino's or Little Caesar's. Although this person may have started as a small-business owner, the growth of the firm resulted from entrepreneurial vision and activity. Thus, the basic distinction between small-business ownership and entrepreneurship is aspiration—the former wants to remain small and support a lifestyle whereas the latter is motivated to grow, expand, and build.

SUCCESS AND FAILURE IN SMALL BUSINESS

For every Henry Ford, Walt Disney, Mary Kay Ash, or Bill Gates—people who transformed small businesses into major corporations—there are many small-business owners and entrepreneurs who fail. Over the last 10 years new business start-ups have numbered between 150,000 and 200,000 per year, with about 150,000 new businesses being launched each year. Over this same period, business failures have run between 50,000 and 100,000, with as many as 70,000 failing in any given year. In this section, we look first at a few key trends in small-business start-ups. Then we examine some of the main reasons for success and failure in small-business undertakings.

Trends in Small-Business Start-Ups

Thousands of new businesses are started in the United States every year. Several factors account for this trend, and in this section we focus on five of them:

- The emergence of e-commerce
- Entrepreneurs who cross over from big business
- Increased opportunities for minorities and women
- New opportunities in global enterprise
- Improved rates of survival among small businesses

Emergence of E-Commerce Clearly, the most significant recent trend in small-business start-ups is the rapid emergence of electronic commerce. Because the Internet has provided fundamentally new ways of doing business, savvy entrepreneurs have been able to create and expand new businesses faster and easier than ever before.[18] Such leading-edge firms as America Online, Amazon.com, E*Trade, and eBay, for example, owe their very existence to the Internet. Figure 4.5 amplifies this point by summarizing the tremendous growth in online commerce from 1997 through 2001.

Crossovers from Big Business Increasingly more businesses are being started by people who have opted to leave big corporations and put their experience and know-how to work for themselves. In some cases, these individuals see great new ideas they want to develop. Often, they get burned out working for a big corporation. Sometimes, they have lost their jobs, only to discover that working for themselves was a better idea anyway. John Chambers, the CEO of Cisco Systems <www.cisco.com>, is acknowledged as one of the best entrepreneurs around. But he spent several years working first at IBM and then at Wang Laboratories <www.wang.com/GLOBAL> before he set out on his own. Under his leadership, Cisco <www.cisco.com> has become one of the largest and most important technology companies in the world.[19]

Opportunities for Minorities and Women In addition to big-business expatriates, more small businesses are being started by minorities and women.[20] For example, the number of businesses owned by African Americans has increased by 46 percent during the most recent five-year period for which data are available and now totals about 620,000. Hispanic-owned businesses have grown at an even faster rate of 76 percent and now number about 862,000. Other ethnic groups are also making their presence felt among U.S. business owners. Business ownership among Asians and Pacific Islanders has increased 56 percent, to over 600,000. Although the number of businesses owned by Native Americans and Alaska Natives is still somewhat small, at slightly over 100,000, the total nevertheless represents a five-year increase of 93 percent.

Finally, the number of women-owned businesses is also growing rapidly. There are now 9.1 million businesses owned by women—38 percent of all businesses in the

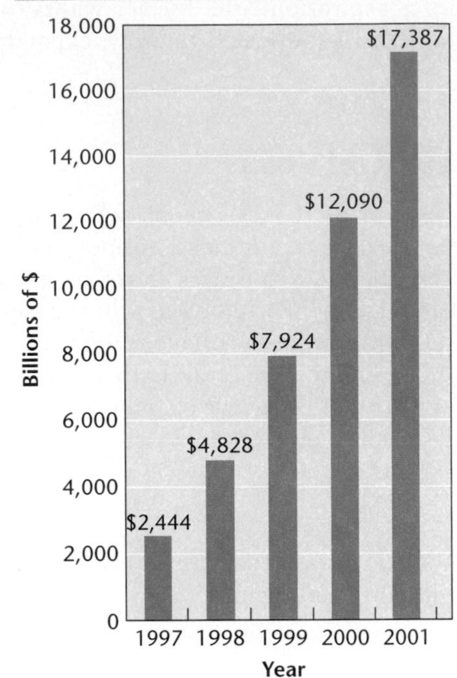

Figure 4.5
Growth of Online Commerce

> *"Women-owned businesses are an economic force that no bank can afford to overlook."*
>
> —Teresa Cavanaugh, director, Women Entrepreneur's Connection at BankBoston

United States. Combined, they generate nearly $4 trillion in revenue a year—an increase of 132 percent since 1992. The number of people employed nationwide at women-owned businesses since 1992 has grown to around 27.5 million—an increase of 108 percent.[21] "Women-owned businesses," says Teresa Cavanaugh, director of the Women Entrepreneur's Connection at BankBoston, "are the largest emerging segment of the small-business market. Women-owned businesses are an economic force that no bank can afford to overlook."[22]

Global Opportunities Many entrepreneurs today are also finding new opportunities in foreign markets.[23] Doug Mellinger, for example, is founder and CEO of PRT Group Inc., a software development company. One of Mellinger's biggest problems was finding enough trained programmers: There are not enough American programmers to go around, and foreign-born programmers face strict immigration quotas. So Mellinger set up shop on Barbados, a Caribbean island eager for economic development. The local government helps him attract foreign programmers and has gone to great lengths to make it easy for him to do business. Today, PRT, which is a part of enherent Corp. <www.enherent.com>, has both customers and suppliers from dozens of nations around the world.

Better Survival Rates Finally, more people are encouraged to test their skills as entrepreneurs because the failure rate among small businesses has been declining in recent years. During the 1960s and 1970s, less than half of all new start-ups survived more than 18 months—only one in five lasted 10 years. Now, however, new businesses have a better chance of surviving. Of new businesses started in the 1980s, for instance, over 77 percent remained in operation for at least three years. Today, the SBA estimates that at least 40 percent of all new businesses can expect to survive for six years.

Reasons for Failure

Unfortunately, 63 percent of all new businesses will not celebrate a sixth anniversary. Why do some succeed and others fail? Although no set pattern has been established, four general factors contribute to small-business failure:

- *Managerial incompetence or inexperience.* Some would-be entrepreneurs assume that they can succeed through common sense, overestimate their own managerial

Rick and Stacy Komendera went straight out of college to Russia in the early 1990s. In June 1999, they opened their first Pizza Picazzo outlet in Moscow, where the number of cafés and fast-food restaurants grew by 30 percent between May 1998 and May 1999. They also found a powerful ally in their first franchisee—BP Amoco, which has refitted several of its 24-hour gas stations in the Russian capital in order to make room for Pizza Picazzos.

acumen, or think that hard work alone will lead to success. If managers do not know how to make basic business decisions or understand the basic concepts and principles of management, they are unlikely to be successful in the long run.

- *Neglect.* Some entrepreneurs try either to launch their ventures in their spare time or to devote only a limited amount of time to a new business. But starting a small business requires an overwhelming time commitment. Entrepreneurs who are not willing to put in the time and effort that a business requires are unlikely to survive.
- *Weak control systems.* Effective control systems are needed to keep a business on track and to help alert entrepreneurs to potential trouble. If control systems do not signal impending problems, managers may be in serious trouble before more visible difficulties alert them.
- *Insufficient capital.* Some entrepreneurs are overly optimistic about how soon they will start earning profits. In most cases, however, it takes months or years before a business is likely to start turning a profit. Amazon.com, for example, has still not earned a profit. Most experts say that a new business should have enough capital to operate at least six months without earning a profit—some recommend enough to last a year.[24]

"Won't all these new rules impact adversely on the viability of small businesses with fewer than fifty employees?"

Reasons for Success

Similarly, four basic factors are typically cited to explain small-business success:

- *Hard work, drive, and dedication.* Small-business owners must be committed to succeeding and be willing to put in the time and effort to make it happen. Gladys Edmunds, a single, teenage mother in Pittsburgh, washed laundry, made chicken dinners to sell to cab drivers, and sold fire extinguishers and Bibles door-to-door to earn money to launch her own business. Today, Edmunds Travel Consultants employs eight people and earns about $6 million in annual revenue.[25]
- *Market demand for the products or services being provided.* Careful analysis of market conditions can help small-business owners assess the probable reception of their products in the marketplace. Whereas attempts to expand local restaurants specializing in baked potatoes, muffins, and gelato have been largely unsuccessful, hamburger and pizza chains continue to have an easier time expanding into new markets.
- *Managerial competence.* Successful small-business owners may acquire competence through training or experience or by using the expertise of others. Few successful entrepreneurs succeed alone or straight out of college. Most spend time working in successful companies or partner with others in order to bring more expertise to a new business.
- *Luck.* Lady Luck also plays a role in the success of some firms. For example, after Alan McKim started Clean Harbors <www.cleanharbors.com>, an environmental cleanup firm based in New England, he struggled to keep his business afloat. Then the U.S. government committed $1.6 billion to toxic waste cleanup—McKim's specialty. He was able to get several large government contracts and put his business on solid financial footing. Had the government fund not been created at just the right time, McKim may well have failed.

STARTING AND OPERATING THE SMALL BUSINESS

The Internet, of course, is rewriting virtually all of the rules for starting and operating a small business. Getting into business is easier and faster than ever before, there are many more potential opportunities than at any time in history, and the ability to gather and assimilate information is at an all-time high. Even so, however, would-be entrepreneurs must still make the right decisions when they start. They must decide precisely how to get into business. Should they buy an existing business or build from the ground up? In addition, would-be entrepreneurs must find appropriate sources of financing and decide when and how to seek the advice of experts.

Starting the Small Business

An old Chinese proverb suggests that a journey of a thousand miles begins with a single step. This is also true of a new business. The first step is the individual's commitment to becoming a business owner. Next comes choosing the goods or services to be offered—a process that means investigating one's chosen industry and market. Making this choice also requires would-be entrepreneurs to assess not only industry trends but also their own skills. Like the managers of big businesses, small-business owners must also be sure that they understand the true nature of the enterprises in which they are engaged.

Buying an Existing Business After choosing a product and making sure that the choice fits their own skills and interests, entrepreneurs must decide whether to buy an existing business or to start from scratch. Consultants often recommend the first approach. Quite simply, the odds are better: If successful, an existing business has already proved its ability to draw customers at a profit. It has also established working relationships with lenders, suppliers, and the community. Moreover, the track record of an existing business gives potential buyers a much clearer picture of what to expect than any estimate of a new business's prospects. Around 30 percent of the new businesses started in the past decade were bought from someone else, as were McDonald's <www.mcdonalds.com> and Starbucks <www.starbucks.com>.

Starting from Scratch Some people seek the satisfaction that comes from planting an idea, nurturing it, and making it grow into a strong and sturdy business. There are also practical reasons to start a business from scratch. A new business does not suffer the ill effects of a prior owner's errors. The start-up owner is also free to choose lenders, equipment, inventories, locations, suppliers, and workers, unbound by a predecessor's commitments and policies. Of the new businesses begun in the past decade, 64 percent were started from scratch.

The risks of starting a business from scratch are greater than those of buying an existing firm. Founders of new businesses can only make predictions and projections about their prospects. Success or failure thus depends heavily on identifying a genuine business opportunity—a product for which many customers will pay well but that is currently unavailable to them. To find openings, entrepreneurs must study markets and answer the following questions:

- Who are my customers?
- Where are they?
- At what price will they buy my product?
- In what quantities will they buy?
- Who are my competitors?
- How will my product differ from those of my competitors?

Financing the Small Business

Although the choice of how to start is obviously important, it is meaningless unless a small-business owner can obtain the money to set up shop. Among the more common sources for funding are family and friends, personal savings, banks and similar lending institutions, investors, and governmental agencies. Lending institutions are more likely to help finance the purchase of an existing business than a new business because the risks are better understood. Individuals starting up new businesses, on the other hand, are more likely to have to rely on their personal resources.

According to a study by the National Federation of Independent Business <www.nfibonline.com>, an owner's personal resources, not loans, are the most important source of money. Including money borrowed from friends and relatives, personal resources account for over two-thirds of all money invested in new small businesses and one-half of that invested in the purchase of existing businesses. When Michael Dorf and his friends decided to launch a New York nightclub dubbed the Knitting Factory <www.knittingfactory.com>, he started with $30,000 of his own money. Within four months of opening, Dorf asked his father to co-sign the first of four consecutive Milwaukee bank loans (for $70,000, $200,000, $300,000, and, to move to a new facility, $500,000, respectively). Dorf and his partners also engaged in creative bartering, such as putting a sound system company's logo on all its advertising in exchange for free equipment. Finally, because the Knitting Factory has become so successful, other investors are now stepping forward to provide funds—$650,000 from one investor and $4.2 million from another.[26]

Although banks, independent investors, and government loans all provide much smaller portions of start-up funds than the personal resources of owners, they are important in many cases. Getting money from these sources, however, requires some extra effort. Banks and private investors usually want to see formal business plans—detailed outlines of proposed businesses and markets, owners' backgrounds, and other sources of funding. Government loans have strict eligibility guidelines.

Other Sources of Investment **Venture capital companies** are groups of small investors seeking to make profits on companies with rapid growth potential. Most of these firms do not lend money: They invest it, supplying capital in return for stock. The venture capital company may also demand a representative on the board of directors.

venture capital company
Group of small investors who invest money in companies with rapid growth potential

New York's Knitting Factory <www.knittingfactory.com> has been host to hundreds of progressive rock and jazz bands since 1987, when CEO Michael Dorf opened it on a $30,000 investment. Within four months, Dorf was able to get over $1 million in bank loans. Once the club became known to local musicians and music followers, he was able to attract venture capital, including $4.2 million from a New York City investment firm. Between 1994 and 1998, revenues skyrocketed from $270,000 to $6 million (an increase of 2,134 percent).

In some cases, managers may even need approval from the venture capital company before making major decisions. Of all venture capital currently committed in the United States, 29 percent comes from true venture capital firms.

small-business investment company (SBIC) Government-regulated investment company that borrows money from the SBA to invest in or lend to a small business

Taking a more balanced approach in their choices than venture capital companies, **small-business investment companies (SBICs)** seek profits by investing in companies with potential for rapid growth. Created by the Small Business Investment Act of 1958, SBICs are federally licensed to borrow money from the SBA and to invest it in or lend it to small businesses. They are themselves investments for their shareholders. Past beneficiaries of SBIC capital include Apple Computer, Intel, and Federal Express. In addition, the government has recently begun to sponsor *minority enterprise small-business investment companies (MESBICs)*. As the name suggests, MESBICs specialize in financing businesses that are owned and operated by minorities.

SBA Financial Programs Since its founding in 1953, the SBA has offered more than 20 financing programs to small businesses that meet standards in size and independence. Eligible firms must also be unable to get private financing at reasonable terms. Under the SBA's *guaranteed loans program*, for example, small businesses can borrow from commercial lenders. The SBA guarantees to repay 75 to 85 percent of the loan amount, not to exceed $750,000. Through the *immediate participation loans program*, the SBA and a bank each put up a share of the loan amount. Under the *local development companies (LDCs) program*, the SBA works with a corporation (either for-profit or not-for-profit) founded by local citizens who want to boost the local economy.

Spurred in large part by the boom in Internet businesses, both venture capital and loans are becoming easier to get. Most small businesses report that it has generally gotten increasingly easier to obtain loans over the last 10 years. The "Wired World" box in this chapter discusses an even more extreme situation: Some technology companies are being offered so much venture capital that they are turning down part of it to keep from diluting their ownership unnecessarily.

Other SBA Programs Even more important than its financing role is the SBA's role in helping small-business owners improve their management skills. It is easy for entrepreneurs to spend money—SBA programs are designed to show them how to spend it wisely. The SBA offers small businesses several major management counseling programs at virtually no cost. For example, a small-business owner who needs help in starting a new business can get it free through the *Service Corps of Retired Executives (SCORE)* <www.score.org>. All SCORE members are retired executives, and all are volunteers.

IT'S A WIRED WORLD

A Wealth of Investors for Picky Start-Ups

Most people wouldn't dream of passing up $30 million, but in Silicon Valley, giving up cash is *de rigueur* for a growing number of tech start-ups. The reason: With so much cash available and banks and venture capital firms clamoring for a piece of the next big thing, start-ups want to ensure they don't give away too much and dilute the company's value.

Competition among investment firms has never been tougher as businesses pick and choose who will supply their seed money. Even companies with no-name CEOs and untested business models are turning away investors:

- I-drive.com, which allows users to store, organize, and share information on the Web, took $17 million but was offered almost $50 million. It refused the extra.
- Linuxcare <www.linuxcare.com>, which provides technical support for companies using Linux, took $32.5 million in investments but spurned offers that totaled nearly $300 million.
- Della.com, an online aggregator of wedding registry sites, and Yodlee.com, which aggregates personalized Web sites, have refused several million dollars in financing.

The access to cash is being fueled by the growth in venture capital firms, which shot up from about 250 in 1992 to at least 850 today, says Todd Carter, an investment banker with Banc Boston Robertson Stephens. "We see a heightened level of competition." Entrepreneurs say the piles of cash are a mixed blessing. "There are great people out there who have money, and you want to have them involved in the company," says Rebecca Patton, CEO of Della.com, "but you can't say yes to everyone."

More companies choose to stick it out until they can go public. An initial public offering is generally a cheaper way to raise funds and keep control of the company. For example, a venture capitalist might offer to give a company $20 million in exchange for 20 percent of the company. But in the public market, the company could likely sell 20 percent of its firm for $200 million.

Jeff Bonforte, CEO of I-drive.com, says picking the right investors is as important as accepting the right amount of cash. "You pick a VC like you pick a girlfriend or a wife," says Bonforte, whose company is funded by Draper Fisher Jurvetson. "You're locked in with these people. . . . A lead investor will make your life hell if you don't go along with what they want."

The newest of the SBA's management counseling projects is its **Small Business Development Center** (**SBDC**) program <www.sba.gov/sbdc>. Begun in 1976, SBDCs are designed to consolidate information from various disciplines and institutions, including technical and professional schools. Then they make this knowledge available to new and existing small businesses.

Small Business Development Center (SBDC)
SBA program designed to consolidate information from various disciplines and make it available to small businesses

FRANCHISING

McDonald's, Taco Bell, Subway, Denny's, 7-Eleven, RE/Max, Ramada, and Blockbuster are all franchised operations, operating under licenses issued by parent companies to local entrepreneurs who own and manage them. A **franchise** is an arrangement that permits the *franchisee* (buyer) to sell the product of the *franchiser* (seller, or parent company). As many would-be businesspeople have discovered, franchising agreements are an accessible doorway to entrepreneurship.[27]

franchise
Arrangement in which a buyer (franchisee) purchases the right to sell the good or service of the seller (franchiser)

Franchisees, for example, can benefit from the selling corporation's experience and expertise, and the franchiser may even supply financing. It may pick the store location, negotiate the lease, design the store, and purchase necessary equipment. It may train the first set of employees and managers and provide standardized policies and procedures. Once the business is open, the franchiser may offer savings by allowing the franchisee to purchase from a central location. Marketing strategy (especially advertising) may also be handled by the franchiser. In short, franchisees receive—that is, invest in—not only their own ready-made businesses but also expert help in running them.

WEB Connection

The SBA Web site is a virtual gold mine of information on starting, financing, and expanding small businesses, as well as on disaster assistance and pertinent legislation and regulation. It also offers links to a wide variety of additional sites.

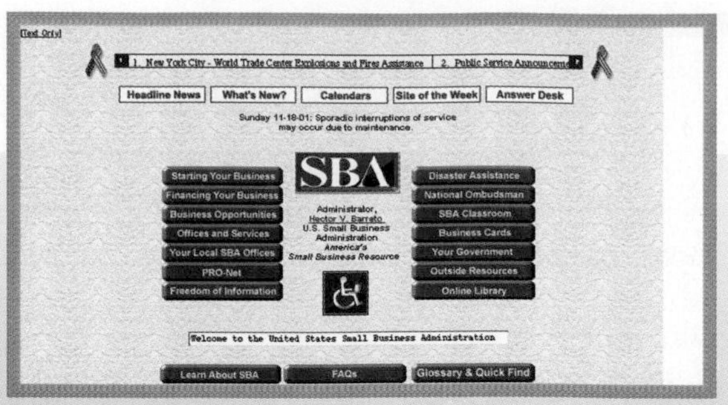

www.sba.gov

Advantages and Disadvantages of Franchising

Franchises offer many advantages to both sellers and buyers. For example, franchisers benefit from the ability to grow rapidly by using the investment money provided by franchisees. For the franchisee, the arrangement combines the incentive of owning a business with the advantage of access to big-business management skills. Unlike the person who starts from scratch, the franchisee does not have to build a business step-by-step. Moreover, because each franchise outlet is probably a carbon copy of every other outlet, the chances of failure are reduced.

Of course owning a franchise also involves certain disadvantages. Perhaps the most significant is the start-up cost. Franchise prices vary widely. Fantastic Sam's <www.fantasticsams.com> hair salon franchise fees are $30,000, but a McDonald's franchise costs at least $650,000 to $750,000, and a professional sports team can cost several hundred million dollars. Franchisees may also have continued obligations to contribute percentages of sales to parent corporations.

Continued from page 88

Tapping Out

From a business standpoint, one of the most significant things about the Internet is its amazing ability to reach and connect people no matter where they are. Little wonder, then, that Garden.com's founders entertained the possibility of buying and selling around the world. Unfortunately, it's not always that easy. Cliff and Lisa Sharples and Jamie O'Neil quickly discovered the constraints that national boundaries can impose on any business. For one thing, agricultural products—growing plants, seeds, chemicals, and the like—are among the most highly regulated goods in the world. In most cases, it's actually illegal to transport them from one country to another. As a practical matter, therefore, virtually all of Garden.com's business had to be conducted within the boundaries of the continental United States.

But does this mean that a start-up firm like Garden.com is forever confined to its home country? By no means. In fact, Garden.com had every intention of entering the European market at the earliest possible opportunity. As early as 1999, a few upstart European e-businesses were already patterning themselves after Garden.com. Thus one option the company considered was buying outright one of the most promising of these firms. Another was launching its own business in Europe. Given the complexities of doing business in the European Union, however, the firm had a clear preference for buying an existing operation—if it could have found just the right company and acquired it for just the right price.

The Internet also makes it possible to personalize versions of a company's Web page according to the interests and purchasing habits of customers and their interactions with the site. To do this, however, Garden.com first had to develop its own information technology—technology that needed continual improvement if it was going to attract new customers and guarantee repeat business. Not surprisingly, the development of this technology was a major area of capital expenditure. Equally expensive was the continuous upgrading of systems for processing customer orders and payments. By mid-1999, Garden.com had counted 4.4 million visitors to its Web site and planned for an increase in the number of Internet users to an estimated 502 million by 2003. Consequently, technology expenses alone totaled $1.9 million in just one fiscal quarter in 2000, while sales revenues were only $2.2 million.

Garden.com's combination of 23,000 items of merchandise, gardening tips, and personalized gardening information—all available from a single site—was a truly unique resource for gardeners. Market growth, however, continued to lag behind the firm's growing expenses. What was the problem? One e-consumer expert at Forrester Research <www.forrester.com> suggests that some of Garden.com's assumptions about its customer base were flawed: Garden products, he argues, "tend to be something that people want to go to the store to buy." At bottom, this reading of the market questions the wisdom of having a wholly online business. Which view is valid? Do gardeners prefer in-store shopping, or would they prefer to use the Internet? The same analyst contends that because most gardening products don't command much brand loyalty, retailers have a rough time competing for repeat sales. Whether for just these or for other reasons, Garden.com posted the following announcement on its Web site on November 21, 2000: "This is not only the best sale of the season, it's our last sale. The doors of our cyber garden center are closing December 1."

Discussion Questions

1. Why did the founders initially choose a partnership form of legal organization? Were there any risks in choosing this form?
2. What advantages were gained from switching from a partnership to a corporation?
3. What were the key start-up decisions made by Cliff and Lisa Sharples and Jamie O'Neill? In retrospect, are there any alternative decisions that might have been better? Explain.
4. Identify the sources of financial aid that were used by this firm. Why do you suppose each of those sources, rather than others, was chosen at various stages in the firm's life?
5. Before its final demise, Garden.com's officers were thinking about acquiring a compatible firm in Europe, but didn't find one. Do you think that such an acquisition or a joint venture abroad could have saved Garden.com? Explain.
6. Identify the main reasons for Garden.com's successes and the main reasons for its eventual failure.

SUMMARY OF LEARNING OBJECTIVES

1 Define *small business*, discuss its importance to the U.S. economy, and explain which *types of small business* best lend themselves to success. A *small business* is independently owned and managed and does not dominate its market. Small businesses are crucial to the economy because they create new jobs, foster *entrepreneurship* and *innovation*, and supply goods and services needed by larger businesses.

Services are the easiest operations for small business owners to start because they require low levels of resources. They also offer high returns on investment and tend to foster innovation. Retailing and wholesaling are more difficult because they usually require some experience, but they are still attractive to many entrepreneurs. Construction and financial and insurance operations are also common sectors for small business. As the most resource-intensive areas of the economy, transportation and manufacturing are the areas least populated by small firms.

2 **Explain *sole proprietorships* and *partnerships* and discuss the advantages and disadvantages of each.** *Sole proprietorships*, the most common form of business, consist of one person doing business. Although sole proprietorships offer freedom and privacy and are easy to form, they lack continuity and present certain financial risks. For one thing, they feature *unlimited liability*: The sole proprietor is liable for all debts incurred by the business. *General partnerships* are proprietorships with multiple owners. *Limited partnerships* allow for limited partners who can invest without being liable for debts incurred by general or active partners. In *master limited partnerships*, master partners can sell shares and pay profits to investors. Partnerships have access to a larger talent pool and more investment money than sole proprietorships, but they may be dissolved if conflicts between partners cannot be settled.

3 **Describe *corporations*, discuss their advantages and disadvantages, and identify different kinds of corporations.** *Corporations* are independent legal entities that are usually run by professional managers. The corporate form is used by most large businesses because it offers continuity and opportunities for raising money. It also features financial protection through *limited liability*: The liability of investors is limited to their personal investments. However, the corporation is a complex legal entity subject to *double taxation:* In addition to taxes paid on corporate profits, investors must pay taxes on earned income. The most common types are *closely held corporations* (also called *private corporations*), *publicly held corporations* (also called *public corporations*), *S corporations*, *limited liability corporations* (*LLCs*), *professional corporations*, and *multinational* or *transnational corporations*.

4 **Describe the *start-up decisions* made by small businesses and identify sources of *financial aid* and *management advice* available to such enterprises.** The Internet is rewriting the rules of business start-up. But in deciding to go into business, the entrepreneur must still first choose between buying an existing business and starting from scratch. Both approaches involve practical advantages and disadvantages. A successful existing business has working relationships with other businesses and has already proved its ability to make a profit. New businesses, on the other hand, allow owners to plan and work with clean slates, but it is hard to make projections about the business's prospects.

Although small business owners generally draw heavily on their own resources for financing, they can get financial aid from venture capital firms, which seek profits from investments in companies with rapid growth potential. *The Small Business Administration (SBA)* also sponsors a variety of loan programs, including *small-business investment companies*. Finally, foreign firms and other nonbank lenders make funds available under various circumstances. Management advice is available from *advisory boards, management consultants, the SBA*, and the practice of *networking* (meeting regularly with people in related businesses to discuss problems and opportunities).

5 **Identify the advantages and disadvantages of *franchising*.** *Franchising* has become a popular form of small-business ownership because the *franchiser* (parent company) supplies financial, managerial, and marketing assistance to the *franchisee*, who buys the right to sell the franchiser's product. Franchising also enables small businesses to grow rapidly. Finally, the risks in franchising are lower than those in starting a new business from scratch. The costs of purchasing a franchise can be quite high, however, and the franchisee sacrifices independence and creativity. In addition, owning franchises provides no guarantee of success.

QUESTIONS AND EXERCISES

Questions for Review

1. Why are small businesses important to the U.S. economy?
2. Why might a closely held corporation choose to remain private? Why might a closely held corporation choose to become a publicly traded corporation?
3. What key factors typically contribute to the success and failure of small businesses?
4. From the standpoint of the franchisee, what are the primary advantages and disadvantages of most franchise arrangements?

Questions for Analysis

5. Go to the library or to the Internet and research a recent merger or acquisition. What factors led to the arrangement? What circumstances characterized the process of completing the arrangement? Were they friendly or unfriendly?

6. If you were going to open a small business, what type would it be? Why?
7. Would you prefer to buy an existing business or start your own business from scratch? Why?
8. Under what circumstances might it be wise for an entrepreneur to turn down venture capital? Under what circumstances might it be advisable to take more venture capital than the entrepreneur actually needs?

Application Exercises

9. Interview the owner-manager of a sole proprietorship or a general partnership. What characteristics of that business form led the owner to choose it? Does he or she ever contemplate changing the form of the business?
10. Select a small local firm that has gone out of business recently. Identify as many factors as you can that led to the company's failure.

EXPLORING THE WEB

Taking a Field Trip to the SBA

One of the most important contacts for most small-business owners is the Small Business Administration (SBA). You can reach the SBA's Web site at the following address:

<www.sbaonline.sba.gov/textonly/>

Begin by examining the sections on "Starting Your Business," "Financing Your Business," and "Expanding Your Business." After you have examined these features, consider the following questions:

1. Assume that you are planning to purchase an existing small business. In the previous areas, what was the most important information that you could find? Identify other sections of the SBA site that might be relevant to you. What useful information did you find by browsing a few of these additional areas?
2. Assume that you are planning to start a new small business from scratch. Again, review the sections of the SBA site that might be most relevant, and report on the available information.
3. Assume that you are already operating a small business but are concerned about increasing competition. In what sections of its Web site does the SBA offer material that might be helpful to you?
4. Use the SBA links to visit the Web sites maintained by your U.S. representative and senator. What specific information on these sites, if any, might be most helpful to a small-business owner?
5. Over all, do you think the SBA site is likely to be more helpful for an existing business or for a new business just starting out? Why?

EXERCISING YOUR ETHICS

Breaking Up Is Hard to Do

THE SITUATION

Connie and Mark began a 25-year friendship after finishing college and discovering their mutual interest in owning a business. Established as a general partnership, their home-furnishings center is a successful business that has for 20 years been sustained by a share-and-share-alike relationship. Start-up cash, daily responsibilities, and profits all have been shared equally. The partners both work four days each week except when busy seasons require both of them to be at work. Their shared goals and compatible personalities have led to a solid give-and-take relationship that helps them overcome numerous business problems while maintaining a happy interpersonal relationship.

The division of work is a natural match because the partners' different but complementary interests meet all the requirements for success. Mark buys the merchandise and maintains up-to-date contacts with suppliers; he also handles personnel matters (hiring and training employees). Connie manages the inventory, buys shipping supplies, keeps the books, and manages the firm's finances. While Mark does more selling, Connie helps with sales only during busy seasons. Both partners share in decisions about advertising and promotions.

THE DILEMMA

Things began changing two years ago as Connie became less interested in the business and got more involved in other activities. As Mark's enthusiasm for the business remained unwavering, travel, recreation, and service on community-service activities increasingly consumed Connie's time. At first, she reduced her work commitment from four to three days a week and then indicated that she wanted to cut back further, to just two days a week. "In that case," Mark replied, "we'll have to make some changes."

Mark insisted that profit sharing be adjusted to reflect his larger role in running the business. He proposed that Connie's monthly salary be cut in half (from \$4,000 to \$2,000). Connie agreed. In addition, Mark recommended that the \$2,000 savings be shifted to his salary because of his increased workload. This time Connie balked, saying that Mark's current \$4,000 salary already compensated him for his contributions.

But to avoid confrontation, Connie proposed that they "split the difference," with Mark getting a $1,000 increase and the other $1,000 going into the firm's cash account. Mark rejected the compromise, insisting on a full $2,000 raise. To avoid a complete falling out, Connie finally conceded to Mark's demand even though she thought it unfair that his salary should increase from $4,000 per month to $6,000. At that point, Connie made a promise to herself: "To even things out, I'll find a way to remove $2,000 worth of inventory for my own personal use each month."

QUESTIONS FOR DISCUSSION

1. Identify the ethical issues, if any, regarding Mark's and Connie's respective positions on Mark's proposed $2,000 monthly salary increase.
2. What kind of salary adjustments for Mark and Connie do you think would be fair in this situation? Explain why.
3. There is, of course, another way for Mark and Connie to solve their differences: Because the terms of participation have changed during recent years, it might make sense to dissolve the existing partnership. What do you recommend in this regard?

BUILDING YOUR BUSINESS SKILLS

Working the Internet

This exercise enhances the following SCANS workplace competencies: demonstrating basic skills, demonstrating thinking skills, exhibiting interpersonal skills, and working with information.

GOAL

To encourage students to define the opportunities and problems for small companies doing business on the Internet.

THE SITUATION

Suppose you and two partners own a gift basket store, specializing in special occasion baskets for individual and corporate clients. Your business is doing well in your community, but you believe there may be opportunity for growth through a virtual storefront on the Internet.

METHOD

Step 1

Join with two other students and assume the role of business partners. Start by researching Internet businesses. Look at books and articles at the library and contact the following Web sites for help:

- Small Business Administration <www.sba.gov>
- IBM Small Business Center <www.businesscenter.ibm.com>
- Apple Small Business Home Page <www.smallbusiness.apple.com>

These sites may lead you to other sites, so keep an open mind.

Step 2

Based on your research, determine the importance of the following small-business issues:

- An analysis of changing company finances as a result of expansion onto the Internet
- An analysis of your new competitive marketplace (the world) and how it affects your current marketing approach, which focuses on your local community
- Identification of sources of management advice as the expansion proceeds
- The role of technology consultants in launching and maintaining the Web site
- Customer service policies in your virtual environment

FOLLOW-UP QUESTIONS

1. Do you think your business would be successful on the Internet? Why or why not?
2. Based on your analysis, how will Internet expansion affect your current business practices? What specific changes are you likely to make?
3. Do you think that operating a virtual storefront will be harder or easier than doing business in your local community? Explain your answer.

CRAFTING YOUR BUSINESS PLAN

Fitting in to the Entrepreneurial Mold

THE PURPOSE OF THE ASSIGNMENT

1. To familiarize students with the ways in which entrepreneurship and small business considerations enter into the business planning framework of *Business PlanPro (BPP)* (Version 4.0).
2. To encourage students to think about how to apply their textbook information on entrepreneurship to the preparation of a small business plan using *BPP*.

FOLLOW-UP ASSIGNMENT

After reading Chapter 4 in the textbook, open the BPP *software and look around for information about planning a new start-up company called* Corporate Fitness. *In the Plan Outline screen, click on* **1.0 Executive Summary** *to familiarize yourself with an overview of this firm. Then respond to the following questions:*

1. Which industry category for small businesses—wholesaling, retailing, services, or manufacturing—best describes the Corporate Fitness line of business?
2. The textbook identifies several characteristics of successful entrepreneurs. Judging by its business plan, do you think the management team of Corporate Fitness has an entrepreneurial orientation? Explain why or why not. [Sites to see in *BPP* for this item: In the Plan Outline screen, click on each of the following: **6.0 Management Summary, 6.2 Management Team,** and **6.3 Management Team Gaps**.]
3. Your textbook identifies several sources of advice for starting and running small businesses. Judging from its business plan, do you think that Corporate Fitness is planning to seek advice from any of those sources in getting started? Do you think it is a good idea to discuss the planned uses of such sources in the business plan? Explain why or why not. [Sites to see in *BPP* for this item: In the Plan Outline screen, explore Corporate Fitness's business plan using your judgment as to where you would expect to find information on start-up advice.]
4. What sources of advice and assistance do you recommend for getting Corporate Fitness off to a sound start? In which areas of the business and for which of its business activities will it benefit the most from outside advice and assistance? Where in its business plan do you recommend reporting its planned use of such assistance?

VIDEO EXERCISE

Doing Business Privately: Amy's Ice Creams

LEARNING OBJECTIVES

The purpose of this video exercise is to help you

1. Recognize the factors that motivate people to open businesses.
2. Understand the advantages and disadvantages of incorporation.
3. Appreciate the role of corporations as employers.

BACKGROUND INFORMATION

Amy's Ice Creams is a privately held corporation formed in 1984 by Amy Miller and owned by Miller and a small group of family members and friends. Based in Austin, Texas, Amy's continues to evolve and now boasts nine stores earning close to $3.5 million. Customers' suggestions for new flavors are welcomed, and quality is never compromised. It is also famous for the zany antics of its behind-the-counter scoopers (just applying for a job is an adventure in creativity).

THE VIDEO

Amy Miller talks about some of the basic issues involved in starting up and running her business, including her philosophy and the marketing and financial savvy that she brings to the task. You'll hear about the advantages and disadvantages of incorporating, and you'll discover some of the ways in which Amy's keeps both employees and customers on their toes.

QUESTIONS FOR DISCUSSION

1. How do Amy's organization and principles differ from those of a publicly held corporation?
2. What are some of the particular advantages of corporate ownership for a firm like Amy's? Are there any disadvantages?
3. How well do you think Amy's is working to ensure its continued survival and success? Looking into the future, what marketing, financial, or other suggestions would you offer the company?

FOLLOW-UP ASSIGNMENT

How do you think a company like Amy's can compete with national ice cream chains like Baskin-Robbins or Carvel? What does Amy's offer its customers that these firms do not? What does it offer its employees? How important are these elements in ensuring any company's continued success? (To find out more about the company, you can visit Amy's Web site at <www.amysicecream.com>.)

FOR FURTHER EXPLORATION

Find out the requirements for incorporating a business in your state. You might begin by typing *incorporation* into the search box at <www.toolkit.cch.com>. If you were going to start a small business yourself, is a corporation the form of business ownership you would choose? Why or why not? Make a list of the pros and cons that incorporation presents for the type of business that you have in mind.

Understanding the Business of Managing

Part II

CHAPTER 5

Managing the Business Enterprise

After reading this chapter, you should be able to:

1. Explain the importance of setting *goals* and formulating *strategies* as the starting points of effective management.
2. Describe the four activities that constitute the *management process.*
3. Identify *types of managers* by level and area.
4. Describe the five basic *management skills.*
5. Describe the development and explain the importance of *corporate culture.*

Grounds for the Defense

In some ways it's like David and Goliath—a small upstart New England coffee retailer called Maine Roasters going toe-to-toe with Starbucks <www.starbucks.com>, the fastest-growing and, arguably, the highest-profile food and beverage company in the United States. To understand the competitive dynamics of this situation, let's first find out how Starbucks became the big kid on the block. It was started in Seattle in 1971 by three coffee aficionados. Their primary business at the time was buying premium coffee beans, roasting them, and then selling the coffee by the pound. The business performed modestly well and soon grew to nine stores, all in the Seattle area. When they thought their business growth had stalled in 1987, the three partners sold Starbucks to a former employee named Howard Schultz. Schultz promptly reoriented, trading in bulk coffee sales for retail coffee sales through the firm's coffee bars.

Today Starbucks is not only the country's largest coffee importer and roaster of specialty beans but also the largest specialty coffee bean retailer in the United States. There are more than 2,100 Starbucks locations in the United States. The firm has revenues of over $1.7 billion a year, annual profits of almost $102 million, and a workforce of more than 37,000 employees.

What is the key to Starbucks' phenomenal growth and success? One important ingredient is its well-conceived and implemented strategy. Starbucks is on a phenomenal growth pace, opening a new coffee shop somewhere almost every day. This growth is planned and coordinated at each step of the way through careful site selection. In addition, through its astute promotional campaigns and commitment to quality, the firm has elevated the coffee-drinking taste of millions of Americans and fueled a significant increase in demand.

Its phenomenal growth rate notwithstanding, Starbucks is also continually on the alert for new

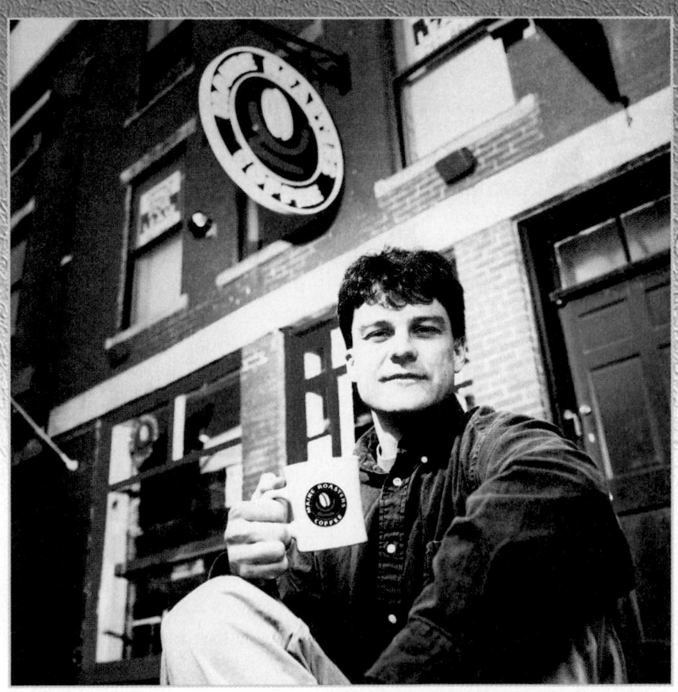

> *"It's Maine versus the national giant."*
>
> —Rand Smith, owner of Maine Roasters, upon hearing that Starbucks was coming to town

business opportunities. One area of growth is the international market, where the company operates about 700 stores and kiosks in Asia, Europe, and the Pacific Rim. Another growth area is brand extension through ventures with other companies. Dreyer's <www.dreyers.com>, for example, distributes five flavors of Starbucks coffee ice cream to grocery freezers across the country. Capital Records <www.hollywoodandvine.com> has produced two special jazz CDs that are available only in Starbucks stores. Redhook Brewery <www.redhook.com> uses Starbucks coffee extract in its double black stout beer.

Given the enormous marketing and financial muscle that a company like Starbucks brings to the table, imagine how Rand Smith, the owner of Maine Roasters <www.maineroasters.qpg.com>, a small coffee shop in Portland, Maine, reacted when he heard that the coffee Goliath was coming to town. "It's Maine versus the national giant," said Smith, who decided to load whatever slingshot he could find.

Smith's strategy was grounded in the passion and loyalty that exist among Maine residents for the sanctity of their home state. He has mounted a finely tuned plan for portraying Starbucks as a big bully from the "outside" and his own upstart operation as the homespun underdog. To promote this image, every morning he dispatches a team of his employees to stand outside the Starbucks restaurant closest to his own store to pass out chocolate drops and to encourage Starbucks customers to "Support a Maine-owned-and-operated company." So far, his efforts are paying off. The local paper, for example, has editorialized against corporate heavyweights, community groups have picketed Starbucks, and there has even been a spate of vandalism against Starbucks, usually involving broken store windows. Smith does not condone such tactics, but he no doubt privately sees each stone being thrown through a Starbucks window as a metaphor for the stone with which David felled Goliath in an earlier time.

Our opening story continues on page 134

All corporations depend on effective management. Whether managers are involved in running a big international corporation like Starbucks or a small local or regional business like Maine Roasters Coffee, they perform many of the same functions, are responsible for many of the same tasks, and have many of the same responsibilities. The work of all managers involves developing strategic and tactical plans. Along with numerous other things, they must analyze their competitive environments and plan, organize, direct, and control day-to-day operations.

By focusing on the learning objectives of this chapter, you will better understand the nature of managing and the range of skills that managers like Howard Schultz and Rand Smith need if they are to compete effectively, and the importance of corporate culture.

Although our focus is on managers in *business* settings, remember that the principles of *management* apply to all kinds of organizations. Managers work in charities, churches, social organizations, educational institutions, and government agencies. The prime minister of Canada, curators at the Museum of Modern Art, the dean of your college, and the chief administrator of your local hospital are all managers. Remember, too, that managers bring to small organizations much the same kinds of skills—the ability to make decisions and respond to a variety of challenges—as they bring to large ones.

Regardless of the nature and size of an organization, managers are among its most important resources. Consider the profiles of the following three managers:

- Jenny Ming is president of Old Navy <www.oldnavy.com>, a division of The Gap Inc. <www.gapinc.com> and one of the fastest-growing retail chains around. After earning her college degree in fashion merchandising at San Jose State, she went to work for Mervyn's, a division of Dayton Hudson Corporation, first as a management trainee and then as a buyer. After he heard a supplier singing Ming's praises, Gap CEO Mickey Drexler lured her away and put her in charge of buying T-shirts for Gap stores. She continued to excel and was named to her present job in early 1999. For some time now, Old Navy has outperformed most of the other retailers including Gap. Much of the credit goes to Ming and the relatively rare combination of skills that enables her to understand and spot the newest fashion trends, instill loyalty and dedication in those who work for her, and run a tightly controlled and focused business enterprise.[1]
- Kenneth Chenault is considered one of the best young senior managers around. He joined American Express <www.americanexpress.com>in 1981 as a marketing specialist and then systematically worked his way up the corporate ladder until he became president in 1997. During the next two years, Chenault presided over a major overhaul at AmEx as the firm sought to undo an ill-fated diversification strategy undertaken by a previous CEO. So impressive was Chenault's performance that in April 2001 he was named chairman and CEO of the company. Having reorganized a huge number of services into four core businesses—Global Financial Services, U.S. Consumer and Small Business Services, Global Corporate Services, and Global Establishment Services and Travelers Cheque Group—Chenault now has to show that AmEx can profitably service 52 million cardholders and 2.3 million financial services customers.[2]
- Twenty years ago, when he was running PepsiCo <www.pepsico.com>, Andrall Pearson was identified as one of the 10 toughest bosses in America. Much of that reputation was based on his ability to humiliate employees and to lead through fear and intimidation. Although he was credited with increasing the firm's revenues from less than $1 billion to over $8 billion, he was also vilified by almost everyone who worked for him. Today, however, Pearson runs Tricon Global Restaurants <www.triconglobal.com> (owners of KFC, Pizza Hut, and Taco Bell) with a much different approach. He remains demanding and results-oriented, but he has become much more concerned about the personal and professional welfare of his employees. Indeed, colleagues describe his current leadership style in terms of his warmth, energy, and charisma.[3]

Although Jenny Ming, Kenneth Chenault, and Andrall Pearson are clearly different people who work in different kinds of organizations and have different approaches to what they do, they also share one fundamental commonality with other high-level managers: responsibility for the performance and effectiveness of business enterprises. Thus, they are accountable to shareholders, employees, customers, and other key constituents. In this chapter, we describe the management process and the skills that managers must develop to perform their functions in organizations. Perhaps you will then have a better feel for the reasons why organizations value good managers so highly.

SETTING GOALS AND FORMULATING STRATEGY

The starting point in effective management is setting **goals**—objectives that a business hopes (and plans) to achieve. Every business needs goals. We begin, therefore, by discussing the basic aspects of organizational goal setting. Remember, however, that deciding what it *intends* to do is only the first step for an organization. Managers must also make decisions about *actions* that will and will not achieve company goals. Decisions cannot be made on a problem-by-problem basis or merely to meet needs as they arise. In most companies, a broad program underlies those decisions. That program is called a **strategy**, which is a broad set of organizational plans for implementing the decisions made for achieving organizational goals.

goal
Objective that a business hopes and plans to achieve

strategy
Broad set of organizational plans for implementing the decisions made for achieving organizational goals

corporate strategy
Strategy for determining the firm's overall attitude toward growth and the way it will manage its businesses or product lines

business (or competitive) strategy
Strategy, at the business-unit or product-line level, focusing on a firm's competitive position

functional strategy
Strategy by which managers in specific areas decide how best to achieve corporate goals through productivity

Types of Strategy Figure 5.1 shows the relationship among the three types of strategy that are usually considered by a company:[4]

- The purpose of **corporate strategy** is to determine the firm's overall attitude toward growth and the way it will manage its businesses or product lines. A company may decide to *grow* by increasing its activities or investment or to *retrench* by reducing them. Under Kenneth Chenault, AmEx corporate strategy calls for strengthening operations through a principle of growth called e-partnering—buying shares of small companies that can provide technology that AmEx itself does not have.
- **Business** (or **competitive**) **strategy**, which takes place at the level of the business unit or product line, focuses on improving the company's competitive position. At this level, AmEx makes decisions about how best to compete in an industry that includes Visa, MasterCard, and other credit card companies. In this respect, the company has committed heavily to expanding its product offerings and serving customers through new technology.
- At the level of **functional strategy**, managers in specific areas decide how best to achieve corporate goals by being as productive as possible. At AmEx, each business unit has considerable autonomy in deciding how to use the single Web site at which the company has located its entire range of services.

We will complete this section by detailing the basic steps in strategy formulation.

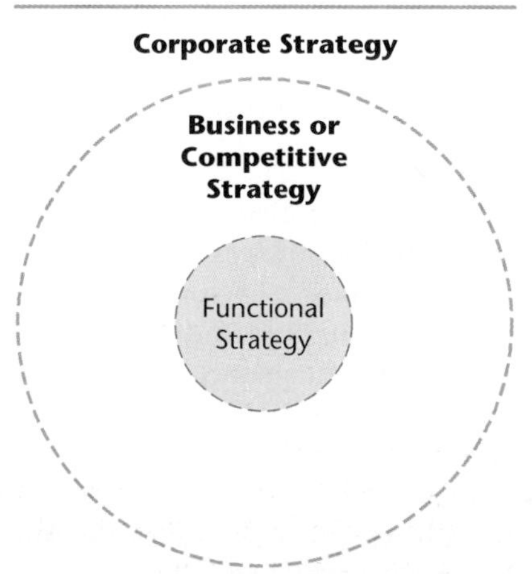

Figure 5.1
Hierarchy of Strategy

Setting Business Goals

Goals are performance targets—the means by which organizations and their managers measure success or failure at every level. For example, Jenny Ming's goals at Old Navy are largely tied to sales increases, profitability, and new store openings. Because her business is a subsidiary of a larger corporation, she has no goals for the stock price of her own operation. However, because AmEx is a publicly traded corporation, in addition to goals for sales and profit margins, Kenneth Chenault must also must focus a great deal of attention on stock price. Andrall Pearson's goals, meanwhile, focus generally on motivating lower-wage workers in a highly competitive business environment while simultaneously leading a major global expansion.

Purposes of Goal Setting An organization functions systematically because it sets goals and plans accordingly. An organization commits its resources on all levels to achieving its goals. Specifically, we can identify four main purposes in organizational goal setting:

"Our management team is 100% focused on growing our core business without distraction from any other initiative."

—Howard Schultz, CEO of Starbucks

1. *Goal setting provides direction and guidance for managers at all levels.* If managers know precisely where the company is headed, there is less potential for error in the different units of the company. Starbucks, for example, has a goal of increasing capital spending by 15 percent, with all additional expenditures devoted to opening new stores. This goal clearly informs everyone in the firm that expansion into new territories is a high priority for the firm.
2. *Goal setting helps firms allocate resources. Areas that are expected to grow will get first priority.* The company allocates more resources to new projects with large sales potential than it allocates to mature products with established but stagnant sales potential. Thus, Starbucks is primarily emphasizing new store expansion, while its e-commerce initiatives are currently given a lower priority. "Our management team," says CEO Howard Schultz, "is 100% focused on growing our core business without distraction . . from any other initiative."
3. *Goal setting helps to define corporate culture.* For years, the goal at General Electric <www.ge.com> has been to push each of its divisions to first or second in its industry. The result is a competitive (and often stressful) environment and a culture that rewards success and has little tolerance for failure. At the same time, however, GE's appliance business, television network (NBC), aircraft engine unit, and financial services business are each among the very best in their respective industries. Eventually, CEO Jack Welch set an even higher companywide standard—to make the firm the most valuable in the world.
4. *Goal setting helps managers assess performance.* If a unit sets a goal of increasing sales by 10 percent in a given year, managers in that unit who attain or exceed the goal can be rewarded. Units failing to reach the goal will also be compensated accordingly. GE has a long-standing reputation for stringently evaluating managerial performance, richly rewarding those who excel, and getting rid of those who do not. Each year the lower 10 percent of GE's managerial force are informed that either they make dramatic improvements in performance or consider alternative directions for their careers.

Kinds of Goals Goals differ from company to company, depending on the firm's purpose and mission. Every enterprise has a *purpose* or a reason for being. Businesses seek profits, universities seek to discover and transmit new knowledge, and government agencies seek to set and enforce public policy. Many enterprises also have missions and **mission statements**—statements of how they will achieve their purposes in the environments in which they conduct their business.

mission statement
Organization's statement of how it will achieve its purpose in the environment in which it conducts its business

A company's mission is usually easy to identify, at least at a basic level. Dell Computer <www.dell.com>, for example, set out to make a profit by selling personal computers directly to consumers. In San Francisco, Platinum Concepts Inc. <www.mousedriver.com> intends to become profitable by developing "unique and innovative products." So far, the company's only product is the MouseDriver, a computer mouse shaped like the head of a golf club, but it expects to sell $1 million worth of MouseDrivers this year.[5]

Businesses often have to rethink their missions as the competitive environment changes. In 1999, for example, Starbucks announced that Internet marketing and sales were going to become core business initiatives. Managers subsequently realized, however, that this initiative did not fit the firm as well as they first thought. As a result, they scaled back this effort and, as we noted, made a clear recommitment to their existing retail business. The demands of change force many companies to rethink their missions and thus revise their statements of what they are and what they do. (We discuss more fully the problems in managing change—as well as some solutions—later in this chapter.)

At many companies, top management drafts and circulates detailed mission statements. Because such a statement reflects a company's understanding of its activities as a *marketer*, it is not easily described. Consider the similarities and differences between Timex and Rolex. Although both firms share a common purpose—to sell watches at a profit—they have very different missions. Timex <www.timex.com> sells low-cost, reliable watches in outlets ranging from department stores to corner drugstores. Rolex <www.rolex.com> sells high-quality, high-priced watches through selected jewelry stores.

Regardless of a company's purpose and mission, however, every firm has long-term, intermediate, and short-term goals:

- **Long-term goals** relate to extended periods of time, typically five years or more. For example, American Express might set a long-term goal of doubling the number of participating merchants during the next 10 years. Kodak might adopt a long-term goal of increasing its share of the 35mm film market by 10 percent during the next eight years.
- **Intermediate goals** are set for a period of one to five years. Companies usually set intermediate goals in several areas. For example, the marketing department's goal might be to increase sales by 3 percent in two years. The production department might want to reduce expenses by 6 percent in four years. Human resources might seek to cut turnover by 10 percent in two years. Finance might aim for a 3-percent increase in return on investment in three years.
- **Short-term goals** are set for perhaps one year and are developed for several different areas. Increasing sales by 2 percent this year, cutting costs by 1 percent next quarter, and reducing turnover by 4 percent over the next six months are examples of short-term goals.

long-term goals
Goals set for an extended time, typically five years or more into the future

intermediate goals
Goals set for a period of one to five years into the future

short-term goals
Goals set for the very near future, typically less than one year

Formulating Strategy

Planning is often concerned with the nuts and bolts of setting goals, choosing tactics, and establishing schedules. In contrast, strategy tends to have a wider scope. It is by definition a "broad program" that describes an organization's intentions. A business strategy outlines how the business intends to meet its goals and includes the organization's responsiveness to new challenges and new needs.

Because a well-formulated strategy is so vital to a business's success, most top managers devote much attention and creativity to this process. **Strategy formulation** involves three basic steps summarized in Figure 5.2.[6]

It is interesting to note at least one change in contemporary thinking about the role of strategy. Once the responsibility of top management, strategy made its way into the everyday world of setting and implementing goals (planning) by means of a fairly rigid top-down process. Today, however, strategy formulation is often a much more democratic process.

Setting Strategic Goals Described as long-term goals, **strategic goals** are derived directly from a firm's mission statement.

For example, Ferdinand Piëch, CEO of Volkswagen <www.vw.com>, has clear strategic goals for the European carmaker. When he took over in 1993, Volkswagen was only marginally profitable, regarded as an also-ran in the industry, and thinking

strategy formulation
Creation of a broad program for defining and meeting an organization's goals

strategic goals
Long-term goals derived directly from a firm's mission statement

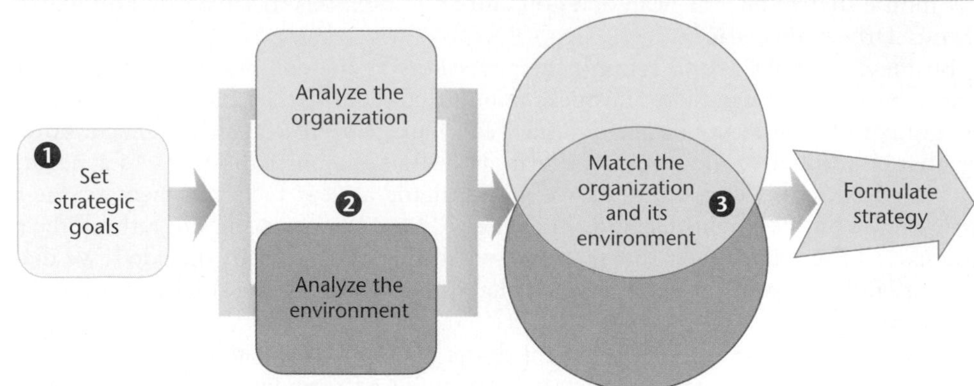

Figure 5.2
Strategy Formulation

> *"For the moment we are happy with the bronze medal. But we want to step up the stairway."*
>
> —Ferdinand Piëch, CEO of Volkswagen, on plans for improving the company's number-three standing in the industry

environmental analysis
Process of scanning the business environment for threats and opportunities

about pulling out of the U.S. market altogether because its sales were so poor. Over the next few years, however, Piëch totally revamped the firm and has it making big profits. Volkswagen is now a much more formidable force in the global automobile industry. It competes with Toyota for the number-three spot in the industry (behind only General Motors and Ford), but Piëch is clearly not finished. "For the moment," he reports, "we are happy with the bronze medal. But we want to step up the stairway."[7]

Analyzing the Organization and Its Environment The term **environmental analysis** involves scanning the environment for threats and opportunities. Changing consumer tastes and hostile takeover offers are *threats*, as are new government regulations. Even more important threats come from new products and new competitors. *Opportunities*, meanwhile, are areas in which the firm can potentially expand, grow, or take advantage of existing strengths.

Consider the case of British entrepreneur Sir Richard Branson and his company, Virgin Group Ltd. <www.virgin.com>. Branson started the firm in 1968, when he was 17, naming it in acknowledgment of his own lack of experience in the business world. Over the years, he has built Virgin into one of the world's best-known brands, comprising a conglomeration of over 200 entertainment, media, and travel companies worldwide. Among the best known of his enterprises are Virgin Atlantic (an international airline), Virgin Megastores (retailing), and V2 Music (record labels). Branson

Since Ferdinand Piëch became chairman of Volkswagen <www.vw.com> in 1993, productivity at plants like this one in Wolfsburg, Germany, have increased sales to 4.7 million vehicles per year and enabled VW to catch Toyota as the world's third-largest carmaker. Piëch (who calls his management style "democratic dictatorship") requires all new projects to be self-financing and gives designers free rein to create new models only as long as they buy parts off a preset purchasing list. Current long-term goals call for matching Audi in quality and marketing high-end VWs against both Audi and Mercedes models.

WEB Connection

British-based Virgin operates businesses ranging from an airline to a chain of megamedia stores to a financial services company. Only recently, however, has its strategy included the expansion of its Web site into an international e-commerce portal. While some critics say the move is too late, Virgin counters that because it already has so many of its own products, it's well-suited to make the entrepreneurial move. To find out more about Virgin's diverse product line, contact the company's Web site.

www.virgin.com

sees potential threats in the form of other competitors such as British Airways <www.britishairways.com> and KLM <nederland.klm.com> for Virgin Atlantic, Tower Records <www.towerrecords.com> (retailing), and the EMI Group <www.emi.fr> (recorded music).

He also sees significant opportunities because of his firm's strong brand name (especially in Europe). One of his most recent ventures is a new e-commerce firm. The business is called Virgin Mobile <www.virginmobile.com> and operates like a cellular telephone company. But in addition to providing conventional cellular service, the Virgin telephone permits the user to press a red button to go directly to a Virgin operator who can sell products, make airline and hotel reservations, and provide numerous other services. A companion Web site also complements the cellular service and its related programs. Virgin Mobile signed up more than a million new customers during its first year of operation and is now one of the market leaders in Great Britain.[8]

organizational analysis
Process of analyzing a firm's strengths and weaknesses

In addition to performing environmental analysis, which is analysis of *external* factors, managers must also examine *internal* factors. The purpose of **organizational analysis** is to better understand a company's strengths and weaknesses. Strengths might include surplus cash, a dedicated workforce, an ample supply of managerial talent, technical expertise, or little competition. The absence of any of these strengths could represent an important weakness.

Branson, for example, started Virgin Mobile in part because he saw so many of his current operations as old-line, traditional businesses that might be at future risk from new forms of business and competition. One strength he employs is the widespread name recognition his businesses enjoy. Another relates to finances. He sold 49 percent of Virgin Atlantic to Singapore Airlines <www.singaporeair.com> for almost $1 billion in cash, retaining ownership control but raising all of the funds he needed to launch his new venture. On the other hand, he also admits that neither he nor many of his senior managers have much experience in or knowledge about e-commerce, which may be a significant weakness.

Matching the Organization and Its Environment The final step in strategy formulation is matching environmental threats and opportunities against corporate strengths and weaknesses. The matching process is the heart of strategy formulation. More than any other facet of strategy, matching companies with their environments lays the foundation for successfully planning and conducting business.

Over the long term, this process may also determine whether a firm typically takes risks or behaves more conservatively. Either strategy can be successful. Blue Bell

<www.bluebell.com>, for example, is one of the most profitable ice–cream makers in the world, even though it sells its products in only a dozen states. Based in Brenham, Texas, Blue Bell controls more than 50 percent of the market in each state in which it does business. The firm, however, has resisted the temptation to expand too quickly. Its success is based on product freshness and frequent deliveries—strengths that may suffer if the company grows too large.

A Hierarchy of Plans Plans can be viewed on three levels: strategic, tactical, and operational. Managerial responsibilities are defined at each level. The levels constitute a hierarchy because implementing plans is practical only when there is a logical flow from one level to the next.

strategic plans
Plans reflecting decisions about resource allocations, company priorities, and steps needed to meet strategic goals

tactical plans
Generally short-range plans concerned with implementing specific aspects of a company's strategic plans

operational plans
Plans setting short-term targets for daily, weekly, or monthly performance

- **Strategic plans** reflect decisions about resource allocations, company priorities, and the steps needed to meet strategic goals. They are usually determined by the board of directors and top management. General Electric's decision that viable businesses must rank first or second within their respective markets is a matter of strategic planning.
- **Tactical plans** are shorter-range plans for implementing specific aspects of the company's strategic plans. They typically involve upper and middle management. Coca-Cola's decision to increase sales in Europe by building European bottling facilities is an example of tactical planning.
- **Operational plans**, which are developed by mid-level and lower-level managers, set short-term targets for daily, weekly, or monthly performance. McDonald's, for example, establishes operational plans when it explains to franchisees precisely how Big Macs are to be cooked, warmed, and served.

Contingency Planning and Crisis Management

Because business environments are often difficult to predict, and because the unexpected can create major problems, most managers recognize that even the best-laid plans sometimes simply do not work out. For instance, when the Walt Disney Co. <www.disney.go.com> announced plans to launch a cruise line replete with familiar Disney characters and themes, managers also began aggressively developing and marketing packages linking three- and four-day cruises with visits to Disney World <www.disney.go.com/DisneyWorld> in Florida. Indeed, the inaugural sailing was sold out more than a year in advance, and the first year was booked solid six months before the ship was launched. Three months before the first sailing, however, the shipyard constructing Disney's first ship (the *Disney Magic*) notified the company that it was behind schedule and that delivery would be several weeks late. When similar problems befall other cruise lines, they can offer to rebook passengers on alternative itineraries. Because Disney had no other ship, it had no choice but to refund the money it had collected as prebooking deposits for its first 15 cruises.

The 20,000 displaced customers were offered big discounts if they rebooked on a later cruise. Many of them, however, could not rearrange their schedules and requested full refunds. Moreover, quite a few blamed Disney, and a few expressed outrage at what they saw as poor planning by the entertainment giant. Fortunately for Disney, however, the *Disney Magic* was eventually launched and has now become very popular and very profitable.[9]

Because managers know such things can happen, they often develop alternative plans in case things go awry. Two common methods of dealing with the unknown and unforeseen are *contingency planning* and *crisis management.*

contingency planning
Identifying aspects of a business or its environment that might entail changes in strategy

Contingency Planning Contingency planning recognizes the need to find solutions to specific aspects of a problem. By its very nature, a contingency plan is a hedge against changes that might occur. **Contingency planning**, then, is planning for change: It seeks to identify in advance important aspects of a business or its market that might change. It also identifies the ways in which a company will respond to changes. Today, many companies use computer programs for contingency planning.

Suppose, for example, that a company develops a plan to create a new division. It expects sales to increase at an annual rate of 10 percent for the next five years and develops a marketing strategy for maintaining that level. But suppose that sales have increased by only 5 percent by the end of the first year. Does the firm abandon the venture, invest more in advertising, or wait to see what happens in the second year? Any of these alternatives is possible. Regardless of the firm's choice, however, its efforts will be more efficient if managers decide in advance what to do in case sales fall below planned levels. Contingency planning helps them do exactly that. Disney learned from its mistake with its first ship, and when the second (the *Disney Wonder*) was launched a year later, managers did several things differently. For one thing, they allowed for an extra two weeks between when the ship was supposed to be ready for sailing and its first scheduled cruise. They also held open a few cabins on the *Disney Magic* as a backup for any especially disgruntled customers who might need accommodations if there were unexpected delays launching the *Disney Wonder*.

Crisis Management A crisis is an unexpected emergency requiring immediate response. **Crisis management** involves an organization's methods for dealing with emergencies. In May 2000, for example, millions of computers around the world were hit by a virus that was quickly dubbed the "Love Bug." The virus came disguised as an e-mail attachment with a tag line indicating that the receiver should open it to see a love note. But once opened, the virus-laden file began damaging files on the receiver's computer and transmitting itself to others via e-mail and the Internet. Among the many organizations seriously affected were not only Ford Motor Co. <www.ford.com>, Bear Stearns <www.bearstearns.com>, and Japan's Nomura Securities <www.nomura.co.jp>, but also the Pentagon <www.defenselink.mil/pubs/pentagon>, the U.S. Congress, the British Parliament, and the whole Danish government. These organizations and numerous others literally had to shut down their electronic communications networks for hours in order to set up new and more effective security procedures. Some organizations were able to get back up and running very quickly, but others took much longer. Warns Steve White, a computer-virus expert at IBM: "Everybody now needs e-mail. Somebody shuts it down and we are significantly out of business."[10]

crisis management
Organization's methods for dealing with emergencies

"Everybody now needs e-mail. Somebody shuts it down and we are significantly out of business."

—Steve White, IBM computer-virus scientist, on the attack of the "Love Bug"

The tragic events of September 11, 2001, further served to underscore the importance of crisis management. In addition to the horrific loss of human life, virtually every business in the United States experienced a drop in income. As a result, more firms than ever before have developed crisis management plans. Unfortunately, however, because it is impossible to forecast the future precisely, no organization can ever be perfectly prepared for every eventuality.

THE MANAGEMENT PROCESS

Management is the process of planning, organizing, directing, and controlling an organization's financial, physical, human, and information resources to achieve its goals. Managers oversee the use of all these resources in their respective firms. All aspects of a manager's job are interrelated. In fact, any given manager is likely to be engaged in each of these activities during the course of any given day.

management
Process of planning, organizing, directing, and controlling an organization's resources to achieve its goals

Planning

Determining what the organization needs to do and how best to get it done requires planning. **Planning** has three main components. As we have seen, it begins when managers determine the firm's goals. Next, they develop a comprehensive strategy for achieving those goals. After a strategy is developed, they design tactical and operational plans for implementing the strategy.

planning
Management process of determining what an organization needs to do and how best to get it done

When Yahoo! <www.yahoo.com> was created, for example, the firm's top managers set a strategic goal of becoming a top firm in the then-emerging market for Internet search engines. But then came the hard part—figuring out how to do it. They started by assessing the ways in which people actually use the Web and concluded that users wanted to be able to satisfy a wide array of needs, preferences, and priorities by going to as few sites as possible to find what they were looking for.

Thus, one key component of Yahoo!'s strategy was to foster partnerships and relationships with other companies so that potential Web surfers could draw upon several sources through a single portal—which would be Yahoo!. Thus, the goal of partnering emerged as one set of tactical plans for moving forward. Yahoo! managers then began fashioning alliances with such diverse partners as Reuters <www.reuters.com>, Standard & Poor's <www.standardpoor.com>, and the Associated Press <www.ap.org> (for news coverage), RE/Max <www.remax.com> (for real estate information), and a wide array of information providers specializing in sports, weather, entertainment, shopping, and travel. The creation of individual partnership agreements with each of these partners represents a form of operational planning.

Organizing

Once one of the leading-edge high-technology firms in the world, Hewlett-Packard <www.hewlett-packard.com> began to lose some of its luster a few years ago. Ironically, one of the major reasons for its slide could be traced back to what had once been a major strength. Specifically, HP had long prided itself on being little more than a corporate confederation of individual businesses. Sometimes, these businesses even ended up competing among themselves. This approach had been beneficial for much of the firm's history: It was easier for each business to make its own decisions quickly and efficiently, and the competition kept each unit on its toes. By the late 1990s, however, problems had become apparent, and no one could quite figure out what was going on.

Enter Ann Livermore, then head of the firm's software and services business. Livermore realized that the structure that had served so well in the past was now holding the firm back. To regain its competitive edge, HP needed an integrated, organization-wide Internet strategy. Unfortunately, the company's highly decentralized organization made that impossible. Livermore led the charge to create one organization to drive a single Internet plan. "I felt we could be the most powerful company in the industry," she said, "if we could get our hardware, software, and services aligned." Eventually, a new team of top managers was handed control of the company, and every major component of the firm's structure was reorganized. Today, under the leadership of new CEO Carly Fiorina, HP is showing signs of recreating the magic from its early years.[11]

This process—determining the best way to arrange a business's resources and activities into a coherent structure—is called **organizing**. (We explore this topic further in Chapter 6.)

organizing
Management process of determining how best to arrange an organization's resources and activities into a coherent structure

directing
Management process of guiding and motivating employees to meet an organization's objectives

Directing

Managers have the power to give orders and demand results. Directing, however, involves more complex activities. When **directing**, a manager works to guide and motivate employees to meet the firm's objectives. Andrall Pearson, for example, has clearly changed his entire approach to directing employees. Gordon Bethune, CEO of Continental Airlines <www.continental.com>, is an excellent example of a manager who excels at motivating his employees. When he took the helm of the troubled carrier in 1994, morale was dismal, most employees hated their jobs, and the company's performance was among the worst in the industry.

Almost immediately, Bethune started listening to his employees to learn about their problems and hear how they thought the company could be improved. He also began to reward everyone when things went well and continued communicating with all Continental employees on a regular basis. Today, the firm is ranked among the best in the industry and is regularly identified as one of the best places to work in the United States. In both 2000 and 2001, Continental was named the highest-quality airline in the United States, based on the J.D. Powers Survey of Customer Satisfaction.[12]

Controlling

Controlling is the process of monitoring a firm's performance to make sure that the firm is meeting its goals. All CEOs must pay close attention to costs and performance. Indeed, skillful controlling, like innovative directing, is one reason that Gordon Bethune has been so successful at Continental. For example, the firm focuses almost relentlessly on numerous indicators of performance that can be constantly measured and adjusted. Everything from on-time arrivals to baggage-handling errors to the number of empty seats on an airplane to surveys of employee and customer satisfaction are regularly and routinely monitored. If on-time arrivals start to slip, Bethune focuses on the problem and gets it fixed. If a manager's subordinates provide less than glowing reviews, that manager loses part of his or her bonus. As a result, no single element of the firm's performance can slip too far before it's noticed and fixed.

controlling
Management process of monitoring an organization's performance to ensure that it is meeting its goals

Figure 5.3 illustrates the control process that begins when management establishes standards, often for financial performance. If, for example, a company wants to increase sales by 20 percent over the next 10 years, then an appropriate standard might be an increase of about 2 percent a year.

Managers then measure actual performance against standards. If the two amounts agree, the organization continues along its present course. If they vary significantly, however, one or the other needs adjustment. If sales have increased 2.1 percent by the end of the first year, things are probably fine. If sales have dropped 1 percent, some revision in plans may be needed. Perhaps the original goal should be lowered or more money should be spent on advertising.

Control can also show where performance is running better than expected and, thus, serve as a basis for providing rewards or reducing costs. For example, when Ford recently introduced the new Explorer SportsTrac (an SUV with a pickup bed), initial

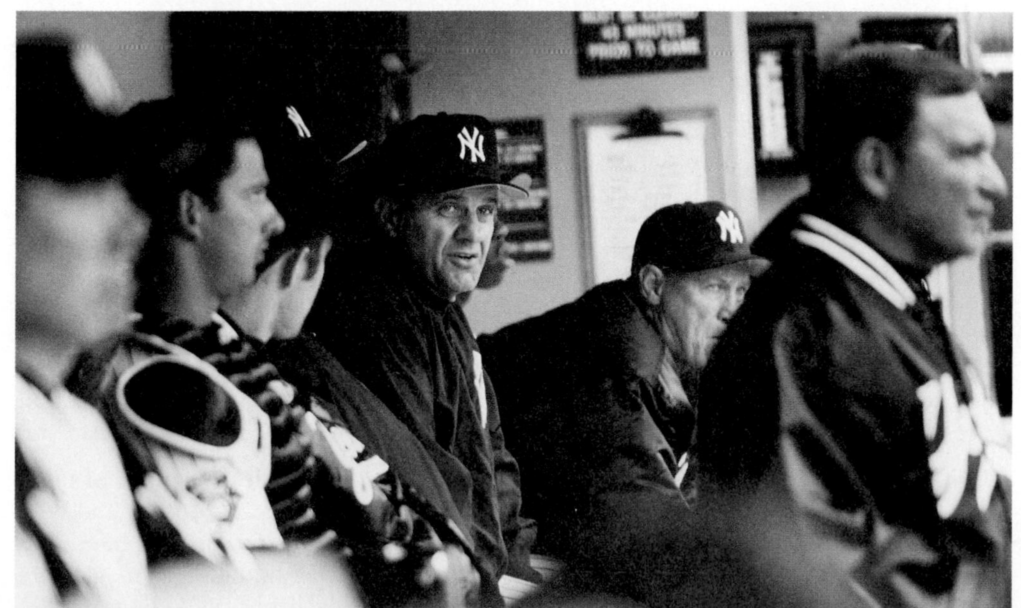

As field boss of the New York Yankees <www.yankees.com>, Joe Torre has managed (since 1996) to hold on to a slippery job (the team has had 21 managers in 24 years). Of course, he's won 4 World Series in a 6-year stretch, and by most accounts, Torre's success as an organizational leader derives from his ability as a motivator. He prefers one-on-one dealings with "subordinates" (multimillion-dollar baseball players) instead of motivational speech making. He tries to make every employee (even well-paid utility players) feel useful, and he sees no reason to punish failure (which is a routine part of a baseball player's job). Many observers—including Torre's boss, George Steinbrenner—think that his approach would be effective in a business setting.

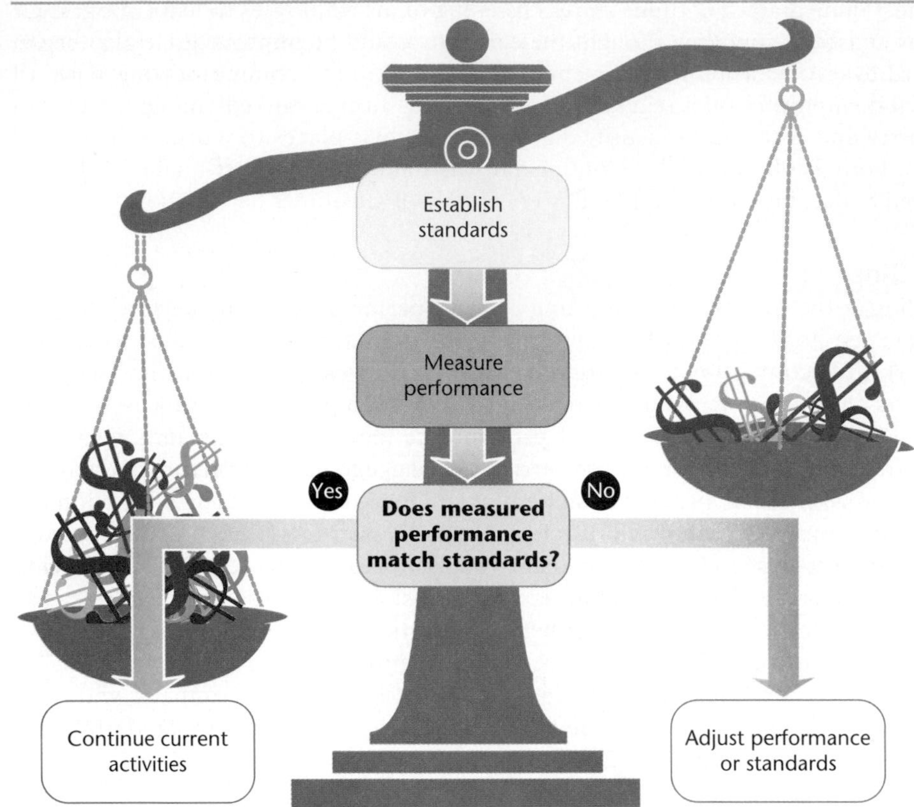

Figure 5.3
The Control Process

sales were so strong the firm was able to delay a major advertising campaign for three months because it was selling all of the vehicles it could make anyway.

TYPES OF MANAGERS

Although all managers plan, organize, direct, and control, not all managers have the same degree of responsibility for these activities. Thus, it is helpful to classify managers according to levels and areas of responsibility.

Levels of Management

The three basic levels of management are *top, middle*, and *first-line management*. Most firms have more middle managers than top managers and more first-line managers than middle managers. Both the power of managers and the complexity of their duties increase as they move up the ladder.

top managers
Managers responsible to the board of directors and stockholders for a firm's overall performance and effectiveness

middle managers
Managers responsible for implementing the strategies, policies, and decisions made by top managers

Top Managers Like Jenny Ming, Kenneth Chenault, and Andrall Pearson, the fairly small number of executives who get the chance to guide the fortunes of most companies are **top managers**. Common titles for top managers include *president, vice president, treasurer, chief executive officer* (CEO), and *chief financial officer* (CFO). Top managers are responsible for the overall performance and effectiveness of the firm. They set general policies, formulate strategies, approve all significant decisions, and represent the company in dealings with other firms and with government bodies.

Middle Managers Just below the ranks of top managers is another group of managers who also occupy positions of considerable autonomy and importance and who are called **middle managers**. Titles such as *plant manager, operations manager*, and *division manager* designate middle-management slots. In general, middle managers are responsible for implementing the strategies, policies, and decisions made by top managers. For example, if top management decides to introduce a new product in 12 months or to cut costs by 5 percent in the next quarter, middle management must decide how to meet these goals. The manager of an American Express service center, an Old Navy distribution center, or a regional collection of Tricon restaurants will likely be a middle manager.

First-Line Managers Those who hold such titles as *supervisor, office manager*, and *group leader* are **first-line managers**. Although they spend most of their time working with and supervising the employees who report to them, first-line managers' activities are not limited to that arena. At a building site, for example, the *project manager* not only ensures that workers are carrying out construction as specified by the architect, but also interacts extensively with materials suppliers, community officials, and middle- and upper-level managers at the home office. The manager of an Old Navy store and the manager for an individual Taco Bell outlet would also be considered first-line managers.

first-line managers
Managers responsible for supervising the work of employees

Areas of Management

In any large company, top, middle, and first-line managers work in a variety of areas including *human resources, operations, marketing, information*, and *finance*. For the most part, these areas correspond to the types of managerial skills described later in this chapter and to the wide range of business principles and activities discussed in the rest of this book.

Human Resource Managers Most companies have *human resource managers* who hire and train employees, who evaluate performance, and who determine compensation. At large firms, separate departments deal with recruiting and hiring, wage and salary levels, and labor relations. A smaller firm may have a single department—or a single person—responsible for all human resource activities. (Some key issues in human resource management are discussed in Part 3.)

Operations Managers As we will see in Chapter 7, the term *operations* refers to the systems by which a firm produces goods and services. Among other duties, operations managers are responsible for production, inventory, and quality control. Manufacturing companies such as Texas Instruments, Ford, and Caterpillar have a strong need for operations managers at many levels. Such firms typically have a *vice president for operations* (top), *plant managers* (middle), and *production supervisors* (first-line managers). In recent years, sound operations management practices have become increasingly important to a variety of service organizations.

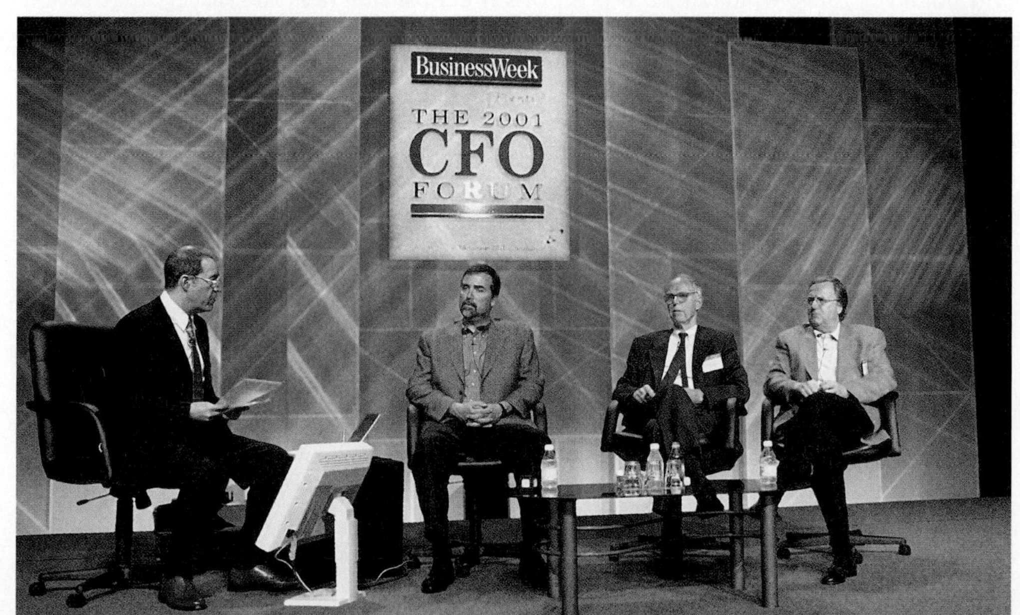

At Business Week's *2001 CFO Forum, participants—including the CFOs of such companies as GE Capital, Toysrus.com, and Oracle Corp.—stressed the fact that a major responsibility of today's CFOs is helping companies fit into a business world that is constantly being changed by technology. In other words, the CFO is no longer just a high-ranking numbers cruncher. Because financing the adoption of a new business model affects a number of managerial areas, CFOs often play a key role in so-called "e-transformation." Among other things, they evaluate new technologies as investment opportunities and promote companywide willingness to change.*

Marketing Managers As we will see in Chapter 10, marketing encompasses the development, pricing, promotion, and distribution of goods and services. Marketing managers are responsible for getting products from producers to consumers. Marketing is especially important for firms that manufacture consumer products, such as Procter & Gamble, Coca-Cola, and Levi Strauss. Such firms often have large numbers of marketing managers at several levels. For example, a large consumer products firm is likely to have a *vice president for marketing* (top), several *regional marketing managers* (middle), and several *district sales managers* (first-line managers). (The different areas of marketing are discussed in Part 4.)

Information Managers Occupying a fairly new managerial position in many firms, information managers design and implement systems to gather, organize, and distribute information. Huge increases in both the sheer volume of information and the ability to manage it have led to the emergence of this important function.

Although relatively few in number, the ranks of *information managers* are growing at all levels. Some firms have a top-management position called a *chief information officer.* Middle managers help design information systems for divisions or plants. Computer systems managers within smaller businesses are usually first-line managers. (Information management is discussed in more detail in Chapter 12.)

Financial Managers Nearly every company has financial managers to plan and oversee its accounting functions and financial resources. Levels of financial management may include *chief financial officer* (CFO) or *vice president for finance* (top), a *division controller* (middle), and an *accounting supervisor* (first-line manager). Some institutions—NationsBank <www.nationsbank.com> and Prudential <www.prudential.com>, for example—have even made effective financial management the company's reason for being. (Financial management is treated in more detail in Part 6.)

Other Managers Some firms also employ other specialized managers. Many companies, for example, have public relations managers. Chemical and pharmaceutical companies such as Monsanto <www.pharmacia.com> and Merck <www.merck.com> have research and development managers. The range of possibilities is wide, and the areas of management are limited only by the needs and imagination of the firm.

BASIC MANAGEMENT SKILLS

Although the range of managerial positions is almost limitless, the success that people enjoy in those positions is often limited by their skills and abilities. Effective managers must develop *technical, human relations, conceptual, decision-making*, and *time management skills*. Unfortunately, these skills are quite complex, and it is the rare manager who excels in every area.

Technical Skills

technical skills
Skills needed to perform specialized tasks

The skills needed to perform specialized tasks are called **technical skills**. A programmer's ability to write code, an animator's ability to draw, and an accountant's ability to audit a company's records are all examples of technical skills. People develop technical skills through a combination of education and experience. Technical skills are especially important for first-line managers. Many of these managers spend considerable time helping employees solve work-related problems, training them in more efficient procedures, and monitoring performance.

Human Relations Skills

human relations skills
Skills in understanding and getting along with people

Effective managers also generally have good **human relations skills**—specifically, skills in understanding and getting along with other people. A manager with poor human relations skills may have trouble getting along with subordinates, cause valuable employees to quit or transfer, and contribute to poor morale. Today, Andrall Pearson works well with people, has fun when he works, and makes everyone feel excited about the work. He also genuinely cares about the welfare of his employees. So, too, does Gordon Bethune, who routinely visits his employees throughout the company. Reports one baggage manager at Continental's Newark, New Jersey, hub: "Anybody who's worked here longer than two months can recognize Gordon."

Although human relations skills are important at all levels, they are probably most important for middle managers, who must often act as bridges between top managers, first-line managers, and managers from other areas of the organization. Managers should possess good communication skills. Many managers have found that being able to understand others, and to get others to understand them, can go a long way toward maintaining good relations in an organization.[13]

"Anybody who's worked here longer than two months can recognize Gordon."

—Baggage manager at Continental's Newark, New Jersey, hub, on the airline's CEO, Gordon Bethune

Conceptual Skills

Conceptual skills refer to a person's ability to think in the abstract, to diagnose and analyze different situations, and to see beyond the present situation. Conceptual skills help managers recognize new market opportunities and threats. They can also help managers analyze the probable outcomes of their decisions. The need for conceptual skills differs at various management levels: Top managers depend most on conceptual skills, first-line managers least. Although the purposes and everyday needs of various jobs differ, conceptual skills are needed in almost any job-related activity.

In many ways, conceptual skills may be the most important ingredient in the success of executives in e-commerce businesses. For example, the ability to foresee how a particular business application will be affected by or can be translated to the Internet is clearly conceptual in nature. The "Wired World" box in this chapter discusses this idea in more detail.

conceptual skills
Abilities to think in the abstract, diagnose and analyze different situations, and see beyond the present situation

Decision-Making Skills

Decision-making skills include the ability to define problems and select the best course of action. Figure 5.4 illustrates the following basic steps in decision making:

decision-making skills
Skills in defining problems and selecting the best courses of action

1. *Define the problem, gather facts, and identify alternative solutions.* Vivendi Universal, for example, is a large French entertainment and media company. The firm's top managers recently decided that they needed a stronger presence in the United States if they were to continue their quest to become a global media powerhouse. Thus, they defined their problem as how to best enter the U.S. media market. They subsequently determined that there were two alternatives: starting a new media business from scratch or buying an existing one.
2. *Evaluate each alternative and select the best one.* Managers at Vivendi Universal realized that it would take many years and a huge cash investment to launch a new media enterprise from scratch. They also recognized that because there was ongoing consolidation in the U.S. media industry, buying an existing firm might be relatively easy. Further analysis identified Houghton Mifflin, one of the last remaining independent publishers, as an attractive acquisition target.
3. *Implement the chosen alternative, periodically following up and evaluating the effectiveness of that choice.* Vivendi Universal executives quietly began negotiating with senior managers at Houghton Mifflin in mid-2001. Within a matter of weeks, the two firms had reached an agreement: Vivendi Universal would acquire

Define the problem
Gather facts and develop alternatives
Evaluate alternatives
Select the best alternative
Implement the chosen alternative
Follow up and evaluate the chosen alternative

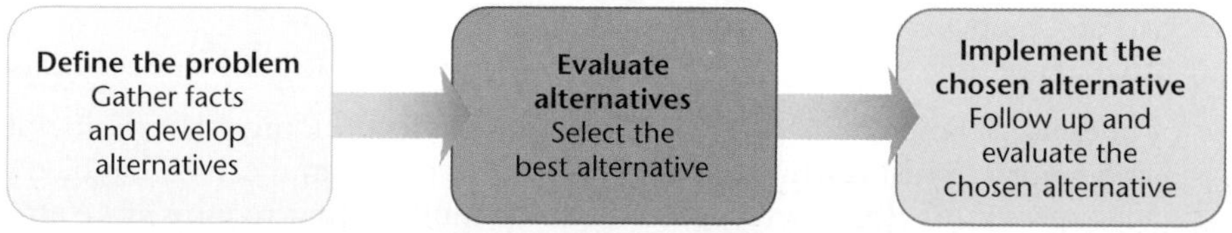

Figure 5.4
The Decision-Making Process

IT'S A WIRED WORLD

How to Spot the E-CEO

Top managers, especially CEOs, have always moved in a fast-paced, stress-filled work environment. But the job of CEO for an e-commerce company seems to be setting new standards for pace, complexity, and stress. CEOs in traditional businesses are generally accustomed to dealing with either tangible products (such as automobiles, shoes, or computer hardware) or relatively well-defined services (accounting, transportation, or retailing operations). Moreover, the rules of the game, established over a period of decades, are relatively clear: Businesses are supposed to make profits, stock price is based on earnings, and so forth.

But the world of electronic commerce has put a few bumps in this well-worn road. Managers in this environment clearly believe that the pace of their work is faster, more complex, and more ambiguous than that of their traditional counterparts. They attribute some of these conditions to the nature of their business (which is based almost solely on information), some to the pace of change in their industries (it occurs very quickly), and some to a new set of business rules (for example, market valuation based more on intuition rather than reality). But all agree on one fundamental thing: They operate at breakneck speed with little or no margin for error. Table 5.1 highlights some of the more fundamental differences between the work of a traditional CEO and an e-CEO.

Traditional CEOs are generally expected to be encouraging, cordial, and fast moving with a dislike for ambiguity. They might also have some anxiety about confronting technology-related issues, and their average age is 57. E-CEOs, on the other hand, are more prone to evangelizing, often brutally frank, and apparently thrive on ambiguity. Furthermore, e-CEOs exhibit more anxiety when they are deprived of technology, and their average age is 38. Finally, while all CEOs are presumed to be rich, well-to-do, or comfortable, successful e-CEOs are likely to be rolling in money.

Table 5.1 Traditional CEOs versus E-CEOs

Traditional CEO	E-CEO
Encouraging	Evangelizing
Alert	Paranoid
Cordial	Brutally frank
Infotech semiliterate (at best)	Infotech literate (at least)
Clearly focused	Intensely focused
Fast moving	Faster moving
Antiambiguity	Proambiguity
Technology-confrontation-anxiety sufferer	Bandwidth-separation-anxiety sufferer
Paragon of good judgment	Paragon of good judgment
Age: 57	Age: 38
Rich	Really rich

100 percent of Houghton Mifflin, thus providing the French company with exactly what it had been seeking—a viable entry into U.S. markets.[14]

Time Management Skills

time management skills Skills associated with the productive use of time

Time management skills refer to the productive use that managers make of their time. In 2000, for example, Prudential Insurance CEO Arthur Ryan was paid $7,187,525 in salary. Assuming that he worked 50 hours a week and took 2 weeks' vacation, Ryan earned $2,875 an hour—about $48 per minute. Any amount of time that Ryan wastes clearly represents a large cost to Prudential and its stockholders. Most managers, of course, receive much smaller salaries than Ryan. Their time, however, is valuable, and poor use of it still translates into costs and wasted productivity. (Actually, this example underestimates Ryan's earnings; he also received additional deferred compensation such as stock options and retirement benefits.)

To manage time effectively, managers must address four leading causes of wasted time:

- *Paperwork.* Some managers spend too much time deciding what to do with letters and reports. Most documents of this sort are routine and can be handled quickly. Managers must learn to recognize those documents that require more attention.

- *Telephone.* Experts estimate that managers get interrupted by the telephone every five minutes. To manage this time more effectively, they suggest having an assistant screen all calls and setting aside a certain block of time each day to return the important ones. Unfortunately, the explosive use of cell phones seems to be making this problem even worse for many managers.
- *Meetings.* Many managers spend as much as four hours a day in meetings. To help keep this time productive, the person handling the meeting should specify a clear agenda, start on time, keep everyone focused on the agenda, and end on time.
- *E-mail.* Increasingly, more and more managers are also relying heavily on e-mail and other forms of electronic communication. Like memos and telephone calls, many e-mail messages are not particularly important—some are even trivial. As a result, time is wasted when managers have to sort through a variety of electronic folders, in-baskets, and archives. As the average number of electronic messages grows, the potential time wasted also increases.[15]

Management Skills for the Twenty-First Century

Although the skills discussed in this chapter have long been an important part of every successful manager's career, new skill requirements continue to emerge. As we enter the twenty-first century, most experts point to the growing importance of skills involving *global management* and *technology*.

Global Management Skills Tomorrow's managers must equip themselves with the special tools, techniques, and skills necessary to compete in a global environment. They will need to understand foreign markets, cultural differences, and the motives and practices of foreign rivals.

On a more practical level, businesses will need managers who are capable of understanding international operations. In the past, most U.S. businesses hired local managers to run their operations in the various countries in which they operated. More recently, however, the trend has been to transfer U.S. managers to foreign locations. This practice helps firms better transfer their corporate cultures to foreign operations. In addition, foreign assignments help managers become better prepared for international competition as they advance within the organization. General Motors <www.gm.com> now has almost 500 U.S. managers in foreign posts.

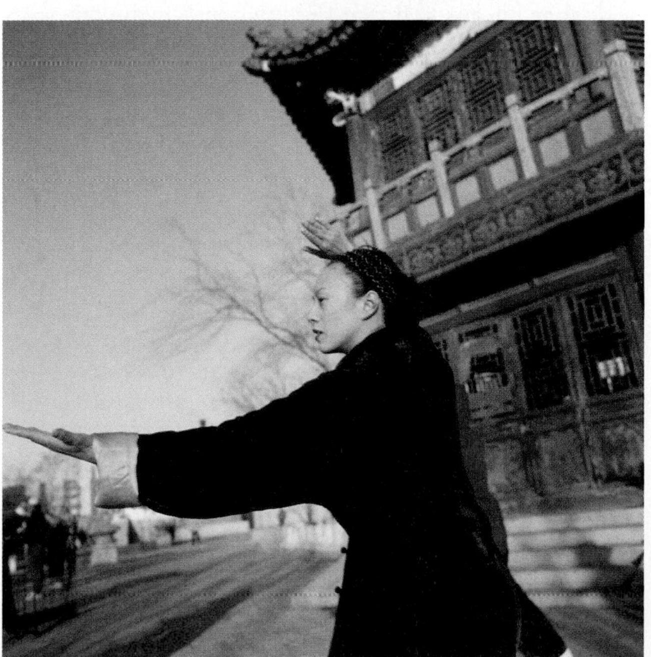

Although more and more U.S. companies are sending American managers to foreign locations, there are still times when it makes much better sense to hire a local person to run foreign operations. What MTV <www.mtv.com> *needed in China was someone who understood both conservative Chinese television regulators and China's young urban elite. They chose 37-year-old Li Yifei, a former Baylor University political science student, United Nations intern, public relations consultant, and tai chi champion. Li has already brought the Chinese equivalent of the MTV awards to state-owned television, and although the show got only a 7.9-percent rating, she's quick to point out that in China, that's 150 million people (about half the U.S. population).*

Management and Technology Skills Another significant issue facing tomorrow's managers is technology, especially as it relates to communication. Managers have always had to deal with information. In today's world, however, the amount of information has reached staggering proportions. In the United States alone, people exchange hundreds of millions of e-mail messages every day. New forms of technology have added to a manager's ability to process information while simultaneously making it even more important to organize and interpret an ever-increasing wealth of input.

Technology has also begun to change the way the interaction of managers shapes corporate structures. Computer networking, for example, exists because it is no longer too expensive to put a computer on virtually every desk in the company. In turn, this elaborate network controls the flow of the firm's lifeblood—information. This information no longer flows strictly up and down through hierarchies. It now flows to everyone simultaneously. As a result, decisions are made more quickly, and more people are directly involved. With e-mail, teleconferencing, and other forms of communication, neither time nor distance—nor such corporate "boundaries" as departments and divisions—can prevent people from working more closely together. More than ever, bureaucracies are breaking down, while planning, decision making, and other activities are beginning to benefit from group building and teamwork.

"E-mail is a major cultural event—it changes the way you run the organization."

—Bill Raduchel, chief information officer, Sun Microsystems

Bill Raduchel, chief information officer of Sun Microsystems <www.sun.com>, goes so far as to say that "e-mail is a major cultural event—it changes the way you run the organization." But, of course, as noted earlier, managers must also work to use information technology wisely and efficiently.

MANAGEMENT AND THE CORPORATE CULTURE

Every organization—big or small, more successful or less successful—has an unmistakable "feel" to it. Just as every individual has a unique personality, so every company has a unique identity, called **corporate culture**: the shared experiences, stories, beliefs, and norms that characterize an organization. This culture helps define the work and business climate that exists in an organization.

corporate culture
The shared experiences, stories, beliefs, and norms that characterize an organization

A strong corporate culture serves several purposes. For one thing, it directs employees' efforts and helps everyone work toward the same goals. Some cultures, for example, stress financial success to the extreme, while others focus more on quality of life. In addition, corporate culture helps newcomers learn accepted behaviors. If financial success is the key to a culture, newcomers quickly learn that they are expected to work long, hard hours and that the "winner" is the one who brings in the most revenue. But if quality of life is more fundamental, newcomers learn that it's more acceptable to spend less time at work and that balancing work and nonwork is encouraged.

Where does a business's culture come from? In some cases it emanates from the days of an organization's founder. Firms such as the Walt Disney Co., Hewlett-Packard, Wal-Mart <www.walmart.com>, and JCPenney <www.jcpenney.com>, for example, still bear the imprint of their founders. In other cases, an organization's culture is forged over a long period of time by a constant and focused business strategy. PepsiCo <www.pepsico.com>, for example, has an achievement-oriented culture tied to its long-standing goal of catching its biggest competitor, Coca-Cola <www.cokecce.com>. Similarly, Apple Computer <www.apple.com> has a sort of "counterculture" culture stemming from its self-styled image as the alternative to the staid IBM <www.ibm.com> corporate model for computer makers.

Communicating the Culture and Managing Change

Corporate culture influences management philosophy, style, and behavior. Managers, therefore, must carefully consider the kind of culture they want for their organization, then work to nourish that culture by communicating with everyone who works there. Wal-Mart, for example, is acutely conscious of the need to spread the message of its culture as it opens new stores in new areas. One of the company's methods is to

"I don't know how it started, either. All I know is that it's part of our corporate culture."

regularly assign veteran managers to lead employees in new territories. Gordon Bethune delivers weekly messages for all Continental employees to update them on what's going on in the firm; the employees can either listen to it on a closed-circuit broadcast or else call an 800 telephone number and hear a recorded version at their own convenience.

Communicating the Culture To use a firm's culture to its advantage, managers must accomplish several tasks, all of which hinge on effective communication. First, managers themselves must have a clear understanding of the culture. Second, they must transmit the culture to others in the organization. Thus, communication is one aim in training and orienting newcomers. A clear and meaningful statement of the organization's mission is also a valuable communication tool. Finally, managers can maintain the culture by rewarding and promoting those who understand it and work toward maintaining it.

Managing Change Organizations must sometimes change their cultures. In such cases, they must also communicate the nature of the change to both employees and customers. According to the CEOs of several companies that have undergone radical change in the last decade or so, the process usually goes through three stages:

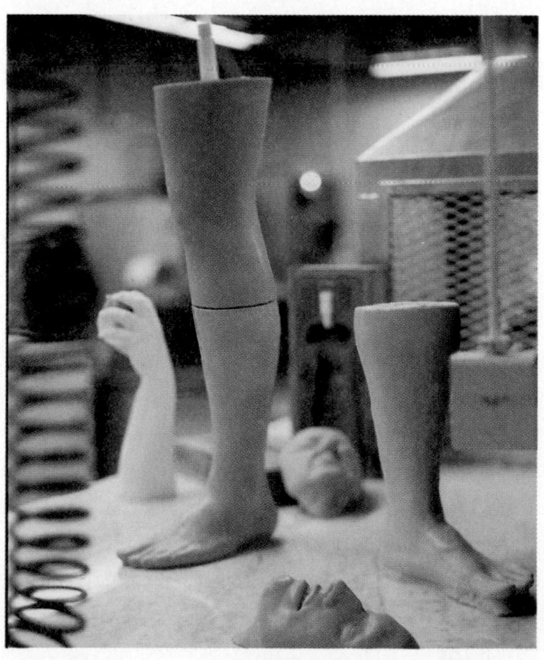

Procter & Gamble <www.pg.com> has been a bastion of conformity for so long that it's been called the home of the "Proctoids"—a place where entrepreneurs and other creative types are systematically squelched. As a result, the Cincinnati-based home-products firm has for several years watched revenues flatten out and famous brands lose market share. Now P&G is betting on bold ideas and new products. A new prototype lab now spends $200 million a year on such projects as testing bandages, cosmetics, and other products on molded body parts.

1. *At the highest level, analysis of the company's environment highlights extensive change as the most effective response to its problems.* This period is typically characterized by conflict and resistance.
2. *Top management begins to formulate a vision of a new company.* Whatever that vision, it must include renewed focus on the activities of competitors and the needs of customers.
3. *The firm sets up new systems for appraising and compensating employees who enforce the firm's new values.* The purpose is to give the new culture solid shape from within the firm.

While some firms like to build on their legacies, others know better. When Gordon Bethune announced his rebuilding plans at Continental, he dubbed it the "Go Forward" program. He stressed that the firm had little to look back on with pride and he wanted everyone to look only to the future. Likewise, Procter & Gamble <www.pg.com> is in the midst of a major overhaul designed to remake its corporate culture into one more suited to today's competitive global business environment. Because its brands have been dominant for such a long time, managers at P&G have been criticized for having tunnel vision—focusing only on the ways they've done things in the past and then trying to repeat them. Procter & Gamble's popular Tide laundry detergent, for example, has been through more than 60 formula upgrades since it was first introduced. A new top-management team, however, is working to shake things up by advocating new approaches, new ways of thinking, and new models of product development.[16]

Continued from page 115

Down East Showdown

Starbucks has become almost synonymous with coffee—people sometimes talk about stopping for some "Starbucks" rather than stopping for coffee. There are currently more than 2,100 Starbucks locations in the United States alone, and the firm has another 700 in other countries. Starbucks also plans to partner with Kraft Foods <www.kraftfoods.com> to distribute its coffee in some 25,000 U.S. grocery stores. To maintain high levels of quality control, Starbucks also refuses to franchise—it owns and operates every one of its stores.

However, a firm like Starbucks is not above reproach. It has been the target of protests at some sites because it buys most of its beans from coffee corporations and plantations in less-developed countries instead of from small independent growers. Other critics take issue with the extra "packaging" that Starbucks uses for a hot cup of coffee—double cups or corrugated bands, large plastic lids, plastic stirring sticks, and so forth. Still others lump Starbucks with other megaretailers, such as Barnes & Noble and Wal-Mart, criticizing them all for overwhelming independent family-owned businesses—businesses like Maine Roasters Coffee.

So far, Maine Roasters is holding its own in its hometown of Portland, Maine. Rand Smith's strategy of pitching his small company as a David to Starbucks' Goliath has attracted considerable local sympathy. But Smith faces some other problems, too. For one thing, even as he pitches his business as a local, down-home operation, his original business plan called for more than 30 stores spread throughout New England. (As of yet, only a handful have been opened.) Smith openly acknowledges the inherent contradiction in his portrayal of Starbucks and his own vision. He also sees the day when he might very well be interested in selling his company—and thinks Starbucks might be the most logical buyer. In an especially ironic twist, he actually credits Starbucks with boosting sales at his coffee shops by educating consumers about specialty coffees and, thus, broadening the local market.

Questions for Discussion

1. Describe the management process at a big international company like Starbucks.
2. Describe the management process at a small local business like Maine Roasters Coffee.
3. Compare and contrast goals and strategies at Starbucks and Maine Roasters.
4. What are the types of managers and areas of management that exist in a firm like Starbucks? How about Maine Roasters?
5. What differences, if any, are likely to exist among the key management skills needed at Starbucks and Maine Roasters?
6. What role does corporate culture play in the operations and activities of these two firms?

SUMMARY OF LEARNING OBJECTIVES

1 **Explain the importance of setting *goals* and formulating *strategies* as the starting points of effective management.** *Goals*—the performance targets of an organization—can be *long term, intermediate*, or *short term*. They provide direction for managers, help managers decide how to allocate limited resources, define the corporate culture, and help managers assess performance. *Strategies*—the methods that a company uses to meet its stated goals—involve three major activities: *setting strategic goals, analyzing the organization and its environment*, and *matching the organization and its environment*. These strategies are translated into *strategic, tactical*, and *operational plans*. To deal with crises or major environmental changes, companies develop *contingency plans* and plans for *crisis management*.

2 **Describe the four activities that constitute the *management process*.** *Management* is the process of planning, organizing, directing, and controlling an organization's financial, physical, human, and information resources to achieve the organization's goals. *Planning* means determining what the company needs to do and how best to get it done. *Organizing* means determining how best to arrange a business's resources and the necessary jobs into an overall structure. *Directing* means guiding and motivating employees to meet the firm's objectives. *Controlling* means monitoring the firm's performance to ensure that it is meeting its goals.

3 **Identify *types of managers* by level and area.** Managers can be differentiated in two ways: by level and by area. By level, *top managers* set policies, formulate strategies, and approve decisions. *Middle managers* implement strategies, policies, and decisions. *First-line managers* usually work with and directly supervise employees. Areas of management include human resources, operations, marketing, information, and finance. Managers at all levels may be found in every area of a company.

4 **Describe the five basic *management skills*.** Most managers agree that five basic management skills are necessary for success. *Technical skills* are associated with performing specialized tasks. *Human relations skills* are associated with understanding and getting along with other people. *Conceptual skills* are the abilities to think in the abstract, to diagnose and analyze different situations, and to see beyond present circumstances. *Decision-making skills* allow managers to define problems and to select the best course of action. *Time management skills* refer to the productive use that managers make of their time. *Global management* and *technology skills* are also becoming increasingly important.

5 **Describe the development and explain the importance of *corporate culture*.** A strong, well-defined culture can help a business reach its goals and can influence management styles. In addition to having a clear understanding of *corporate culture*, managers must be able to communicate it effectively to others. Communication is especially important when organizations find it necessary to make changes in the culture. Top management must establish new values that reflect a vision of a new company, and these values must play a role in appraising and compensating employee performance.

QUESTIONS AND EXERCISES

Questions for Review

1. What are the four main purposes of setting goals in an organization?
2. Identify and explain the three basic steps in strategy formulation.
3. Relate the five basic management skills to the four activities in the management process. For example, which skills are most important in directing?
4. What is corporate culture? How is it formed? How is it sustained?

Questions for Analysis

5. Select any group of which you are a member (your company, your family, or a club or organization, for example). Explain how planning, organizing, directing, and controlling are practiced in that group.
6. Identify managers by level and area at your school, college, or university.
7. In what kind of company would the technical skills of top managers be more important than human relations or conceptual skills? Are there organizations in which conceptual skills are not important?
8. What differences might you expect to find in the corporate cultures of a 100-year-old manufacturing firm based in the Northeast and a 1-year-old e-commerce firm set in Silicon Valley?

Application Exercises

9. Interview the manager at any level of a local company. Identify that manager's job according to level and area. Show how planning, organizing, directing, and controlling are part of this person's job. Inquire about the manager's education and work experience. Which management skills are most important for this manager's job?
10. Compare and contrast the corporate cultures of two companies that do business in most communities. Be sure to choose two companies in the same industry—for example, a Sears department store and a Wal-Mart discount store.

EXPLORING THE WEB

There's Coffee, and Then There's Coffee

This chapter's opening case profiles Starbucks and a small, locally owned competitor named Maine Roasters Coffee. Start this exercise by visiting and exploring each firm's Web site:

<www.starbucks.com>

<www.maineroasters.qpg.com>

After reviewing each site, consider the following questions:

1. Judging from the two Web sites, what differences in corporate strategies can you determine?
2. List all the things you can learn about each company from its Web site. Precisely, how do the two companies differ? How do you account for the major differences?
3. Does Maine Roasters Coffee's Web site make any reference to Starbucks? Do you think this tactic should change?
4. Again, judging from the Web sites, can you make any conjectures about the corporate cultures at the two firms?
5. What advice, if any, would you give to these two firms to enhance or improve their respective Web sites?

EXERCISING YOUR ETHICS

Making Room for Alternative Actions

THE SITUATION

Assume that you are the manager of a large hotel adjacent to a medical center in a major city. The medical center itself consists of 10 major hospitals and research institutes. Two of the hospitals are affiliated with large universities and two with churches. Three are public and three are private. The center has an international reputation and attracts patients from around the world.

Because so many patients and their families travel great distances to visit the medical center and often stay for days or weeks, there are also eight large hotels in the area, including three new ones. The hotel that you manage is one of the older ones and, frankly, is looking a bit shabby. Corporate headquarters has told you that the hotel will either be closed or undergo a major remodeling in about two years. In the meantime, you are expected to wring every last cent of profit out of the hotel.

THE DILEMMA

A tropical storm has just struck the area and brought with it major flooding and power outages. Three of the medical center hospitals have been shut down indefinitely, as have six of the nearby hotels. Fortunately, your hotel sustained only minor damage and is fully functional. You have just called a meeting with your two assistant managers to discuss what actions, if any, you should take.

One assistant manager has urged you to cut room rates immediately for humanitarian purposes. This manager also wants you to open the hotel kitchens 24 hours a day to prepare free food for rescue workers and meals to donate to the hospitals, whose own food service operations have been disrupted. The other assistant manager, meanwhile, has urged just the opposite approach: raise room rates by at least 20 percent and sell food to rescue workers and hospitals at a premium price. Of course, you can also choose to follow the advice of neither and continue doing business as usual.

QUESTIONS FOR DISCUSSION

1. What are the ethical issues in this situation?
2. What do you think most managers would do in this situation?
3. What would you do?

BUILDING YOUR BUSINESS SKILLS

Speaking with Power

This exercise enhances the following SCANS workplace competencies: demonstrating basic skills, demonstrating thinking skills, exhibiting interpersonal skills, and working with information.

GOAL

To encourage students to appreciate effective speaking as a critical human relations skill.

BACKGROUND

A manager's ability to understand and get along with supervisors, peers, and subordinates is a critical human relations skill. At the heart of this skill, says Harvard University professor of education Sarah McGinty, is the ability to speak with power and control. McGinty defines "powerful speech" in terms of the following characteristics:

- The ability to speak at length and in complete sentences
- The ability to set a conversational agenda
- The ability to deter interruptions
- The ability to argue openly and to express strong opinions about ideas, not people
- The ability to make statements that offer solutions rather than pose questions
- The ability to express humor

Taken together, says McGinty, "all this creates a sense of confidence in listeners."

METHOD

Step 1
Working alone, compare your own personal speaking style with McGinty's description of powerful speech by taping yourself as you speak during a meeting with classmates or during a phone conversation. (Tape both sides of the conversation only if the person to whom you are speaking gives permission.) Listen for the following problems:

- Unfinished sentences
- An absence of solutions
- Too many disclaimers ("I'm not sure I have enough information to say this, but . . .")
- The habit of seeking support from others instead of making definitive statements of personal conviction (saying, "I recommend consolidating the medical and fitness functions," instead of, "As Emily stated in her report, I recommend consolidating the medical and fitness functions")
- Language fillers (saying, "you know," "like," and "um" when you are unsure of your facts or uneasy about expressing your opinion)

Step 2
Join with three or four other classmates to evaluate each other's speaking styles. Finally:

- Have a 10-minute group discussion on the importance of human relations skills in business.
- Listen to other group members and take notes on the "power" content of what you hear.
- Offer constructive criticism by focusing on what speakers say rather than on personal characteristics (say, "Bob, you sympathized with Paul's position, but I still don't know what you think," instead of, "Bob, you sounded like a weakling").

FOLLOW-UP QUESTIONS

1. How do you think the power content of speech affects a manager's ability to communicate? Evaluate some of the ways in which effects may differ among supervisors, peers, and subordinates.
2. How do you evaluate yourself and group members in terms of powerful and powerless speech? List the strengths and weaknesses of the group.
3. Do you agree or disagree with McGinty that business success depends on gaining insight into your own language habits? Explain your answer.

4. In our age of computers and e-mail, why do you think personal presentation continues to be important in management?
5. McGinty believes that power language differs from company to company and that it is linked to the corporate culture. Do you agree, or do you believe that people express themselves in similar ways no matter where they are?

CRAFTING YOUR BUSINESS PLAN

Furnishing Yourself with Management Skills

THE PURPOSE OF THE ASSIGNMENT

1. To familiarize students with management-related issues that a firm must address in developing its business plan, in the planning framework of *Business PlanPro (BPP)* (Version 4.0).
2. To demonstrate how three chapter topics—business goals, business strategies, and management skills—can be integrated as components in the *BPP* planning environment.

ASSIGNMENT

After reading Chapter 5 in the textbook, open the BPP *software and look around for information about business goals, business strategies, and management skills as they apply to a sample firm:* Furniture Manufacturer *(Sample Furniture). Then respond to the following questions:*

1. Evaluate Sample Furniture's business objectives. Are they clearly stated? Are they measurable? [Sites to see in *BPP* for this item: In the Plan Outline screen, click on **1.1 Objectives.**]
2. Evaluate Sample Furniture's mission and strategy statements. Do they clearly state how Sample Furniture intends to achieve its purposes? [Sites to see in *BPP* for this item: In the Plan Outline screen, click on **1.0 Executive Summary**. Then click on **1.2 Mission**. Next click on **5.0 Strategy and Implementation**, then on **5.1 Strategy Pyramids.**]
3. In what areas of the business does each of Sample Furniture's top managers work? [Sites to see in *BPP* for this item: In the Plan Outline screen, click on **6.0 Management Summary**. Now click on **6.1 Organization Structure** and then on **6.2 Management Team.**]
4. What management skills areas are lacking in Sample Furniture's management team? Would you classify the missing skills as technical, human resources, conceptual, or decision-making skills? [Sites to see in *BPP* for this item: In the Plan Outline screen, click on **6.3 Management Team Gaps.**]

VIDEO EXERCISE

The Management Picture: Quick Takes Video (I)

LEARNING OBJECTIVES

The purpose of this video exercise is to help you

1. Appreciate the goal-setting process.
2. Understand the management process.
3. Observe some of the ways in which corporate culture is shaped and communicated.

BACKGROUND INFORMATION

Based on a real company in the same line of business, Quick Takes Video is a fictitious firm that produces corporate, industrial, and training videos and video news releases. It was founded by Hal Boylston and Karen Jarvis, and the management team includes a production coordinator, who oversees the producers responsible for the actual filming and editing of the firm's products. The production coordinator forecasts staff and equipment needs for each shoot, coordinates the use of the company's physical resources, manages producers, and keeps the shoots on schedule and on budget. Planning, organizing, leading, and controlling are all part of the production coordinator's job.

THE VIDEO

John Switzer has just been hired as Quick Takes' new production coordinator, and it is his first day on the job. After settling into his new office, he meets with Boylston and Jarvis to discuss their views of the company's future and to bring up a few questions and suggestions of his own. By attending this meeting, you'll see how the four management functions apply to Switzer's new job.

QUESTIONS FOR DISCUSSION

1. What information about the Quick Takes culture does John receive on his first day? How does he receive it?
2. How does Quick Takes set goals? Could its managers do a better job of goal setting?
3. Which of John's questions most clearly reflect one (or more) of the four management functions?

FOLLOW-UP ASSIGNMENT

Select one of the following managers and determine, in as much detail as you can, the specific tasks that make up the four management activities (planning, organizing, directing, controlling) for each:

- The president of your college or university
- The supervisor of online software support for Dell Computer Corp.
- The manager of a Gap clothing store
- The vice president of manufacturing for Virgin Records
- An entrepreneur setting up an online retail business

FOR FURTHER EXPLORATION

Select a media firm, such as a filmmaker, a recording company, an ad agency, a newspaper, or a magazine. Visit the company's Web site and try to draw some conclusions about its corporate culture. (*Hint*: Find the page for employment opportunities.) What do you notice about the firm's culture? How would you describe it? Is the image here consistent with the impression you get about the company from its products? Is it a culture in which you would like to work? Why or why not?

CHAPTER 6

Organizing the Business Enterprise

After reading this chapter, you should be able to:

1. Discuss the elements that influence a firm's *organizational structure.*
2. Explain *specialization* and *departmentalization* as the building blocks of organizational structure.
3. Distinguish between *responsibility, authority, delegation,* and *accountability,* and explain the differences between decision making in *centralized* and *decentralized organizations.*
4. Explain the differences between *functional, divisional, matrix,* and *international organizational structures.*
5. Describe the *informal organization* and discuss *intrapreneuring.*

Forging E-Connections

Construction is one of the world's oldest jobs. Ever since they lived in caves, people have been continually crafting newer, bigger, safer, and more functional places to live, work, and play. But if any industry seems tailor-made for the Internet, it just might be construction.

Construction has always been a job that encourages specialization. Very different kinds of skills and expertise are needed to create a foundation from concrete, erect walls from brick, wood, or steel, fabricate networks of pipes for plumbing and wire for electricity, construct a weatherproof roof, and finish off an interior with a high-quality appearance. There are even craft specialists within specialties—building a wall from steel, for example, or a roof from shingles is far different from building a wooden wall or a metal roof.

Putting all these pieces together, then, can be a big and complicated job. Consider just a few of the complexities in building a simple wood-frame house. Shortly after the concrete foundation has been poured and set, a supplier should deliver a load of wooden studs for constructing the frame. If the wood is delivered too early, it may get damaged, scattered, or even stolen. If it comes too late, delays will result. Quantity is also important: Too much wood means needless cost overruns, and too little wood means more delays. The contractor faces the same issues when it comes to the framing crew: They need to arrive on a certain day and finish on a certain day. Complicating things even further is the homeowner. As the project takes shape, the homeowner may decide to move a wall, add a door, or change the color of the walls.

In short, someone has to organize the overall process, ensuring—to some extent—that the right materials in the right quantities and the right people are at the job site at the right time. This individual is generally called the *contractor*. Each one of the specialists hired to

> *"Construction has always been a very fragmented industry because it's so local."*
>
> —Kent Allen, e-commerce consultant

perform certain specific tasks required by the overall project—roofers, plumbers, electricians, painters, and so forth—is called a *subcontractor*. Construction, says Kent Allen, a Boston e-commerce consultant, "has always been a very fragmented industry because it's so local."

All told, a house like the one we just described will probably require a dozen or more subcontractors. But what about a major construction project—a high-rise building or an office complex? These projects will call for hundreds of separate subcontractors working at different times over periods spanning several months or even years. The complexities of organizing such a massive project are significant indeed. A well-organized project can make the difference between a profit and a loss for the contractor.

Until recently, organizing most building projects relied on paper—architects drew up blueprints, contractors drew up schedules, and paperwork flowed freely between contractors and subcontractors as materials were requested and ordered and work completed and billed. But a simple change—a redesigned doorway—or one delay—one late order of materials—could have a domino effect on dozens of other subcontractors. On top of everything else, someone had to monitor the project continually, make scheduling and delivery adjustments as needed, and then notify suppliers and subcontractors.

Slowly but surely, however, Internet technology is creeping into the construction industry. As it does, it's revolutionizing the way contractors and subcontractors work and interact with one another. It's also showing signs of enormous potential for lowering costs, shortening schedules, and improving overall efficiency. Big construction firms like the Turner Corp. <www.turnerconstruction.com> and the Bechtel Group <www.bechtel.com> have started partnering with such e-commerce companies as Bidcom <www.bidcom.com> and Cephren <www.cephren.com> to use Web technology to communicate with suppliers and subcontractors.

Now blueprints can be posted online, suppliers and subcontractors can review their respective parts of the project online, including scheduling details, e-mail can be sent to everyone involved, work schedules issued, and bid requests sent to potential suppliers, all with the push of a button or click of a mouse. The advent of newer handheld computers is also accelerating change because they allow contractors, subcontractors, supervisors, and workers to access information at the construction project.

Our opening story continues on page 160

For companies in the construction industry, the issues involved in organizing projects and creating networks can affect operations and profits in dramatic ways. Whether a contractor or subcontractor employs five people or 50,000, a number of fundamental organizational issues determine how well a business will function. In this chapter, we consider the elements of business organization and the basic structures that firms typically use.

By focusing on the learning objectives of this chapter, you will better understand the importance of business organization and the ways in which both formal and informal aspects of its structure affect the decisions that a business makes.

WHAT IS ORGANIZATIONAL STRUCTURE?

What do we mean by the term *organizational structure*? Consider a simple analogy. In some ways, a business is like an automobile. All cars have engines, four wheels, fenders, and other structural components. They all have passenger compartments, storage areas, and various operating systems (fuel, braking, climate control). Although each component has a distinct purpose, it must also work in accord with the others. In addition, although the ways they look and fit may vary widely, all automobiles have the same basic components.

Similarly, all businesses have common structural and operating components, each composed of a series of *jobs to be done* and each with a *specific overall purpose*. From company to company these components look different and fit together differently, but in every organization components have the same fundamental purpose—each must perform its own function while working in concert with the others.

Although all organizations feature the same basic elements, each must develop the structure that is most appropriate for it. What works for Texas Instruments will not work for Shell Oil, Amazon.com, or the U.S. Department of Justice. The structure of the American Red Cross will probably not work for Union Carbide or the University of Minnesota. We define **organizational structure** as the specification of the jobs to be done within an organization and the ways in which those jobs relate to one another.

organizational structure
Specification of the jobs to be done within an organization and the ways in which they relate to one another

Determinants of Organization

How is an organization's structure determined? Does it happen by chance, or is there some logic that managers use to create structure? Does it develop by some combination of circumstance and strategy? Ideally, managers carefully assess a variety of important factors as they plan for and then create a structure that will allow their organization to function efficiently.

Many elements work together to determine an organization's structure. Chief among these are the organization's *purpose, mission*, and *strategy*. A dynamic and rapidly growing enterprise, for example, achieved that position because of its purpose and successful strategies for achieving it. Such a firm will need a structure that contributes to flexibility and growth. A stable organization with only modest growth will function best with a different structure.

Size, technology, and changes in environmental circumstances also affect structure. A large manufacturer operating in a strongly competitive environment—say, Boeing or Hewlett-Packard—requires a different structure than a local barbershop or video store. Moreover, even after a structure has been created, it is rarely free from tinkering—or even outright re-creation. Most organizations change their structures on an almost continuing basis.

As we saw in Chapter 5, organizing is a function of managerial planning. As such, it is conducted with an equal awareness of both a firm's external and internal environments. Since it was first incorporated in 1903, Ford Motor Co. <www.ford.com> has undergone literally dozens of major structural changes, hundreds of moderate changes, and thousands of minor changes.

In the last 10 years alone, Ford has initiated several major structural changes. In 1994, for instance, the firm announced a major restructuring plan called Ford 2000, which was intended to integrate all of Ford's vast international operations into a single,

IT'S A WIRED WORLD

Hot-Wiring Ford

Imagine going to a Web page to buy a new car. You specify the car online just as you want it—color, engine size, options—and electronically negotiate the price. Then you click "OK." Your simple action transmits a slew of information directly to a local dealer, to a financial broker, to your insurance agent, to the factory that will build your car, to the suppliers that provide the components, and to the Ford designers working on next year's models. A few days later, your new car is delivered to your driveway.

Fantasy? Not if Ford CEO William Ford has his way. He and his managers at Ford are rushing headlong toward his vision of the automobile-buying future. To get there, Ford is convinced that the firm must systematically absorb the Internet into every element of its organization. Experts agree that Ford stands at the forefront of old-line manufacturers who are working to absorb Web technology. Recall, for instance, our "Wired World" box in Chapter 1, where we described Ford's participation in an electronic marketplace for auto parts and supplies.

Another major initiative at Ford rests on its comprehensive and integrated corporate intranet. One official goes so far as to describe it as the backbone of Ford's business today. To weave one major strand in the Ford intranet, managers are strongly encouraged to create all reports on line. Managers want to deliver a clear message: namely, Ford manages itself on the intranet and interacts with stakeholders on the Internet.

Ford also believes that if the firm is to embrace the Internet fully, each and every one of its employees must "think Internet." Toward that end, Ford announced in early 2000 that it would provide all of its 350,000 global employees with a home computer, a printer, and $5 a month for Internet access.

Ford is also working to integrate Web technology into its cars. Designers are trying to figure out the best way to wire cars for e-mail and news, voice-recognition systems, and satellite phone services. Ford executives are clearly gambling on the future. If they're right, they may well become the car of choice for the Internet generation.

unified structure by the year 2000. By 1998, however, midway through implementation of the grand plan, top Ford executives announced major modifications indicating that (1) additional changes would be made, (2) some previously planned changes would not be made, and (3) some recently realigned operations would be changed again. In early 1999, managers announced another set of changes intended to eliminate corporate bureaucracy, speed decision making, and improve communication and working relationships among people at different levels of the organization.[1] Early in 2001, Ford announced yet more sweeping changes intended to boost the firm's flagging bottom line and stem a decline in product quality.[2]

The "Wired World" box in this chapter shows how Ford's e-commerce initiatives are affecting its structure in still other ways.

Chain of Command

Most businesses prepare **organization charts** to clarify structure and to show employees where they fit into a firm's operations. Figure 6.1 is an organization chart for Contemporary Landscape Services Inc. <www2.cy-net/~clsinc/cls>, a small but thriving business in Bryan, Texas. Each box in the chart represents a job. The solid lines define the **chain of command**, or *reporting relationships*, within the company. For example, the retail shop, nursery, and landscape operations managers all report to the owner and president, Mark Ferguson. Within the landscape operation is one manager for residential accounts and another for commercial accounts. Similarly, there are other managers in the retail shop and the nursery.

The organization charts of large firms are far more complex and include individuals at many more levels than those shown in Figure 6.1. Size prevents many large firms from drawing charts that include all their managers. Typically, they create one organization chart showing overall corporate structure and separate charts for each division.

organization chart
Diagram depicting a company's structure and showing employees where they fit into its operations

chain of command
Reporting relationships within a company

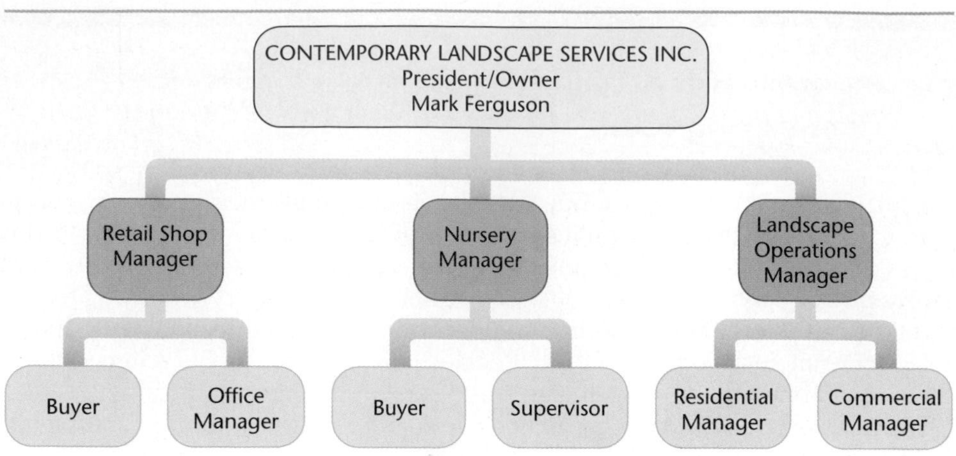

Figure 6.1
The Organization Chart

THE BUILDING BLOCKS OF ORGANIZATIONAL STRUCTURE

The first step in developing the structure of any business, large or small, involves two activities:

- *Specialization*: determining who will do what
- *Departmentalization*: determining how people performing certain tasks can best be grouped together

These two activities are the building blocks of all business organizations.[3]

Specialization

job specialization
The process of identifying the specific jobs that need to be done and designating the people who will perform them

The process of identifying the specific jobs that need to be done and designating the people who will perform them leads to **job specialization.** In a sense, all organizations have only one major job, such as making cars (Ford), selling finished goods to consumers (Wal-Mart), or providing telecommunications services (AT&T). Usually, the job is more complex in nature. For example, the job of Chaparral Steel <www.txi.com/steel> is converting scrap steel, such as wrecked automobiles, into finished steel products such as beams and reinforcement bars.

To perform this one overall job, managers actually break it down, or specialize it, into several smaller jobs. Thus, some workers transport the scrap steel to the company's mill in Midlothian, Texas. Others operate shredding equipment before turning raw materials over to the workers who then melt them into liquid form. Other specialists oversee the flow of the liquid into molding equipment in which it is transformed into new products. Finally, other workers are responsible for moving finished products to a holding area before they are shipped out to customers. When the overall job of the organization is thus broken down, workers can develop real expertise in their jobs, and employees can better coordinate their work with that done by others.

Specialization and Growth In a very small organization the owner may perform every job. As the firm grows, however, so does the need to specialize jobs so that others can perform them. To see how specialization can evolve in an organization, consider the case of the Walt Disney Co. <www.disney.go.com>. When Walt Disney first opened his studio, he and his brother Roy did everything. For example, when they created the very first animated feature, *Steamboat Willy*, they wrote the story, drew the pictures, transferred the pictures to film, provided the voices, and then went out and sold the cartoon to theater operators.

Today, by sharp contrast, a Disney animated feature is made possible only through the efforts of hundreds of creators. The job of one cartoonist may be to draw the face of a single character throughout an entire feature. Another artist may be charged with erasing stray pencil marks inadvertently made by other illustrators. People other than artists are responsible for the subsequent operations that turn individual animated cells into a moving picture or for the marketing of the finished product.

Job specialization is a natural part of organizational growth. It also has certain advantages. For example, specialized jobs are learned more easily and can be performed more efficiently than nonspecialized jobs, and it is also easier to replace people who leave an organization. However, jobs at lower levels of the organization are especially susceptible to overspecialization. If such jobs become too narrowly defined, employees may become bored and careless, derive less satisfaction from their jobs, and lose sight of their roles in the organization.[4]

Departmentalization

After jobs are specialized, they must be grouped into logical units, which is the process of **departmentalization**. Departmentalized companies benefit from the division of activities. Control and coordination are narrowed and made easier, and top managers can see more easily how various units are performing.

departmentalization
Process of grouping jobs into logical units

profit center
Separate company unit responsible for its own costs and profits

Departmentalization allows the firm to treat a department as a **profit center**—a separate unit responsible for its own costs and profits. Thus, Sears <www.sears.com> can calculate the profits it generates from men's clothing, appliances, home furnishings, and every other department within a given store. Managers can then use this information in making decisions about advertising and promotional events, space allocation, and so forth.

In an effort to improve competitiveness, Lucent Technologies <www.lucent.com>, the world's largest telephone equipment maker, recently created four new departments. These departments represent activities that have grown so large within existing departmental arrangements that they now warrant separate units. One department will focus on optical networking; another on wireless communications; a third will be responsible for semiconductor operations; and a fourth will address Lucent's e-business initiatives. Lucent managers believe that these new departments will sharpen the company's focus on these four high-growth areas.[5] "This new organization," explains one Lucent executive, "will allow Lucent to move forward in a more aggressive and flexible way as we continue to expand into new markets." Unfortunately, Lucent has continued to struggle and is currently undergoing more major organizational changes, the most radical of which would have been a proposed merger with French telecom company Alcatel that fell through in May 2001.[6]

Obviously, managers do not departmentalize jobs randomly. They group them logically, according to some common thread or purpose. In general, departmentalization may occur along *customer, product, process, geographic*, or *functional lines* (or any combination of these).

Whether they are produced manually or digitally, the drawings that comprise a full-length cartoon such as Disney's Atlantis *are the result of highly coordinated job specialization. A lead animator, for example, may provide a rough pencil sketch that is then refined by one or more artists. Other teams scan clean drawings into a computer and color them according to a plan devised by the art director. The process is a far cry from the one pioneered by Walt and Roy Disney, who did virtually everything themselves in the 1930s.*

customer departmentalization Departmentalization according to types of customers likely to buy a given product

product departmentalization Departmentalization according to specific products being created

process departmentalization Departmentalization according to production processes used to create a good or service

Customer Departmentalization Stores such as Sears and Macy's <www.macys.com> are divided into departments—a men's department, a women's department, a luggage department, and so on. Each department targets a specific customer category (men, women, people who want to buy luggage). **Customer departmentalization** makes shopping easier by providing identifiable store segments. Thus, a customer shopping for a baby's playpen can bypass Lawn and Garden Supplies and head straight for Children's Furniture. Stores can also group products in locations designated for deliveries, special sales, and other service-oriented purposes. In general, the store is more efficient and customers get better service because salespeople tend to specialize and gain expertise in their departments.

Product Departmentalization Manufacturers and service providers often opt for **product departmentalization**—dividing an organization according to the specific product or service being created. This approach is consistent with what Lucent Technologies has tried to do. For example, the wireless communications department focuses on cellular telephones and services, while the optical networking department focuses on fiber optical and other cable and communications technologies. Because each of these represents a defined group of products or services, Lucent managers are able—in theory—to focus on specific product lines in a clear and defined way.

Process Departmentalization Other manufacturers favor **process departmentalization**, in which the organization is divided according to production processes. This principle is logical for the pickle maker Vlasic <www.vlasic.com>, which has separate departments to transform cucumbers into fresh-packed pickles, pickles cured in brine, and relishes. Cucumbers destined to become fresh-packed pickles must be packed into jars immediately, covered with a solution of water and vinegar, and prepared for sale. Those slated for brined pickles must be aged in brine solution before packing. Relish cucumbers must be minced and combined with a host of other ingredients. Each process requires different equipment and worker skills.

Geographic Departmentalization Some firms are divided according to the areas of the country, or the world, that they serve. Levi Strauss, for instance, has one division for the United States <www.levi.com>, one for Europe <www.eu.levi.com>, one for the Asia Pacific region <www.levi.co.kr>, and one for Latin America <www.levi.com/lar>.

This truck-frame plant in Stockton, California, represents the commitment of Toyota Motor Co. <www.global.toyota.com> to geography as one factor in the division of its activities. Operating in North America requires Toyota to forge relationships with such U.S. suppliers as Dana Corp. <www.dana.com>, an Ohio-based firm that furnishes Toyota with frame assemblies from its Parish Structural Products facility, also located in Stockton. Dana, therefore, also practices geographic departmentalization. Meanwhile, Toyota also combines product with geographic departmentalization: At Stockton, it makes frames for its Tacoma-model trucks, not for its Highlander SUVs, Camry passenger cars, or even Tundra-model trucks.

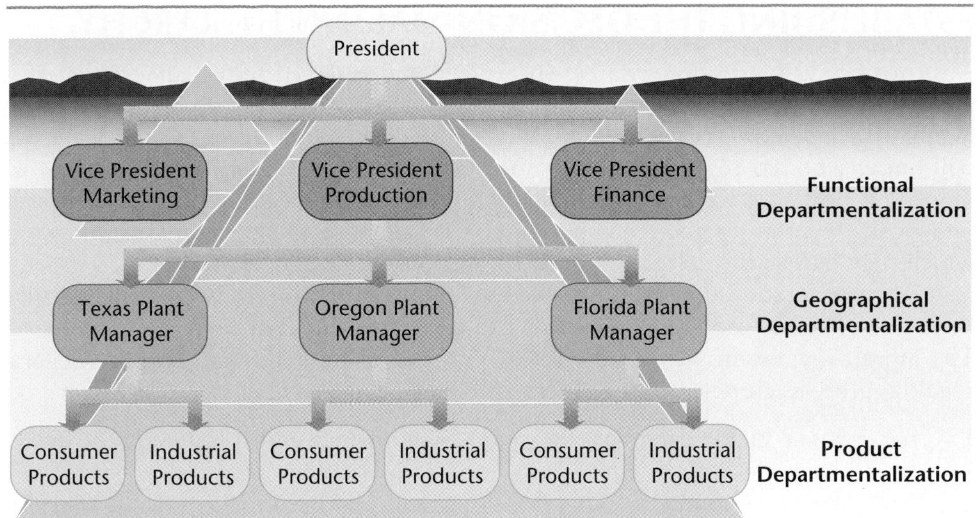

Figure 6.2
Multiple Forms of Departmentalization

Within the United States, **geographic departmentalization** is common among utilities. Pacific Power and Light is organized as four geographic departments—Southwestern, Columbia Basin, Mid-Oregon, and Wyoming.

geographic departmentalization
Departmentalization according to areas served by a business

Functional Departmentalization Many service and manufacturing companies, especially smaller ones, develop departments according to a group's functions or activities—a form of organization known as **functional departmentalization**. Such firms typically have production, marketing and sales, human resources, and accounting and finance departments. Departments may be further subdivided. For example, the marketing department might be divided geographically or into separate staffs for market research and advertising.

functional departmentalization
Departmentalization according to groups' functions or activities

Because different forms of departmentalization have different advantages, larger companies tend to adopt different types of departmentalization for various levels. The company illustrated in Figure 6.2 uses functional departmentalization at the top level. At the middle level, production is divided along geographic lines. At a lower level, marketing is departmentalized by product group.

WEB Connection

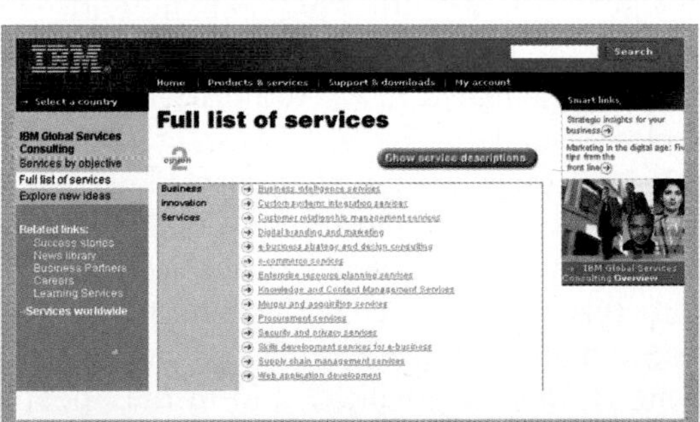

IBM's Global Services unit provides a wide range of Internet-related services, including business consulting, systems management, and outsourcing services. Recent additions to the product line include privacy consulting and an online service specially designed for small and midsize businesses. IBM still builds and sells computers and software, but the growth of such units as Global Services reflects some dramatic changes in the company's approach to functional departmentalization.

www-1.ibm.com/services/fullservice.html

ESTABLISHING THE DECISION-MAKING HIERARCHY

After jobs have been appropriately specialized and grouped into manageable departments, the next step in organizing is to establish the decision-making hierarchy. That is, managers must explicitly define reporting relationships among positions so everyone will know who has responsibility for various decisions and operations. The goal is to figure out how to structure and stabilize the organizational framework so that everyone works together to achieve common goals. Companies vary greatly in the ways in which they handle the delegation of tasks, responsibility, and authority.

A major question that must be asked about any organization is: *Who makes which decisions?* The answer almost never focuses on an individual or even on a small group. The more accurate answer usually refers to the decision-making hierarchy. Generally speaking, the development of this hierarchy results from a three-step process:

1. *Assigning tasks:* determining who can make decisions and specifying how they should be made
2. *Performing tasks:* implementing decisions that have been made
3. *Distributing authority*: determining whether the organization is to be centralized or decentralized

For example, when Jack Greenberg took over as CEO of McDonald's <www.mcdonalds.com>, he immediately implemented several changes in the firm's decision-making hierarchy. McDonald's has always been, and continues to be, highly centralized. But Greenberg restructured both the company's decision-making process and its operations. He reduced staff at corporate headquarters in Oak Brook, Illinois, and established five regional offices throughout the United States. Now many decisions are made at the regional level.

"For 40 years, all we did was open restaurants. That's not enough anymore."

—Jack Greenberg, CEO of McDonald's

Greenberg also clamped a lid on domestic growth and increased international expansion. In addition, he purchased stakes in three new restaurant chains with an eye on expansion: Donatos Pizza <www.donatos.com>, Chipotle Mexican Grill <www.chipotle.com>, and Aroma, a British coffee chain. Greenberg then installed four new managers, one to head up international operations and the others to oversee the three new restaurant partner groups. All four of these executives report directly to Greenberg. Why the changes? "Maybe it was arrogance," says Greenberg. "For 40 years, all we did was open restaurants. That's not enough anymore."[7]

Assigning Tasks: Responsibility and Authority

The question of who is *supposed* to do what and who is entitled to do what in an organization is complex. In any company with more than one person, individuals must work out agreements about responsibilities and authority. **Responsibility** is the duty to perform an assigned task. **Authority** is the power to make the decisions necessary to complete the task.

responsibility
Duty to perform an assigned task

authority
Power to make the decisions necessary to complete a task

delegation
Assignment of a task, responsibility, or authority by a manager to a subordinate

accountability
Liability of subordinates for accomplishing tasks assigned by managers

For example, imagine a midlevel buyer for Macy's department store who encounters an unexpected opportunity to make a large purchase at an extremely good price. Assume that an immediate decision is absolutely necessary—a decision that this buyer has no authority to make without confirmation from above. The company's policies on delegation and authority are inconsistent because the buyer is *responsible* for purchasing the clothes that will be sold in the upcoming season, but lacks the *authority* to make the needed purchases.

Performing Tasks: Delegation and Accountability

Trouble occurs when appropriate levels of responsibility and authority are not clearly delineated in the working relationships between managers and subordinates. Here the issues become delegation and accountability. **Delegation** begins when a manager assigns a task to a subordinate. **Accountability** falls to the subordinate, who must then complete the task. If tasks are effectively delegated and performed, the organization will function smoothly. But if the subordinate does not perform the task as assigned—perhaps doing a poor job or not getting the work done on time—problems can arise. The work unit may suffer and the employee's performance abilities or motivation may be called into question.

Fear of Delegating Unfortunately, many managers actually have trouble delegating tasks to others.[8] This is especially true in small businesses where the owner-manager started out doing everything. Delegating responsibility has been especially difficult for Rene Reiser, owner of Paradise Candles, a three-employee candle manufacturer in Idaho. Reiser believes that it was her personal creative style that built her company. It took her years to develop a specialized production process, and she has found it hard to let others take charge of it. "Eventually," she concedes, "I'll have to teach someone else to do it. It makes me nervous, and I wonder, 'Will they do it in my style?' "[9]

Experts pinpoint certain reasons why some small-business managers may have trouble delegating effectively:[10]

- The feeling that employees can never do anything as well as you can
- The fear that something will go wrong if someone else takes over a job
- The lack of time for long-range planning because you are bogged down in day-to-day operations
- The sense of being in the dark about industry trends and competitive products because of the time you devote to day-to-day operations

To overcome these tendencies, small-business owners must begin by admitting that they can never go back to running the entire show and that they can in fact prosper—with the help of their employees—if they learn to let go. This problem, however, isn't always confined to small businesses. Some managers in big companies also don't delegate as much or as well as they should. There are also several reasons for this problem:

- The fear that subordinates don't really know how to do the job
- The fear that a subordinate might "show the manager up" in front of others by doing a superb job
- The desire to keep as much control as possible over how things are done
- A simple lack of ability as to how to effectively delegate to others

The remedies in these instances are a bit different. First, all managers should recognize that they can't do everything themselves. Second, if subordinates can't do a job, they should be trained so that they can assume more responsibility in the future. Third, managers should actually recognize that if a subordinate performs well it also reflects favorably on the manager. Finally, a manager who simply doesn't know how to delegate might need specialized training in how to divide up and assign tasks to others.

Distributing Authority: Centralization and Decentralization

Delegation involves a specific relationship between managers and subordinates. Most businesses must also make decisions about general patterns of authority throughout the company. This pattern may be largely *centralized* or *decentralized* (or, usually, somewhere in between).

Centralized Organizations In a **centralized organization**, most decision-making authority is held by upper-level managers. Most lower-level decisions must be approved by upper management before they can be implemented.[11] As we noted earlier, McDonald's practices centralization as a way to maintain standardization. All restaurants must follow precise steps in buying products and making and packaging burgers and other menu items. Most advertising is handled at the corporate level, and any local advertising must be approved by a regional manager. Restaurants even have to follow prescribed schedules for facilities' maintenance and upgrades like floor polishing and parking lot cleaning.[12] Similarly, the new CEO of JCPenney, Allen

centralized organization
Organization in which most decision-making authority is held by upper-level management

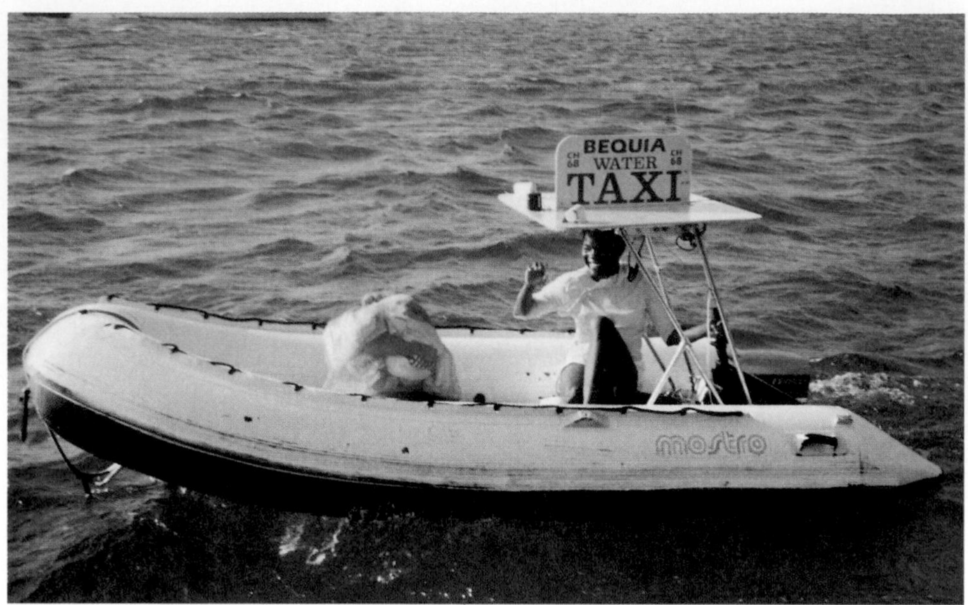

Daffodil Harris's first business required only a dinghy and a washing machine: She ran a laundry business out of an open boat, picking up and returning soggy clothes from yachts moored at the Caribbean island of Bequia. Eight years later, she was also operating Daffodil's Marine Service (to rent and repair equipment), a grocery store, a Chinese take-out restaurant, and Bequia Water Taxi. She now has 23 employees, but the multidivisional enterprise, like many small businesses, remains highly centralized, with Harris personally overseeing all of her service operations.

Questrom, has been systematically centralizing decision making as part of his efforts to revive the venerable retailer.[13] Centralized authority is also typical of small businesses.

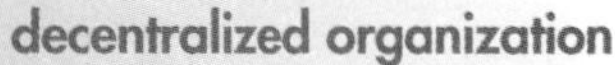

decentralized organization Organization in which a great deal of decision-making authority is delegated to levels of management at points below the top

Decentralized Organizations As a company gets larger, increasingly more decisions must be made; thus, the company tends to adopt a more decentralized pattern. In a **decentralized organization**, much decision-making authority is delegated to levels of management at various points below the top. The purpose of decentralization is to make a company more responsive to its environment by breaking the company into more manageable units, ranging from product lines to independent businesses. Reducing top-heavy bureaucracies is also a common goal. Jack Welch, former CEO of General Electric <www.ge.com/businesses>, is a longtime proponent of decentralized management. As he put it, "If you don't let managers make their own decisions, you're never going to be anything more than a one-person business." This logic also explains why cereal maker Kellogg Co. has been decentralizing. Top managers realize that in order to keep pace with today's "eat-on-the-run" lifestyles, lower-level managers need more autonomy to make decisions and rush new products to market.[14]

"If you don't let managers make their own decisions, you're never going to be anything more than a one-person business."

—Jack Welch, former CEO of General Electric

flat organizational structure Characteristic of decentralized companies with relatively few layers of management and relatively wide spans of control

tall organizational structure Characteristic of centralized companies with multiple layers of management and relatively narrow spans of control

Tall and Flat Organizations Related to the concept of centralized or decentralized authority are the concepts of tall and flat organizational structures. With relatively fewer layers of management, decentralized firms tend to reflect a **flat organizational structure** like that of the hypothetical law firm described in Figure 6.3(a). In contrast, companies with centralized authority systems typically require multiple layers of management and thus **tall organizational structures**. As you can see from Figure 6.3(b), the United States Army is a good example. Because information, whether upward or downward bound, must pass through so many organizational layers, tall structures are prone to delays in information flow.

As organizations grow in size, it is both normal and necessary that they become at least somewhat taller. For instance, a small firm with only an owner-manager and a few employees is likely to have two layers—the owner-manager and the employees who report to that person. But as the firm grows, more layers will be needed. Born Information Services <www.born.com>, for instance, is a small consulting firm created and run by Rick Born. At first, all his employees reported to him. But when the size of his firm had grown to more than 20 people, Born knew that he needed help in supervising and coordinating projects. As a result, he added a layer of management consisting of what he termed *staff managers* to serve as project coordinators. This

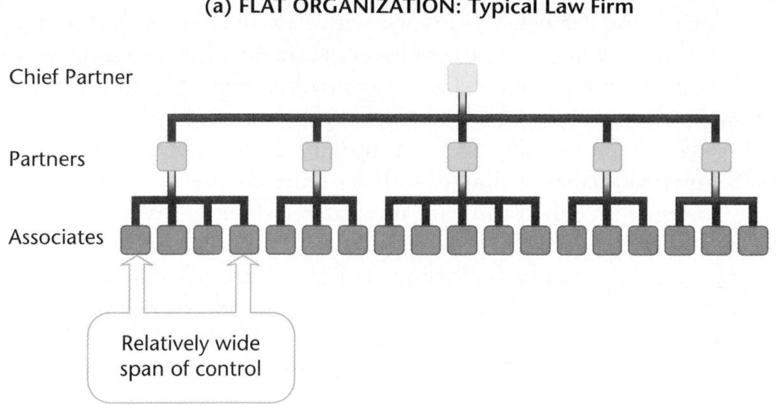

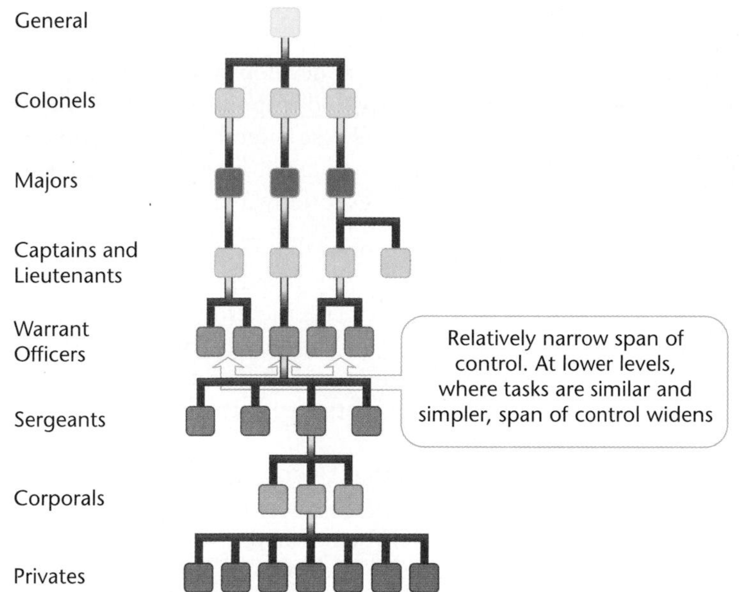

Figure 6.3
Organizational Structure and Span of Control

move freed up time for Born to seek new business clients.[15] Like other managers, however, Born must ensure that he has only the number of layers his firm needs. Too few layers can create chaos and inefficiency, whereas too many layers can create rigidity and bureaucracy.

Span of Control As you can see from Figure 6.3, the distribution of authority in an organization also affects the number of people who work for any individual manager. In a flat organizational structure, the number of people managed by one supervisor—the manager's **span of control**—is usually wide. In tall organizations, span of control tends to be relatively narrower. Span of control, however, depends on many factors. Employees' abilities and the supervisor's managerial skills help determine whether span of control is wide or narrow, as do the similarity and simplicity of tasks performed under the manager's supervision and the extent to which they are interrelated.[16]

span of control
Number of people supervised by one manager

If lower-level managers are given more decision-making authority, their supervisors will thus have less work to do because some of the decisions they previously made will be transferred to their subordinates. By the same token, these managers may then be able to oversee and coordinate the work of more subordinates, resulting in an increased span of control. We have already seen that at McDonald's, the creation of five regional offices freed up time for the CEO, Jack Greenberg. In turn, reorganization allowed him to then create four new executive positions, one to oversee international expansion and the others to work with new restaurant partners.

Similarly, when several employees perform either the same simple task or a group of interrelated tasks, a wide span of control is possible and often desirable. For instance, because all the jobs are routine, one supervisor may well control an entire assembly line. Moreover, each task depends on another. If one station stops, everyone stops. Having one supervisor ensures that all stations receive equal attention and function equally well.

In contrast, when jobs are more diversified or prone to change, a narrow span of control is preferable. In Racine, Wisconsin, for example, the Case Corp. <www.casecorp.com> factory makes farm tractors exclusively to order in five to six weeks. Farmers can select from among a wide array of options, including engines, tires, power trains, and even a CD player. A wide assortment of machines and processes is used to construct each tractor. Although workers are highly skilled operators of their assigned machines, each machine is different. In this kind of setup, the complexities of each machine and the advanced skills needed by each operator mean that one supervisor can oversee only a small number of employees.[17]

Three Forms of Authority

Whatever type of structure a company develops it must decide who will have authority over whom. As individuals are delegated responsibility and authority in a firm, a complex web of interactions develops. These interactions may take one of three forms of authority: *line, staff*, or *committee and team*. Like departmentalization, all three forms may be found in a given company, especially a large one.

line authority
Organizational structure in which authority flows in a direct chain of command from the top of the company to the bottom

line department
Department directly linked to the production and sales of a specific product

staff authority
Authority based on expertise that usually involves advising line managers

staff members
Advisers and counselors who aid line departments in making decisions but do not have the authority to make final decisions

committee and team authority
Authority granted to committees or work teams involved in a firm's daily operations

Line Authority The type of authority that flows up and down the chain of command is **line authority**. Most companies rely heavily on **line departments**—those directly linked to the production and sales of specific products. For example, Clark Equipment Corp. has a division that produces forklifts and small earthmovers. In this division, line departments include purchasing, materials handling, fabrication, painting, and assembly (all of which are directly linked to production) along with sales and distribution (both of which are directly linked to sales).

Each line department is essential to an organization's success. Line employees are the doers and producers in a company. If any line department fails to complete its task, the company cannot sell and deliver finished goods. Thus, the authority delegated to line departments is important. A bad decision by the manager in one department can hold up production for an entire plant. Say, for example, that the painting department manager at Clark Equipment changes a paint application on a batch of forklifts, which then show signs of peeling paint. The batch will have to be repainted (and perhaps partially reassembled) before the machines can be shipped.

Staff Authority Most companies also rely on **staff authority**, which is based on special expertise and usually involves counseling and advising line managers. Common staff members include specialists in areas such as law, accounting, and human resource management. A corporate attorney, for example, may be asked to advise the marketing department as it prepares a new contract with the firm's advertising agency. Legal staff, however, do not actually make decisions that affect how the marketing department does its job. **Staff members**, therefore, aid line departments in making decisions but do not have the authority to make final decisions.

Typically, the separation between line authority and staff responsibility is clearly delineated. As Figure 6.4 shows, this separation is usually indicated in organization charts by solid lines (line authority) and dotted lines (staff responsibility). It may help to understand this separation by remembering that whereas staff members generally provide services to management, line managers are directly involved in producing the firm's products.

Committee and Team Authority Recently, more and more organizations have started to use **committee and team authority**—authority granted to committees or work teams that play central roles in the firm's daily operations.[18] A committee, for

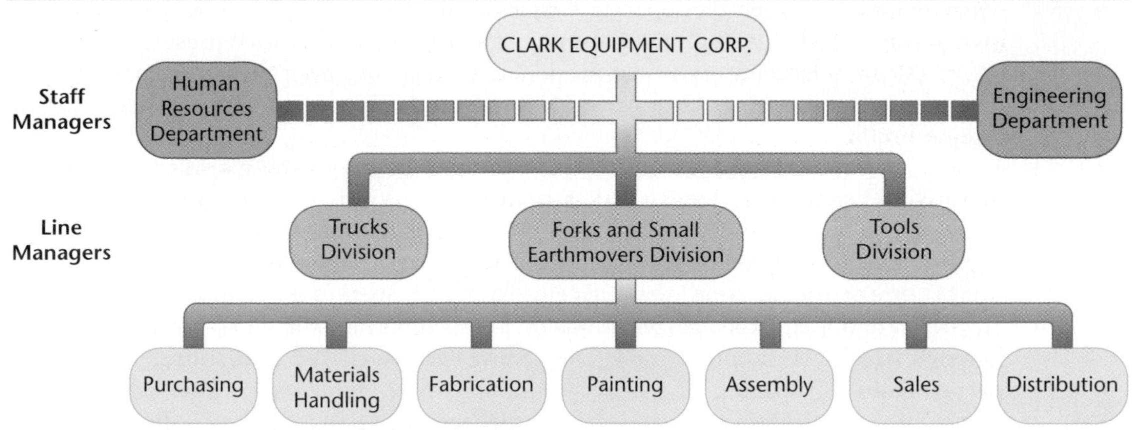

Figure 6.4
Line and Staff Organization

example, may consist of top managers from several major areas. If the work of the committee is especially important, and if the committee will be working together for an extended time, the organization may even grant it special authority as a decision-making body that goes beyond the individual authority possessed by each of its members.

At the operating level, many firms today are also using work teams—groups of operating employees who are empowered to plan and organize their own work and to perform that work with a minimum of supervision. As with permanent committees, the organization will usually find it beneficial to grant special authority to work teams so that they may function more effectively.

BASIC FORMS OF ORGANIZATIONAL STRUCTURE

Organizations can structure themselves in an almost infinite number of ways—according to specialization, for example, or departmentalization or the decision-making hierarchy.[19] Nevertheless, it is possible to identify four basic forms of organizational structure that reflect the general trends followed by most firms: *functional, divisional, matrix*, and *international*.

Functional Organization

Functional organization is the approach to organizational structure used by most small to medium-size firms. Such organizations are usually structured around basic business functions (marketing, operations, finance). Thus, within the company there is a marketing department, an operations department, and a finance department. The benefits of this approach include specialization within functional areas and smoother coordination among them. Experts with specialized training, for example, are hired to work in the marketing department, which handles all marketing for the firm.

In large firms, coordination across functional departments becomes more complicated. Functional organization also fosters centralization (which may possibly be desirable) and makes accountability more difficult. As organizations grow, therefore, they tend to shed this form and move toward one of the other three structures.

Divisional Organization

A **divisional organization** relies on product departmentalization. The firm creates product-based divisions, each of which may then be managed as a separate enterprise. Organizations using this approach are typically structured around several **divisions**—

functional organization
Form of business organization in which authority is determined by the relationships between group functions and activities

divisional organization
Organizational structure in which corporate divisions operate as autonomous businesses under the larger corporate umbrella

division
Department that resembles a separate business in producing and marketing its own products

departments that resemble separate businesses in that they produce and market their own products. The head of each division may be a corporate vice president or, if the organization is large, a divisional president. In addition, each division usually has its own identity and operates as a relatively autonomous business under the larger corporate umbrella.

H. J. Heinz <www.heinz.com>, for example, is one of the world's largest food-processing companies. Heinz makes literally thousands of different products and markets them around the world. The firm is organized into seven basic divisions: food service (selling small packaged products such as mustard and relish to restaurants), infant foods, condiments (Heinz ketchup, steak sauce, and tomato sauce), Star-Kist tuna, pet foods, frozen-foods division, and one division that handles miscellaneous products including new lines being test-marketed and soups, beans, and pasta products. Because of its divisional structure, Heinz can evaluate the performance of each division independently. Until recently, Heinz also had a division for its Weight Watchers business. But because this business was performing poorly, the company sold the Weight Watchers classroom program and folded its line of frozen foods into its existing frozen-foods division.[20] Because divisions are relatively autonomous, a firm can take such action with minimal disruption to its remaining business operations.

Like Heinz, other divisionalized companies are free to buy, sell, create, and disband divisions without disrupting the rest of their operations. Divisions can maintain healthy competition among themselves by sponsoring separate advertising campaigns, fostering different corporate identities, and so forth. They can also share certain corporate-level resources (such as market research data). Of course, if too much control is delegated to divisional managers, corporate managers may lose touch with daily operations. Competition between divisions can also become disruptive, and efforts in one division may be duplicated by those of another.

Matrix Organization

matrix structure
Organizational structure in which teams are formed and team members report to two or more managers

In a **matrix structure**, teams are formed in which individuals report to two or more managers. One manager usually has functional expertise, while the other has more of a product or project orientation. This structure was pioneered by the National Aeronautics and Space Administration (NASA) <www.nasa.gov> for use in developing specific programs. It is a highly flexible form that is readily adaptable to changing circumstances. Matrix structures rely heavily on committee and team authority.

In some companies, the matrix organization is a temporary measure, installed to complete a specific project and affecting only one part of the firm. In these firms, the end of the project usually means the end of the matrix—either a breakup of the team or a restructuring to fit it into the company's existing line-and-staff structure. Ford, for example, uses a matrix organization to design new models such as the Ford

"Hey, can I get back to you? I think the restructuring has begun."

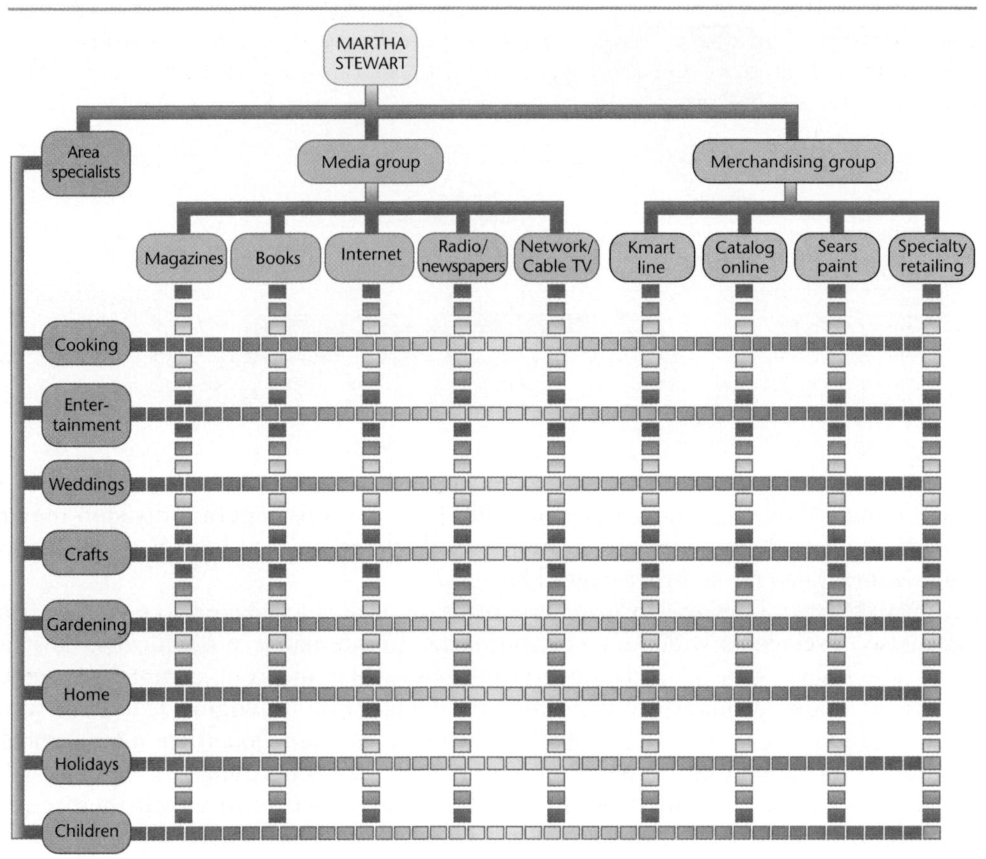

Figure 6.5
Matrix Organization at Martha Stewart

Thunderbird, which was launched in 2001. A design team comprised of people from engineering, marketing, operations, and finance was created to design the new car. After its work was done, the team members moved back to their permanent functional jobs. In other settings the matrix organization is a semipermanent fixture.

Figure 6.5 shows how Martha Stewart Living Omnimedia, Inc. <www.marthastewart.com> has created a matrix organization for its burgeoning lifestyle business. As you can see, the company is organized broadly into media and merchandising groups, each of which has specific product and product groups. Layered on top of this structure are teams of lifestyle experts organized into groups such as cooking, crafts, weddings, and so forth. Although each group targets specific customer needs, they all work, as necessary, across all product groups. A wedding expert, for example, might contribute to an article on wedding planning for a Martha Stewart magazine, contribute a story idea for a Martha Stewart cable television program, and supply content for a Martha Stewart Web site. This same individual might also help select fabrics suitable for wedding gowns to be retailed.[21]

International Organization

As we saw in Chapter 2, many businesses today manufacture, purchase, and sell in the world market. Thus, several different **international organizational structures** have emerged. Moreover, as competition on a global scale becomes more complex, companies often find that they must experiment with the ways in which they respond.[22]

international organizational structures
Approaches to organizational structure developed in response to the need to manufacture, purchase, and sell in global markets

For example, when Wal-Mart <www.walmart.com> opened its first store outside the United States in 1992, it set up a special projects team to handle the logistics. As more stores were opened abroad in the mid-1990s, the firm created a small international department to handle overseas expansion. By 1999, however, international sales and expansion had become such a major part of Wal-Mart's operations that the firm created a separate international division headed up by a senior vice president.

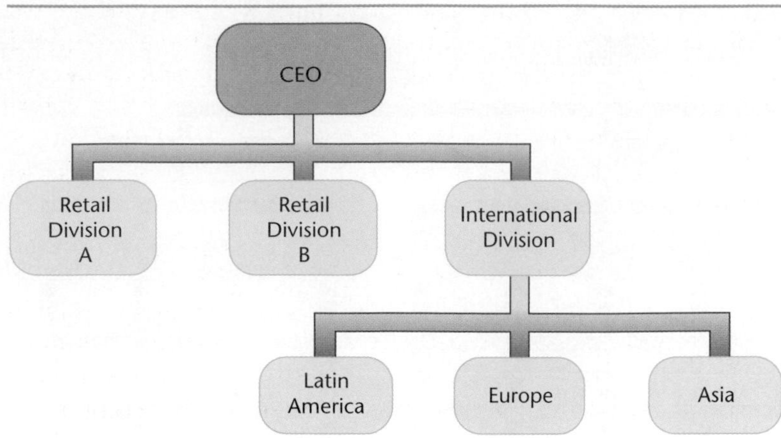

Figure 6.6
International Division Structure

Interestingly, Wal-Mart now envisions the day when this separate division may no longer be needed, simply because international operations will have become so thoroughly integrated in the firm's overall business.[23]

Wal-Mart typifies the form of organization outlined in Figure 6.6. Other firms have also developed a wide range of approaches to international organizational structure. The French food giant Danone Group <www.danonegroup.com>, for instance, has three major product groups: dairy products (Danone yogurts), bottled water (Evian), and cookies (Pim's). Danone's structure does not differentiate internationally but rather integrates global operations within each product group.[24]

Finally, some companies adopt a truly global structure in which they acquire resources (including capital), produce goods and services, engage in research and development, and sell products in whatever local market is appropriate, without any consideration of national boundaries. Until a few years ago, General Electric kept its international business operations as separate divisions. Now, however, the company functions as one integrated global organization. GE businesses around the world connect and interact with each other constantly, and managers freely move back and forth among them. This integration is also reflected in the top management team: The head of GE's audit team is French, the head of quality control is Dutch, and a German runs one of GE's core business groups.[25]

Organizational Design for the Twenty-First Century

As the world grows increasingly complex and fast-paced, organizations also continue to seek new forms of organization that permit them to compete effectively. Among the most popular of these new forms are the *boundaryless organization*, the *team organization*, the *virtual organization*, and the *learning organization*.

Boundaryless Organization The *boundaryless organization* is one in which traditional boundaries and structures are minimized or eliminated altogether. For example, General Electric's fluid organization structure, in which people, ideas, and information flow freely between businesses and business groups, approximates this concept. Similarly, as firms partner with their suppliers in more efficient ways, external boundaries disappear. Some of Wal-Mart's key suppliers are tied directly into the retailer's vaunted information system. As a result, when Wal-Mart distribution centers start running low on Wrangler blue jeans, the manufacturer gets the information as soon as the retailer. Wrangler proceeds to manufacture new inventory and restock the distribution center without Wal-Mart's having to place a new order.

Team Organization *Team organization* relies almost exclusively on project-type teams, with little or no underlying functional hierarchy. People "float" from project to project as dictated by their skills and the demands of those projects. At Cypress Semiconductor <www.cypress.com>, T. J. Rodgers refuses to allow the organization to grow so large that it can't function this way. Whenever a unit or group starts getting too large, he simply splits it into smaller units. Therefore, the organization is composed entirely of small units. This strategy allows each unit to change direction, explore new ideas, and try new methods without having to deal with a rigid bureaucratic superstructure. Although few large organizations have actually reached this level of adaptability, Apple Computer <www.apple.com> and Xerox <www.xerox.com> are among those moving toward it.

Virtual Organization Closely related to the team organization is the *virtual organization*. A virtual organization has little or no formal structure. Typically, it has only a handful of permanent employees, a very small staff, and a modest administrative facility. As the needs of the organization change, its managers bring in temporary workers, lease facilities, and outsource basic support services to meet the demands of each unique situation. As the situation changes, the temporary workforce changes in parallel, with some people leaving the organization and others entering. Facilities and the subcontracted services also change. In other words, the virtual organization exists only in response to its own needs.[26]

Global Research Consortium (GRC) <www.worldvest.com> is a virtual organization. GRC offers research and consulting services to firms doing business in Asia. As clients request various services, GRC's staff of three permanent employees subcontracts the work to an appropriate set of several dozen independent consultants and researchers with whom it has relationships. At any given time, therefore, GRC may have several projects under way with 20 or 30 people working on various projects. As the projects change, so too does the composition of the organization. Figure 6.7 illustrates a hypothetical virtual organization.

Learning Organization The so-called *learning organization* works to integrate continuous improvement with continuous employee learning and development. Specifically, a learning organization works to facilitate the lifelong learning and personal development of all of its employees while continually transforming itself to respond to changing demands and needs.

While managers might approach the concept of a learning organization from a variety of perspectives, the most frequent goals are improved quality, continuous improvement, and performance measurement. The idea is that the most consistent and logical strategy for achieving continuous improvement is constantly upgrading

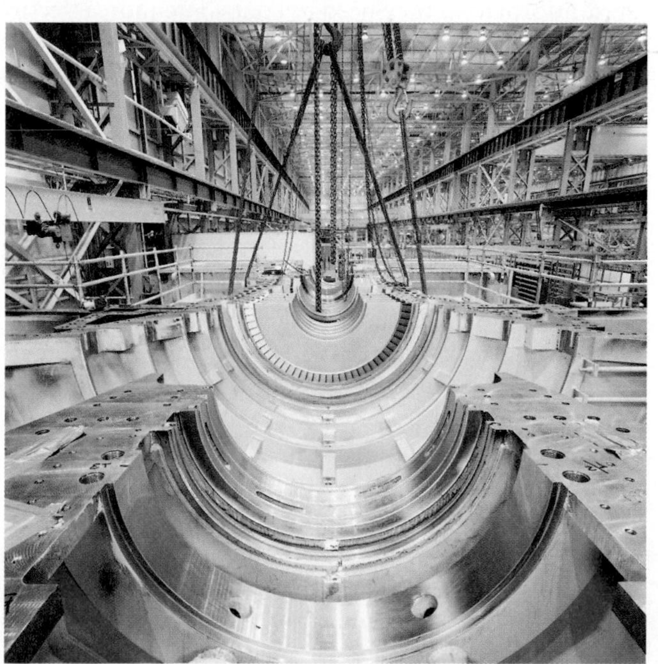

As the term suggests, the boundaryless organization is one that has erased certain boundaries. GE Power Systems <www.gepower.com/en_us>, *which sells electricity-generating turbines, uses the Internet to eliminate a boundary that once separated its traditional functions from those of its customers. Using the Web to connect with GE's so-called turbine optimizer, any operator of a GE turbine can compare its performance with other turbines of the same model located anywhere in the world. GE will also calculate the long-term savings of a given improvement—another task that, in the pre–e-business era, would have been performed by the buyer-operator.*

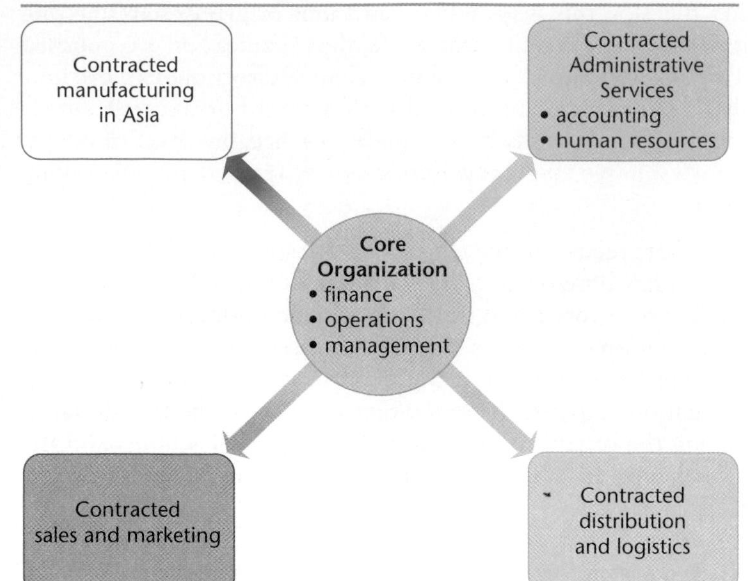

Figure 6.7
The Virtual Organization

employee talent, skill, and knowledge. For example, if each employee in an organization learns one new thing each day and can translate that knowledge into work-related practice, continuous improvement will logically follow. Indeed, organizations that wholeheartedly embrace this approach believe that only through constant employee learning can continuous improvement really occur.

In recent years, many different organizations have implemented this approach on various levels. Shell Oil Company <www.countonshell.com>, for example, recently purchased an executive conference center north of its headquarters in Houston. Called the Shell Learning Center, the facility boasts state-of-the-art classrooms and instructional technology, lodging facilities, a restaurant, and recreational amenities, such as a golf course, swimming pool, and tennis courts. Line managers at the firm rotate through the Center and serve as teaching faculty. Teaching assignments last anywhere from a few days to several months. At the same time, all Shell employees routinely attend training programs, seminars, and related activities, all the while gathering the latest information they need to contribute more effectively to the firm. Recent seminar topics have included time management, implications of the Americans with Disabilities Act, balancing work and family demands, and international trade theory.[27]

INFORMAL ORGANIZATION

Much of our discussion has focused on the organization's *formal structure*—its official arrangement of jobs and job relationships. In reality, however, all organizations also have another dimension—an *informal* organization within which people do their jobs in different ways and interact with other people in ways that do not follow formal lines of communication.

Formal Versus Informal Organizational Systems

informal organization
Network, unrelated to the firm's formal authority structure, of everyday social interactions among company employees

The formal organization of a business is the part that can be seen and represented in chart form. The structure of a company, however, is by no means limited to the organization chart and the formal assignment of authority. Frequently, the **informal organization**—everyday social interactions among employees that transcend formal jobs and job interrelationships—effectively alters a company's formal structure. Indeed, this level of organization is sometimes just as powerful, if not more powerful, than the formal structure.

On the negative side, the informal organization can reinforce office politics that put the interests of individuals ahead of those of the firm.[28] Likewise, a great deal of harm can be caused by distorted or inaccurate information communicated without management input or review. For example, if the informal organization is highlighting false information about impending layoffs, valuable employees may act quickly (and unnecessarily) to seek other employment. Among the more important elements of the informal organization are *informal groups* and the *organizational grapevine.*

Informal Groups *Informal groups* are simply groups of people who decide to interact among themselves. They may be people who work together in a formal sense or who just get together for lunch, during breaks, or after work. They may talk about business, the boss, or nonwork-related topics like families, movies, or sports. Their impact on the organization may be positive (if they work together to support the organization), negative (if they work together in ways that run counter to the organization's interests), or irrelevant (if what they do is unrelated to the organization).

Organizational Grapevine The **grapevine** is an informal communication network that can run through an entire organization.[29] Grapevines are found in all organizations except the very smallest, but they do not always follow the same patterns as formal channels of authority and communication, nor do they necessarily coincide with them. Moreover, because the grapevine typically passes information orally, it often becomes distorted in the process.

grapevine
Informal communication network that runs through an organization

Attempts to eliminate the grapevine are fruitless, but, fortunately, managers do have some control over it. By maintaining open channels of communication and responding vigorously to inaccurate information, they can minimize the damage the grapevine can do. In fact, the grapevine can actually be an asset. By getting to know the key people in the grapevine, for example, the manager can partially control the information they receive and use the grapevine to sound out employee reactions to new ideas (for example, a change in human resource policies or benefit packages). The manager can also get valuable information from the grapevine and use it to improve decision making.

Intrapreneuring

Sometimes organizations actually take steps to encourage the informal organization. They do so for a variety of reasons, two of which we have already discussed. First, most experienced managers recognize that the informal organization exists whether they want it or not. Second, many managers know how to use the informal organization to reinforce the formal organization. Perhaps more important, however, the energy of the informal organization can be harnessed to improve productivity.

Many firms, including Compaq Computer, Rubbermaid, 3M, and Xerox, support a process called **intrapreneuring**: creating and maintaining the innovation and flexibility of a small-business environment within the confines of a large, bureaucratic structure. The concept is basically sound. Historically, most innovations have come from individuals in small businesses (see Chapter 4). As businesses increase in size, however, innovation and creativity tend to become casualties in the battle for more sales and profits. In some large companies, new ideas are even discouraged, and champions of innovation have been stalled in midcareer.

intrapreneuring
Process of creating and maintaining the innovation and flexibility of a small-business environment within the confines of a large organization

Compaq <www.compaq.com> is an excellent example of how intrapreneuring works to counteract this trend. The firm has one major division called the New Business Group. When a manager or engineer has an idea for a new product or product application, the individual takes it to the New Business Group and "sells" it. The managers in the group itself are then encouraged to help the innovator develop the idea for field testing. If the product takes off and does well, it is then spun off into its own new business group or division. If it doesn't do as well as hoped, it may still be maintained as part of the New Business Group or may be phased out.

Continued from page 141

Building on Cybersites

As we noted at the beginning of this story, Cephren and Bidcom are at the forefront in applying Web technology to construction projects. Cephren, for example, has created a software network that serves as a communications system for the contractors and subcontractors who are working together on a project. Clients pay a start-up fee of $750 and a monthly fee of $1,250 to use the Cephren system, plus an initial $1,500 training fee. Each member of the construction team receives a password that allows access to the facet of the project that is relevant to the respective team member's work. Thus, a middle manager working at the construction site might need access to blueprints but not to the minutes of the senior management team's last meeting.

Bidcom is another emerging player in this new construction model. While Cephren focuses primarily on organizing construction projects more efficiently, Bidcom focuses more tightly on the job of linking contractors and suppliers. Using the Bidcom system, for example, a contractor can put out a call for bids on 100 steel doors or 500 windows, with corresponding specifications and delivery details. Suppliers, meanwhile, can review the call and submit bids directly to the contractor. This overall improvement in efficiency can potentially save thousands of dollars on a big construction project.

Of course, not everyone is rushing to this new way of doing business. But all the major companies are at least taking steps in this direction. Experts forecast that by the year 2004, at least 10 percent of all construction-industry business will be conducted online. One major construction firm, WebCor <www.webcor.com>, indicates that in two years it will do business only with subcontractors and suppliers who are able to work online. We may never live and work in virtual buildings, but, increasingly, the construction of old-fashioned brick-and-mortar facilities is taking place in cyberspace.

Questions for Discussion

1. What elements of organizational structure are most relevant to the construction industry?
2. Why do you think some firms are so eager and some reluctant to adopt this new technology?
3. What new pitfalls might exist for a construction project being managed totally online?
4. Are the organizational effects of new technology more likely to be felt within a given construction company or in the way that construction companies relate to one another? Why?
5. In what ways, if any, might new technology affect the informal organization that exists at a construction site?

SUMMARY OF LEARNING OBJECTIVES

1 **Discuss the elements that influence a firm's *organizational structure*.** Every business needs structure to operate. *Organizational structure* varies according to a firm's mission, purpose, and strategy. Size, technology, and changes in environmental circumstances also influence structure. In general, although all organizations have the same basic elements, each develops the structure that contributes to the most efficient operations.

2 **Explain *specialization* and *departmentalization* as the building blocks of organizational structure.** The building blocks of organizational structure are *job specialization* and *departmentalization*. As a firm grows, it usually has a greater need for people to perform specialized tasks (specialization). It also has a greater need to group types of work into logical units (departmentalization). Common forms of departmentalization are *customer, product, process, geographic*, and *functional*. Large businesses often use more than one form of departmentalization.

3 **Distinguish between *responsibility, authority, delegation*, and *accountability*, and explain the differ-**

ences between decision making in *centralized* and *decentralized organizations*. *Responsibility* is the duty to perform a task; *authority* is the power to make the decisions necessary to complete tasks. *Delegation* begins when a manager assigns a task to a subordinate; *accountability* means that the subordinate must complete the task. *Span of control* refers to the number of people who work for any individual manager. The more people supervised, the wider the span of control. Wide spans are usually desirable when employees perform simple or unrelated tasks. When jobs are diversified or prone to change, a narrower span is generally preferable.

In a *centralized organization*, only a few individuals in top management have real decision-making authority. In a *decentralized organization*, much authority is delegated to lower-level management. When both *line* and *line-and-staff systems* are involved, line departments generally have authority to make decisions, whereas *staff departments* have a responsibility to advise. A relatively new concept, *committee and team authority*, empowers committees or work teams involved in a firm's daily operations.

4 Explain the differences between *functional, divisional, matrix*, and *international organizational structures*. In a *functional organization*, authority is usually distributed among such basic functions as marketing and finance. In a *divisional organization*, the various divisions of a larger company, which may be related or unrelated, operate in a relatively autonomous fashion. In a *matrix organization*, in which individuals report to more than one manager, a company creates teams to address specific problems or to conduct specific projects. A company that has divisions in many countries may require an additional level of *international organization to coordinate those operations.*

5 Describe the *informal organization* and discuss *intrapreneuring*. The *informal organization* consists of the everyday social interactions among employees that transcend formal jobs and job interrelationships. To foster the innovation and flexibility of a small business within the big-business environment, some large companies encourage *intrapreneuring*—creating and maintaining the innovation and flexibility of a small-business environment within the confines of a large bureaucratic structure.

QUESTIONS AND EXERCISES

Questions for Review

1. What is an organization chart? What purpose does it serve?
2. Explain the significance of size as it relates to organizational structure. Describe the changes that are likely to occur as an organization grows.
3. What is the difference between responsibility and authority?
4. Why do some managers have difficulties in delegating authority? Why does this problem tend to plague smaller businesses?
5. Why is a company's informal organization important?

Questions for Analysis

6. Draw up an organization chart for your college or university.
7. Describe a hypothetical organizational structure for a small printing firm. Describe changes that might be necessary as the business grows.
8. Compare and contrast the matrix and divisional approaches to organizational structure. How would you feel personally about working in a matrix organization in which you were assigned simultaneously to multiple units or groups?

Application Exercises

9. Interview the manager of a local service business—a fast-food restaurant. What types of tasks does this manager typically delegate? Is the appropriate authority also delegated in each case?
10. Using books, magazines, or personal interviews, identify a person who has succeeded as an intrapreneur. In what ways did the structure of the intrapreneur's company help this individual succeed? In what ways did the structure pose problems?

EXPLORING THE WEB

How to Organize a Magic Kingdom

This chapter alludes to the years when Walt Disney and his brother Roy first opened their studio. To introduce the concept of job specialization, we describe the opposite practice—a few people doing just about everything. As their jobs grew more complex, the Disney brothers found it increasingly necessary to assign facets of their jobs to other people. Today, the Walt Disney Co. is a multinational entertainment empire. The company's Web site can be found at:

<www.disney.go.com>

Browse this Web site and then consider the following questions and activities:

1. Using the Disney Web site as a guide, diagram an organization structure that might make sense for the firm. Make your diagram as detailed as possible.
2. What base of departmentalization does Disney apparently use?
3. Disney has a history of being relatively centralized. What impact would this practice likely have on the firm's current structure?
4. Can you draw any implications from your diagram about the firm's span of control?
5. Disney employs people it calls "Imagineers." See what you can learn about the jobs performed by these people, and compare them with the various roles played by intrapreneurs.
6. Research Disney's "real" organizational structure. Compare and contrast it with the one you diagrammed. What basic factors might account for major differences?

EXERCISING YOUR ETHICS

Minding Your Own Business

THE SITUATION

Assume that you have recently gone to work for a large high-tech company. You have discovered an interesting arrangement in which one of your co-workers is engaging. Specifically, he blocks his schedule for the hour between 11:00 and 12:00 each day and does not take a lunch break. During this two-hour interval, he is actually running his own real estate business.

THE DILEMMA

You recently asked him how he manages to pull this off. "Well," he responded, "the boss and I never talked about it, but she knows what's going on. They know they can't replace me, and I always get my work done. I don't use any company resources. So, what's the harm?" Interestingly, you also have a business opportunity that could be pursued in the same way.

QUESTIONS FOR DISCUSSION

1. What are the ethical issues in this situation?
2. What do you think most people would do in this situation?
3. What would you do in this situation?

BUILDING YOUR BUSINESS SKILLS

Getting with the Program

This exercise enhances the following SCANS workplace competencies: demonstrating basic skills, demonstrating thinking skills, exhibiting interpersonal skills, and working with information.

GOAL

To encourage students to understand the relationship between organizational structure and a company's ability to attract and keep valued employees.

SITUATION

You are the founder of a small but growing high-technology company that develops new computer software. With your current workload and new contracts in the pipeline, your business is thriving except for one problem: You cannot find computer programmers for product development. Worse yet, current staff members are being lured away by other high-tech firms. After suffering a particularly discouraging personnel raid in which competitors captured three of your most valued employees, you schedule a meeting with your director of human resources to plan organizational changes designed to encourage worker loyalty. You already pay top dollar, but the continuing exodus tells you that programmers are looking for something more.

METHOD

Working with three or four classmates, identify some ways in which specific organizational changes might improve the working environment and encourage employee loyalty. As you analyze the following factors, ask yourself the obvious question: If I were a programmer, what organizational changes would encourage me to stay?

- *Level of job specialization.* With many programmers describing their jobs as tedious because of the focus on detail in a narrow work area, what changes, if any, would you make in job specialization? Right now, for instance, few of your programmers have any say in product design.
- *Decision-making hierarchy.* What decision-making authority would encourage people to stay? Is expanding employee authority likely to work better in a centralized or decentralized organization?
- *Team authority.* Can team empowerment make a difference? Taking the point of view of the worker, describe the ideal team.
- *Intrapreneuring.* What can your company do to encourage and reward innovation?

FOLLOW-UP QUESTIONS

1. With the average computer programmer earning nearly $70,000, and with all competitive firms paying top dollar, why might organizational issues be critical in determining employee loyalty?
2. If you were a programmer, what organizational factors would make a difference to you? Why?
3. As the company founder, how willing would you be to make major organizational changes in light of the shortage of qualified programmers?

CRAFTING YOUR BUSINESS PLAN

Doctoring the Organization

THE PURPOSE OF THE ASSIGNMENT

1. To provide an example that illustrates ways in which organizational options can be presented in a business plan, using the planning framework of *Business PlanPro (BPP)* (Version 4.0).
2. To demonstrate how three chapter topics—organization structure, departmentalization, and authority and responsibility—can be integrated as components in the *BPP* planning environment.

ASSIGNMENT

After reading Chapter 6 in the textbook, open the BPP *software and look around for information about organizational structure, departmentalization, and authority and responsibility as they apply to a sample firm:* Medical Equipment Development *(Medquip, Inc.). Then respond to the following items*:

1. Construct an organization chart for Medquip, Inc. [Sites to see in *BPP* for this item: In the Plan Outline screen, click on each of the following, in turn: **6.0 Management Summary**; **6.1 Organizational Structure**; **6.2 Management Team**; and **Table: Personnel** (located beneath **6.4 Personnel Plan** on the Plan Outline screen.]
2. Explain how Medquip's organizational structure is set up to take advantage of its competitor's weakness in product innovation. [Sites to see in *BPP* for this item: In the Plan Outline screen, click on **4.2.4 Main Competitors**.]
3. Which type of departmentalization—customer, product, functional, or process—does Medquip use? Give examples from Medquip's business plan to support your answer.
4. For each job position at Medquip, how clearly are its authority and responsibility delineated in the business plan?

VIDEO EXERCISE

The Management Picture: Quick Takes Video (II)

LEARNING OBJECTIVES

The purpose of this video exercise is to help you

1. Recognize the difference between responsibility and authority.
2. Understand the decision-making process.
3. Understand the three forms of authority.

BACKGROUND INFORMATION

Based on a real company in the same line of business, Quick Takes Video is a fictitious firm that produces corporate, industrial, and training videos and video news releases. It was founded by Hal Boylston and Karen Jarvis, and the management team includes a production coordinator, who oversees the producers responsible for the actual filming and editing of the firm's products. The production coordinator forecasts staff and equipment needs for each shoot, coordinates the use of the company's physical resources, manages producers, and keeps the shoots on schedule and on budget. The new production coordinator, John Switzer, reports to Hal Boylston.

THE VIDEO

In this segment, Switzer runs into trouble with a producer named Susan, who reports to him. She disagrees with his decision to give her a freelance crew instead of a staff crew for a shoot that she considers very important. Switzer discusses the problem with Boylston, to whom Susan used to report, and wonders whether Susan will make a habit of taking her complaints to Boylston or will get used to reporting to Switzer, her new supervisor.

QUESTIONS FOR DISCUSSION

1. In what ways might Switzer have contributed to the disagreement with Susan? How could Susan have helped to avoid the confrontation?
2. What kind of authority does Switzer have (line, staff, or committee)? What does that kind of authority imply about his working relationship with Susan?
3. Boylston advises Switzer to give Susan time to get used to a new manager and to accept the fact that she is somewhat spoiled. What do you think of this advice?

FOLLOW-UP ASSIGNMENT

Have you ever disagreed with the decision of a boss (or perhaps an instructor or other supervisor)? How did you deal with the problem? Did you consult others in the organization? What kinds of reporting hierarchy existed in the organization, and how did that hierarchy affect the outcome of the disagreement? Would you take the same action if you had it to do over? Why or why not?

FOR FURTHER EXPLORATION

Choose a formal organization with which you are familiar, such as your college, your employer, or a club or other organization to which you belong. Draw an organization chart for this entity, including appropriate lines of authority. Decide whether it closely resembles a functional, divisional, matrix, or perhaps even an international organization. Determine whether relationships of responsibility and authority are consistent in this organization.

Managing Operations and Improving Quality

After reading this chapter, you should be able to:

1. Explain the meaning of the term *operations* and describe the four kinds of *utility* operations processes provide.
2. Identify the characteristics that distinguish *service operations* from *goods production* and explain the main objects of the *service focus.*
3. Describe the decision areas involved in *operations planning.*
4. Identify some of the key tools for *total quality management,* including strategies for getting closer to the customer.
5. Explain how a *supply chain strategy* differs from traditional strategies for coordinating operations among firms.

"Speed Is Everything"

Dell Computer Corp. has never done business in quite the same way that other computer makers have. One of the country's fastest-growing high-tech firms, Dell sells computers directly to customers, and it is making a big splash on the Internet, writing up to $40 million worth of orders a day from its Web site <www.dell.com>. It is now the number-one PC retailer on the Web, with sales continuing to grow at an astounding rate of 54 percent per year for the last 10 years. "We've become the poster boy for the Internet," says company founder Michael Dell. In fact, Dell's company has led the way to a whole new world of selling: In the last quarter of its 2001 fiscal year, direct sales accounted for about half of Dell's $8.6 billion in new PC sales, and growth for the year is 250 percent higher than the industry average.

What's the secret of Dell's success? Michael Dell, chairman and CEO, has stressed a few key production principles that sustain productivity and keep costs and inventories low. For one thing, information is replacing inventory: By keeping up-to-the-minute information on supplies, customer orders, and production status, Dell keeps 10 times less inventory than its competitors and passes the savings along to customers. By redesigning its products—in particular, simplifying them with fewer parts—Dell has made production faster and, of course, has to purchase fewer parts.

Perhaps the most important principle at Dell is speed. Just-in-time manufacturing has always been a key tenet at the firm, and Dell has recently extended it to suppliers. Dell now requires its supply chain to warehouse most computer components within 15 minutes of Dell's factories in Texas, Ireland, and Malaysia,

"Speed is everything in this business. We're setting the pace for the industry."

—Michael Dell,
CEO of Dell Computer

and it has dropped suppliers that can't comply. Dell doesn't even buy components until it's received an order for at least one unit of a computer, thus realizing big savings on parts whose prices can drop almost overnight. When it gets a customer order, Dell quickly relays the information to its suppliers, which are committed to quick delivery. Despite the squeeze on suppliers, the firm can still book a custom order and ship a finished machine within 48 hours.

Dell also collects on sales faster than the competition, averaging 24 hours from order to cash. That's days sooner than rivals Gateway <www.gateway.com> and Compaq <www.compaq.com>. "Speed is everything in this business," says CEO Dell. "We're setting the pace for the industry." With the firm's stock price continuing to climb faster than competitors', it seems that investors as well as customers must agree that Dell has figured out how to achieve an enviable mix of productivity and quality.

Our opening story continues on page 188

GOODS AND SERVICES OPERATIONS

Everywhere you go today, you encounter business activities that provide goods and services. You wake up in the morning to the sound of your favorite radio station. You stop at the corner newsstand for a newspaper on your way to the bus stop, where you catch the bus to work or school. Your instructors, the bus driver, the clerk at the 7-Eleven store, and the morning radio announcer are all examples of people who work in **service operations**. They provide you with tangible and intangible service products, such as entertainment, transportation, education, and food preparation. Firms that make tangible products—radios, newspapers, buses, textbooks—are engaged in **goods production.**

service operations
Produces tangible and intangible services, such as entertainment, transportation, and education

goods production
Produces tangible products, such as radios, newspapers, buses, and textbooks

Growth in the Service and Goods Sectors

Although the term *production* has historically referred to companies engaged in goods production, the concept as we now use it means services as well as goods. An abundance of necessities and conveniences on which we rely, from fire protection and health care to mail delivery and fast food, is all produced by service operations. Traditionally, service sector managers have focused less on such manufacturing-centered goals as equipment and technology. Rather, they have stressed the human element in their activities. Why? Because success or failure depends on contact with the customer during service delivery. The provider's employees—its human resources—who deal directly with its customers affect the customer's feelings about the service.

Manufacturing industries today still account for about 23 percent of all private sector jobs in the United States—while the number of manufacturing jobs has remained steady for the past four decades. Nevertheless, the economic significance of manufacturing activity is rising. For example, real income from manufacturing has been rising steadily, increasing by over 30 percent in the past 10 years. So effective are new manufacturing methods—and so committed are U.S. manufacturers to using them—that in 2000 the United States remained ahead of Germany and Japan in manufactured exports, retaining the number-one spot for the seventh consecutive year.

Naturally, both goods and service industries are important to the economy. As you can see from Figures 7.1 and 7.2, services have grown far more rapidly since 1984. For one thing, employment has risen significantly in the service sector while remaining stagnant in goods production (Figure 7.1). In fact, by 2000 employment in service industries accounted for nearly 81 percent of the total U.S. workforce—106 million

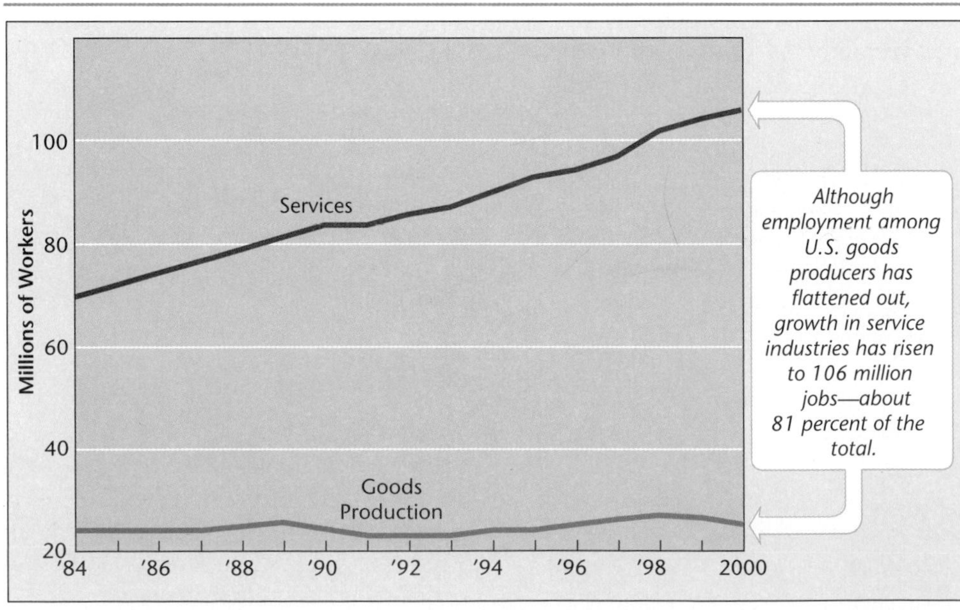
Millions of Workers
100
80
60
40
20
Services
Goods Production
'84
'86
'88
'90
'92
'94
'96
'98
2000
Although employment among U.S. goods producers has flattened out, growth in service industries has risen to 106 million jobs—about 81 percent of the total.

Figure 7.1
Employment in Goods and Service Sectors

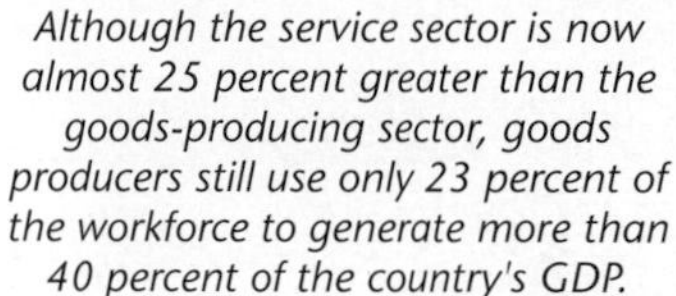

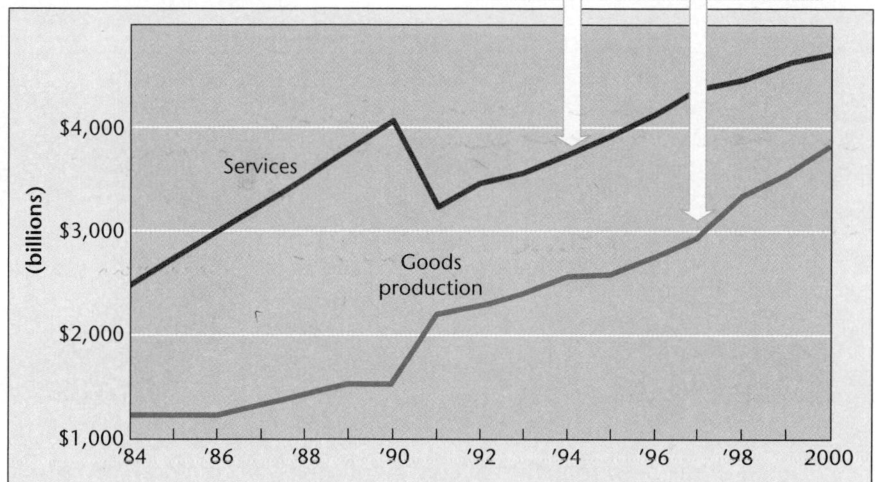

Figure 7.2
GDP from Goods and Services

jobs. Much of this growth comes from new e-commerce jobs and from the business services, social services, health care, amusement and recreation, and educational industries. Employment projections indicate that services will remain the faster-growing employment source in the immediate future.[1] With this growth, the gap in average wages between the two sectors has closed to just $19 per week more for goods-producing workers. More importantly, the distribution of high-paying and low-paying jobs in each sector is now equal.

By 2000, the service sector also provided nearly 56 percent of national income, as opposed to just over 50 percent in 1947. As Figure 7.2 shows, the service sector's share of the U.S. gross domestic product (GDP)—the value of all the goods and services produced by the economy, excluding foreign income—has climbed since 1984 until it is now nearly 25 percent greater than that of the goods-producing sector. At the same time, the 23 percent of the U.S. workforce in manufacturing produces more than 40 percent of the nation's GDP.[2] In China, by contrast, manufacturing employs 70 percent of the urban labor force but produces only 30 percent of the country's national income.[3]

Remember that although companies are typically classified as either goods producers or service providers, the distinction is often blurred. For one thing, all businesses are service operations to some extent. Consider General Electric <www.ge.com>, which popularly conjures up thoughts of appliances for laundry and kitchen (and jet engines). But GE is not just a goods producer. According to its own annual report, "The General Electric Company is the world's largest diversified services company as well as a provider of high-quality, high-technology industrial and consumer products."[4] GE's many service operations include broadcasting (NBC), commercial and consumer finance, reinsurance of primary insurers, equity investing, real estate, and aviation services.

The Growth of Global Operations

Many countries have joined in the global competition that has reshaped production into a faster-paced, more complex business activity. Although the factory remains the centerpiece for manufacturing, it is virtually unrecognizable when compared with its counterpart of even just a decade ago. The smoke, grease, and danger have been replaced in many companies by glistening high-tech machines, computers, and "clean rooms" that are contaminant-free and carefully controlled for temperature.

VF Corp. <www.vfc.com> sells more jeans—Lee, Wrangler, and other brands—than anybody else in the world. In 1995, the company began developing its Data Services Control Center in Greensboro, North Carolina. The idea was to aggregate key data—demographics, point-of-sale information on sizes and colors—so that managers could pinpoint the precise mix of products that was likely to sell at a particular retail location. Today, VF's corporate-level system also runs software to handle all financial operations as well as order-management and materials-management functions.

Instead of the need to maintain continuous mass production, firms today face constant change. New technologies are allowing machines to run cleaner, faster, and safer and to operate on a global scale. For online manufacturing, industrial machines can log on to the Internet, adjust their own settings, and make minor decisions without human help. They can communicate both with other machines in the company (via an intranet) and with other companies' machines (via the Internet). With the Internet, producers of both services and goods are integrating their production activities with those of far-off suppliers and customers.

CREATING VALUE THROUGH OPERATIONS

To understand the production processes of a firm we need to know how to measure the value of services and goods. Products provide businesses with economic results: profits, wages, and goods purchased from other companies. At the same time, they provide consumers with **utility**—the ability of a product to satisfy a human want.

utility
A product's ability to satisfy a human want

There are four basic kinds of production-based utility:

- When a company turns out ornaments in time for Christmas, it creates *time utility*; that is, it makes products available when consumers want them.
- When a department store opens its annual Trim-a-Tree department, it creates *place utility*: It makes products available where they are convenient for consumers.
- By making a product available for consumers to own and use, production creates *ownership* or *possession utility*, which customers enjoy when they buy boxes of ornaments and decorate their trees.
- Production makes products available in the first place: By turning raw materials into finished goods, production creates *form utility*, as when an ornament maker combines glass, plastic, and other materials to create tree decorations.

operations (or production) management
Systematic direction and control of the processes that transform resources into finished products

operations (or production) managers
Managers responsible for production, inventory, and quality control

Because the term *production* was historically associated just with manufacturing, writers have recently replaced it with *operations*, a term that reflects both service and goods production. **Operations** (or **production**) **management** is the systematic direction and control of the processes that transform resources into finished services and goods. Thus, **operations** (or **production**) **managers** are ultimately responsible for creating utility for customers.

As Figure 7.3 shows, operations managers must draw up plans to transform resources into products. First, they must bring together basic resources: knowledge, physical materials, equipment, and labor. Naturally, they must put those resources to

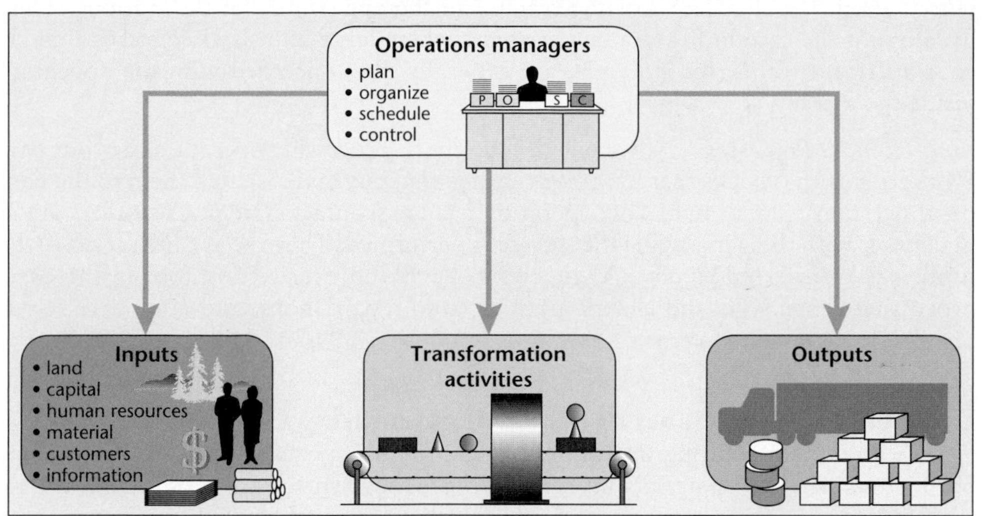

Figure 7.3
Resource Transformation Process

effective use in the production facility. As demand for a product increases, managers must schedule and control work to produce the required amounts of products. Finally, they must also control costs, quality levels, inventory, and facilities and equipment.

Although some operations managers work in factories, others work in offices and retail stores. Farmers are also operations managers. They create utility by transforming soil, seeds, fuel, and other inputs into soybeans, milk, and other outputs. As production managers, they may employ crews of workers to plant and harvest. Or they may opt for automated machinery or some combination of workers and machinery. These decisions affect costs, the role of buildings and equipment in their operations, and the quality and quantity of goods that they produce.

Operations Processes

An **operations process** is a set of methods and technologies used in the production of a good or a service. We classify various types of production according to differences in their operations processes. We can describe goods according to whether their operations process combines resources or breaks them into component parts. We can describe services according to the *extent of customer contact* required.

operations process
Set of methods used in the production of a good or service

Goods-Manufacturing Processes: Analytic Versus Synthetic Processes All goods-manufacturing processes can be classified by the *analytic* or *synthetic* nature of the transformation process. An **analytic process** breaks down resources into components. Tyson reduces incoming whole chickens to the packaged parts we find at the meat counter. The reverse approach, a **synthetic process**, combines raw materials to produce a finished product. General Electric uses this approach in manufacturing refrigerators. It forms and shapes steel to produce the basic refrigerator, then it adds motors, lightbulbs, trays, and shelves. Finally, it packages the refrigerator in a shipping carton and delivers it to an appliance store.

analytic process
Production process in which resources are broken down into components to create finished products

synthetic process
Production process in which resources are combined to create finished products

Service Processes: Extent of Customer Contact One way of classifying services is to ask whether a given service can be provided without the customer's being part of the production system. In answering this question, we classify services according to the *extent of customer contact.*[5]

High-Contact Processes Think for a moment about your local public transit system. The service provided is transportation, and when you purchase transportation, you must board a bus or train. The Bay Area Rapid Transit System (BART) <www.bart.gov> connects San Francisco with many of its outlying suburbs. Like all public transportation systems, BART is a **high-contact system:** To receive the service, the customer must be a part of the system. For this reason, BART managers must

high-contact system
Level of customer contact in which the customer is part of the system during service delivery

worry about the cleanliness of the trains and the appearance of the stations. This is usually not the case in low-contact systems, where large industrial concerns that ship coal in freight trains, for example, are generally not concerned with the appearance inside those trains.

low-contact system
Level of customer contact in which the customer need not be a part of the system to receive the service

Low-Contact Processes Now consider the check-processing operations at your bank. Workers sort the checks that have been cashed that day and dispatch them to the banks on which they were drawn. This operation is a **low-contact system:** Customers are not in contact with the bank while the service is performed. They receive the service—their funds are transferred to cover their checks—without ever setting foot in the check-processing center. Gas and electric utilities, auto repair shops, and lawn care services are also low-contact systems.

Differences Between Service and Manufacturing Operations

Service and manufacturing operations share several important features. For example, both transform raw materials into finished products. In service production, the raw materials, or inputs, are not glass or steel. Rather, they are people who choose among sellers because they have either unsatisfied needs or possessions for which they need some form of care or alteration. In service operations, then, "finished products" or "outputs" are people with needs met and possessions serviced.[6]

Focus on Performance Thus, at least one very obvious difference exists between service and manufacturing operations: Whereas goods are produced, services are performed. Therefore, customer-oriented performance is a key factor in measuring the effectiveness of a service company.

Wal-Mart <www.walmart.com> sells to millions of people from California to China to Argentina out of nearly 4,200 stores. Its superstar status stems from an obsession with speedy product delivery that it measures not in days or even hours but in minutes and seconds. Wal-Mart's keen customer focus emphasizes avoiding unnecessary inventories, getting fast responses from suppliers, streamlining transactions processes, and knowing accurately the sales and restocking requirements for keeping the right merchandise moving from warehouses to store shelves. To implement this strategy, Wal-Mart has made technology—namely, its vaunted computer and telecommunications system—a core competency.[7]

In many ways, the focus of service operations is more complex than that of goods production. First, service operations feature a unique link between production and consumption—between process and outcome. Second, services are more intangible and more customized and less storable than most products. Finally, quality considerations must be defined and managed differently in the service sector than in manufacturing operations.

Focus on Process and Outcome As we saw earlier, manufacturing operations focus on the outcome of the production process. The products offered by most service operations, however, are actually combinations of goods and services. Services, therefore, must focus on both the transformation *process* and its outcome—both on making a pizza and on delivering it to the buyer.[8] Service operations thus require different skills from manufacturing operations. Local gas company employees may need the interpersonal skills necessary to calm and reassure frightened customers who have reported gas leaks. The job, therefore, can mean more than just repairing defective pipes. Factory workers who install gas pipes while assembling mobile homes are far less likely to need such skills.

Focus on Service Characteristics Service companies' transactions always reflect the fact that service products are characterized by three key qualities: *intangibility, customization*, and *unstorability*.

Intangibility Often services cannot be touched, tasted, smelled, or seen. An important value, therefore, is the *intangible* value that the customer experiences in the form of pleasure, satisfaction, or a feeling of safety. When you hire an attorney to resolve a problem, you purchase not only the intangible quality of legal expertise but also the

WEB Connection

If your company's Web site uses Lightning Rod Software, a customer can click on a "callback" button. A form will appear asking the prospective buyer to type in a name and telephone number. Your server then sends the information to your next available sales rep, who calls it up and phones the customer. To find out more about Lightning Rod Software, access the company at its Web site.

www.lightrodsoft.com

equally intangible reassurance that help is at hand. Although all services have some degree of intangibility, some provide tangible elements as well. Your attorney can draw up the living will that you want to keep in your safe-deposit box.

Customization When you visit a physician, you expect to be examined for your symptoms. Likewise, when you purchase insurance, get your pet groomed, or have your hair cut, you expect these services to be designed for your needs. Therefore, services are *customized*.

Unstorability Services such as rubbish collection, transportation, child care, and house cleaning cannot be produced ahead of time and then stored. If a service is not used when available, it is usually wasted. Services, then, are typically characterized by a high degree of *unstorability*.

Focus on the Customer-Service Link Because they transform customers or their possessions, service operations often acknowledge the customer as part of the operations process itself. For example, to purchase a haircut you must usually go to the barbershop or beauty salon.

As physical participants in the operations process, service consumers have a unique ability to affect that process. In other words, as the customer, you expect the salon to be conveniently located, to be open for business at convenient times, to offer needed services at reasonable prices, and to extend prompt service. Accordingly, the manager adopts hours of operation, available services, and an appropriate number of employees to meet the requirements of the customer.

E-Commerce: The "Virtual Presence" of the Customer The growth of e-commerce has introduced a "virtual presence," as opposed to a physical presence, of customers in the service system. Consumers interact electronically, in real time, with sellers, collecting information about product features, delivery availability, and after-sales service. They get around-the-clock access to information via automated call centers, and those who want human interaction can talk with live respondents or log on to chat rooms. Many companies have invited "the virtual customer" into their service systems by building customer-communications relationships. The online travel agency Expedia.com responds to your personalized profile with a welcome e-mail letter, presents you with a tailor-made Web page the next time you sign on, offers chat rooms in which you can compare notes with other customers, and notifies you of upcoming special travel opportunities.[9]

Focus on Service Quality Considerations Consumers use different criteria to judge services and goods. Service managers must understand that quality of work and quality of service are not necessarily synonymous. For example, although your car may have been flawlessly repaired, you might feel dissatisfied with the service if you were forced to pick it up a day later than promised.

OPERATIONS PLANNING

Now that we've contrasted goods and services we can return to a more general consideration of production encompassing both goods and services. Like all good managers, we start with planning. Managers from many departments contribute to the firm's decisions about operations management. As Figure 7.4 shows, however, no matter how many decision makers are involved, the process can be described as a series of logical steps. The success of any firm depends on the final result of this logical sequence of decisions.

The overall business plan and forecasts developed by a company's top executives guide operations planning. The business plan outlines the firm's goals and objectives, including the specific goods and services that it will offer in the upcoming years. In this section, we survey the development of the main parts of operations planning. We discuss the key planning activities that fall into one of five major categories: *capacity, location, layout, quality*, and *methods planning*.

Capacity Planning

capacity
Amount of a product that a company can produce under normal working conditions

The amount of a product that a company can produce under normal working conditions is its **capacity**. The capacity of a goods or service firm depends on how many people it employs and the number and size of its facilities. Long-range planning must take into account both current and future capacity.[10]

Capacity Planning for Producing Goods Capacity planning for goods means ensuring that a manufacturing firm's capacity slightly exceeds the normal demand for its product. To see why this policy is best, consider the alternatives. If capacity is too

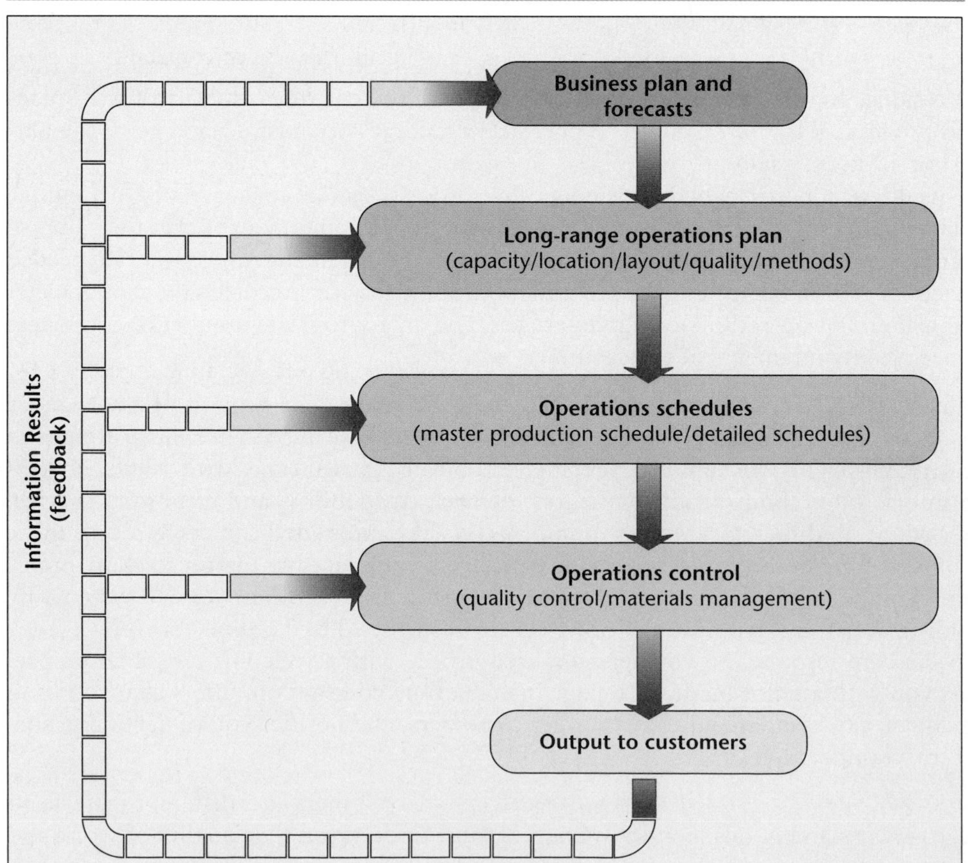

Figure 7.4
Operations Planning and Control

small to meet demand, the company must turn away customers—a situation that not only cuts into profits but also alienates both customers and salespeople. If capacity greatly exceeds demand, then the firm is wasting money by maintaining a plant that is too large, by keeping excess machinery on-line, or by employing too many workers.

The stakes are high in the company's capacity decisions: While expanding fast enough to meet future demand and to protect market share from competitors, it must also weigh the increased costs of expanding. One reason that Intel Corp. <www.intel.com> enjoys more than 70-percent market share in the worldwide semiconductor business is the $11 billion it invested in capacity expansion between 1991 and 1995 (including $1.8 billion for its plant in Rio Rancho, New Mexico) and the additional $625 million to buy Digital Equipment's Hudson, Massachusetts, semiconductor plant in 1998. Will demand for semiconductors continue to grow even further? Was the industry's 2000–2001 downturn just a temporary setback? With so much invested thus far, Intel must decide whether the risks of additional capacity are worth the potential gains.[11]

Capacity Planning for Producing Services In low-contact processes, maintaining inventory lets managers set capacity at the level of *average demand.* The JCPenney <www.jcpenney.com> catalog sales warehouse may hire enough order fillers to handle 1,000 orders each day. When daily orders exceed this average demand, some orders are placed in inventory—set aside in a "to be done" file—to be processed on a day when fewer than 1,000 orders are received.

In high-contact processes, managers must plan capacity to meet *peak demand.* A supermarket, for instance, has far more cash registers than it needs on an average day, but on a Saturday morning or during the three days before Thanksgiving, all registers will be running full speed.

Location Planning

Because the location of a factory, office, or store affects its production costs and flexibility, sound location planning is crucial. Depending on the site of its facility, a company may be capable of producing a low-cost product or may find itself at an extreme cost disadvantage relative to its competitors.[12]

Location Planning for Producing Goods Managers in goods-producing operations must consider many factors in location planning. Their location decisions are influenced by proximity to raw materials and markets, availability of labor, energy and transportation costs, local and state regulations and taxes, and community living conditions.

In 2000, General Motors <www.gm.com> launched its $554 million "Blue Macaw" car project in Brazil's southern-most state of Rio Grande do Sol. Working together, GM do Brazil and its suppliers created a new arrangement to increase assembly productivity and competitiveness. This agile, highly efficient assembly plant relies on outside producers to supply large components such as fully assembled dashboards, stamped hoods, and other body parts. GM gains production efficiencies because each supplier specializes in making just one major component. To resupply the GM assembly plant quickly and to reduce transportation costs, 16 suppliers have located their factories onsite, where they share a large floor space. They reduce needless inventory by delivering customized modules in just-in-time sequence to the nearby final assembly line.[13]

Location Planning for Producing Services In planning low-contact services, companies have some options: Services can be located near resource supplies, labor, or transportation outlets. The typical Wal-Mart distribution center is located near the hundreds of Wal-Mart stores it supplies, not the companies that supply the distribution center. Distribution managers regard Wal-Mart stores as their customers. To better serve them, distribution centers are located so that truckloads of merchandise flow quickly to the stores.

On the other hand, high-contact services are more restricted. They must locate near the customers who are a part of the system. Accordingly, fast-food restaurants such as Taco Bell, McDonald's, and Burger King have begun moving into nontraditional locations with high traffic—dormitories, hospital cafeterias, and shopping malls. They can also be found in Wal-Mart outlets and Meijer Supermarkets that draw large crowds. Similarly, some McDonald's are located on interstate highway rest stops, and Domino's Pizza and KFC restaurants can be found on military bases.

Layout Planning

Once a site has been selected, managers must decide on plant layout. Layout of machinery, equipment, and supplies determines whether a company can respond quickly and efficiently to customer requests for more and different products or finds itself unable to match competitors' production speed or convenience of service.[14]

Layout Planning for Producing Goods In facilities that produce goods, layout must be planned for three different types of space:

productive facility
Workstation or equipment for transforming raw materials

- **Productive facilities:** workstations and equipment for transforming raw materials, for example
- *Nonproductive facilities*: storage and maintenance areas
- *Support facilities*: offices, restrooms, parking lots, cafeterias, and so forth

In this section, we focus on productive facilities. Alternatives include *process, product*, and *cellular layouts*.

process layout
Spatial arrangement of production activities that groups equipment and people according to function

product layout
Spatial arrangement of production activities designed to move resources through a smooth, fixed sequence of steps

assembly line
Product layout in which a product moves step-by-step through a plant on conveyor belts or other equipment until it is completed

Process Layouts In a **process layout**, which is well suited to job shops specializing in custom work, equipment and people are grouped according to function. In a custom cake bakery, for instance, machines blend batter in an area devoted to mixing, baking occurs in the oven area, and cakes are decorated on tables in a finishing area before boxing. Machine, woodworking, and dry cleaning shops often feature process layouts.

Product Layouts In a **product layout**, equipment and people are set up to produce one type of product in a fixed sequence of steps and are arranged according to its production requirements. Product layouts are efficient for producing large volumes of product quickly and often use **assembly lines:** A partially finished product moves step-by-step through the plant on conveyor belts or other equipment, often in a straight line, until the product is completed. Automobile, food-processing, and television-assembly plants use product layouts.

Product layouts are efficient because the work skill is built into the equipment—simplified work tasks can then use unskilled labor. They tend to be inflexible because, traditionally, they have required a heavy investment in specialized equipment that is hard to rearrange for new applications. In addition, workers are subject to boredom, and when someone is absent or overworked, those farther down the line cannot help out.

cellular layout
Spatial arrangement of production facilities designed to move families of products through similar flow paths

Cellular Layouts Another workplace arrangement for some applications is called the **cellular layout.** Cellular layouts are used when a family of products (a group of similar products) follow a fixed flow path. A clothing manufacturer may establish a cell, or designated area, dedicated to making a family of pockets—pockets for shirts, coats, blouses, trousers, and slacks. Although each type of pocket is unique in shape, size, and style, all go through the same production steps. Within the cell, various types of equipment (for cutting, trimming, and sewing) are arranged close together in the appropriate sequence. All pockets pass stage by stage through the cell from beginning to end in a nearly continuous flow.

Cellular layouts have several advantages. Because similar products require less machine adjustment, equipment setup time in the cell is reduced, as compared with setup times in process layouts. Because flow distances are usually shorter, there is less

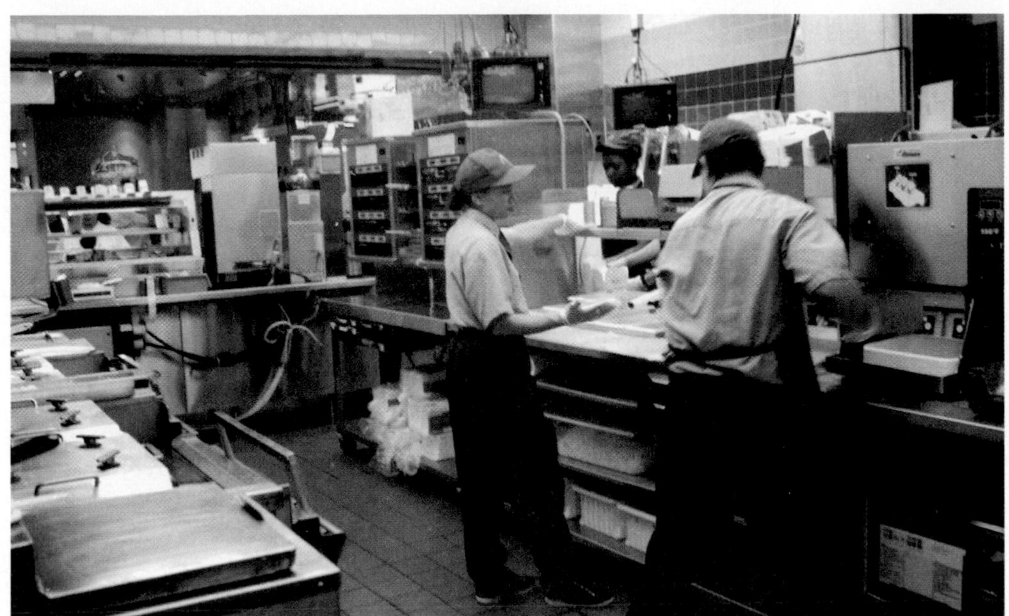

McDonald's <www.mcdonalds.com> claims that a new wrinkle in layout planning ranks with indoor seating and drive-through windows among the most important innovations in the company's first half century. The change is in the kitchen, where such nonmeat ingredients as bread, onions, and lettuce are now spared the wilting heat of holding bins and the microwave. Now only the meat is kept warm, and everything else is added after microwaving. McDonald's expects to save $100 million per year in food costs.

material handling and transit time. Finally, inventories of goods in progress are lower and paperwork is simpler because material flows are more orderly.

Layout Planning for Producing Services Service firms use some of the same layouts as goods-producing firms. In a low-contact system, for instance, the facility should be arranged to enhance the production of the service. A mail-processing facility at UPS or Federal Express, therefore, looks very much like a product layout in a factory: Machines and people are arranged in the order in which they are used in the mass processing of mail. In contrast, Kinko's Copy Centers <www.kinkos.com> use process layouts for different custom jobs: Specific functions such as photocopying, computing, binding, photography, and laminating are performed in specialized areas of the store.

High-contact systems should be arranged to meet customer needs and expectations. Piccadilly Cafeterias <www.piccadilly.com> focuses both layout and services on the groups that constitute its primary market: families and elderly people. As you can see in Figure 7.5, families enter to find an array of high chairs and rolling baby beds that make it convenient to wheel children through the line. Servers are willing to carry trays for elderly people and for those pushing strollers. Note that customers must pass by the whole serving line before making selections. Not only does this layout help them make up their minds; it also tempts them to select more.

Quality Planning

In planning production systems and facilities, managers must keep in mind the firm's quality goals. Thus, any complete operations plan must ensure that products are produced to meet the firm's standards of quality. The American Society for Quality defines

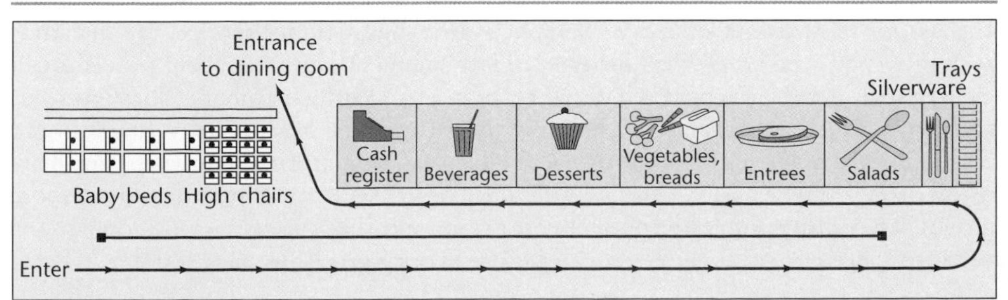

Figure 7.5

Layout of a Typical Piccadilly Cafeteria

quality as "the totality of features and characteristics of a product or service that bear on its ability to satisfy stated or implied needs."

Such features may include a product's reasonable price and its consistent performance in delivering the benefit it promises. Perrigo <www.perrigo.com>, the largest U.S. manufacturer of over-the-counter pharmaceuticals and personal-care products, treats quality planning as a central part of its competitive strategy. Quality is enhanced through the continuous improvement of manufacturing methods, the careful control of every step in production and packaging, and a quality improvement program that empowers employees to reduce waste and increase production capabilities.

Methods Planning

In designing operations systems, managers must clearly identify every production step and the specific methods for performing them. They can then work to reduce waste, inefficiency, and poor performance by examining procedures on a step-by-step basis—an approach sometimes called *methods improvement*.

Methods Improvement in Goods Improvement of production for goods begins when a manager documents the current method. A detailed description, often using a diagram called the *process flowchart*, is usually helpful for organizing and recording all information. The process flowchart identifies the sequence of production activities, movements of materials, and work performed at each stage as the product flows through production. The flow can then be analyzed to identify wasteful activities, sources of delay in production flows, and other inefficiencies. The final step is implementing improvements.

Mercury Marine <www.mercurymarine.com> used methods improvement to streamline the production of stern-drive units for power boats. Examination of the process flow from raw materials to assembly (the final production step) revealed numerous wastes and inefficiencies. Each product passed through 122 steps, traveled nearly 21,000 feet (almost four miles) in the factory, and was handled by 106 people. Analysis revealed that only 27 steps actually added value to the product (for example, drilling, painting). Work methods were revised to eliminate nonproductive activities. Mercury ultimately identified potential savings in labor, inventory, paperwork, and space requirements. Because production lead time was also reduced, customer orders were filled faster.

Methods Improvement in Services In a low-contact process, managers can use methods improvements to speed services ranging from mowing lawns to filling prescriptions and drawing up legal documents. Dell Computer <www.dell.com>, for example, sells its computers online and over the phone, mostly to medium and large companies. Methods analysis eliminates unnecessary steps so that orders can be processed quickly for production and delivery. Dell's emphasis on efficient selling by means of electronic technology speeds its response time to provide customers with a specific value—extremely fast delivery service. The "Wired World" box in this chapter explains how employees in sales operations at another company were not ready for a changeover to newer online sales methods.

Design for Customer Contact in Services In a high-contact service, the demands on system designs are somewhat different. Here managers must develop procedures that clearly spell out the ways in which workers interact with customers. These procedures must cover such activities as exchanging information or money, delivering and receiving materials, and even making physical contact. The next time you visit your dentist's office, for instance, notice the way dental hygienists scrub up and wear disposable gloves. They also scrub after patient contact, even if they intend to work on equipment or do paperwork, and they rescrub before working on the next patient. The high-

IT'S A WIRED WORLD
Selling the Idea of Culture Shift

When a firm decides to trade in its traditional operations for high-tech processes, there's more involved than just financial and technical considerations. Consider a company with successful sales procedures established long before today's electronic sales processes were available. What problems does it face in moving from its established (and highly personalized) sales process into the realm of Internet sales?

That's the issue at Mercury Marine <www.mercurymarine.com>, the market leader in recreational boat engines. With various choices of engine types, horsepower ratings, and "salt water" versus "blue water" options, Mercury sells about 400 different outboard engines and enjoys a 40-percent share of the U.S. market. Sales are even better for inboard engines and stern drives, where Mercury's market share is over 70 percent. Mercury's $1.4 billion annual sales are vital to its parent company, Brunswick Corp. <www.brunswickcorp.com>.

Mercury's markets consist of two kinds of customers:

1. Outboard motors are sold mainly to distributors and boat dealers, who resell them.
2. Inboard engines and stern drives are sold to boatbuilders.

In addition to its current person-to-person selling process, Mercury wants to sell motors to outboard dealers and boatbuilders over the Internet. Mercury wants to use technology as a competitive weapon by making it easier for customers to do business with Mercury. Internet access can increase sales productivity and promote better service quality for customers. So what's the problem? Resistance from the sales department. With person-to-person sales, Mercury's salespeople get to know the customers, and *up-selling* and *cross-selling* are important sales tools that would be threatened by the changeover. Currently, salespeople can explain to customers the advantages of upgrading to a more expensive motor (up-selling), thus increasing Mercury's sales revenues. They can also talk customers into buying some of Mercury's complementary products (cross-selling), such as propellers, inflatable boats, and other accessories, all of which increase sales revenues. Admits Geof Storm, Mercury's chief information officer: "There are a lot of culture changes involved when tightening the supply chain." Although the sales department still prefers the more personal touch, some of its resistance is being overcome—Mercury has decided to proceed with Internet sales of inboard engines to boatbuilders. But until the climate changes further, the decision to sell outboards on the Internet is likely to remain on hold.

contact system in a dental office consists of very strict procedures designed to avoid contact that can transmit disease.

OPERATIONS SCHEDULING

Once plans identify needed resources and how they will be used to reach a firm's goals, managers must develop timetables for acquiring resources for production. This aspect of operations is called *scheduling*.

Scheduling Goods Operations

Scheduling of goods production occurs on different levels within the firm. First, a top-level or **master production schedule** shows which products will be produced, when production will occur, and what resources will be used during specified time periods. Consider the case of Logan Aluminum, Inc. Logan produces coils of aluminum that its main customers, Atlantic Richfield and Alcan Aluminum, use to produce aluminum cans. Logan's master schedule extends out to 60 weeks and shows how many coils will be made each week. For various types of coils, the master schedule specifies how many of each will be produced. "We need this planning and scheduling system," says material manager Candy McKenzie, "to determine how much of what product we can produce each and every month."

master production schedule
Schedule showing which products will be produced, when production will take place, and what resources will be used

This information is not complete. Manufacturing personnel must also know the location of all coils on the plant floor and their various stages of production. Start-up and stop times must be assigned, and employees must be given scheduled work assignments. Short-term detailed schedules fill in these blanks on a daily basis. These schedules use incoming customer orders and information about current machine conditions to update the sizes and variety of coils to make each day.

Scheduling Service Operations

Service scheduling may involve both work and workers. In a low-contact service, work scheduling may be based either on desired completion dates or on the time of order arrivals. For example, several cars may be scheduled for repairs at a local garage. If your car is not scheduled for work until 3:30, it may sit idle for several hours even if it was the first to be dropped off. In such businesses, reservations and appointments systems can help smooth ups and downs in demand.

In contrast, if a hospital emergency room is overloaded, patients cannot be asked to make appointments and come back later. As we have seen, in high-contact services, the customer is part of the system and must be accommodated. Thus, precise scheduling of services may not be possible in high-contact systems.

In scheduling workers, managers must also consider efficiency and costs. McDonald's, for example, guarantees workers that they will be scheduled for at least four hours at a time. To accomplish this goal without having workers idle, McDonald's uses overlapping shifts—the ending hours for some employees overlap the beginning hours for others. The overlap provides maximum coverage during peak periods. McDonald's also trains employees to put off minor tasks, such as refilling napkin dispensers, until slow periods.

OPERATIONS CONTROL

operations control
Process of monitoring production performance by comparing results with plans

follow-up
Production control activity for ensuring that production decisions are being implemented

Once long-range plans have been put into action and schedules have been drawn up, **operations control** requires production managers to monitor production performance by comparing results with detailed plans and schedules. If schedules or quality standards are not met, these managers must take corrective action. **Follow-up**—checking to ensure that production decisions are being implemented—is an essential and ongoing facet of operations control.

Operations control features *materials management* and *production process control*. Both activities ensure that schedules are met and that production goals are fulfilled, both in quantity and in quality. In this section, we consider the nature of materials management and look at some important methods of process control.

Materials Management

materials management
Planning, organizing, and controlling the flow of materials from design through distribution of finished goods

standardization
Use of standard and uniform components in the production process

Both goods-producing and service companies use materials. For many manufacturing firms, material costs account for 50 to 75 percent of total product costs. For goods whose production uses little labor, such as petroleum refining, this percentage is even higher. Thus, companies have good reasons to emphasize materials management.

The process of **materials management** not only controls but also plans and organizes the flow of materials. Even before production starts, materials management focuses on product design by emphasizing materials **standardization**—the use of standard and uniform components rather than new or different components.[15] Law firms maintain standardized forms and data files for estate wills, living wills, trust agreements, and various contracts that can be adjusted easily to meet your individual needs. In manufacturing, Ford's engine plant in Romeo, Michigan, uses common parts for several different kinds of engines rather than unique parts for each. Once components were standardized, the total number of different parts was reduced by 25 percent.

Standardization also simplifies paperwork, reduces storage requirements, and eliminates unnecessary material flows.

Once the product has been designed, materials managers purchase the necessary materials and monitor the production process through the distribution of finished goods. There are five major areas in materials management:

- *Transportation* includes the means of transporting resources to the company and finished goods to buyers.
- *Warehousing* is the storage of both incoming materials for production and finished goods for physical distribution to customers.
- **Purchasing** is the acquisition of all the raw materials and services that a company needs to produce its products; most large firms have purchasing departments to buy proper materials in the amounts needed.
- **Supplier selection** means finding and choosing suppliers of services and materials to buy from. It includes evaluating potential suppliers, negotiating terms of service, and maintaining positive buyer-seller relationships.
- **Inventory control** includes the receiving, storing, handling, and counting of all raw materials, partly finished goods, and finished goods. It ensures that enough materials inventories are available to meet production schedules.

purchasing
Acquisition of the raw materials and services that a firm needs to produce its products

supplier selection
Process of finding and selecting suppliers from whom to buy

inventory control
In materials management, receiving, storing, handling, and counting of all raw materials, partly finished goods, and finished goods

Tools for Operations Process Control

Numerous tools assist managers in controlling operations. Chief among these are *worker training, just-in-time production systems, material requirements planning*, and *quality control*.

Worker Training Customer satisfaction is closely linked to the employees who provide the service. Says Kip Tindell, chief operating officer at the Container Store <www.containerstore.com>, a Dallas-based retailer of storage products: "We are just wild-eyed fanatics when it comes to human resources and training." Naturally, effective customer relationships do not come about by accident: Service workers can be trained and motivated in customer-oriented attitudes and behavior. In service-product design, it is important to remember that most services are delivered by people: That is, service system employees are both the producers of the product and the salespeople.

Human relations skills are vital in anyone who has contact with the public. Tindell, who attributes the Container Store's high profits to effective employees, contends that human resources and training are "the most difficult and the most joyous part of the retail business." Like Tindell, more and more human resource experts now realize that without employees' trained relationship skills for pleasing their clients, businesses such as airlines, employment agencies, and hotels can lose customers to better-prepared competitors.

"Human resources and training are the most difficult and the most joyous part of the retail business."

—Kip Tindell, chief operating officer, Container Store

Just-in-Time Production Systems To minimize manufacturing inventory costs, some managers use **just-in-time (JIT) production systems.** JIT brings together all the needed materials and parts at the precise moment they are required for each production stage, not before. All resources are continuously flowing, from their arrival as raw materials to subassembly, final completion, and shipment of finished products. JIT reduces to practically nothing the number of goods in process (that is, goods not yet finished) and saves money by replacing stop-and-go production with smooth movement. Once smooth movements become the norm, disruptions become more visible and thus get resolved more quickly. Finding and eliminating disruptions by continuous improvement of production is a major objective of JIT.[16]

just-in-time (JIT) production
Production method that brings together all materials and parts needed at each production stage at the precise moment they are required

By implementing JIT, Harley-Davidson <www.harley-davidson.com> reduced its inventories by over 40 percent, improved production work flows, and reduced its costs of warranty work, rework, and scrap by 60 percent. In addition, Harley motorcycles have retained their coveted quality reputation: The annual number of shipments more

When American manufacturers turned to leaner operations to counter foreign competition in the 1990s, they shifted to just-in-time inventory methods and cut workforces—and capacity. Today, economic good times mean accelerated demand and hard-pressed, understaffed assembly lines at many firms. At General Electric's locomotive plant in Erie, Pennsylvania <www.getransporation.com>, *managers have tried to head off problems by relying on certified parts supplied on time and in full quantities only by carefully monitored subcontractors.*

than doubled from 1988 to 1996. With the help of JIT, the company's Plan 2003 calls for another doubling of production for Harley's 100th anniversary in 2003.[17]

material requirements planning (MRP)
Production method in which a bill of materials is used to ensure that the right amounts of materials are delivered to the right place at the right time

bill of materials
Production control tool that specifies the necessary ingredients of a product, the order in which they should be combined, and how many of each are needed to make one batch

quality control
Management of the production process designed to manufacture goods or supply services that meet specific quality standards

Material Requirements Planning Like JIT, **material requirements planning (MRP)** seeks to deliver the right amounts of materials at the right place and the right time for goods production. MRP uses a **bill of materials** that is basically a recipe for the finished product. It specifies the necessary ingredients (raw materials and components), the order in which they should be combined, and the quantity of each ingredient needed to make one batch of the product (for example, 2,000 finished telephones). The recipe is fed into a computer that controls inventory and schedules each stage of production. The result is fewer early arrivals, less frequent stock shortages, and lower storage costs. MRP is most popular among companies whose products require complicated assembly and fabrication activities, such as automobile manufacturers, appliance makers, and furniture companies.

Quality Control Another operation control tool is **quality control**—the management of the operations process in order to manufacture goods or supply services that meet specific quality standards. United Parcel Service, Inc. (UPS) <www.ups.com> delivers 13 million packages every day, and all of them are promised to arrive on strict delivery schedules, mostly for business clients. Quality control is essential because delivery reliability—namely, avoiding late deliveries—is critical for customer satisfaction. UPS tracks the locations, time schedules, and on-time performance for some 500 aircraft and 150,000 vehicles as they carry packages through the delivery system. Its record in quality control is one reason why *Fortune* magazine rates UPS as America's most admired company in the mail, package, and freight-delivery category.[18]

Because quality is an inherent part of operations, we next turn our attention to a more detailed discussion on managing for quality.

QUALITY IMPROVEMENT

It is not enough to measure performance in terms of numbers of items produced. We must also take quality into account. For the past 50 years, the American Society for Quality (ASQ) <www.asq.org> has maintained standards for quality and provided ser-

WEB Connection

Founded in 1946, ASQ helps organizations improve customer satisfaction by identifying and promoting high-quality goods and services. To find out more about ASQ's "Mission, Vision, Objectives," as well as its quality-oriented awards and programs, log on to the organization's Web site.

www.asq.org

vices to assist U.S. industry's quality efforts. The "quality revolution" that continues today ranks among the most profound business developments in the history of modern commerce. U.S. companies today are increasingly customer-driven; all employees, rather than just managers, participate in quality efforts; and quality improvement has become a continuous way of life, rather than an occasional activity.

Managing for Quality

Total quality management (**TQM**) (sometimes called **quality assurance**) includes all of the activities necessary for getting high-quality goods and services into the marketplace. It must consider all parts of the business, including customers, suppliers, and employees. Says John Kay, director of Oxford University's School of Management: "You can't run a successful company if you don't care about customers and employees, or if you are systematically unpleasant to suppliers."[19] To bring the interests of all these stakeholders together, TQM involves planning, organizing, directing, and controlling.

Planning for Quality Planning for quality begins before products are designed or redesigned. To ensure that their needs are not overlooked, customers may be invited to participate in the planning process. In the predesign stage, managers must set goals for both performance quality and quality reliability. **Performance quality** refers to the *performance features* of a product. Maytag <www.maytagcorp.com> gets premium prices for its appliances because it is perceived as offering more advanced features and a longer life than competing brands. Through its advertising, the firm has made sure that consumers recognize the Maytag repairman as the world's loneliest service professional.

Performance quality may be related to a product's **quality reliability**—the *consistency* of product quality from unit to unit.[20] Toyotas, for example, enjoy high quality reliability—the firm <www.toyota.com> has a reputation for producing very few "lemons." For both goods and services, consistency is achieved by controlling the quality of raw materials, encouraging conscientious work, and keeping equipment in good working order.

Some products offer both high quality reliability and high performance quality. Kellogg's <www.kelloggs.com> has a reputation for consistently producing cereals made of high-quality ingredients. To achieve any form of high quality, managers must plan for production processes (equipment, methods, worker skills, and materials) that will result in high-quality products.

Organizing for Quality Perhaps most important to the quality concept is the belief that producing high-quality goods and services requires an effort from all parts of the organization. Having a separate "quality control" department is no longer enough.

total quality management (TQM) (or quality assurance)
The sum of all activities involved in getting high-quality products into the marketplace

"You can't run a successful company if you don't care about customers and employees, or if you are systematically unpleasant to suppliers."

—John Kay, director, Oxford University's School of Management

performance quality
The performance features offered by a product

quality reliability
Consistency of a product's quality from unit to unit

Everyone from the chairperson of the board to the part-time clerk—purchasers, engineers, janitors, marketers, machinists, and other personnel—must work to ensure quality. At Merrill Lynch Credit Corp. <www.ml.com> all employees are responsible for taking initiative and responsibility in responding to customers' credit needs. They are also encouraged to be flexible in helping customers and in the development of their own employee skills. The overall goal is to reduce problems to a minimum by providing credit selectively and skillfully right from the beginning. As a result, the number of loans and market share are increasing while loan delinquencies are decreasing.

Although everyone in a company contributes to product quality, responsibility for specific aspects of total quality management is often assigned to specific departments and jobs. In fact, many companies have quality assurance or quality control departments staffed by quality experts. These people may be called in to help solve quality-related problems in any of the firm's other departments. They keep other departments informed of the latest developments in equipment and methods for maintaining quality. In addition, they monitor all quality control activities to identify areas for improvement.

Directing for Quality Too often, firms fail to take the initiative in making quality happen. Directing for quality means that managers must motivate employees throughout the company to achieve quality goals. Managers companywide must help employees see how they affect quality and how quality affects both their jobs and the company.[21] General Electric past-chairman John F. Welch led the changeover to such a quality program by committing more than $1 billion and three years of effort to converting all of GE's divisions <www.ge.com>. The program, says Welch, "has galvanized our company with an intensity the likes of which I have never seen in my 40 years at GE."[22] Welch's willingness to take drastic action to ensure the program's success was a visible display of a quality emphasis that had the added value of raising the quality consciousness of all GE's employees.

Like Welch, leaders must continually find ways to foster a quality orientation by training employees, encouraging involvement, and tying compensation to work quality. Ideally, if managers succeed, employees will ultimately accept **quality ownership**: the idea that quality belongs to each person who creates it while performing a job.

quality ownership
Principle of total quality management that holds that quality belongs to each person who creates it while performing a job

Controlling for Quality By monitoring its products and services, a company can detect mistakes and make corrections. First, however, managers must establish specific

"That's settled, then. We'll lower our standards to meet the competition."

quality standards and measurements. For example, the control system for a bank's teller services might use the following procedure. Supervisors periodically observe the tellers' work and evaluate it according to a checklist. Specific aspects of each teller's work—appearance, courtesy, efficiency—are recorded. The results are reviewed with employees and either confirm proper performance or indicate changes needed to bring performance up to standards.

Tools for Total Quality Management

Many companies rely on proven tools to manage quality. Often ideas for improving both the product and the production process come from competitive product analysis. Toshiba might take apart a Xerox copier and test each component. Test results will then help managers decide which Toshiba product features are satisfactory, which features should be upgraded, and which operations processes need improvement.

In this section, we will survey four of the most commonly used tools for total quality management: *statistical process control*, *quality/cost studies*, *getting closer to the customer*, and *business process reengineering*.

Statistical Process Control Although every company would like complete uniformity in its output, the goal is unattainable: Every business experiences unit-to-unit variations in products and services. Firms can better control product quality by understanding sources of variation. **Statistical process control** (SPC) refers to methods by which employees can gather data and analyze variations in production activities to determine when adjustments are needed. The Glidden Co. <www.icidecorativepaints.com> uses SPC to control paint-making processes more effectively. Litton Precision Gear uses SPC to ensure the quality of transmission gears installed in military helicopters. At Farbex, a plastics manufacturer, SPC analysts spot-check numerous standards such as the weight of samples of plastic pellets at several different points in the production process. Forty percent of all North American pulp and paper mills use SPC to reduce waste and increase productivity during production.

statistical process control (SPC)
Methods for gathering data to analyze variations in production activities to see when adjustments are needed

control chart
Process control method that plots test sampling results on a diagram to determine when a process is beginning to depart from normal operating conditions

Control Charts One of the most common SPC methods is the use of **control charts**. These charts are helpful for monitoring the production process to prevent it from going

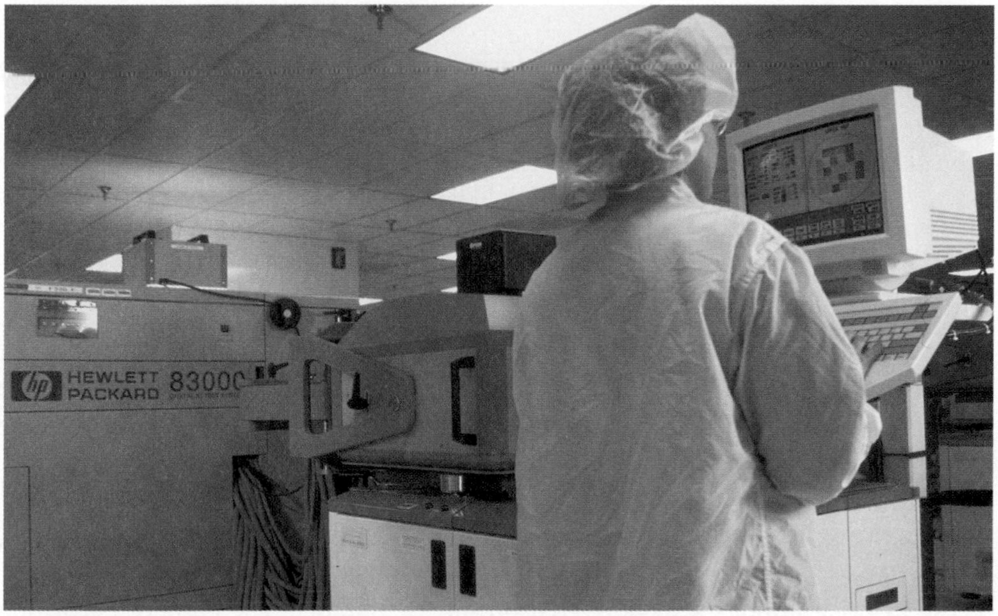

At Hewlett-Packard <www.hp.com>, *testing machines use miniscule probes to ensure that the electronic characteristics of every semiconductor are correct. Such systems are designed to check primarily for so-called "class defects"—problems that can affect a whole parade of products on the assembly line. One bad wafer at the end of the line can represent a waste of $10,000 in costs, and its commercial value is $0.00.*

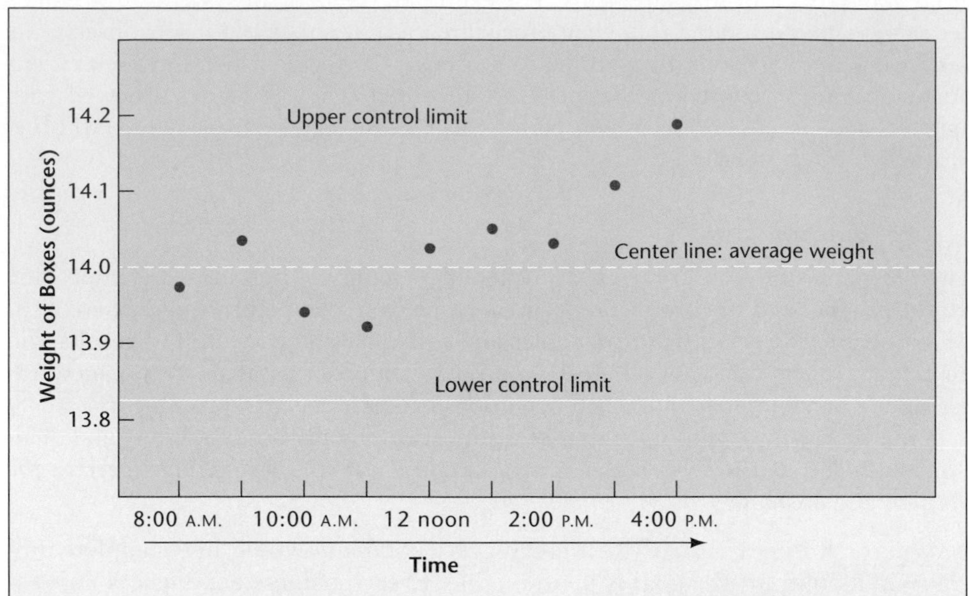

Figure 7.6
Process Control Chart at Honey Nuggets Cereal

awry. To detect the beginning of departures from normal conditions, employees can check production periodically and plot the results on a control chart. Three or four times a day a machine operator at Honey Nuggets might weigh several boxes of cereal together to determine the average weight. That average is then plotted on the control chart.

Figure 7.6 shows the control chart for Machine A at the Honey Nuggets plant. As you can see, the first five points are randomly scattered around the center line, indicating that the machine was operating well from 8 A.M. until noon. However, the points for samples 5 through 9 are all above the center line, indicating that something caused boxes to overfill. The last point falls outside the upper control limit, confirming that the process is out of control. At this point, the machine must be shut down so that an operator can investigate the cause of the problem, be it equipment, people, materials, or work methods. Control is completed when the problem is corrected and the process is restored to normal.

Quality/Cost Studies Statistical process controls help keep operations up to existing capabilities. But in today's competitive environment, firms must consistently raise quality capabilities. However, any improvement in products or production processes means additional costs, whether for new facilities, equipment, training, or other changes. Managers thus face the challenge of identifying the improvements that offer the greatest promise. **Quality/cost studies** are useful because they not only identify a firm's current costs but also reveal areas with the largest cost-savings potential.[23]

quality/cost study
Method of improving quality by identifying current costs and areas with the greatest cost-saving potential

internal failures
Reducible costs incurred during production and before bad products leave a plant

external failures
Reducible costs incurred after defective products have left a plant

Quality costs are associated with making, finding, repairing, or preventing defective goods and services. All of these costs should be analyzed in a quality/cost study. For example, Honey Nuggets must determine its costs for **internal failures**. These are expenses including the costs of overfilling boxes and the costs of sorting out bad boxes incurred during production and before bad products leave the plant. Studies indicate that many U.S. manufacturers incur costs for internal failures up to 50 percent of total costs.

Despite quality control procedures, however, some bad boxes may get out of the factory, reach the customer, and generate complaints from grocers and consumers. These **external failures** are discovered outside the factory. The costs of correcting

WEB Connection

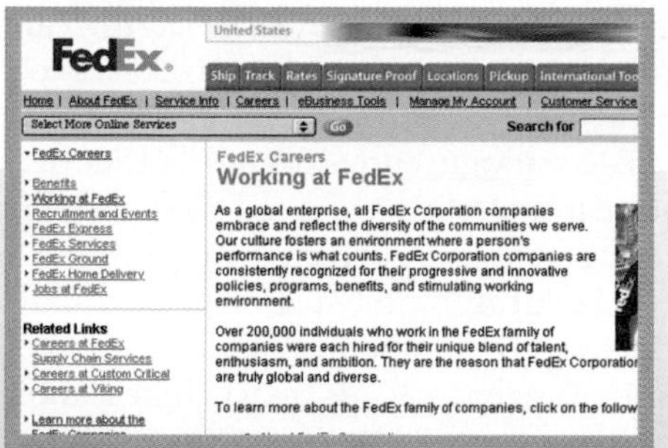

FedEx refers to its policy for satisfying both customers and employees as "PSP," for "People—Service—Profit." The idea is that the customers of a service company deal directly with its employees and that satisfied employees will be more committed to its customers. For other firms, the FedEx PSP is a benchmark in workplace culture. To find out more about PSP, access the FedEx Web site.

www.fedex.com/us/careers/working.html

them (refunds to customers, transportation costs to return bad boxes to the factory, possible lawsuits, and factory recalls) should also be tabulated in the quality/cost study.

The percentage of costs in the different categories varies widely from company to company. Thus, every firm must conduct systematic quality/cost studies to identify the most costly and often the most vital areas of its operations. These areas should be targets for improvement. Too often, however, firms substitute hunches and guesswork for data and analysis.

Getting Closer to the Customer As one advocate of quality improvement has put it, "Customers are an economic asset. They're not on the balance sheet, but they should be." One of the themes of this chapter has been that struggling companies have often lost sight of customers as the driving force for all business activity. Perhaps they waste resources designing products that customers do not want. Sometimes they ignore customer reactions to existing products or fail to keep up with changing consumer tastes. By contrast, the most successful businesses keep close to their customers and know what they want in the products they consume.

> *"Customers are an economic asset. They're not on the balance sheet, but they should be."*
>
> —Claess Fornell, quality improvement advocate

MBNA <www.mbnainternational.com>, a Wilmington, Delaware, credit card company, has learned that speed of service is vital to its customers. Accordingly, MBNA continually monitors its own performance using 15 measures, many of them relating to speed of service. The phone must be picked up within two rings, incoming calls at the switchboard must be transferred within 21 seconds to the correct party, and customer address changes must be processed in one day. By placing the customer at the head of its organizational culture, MBNA is able to retain a remarkable 98 percent of its profitable customers and its common stock price has increased 600 percent in five years.

Process Reengineering Every business consists of processes—activities that it performs regularly and routinely in conducting business. Examples abound: receiving and storing materials from suppliers, billing patients for medical treatment, processing insurance claims for auto accidents, inspecting property for termite infestation, opening checking accounts for new customers, filling customer orders from Internet sales. In each instance, any business process can add value and customer satisfaction if performed well. By the same token, it can disappoint customers and irritate business partners if done improperly.

Business process reengineering focuses on improving both the productivity and quality of business processes—rethinking each step of an organization's operations by

> **business process reengineering**
> Redesigning of business processes to improve quality, performance, and customer service

starting from scratch. *Reengineering* can be defined as the fundamental rethinking and radical redesign of business processes to achieve dramatic improvements in measures of performance, such as cost, quality, service, and speed. The calling-services company GTE <www.gte.com> found that its over-the-phone service was not very user friendly for customers who wanted to make different kinds of transactions, such as getting a service problem corrected or getting a billing question answered. To give customers fast, accurate "one-stop" service, GTE reengineered its call-in–service process by improving equipment, retraining employees, and connecting software into corporate databases that were formerly inaccessible.

The bottom line in every reengineering process is redesigning systems to better serve the needs of customers and to adopt a customer-first value system throughout the company. Redesign is dominated by a desire to improve operations so that goods and services are produced at the lowest possible cost and at the highest value for the customer.

ADDING VALUE THROUGH SUPPLY CHAINS

Managers sometimes forget that a company does not act alone but is instead part of a network of firms that must coordinate their activities. The term *supply chain* refers to the group of companies and stream of activities that operate together to create a product. A **supply chain** for any product is the flow of information, materials, and services that starts with raw-materials suppliers and continues through other stages in the operations process until the product reaches the end customer.[24]

supply chain
Flow of information, materials, and services that starts with raw-materials suppliers and continues through other stages in the operations process until the product reaches the end customer

Figure 7.7 shows the supply chain activities involved in supplying baked goods to consumers. Each stage in the chain adds value for the final customer. Although a typical beginning stage is product design, our bakery example begins with raw materials (grain harvested from the farm). It also includes additional storage and transportation activities, factory operations that bake and wrap the bread, and shipment distributors who supply retailers. Each stage in the supply chain depends on the others for success in getting fresh-baked goods to consumers.

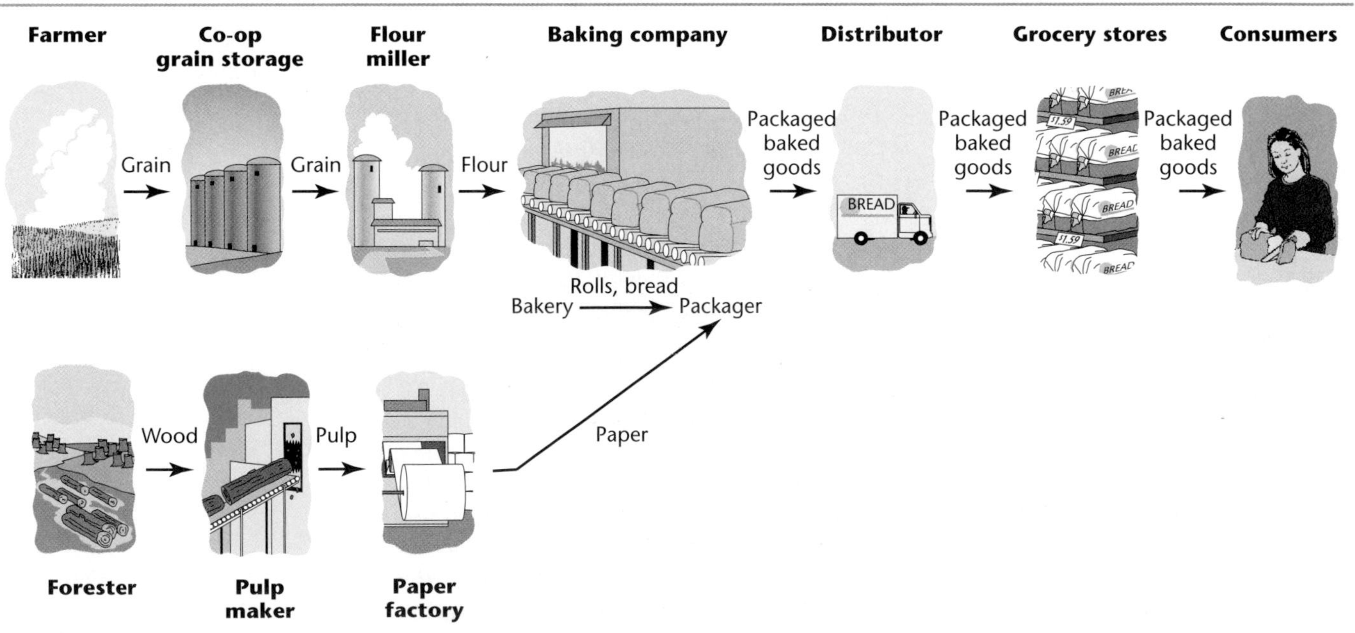

Figure 7.7
Supply Chain for Baked Goods

The Supply Chain Strategy

Traditional strategies assume that companies are managed as individual firms rather than as members of a coordinated supply system. In contrast, supply chain strategy is based on the idea that members of the supply chain, working as a coordinated unit rather than acting alone, will gain competitive advantage. Although each company looks out for its own interests, it works closely with suppliers and customers throughout the chain. The focus is on the entire chain of relationships rather than just on the next stage in the chain.[25]

A traditionally managed bakery, for example, would focus simply on getting production inputs from flour millers and paper suppliers and supplying baked goods to distributors. Unfortunately, this approach limits the chain's performance and doesn't allow for improvements that are possible when activities are more carefully coordinated. Supply chain management can improve performance and, as a result, provide higher-quality bread at lower prices.

Supply Chain Management **Supply chain management** (SCM) looks at the chain as a whole in order to improve the overall flow through the system composed of companies that are working together. Because customers ultimately receive better value, SCM gains competitive advantage for each member of the supply chain.[26]

supply chain management (SCM)
Principle of looking at the supply chain as a whole in order to improve the overall flow through the system

Dell Computer's supply chain, for example, improves performance by sharing information. Dell shares its long-term production plans and up-to-the-minute sales data with suppliers via Internet linkages. Customer orders are automatically translated into updated production schedules on the factory floor. These schedules are used not only by operations managers at Dell but also by such suppliers as Sony, which adjust its own production and shipping activities to better meet Dell's production needs. In turn, suppliers' updated schedules are transmitted to their materials suppliers, and so on, along the supply chain. As Dell's production requirements change, suppliers synchronize their production and shipping schedules so that the right materials and parts are produced efficiently.

The smooth flow of accurate information along the entire chain reduces unwanted inventories, avoids delays, and cuts supply times so that materials move faster to business customers and individual consumers. For both, the efficiency of SCM means faster deliveries and lower costs than they could get if each stage in the supply chain acted only according to its own operations requirements.

Reengineering Supply Chains for Better Results

Process improvements and reengineering are often used for improving supply chains to lower costs, speed up service, or better coordinate flows of information and materials. Consider, for example, some changes in the supply chain for transistor radios. For a long time, radio components manufactured in both the United States and Asia were imported by Li&Fung, the largest export trading company in Hong Kong. After supplying components to a Hong Kong assembly factory, Li&Fung would then ship finished radios to distributors in the United States and Europe. Li&Fung, however, eventually felt pressured by rising wage rates in Hong Kong and feared that increases in assembly expenses would reduce profits and market share. To meet the challenge, Li&Fung changed the supply chain in three ways. First, the company added a new stage into the supply chain: It created little kits—plastic bags filled with all the components needed to make a radio. Second, one of the supply chain links was replaced: The little plastic kits were then shipped to a new assembler in southern China instead of the old factory in Hong Kong. Finally, another stage was added into the chain: After the Chinese supplier had completed the labor-intensive, low-wage assembly process in China, finished radios were shipped back to Hong Kong for final inspection and testing by Li&Fung before being shipped to customers. The result of this change was lower prices for customers and increased business for companies throughout the supply chain.

Continued from page 165

Got a Problem with Your Peripheral? Ask Dudley

Dell's success stems in no small way from its strong customer orientation: Knowing what customers want and helping them feel comfortable while visiting a Web site that has been designed to provide customers with services they really need increase customer loyalty. Thus, Dell's service operations are as important as the computers the company sells. Originally, the Dell site was intended to be a reference for technical information. But by the beginning of 2000, the seven-year-old site had emerged as a multifaceted source of customer assistance. Whether individual consumers or large firms with thousands of computers, customers can ask questions, exchange messages with technicians, and chat online with each other. Each Dell product, for example, has a unique service code. When a customer calls in for help, a customer rep accesses Dell's database for a specific code number. With that number, the rep can look at every detail of the customer's system and provide tailor-made advice.

Another feature is an information database called "Ask Dudley," which customers can search when they have technical questions. "Ask Dudley" was developed after a series of focus group studies on the ways customers actually search the Dell site. Dell found that customers don't mind spending several minutes searching the site as long as they can ask a few questions. They do not, however, like to spend hours searching for something. Dudley allows users to ask natural-language questions and searches through mounds of technical content supplied by experienced Dell technicians (based, in turn, on questions received by the technicians in past years). Finally, Dudley sends a response. Currently, Dudley handles about 150,000 questions a week.

Yet another feature to be found at <www.dell.com> is "Dell Talk"—a chat room in which more than 200,000 registered customers can post messages. Postings are not just social messages. Several Dell owners have banded together as a problem-solving group to help other Dell owners. For customer-to-technician assistance, the site receives more than 25,000 messages each week, to which it sends professional responses via e-mail.

In addition to quality, Dell also wants high productivity in providing customer assistance. Responses for the customer-to-technician service are now answered within 24 hours. The current goal is to get the staff up to the point at which responses are issued within 12 hours. As technology continues to improve, self-help and automated services, such as "Ask Dudley," will further reduce the need for human assistance on tech-support phone calls. Technicians will then be able to spend their time solving the most complex customer problems.

Questions for Discussion

1. Why do you suppose lower inventory levels can cause productivity to increase?
2. Explain how product redesign and product simplification can improve productivity. How might they improve quality at Dell?
3. How do its relationships with suppliers affect Dell's quality?
4. Explain how Dell's service productivity would be affected if "Ask Dudley" were replaced by live customer-response personnel.
5. List some of the methods that Dell uses to "keep close" to its customers.

SUMMARY OF LEARNING OBJECTIVES

1 **Explain the meaning of the term *operations* and describe the four kinds of *utility* that operations processes provide.** *Operations* (or *production*) refers to the process and activities for transforming resources into finished services and goods for customers. Resources include knowledge, physical materials, equipment, and labor that are systematically combined in a production facility to create four kinds of *utility* for customers: *time utility* (which makes products available when customers want them), *place utility* (which makes products available where they are convenient for customers), *possession* or *ownership utility* (by which customers benefit from possessing and using the product), and *form utility* (which results from the creation of the product).

2 **Identify the characteristics that distinguish *service operations* from *goods production* and explain the main objects of the *service focus*.** Although the creation of both goods and services involves resources, transformations, and finished products, service operations differ from goods manufacturing in several important ways. In service production, the raw materials are not, say, glass or steel, but rather people who choose among sellers because they have unsatisfied needs or possessions in need of care or alteration. Therefore, whereas services are typically performed, goods are physically produced. In addition, services are largely *intangible*, more likely than physical goods to be *customized* to meet the purchaser's needs, and more *unstorable* than most products. Service businesses, therefore, focus explicitly on these characteristics of their products. Because services are intangible, for instance, providers work to ensure that customers receive value in the form of pleasure, satisfaction, or a feeling of safety. Often they also focus on both the transformation process and the final product (say, making the loan interview a pleasant experience as well as providing the loan itself). Finally, service providers typically focus on the *customer service link*, often acknowledging the customer as part of the operations process.

3 **Describe the decision areas involved in *operations planning*.** *Operations planning* involves the analysis of five key factors. In *capacity planning*, the firm analyzes how much of a product it must be able to produce. In high-contact services, managers must plan capacity to meet peak demand. Capacity planning for goods means ensuring that manufacturing capacity slightly exceeds the normal demand for its product. *Location planning* for goods and for low-contact services involves analyzing proposed facility sites in terms of proximity to raw materials and markets, availability of labor, and energy and transportation costs. Location planning for high-contact services involves locating the service near customers, who are part of the system. *Layout planning* involves designing a facility so that customer needs are supplied for high-contact services and to enhance production efficiency. Layout alternatives include product, process, and cellular configurations. In *quality planning*, systems are developed to ensure that products meet a firm's quality standards. Finally, in *methods planning*, specific production steps and methods for performing them are identified. In methods planning, *process flowcharts* are helpful for identifying all operations activities and eliminating wasteful steps from production.

4 **Identify some of the key *tools for total quality management*, including strategies for getting closer to the customer.** *Total quality management (TQM)* includes any activity for getting quality products to the marketplace. TQM tools include *statistical process control (SPC)*—methods whereby employees gather data and analyze variations in production activities. The purpose of SPC is to identify needed adjustments. One SPC tool is the *control chart*, which plots the results of sample measurements from operations to identify when a process is beginning to depart from normal conditions, so that corrections can be made. *Quality/cost studies* are useful because improvements in products or production processes always entail additional costs. This method helps identify areas in which quality can be maintained with the greatest cost savings from making, finding, repairing, or preventing defective goods and services. Getting *closer to the customer* involves maintaining contact so that the company knows what customers want in the products they consume. It involves communicating with customers so that products are designed to meet their needs. Finally, *business process reengineering* focuses on improving both the productivity and quality of business practices. It involves the fundamental rethinking and radical redesign of business processes to gain dramatic performance improvement.

5 **Explain how a *supply chain strategy* differs from traditional strategies for coordinating operations among firms.** The *supply chain strategy* is based on

the idea that members of the *supply chain*—the stream of all activities and companies that create a product—can gain competitive advantage by working together as a coordinated system of units. In contrast, traditional strategies assume that companies are managed as individual firms, each acting in its own interest. By managing the chain as a whole—using *supply chain management*—companies can more closely coordinate activities in the chain. By sharing information, overall costs and inventories can be reduced, and deliveries to customers can be faster. Provided with better service and at lower prices, the supply chain's products are preferred, with supply chain members gaining an advantage over competitors whose operations are less effective.

QUESTIONS AND EXERCISES

Questions for Review

1. What are the four different kinds of production-based utility?
2. What are the major differences between goods-production operations and service operations?
3. What are the five major categories of operations planning?
4. What activities are involved in total quality management?
5. What is supply chain management?

Questions for Analysis

6. What are the resources and finished products of the following services?
   - Real estate firm
   - Child care facility
   - Bank
   - City water and electric department
   - Hotel
7. Analyze the layout of a local firm with which you do business—perhaps a restaurant or a supermarket. What problems do you see and what recommendations would you make to management?
8. Select one of your favorite products and identify the supply chain that provides it. How many different firms contribute to the development and delivery of the product from beginning to end?

Application Exercises

9. Interview the owner of a local, small manufacturing firm. Classify the firm's operations processes and then identify its major operations problems. Propose some solutions to these problems.
10. Using a local company as an example, show how you would conduct a quality/cost study. Identify the cost categories and give some examples of the costs in each category. Which categories do you expect to have the highest and lowest costs? Why?

EXPLORING THE WEB

Copying a Formula for Efficient Service

Today, nearly everyone needs documents for communications in both their personal and professional lives. Various documents can sometimes be created in routine formats but, at other times, special formats are more appropriate. Moreover, we typically want to get our documents quickly and conveniently. A number of companies are available to help meet these needs. Perhaps the best known is Kinko's. To learn more about the company's operations, log on to the Kinko's Web site at

<www.kinkos.com/main>

First, browse the home page. Then explore the page entitled *Find Products and Services*. For each product/service category, examine descriptions for various offerings and think about each from the perspective of the operations involved in creating and delivering it. Look also at the page entitled *Kinkos.com*. Again, think about the company's production operations. Finally, consider the following items:

1. Who are Kinko's customers? Are they mostly consumers or other businesses? Explain.
2. Is Kinko's product line primarily goods or services? Explain using examples.
3. Think about location planning for Kinko's facilities. Identify the main factors that must be considered in location planning for Kinko's.
4. From the page entitled *Find Products and Services*, choose any three Kinko's services and for each identify its input resources, describe the steps in its transformation process, and describe the outputs from the transformation.
5. From the page entitled *Find Products and Services*, choose three contrasting products and identify the amount of customer contact in the production system. Is it high contact or low contact? In answering, explain the customer's role in production. How will the amount of customer contact affect the in-store operations?

6. After looking at the page entitled *Kinkos.com*, describe the product(s) it offers. Identify the elements in the conversion process of each product. What role does the customer play in the production system? Is this a high- or low-contact conversion process?
7. Identify the materials requirements for each of three Kinko's services. In what quantities does Kinko's probably purchase those materials? Describe the flow paths of materials through the facility for the three services.
8. Is production scheduling involved in Kinko's operations? Explain.
9. For on-site services, identify key operations items that will determine product quality. In other words, what production activities are most critical for determining quality?

EXERCISING YOUR ETHICS

Calculating the Cost of Conscience

THE SITUATION

Product quality and cost are basic concerns that affect every firm's reputation and profitability as well as the satisfaction of its customers. This exercise will expose you to some ethical considerations that pertain to certain cost and service decisions that must be made by operations managers.

THE DILEMMA

As director of quality for a major appliance manufacturer, Ruth was reporting to the executive committee on the results of a recent program for correcting problems with a newly redesigned rotary compressor that the company recently began putting in its refrigerators. After receiving several customer complaints, the quality lab and the engineering department had determined that some of the new compressor units ran more loudly than expected. Some remedial action was needed. Ruth's department initiated a program for contacting all customers who had purchased refrigerators containing the new compressor. An alternative course of action, however, had been considered: namely, waiting until customers complained and responding to each complaint if and when it occurred. Ruth decided that such an approach was inconsistent with the company's policy of offering the highest quality in the industry; she felt that the firm's reputation called for a proactive, "pro-quality" approach.

Unfortunately, her "quality-and-customers-first" policy was expensive: Local service representatives throughout the United States phoned every customer in each area, made appointments for home visits, and replaced original compressors with a newer model. Because replacement time was only one-half hour, customers were hardly inconvenienced and food stayed refrigerated without interruption. Customer response to the replacement program was overwhelmingly favorable.

Near the end of Ruth's report, an executive vice president was overheard to comment, "Ruth's program has cost this company $400 million in service expenses." Two weeks later Ruth was fired.

QUESTIONS FOR DISCUSSION

1. What are the underlying ethical issues in this situation?
2. What are the respective roles of profits, obligations to customers, and employee considerations for the appliance firm in this situation?
3. Suppose that you were an employee who realized that your company was selling defective appliances. Suppose that the cost of correction might put the firm out of business. What would you do?

BUILDING YOUR BUSINESS SKILLS

The One-on-One Entrepreneur

This exercise enhances the following SCANS workplace competencies: demonstrating basic skills, demonstrating thinking skills, exhibiting interpersonal skills, and working with information.

GOAL

To encourage students to apply the concept of customization to an entrepreneurial idea.

THE SITUATION

Imagine that you are an entrepreneur with the desire to start your own service business. You are intrigued with the idea of creating some kind of customized one-on-one service that would appeal to baby boomers, who traditionally have been pampered, and working women, who have little time to get things done.

METHOD

STEP 1

Get together with three or four other students to brainstorm business ideas that would appeal to harried working people. Among the ideas to consider are the following:

- A concierge service in office buildings that would handle such personal and business services as

arranging children's birthday parties and booking guest speakers for business luncheons.
- A personal image consultation service aimed at helping clients improve their appearance, personal etiquette, and presentation style.
- A mobile pet care network in which veterinarians and personal groomers make house calls.

STEP 2
Choose an idea from these or others you might think of. Then write a memo explaining why you think your idea will succeed. Research may be necessary as you target any of the following:

- A specific demographic group or groups. (Who are your customers and why would they buy your service?)
- The features that make your service attractive to this group.
- The social factors in your local community that would lead to success.

FOLLOW-UP QUESTIONS

1. Why is the customization of and easy access to personal services so attractive in the twenty-first century?
2. As services are personalized, do you think quality will become more or less important? Why?
3. Why does the trend to personalized, one-on-one service present unique opportunities for entrepreneurs?
4. In a personal one-on-one business, how important are the human relations skills of those delivering the service? Can you make an argument that they are more important than the service itself?

CRAFTING YOUR BUSINESS PLAN

Getting on a Par with Customers

THE PURPOSE OF THE ASSIGNMENT

1. To familiarize students with the ways in which operations considerations enter into an example company's business plan, using the planning framework of *Business PlanPro (BPP)* (Version 4.0).
2. To stimulate students' thinking about the application of textbook information on operations management to the preparation of a *BPP* business plan.

FOLLOW-UP ASSIGNMENT

After reading Chapter 7 in the textbook, open the BPP *software and look around for information about the plans for managing operations as it applies to a sample firm:* Golf Pro Shop *(Golf Master Pro Shops, Inc.). Then respond to the following items:*

1. What type of product—physical good or service—is Golf Master Pro Shops creating in its operations process? Explain. [Sites to see in *BPP* for this item: In the Plan Outline screen, click on each of the following in turn: **1.0 Executive Summary, 1.1 Objectives, 1.2 Mission, 3.2 Competitive Comparison,** and **5.1 Marketing Strategy.**]
2. Describe the characteristics of the transformation (operations) process that produces this company's products. [Sites to see in *BPP* for this item: In the Plan Outline screen, click on **2.0 Company Summary** and **2.2 Start-Up Summary.** After returning to the Plan Outline screen, click on each of the following in turn: **3.2 Competitive Comparison** and **6.1 Organizational Structure.**]
3. How many Golf Master stores are planned for the future? What steps can be taken for quality to ensure that the same consistent services are given to all customers regardless of store location? [Sites to see in *BPP* for this item: In the Plan Outline screen, click on **1.0 Executive Summary.** Then click on each of the following in turn: **1.1 Objectives, 3.1 Product and Service Description, 3.2 Competitive Comparison,** and **6.3 Management Team Gaps.**]

VIDEO EXERCISE

Channeling Resources: Regal Marine

LEARNING OBJECTIVES

The purpose of this video is to help you:

1. Recognize the relationship between supply chain management and quality control.
2. Understand how the purchasing process contributes to supply chain management.
3. Understand some of the ways in which firms can manage relationships with supply chain partners.

BACKGROUND INFORMATION

Regal Marine Industries is a family-owned and-operated manufacturer of luxury performance boats and yachts that employs about 680 people in its Orlando, Florida, headquarters and plant. The award-winning firm competes in a multibillion dollar industry and relies on top-quality suppliers and distributors in 45 different countries. Since the filming of this video episode, the company has achieved ISO 9002 certification.

THE VIDEO

Explaining how the company manages its supply chain to ensure the highest quality at the lowest possible costs, director of materials Marty Clement discusses the link between purchasing, cost control, and parts inventory. Some of the strategies and techniques he specifies include supplier partnerships, continuous improvement (both within the firm and among its suppliers), an industry buying group, and close interaction between suppliers and shop floor employees. With purchasing running at about 60 percent of sales, the firm depends heavily on its suppliers to help it control costs.

QUESTIONS FOR DISCUSSION

1. What role do supplier partnerships play in Regal's quest for quality?
2. Regal's suppliers take parts orders directly from shop floor workers and deliver supplies directly to the same employees within a week. Can you think of any other kinds of organizations in which such close cooperation between front-line employees and corporate suppliers could be achieved? Are there any disadvantages to such a strategy?
3. What is the role of Regal's distributors in its supply chain management strategy?

FOLLOW-UP ASSIGNMENT

Research the International Organization for Standardization, which is the parent organization of the ISO certification. You can start at <http://www.iso.ch/>. Look, for instance, at the pages entitled "About ISO" and "ISO 9000." What are the goals of this organization? How does certification benefit a company? What particular relevance do you think ISO 9000 certification has to manufacturing firms and to their supply chain management strategies?

FOR FURTHER EXPLORATION

Visit Regal Marine's Web site at <http://www.regalboats.com> and look in particular at the online factory tour. How does the firm use its Web site to transform its supply chain strategies into marketing tools? Do you think this is an effective strategy? Note that on-site factory tours are also offered with no appointment necessary. What does this policy suggest about the strength of the firm's supplier partnerships?

Understanding People in Organizations

Part III

CHAPTER 8

Motivating, Satisfying, and Leading Employees

After reading this chapter, you should be able to:

1. Describe the nature and importance of *psychological contracts* in the workplace.
2. Discuss the importance of *job satisfaction* and *employee morale* and summarize their roles in human relations in the workplace.
3. Identify and summarize the most important *theories of employee motivation.*
4. Describe some of the strategies used by organizations to improve *job satisfaction* and *employee motivation.*
5. Discuss different managerial styles of *leadership* and their impact on human relations in the workplace.

A New Deal in the Workplace

Back in the "good old days," businesses and workers operated according to a fairly well-defined and clearly understood set of agreements about what each offered to the other in the employment deal. For their part, businesses provided employees with a comfortable salary and benefit package and a secure job that they could expect to keep as long as they worked hard and stayed out of trouble. Employees, meanwhile, contributed their time, talent, and energy, along with steadfastness. Many people worked for the same company for 30 or 40 years or longer. Losing your job bordered on disgrace and changing jobs to work for a competitor was almost on a par with treason. This relationship was even immortalized in a classic book of the 1950s simply called *The Organization Man*, a phrase that quickly embedded itself in the vernacular of popular culture.

Over the last decade or so, all this has changed radically. Most experts agree that the revolution in employment relationships started in the late 1980s, when major corporations all across the United States laid off longtime and dedicated employees by the thousands. For their part, workers contributed to the trend by embracing a philosophy that extolled job-hopping as the best way to get ahead. As a consequence of these trends, the old employment contract has fundamentally changed in business after business.

Consider the case of BMC Software <www.bmc.com>, a Houston-based high-tech company with annual revenues of about $1.2 billion. BMC is a fast-growing enterprise with about 4,500 employees, many of them just recently out of school. BMC employees routinely work 10- to 12-hour days—most work several nights a week, and many report that vacations just never seem to happen. "This place isn't for wimps,"

"*This place isn't for wimps.*"

—BMC Software employee

reports one employee. Surprisingly, however, BMC is ranked number 56 on *Fortune*'s list of the "100 Best Companies to Work For."

Why the apparent contradiction? Maybe it has something to do with BMC's lavish benefits package. The list seems to go on forever—hammocks stretched between trees in a beautifully landscaped office park, an on-site gym, a putting green, a basketball court, a horseshoe pit, and a beach volleyball court. An herb garden to supply the kitchen with fresh ingredients for each day's free gourmet lunch. Free snack areas with big-screen televisions, comfortable seating areas, and free sodas, coffee, tea, and popcorn. On-site massage therapy. A bank, a sundries store, a dry cleaner, a hair salon, and a nail salon. A piano player greeting workers each morning on the company Steinway. Says 30-year-old Christine Choi: "You never have to leave the place."

BMC employees also make above-average salaries, and most have generous stock options or stock-purchase plans. They also describe their work as fun and their employer as the next best thing to a member of the family. Have "the good old days" returned? Quite the contrary. BMC still has a problem keeping its best employees (there's a 14-percent turnover per year) and makes it clear to people that although they enjoy job security right now, there's no guarantee about the future. Instead of resurrecting bygone ways of doing things, BMC reflects a "new deal" between organizations and their employees.

Our opening story continues on page 215

The foundation of good **human relations**—the interactions between employers and employees and their attitudes toward one another—is a satisfied and motivated workforce.[1] But satisfaction and motivation usually are based on what some people call the "psychological contract" that exists between organizations and employees. Thus, we begin our discussion by examining the nature and meaning of *psychological contracts.*

human relations
Interactions between employers and employees and their attitudes toward one another

psychological contract
Set of expectations held by an employee concerning what he or she will contribute to an organization (referred to as *contributions*) and what the organization will in return provide the employee (referred to as *inducements*)

PSYCHOLOGICAL CONTRACTS IN ORGANIZATIONS

Whenever we buy a car or sell a house, both buyer and seller sign a contract that specifies the terms of the agreement—who pays what to whom, when it's paid, and so forth. In some ways, a psychological contract resembles a legal contract. On the whole, however, it's less formal and less rigidly defined. A **psychological contract** is the set of expectations held by employees concerning what they will contribute to an organization (referred to as *contributions*) and what the organization will provide the employees (referred to as *inducements*) in return.[2]

BMC Software's Christine Choi contributes her education, skills, effort, time, and energy. In return for these contributions, BMC provides inducements for her to remain with the firm. As we saw in our opening story, BMC's inducement package includes a good place to work, lavish benefits, and a nice salary. Both BMC and Choi seem to be satisfied with the relationship and are thus likely to maintain it, at least for the time being.

In other situations, however, things might not work out as well. If either party perceives an inequity in the contract, that party may seek a change. The employee, for example, might ask for a pay raise, promotion, or a bigger office. Also, the employee might put forth less effort or look for a better job elsewhere. The organization can also initiate change by training workers to improve their skills, transferring them to new jobs, or terminating them.

All organizations face the basic challenge of managing psychological contracts. They want value from their employees, and they must give employees the right inducements. Valuable but underpaid employees may perform below their capabilities or leave for better jobs. Conversely, overpaying employees who contribute little incurs unnecessary costs.

If psychological contracts are created, maintained, and managed effectively, the result is likely to be workers who are satisfied and motivated. On the other hand, poorly managed psychological contracts may result in dissatisfied, unmotivated workers. Although most people have a general idea of what job satisfaction is, both job satisfaction and high morale can be elusive in the workplace. Because they are critical to an organization's success, we now turn our attention to discussing their importance.

THE IMPORTANCE OF SATISFACTION AND MORALE

job satisfaction
Degree of enjoyment that people derive from performing their jobs

morale
Overall attitude that employees have toward their workplace

Broadly speaking, **job satisfaction** is the degree of enjoyment that people derive from performing their jobs. If people enjoy their work, they are relatively satisfied; if they do not enjoy their work, they are relatively dissatisfied. In turn, satisfied employees are likely to have high **morale**—the overall attitude that employees have toward their workplace. Morale reflects the degree to which they perceive that their needs are being met by their jobs. It is determined by a variety of factors, including job satisfaction and satisfaction with such things as pay, benefits, coworkers, and promotion opportunities.[3]

Companies can improve morale and job satisfaction in a variety of ways. Some large firms, for example, have instituted companywide programs designed specifically to address employees' needs. The numerous benefits provided by BMC Software clearly fit into this category. Forty-six of *Fortune*'s "100 Best Companies to Work For" offer take-home meals for employees who don't have time to cook. Another 26 provide personal concierge services to help harried employees with everything from buying birthday gifts and organizing social events to planning vacations and maintaining cars.[4] Managers at Hyatt Hotels <www.hyatt.com> report that conducting frequent surveys of employee attitudes, soliciting employee input, and—most important—acting

When Curtis Barthold needed 7 months to stay at home and care for a terminally ill wife and 2 small children, he was able to make the necessary arrangements with his employer, investment broker Charles Schwab & Co. <www.schwab.com>*. As a member of Schwab's Life-Threatening Illness program, Barthold was able to take a 2-month sabbatical and use 5 months of unused sick and vacation days donated by co-workers. The program obviously promotes loyalty among Schwab employees, 90 percent of whom say that they can count on co-workers for help in time of need.*

on that input give the company an edge in recruiting and retaining productive workers. Managers of smaller businesses realize that the personal touch can reap big benefits in employee morale. For example, First Tennessee <www.ftb.com>, a midsize regional bank, believes that work and family are so closely related that family considerations should enter into job design. Thus, it offers such benefits as on-site child care.

When workers are satisfied and morale is high, the organization benefits in many ways. Compared with dissatisfied workers, for example, satisfied employees are more committed and loyal. Such employees are more likely to work hard and to make useful contributions. In addition, they tend to have fewer grievances and engage in fewer negative behaviors (complaining, deliberately slowing their work pace, and so forth) than dissatisfied counterparts. Finally, satisfied workers tend not only to come to work every day but also to remain with the organization. By promoting satisfaction and morale, then, management is working to ensure more efficient operations.

WEB Connection

According to Kip Tindell, CEO and president of The Container Store, "A funny thing happens when you take the time to educate your employees, pay them well, and treat them as equals. You end up with extremely motivated and enthusiastic people."

The Container Store, the nation's leading retailer of storage and organization products, was selected by *Fortune* magazine as the "Best Company to Work For in America" two years in a row. In addition to paying its employees 50 to 100 percent higher than industry average, the company provides all first-year, full-time employees with more than 235 hours of formal training.

www.containerstore.com

turnover
Annual percentage of an organization's workforce who leave and must be replaced

Conversely, the costs of dissatisfaction and poor morale are high.[5] Dissatisfied workers are far more likely to be absent for minor illnesses, personal reasons, or a general disinclination to go to work. Low morale may also result in high **turnover**—the percentage of an organization's workforce who leave and must be replaced. High levels of turnover have many negative consequences including the disruption of production schedules, high retraining costs, and decreased productivity. On the other hand, a moderate level of turnover may be beneficial: Organizations can eliminate the jobs of low-performing workers and/or bring in new ideas and fresh talent.

Recent Trends in Managing Satisfaction and Morale

Achieving high levels of job satisfaction and morale seems like a reasonable organizational goal, especially given their potential impact on organizational performance. From the late 1980s through the mid-1990s, many major companies went through periods of massive layoffs and cutbacks. AT&T <www.att.com>, for example, eliminated 40,000 jobs. Although this case is extreme, such firms as Nabisco <www.nabisco.com>, Apple Computer <www.apple.com>, ConAgra <www.conagra.com>, ExxonMobil <www.exxonmobil.com>, and Delta Airlines <www.delta-air.com> also cut thousands of jobs. Even in more recent—and prosperous—times, Chubb Corp. <www.chubb.com>, Eastman Kodak <www.kodak.com>, and Entergy Corp. <www.entergy.com> have cut jobs. Not surprisingly, then, satisfaction and morale plummeted in many companies. Workers feared for their job security, and even those who kept their jobs were unhappy about their less fortunate colleagues and friends.

In the late 1990s, however, things changed dramatically. A booming economy and the creation of thousands of new jobs led to low unemployment in most industries and regions. As a result, companies suddenly found themselves having to work harder not only to retain current employees who were being courted by other employers, but also to offer creative incentives to secure new employees, many of whom had multiple job opportunities to consider.

In the process, many leading firms came up with innovative benefits and "perks" designed to keep employees happy, boost satisfaction, and enhance morale. Figure 8.1 shows some recent trends in the area of benefits. In 1994, for example, no major

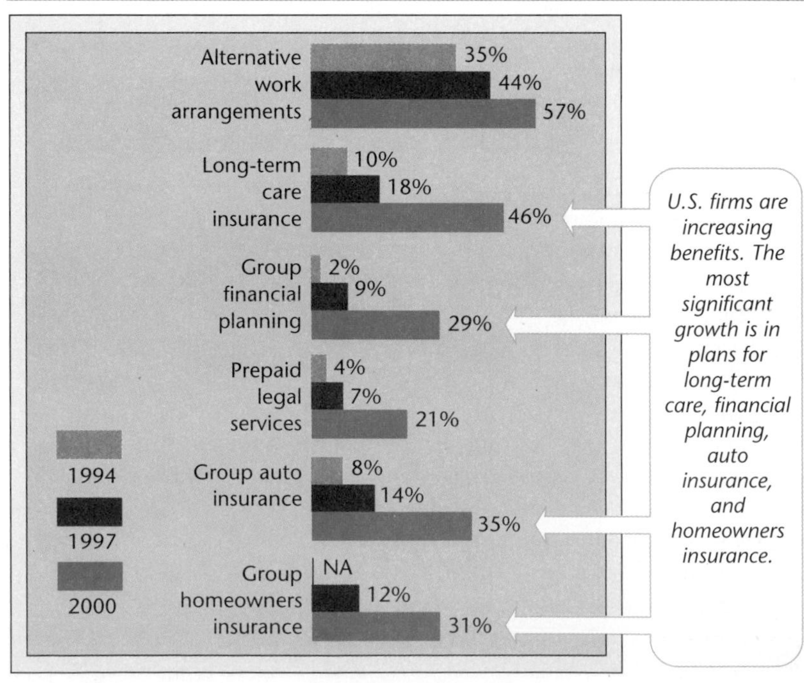

Figure 8.1
Expansion of Benefits

employer reported offering employees group homeowners insurance. By 1997, 12 percent had such plans; and by 2000, about one-third were offering this benefit. Virtually all of this expansion in benefits and perks results from the desire of businesses to make themselves more attractive workplaces by maintaining job satisfaction and employee morale.[6]

In 2001, however, things took another reversal. Many large firms either downsized again or else simply stopped hiring. For example, Compaq Computer eliminated 4,000 jobs, while Hewlett-Packard cut 2,500. As a result, the expansion of new benefits also slowed and many employers were once again in the driver's seat.[7]

MOTIVATION IN THE WORKPLACE

Although job satisfaction and morale are important, employee motivation is even more critical to a firm's success. As we saw in Chapter 5, **motivation** is one part of the managerial function of directing. Broadly defined, motivation is the set of forces that cause people to behave in certain ways. One worker may be motivated to work hard to produce as much as possible, whereas another may be motivated to do just enough to survive. Managers must understand these differences in behavior and the reasons for them.

motivation
The set of forces that cause people to behave in certain ways

Over the years, a steady progression of theories and studies has attempted to address these issues. In this section, we survey the major studies and theories of employee motivation. In particular, we focus on three approaches to human relations in the workplace that reflect a basic chronology of thinking in the area: *classical theory* and *scientific management*, *behavior theory*, and *contemporary motivational theories*.[8]

Classical Theory

According to the so-called **classical theory of motivation**, workers are motivated solely by money. In his seminal book, *The Principles of Scientific Management*, industrial engineer Frederick Taylor (1911) proposed a way for both companies and workers to benefit from this widely accepted view of life in the workplace. If workers are motivated by money, Taylor reasoned, then paying them more should prompt them to produce more. Meanwhile, the firm that analyzed jobs and found better ways to perform them would be able to produce goods more cheaply, make higher profits, and thus pay and motivate workers better than its competitors.

classical theory of motivation
Theory holding that workers are motivated solely by money

Taylor's approach is known as *scientific management*. His ideas captured the imagination of many managers in the early twentieth century. Soon plants across the United States were hiring experts to perform *time and motion studies*: Industrial engineering techniques were applied to each facet of a job in order to determine how to perform it most efficiently. These studies were the first scientific attempts to break down jobs into easily repeated components and to devise more efficient tools and machines for performing them.

Behavior Theory: The Hawthorne Studies

In 1925, a group of Harvard researchers began a study at the Hawthorne Works of Western Electric outside Chicago. With an eye to increasing productivity, they wanted to examine the relationship between changes in the physical environment and worker output.

The results of the experiment were unexpected, even confusing. For example, increased lighting levels improved productivity. For some reason, however, so did lower lighting levels. Moreover, against all expectations, increased pay *failed* to increase productivity. Gradually, the researchers pieced together the puzzle. The explanation lay in the workers' response to the attention that they were receiving. The researchers concluded that productivity rose in response to almost any management action that workers interpreted as special attention. This finding, known widely today as the **Hawthorne effect**, had a major influence on human relations theory, although in many cases it amounted simply to convincing managers that they should pay more attention to employees.

Hawthorne effect
Tendency for productivity to increase when workers believe they are receiving special attention from management

Table 8.1
Theory X and Theory Y

Theory X	Theory Y
People are lazy.	People are energetic.
People lack ambition and dislike responsibility.	People are ambitious and seek responsibility.
People are self-centered.	People can be selfless.
People resist change.	People want to contribute to business growth and change.
People are gullible and not very bright.	People are intelligent.

Contemporary Motivational Theories

Following the Hawthorne studies, managers and researchers alike focused more attention on the importance of good human relations in motivating employee performance. Stressing the factors that cause, focus, and sustain workers' behavior, most motivation theorists are concerned with the ways in which management thinks about and treats employees. The major motivation theories include the *human resources model*, the *hierarchy of needs model*, *two-factor theory*, *expectancy theory*, and *equity theory*.

Human Resources Model: Theories X and Y In an important study, behavioral scientist Douglas McGregor concluded that managers had radically different beliefs about how best to use the human resources employed by a firm. He classified these beliefs into sets of assumptions that he labeled "Theory X" and "Theory Y." The basic differences between these two theories are highlighted in Table 8.1.

Theory X
Theory of motivation holding that people are naturally irresponsible and uncooperative

Theory Y
Theory of motivation holding that people are naturally responsible, growth oriented, self-motivated, and interested in being productive

hierarchy of human needs model
Theory of motivation describing five levels of human needs and arguing that basic needs must be fulfilled before people work to satisfy higher-level needs

Managers who subscribe to **Theory X** tend to believe that people are naturally lazy and uncooperative and must therefore be either punished or rewarded to be made productive. Managers who are inclined to accept **Theory Y** tend to believe that people are naturally energetic, growth oriented, self-motivated, and interested in being productive.

McGregor generally favored Theory Y beliefs. Thus, he argued that Theory Y managers are more likely to have satisfied and motivated employees. Of course, Theory X and Y distinctions are somewhat simplistic and offer little concrete basis for action. Their value lies primarily in their ability to highlight and classify the behavior of managers in light of their attitudes toward employees.

Maslow's Hierarchy of Needs Model Psychologist Abraham Maslow's **hierarchy of human needs model** proposed that people have several different needs that they attempt to satisfy in their work. He classified these needs into five basic types and suggested that they be arranged in the hierarchy of importance as shown in Figure 8.2. According to Maslow, needs are hierarchical because lower-level needs must be met before a person will try to satisfy higher-level needs.

Once a set of needs has been satisfied, it ceases to motivate behavior. This is the sense in which the hierarchical nature of lower- and higher-level needs affects employee motivation and satisfaction. For example, if you feel secure in your job, a new pension plan will probably be less important to you than the chance to make new friends and join an informal network among your coworkers.

If, however, a lower-level need suddenly becomes unfulfilled, most people immediately refocus on that lower level. Suppose, for example, that you are seeking to meet your self-esteem needs by working as a divisional manager at a major company. If you learn that your division and, consequently, your job may be eliminated, you might very well find the promise of job security at a new firm as motivating as a promotion once would have been at your old company.

Maslow's theory recognizes that because different people have different needs, they are motivated by different things. Unfortunately, it provides few specific guidelines for action in the workplace. Furthermore, research has found that the hierarchy varies widely, not only for different people but across different cultures.

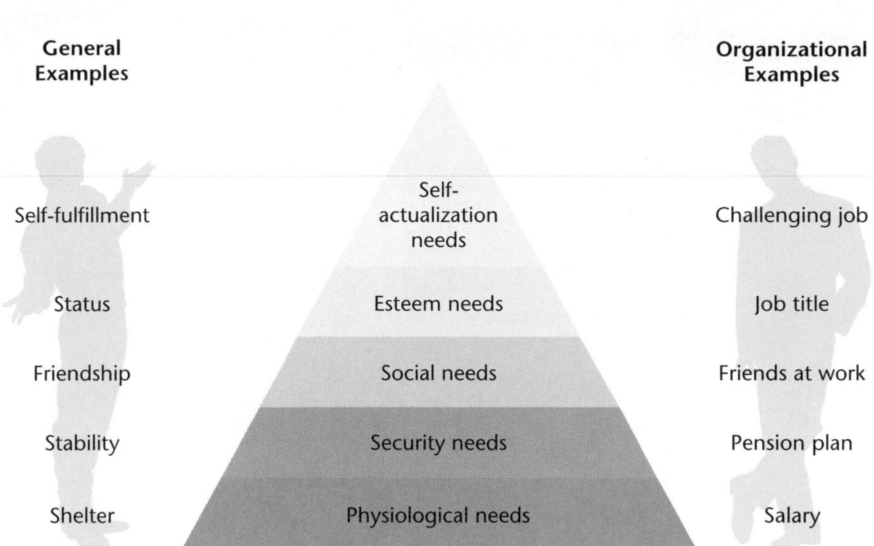

Figure 8.2
Maslow's Hierarchy of Needs

Two-Factor Theory After studying a group of accountants and engineers, psychologist Frederick Herzberg concluded that job satisfaction and dissatisfaction depend on two factors: *hygiene factors*, such as working conditions, and *motivation factors*, such as recognition for a job well done.

According to the **two-factor theory**, hygiene factors affect motivation and satisfaction only if they are absent or fail to meet expectations. For example, workers will be dissatisfied if they believe that they have poor working conditions. If working conditions are improved, however, they will not necessarily become satisfied; they will simply not be dissatisfied. If workers receive no recognition for successful work, they may be neither dissatisfied nor satisfied. If recognition is provided, they will likely become more satisfied.

two-factor theory
Theory of motivation holding that job satisfaction depends on two types of factors, hygiene and motivation

Figure 8.3 illustrates the two-factor theory. Note that motivation factors lie along a continuum from *satisfaction* to *no satisfaction*. Hygiene factors, in contrast, are likely to produce feelings that lie on a continuum from *dissatisfaction* to *no dissatisfaction*. Whereas motivation factors are directly related to the work that employees actually perform, hygiene factors refer to the environment in which they perform it.

This theory thus suggests that managers should follow a two-step approach to enhancing motivation. First, they must ensure that hygiene factors—working conditions, clearly stated policies—are acceptable. This practice will result in an absence of dissatisfaction. Then they must offer motivation factors—recognition, added responsibility—as means of improving satisfaction and motivation.

Research suggests that although two-factor theory works in some professional settings, it is less effective in clerical and manufacturing settings. (Herzberg's research was limited to accountants and engineers.) In addition, one person's hygiene factor may be another person's motivation factor. For example, if money represents nothing more than pay for time worked, it may be a hygiene factor for one person. For another person, however, money may be a motivation factor because it represents recognition and achievement.

Expectancy Theory The **expectancy theory** suggests that people are motivated to work toward rewards that they want and that they believe they have a reasonable chance—or expectancy—of obtaining. A reward that seems out of reach is likely to be undesirable even if it is intrinsically positive. Figure 8.4 illustrates expectancy theory in terms of issues that are likely to be considered by an individual employee. Consider the case of an assistant department manager who learns that her firm needs to replace a retiring division manager two levels above her in the organization. Even though she wants the job, she does not apply because she doubts that she will be selected. In this case, she raises the *performance–reward issue*: For some reason, she believes that her

expectancy theory
Theory of motivation holding that people are motivated to work toward rewards that they want and that they believe they have a reasonable chance of obtaining

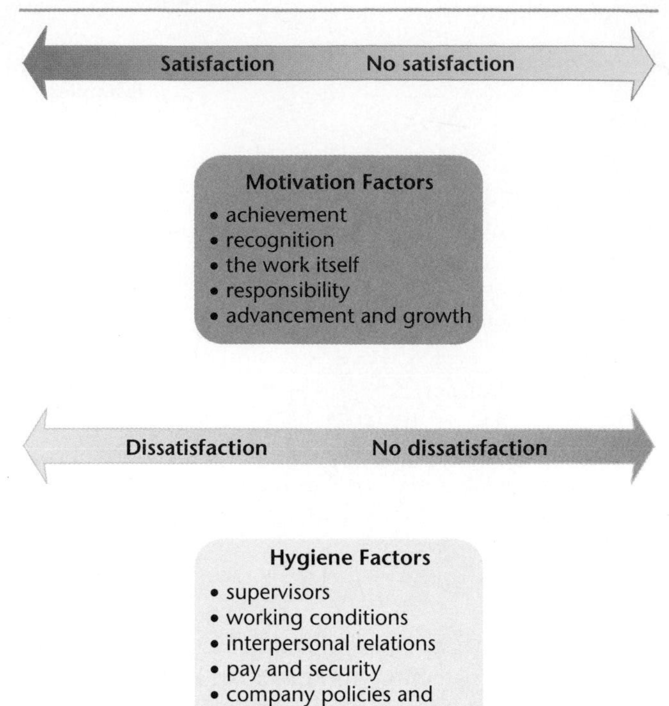

Figure 8.3
Two-Factor Theory of Motivation

performance will not get her the position. Note that she may think that her performance merits the new job but that performance alone will not be enough; perhaps she expects the reward to go to someone with more seniority.

Assume that our employee also learns that the firm is looking for a production manager on a later shift. She thinks that she could get this job but does not apply because she does not want to change shifts. In this instance, she raises the *rewards–personal goals issue*. Finally, she learns of an opening one level higher—department manager—in her own division. She may well apply for this job because she both wants it and thinks that she has a good chance of getting it. In this case, her consideration of all the issues has led to an expectancy that she can reach a given goal.

Expectancy theory helps explain why some people do not work as hard as they can when their salaries are based purely on seniority. Paying employees the same whether they work very hard or just hard enough to get by removes the financial incentive for them to work harder. In other words, they ask themselves, "If I work harder, will I get a pay raise?" and conclude that the answer is no. Similarly, if hard work will result in one or more undesirable outcomes—say, a transfer to another location or a promotion to a job that requires unpleasant travel—employees will not be motivated to work hard. The "Wired World" box in this chapter examines ways in which the expectancy theory of motivation has been instrumental at a dot-com business called TixToGo.

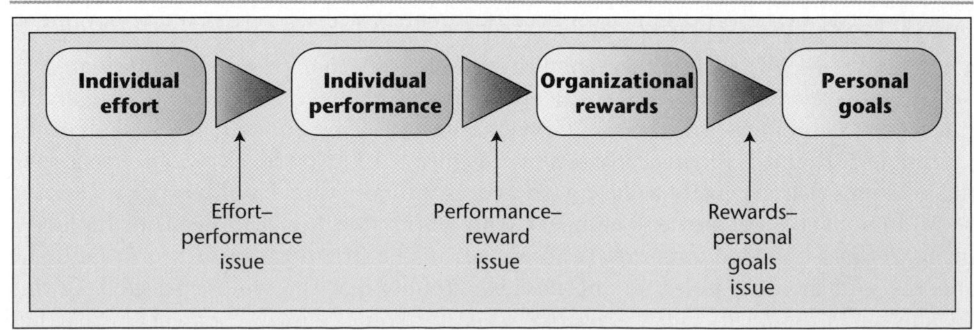

Figure 8.4
Expectancy Theory Model

IT'S A WIRED WORLD

The Future of Compensation?

What would it take to get someone to work for free? Let's rephrase the question in more realistic terms: What would it take to get someone to work for no income today but with the potential for a big payoff in the future? That's the question that a Silicon Valley start-up company recently asked. The answers that it got may be surprising. The company found that the right people would actually be quite enthusiastic about this prospect—as long as the potential rewards were substantial and the probability of getting them within reason.

The company in question is TixToGo <www.tixtogo.com> (now known as Acteva <www.acteva.com>) which sells events and activities, such as tours and programs, for other vendors. The firm was actually a fledgling Internet site when its founder approached Lu Cordova, head of a consulting company and acting director of another Internet start-up firm, with an offer to become CEO. He wanted Cordova to run the firm while he devoted more time to looking for new funding. The only problem was that TixToGo only had $12,000 in the bank and, with four other full-time employees, had no money to pay Cordova. Although she was intrigued with the firm's prospects, Cordova wasn't excited about working for free. So, she devised her own compensation plan, which revolved around the promise that she would be given an attractive salary retroactive to her start date, payable in cash or equity, if the firm was successful in obtaining new funding.

Now, just because Cordova was willing to buy into this plan, it did not follow that anyone else at TixToGo was interested. The skeptics were quickly proven wrong, however, when Cordova was able to attract six full-time employees, two part-timers, and eight outside consultants and contractors—all for deferred pay. Moreover, each individual was given the option of taking his or her deferred pay in cash or stock. Actually, however, "deferred pay" might have been a misnomer. After all, if TixToGo never gets the funding it needs, no one, starting with Cordova, will ever be paid a cent, deferred or otherwise.

Why would someone accept this deal? One major reason is the potential payoff. Many of the new TixToGo employees have taken their future compensation in stock. The number of shares received by each is determined by dividing the dollar amount of the employee's salary by the per-share valuation used in determining the venture capitalists' stake ($11 per share). As a result, an individual could end up with several thousand shares of stock. If the firm then subsequently goes public, a truly big payoff would be in the offing.

Outside consultants and contractors also bought in. They took part of their fees in cash, generally just enough to cover costs, and the rest in stock based on the same per-share valuation estimate offered to employees. One contractor, for example, put together a television ad for TixToGo. The normal fee would have been $250,000. In this instance, however, the contractor took $70,000 in cash and $20,000 in stock. Like employees, contractors stand to make a bundle if the stock price takes off.

At this point, we are left with one significant question: How realistic is it for employees and contractors to expect a big payday in the future? Given the recent spate of successful high-technology public offerings and the initial interest shown by investors, TixToGo appears to have a promising future. One investor, for instance, wrote Cordova a check for $50,000 on the basis of its compensation system alone—without even seeing a business plan. Because TixToGo also attracted the attention of several other big-time investment groups, the prospects for success seem to be quite promising.

Equity Theory The **equity theory** focuses on social comparisons—people evaluating their treatment by the organization relative to the treatment of others. This approach holds that people begin by analyzing *inputs* (what they contribute to their jobs in terms of time, effort, education, experience) relative to *outputs* (what they receive in return—salary, benefits, recognition, security). The result is a ratio of contribution to return. Then they compare their own ratios with those of other employees: They ask whether their ratios are *equal to*, *greater than*, or *less than* those of the people with whom they are comparing themselves. Depending on their assessments, they experience feelings of equity or inequity. Figure 8.5 illustrates the three possible results of such an assessment.

equity theory
Theory of motivation holding that people evaluate their treatment by employers relative to the treatment of others

For example, suppose a new college graduate gets a starting job at a large manufacturing firm. His starting salary is $35,000 a year, he gets a compact company car, and he

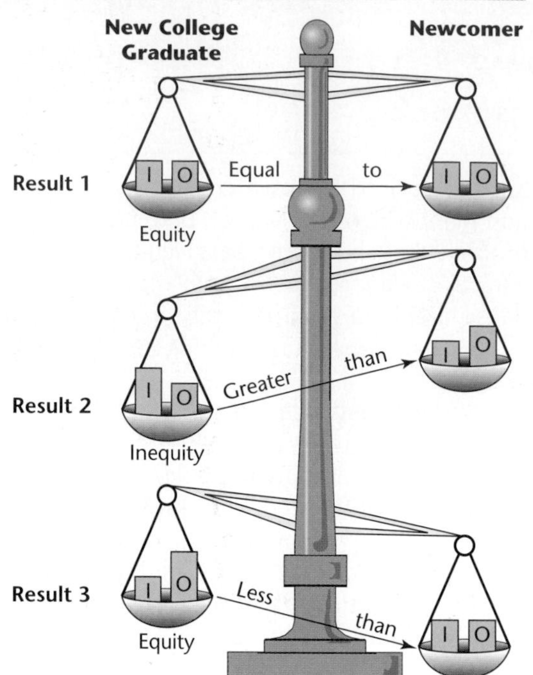

Figure 8.5
Equity Theory: Possible Assessments

shares an office with another new employee. If he later learns that another new employee has received the same salary, car, and office arrangement, he will feel equitably treated. If the other newcomer, however, has received $40,000, a full-size company car, and a private office, he may feel inequitably treated (see Result 2 in Figure 8.5).

Note, however, that for an individual to feel equitably treated, the two ratios do not have to be the same, only *fair*. Assume, for instance, that our new employee has a bachelor's degree and two years of work experience. Perhaps he learns subsequently that the other new employee has an advanced degree and 10 years of experience. After first feeling inequity, the new employee may conclude that the person with whom he compared himself is actually contributing more to the organization. That employee is equitably entitled, therefore, to receive more in return (Result 3).

When people feel they are being inequitably treated, they may do various things to restore fairness. For example, they may ask for raises, reduce their efforts, work shorter hours, or just complain to their bosses. They may also rationalize ("Management succumbed to pressure to promote a woman/Asian American"), find different people with whom to compare themselves, or leave their jobs.

Virtually perfect examples of equity theory at work can be found in professional sports. Each year, for example, rookies, sometimes fresh out of college, are often signed to lucrative contracts. No sooner than the ink is dry do veteran players start grumbling about raises or revised contracts.

STRATEGIES FOR ENHANCING JOB SATISFACTION AND MORALE

Deciding what provides job satisfaction and motivates workers is only one part of human resource management. The other part is applying that knowledge. Experts have suggested—and many companies have implemented—a range of programs designed to make jobs more interesting and rewarding and to make the work environment more pleasant.

Reinforcement/Behavior Modification Theory

Many companies try to control, and even alter or modify, workers' behavior through systematic rewards and punishments for specific behaviors. In other words, they first try to define the specific behaviors that they want their employees to exhibit (working

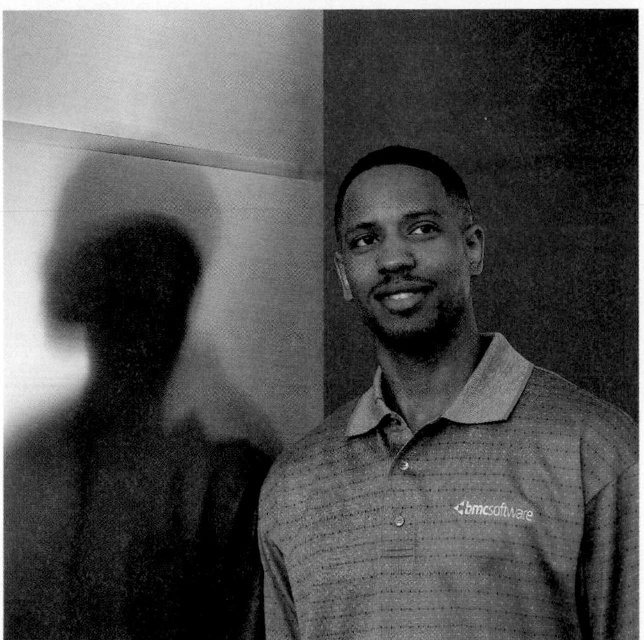

Brian Stevens started out at BMC Software Inc. as a temporary worker in a non-tech job but took advantage of company-sponsored free software training. After some hard work, he was rewarded with positive reinforcement: He was promoted to a permanent position in quality assurance. Regarded as one of America's 100 Best Companies to work for, Houston-based BMC <www.bmc.com> *also offers top salaries, good benefits, and attractive on-site amenities (such as a full-service gym, two restaurants, and a car wash).*

hard, being courteous to customers, stressing quality) and the specific behaviors they want to eliminate (wasting time, being rude to customers, ignoring quality). Then they try to shape employee behavior by linking reinforcement with desired behaviors and punishment with undesired behaviors.

reinforcement
Theory that behavior can be encouraged or discouraged by means of rewards or punishments

Reinforcement is used when a company pays *piecework* rewards—when workers are paid for each piece or product completed. In reinforcement strategies, rewards refer to all the positive things that people get for working (pay, praise, promotions, job security, and so forth). When rewards are tied directly to performance, they serve as *positive reinforcement.* For example, paying large cash bonuses to salespeople who exceed quotas prompts them to work even harder during the next selling period. John Deere <www.deere.com> has recently adopted a new reward system based on positive reinforcement. The firm now gives pay increases when its workers complete college courses and demonstrate mastery of new job skills.

Punishment is designed to change behavior by presenting people with unpleasant consequences if they fail to change in desirable ways. Employees who are repeatedly late to work, for example, may be suspended or have their pay docked. Similarly, when the National Football League or Major League Baseball fines or suspends players found guilty of substance abuse, the organization is seeking to change players' behavior.

Extensive rewards work best when people are learning new behavior, new skills, or new jobs. As workers become more adept, rewards can be used less frequently. Because such actions contribute to positive employer–employee relationships, managers generally prefer giving rewards and placing positive value on performance. Conversely, most managers dislike doling out punishment, partly because workers may respond with anger, resentment, hostility, or even retaliation. To reduce this risk, many managers couple punishment with rewards for good behavior.

Management by Objectives

management by objectives (MBO)
Set of procedures involving both managers and subordinates in setting goals and evaluating progress

Management by objectives (MBO) is a system of collaborative goal setting that extends from the top of an organization to the bottom. As a technique for managing the planning process, MBO is concerned mainly with helping managers implement and carry out their plans. As you can see from Figure 8.6, MBO involves managers and subordinates in setting goals and evaluating progress. Once the program is set up, the first step is establishing overall organizational goals. It is also these goals that will ultimately be evaluated to determine the success of the program. At the same time,

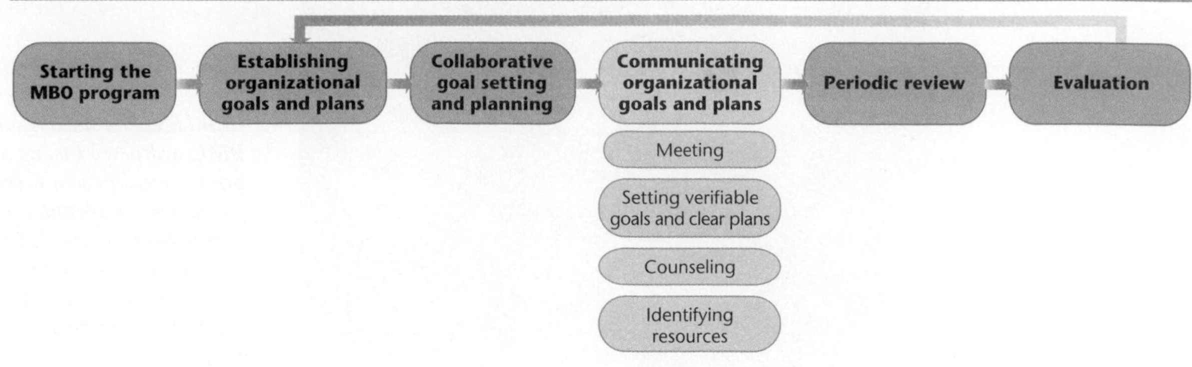

Figure 8.6
Management by Objectives

however, collaborative activity—communicating, meeting, controlling, and so forth—is the key to MBO. Therefore, it can also serve as a program for improving satisfaction and motivation.

According to many experts, motivational impact is the biggest advantage of MBO. When employees sit down with managers to set upcoming goals, they learn more about companywide objectives, come to feel that they are an important part of a team, and see how they can improve companywide performance by reaching their own goals. If an MBO system is used properly, employees should leave meetings not only with an understanding of the value of their contributions, but also with fair rewards for their performances. They should also accept and be committed to the moderately difficult and specific goals they have helped set for themselves.

Participative Management and Empowerment

participative management and empowerment Method of increasing job satisfaction by giving employees a voice in the management of their jobs and the company

In **participative management and empowerment**, employees are given a voice in how they do their jobs and how the company is managed—they become *empowered* to take greater responsibility for their own performance. Not surprisingly, participation and empowerment make employees feel more committed to organizational goals they have helped to shape.

Participation and empowerment can be used in large firms or small firms, both with managers and operating employees. For example, managers at General Electric <www.ge.com> who once needed higher-level approval for any expenditure over $5,000 have the autonomy to make their own expense decisions up to as much as $50,000. At Adam Hat Co., a small firm that makes men's dress, military, and cowboy hats, workers who previously had to report all product defects to supervisors now have the freedom to correct problems themselves or even return products to the workers who are responsible for them.

Team Management At one level, employees may be given decision-making responsibility for certain narrow activities, such as when to take lunch breaks or how to divide assignments with coworkers. On a broader level, employees are also being consulted on such decisions as production scheduling, work procedures and schedules, and the hiring of new employees. Among the many organizations actively using teams today are Texas Instruments <www.ti.com>, Lucent Technologies <www.lucent.com>, Ford Motor Co. <www.ford.com>, and Shell Oil <www.countonshell.com>.

Although some employees thrive in participative programs, such programs are not for everyone. Many people will be frustrated by responsibilities they are not equipped to handle. Moreover, participative programs may actually result in dissatisfied employees if workers see the invitation to participate as more symbolic than substantive. One key, say most experts, is to invite participation only to the extent that employees want to have input and only if participation will have real value for an organization.

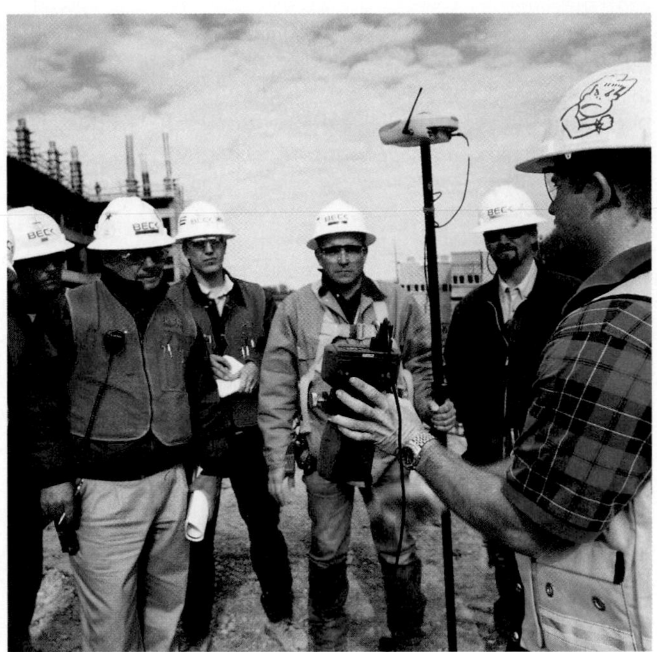

When employees of the Beck Group <www.beckgroup.com>, a Dallas-based construction and real estate development company, go to work on a project, they are given a great deal of autonomy in applying their decision-making and other skills. The approach works because the company both mandates and encourages continuous training, reimbursing workers up to $4,500 a year for higher-education courses. Bonuses are paid out when customers are happy, and apparently the job satisfaction of Beck employees translates into customer satisfaction: 80% of the firm's clients are repeats.

Managers, therefore, should remember that teams are not for everyone. Levi Strauss <www.levi.com>, for example, has encountered major problems in its efforts to use teams. Previously, individual workers performed repetitive, highly specialized tasks, such as sewing zippers into jeans, and were paid according to the number of jobs they completed each day. In an attempt to boost productivity, company management reorganized everyone into teams of 10 to 35 workers and assigned tasks to the entire group. Each team member's pay was determined by the team's level of productivity. In practice, however, faster workers became resentful of slower workers because they reduced the group's total output. Slower workers, meanwhile, resented the pressure put on them by faster-working coworkers. As a result, motivation, satisfaction, and morale all dropped, and Levi's eventually abandoned the teamwork plan altogether.[9]

By and large, however, participation and empowerment in general, and team management in particular, continue to be widely used as enhancers of employee motivation and company performance. Although teams are often less effective in traditional and rigidly structured bureaucratic organizations, they often help smaller, more flexible organizations make decisions more quickly and effectively, enhance companywide communication, and encourage organizational members to feel more like a part of an organization. In turn, these attitudes usually lead to higher levels of both employee motivation and job satisfaction.[10]

Job Enrichment and Job Redesign

Whereas MBO programs and empowerment can work in a variety of settings, *job enrichment* and *job redesign programs* are generally used to increase satisfaction in jobs significantly lacking in motivating factors.[11]

job enrichment
Method of increasing job satisfaction by adding one or more motivating factors to job activities

Job Enrichment Programs **Job enrichment** is designed to add one or more motivating factors to job activities. For example, *job rotation programs* expand growth opportunities by rotating employees through various positions in the same firm. Workers gain not only new skills but also broader overviews of their work and their organization. Other programs focus on increasing responsibility or recognition. At Continental Airlines <www.continental.com>, for example, flight attendants now have more control over their own scheduling. The jobs of flight service managers were enriched when they were given more responsibility and authority for assigning tasks to flight crew members.

job redesign
Method of increasing job satisfaction by designing a more satisfactory fit between workers and their jobs

Job Redesign Programs Job redesign acknowledges that different people want different things from their jobs. By restructuring work to achieve a more satisfactory fit between workers and their jobs, **job redesign** can motivate individuals with strong needs for career growth or achievement. Job redesign is usually implemented in one of three ways: through *combining tasks*, *forming natural work groups*, or *establishing client relationships*.

Combining Tasks The job of combining tasks involves enlarging jobs and increasing their variety to make employees feel that their work is more meaningful. In turn, employees become more motivated. For example, the job done by a programmer who maintains computer systems might be redesigned to include some system design and system development work. While developing additional skills, then, the programmer also gets involved in the overall system package.

Forming Natural Work Groups People who do different jobs on the same projects are candidates for natural work groups. These groups are formed to help employees see the place and importance of their jobs in the total structure of the firm. They are valuable to management because the people working on a project are usually the most knowledgeable about it and thus the most capable problem solvers.

Establishing Client Relationships Establishing client relationships means letting employees interact with customers. This approach increases job variety. It gives workers both a greater sense of control and more feedback about performance than they get when their jobs are not highly interactive.

For example, software writers at Microsoft <www.microsoft.com> watch test users work with programs and discuss problems with them directly rather than receive feedback from third-party researchers. In Fargo, North Dakota, Great Plains Software <www.greatplains.com> has employee turnover of less than 7 percent, compared with an industry average of 15 to 20 percent. The company recruits and rewards in large part according to candidates' customer service skills and their experience with customer needs and complaints.

Modified Work Schedules

As another way of increasing job satisfaction, many companies are experimenting with *modified work schedules*—different approaches to working hours and the workweek. The two most common forms of modified scheduling are *work-share programs* and *flextime programs*, including *alternative workplace strategies*.[12]

work sharing (or job sharing)
Method of increasing job satisfaction by allowing two or more people to share a single full-time job

Work-Share Programs At Steelcase Inc. <www.steelcase.com>, the country's largest maker of office furnishings, two very talented women in the marketing division both wanted to work only part-time. The solution: They now share a single full-time job. With each working 2.5 days a week, both got their wish and the job gets done—and done well.[13] In another situation, one person might work mornings and the other afternoons. The practice, known as **work sharing** (or **job sharing**), has "brought sanity back to our lives," according to at least one Steelcase employee.

"Work sharing brought sanity back to our lives."

—Steelcase employee

Job sharing usually benefits both employees and employers. Employees, for instance, tend to appreciate the organization's attention to their personal needs. At the same time, the company can reduce turnover and save on the cost of benefits. On the negative side, job-share employees generally receive fewer benefits than their full-time counterparts and may be the first to be laid off when cutbacks are necessary.

flextime programs
Method of increasing job satisfaction by allowing workers to adjust work schedules on a daily or weekly basis

Flextime Programs and Alternative Workplace Strategies **Flextime programs** allow people to choose their working hours by adjusting a standard work schedule on a daily or weekly basis. Indeed, there was a significant boom in flextime programs in the late 1990s as part of the escalation of employee benefits that we mentioned before.

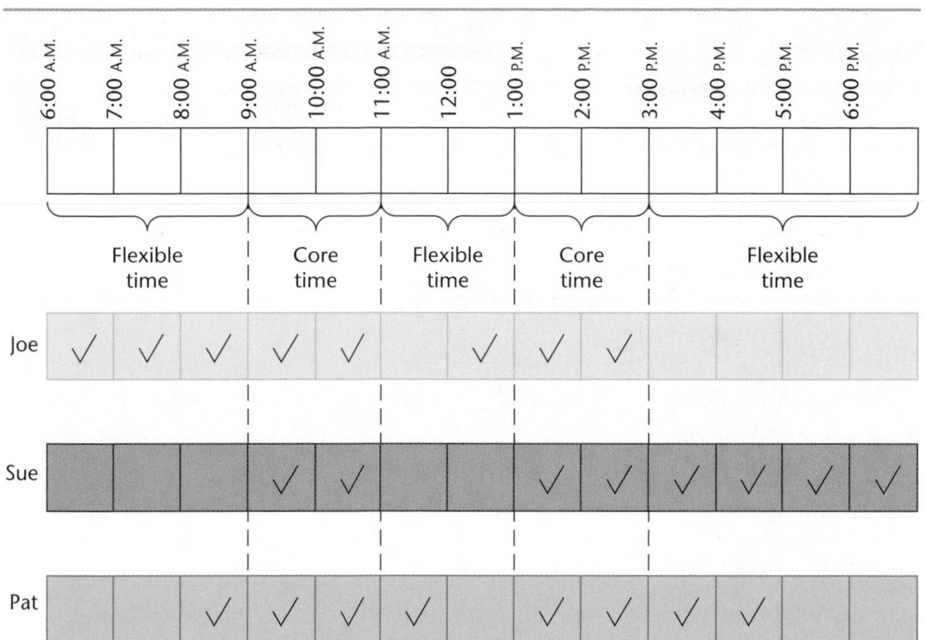

Figure 8.7
Sample Flextime Schedule

There are, of course, limits. The Steelcase program, for instance, requires all employees to work certain core hours. This practice allows everyone to reach coworkers at a specified time of day. Employees can then decide whether to make up the rest of the standard eight-hour day by coming in and leaving early (by working 6:00 A.M. to 2:00 P.M. or 7:00 A.M. to 3:00 P.M.) or late (9:00 A.M. to 5:00 P.M. or 10:00 A.M. to 6:00 P.M.).

Figure 8.7 shows a hypothetical flextime system that could be used by three different people. The office is open from 6:00 A.M. until 7:00 P.M. Core time is 9:00 A.M. to 11:00 A.M. and 1:00 P.M. to 3:00 P.M. Joe, an early riser, comes in at 6:00, takes an hour for lunch between 11:00 and noon, and finishes his day by 3:00. Sue, a working mother, prefers a later day. She comes in at 9:00, takes a long lunch from 11:00 to 1:00, and then works until 7:00. Pat works a more traditional 8-to-5 schedule.

In one variation, companies may also allow employees to choose four, five, or six days on which to work each week. Some, for instance, may choose Monday through Thursday, others Tuesday through Friday. Still others may work Monday–Tuesday and Thursday–Friday and take Wednesday off. By working 10 hours over four workdays, employees still complete 40-hour weeks.

Telecommuting and Virtual Offices Kelly Ramsey-Dolson is an accountant employed by Ernst & Young <www.ey.com>. Because she has a young son, she does not want to be away from home more than she absolutely must. Ramsey-Dolson and the company have worked out an arrangement whereby she works at home two or three days a week and comes into the office the other days. Her home office is outfitted with a PC, modem, and fax machine, and she uses this technology to keep abreast of everything going on at the office.

Ramsey-Dolson is one of a rapidly growing number of U.S. workers who do a significant portion of their work by a relatively new version of flextime known as **telecommuting**—performing some or all of a job away from standard office settings. Among salaried employees, the telecommuter workforce grew by 21.5 percent in 1994, to 7.6 million, and then to 11 million in 1997; the number of telecommuters now exceeds 25 million employees.

telecommuting
Form of flextime that allows people to perform some or all of a job away from standard office settings

The key to telecommuting is technology. The availability of networked computers, fax machines, cellular telephones, and overnight-delivery services makes it possible for many professionals to work at home or while traveling. Cisco Systems

WEB Connection

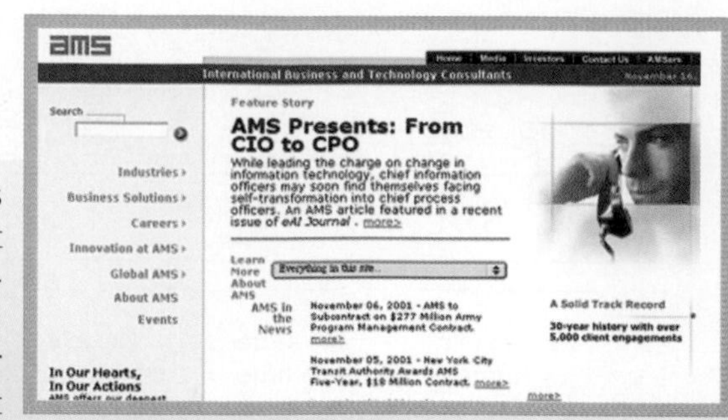

Ninety percent of the employees of American Management Systems, a Virginia-based technology-consulting firm, use flextime; 30 percent telecommute. Other benefits and programs aimed at "balancing work and personal life" include free child care, elder care, and adoption counseling services. To learn more about the company's approach to employee motivation, log on to its Web site.

www.ams.com

"The work environment was designed around the concept that one's best thinking isn't necessarily done at a desk or in an office. Sometimes it's done in a conference room with other people. Other times it's done on a ski slope or driving to a client's office."

—Director of Operations Adelaide Horton, Chiat Day Mojo advertising firm

<www.cisco.com>, the Internet networking giant, is at the forefront of telecommuting arrangements for its workers. The firm estimates that by allowing employees to do some of their work at home, it has boosted productivity by 25 percent, lowered overhead costs by $1 million, and achieved a higher retention rate among key knowledge workers who might have otherwise left for more flexibility elsewhere.[14]

Other companies have experimented with so-called *virtual offices*. They have redesigned conventional office space to accommodate jobs and schedules that are far less dependent on assigned spaces and personal apparatus. At the advertising firm of Chiat Day Mojo <www.chiatday.com> in Venice, California, only about one-third of the salaried workforce is in the office on any given day. The office building features informal work carrels or nooks and open areas available to every employee. "The work environment," explains Director of Operations Adelaide Horton, "was designed around the concept that one's best thinking isn't necessarily done at a desk or in an office. Sometimes it's done in a conference room with other people. Other times it's done on a ski slope or driving to a client's office."

Advantages and Disadvantages of Modified Schedules and Alternative Workplaces Flextime gives employees more freedom in their professional and personal lives. It allows workers to plan around the work schedules of spouses and the school schedules of young children. Studies show that the increased sense of freedom and control reduces stress and thus improves individual productivity.

Companies also benefit in other ways. In urban areas, for example, such programs can reduce traffic congestion and similar problems that contribute to stress and lost work time. Furthermore, employers benefit from higher levels of commitment and job satisfaction. John Hancock Insurance <www.jhancock.com>, Atlantic Richfield <www.arco.com>, and Metropolitan Life <www.metlife.com> are among the major American corporations that have successfully adopted some form of flextime.

Conversely, flextime sometimes complicates coordination because people are working different schedules. In the schedules shown in Figure 8.7, for instance, Sue may need some important information from Joe at 4:30 P.M., but because Joe is working an earlier schedule, he leaves for the day at 3:00. In addition, if workers are paid by the hour, flextime may make it difficult for employers to keep accurate records of when employees are actually working.

As for telecommuting and virtual offices, although they may be the wave of the future, they may not be for everyone. For example, consultant Gil Gordon points out that telecommuters are attracted to the ideas of "not having to shave and put on makeup or go through traffic, and sitting in their blue jeans all day." However, he suggests that would-be telecommuters ask themselves several other questions: "Can I manage deadlines? What will it be like to be away from the social context of the office five

One of the most conspicuous features of the "new company town" is the presence of workplace amenities. At the Kansas City architectural firm of Gould Evans Goodman Associates <www.geaf.com>, pooped employees can escape to one of three "spent tents"—retreats with sleeping bags, pillows, alarm clocks, and soothing music. The principle is to ease overwork by making the workplace—or certain alternative areas of it—as comfortable as home. In theory, such amenities renew the body and spirit so that an employee is more productive during the time he or she spends at a workstation.

days a week? Can I renegotiate the rules of the family, so my spouse doesn't come home every night expecting me to have a four-course meal on the table?" One study has shown that even though telecommuters may be producing results, those with strong advancement ambitions may miss networking and rubbing elbows with management on a day-to-day basis.

Another obstacle to establishing a telecommuting program is convincing management that it can be beneficial for all involved. Telecommuters may have to fight the perception, from both bosses and coworkers, that if they are not being supervised, they are not working. Managers, admits one experienced consultant, "usually have to be dragged kicking and screaming into this. They always ask, 'How can I tell if someone is working when I can't see them?' " By the same token, he adds, "that's based on the erroneous assumption that if you can see them they are working." Most experts agree that reeducation and constant communication are requirements of a successful telecommuting arrangement. Both managers and employees must determine expectations in advance.

"Managers always ask, 'How can I tell if someone is working when I can't see them?' That's based on the erroneous assumption that if you can see them they are working."

—HR consultant on managerial qualms about telecommuting

"Good grief, Bradbury! How long have you been working at home?"

MANAGERIAL STYLES AND LEADERSHIP

In trying to enhance morale, job satisfaction, and motivation, managers can use many different styles of leadership. **Leadership** is the process of motivating others to work to meet specific objectives. Leading is also one of the key aspects of a manager's job and an important component of the directing function.[15]

leadership
Process of motivating others to work to meet specific objectives

Joe Liemandt, for example, dropped out of Stanford in 1990 to start a software company in Austin, Texas. As part of his strategy, he was determined to develop and maintain a workforce of creative people who worked well in teams, adapted to rapid change, and felt comfortable taking risks. A decade later, people with these qualities—now numbering nearly 1,000—have helped build Liemandt's company, Trilogy Software, Inc. <www.trilogy.com>, into a rapidly growing maker of industry-leading software for managing product pricing, sales plans, and commissions.

When Trilogy hires a new group of employees, Liemandt himself oversees their training. He sees himself as the firm's leader and believes that, as such, it is his responsibility to ensure that every employee shares his vision and understands his way of doing business. Training takes several weeks, starting with a series of classes devoted to the technical aspects of Trilogy's products and methods of software development. Then recruits move into areas in which Liemandt truly believes they make a real difference—developing risk-taking skills and the ability to recognize new opportunities.

Recruits are formed into teams, and each team is given three weeks to complete various projects, ranging from the creating of new products to the developing of marketing campaigns for existing products. Teams actually compete with one another and are scored on such criteria as risk and innovation, goal setting, and goal accomplishment. Evaluations are completed by Liemandt, other Trilogy managers, and some of the firm's venture capital backers. Winners get free trips to Las Vegas. Losers go straight to work.

Liemandt's leadership doesn't stop there, even for those who go to Las Vegas, where Liemandt challenges everyone to place a $2,000 bet at the roulette wheel. He argues that $2,000 is a meaningful sum, and one that can cause real pain, but not so much that it will cause financial disaster for anyone. Actually, Liemandt puts up the money, which losers pay back through payroll deductions of $400 over five months. Not everyone, of course, decides to take the chance, but enough do to make the message clear: Liemandt aims to succeed by taking chances, and he expects employees to share the risks. Those who do stand to earn bigger returns on more intrepid investments.[16]

In this section, we begin by describing some of the basic features of and differences in managerial styles and then focus on an approach to managing and leading that, like Joe Liemandt's, understands those jobs as responses to a variety of complex situations.

Managerial Styles

managerial style
Pattern of behavior that a manager exhibits in dealing with subordinates

autocratic style
Managerial style in which managers generally issue orders and expect them to be obeyed without question

democratic style
Managerial style in which managers generally ask for input from subordinates but retain final decision-making power

Early theories of leadership tried to identify specific traits associated with strong leaders. For example, physical appearance, intelligence, and public speaking skills were once thought to be "leadership traits." Indeed, it was once believed that taller people made better leaders than shorter people. The trait approach, however, proved to be a poor predictor of leadership potential. Ultimately, attention shifted from managers' traits to their behaviors, or **managerial styles**—patterns of behavior that a manager exhibits in dealing with subordinates. Managerial styles run the gamut from autocratic to democratic to free rein. Naturally, most managers do not clearly conform to any one style, but these three major types of styles involve very different kinds of responses to human relations problems. Under different circumstances, any given style or combination of styles may prove appropriate.[17]

- Managers who adopt an **autocratic style** generally issue orders and expect them to be obeyed without question. The military commander prefers and usually needs the autocratic style on the battlefield. Because no one else is consulted, the autocratic style allows for rapid decision making. It may, therefore, be useful in situations testing a firm's effectiveness as a time-based competitor.
- Managers who adopt a **democratic style** generally ask for input from subordinates before making decisions but retain final decision-making power. For exam-

ple, the manager of a technical group may ask other group members to interview and offer opinions about job applicants. The manager, however, will ultimately make the hiring decision.

- Managers who adopt a **free-rein style** typically serve as advisers to subordinates who are allowed to make decisions. The chairperson of a volunteer committee to raise funds for a new library may find a free-rein style most effective.

free-rein style
Managerial style in which managers typically serve as advisers to subordinates who are allowed to make decisions

According to many observers, the free-rein style of leadership is currently giving rise to an approach that emphasizes broad-based employee input into decision making and the fostering of workplace environments in which employees increasingly determine what needs to be done and how.

Regardless of theories about the ways in which leaders ought to lead, the relative effectiveness of any leadership style depends largely on the desire of subordinates to share input or to exercise creativity. Whereas some people, for example, are frustrated, others prefer autocratic managers because they do not want a voice in making decisions. The democratic approach, meanwhile, can be disconcerting both to people who want decision-making responsibility and to those who do not. A free-rein style lends itself to employee creativity and thus to creative solutions to pressing problems. This style also appeals to employees who like to plan their own work. Not all subordinates, however, have the necessary background or skills to make creative decisions. Others are not sufficiently self-motivated to work without supervision.

The Contingency Approach to Leadership

Because each managerial style has both strengths and weaknesses, most managers vary their responses to different situations. Flexibility, however, has not always characterized managerial style or responsiveness. For most of the twentieth century, in fact, managers tended to believe that all problems yielded to preconceived, pretested solutions. If raising pay reduced turnover in one plant, for example, it followed that the same tactic would work equally well in another.

More recently, however, managers have begun to adopt a **contingency approach to managerial style**. They have started to view appropriate managerial behavior in any situation as dependent, or contingent, on the elements unique to that situation. This change in outlook has resulted largely from an increasing appreciation of the complexity of managerial problems and solutions. For example, pay raises may reduce turnover when workers have been badly underpaid. The contingency approach, however, recognizes that raises will have little effect when workers feel adequately paid but ill-treated by management. This approach also recommends that training managers in human relations skills may be crucial to solving the problem in the second case.[18]

contingency approach to managerial style
Approach to managerial style holding that the appropriate behavior in any situation is dependent (contingent) on the unique elements of that situation

WEB Connection

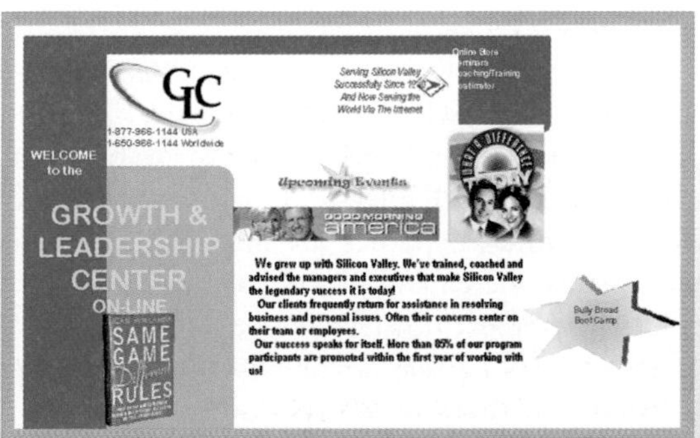

Located in Mountain View, California, the Growth & Leadership Center offers professional and psychological assistance to Silicon Valley executives who are feeling the pressures of increasing workloads and stress levels. Using a variety of techniques, the company helps managers from such companies as Lucent Technologies, Sun Microsystems, Netscape, and Intel develop the patterns of behavior and communication that make them more valuable leaders to their employers.

www.glcweb.com

The contingency approach also acknowledges that people in different cultures behave differently and expect different things from their managers. A certain managerial style, therefore, is more likely to be successful in some countries than in others. Japanese workers, for example, generally expect managers to be highly participative and to give them input in decision making. In contrast, many South American workers actually balk at participation and want take-charge leaders. The basic idea, then, is that managers will be more effective when they adapt their styles to the contingencies of the situations they face.[19]

Motivation and Leadership in the Twenty-First Century

Motivation and leadership remain critically important areas of organizational behavior. As times change, however, so do the ways managers motivate and lead their employees.

Changing Patterns of Motivation From the motivational side, today's employees want rewards that are often quite different from those valued by earlier generations. Money, for example, is no longer the prime motivator for most people. In addition, because businesses today cannot offer the degree of job security that many workers want, motivating employees to strive toward higher levels of performance requires skillful attention from managers.

One recent survey asked workers to identify those things they most wanted at work. Among the things noted were flexible working hours (67%), casual dress (56%), unlimited Internet access (51%), opportunities to telecommute (43%), nap time (28%), massages (25%), day care (24%), espresso machines (23%), and the opportunity to bring a pet to work (11%). In another study focusing on fathers, many men also said they wanted more flexible working hours in order to spend more time with their families. Managers, then, must recognize the fact that today's workers have a complex set of needs and must be motivated in increasingly complicated ways.

Finally, the diversity inherent in today's workforce also makes motivating behavior more complex. The reasons why people work reflect more varying goals than ever before, and the varying lifestyles of diverse workers mean that managers must first pay closer attention to what their employees expect to get for their efforts and then try to link rewards with job performance.[20]

Changing Patterns of Leadership Leadership, too, is taking different directions as we head into the twenty-first century. For one thing, today's leaders are finding it necessary to change their own behavior. As organizations become flatter and workers more empowered, managers naturally find it less acceptable to use the autocratic approach to leadership. Instead, many are becoming more democratic—functioning more as "coaches" than as "bosses." Just as an athletic coach teaches athletes how to play and then steps back to let them take the field, many leaders now try to provide workers with the skills and resources to perform at their best before backing off to let them do their work with less supervision.

Diversity, too, is also affecting leadership processes. In earlier times, most leaders were white males who were somewhat older than the people they supervised—people who were themselves relatively similar to one another. But as organizations become more and more diverse, leaders are also becoming increasingly diverse—women, African Americans, and Hispanics are entering the managerial ranks in ever greater numbers. They are also increasingly likely to be younger than some of the people they are leading. Leaders, therefore, must have greater sensitivity to the values, needs, and motives of a diverse group of people as they examine their own behavior in its relation to other people.

Finally, leaders must also adopt more of a "network" mentality rather than a "hierarchical" one. As long as people worked in the same place at the same time, the organizational hierarchy had a clear vertical chain of command and lines of communication. But now people work in different places and at different times. New forms of organization design may call for one person to be the leader on one project and a team member on another. Thus, people need to get comfortable with leadership based more on expertise than on organizational position and with interaction patterns not tied to specific places or times. The leader of tomorrow, then, will need a different set of skills and a different point of view than did the leader of yesterday.[21]

Continued from page 195

What Did You Expect?

So, how does a hard-charging business that pushes its employees to the limit come to be known as one of the best places to work? At BMC Software, as at many other businesses today, it's mostly a matter of the "new deal" that has been forged between businesses and employees. Gone is the lifetime employment security once offered by businesses. Gone, too, is the steadfast employee loyalty that once kept a worker with a single employer for an entire career. In their places are new bargaining positions for both employer and employee that are fundamental to the new employment contract.

Employees now offer a new set of contributions and have different expectations. They are generally willing to work long, hard hours and put their jobs at or near the top of their priorities. Often they also have cutting-edge skills and a solid understanding of how businesses, markets, and technology fit together. In return, they expect employers to provide an increasingly diverse set of benefits and perks and want to share in the organization's successes.

Business has also learned to expect and offer different things than in the past. They often meet the challenges of a tight labor market by offering lavish signing bonuses for the very best talent, high salaries, stock options, and benefits only dreamed of a few years ago. But they offer little or no job security. Instead, they offer ample opportunity for employees to keep current in their fields and to learn more advanced skills. Thus, while they don't promise job security, they do offer "employability," giving workers the tools to find jobs elsewhere if their current employers can't keep them. In return, they expect—explicitly or implicitly—that employees will devote a large proportion of their waking hours to the company's success.

Questions for Discussion

1. Which sounds better to you personally—the "old deal" or the "new deal"?
2. In what industries, markets, and kinds of businesses is the new deal most likely to exist? In what industries, markets, and kinds of businesses is the old deal most likely to still remain in place?
3. Aside from the factors noted in the case, what other changes may have contributed to this new employment relationship?
4. Under what circumstances might employment relationships change again? Would this change more likely be a reversion to the old relationship or to a new one altogether?
5. What are the most fundamental risks that a business takes in adopting the new employment relationship?
6. What are the most fundamental risks an individual employee takes in adopting the new employment relationship?

SUMMARY OF LEARNING OBJECTIVES

1 **Describe the nature and importance of *psychological contracts* in the workplace.** A *psychological contract* is the set of expectations held by employees concerning what they will contribute to an organization (referred to as *contributions*) and what the organization will in return provide to the employees (referred to as *inducements*). Until the last decade or so, businesses generally offered their employees high levels of job security and employees were very loyal to their employers. More recently, however, new psychological contracts have been created in many sectors. Now organizations offer less security but more benefits. In turn, employees are often willing to work longer hours but also are more willing to leave an employer for a better opportunity elsewhere.

2 **Discuss the importance of *job satisfaction* and *employee morale* and summarize their roles in human relations in the workplace.** Good *human relations*—the interactions between employers and employees and their attitudes toward one another—are important to

business because they lead to high levels of *job satisfaction* (the degree of enjoyment that workers derive from their jobs) and *morale* (workers' overall attitudes toward their workplaces). Satisfied employees generally exhibit lower levels of absenteeism and turnover. They also have fewer grievances and engage in fewer negative behaviors.

3 **Identify and summarize the most important *theories of employee motivation*.** Views of employee motivation have changed dramatically over the years. The *classical theory* holds that people are motivated solely by money. *Scientific management* tried to analyze jobs and increase production by finding better ways to perform tasks. The *Hawthorne studies* were the first to demonstrate the importance of making workers feel that their needs were being considered. The *human resources model* identifies two kinds of managers—*Theory X managers*, who believe that people are inherently uncooperative and must be constantly punished or rewarded, and *Theory Y managers*, who believe that people are naturally responsible and self-motivated to be productive.

Maslow's *hierarchy of needs model* proposes that people have several different needs (ranging from physiological to self-actualization), which they attempt to satisfy in their work. People must fulfill lower-level needs before seeking to fulfill higher-level needs. *Two-factor theory* suggests that if basic hygiene factors are not met, workers will be dissatisfied. Only by increasing more complex motivation factors can companies increase employees' performance.

Expectancy theory holds that people will work hard if they believe that their efforts will lead to desired rewards. *Equity theory* says that motivation depends on the way employees evaluate their treatment by an organization relative to its treatment of other workers.

4 **Describe some of the strategies used by organizations to improve *job satisfaction* and *employee motivation*.** Managers can use several strategies to increase employee satisfaction and motivation. The principle of *reinforcement*, or *behavior modification theory*, holds that reward and punishment can control behavior. *Rewards*, for example, are positive reinforcement when they are tied directly to desired or improved performance. *Punishment* (using unpleasant consequences to change undesirable behavior) is generally less effective.

Management by objectives (a system of collaborative goal setting) and *participative management and empowerment* (techniques for giving employees a voice in management decisions) can improve human relations by making an employee feel like part of a team. *Job enrichment, job redesign*, and *modified work schedules* (including *work-share programs, flextime*, and *alternative workplace strategies*) can enhance job satisfaction by adding motivation factors to jobs in which they are normally lacking.

5 **Discuss different managerial styles of *leadership* and their impact on human relations in the workplace.** Effective *leadership*—the process of motivating others to meet specific objectives—is an important determinant of employee satisfaction and motivation. Generally speaking, managers practice one of three basic managerial styles. *Autocratic managers* generally issue orders that they expect to be obeyed. *Democratic managers* generally seek subordinates' input into decisions. *Free-rein managers* are more likely to advise than to make decisions. The *contingency approach to leadership* views appropriate managerial behavior in any situation as dependent on the elements of that situation. Managers thus need to assess situations carefully, especially to determine the desire of subordinates to share input or exercise creativity. They must also be aware of the changing nature of both motivation and leadership as we move into the twenty-first century.

QUESTIONS AND EXERCISES

Questions for Review

1. Describe the psychological contract you currently have or have had in the past with an employer. If you have never worked, describe the psychological contract that you have with the instructor in this class.
2. Do you think that most people are relatively satisfied or dissatisfied with their work? Why are they mainly satisfied or dissatisfied?
3. Compare and contrast Maslow's hierarchy of needs with the two-factor theory of motivation.
4. How can participative management programs enhance employee satisfaction and motivation?

Questions for Analysis

5. Some evidence suggests that recent college graduates show high levels of job satisfaction. Levels then drop dramatically as they reach their late twenties, only to increase gradually once they get older. What might account for this pattern?
6. As a manager, under what sort of circumstances might you apply each of the theories of motivation discussed in this chapter? Which would be easiest to use? Which would be hardest? Why?

7. Suppose you realize one day that you are dissatisfied with your job. Short of quitting, what might you do to improve your situation?
8. List five U.S. managers who you think would also qualify as great leaders.

Application Exercises

9. At the library, research the manager or owner of a company in the early twentieth century and the manager or owner of a company in the 1990s. Compare and contrast the two in terms of their times, leadership styles, and views of employee motivation.
10. Interview the manager of a local manufacturing company. Identify as many different strategies for enhancing job satisfaction at that company as you can.

EXPLORING THE WEB

The Satisfaction of Surveying

This chapter stresses the fact that employee satisfaction and morale are important to any organization. However, it is also quite difficult for managers to know for sure just how satisfied and motivated their employees actually are. In most cases, managers interested in assessing satisfaction and morale do so with surveys. Employees are asked to respond to various questions about how they feel about their work, and their responses are scored to provide an indication of their satisfaction and morale. To examine such a survey, visit the Web site at:

<www.quicken.com/small_business/cch/tools/?article5satsrv_m>

After you have examined the satisfaction questionnaire at this site, consider the following questions:

1. For whose use is this questionnaire geared? Can you identify two or three key principles of instruments like this one?
2. At face value, how valid does this survey instrument seem to be?
3. Fill out the survey and then analyze your responses. (Total the number of positive, negative, and neutral responses you've given, for instance.)
4. What appear to be the biggest strengths and weaknesses of this particular survey? Assuming this questionnaire to be typical, what would you judge to be the strengths and weaknesses of job satisfaction surveys in general?
5. Try writing a survey yourself. Focus it on job satisfaction in your present job, in a previous job, or in this class. What information do you most want to elicit? What aspect of this information is hardest to elicit? Why?

EXERCISING YOUR ETHICS

Practicing Controlled Behavior

THE SITUATION

As we noted in the text, some companies try to control—and even alter—workers' behavior through systematic rewards and punishments for specific behaviors. In other words, they first try to define the specific behaviors that they want their employees to exhibit (such as working hard, being courteous to customers, stressing quality) and the specific behaviors they want to eliminate (wasting time, being rude to customers, ignoring quality). Then they try to shape employee behavior by linking reinforcement to desired behaviors and punishment to undesired behaviors.

THE DILEMMA

Assume that you are the new human resources manager in a medium-size organization. Your boss has just ordered you to implement a behavior-modification program by creating an intricate network of rewards and punishments to be linked to specific desired and undesired behaviors. You, however, are uncomfortable with this approach: You regard behavior modification policies as much like experiments on laboratory rats. Instead, you would prefer to use rewards in a way that is consistent with expectancy theory—that is, by letting employees know in advance how they can most effectively reach the rewards they most want. You have tried to change your boss' mind, but to no avail. She says to proceed with behavior modification with no further discussion.

QUESTIONS FOR DISCUSSION

1. What are the ethical issues in this case?
2. What do you think most managers would do in this situation?
3. What would you do?

BUILDING YOUR BUSINESS SKILLS

Too Much of a Good Thing

This exercise enhances the following SCANS workplace competencies: demonstrating basic skills, demonstrating thinking skills, exhibiting interpersonal skills, working with information, and applying systems knowledge.

GOAL

To encourage students to apply different motivational theories to a workplace problem involving poor productivity.

BACKGROUND

For years, working for the George Uhe Co., a small chemicals broker in Paramus, New Jersey, made employees feel as if they were members of a big family. Unfortunately, this family was going broke because too few members were working hard enough to make money for it. They were happy, comfortable, complacent—and lazy.

With sales dropping in the pharmaceutical and specialty-chemicals division, Uhe brought in management consultants to analyze the situation and make recommendations. The outsiders quickly identified a motivational problem affecting the sales force: Reps were paid a handsome salary and received automatic, year-end bonuses regardless of performance. They were also treated to bagels every Friday and regular group birthday lunches that cost as much as $200. Employees felt satisfied but had little incentive to work very hard.

Eager to return to profitability, Uhe's owners waited to hear the consultants' recommendations.

METHOD

STEP 1

In groups of four, step into the role of Uhe's management consultants. Start by analyzing your client's workforce-motivation problems from the following perspectives (our questions focus on key motivational issues):

- *Job satisfaction and morale*. As part of a 77-year-old family-owned business, Uhe employees were happy and loyal, in part, because they were treated so well. Can high morale have a downside? How can it breed stagnation, and what can managers do to prevent stagnation from taking hold?
- *Theory X versus Theory Y*. Although the behavior of these workers seems to make a case for Theory X, why is it difficult to draw this conclusion about a company that focuses more on satisfaction than on sales and profits?
- *Two-factor theory*. Analyze the various ways in which improving such motivational factors as recognition, added responsibility, advancement, and growth might reduce the importance of hygiene factors, including pay and security.
- *Expectancy theory*. Analyze the effect on productivity of redesigning the company's sales force compensation structure: namely, by paying lower base salaries while offering greater earnings potential through a sales-based incentive system. Why would linking performance with increased pay that is achievable through hard work motivate employees? Why would the threat of a job loss also motivate greater effort?

STEP 2

Writing a short report based on your analysis, make recommendations to Uhe's owners. The goal of your report is to change the working environment in ways that will motivate greater effort and generate greater productivity.

FOLLOW-UP QUESTIONS

1. What is your group's most important recommendation? Why do you think it is likely to succeed?
2. Changing the corporate culture to make it less paternalistic may reduce employees' sense of belonging to a family. If you were an employee, would you consider a greater focus on profits to be an improvement or a problem? How would it affect your motivation and productivity?
3. What steps would you take to improve the attitude and productivity of longtime employees who resist change?

CRAFTING YOUR BUSINESS PLAN

Making Reservations and Other Plans

1. To familiarize students with the ways in which employee considerations (morale, motivation, and job satisfaction) enter into the development of a sample business plan, using the planning framework of *Business PlanPro (BPP)* (Version 4.0).
2. To stimulate students' thinking about the application of textbook information on employee morale, motivation, job satisfaction, and leadership to the preparation of a *BPP* business plan.

FOLLOW-UP ASSIGNMENT

After reading Chapter 8 in the textbook, open the BPP *software and look around for information about the plans being made by a sample firm:* Puddle Jumpers Airline. *Familiarize yourself with this firm by clicking on* ***1.0 Executive Summary****. Then respond to the following questions*:

1. Consider Puddle Jumpers' plans to lower costs by using its flight crews more effectively than its competition does. If implemented, how might these plans affect employee morale? Job satisfaction? [Sites to see in *BPP* for this item: In the Plan Outline screen, click on each of the following, in turn: **1.2 Mission** and **1.3 Keys to Success**. After returning to the Plan Outline screen, click on **3.2 Competitive Comparison**. Finally, return to the Plan Outline screen and explore any listed categories in which you would expect to find information about employee motivation and job satisfaction.]

2. Consider both Puddle Jumpers' plans for dealing with the high turnover among airline reservationists and its plans for training reservationists. Do you think the planned redesign will enrich the reservationist's job? Will it affect job satisfaction? Explain. [Sites to see in *BPP* for this item: In the Plan Outline screen, click on each of the following, in turn: **3.2 Competitive Comparison** and **3.5 Technology**. After returning to the Plan Outline screen, click on **5.0 Strategy and Implementation Summary**.]
3. Consider the qualifications of Judy Land, director of reservations. Based on her background, would you say that she is qualified to lead and motivate employees under the new reservations system? Explain. [Sites to see in *BPP* for this item: In the Plan Outline screen, click on **6.2 Management Team**.]

VIDEO EXERCISE

Learning to Motivate: Student Advantage

LEARNING OBJECTIVES

The purpose of this video is to help you

1. Identify some of the varied ways in which managers can motivate employees.
2. Recognize the role of empowerment in motivating employees.
3. Appreciate the connections between achievable goals, job satisfaction, and motivation.

BACKGROUND INFORMATION

Student Advantage Inc. is a membership organization whose mission is to help other firms market products to the 15 million high school, college, and graduate students on the country's 4,000 different campuses. It uses its growing student base to achieve member discounts on transportation and brand-name consumer goods and services. Student Advantage was founded in Boston in 1992 and has expanded mainly by acquisition to a nationwide staff of about 450 employees in 10 different locations across the United States.

THE VIDEO

Among other employees, CEO Ray Sozzi and Vice President of Human Resources Kevin Roche discuss some of the ways in which each company motivates employees, beginning with Sozzi's desire for his "partners," as he calls them, to feel and act as if they were owners of the firm, willing and able to do things that aren't in their job descriptions. In fact, "ownership" is one of the company's five core values, and empowerment is a key to allowing employees to handle the relatively high degree of autonomy and responsibility they are given on the job. Listen for some of the other ways in which employees are given the means to "make a difference."

QUESTIONS FOR DISCUSSION

1. How many different ways can you find in which Student Advantage employees are being motivated?
2. What motivational problems do you think might be associated with a growth-by-acquisition strategy like that of Student Advantage?
3. Chief technology officer Craig McFarlane says in the video that he doesn't want to work in a place where "the job is already done." What does he mean? How does a company motivate someone with this approach to the job?

FOLLOW-UP ASSIGNMENT

Do some research into an organization whose mission parallels that of Student Advantage—namely, the American Association of Retired People, or AARP <www.aarp.com>. How do this organization's mission and goals differ from those of Student Advantage? What do you think is the resulting difference in the kind of people that AARP seeks as employees? In the ways in which it motivates them?

FOR FURTHER EXPLORATION

Visit the Student Advantage Web site <www.studentadvantage.com> and look at the "About Us" page and job listings. What specific things can you discover about the company that, as an employer, should be especially helpful in its efforts to motivate employees? Are these benefits of working at Student Advantage attractive to you in particular? Why or why not? What types of people do you think the firm tries to attract as employees? Why?

CHAPTER 9

Managing Human Resources and Labor Relations

After reading this chapter, you should be able to:

1. Define *human resource management* and explain how managers plan for human resources.
2. Identify the issues involved in *staffing* a company and discuss ways in which organizations develop human resources and evaluate employee performance.
3. Discuss the importance of *wages and salaries, incentives,* and *benefit programs* in attracting and keeping skilled workers.
4. Describe some of the key legal issues involved in hiring, compensating, and managing workers in today's workplace.
5. Discuss *workforce diversity,* the management of *knowledge workers,* and the use of a *contingent workforce* as important changes in the contemporary workplace.
6. Explain why workers organize and identify the steps in the *collective bargaining process.*

And All the M&Ms You Can Eat . . .

Imagine working for a company with its own on-site cafeteria and medical and day care facilities. Imagine working for a company that provides free on-site dental care and massage therapy. Imagine working for a company that has a lavish on-site exercise facility. How about one that launders your dirty exercise clothes after your workout session? Imagine working for a company that offers unlimited sick days. Imagine working for a company that provides free soda, coffee, tea, and juice. Imagine working for a company that actually encourages you to go home at the end of the day. If that's not enough, imagine working for a company that gives everyone free M&Ms every Wednesday of the year. Nirvana? No, it's a real company—SAS Institute, Inc.

Based in rural North Carolina, SAS Institute <www.sas.com> is perhaps the least well-known major software company in the world today. SAS got its start in 1976 when two North Carolina State University professors, James Goodnight and John Sall, created a unique software package to analyze agricultural data around the state. They called their software the Statistical Analysis System, or SAS for short. Goodnight and Sall quickly found numerous new applications for their product and left NC State to start their own business, which eventually became known simply as SAS Institute.

SAS designs complex statistical software that helps big companies better manage, analyze, and interpret especially large quantities of data and information.

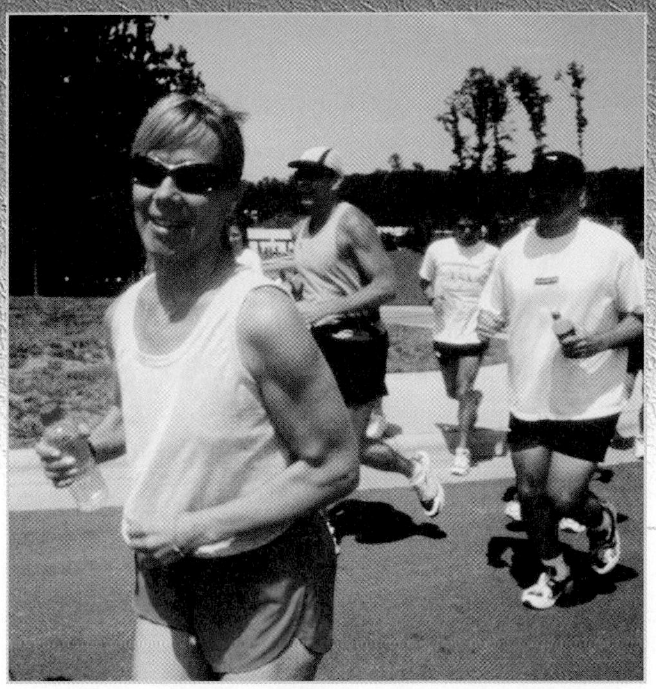

"The idea is that if you hire adults and treat them like adults, then they'll behave like adults."

—David Russo, head of human resources at SAS Institute

Marriott Hotels, for example, uses SAS software to manage its frequent-visitor program and to track occupancy rates and patterns in all its hotels. The U.S. government uses SAS software to compute the Consumer Price Index and other complex economic measures. Giant pharmaceutical companies such as Pfizer and Merck use SAS software to compare near-infinite combinations of elements as they develop new drugs.

Because SAS is a private firm, the general public knows little about its revenues and profits. A few details are illuminating, however. For one thing, Jim Goodnight, who owns two-thirds of the company and serves as CEO, is listed by *Forbes* magazine as the 43rd richest individual in the United States, with a personal net worth of $3 billion. Senior vice president John Sall owns the other third and he still spends much of his time writing code. SAS also hires several hundred new employees each year—a clear indicator that it's consistently growing at a strong pace. The firm also continues to invest in impressive—and clearly expensive—buildings and related facilities.

But SAS is even more interesting beneath the surface. Even though it pays salaries that are merely competitive for the industry, the firm's employees are almost fanatical in their devotion to SAS in general and to Jim Goodnight in particular. As a result, annual turnover at SAS is less than 4 percent—far below that of other firms in the industry—and employees are constantly coming up with new and better ways of doing things. Both insiders and outside experts agree that the key to all this loyalty and creativity is the way Goodnight treats his employees. Says human resources head David Russo: "Jim's idea is that if you hire adults and treat them like adults, then they'll behave like adults."

All SAS employees get unlimited sick days—which they can use to stay home and care for a sick family member. To keep work from interfering with employees' family lives, SAS also operates the largest child care facility in the state. Company cafeterias stock baby seats and high chairs so that employees can eat with their children. SAS has also adopted a seven-hour workday—the switchboard shuts down at 5:00 P.M., and the front gate is locked at 6:00 P.M. Unlike executives at many high-tech firms in other parts of the country, Goodnight doesn't want his employees working late or coming back to the office on weekends. He himself never checks his e-mail or voice messages in the evenings or on weekends.

If they want, however, employees can come in early—to work out in a lavish 36,000-square-foot gym and health center. The center also offers massages several times a week, as well as classes in golf, tennis, tai chi, and African dance. The staff even launders dirty workout clothes at the end of the day and returns them clean and neatly folded. SAS provides unlimited free soda, coffee, tea, and juice, and has live piano music in the cafeteria. The company shuts down for the week between Christmas and New Year's Day each year, but everyone still gets paid. An on-site health clinic has two full-time physicians and six nurses, and health insurance is free for everyone. Every Wednesday, bowls of free M&Ms are set out all over the company. All told, SAS buys 22.5 tons of M&Ms each year.

All this largesse issues from Jim Goodnight's most fundamental philosophic principle: If you treat people with dignity and respect and reward them for their contributions, they will treat you the same way in return. When this relationship can be established and maintained within the context of a business, everyone wins.

Our opening story is continued on page 244

THE FOUNDATIONS OF HUMAN RESOURCE MANAGEMENT

Human resource management (HRM) is the set of organizational activities directed at attracting, developing, and maintaining an effective workforce. Human resource management takes place within a complex and ever-changing environmental context and is increasingly being recognized for its strategic importance.[1]

human resource management (HRM)
Set of organizational activities directed at attracting, developing, and maintaining an effective workforce

The Strategic Importance of HRM

Human resources are critical for effective organizational functioning. HRM (or *personnel*, as it is sometimes called) was once relegated to second-class status in many organizations, but its importance has grown dramatically in the last two decades. This new importance stems from increased legal complexities, the recognition that human resources are a valuable means for improving productivity, and the awareness today of the costs associated with poor human resource management.

Indeed, managers now realize that the effectiveness of their HR function has a substantial impact on a firm's bottom-line performance. Poor human resource planning can result in spurts of hiring followed by layoffs—costly in terms of unemployment compensation payments, training expenses, and morale. Haphazard compensation systems do not attract, keep, and motivate good employees, and outmoded recruitment practices can expose the firm to expensive and embarrassing legal action. Consequently, the chief human resource executive of most large businesses is a vice president directly accountable to the CEO, and many firms are developing strategic HR plans that are integrated with other strategic planning activities.

Human Resource Planning

As you can see in Figure 9.1, the starting point in attracting qualified human resources is planning. In turn, HR planning involves job analysis and forecasting the demand for and supply of labor.

Job Analysis **Job analysis** is a systematic analysis of jobs within an organization.[2] A job analysis is made up of two parts:

- The **job description** lists the duties of a job, its working conditions, and the tools, materials, and equipment used to perform it.
- The **job specification** lists the skills, abilities, and other credentials needed to do the job.

job analysis
Systematic analysis of jobs within an organization

job description
Outline of the duties of a job, working conditions, and the tools, materials, and equipment used to perform it

job specification
Description of the skills, abilities, and other credentials required by a job

Job analysis information is used in many HR activities. For instance, knowing about job content and job requirements is necessary to develop appropriate selection methods and job-relevant performance appraisal systems and to set equitable compensation rates.

Forecasting HR Demand and Supply After managers fully understand the jobs to be performed within an organization, they can start planning for the organization's future HR needs. The manager starts by assessing trends in past HR usage, future organizational plans, and general economic trends. A good sales forecast is often the foundation, especially for smaller organizations. Historical ratios can then be used to predict demand for types of employees, such as operating employees and sales representatives. Large organizations use much more complicated models to predict HR needs.

Forecasting the supply of labor is really two tasks:

- Forecasting *internal supply*—the number and type of employees who will be in the firm at some future date.
- Forecasting *external supply*—the number and type of people who will be available for hiring from the labor market at large.

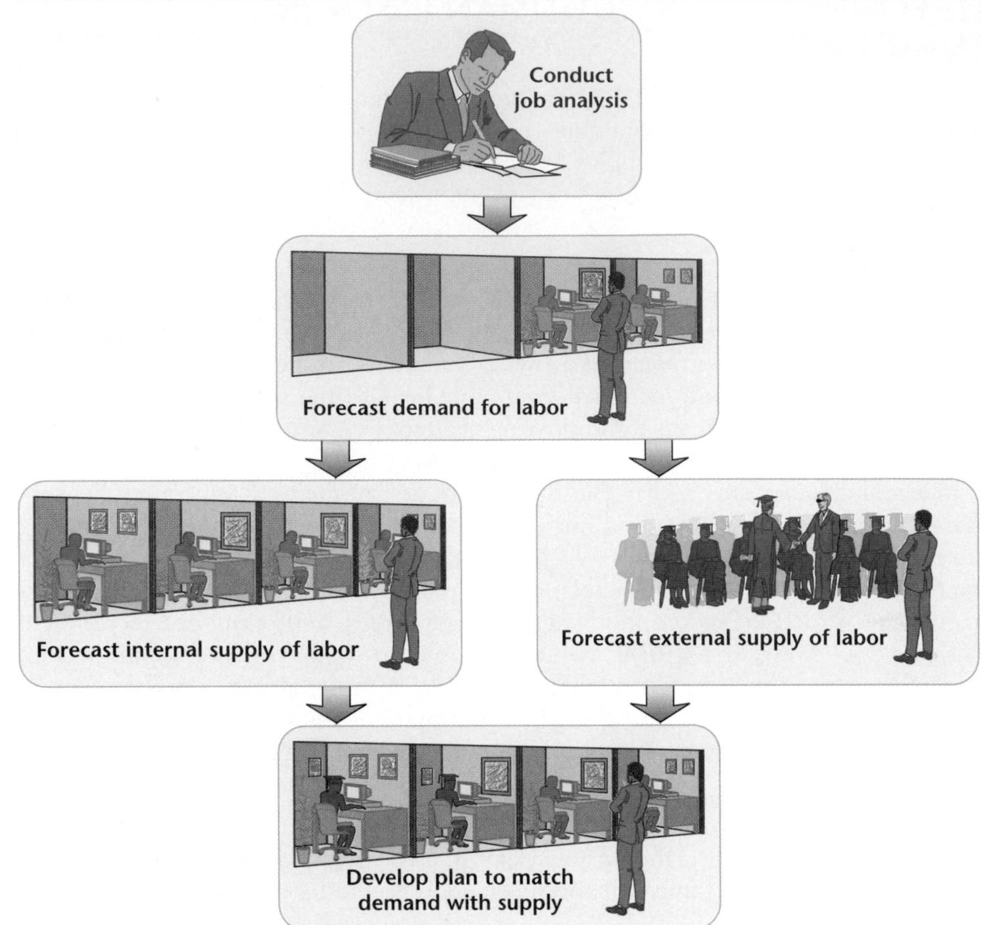
Conduct job analysis
Forecast demand for labor
Forecast internal supply of labor
Forecast external supply of labor
Develop plan to match demand with supply

Figure 9.1
The Human Resource Planning Process

The simplest approach merely adjusts present staffing levels for anticipated turnover and promotions. Again, however, large organizations use extremely sophisticated models to make these forecasts.

replacement chart
List of each management position, who occupies it, how long that person will likely stay in the job, and who is qualified as a replacement

employee information system (skills inventory)
Computerized system containing information on each employee's education, skills, work experiences, and career aspirations

Replacement Charts At higher levels of the organization, managers plan for specific people and positions. The technique most commonly used is the **replacement chart**, which lists each important managerial position, who occupies it, how long that person will probably stay in it before moving on, and who (by name) is now qualified or soon will be qualified to move into it. This technique allows ample time to plan developmental experiences for people identified as potential successors to critical managerial jobs.[3] Charles Knight, CEO of Emerson Electric Co. <www.emersonelectric.com>, maintains an entire room for posting the credentials of his top 700 executives.

Skills Inventories To facilitate both planning and identifying people for transfer or promotion, some organizations also have **employee information systems**, or **skills inventories**. These systems are usually computerized and contain information on each employee's education, skills, work experience, and career aspirations. Such a system can quickly locate every employee who is qualified to fill a position requiring, for example, a degree in chemical engineering, three years of experience in an oil refinery, and fluency in Spanish.

Forecasting the external supply of labor is a different problem altogether. How does a manager, for example, predict how many electrical engineers will be seeking work in California or Florida three years from now? To get an idea of the future availability of labor, planners must rely on information from outside sources such as state employment commissions, government reports, and figures supplied by colleges on the number of students in major fields.

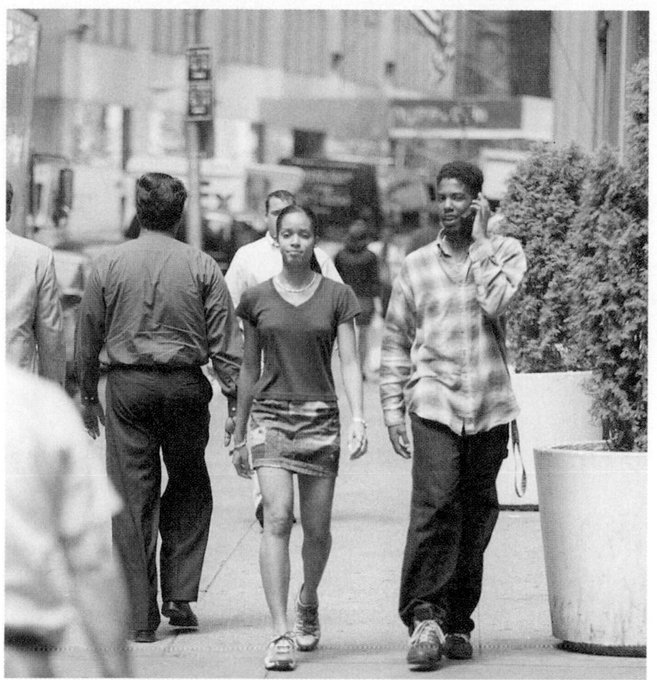

It's no secret that Internet start-ups have proliferated, and both software and hardware companies continue to grow. One result is rapidly growing demand for computer-savvy young people, and many companies have realized that focusing only on college juniors and seniors means ignoring too much talent. Interns Shamarrah Broadus, 18, and Henry Fabian, 16, have Wall Street offices at Market Technologies Group <www.mtgny.com>, a small software-training company in New York. And they don't make minimum wage: such internships pay from $4,000 to $10,000 for a summer.

Matching HR Supply and Demand After comparing future demand and internal supply, managers can make plans to manage predicted shortfalls or overstaffing. If a shortfall is predicted, new employees can be hired, present employees can be retrained and transferred into understaffed areas, individuals approaching retirement can be convinced to stay on, or labor-saving or productivity-enhancing systems can be installed.

If the organization needs to hire, the external labor-supply forecast helps managers plan how to recruit according to whether the type of person needed is readily available or scarce in the labor market. The use of temporary workers also helps managers in staffing by giving them extra flexibility. If overstaffing is expected to be a problem, the main options are transferring the extra employees, not replacing individuals who quit, encouraging early retirement, and laying people off.[4]

STAFFING THE ORGANIZATION

When managers have determined that new employees are needed, they must then turn their attention to recruiting and hiring the right mix of people. Staffing the organization is one of the most complex and important tasks of good HR management. In this section, we will describe both the process of acquiring staff from outside the company (*external staffing*) and the process of promoting staff from within (*internal staffing*). Both external and internal staffing, however, start with effective *recruiting*.

Recruiting Human Resources Once an organization has an idea of its future HR needs, the next phase is usually recruiting new employees. **Recruiting** is the process of attracting qualified persons to apply for the jobs that are open. Where do recruits come from? Some recruits are found internally while others come from outside of the organization.

recruiting
Process of attracting qualified persons to apply for jobs an organization is seeking to fill

internal recruiting
Considering present employees as candidates for openings

Internal Recruiting **Internal recruiting** means considering present employees as candidates for openings. Promotion from within can help build morale and keep high-quality employees from leaving. In unionized firms, the procedures for notifying employees of internal job-change opportunities are usually spelled out in the union contract. For higher-level positions, a skills inventory system may be used to identify internal candidates or managers may be asked to recommend individuals who should be considered.

external recruiting
Attracting persons outside the organization to apply for jobs

External Recruiting **External recruiting** involves attracting people outside the organization to apply for jobs. External recruiting methods include advertising, campus interviews, employment agencies or executive search firms, union hiring halls, referrals by present employees, and hiring "walk-ins" or "gate-hires" (people who show up without being solicited). A manager must select the most appropriate method for each job. The manager might, for instance, use the state employment service to find a maintenance worker but not a nuclear physicist. Private employment agencies can be a good source of clerical and technical employees, and executive search firms specialize in locating top-management talent. Newspaper ads are often used because they reach a wide audience and thus allow minorities equal opportunity to find out about and apply for job openings.

During the late 1990s recruiters faced a difficult job as unemployment plummeted. By early 1998, for example, unemployment had dropped to a 23-year low of 4.6 percent. As a result, recruiters at firms such as Sprint, PeopleSoft, and Cognex had to stress how much "fun" it was to work for them, reinforcing this message with ice cream socials, karaoke contests, softball leagues, and free-movie nights. The "Wired World" box in this chapter shows how some companies have also used the Internet to recruit prospective employees.

IT'S A WIRED WORLD

Companies Put Web to Work as Recruiter

At DVCi Technologies' office in New York, employees never know who's looking over their shoulders. Their moves are broadcast live to the world via a Webcam as part of the company's effort to attract new hires by giving them a glimpse behind the scenes.

The video show is the latest example of how companies are using Web sites as an increasingly creative recruiting tool. It's no longer enough to post jobs on the Internet. Employers today are attracting candidates with such tactics as downloaded video and audio feeds, online employment tests, and real-time chats with recruiters.

"We had to differentiate ourselves," says Haim Ariav at DVCi Technologies <www.dvci-muffinhead.com>, a provider of Internet solutions. His movements—a wave, pen chewing, typing—are broadcast online at www.recruitcam.com. "It's been phenomenal. We've hired a lot of people through it, and we're still getting e-mail."

How others are using Web sites:

- *Giving visitors a behind-the-scenes look.* The U.S. Army's Web site <www.army.mil> includes a virtual tour of barracks. Visitors can click and drag their computer mouse to see sweeping views of bedrooms, laundry rooms, and courtyard. Visitors can also chat with online cyber-recruiters or download a video of an Abrams M1A2 tank.
- *Letting job candidates "meet" current employees.* Visitors to Chicago-based Andersen Consulting's Web site <www.arthurandersen. com> can view pictures of employees and read messages. Entries range from "I love water skiing" to "my job gives me satisfaction and balance." At San Jose, California–based Cisco Systems <www.cisco.com>, visitors can join in an online program called "Make Friends at Cisco." Job candidates can ask to get in touch with current workers to grill them about what it's like to work there.
- *Staying in touch with potential hires.* At Sprint's site <www.sprint.com>, job seekers can send e-mail about their ideal job. The company will send automatic e-mail if future job postings match the criteria. "There are a lot of ways to establish long-term relationships with this tool," says Sonja Ambur, national staffing director in Kansas City, Missouri. "Every company is looking at ways to maximize the Internet as a recruiting tool."

Some job seekers say the tactics work. Marta Sant, 28, took a job with DVCi Technologies after viewing the company through its Webcam. "I looked at the pictures and thought it was fun," says Sant, senior art director. "I e-mail my friends and family, and they can see me."

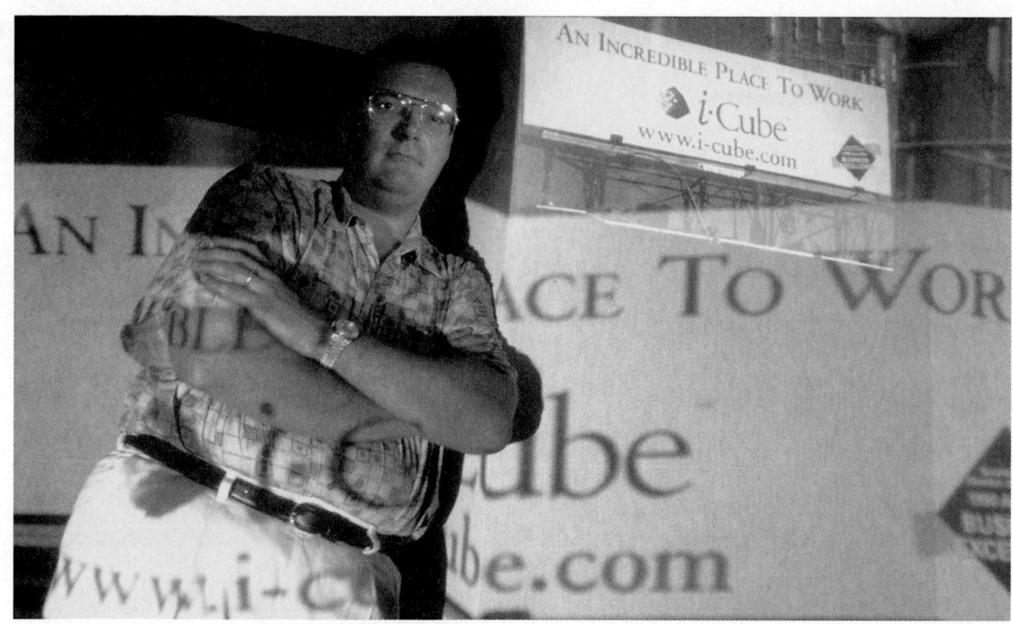

Michael Pehl, CEO of I-Cube <www.icube.com>, an IT-consulting-services company, needs employees—good employees—in the worst way. He's willing to pay $15,000 for billboards touting I-Cube as "An Incredible Place to Work," and he has launched a variety of incentives to motivate current employees as recruiters. Anyone making a successful referral may get $2,000, a 32-inch TV, and a VCR. Eight successful referrals in a calendar year can be worth as much as a Jeep Wrangler.

By 2001, however, the situation had begun to change. Unemployment began to creep back up, many larger employers (such as Compaq Computer and Hewlett-Packard) announced major job cutbacks, and recruiters were again able to attract highly qualified employees. While most companies maintained the innovative benefits programs that they had inaugurated in the 1990s, they were also able to avoid costly new programs and could afford to be more selective in the employees they chose to hire.[5]

Selecting Human Resources

Once the recruiting process has attracted a pool of applicants, the next step is to select someone to hire. The intent of the selection process is to gather from applicants information that will predict their job success and then to hire the candidates likely to be most successful. Of course, the organization can only gather information about factors that are predictive of future performance. The process of determining the predictive value of information is called **validation.**[6]

validation
Process of determining the predictive value of a selection technique

Application Forms The first step in selection is usually asking the candidate to fill out an application. An application form is an efficient method of gathering information about the applicant's previous work history, educational background, and other job-related demographic data. It should not contain questions about areas unrelated to the job such as gender, religion, or national origin. Application form data are generally used informally to decide whether a candidate merits further evaluation, and interviewers use application forms to familiarize themselves with candidates before interviewing them.

Tests Tests of ability, skill, aptitude, or knowledge that is relevant to a particular job are usually the best predictors of job success, although tests of general intelligence or personality are occasionally useful as well. In addition to being validated, tests should be administered and scored consistently. All candidates should be given the same directions, allowed the same amount of time, and offered the same testing environment (temperature, lighting, distractions).[7]

Interviews Although a popular selection device, the interview is sometimes a poor predictor of job success. For example, biases inherent in the way people perceive and judge others on first meeting affect subsequent evaluations. Interview validity can be improved by training interviewers to be aware of potential biases and by increasing the

WEB Connection

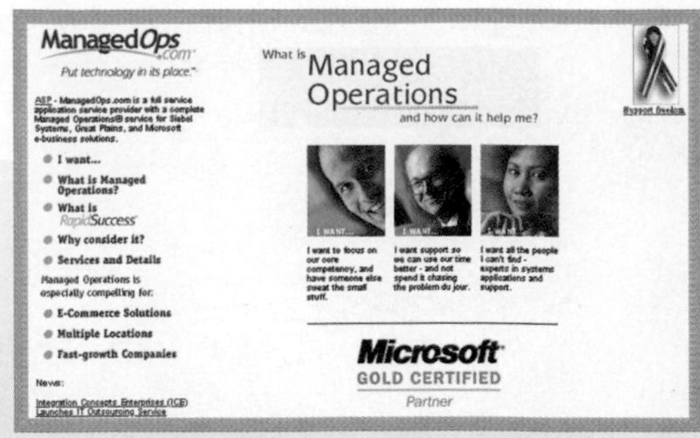

At ManagedOps, an application service provider (ASP) located in Bedford, New Hampshire, hiring new employees is serious business. It's also a methodical—indeed, intensive—process designed to make just the right person–job fit. To find out more about the company—and to hear from some employees who were hired after as many as eight interviews—log on to the ManagedOps Web site at www.managedops.com/corporate/careers.asp

www.managedops.com

structure of the interview. In a structured interview, questions are written in advance and all interviewers follow the same question list with each candidate. Such structure introduces consistency into the interview procedure and allows the organization to validate the content of the questions. For interviewing managerial or professional candidates, a somewhat less structured approach can be used. Although question areas and information-gathering objectives are still planned in advance, specific questions vary with the candidates' backgrounds.

Other Techniques Organizations also use other selection techniques that vary with circumstances. Polygraph tests, once popular, are declining in popularity. On the other hand, organizations occasionally require that applicants take physical exams (being careful that their practices are consistent with the Americans with Disabilities Act). More organizations are using drug tests, especially in situations in which drug-related performance problems could create serious safety hazards. Applicants at a nuclear power plant, for example, will probably be tested for drugs. Some organizations also run credit checks on prospective employees.

DEVELOPING THE WORKFORCE

After a company has hired new employees, it must acquaint them with the firm and their new jobs. Managers also take steps to train employees and further develop necessary job skills. In addition, every firm has some system for performance appraisal and feedback. Unfortunately, the results of these assessments sometimes require procedures for demoting or terminating employees.

Training

As its name suggests, **on-the-job training** occurs while the employee is at work. Much of this training is informal, as when one employee shows another how to use the photocopier. In other cases, it is quite formal. For example, a trainer may teach secretaries how to operate a new e-mail system from their workstations.

on-the-job training Training, sometimes informal, conducted while an employee is at work

off-the-job training Training conducted in a controlled environment away from the work site

Off-the-job training takes place at locations away from the work site. This approach offers a controlled environment and allows focused study without interruptions. For example, the petroleum equipment manufacturer Baker-Hughes uses classroom-based programs to teach new methods of quality control. Chaparral Steel's training program includes four hours a week of classroom training in areas such as basic math and grammar.

Other firms use **vestibule training**, in simulated work environments, to make off-the-job training more realistic. American Airlines, for example, trains flight attendants through vestibule training, and AT&T uses it to train telephone operators. Finally, many organizations today are exploring computerized and/or Web-based training.[8]

vestibule training
Off-the-job training conducted in a simulated environment

performance appraisal
Evaluation of an employee's job performance in order to determine the degree to which the employee is performing effectively

Performance Appraisal

In some small companies, **performance appraisal** takes place when the owner tells an employee, "You're doing a good job." In larger firms, performance appraisals are designed to show more precisely how well workers are doing their jobs. Typically, the appraisal process involves a written assessment issued on a regular basis. As a rule, however, the written evaluation is only one part of a multistep process.

The appraisal process begins when a manager defines performance standards for an employee. The manager then observes the employee's performance. If the standards are clear, the manager should have little difficulty comparing expectations with performance. For some jobs, a rating scale like the abbreviated one in Figure 9.2 is useful in providing a basis for comparisons. In addition to scales for initiative, punctuality, and cleanliness, a complete form will include several other scales directly related to performance. Comparisons drawn from such scales form the basis for written appraisals and for decisions about raises, promotions, demotions, and firings. The process is completed when manager and employee meet to discuss the appraisal.[9]

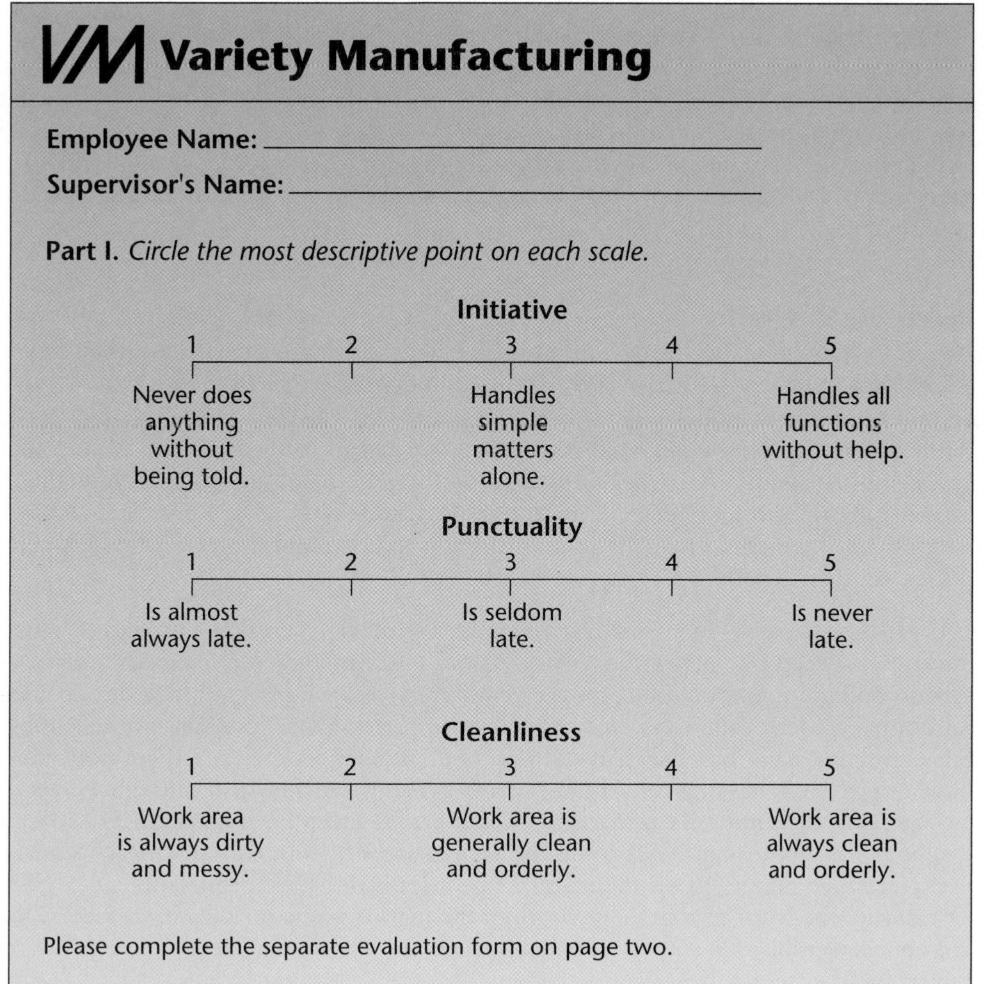
VM Variety Manufacturing

Employee Name: __________

Supervisor's Name: __________

Part I. *Circle the most descriptive point on each scale.*

Initiative

1	2	3	4	5
Never does anything without being told.		Handles simple matters alone.		Handles all functions without help.

Punctuality

1	2	3	4	5
Is almost always late.		Is seldom late.		Is never late.

Cleanliness

1	2	3	4	5
Work area is always dirty and messy.		Work area is generally clean and orderly.		Work area is always clean and orderly.

Please complete the separate evaluation form on page two.

Figure 9.2
Performance Rating Scale

COMPENSATION AND BENEFITS

Most workers today also expect certain benefits from their employers. Indeed, a major factor in retaining skilled workers is a company's **compensation system**—the total package that it offers employees in return for their labor.[10]

compensation system
Set of rewards that organizations provide to individuals in return for their willingness to perform various jobs and tasks within the organization

Although wages and salaries are key parts of all compensation systems, most also include *incentives* and *employee benefits programs*. We discuss these and other types of employee benefits in this section. Remember, however, that finding the right combination of compensation elements is always complicated by the need to make employees feel valued while holding down company costs. Thus, compensation systems differ widely, depending on the nature of the industry, the company, and the types of workers involved.

Wages and Salaries

wages
Compensation in the form of money paid for time worked

salary
Compensation in the form of money paid for discharging the responsibilities of a job

Wages and salaries are the dollar amounts paid to employees for their labor. **Wages** are paid for time worked. For example, workers who are paid by the hour receive wages. A **salary** is paid for discharging the responsibilities of a job. A salaried executive earning $100,000 per year is paid to achieve results even if that means working 5 hours one day and 15 the next. Salaries are usually expressed as an amount paid per year.

In setting wage and salary levels, a company may start by looking at its competitors' levels. A firm that pays less than its rivals knows that it runs the risk of losing valuable personnel. Conversely, to attract top employees, some companies pay more than their rivals. M&M/Mars, for example, pays managerial salaries about 10 percent above the average in the candy and snack food industry.

A firm must also decide how its internal wage and salary levels will compare for different jobs. For example, Sears must determine the relative salaries of store managers, buyers, and advertising managers. In turn, managers must decide how much to pay individual workers within the company's wage and salary structure. Although two employees may do exactly the same job, the employee with more experience may earn more. Moreover, some union contracts specify differential wages based on experience.

Incentive Programs

Naturally, employees feel better about their companies when they believe that they are being fairly compensated; however, studies and experience have shown that beyond a certain point, more money will not produce better performance. Indeed, neither across-the-board nor cost-of-living wage increases cause people to work harder. Money motivates employees only if it is tied directly to performance. The most common method of establishing this link is the use of **incentive programs**—special pay programs designed to motivate high performance. Some programs are available to individuals, whereas others are distributed on a companywide basis.[11]

incentive program
Special compensation program designed to motivate high performance

bonus
Individual performance incentive in the form of a special payment made over and above the employee's salary

merit salary system
Individual incentive linking compensation to performance in nonsales jobs

Individual Incentives A sales bonus is a typical incentive: Employees receive **bonuses**—special payments above their salaries—when they sell a certain number or certain dollar amount of goods for the year. Employees who fail to reach this goal earn no bonuses. **Merit salary systems** link raises to performance levels in nonsales jobs.[12] For example, many baseball players have contract clauses that pay them bonuses for hitting over .300, making the All-Star team, or being named Most Valuable Player.

Executives commonly receive stock options as incentives. Disney CEO Michael Eisner, for example, can buy several thousand shares of company stock each year at a predetermined price.[13] If his managerial talent leads to higher profits and stock prices, he can buy the stock at a price lower than the market value for which, in theory, he is largely responsible. He is then free to sell them at market price, keeping the profits for himself.

A newer incentive plan is called **pay for performance**, or **variable pay**. In essence, middle managers are rewarded for especially productive output—for producing earnings that significantly exceed the cost of bonuses. Such incentives have long been common among top-level executives and factory workers, but variable pay goes to middle managers on the basis of companywide performance, business unit performance, personal record, or all three factors.

The number of variable pay programs in the United States has been growing consistently for the last decade, and most experts predict that they will continue to grow in popularity. Eligible managers must often forgo merit or "entitlement" raises (increases for staying on and reporting to work every day), but many firms say that variable pay is a better motivator because the range between generous and mediocre merit raises is usually quite small anyway. Merit raises also increase fixed costs: They are added to base pay and increase the base pay used to determine the retirement benefits that the company must pay out.

pay for performance (or variable pay)
Individual incentive that rewards a manager for especially productive output

Companywide Incentives Some incentive programs apply to all the employees in a firm.[14] Under **profit-sharing plans**, for example, profits earned above a certain level are distributed to employees. Conversely, **gainsharing plans** distribute bonuses to employees when a company's costs are reduced through greater work efficiency. **Pay-for-knowledge plans** encourage workers to learn new skills and to become proficient at different jobs. They receive additional pay for each new skill or job that they master.

profit-sharing plan
Incentive plan for distributing bonuses to employees when company profits rise above a certain level

gainsharing plan
Incentive plan that rewards groups for productivity improvements

pay-for-knowledge plan
Incentive plan to encourage employees to learn new skills or become proficient at different jobs

Benefits Programs

A growing part of nearly every firm's compensation system is its benefits program. **Benefits**—compensation other than wages and salaries offered by a firm to its workers—comprise a large percentage of most compensation budgets. Most companies are required by law to provide social security retirement benefits and **workers' compensation insurance** (insurance for compensating workers injured on the job). Most businesses also voluntarily provide health, life, and disability insurance. Many also allow employees to use payroll deductions to buy stock at discounted prices. Another common benefit is paid time off for vacations and holidays. Counseling services for employees with alcohol, drug, or emotional problems are also becoming more common. On-site child care centers are also becoming popular.[15]

benefits
Compensation other than wages and salaries

workers' compensation insurance
Legally required insurance for compensating workers injured on the job

Retirement Plans Retirement plans are also an important, and sometimes controversial, benefit that is available to many employees. Most company-sponsored retirement plans are set up to pay pensions to workers when they retire. In some cases, the company contributes all the money to the pension fund. In others, contributions are made by both the company and employees. Currently, about 60 percent of U.S. workers are covered by pension plans of some kind.

Containing the Costs of Benefits As the range of benefits has grown, so has concern about containing their costs. Many companies are experimenting with cost-cutting plans under which they can still attract and retain valuable employees. One approach is the **cafeteria benefits plan**: A certain dollar amount of benefits per employee is set aside so that each employee can choose from a variety of alternatives.

cafeteria benefit plan
Benefit plan that sets limits on benefits per employee, each of whom may choose from a variety of alternative benefits

Another area of increasing concern is health care costs. Medical procedures that once cost several hundred dollars now cost several thousand dollars. Medical expenses have increased insurance premiums, which in turn have increased the cost to employers of maintaining benefits plans.

Many employers are looking for new ways to cut those costs. One increasingly popular approach is for organizations to create their own networks of health care providers. These providers agree to charge lower fees for services rendered to employees of member organizations. In return, they enjoy established relationships with large employers and thus more clients and patients. Because they must make lower reimbursement payments, insurers also charge less to cover the employees of network members.

THE LEGAL CONTEXT OF HR MANAGEMENT

As much or more than any area of business, HR management is heavily influenced by federal law and judicial review. In this section, we summarize some of the most important and far-reaching areas of HR regulation.

Equal Employment Opportunity

equal employment opportunity Legally mandated nondiscrimination in employment on the basis of race, creed, sex, or national origin

The basic goal of all **equal employment opportunity** regulation is to protect people from unfair or inappropriate discrimination in the workplace.[16] Let's begin by noting that discrimination in itself is not illegal. Whenever one person is given a pay raise and another is not, for example, the organization has made a decision to distinguish one person from another. As long as the basis for this discrimination is purely job related (made, for instance, on the basis of performance or seniority) and is applied objectively and consistently, the action is legal and appropriate.

Problems arise when distinctions among people are not job related. In such cases, the resulting discrimination is illegal. Various court decisions, coupled with interpretations of the language of various laws, suggest that illegal discrimination actions by an organization or its managers cause members of a "protected class" to be unfairly differentiated from other members of the organization.

Protected Classes in the Workplace Illegal discrimination is based on a stereotype, belief, or prejudice about classes of individuals. At one time, for example, common stereotypes regarded black employees as less dependable than white employees, women as less suited to certain types of work than men, and disabled individuals as unproductive employees.

Based on these stereotypes, some organizations routinely discriminated against blacks, women, and the disabled. To combat discrimination, laws have been passed to protect various classes of individuals. A **protected class** consists of all individuals who share one or more common characteristics as indicated by a given law. The most common criteria for defining protected classes include race, color, religion, gender, age, national origin, disability status, and status as a military veteran.[17]

protected class Set of individuals who by nature of one or more common characteristics are protected under the law from discrimination on the basis of that characteristic

Equal Employment Opportunity Commission (EECO) Federal agency enforcing several discrimination-related laws

affirmative action plan Practice of recruiting qualified employees belonging to racial, gender, or ethnic groups who are underrepresented in an organization

Enforcing Equal Employment Opportunity The enforcement of equal opportunity legislation is handled by two agencies. The **Equal Employment Opportunity Commission**, or **EEOC** <www.eeoc.gov>, is a division of the Department of Justice. It was created by Title VII of the 1964 Civil Rights Act and has specific responsibility for enforcing Title VII, the Equal Pay Act, and the Americans with Disabilities Act.

The other agency charged with monitoring equal employment opportunity legislation is the Office of Federal Contract Compliance Programs, or OFCCP <www.dol.gov/dol/esa/public/of org.htm>. The OFCCP is responsible for enforcing executive orders that apply to companies doing business with the federal government. A business with government contracts must have on file a written **affirmative action plan**: that is, a written statement of how the organization intends to actively recruit, hire, and develop members of relevant protected classes.

Legal Issues in Compensation As we noted earlier, most employment regulations are designed to provide equal employment opportunity. Some legislation, however, goes beyond equal employment opportunity and really deals more substantively with other issues. One such area is legislation covering compensation.

Contemporary Legal Issues in HR Management

In addition to these established areas of HR legal regulation, there are several emerging legal issues that will likely become more and more important with the passage of time. These include employee safety and health, various emerging areas of discrimination law, employee rights, employment-at-will, and ethics and human resource management.

Employee Safety and Health The **Occupational Safety and Health Act of 1970**, or **OSHA** <www.osha.gov>, is the single most comprehensive piece of legislation ever passed regarding worker safety and health. OSHA holds that every employer has an obligation to furnish each employee with a place of employment that is free from hazards that cause or are likely to cause death or physical harm. It is generally enforced through inspections of the workplace by OSHA inspectors. If an OSHA compliance officer believes that a violation has occurred, a citation is issued. Nonserious violations may result in fines of up to $1,000 for each incident. Serious or willful and repeated violations may incur fines of up to $10,000 per incident.

Occupational Safety and Health Act of 1970 (OSHA)
Federal law setting and enforcing guidelines for protecting workers from unsafe conditions and potential health hazards in the workplace

Emerging Areas of Discrimination Law There are also several emerging areas of discrimination law that managers must also be familiar with. In this section, we will discuss some of the most important.

AIDS in the Workplace Although AIDS is considered a disability under the Americans with Disabilities Act of 1990, the AIDS situation itself is sufficiently severe enough that it warrants special attention. Employers cannot legally require an AIDS or any other medical examination as a condition for making an offer of employment. Organizations must treat AIDS like any other disease covered by law. They must maintain the confidentiality of all medical records. They cannot discriminate against a person with AIDS, and they should try to educate coworkers about AIDS. They cannot discriminate against AIDS victims in training or in consideration for promotion, and they must accommodate or make a good-faith effort to accommodate AIDS victims.

Sexual Harassment Sexual harassment has been a problem in organizations for a long time and is a violation of Title VII of the Civil Rights Act of 1964. **Sexual harassment** is defined by the EEOC as unwelcome sexual advances in the work environment. If the conduct is indeed unwelcome and occurs with sufficient frequency to create an abusive work environment, the employer is responsible for changing the environment by warning, reprimanding, or perhaps firing the harasser.[18]

sexual harassment
Practice or instance of making unwelcome sexual advances in the workplace

The courts have ruled and defined that there are two types of sexual harassment:

- In cases of **quid pro quo harassment**, the harasser offers to exchange something of value for sexual favors. A male supervisor, for example, might tell or suggest to a female subordinate that he will recommend her for promotion or give her a raise in exchange for sexual favors.
- The creation of a **hostile work environment** is a subtler form of sexual harassment. A group of male employees who continually make off-color jokes and lewd comments and perhaps decorate the work environment with inappropriate photographs may create a hostile work environment for a female colleague, who becomes uncomfortable working in that environment. As we noted earlier, it is the organization's responsibility for dealing with this sort of problem.

quid pro quo harassment
Form of sexual harassment in which sexual favors are requested in return for job-related benefits

hostile work environment
Form of sexual harassment deriving from off-color jokes, lewd comments, and so forth

Regardless of the pattern, the same bottom-line rules apply: Sexual harassment is illegal and the organization is responsible for controlling it.

Employment-at-Will The concept of **employment-at-will** holds that both employer and employee have the mutual right to terminate an employment relationship anytime for any reason and with or without advance notice to the other. Specifically, it holds that an organization employs an individual at its own will and can, therefore, terminate that employment at any time for any reason. Over the last two decades, however, terminated employees have challenged the employment-at-will doctrine by filing lawsuits against former employers on the grounds of wrongful discharge.

employment-at-will
Principle, increasingly modified by legislation and judicial decision, that organizations should be able to retain or dismiss employees at their discretion

In the last several years, such suits have put limits on employment-at-will provisions in certain circumstances. In the past, for example, organizations were guilty of firing employees who filed workers' compensation claims or took excessive time off to serve on jury duty. More recently, however, the courts have ruled that employees may not be fired for exercising rights protected by law.

NEW CHALLENGES IN THE CHANGING WORKPLACE

As we have seen throughout this chapter, human resource managers face several ongoing challenges in their efforts to keep their organizations staffed with effective workforces. To complicate matters, new challenges arise as the economic and social environments of business change. We conclude this chapter with a look at several of the most important human resource management issues facing business today.

Managing Workforce Diversity

workforce diversity
Range of workers' attitudes, values, and behaviors that differ by gender, race, and ethnicity

One extremely important set of human resource challenges centers on **workforce diversity**—the range of workers' attitudes, values, beliefs, and behaviors that differ by gender, race, age, ethnicity, physical ability, and other relevant characteristics. In the past, organizations tended to work toward homogenizing their workforces, getting everyone to think and behave in similar ways. Partly as a result of affirmative action efforts, however, many U.S. organizations are now creating more diverse workforces, embracing more women, ethnic minorities, and foreign-born employees than ever before.

Figure 9.3 helps put the changing U.S. workforce into perspective by illustrating changes in the percentages of different groups of workers—males and females, whites, blacks, Hispanics, Asians, and others—in the total workforce in the years 1986, 1996, and (as projected) 2006. The picture is clearly one of increasing diversity. By 2006, say

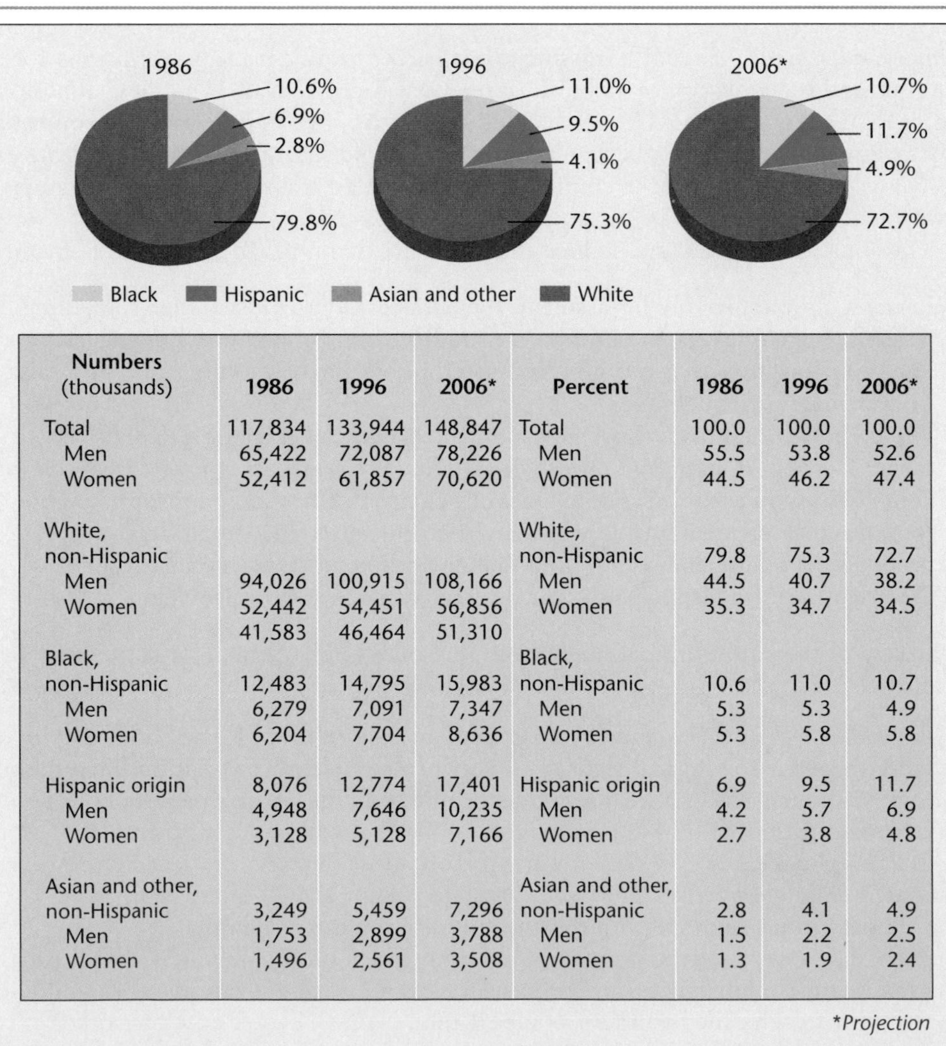

Numbers (thousands)	1986	1996	2006*	Percent	1986	1996	2006*
Total	117,834	133,944	148,847	Total	100.0	100.0	100.0
Men	65,422	72,087	78,226	Men	55.5	53.8	52.6
Women	52,412	61,857	70,620	Women	44.5	46.2	47.4
White,				White,			
non-Hispanic				non-Hispanic	79.8	75.3	72.7
Men	94,026	100,915	108,166	Men	44.5	40.7	38.2
Women	52,442	54,451	56,856	Women	35.3	34.7	34.5
	41,583	46,464	51,310				
Black,				Black,			
non-Hispanic	12,483	14,795	15,983	non-Hispanic	10.6	11.0	10.7
Men	6,279	7,091	7,347	Men	5.3	5.3	4.9
Women	6,204	7,704	8,636	Women	5.3	5.8	5.8
Hispanic origin	8,076	12,774	17,401	Hispanic origin	6.9	9.5	11.7
Men	4,948	7,646	10,235	Men	4.2	5.7	6.9
Women	3,128	5,128	7,166	Women	2.7	3.8	4.8
Asian and other,				Asian and other,			
non-Hispanic	3,249	5,459	7,296	non-Hispanic	2.8	4.1	4.9
Men	1,753	2,899	3,788	Men	1.5	2.2	2.5
Women	1,496	2,561	3,508	Women	1.3	1.9	2.4

*Projection

Figure 9.3
Changing Composition of the U.S. Workforce

experts, almost half of all workers in the labor force will be women and almost one-third will be blacks, Hispanics, Asian Americans, and others.

Today, organizations are recognizing not only that they should treat everyone equitably, but also that they should acknowledge the individuality of each person they employ. They are also recognizing that diversity can be a competitive advantage.[19] For example, by hiring the best people available from every single group rather than hiring from just one or a few groups, a firm can develop a higher-quality labor force. Similarly, a diverse workforce can bring a wider array of information to bear on problems and can provide insights on marketing products to a wider range of consumers. Says the head of workforce diversity at IBM: "We think it is important for our customers to look inside and see people like them. If they can't . . . the prospect of them becoming or staying our customers declines."

"We think it is important for our customers to look inside and see people like them. If they can't, the prospect of them becoming or staying our customers declines."

—Head of workforce diversity at IBM

Managing Knowledge Workers

Traditionally, employees added value to organizations because of what they did or because of their experience. In the "information age," however, many employees add value because of what they know.[20]

The Nature of Knowledge Work These employees are usually called **knowledge workers,** and the skill with which they are managed is a major factor in determining which firms will be successful in the future. Knowledge workers, including computer scientists, engineers, and physical scientists, provide special challenges for the HR manager. They tend to work in high-technology firms and are usually experts in some abstract knowledge base. They often like to work independently and tend to identify more strongly with their professions than with any organization—even to the extent of defining performance in terms recognized by other members of their professions.

knowledge workers
Employees who are of value because of the knowledge they possess

As the importance of information-driven jobs grows, the need for knowledge workers continues to grow as well. But these employees require extensive and highly specialized training, and not every organization is willing to make the human capital investments necessary to take advantage of these jobs. In fact, even after knowledge workers are on the job, retraining and training updates are critical to prevent their skills from becoming obsolete. It has been suggested, for example, that the "half-life" of a technical education in engineering is about three years. The failure to update such skills will not only result in the loss of competitive advantage but will also increase the likelihood that the knowledge worker will go to another firm that is more committed to updating the worker's skills.

Knowledge Worker Management and Labor Markets In recent years, the demand for knowledge workers has been growing at a dramatic rate. Even the economic downturn in 2001 had little effect on the demand for highly skilled knowledge workers. As a result, organizations that need these workers must introduce regular market adjustments (upward) in order to pay them enough to keep them. This is especially critical in areas in which demand is growing, since even entry-level salaries for these employees are skyrocketing. Once an employee accepts a job with a firm, the employer faces yet another dilemma. Once hired, workers are more subject to the company's internal labor market, which is not likely to be growing as quickly as the external market for knowledge workers as a whole. Consequently, the longer employees remain with a firm, the further behind the market their pay falls—unless it is regularly adjusted upward.

The growing demand for these workers has inspired some fairly extreme measures for attracting them in the first place.[21] High starting salaries and sign-on bonuses are common. British Petroleum Exploration <www.bpamoco.com> was recently paying starting petroleum engineers with undersea platform-drilling knowledge—not experience, just knowledge—salaries in the six figures, plus sign-on bonuses of over $50,000 and immediate profit sharing. Even with these incentives, HR managers complain that in the Gulf Coast region, they cannot retain specialists because young engineers soon leave

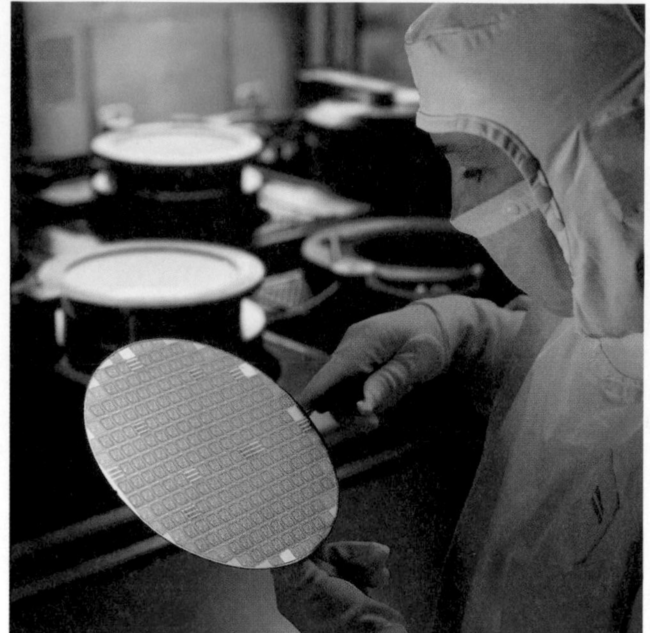

Every year the toy industry sells about 10 million scientific toys, such as chemistry sets. It also sells about 30 million electronic toys. These discrepancies help account for the fact that more and more science-minded college students—like this Power PC chip builder at Intel Corp. <www.intel.com>—are opting for computer-industry jobs instead of jobs in the traditional hard sciences, such as chemistry. Many experts predict that the current lure of quick financial solvency will result in a future shortage of science researchers and teachers.

to accept sign-on bonuses with competitors. Laments one HR executive: "We wind up six months after we hire an engineer having to fight off offers for that same engineer for more money."[22]

Contingent and Temporary Workers

A final contemporary HR issue of note involves the use of contingent and temporary workers. Indeed, recent years have seen an explosion in the use of such workers by organizations.

contingent worker
Employee hired on something other than a full-time basis to supplement an organization's permanent workforce

Trends in Contingent and Temporary Employment In recent years, the number of contingent workers in the workforce has increased dramatically. A **contingent worker** is a person who works for an organization on something other than a permanent or full-time basis. Categories of contingent workers include independent contractors, on-call workers, temporary employees (usually hired through outside agencies), and contract and leased employees. Another category is part-time workers. The financial services giant Citigroup <www.citigroup.com>, for example, makes extensive use of part-time sales agents to pursue new clients. About 10 percent of the U.S. workforce currently uses one of these alternative forms of employment relationships. Experts suggest, however, that this percentage is increasing at a consistent pace.

Managing Contingent and Temporary Workers Given the widespread use of contingent and temporary workers, HR managers must understand how to use such employees most effectively. That is, they need to understand how to manage contingent and temporary workers.

One key is careful planning. Even though one of the presumed benefits of using contingent workers is flexibility, it still is important to integrate such workers in a coordinated fashion. Rather than having to call in workers sporadically and with no prior notice, organizations try to bring in specified numbers of workers for well-defined periods of time. The ability to do so comes from careful planning.

A second key is understanding contingent workers and acknowledging their advantages and disadvantages. That is, the organization must recognize what it can and can't achieve from the use of contingent and temporary workers. Expecting too much from such workers, for example, is a mistake that managers should avoid.

Third, managers must carefully assess the real cost of using contingent workers. We noted previously that many firms adopt this course of action to save labor costs. The organization should be able to document precisely its labor-cost savings. How much would it be paying people in wages and benefits if they were on permanent staff? How does this cost compare with the amount spent on contingent workers? This difference, however, could be misleading. We also noted, for instance, that contingent workers might be less effective performers than permanent and full-time employees. Comparing employee for employee on a direct-cost basis, therefore, is not necessarily valid. Organizations must learn to adjust the direct differences in labor costs to account for differences in productivity and performance.

Finally, managers must fully understand their own strategies and decide in advance how they intend to manage temporary workers, specifically focusing on how to integrate them into the organization. On a very simplistic level, for example, an organization with a large contingent workforce must make some decisions about the treatment of contingent workers relative to the treatment of permanent full-time workers. Should contingent workers be invited to the company holiday party? Should they have the same access to such employee benefits as counseling services and child care? There are no right or wrong answers to such questions. Managers must understand that they need to develop a strategy for integrating contingent workers according to some sound logic and then follow that strategy consistently over time.[23]

DEALING WITH ORGANIZED LABOR

A **labor union** is a group of individuals working together to achieve shared job-related goals, such as higher pay, shorter working hours, more job security, greater benefits, or better working conditions.[24] **Labor relations** describes the process of dealing with employees who are represented by a union.

labor union
Group of individuals working together to achieve shared job-related goals, such as higher pay, shorter working hours, more job security, greater benefits, or better working conditions

labor relations
Process of dealing with employees who are represented by a union

Labor unions grew in popularity in the United States in the nineteenth and early twentieth centuries. The labor movement was born with the Industrial Revolution, which also gave birth to a factory-based production system that carried with it enormous economic benefits. Job specialization and mass production allowed businesses to create ever greater quantities of goods at ever lower costs.

But there was also a dark side to this era. Workers became more dependent on their factory jobs. Eager for greater profits, some owners treated their workers like other raw materials: resources to be deployed with little or no regard for the individual worker's well-being. Many businesses forced employees to work long hours—60-hour weeks were common, and some workers were routinely forced to work 12 to 16 hours a day. With no minimum-wage laws or other controls, pay was also minimal and safety standards virtually nonexistent. Workers enjoyed no job security and received few benefits. Many companies, especially textile mills, employed large numbers of children at poverty wages. If people complained, nothing prevented employers from firing and replacing them at will.

Unions appeared and ultimately prospered because they constituted a solution to the worker's most serious problem: They forced management to listen to the complaints of all their workers rather than to just the few who were brave (or foolish) enough to speak out. The power of unions, then, comes from collective action. **Collective bargaining** (which we discuss more fully later in this chapter) is the process by which union leaders and managers negotiate common terms and conditions of employment for the workers represented by unions. Although collective bargaining does not often occur in small businesses, many midsize and larger businesses must engage in the process.

collective bargaining
Process by which labor and management negotiate conditions of employment for union-represented workers

Unionism Today

While understanding the historical context of labor unions is important, so too is appreciating the role of unionism today, especially trends in union membership, union–management relations, and bargaining perspectives. We discuss these topics in the sections that follow.

Trends in Union Membership Since the mid-1950s, U.S. labor unions have experienced increasing difficulties in attracting new members. As a result, although millions of workers still belong to labor unions, union membership *as a percentage of the total workforce* has continued to decline at a very steady rate. In 1977, for example, over 26 percent of U.S. wage and salary employees belonged to labor unions. Today, that figure is about 14 percent. Figure 9.4(a) traces the decades-long decline in union membership. Moreover, if public employees are excluded from consideration, then only around 11 percent of all private industry wage and salary employees currently belong to labor unions. Figure 9.4(b) illustrates the different trends in membership for public employees versus private nonfarm employees.

Furthermore, just as union membership has continued to decline, so has the percentage of successful union-organizing campaigns. In the years immediately following World War II and continuing through the mid-1960s, most unions routinely won certification elections. In recent years, however, labor unions have been winning certification fewer than 50 percent of the time in which workers are called upon to vote. By the same token, of course, unions still do win. Meat cutters at a Florida Wal-Mart store recently voted to unionize—the first-ever successful organizing campaign against the retailing giant. "You'll see a lot more attention to Wal-Mart now," exulted one AFL-CIO official. "It's not like Wal-Mart stands out as some unattainable goal."[25]

From most indications, however, the power and significance of U.S. labor unions, while still quite formidable, are also measurably lower than they were just a few decades ago.

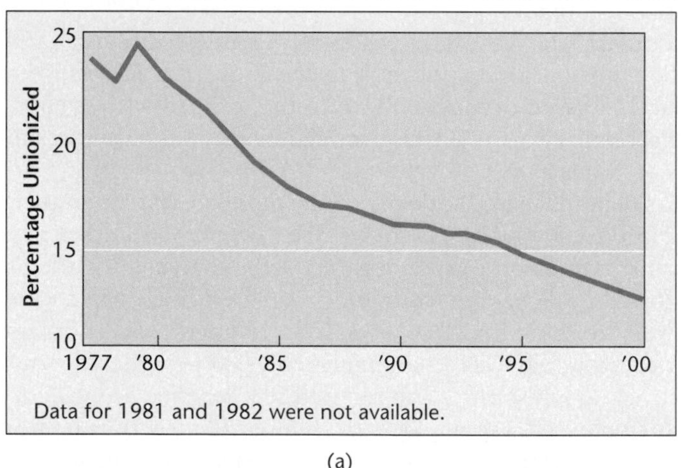

(a)

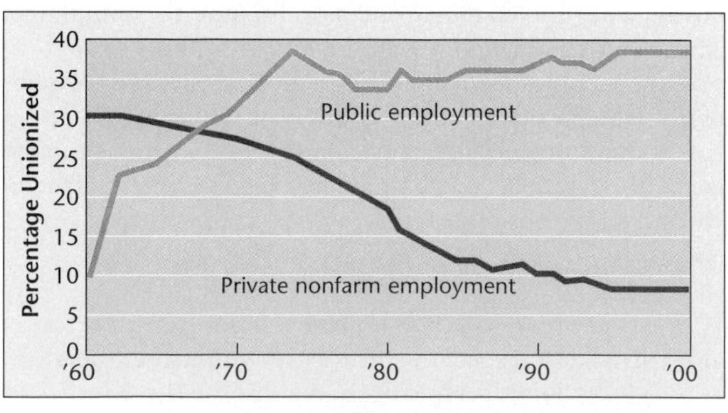

(b)

Figure 9.4

Trends in Union Membership

"Actually, Tommy, we're just about full-blooded management, except for your grandfather on your mom's side, who was one-quarter labor."

Trends in Union–Management Relations The gradual decline in unionization in the United States has been accompanied by some significant trends in union–management relations. In some sectors of the economy, perhaps most notably the automobile and steel industries, labor unions still remain quite strong. In these areas, unions have large memberships and considerable power in negotiating with management. The UAW, for example, is still one of the strongest unions in the United States.

In most sectors, however, unions are clearly in a weakened position, and as a result, many have taken much more conciliatory stances in their relations with management. This situation contrasts sharply with the more adversarial relationship that once dominated labor relations in this country. Increasingly, for instance, unions recognize that they don't have as much power as they once held and that it is in their own best interests, as well as in those of the workers that they represent, to work with management instead of working against it. Ironically, then, union–management relations are in many ways better today than they have been in many years. Admittedly, the improvement is attributable in large part to the weakened power of unions. Even so, however, most experts agree that improved union–management relations have benefited both sides.

Trends in Bargaining Perspectives Given the trends described in the two previous sections, we should not be surprised to find changes in bargaining perspectives as well. In the past, most union–management bargaining situations were characterized by union demands for dramatic increases in wages and salaries. A secondary issue was usually increased benefits for members. Now, however, unions often bargain for different benefits, such as job security. Of particular interest in this area is the trend toward relocating jobs to take advantage of lower labor costs in other countries. Unions, of course, want to restrict job movement, whereas companies want to save money by moving facilities—and jobs—to other countries.

As a result of organizational downsizing and several years of relatively low inflation in this country, many unions today find themselves, rather than striving for wage increases, fighting against wage cuts. Similarly, as organizations are more likely to seek lower health care and other benefits, a common goal of union strategy is preserving what's already been won. Unions also place greater emphasis on improved job security. A trend that has become especially important in recent years is toward improved pension programs for employees.

Unions have also begun increasingly to set their sights on preserving jobs for workers in the United States in the face of business efforts to relocate production in some sectors to countries where labor costs are lower. For example, the AFL-CIO has been

As part of a massive cost-cutting drive, General Electric <www.ge.com> *has begun urging its suppliers to move to Mexico, where the labor is cheaper. The company even sponsors "supplier migration" conferences to help companies work out the logistics of moving. At Ametek Inc.* <www.ametek.com>*, a supplier of parts of GE's jet engine plant in Lynn, Massachusetts, members of the International Union of Electronic Workers protest the export of U.S. jobs across the border. Since 1986, GE's domestic workforce has decreased by 50 percent while foreign employment has nearly doubled.*

an outspoken opponent of efforts to normalize trade relations with China, fearing that more businesses might be tempted to move jobs there. General Electric <www.ge.com> has been targeted for union protests recently because of its strategy to move many of its own jobs—and those of key suppliers—to Mexico.[26]

The Future of Unions Despite declining membership and some loss of power, labor unions remain a major factor in the U.S. business world. The 86 labor organizations in the AFL-CIO, as well as independent major unions such as the Teamsters and the National Education Association, still play a major role in U.S. business. Moreover, some unions still wield considerable power, especially in the traditional strongholds of goods-producing industries. Labor and management in some industries, notably airlines and steel, are beginning to favor contracts that establish formal mechanisms for greater worker input into management decisions. Inland Steel <www.inland.com>, for instance, recently granted its major union the right to name a member to the board of directors. Union officers can also attend executive meetings.

COLLECTIVE BARGAINING

When a union has been legally certified, it assumes the role of official bargaining agent for the workers whom it represents. Collective bargaining is an ongoing process involving both the drafting and the administering of the terms of a labor contract.[27]

Reaching Agreement on Contract Terms

The collective bargaining process begins when the union is recognized as the exclusive negotiator for its members. The bargaining cycle itself begins when union leaders meet with management representatives to agree on a contract. By law, both parties must sit down at the bargaining table and negotiate in good faith.

When each side has presented its demands, sessions focus on identifying the *bargaining zone*. The process is shown in Figure 9.5. For example, although an employer may initially offer no pay raise, it may expect to grant a raise of up to 6 percent. Likewise, the union may initially *demand* a 10-percent pay raise while *expecting* to accept a raise as low as 4 percent. The bargaining zone, then, is a raise between 4 and 6 percent. Ideally, some compromise is reached between these levels and the new agreement submitted for a ratification vote by union membership.

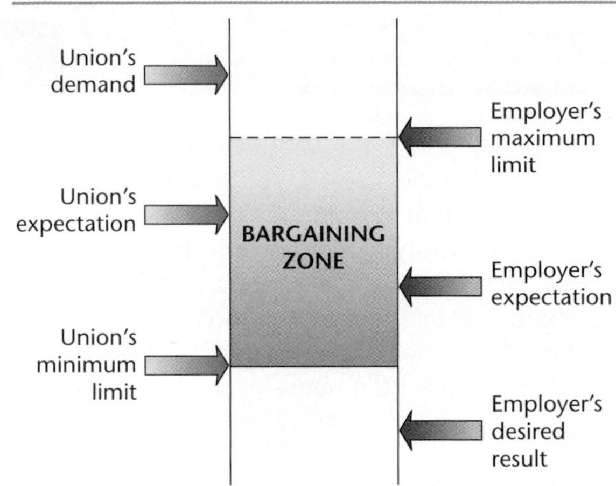

Figure 9.5
The Bargaining Zone

Sometimes this process goes quite smoothly. At other times, however, the two sides cannot—or will not—agree. The speed and ease with which such an impasse is resolved depend in part on the nature of the contract issues, the willingness of each side to use certain tactics, and the prospects for mediation or arbitration.[28]

Contract Issues

The labor contract itself can address an array of different issues. Most of these concern demands that unions make on behalf of their members. In this section we will survey the categories of issues that are typically most important to union negotiators: *compensation, benefits*, and *job security*. Although few issues covered in a labor contract are company sponsored, we will also describe the kinds of management rights that are negotiated in most bargaining agreements.

Compensation The most common issue is compensation. One aspect of compensation is current wages. Obviously, unions generally want their employees to earn higher wages and try to convince management to raise hourly wages for all or some employees.

Of equal concern to unions is future compensation: wage rates to be paid during subsequent years of the contract. One common tool for securing wage increases is a **cost-of-living adjustment (COLA)**. Most COLA clauses tie future raises to the *Consumer Price Index* (CPI), a government statistic that reflects changes in consumer purchasing power. The premise is that as the CPI increases by a specified amount during a given period of time, wages will automatically be increased. Almost half of all labor contracts today include COLA clauses.

cost-of-living adjustment (COLA)
Labor contract clause tying future raises to changes in consumer purchasing power

wage reopener clause
Clause allowing wage rates to be renegotiated during the life of a labor contract

Wage reopener clauses are now included in almost 10 percent of all labor contracts. Such a clause allows wage rates to be renegotiated at preset times during the life of the contract. For example, a union might be uncomfortable with a long-term contract based solely on COLA wage increases. A long-term agreement might be more acceptable, however, if management agrees to renegotiate wages every two years.

Benefits Employee benefits are also an important component in most labor contracts. Unions typically want employers to pay all or most of the costs of insurance for employees. Other benefits commonly addressed during negotiations include retirement benefits, paid holidays, and working conditions.

Job Security Nevertheless, the UAW's top priority in its most recent negotiations with U.S. automakers has been job security, an increasingly important agenda item in many bargaining sessions today. In some cases, demands for job security entail the promise that a company not move to another location. In others, the contract may dictate that if the workforce is reduced, seniority will be used to determine which employees keep their jobs.

WEB Connection

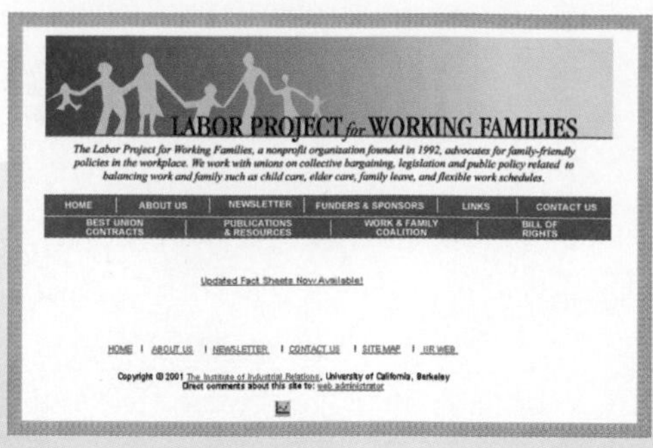

Founded in 1992, the Labor Project for Working Families works with unions to develop family-oriented policies—including family leave, flexible hours, dependent care, and domestic partner benefits—at the workplace. The organization then helps unions negotiate contracts that reflect the needs of working families.

violet.berkeley.edu/~iir/workfam/home.html

Other Union Issues Other possible issues might include such things as working hours, overtime policies, rest period arrangements, differential pay plans for shift employees, the use of temporary workers, grievance procedures, and allowable union activities (dues collection, union bulletin boards, and so forth).

Management Rights Management wants as much control as possible over hiring policies, work assignments, and so forth. Unions, meanwhile, often try to limit management rights by specifying hiring, assignment, and other policies. At a DaimlerChrysler plant in Detroit, for example, the contract stipulates that three workers are needed to change fuses in robots: a machinist to open the robot, an electrician to change the fuse, and a supervisor to oversee the process. As in this case, contracts often bar workers in one job category from performing work that falls in the domain of another. Unions try to secure jobs by defining as many different categories as possible (the DaimlerChrysler plant has over 100). Of course, management resists the practice, which limits flexibility and makes it difficult to reassign workers.

When Bargaining Fails

An impasse occurs when, after a series of bargaining sessions, management and labor have failed to agree on a new contract or a contract to replace an agreement that is about to expire. Although it is generally agreed that both parties suffer when an impasse is reached and action is taken, each side can use several tactics to support its cause until the impasse is resolved.[29]

Union Tactics When their demands are not met, unions may bring a variety of tactics to the bargaining table. Chief among these is the *strike*, which may be supported by *pickets*, *boycotts*, or both.

strike
Labor action in which employees temporarily walk off the job and refuse to work

economic strike
Strike usually triggered by stalemate over one or more mandatory bargaining items

The Strike A **strike** occurs when employees temporarily walk off the job and refuse to work. Most strikes in the United States are **economic strikes**, triggered by stalemates over mandatory bargaining items, including such noneconomic issues as working hours. For example, the Teamsters union struck United Parcel Service (UPS) a few years ago over several noneconomic issues. Specifically, the union wanted the firm to transform many of its temporary and part-time jobs into permanent and full-time jobs. Strikers returned to work only when UPS agreed to create 10,000 new jobs. More recently, the same union struck Union Pacific Corp. <www.up.com> in January 2000 over wages and new jobs. In April 2000, machinists at a Lockheed-Martin <www.lmco.com> plant in Fort Worth, Texas, staged a two-week strike. Reflected the

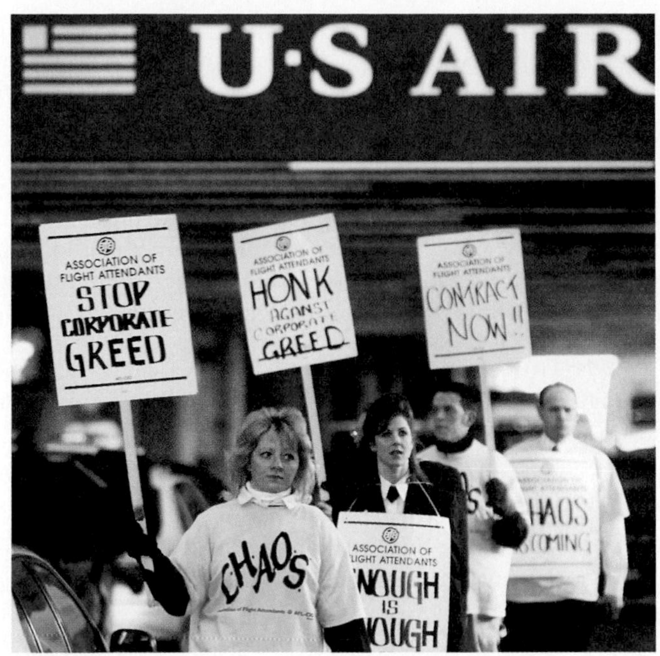

The tactic is called CHAOS—Creating Havoc Around Our System. It isn't typically union-ordered, but it's often effective because, at least in the airline business, it hits employers where it hurts the most—in passenger service. CHAOS consists of a series of service disruptions, which in the airline industry means intermittent strikes against individual flights. In 2000, when U.S. Airways <www.usair.com> *demanded a 5-percent cut in pay and benefits, members of the Association of Flight Attendants* <www.flightattendants-afa.org> *resorted to CHAOS and won an 11-percent pay hike.*

president of the union local: "I think our people gained a lot of respect for taking a stand. We had a good strike."

Still, there are far fewer strikes today than there were in previous years. For example, there were 222 strikes in the United States in 1960 involving a total of 896,000 workers. In 1970, 2,468,000 workers took part in 381 strikes. But in 1990 there were only 44 strikes involving 185,000 workers. Since 1990, the annual number of strikes has ranged from a high of 45 (in 1994) to a low of 29 (in 1997).[30]

Not all strikes are legal. **Sympathy strikes** (also called **secondary strikes**), which occur when one union strikes in sympathy with action initiated by another, may violate the sympathetic union's contract. **Wildcat strikes**—strikes unauthorized by the union that occur during the life of a contract—deprive strikers of their status as employees and thus of the protection of national labor law.

Other Labor Actions To support a strike, a union faced with an impasse has recourse to additional legal activities:

- In **picketing**, workers march at the entrance to the employer's facility with signs explaining their reasons for striking.
- A **boycott** occurs when union members agree not to buy the products of a targeted employer. Workers may also urge consumers to boycott the firm's products.
- Another alternative to striking is a work **slowdown**. Instead of striking, workers perform their jobs at a much slower pace than normal. A variation is the sickout, during which large numbers of workers call in sick. Pilots at American Airlines engaged in a massive "sickout" in early 1999, causing the airline to cancel thousands of flights before a judge ordered them back into the cockpit.

Management Tactics Like workers, management can respond forcefully to an impasse:

- **Lockouts** occur when employers deny employees access to the workplace. Lockouts are illegal if they are used as offensive weapons to give management a bargaining advantage. However, they are legal if management has a legitimate business need (for instance, avoiding a buildup of perishable inventory).

sympathy strike (or secondary strike)
Strike in which one union strikes to support action initiated by another

wildcat strike
Strike that is unauthorized by the strikers' union

picketing
Labor action in which workers publicize their grievances at the entrance to an employer's facility

boycott
Labor action in which workers refuse to buy the products of a targeted employer

slowdown
Labor action in which workers perform jobs at a slower than normal pace

lockout
Management tactic whereby workers are denied access to the employer's workplace

strikebreaker
Worker hired as permanent or temporary replacement for a striking employee

mediation
Method of resolving a labor dispute in which a third party suggests, but does not impose, a settlement

voluntary arbitration
Method of resolving a labor dispute in which both parties agree to submit to the judgment of a neutral party

compulsory arbitration
Method of resolving a labor dispute in which both parties are legally required to accept the judgment of a neutral party

Although rare today, ABC <www.abc.go.com> locked out its off-camera employees in 1998 because they staged an unannounced one-day strike during a critical broadcasting period. Likewise, almost half of the 1998–1999 NBA season was lost when team owners <www.nba.com> locked out their players over contract issues.

- A firm can also hire temporary or permanent replacements called **strikebreakers**. However, the law forbids the permanent replacement of workers who strike because of unfair practices. In some cases, an employer can also obtain legal injunctions that either prohibit workers from striking or prohibit a union from interfering with its efforts to use replacement workers.

Mediation and Arbitration Rather than wield these often unpleasant weapons against one another, labor and management can agree to call in a third party to help resolve the dispute:

- In **mediation**, the neutral third party (the mediator) can advise but cannot impose a settlement on the other parties.
- In **voluntary arbitration**, the neutral third party (the arbitrator) dictates a settlement between the two sides, which have agreed to submit to outside judgment.
- In some cases, arbitration is legally required to settle bargaining disputes. **Compulsory arbitration** is used to settle disputes between the government and public employees such as firefighters and police officers.[31]

Continued from page 222

How Paternal is too Paternal?

Jim Goodnight's HR strategy has paid major dividends for SAS Institute. The firm has a loyal and dedicated workforce and phenomenally low turnover for a firm in its industry. It continues to receive accolades for being one of the very best employers in the United States.

But SAS and Jim Goodnight do have their critics. For one thing, some observers feel that the place is almost too perfect. They say that it conjures up images of Stepford, the fictional town created by novelist Ira Levin in *The Stepford Wives* where "disobedient" or "nonconformist" spouses were replaced by androids. This criticism resurfaced when Goodnight developed a housing subdivision adjacent to the SAS campus so that employees could buy discounted homes with mortgages financed through the company.

Critics also allege that SAS's lavish benefit packages smack of paternalism—that the company treats employees as if they can't take care of their own lives without the company's help. They also point to one glaring omission in SAS's reward system—stock and stock options for employees. While most growing high-tech companies give their employees a chance to prosper along with the company through stock ownership, Jim Goodnight and John Sall retain full ownership of SAS.

Even though these may be legitimate reservations, most observers and employees feel that the criticism is unwarranted. After all, no company can provide everything for its employees, and no one is "forced" to accept the benefits that SAS does provide. Perhaps more importantly, most observers and employees continue to view SAS as a model employer.

Questions for Discussion

1. Evaluate SAS Institute's employment practices from a strict business perspective.
2. How does the history of the firm affect its employment practices?

3. Which SAS benefits appeal most to you personally? Which appeal least to you?
4. Would you have an interest in working for SAS? Why or why not?
5. Are there potential pitfalls or problems with the firm's approach to HR management that might arise in the future?
6. How would you respond to the critics of SAS?

SUMMARY OF LEARNING OBJECTIVES

1 **Define *human resource management* and explain how managers plan for human resources.** *Human resource management*, or *HRM*, is the set of organizational activities directed at attracting, developing, and maintaining an effective workforce. Planning for human resource needs entails several steps. Conducting a *job analysis* enables managers to create detailed, accurate job descriptions and specifications. After analysis is complete, managers must *forecast* demand and supply for both the numbers and types of workers they will need. Then they consider steps to match supply with demand.

2 **Identify the issues involved in *staffing* a company and discuss ways in which organizations develop human resources and evaluate employee performance.** *Recruiting* is the process of attracting qualified persons to apply for jobs that an organization has open. *Internal recruiting* involves considering present employees for new jobs. This approach helps build morale and rewards an organization's best employees. *External recruiting* means attracting people from outside the organization to apply for openings. When organizations are actually selecting people for jobs, they generally use such selection techniques as *application forms, tests*, and *interviews*. Regardless of what selection techniques are used, they must be valid predictors of an individual's expected performance in the job.

If a company is to get the most out of its workers, it must develop both those workers and their skills. *Performance appraisals* help managers decide who needs training and who should be promoted. Appraisals also tell employees how well they are meeting expectations. Although a variety of alternatives are available for appraising performance, employee supervisors are most commonly used. No matter who does the evaluation, however, feedback to the employee is very important. Managers can select from a variety of *ranking* and *rating methods* for use in performance appraisal.

3 **Discuss the importance of *wages and salaries, incentives*, and *benefit programs* in attracting and keeping skilled workers.** *Wages and salaries, incentives*, and *benefit packages* may all be parts of a company's *compensation program*. By paying its workers as well as or better than competitors, a business can attract and keep qualified personnel. Incentive programs can also motivate people to work more productively. *Indirect compensation* also plays a major role in effective and well-designed compensation systems.

4 **Describe some of the key legal issues involved in hiring, compensating, and managing workers in today's workplace.** In hiring, compensating, and managing workers, managers must obey a variety of federal laws. *Equal employment opportunity* and equal pay laws forbid discrimination other than action based on legitimate job requirements. The concept of *comparable worth* holds that different jobs requiring equal levels of training and skill should pay the same. Firms are also required to provide employees with safe working environments, as set down by the guidelines of the *Occupational Safety and Health Administration*. Managers must consider employment-at-will issues (that is, limitations on their rights to hire and fire at their own discretion). AIDS and *sexual harassment* are other key contemporary legal issues in business.

5 **Discuss *workforce diversity*, the management of *knowledge workers*, and the use of *contingent* and *temporary workers* as important changes in the contemporary workplace.** *Workforce diversity* refers to the range of workers' attitudes, values, beliefs, and behaviors that differ by gender, race, ethnicity, age, and physical ability. Today, many U.S. businesses are working to create workforces that reflect the growing diversity of the population as it enters the labor pool. Although many firms see the diverse workforce as a competitive advantage, not all are equally successful in or eager about implementing diversity programs.

Many firms today also face challenges in managing *knowledge workers*. The recent boom in high-technology companies has led to rapidly increasing salaries and high turnover among the workers who are best prepared to work in those companies. *Contingent workers* are temporary and part-time employees hired to supplement an organization's permanent workforce. Their numbers have grown significantly since the early 1980s and are expected to rise further. The practice of hiring contingent workers is gaining in popularity because it gives managers more flexibility and because temps are usually not covered by employers' benefit programs.

6 **Explain why workers unionize and identify the steps in the *collective bargaining process*.** The Industrial Revolution and the emergence of a factory-based production system made many workers dependent on continuing factory employment. The treatment of labor as a raw material led to such abuses as minimal pay, long workdays and weeks, unsafe working conditions, and even child labor. Individuals had little recourse in rectifying problems. By organizing into labor unions, however, workers are able to act collectively to improve work conditions. Most importantly, acting as a group, they can engage in *collective bargaining* for higher wages, greater benefits, or better working conditions.

Once certified, the union engages in collective bargaining with the organization. The initial step in collective bargaining is reaching agreement on a *labor contract*. Contract demands usually involve wages, job security, or management rights.

Both labor and management have several tactics that can be used against the other if negotiations break down. Unions may attempt a *strike* or a *boycott* of the firm or may engage in a *slowdown*. Companies may hire replacement workers (*strikebreakers*) or *lock out* all workers. In extreme cases, *mediation* or *arbitration* may be used to settle disputes. Once a contract has been agreed on, union and management representatives continue to interact to settle worker grievances and interpret the contract.

QUESTIONS AND EXERCISES

Questions for Review

1. What are the advantages and disadvantages of internal and external recruiting? Under what circumstances is each more appropriate?
2. Why is the formal training of workers so important to most employers? Why don't employers simply let people learn about their jobs as they perform them?
3. What different forms of compensation do firms typically use to attract and keep productive workers?
4. Why do workers in some companies unionize whereas workers in others do not?

Questions for Analysis

5. What are your views on drug testing in the workplace? What would you do if your employer asked you to submit to a drug test?
6. Workers at Ford, GM, and DaimlerChrysler are represented by the United Auto Workers (UAW). However, the UAW has been unsuccessful in its attempts to unionize U.S. workers employed at Toyota, Nissan, and Honda plants in the United States. Why do you think this is so?
7. What training do you think you are most likely to need when you finish school and start your career?
8. How much will benefit considerations affect your choice of an employer after graduation?

Application Exercises

9. Interview an HR manager at a local company. Focus on a position for which the firm is currently recruiting applicants and identify the steps in the selection process.
10. Interview the managers of two local companies, one unionized and one nonunionized. Compare the wage and salary levels, benefits, and working conditions of employees at the two firms.

EXPLORING THE WEB

Keeping the Internet on Retainer

One of the most important issues facing managers today is compliance with various legal regulations. The following Web site summarizes many employment cases that were resolved by arbitration:

<www.lawmemo.com/emp/sum/subjects/arbitration/bytopic.htm>

Visit the site and review some of the cases. Choose two or three that seem interesting to you and write a brief description of each. Describe the potential implications for HR managers and respond to the following questions:

1. How useful is the Internet in keeping human resource managers informed about legal actions that may affect them?
2. Does relying on the Internet for legal information pose any risks?
3. What other legal information about HRM might be useful to have on the Internet?

EXERCISING YOUR ETHICS

Operating Tactically

THE SITUATION

Assume that you work as a manager for a medium-size nonunion company that is facing its most serious union organizing campaign in years. Your boss, who is determined to keep the union out, has just given you a list of things to do in order to thwart the efforts of the organizers. For example, he has suggested each of the following tactics:

- Whenever you learn about a scheduled union meeting, you should schedule a "worker appreciation" event at the same time. He wants you to offer free pizza and barbecue and give cash prizes (that winners have to be present to receive).
- He wants you to look at the most recent performance evaluations of the key union organizers and to terminate the one with the lowest overall evaluation.
- He wants you to make an announcement that the firm is seriously considering such new benefits as on-site child care, flexible work schedules, telecommuting options, and exercise facilities. Although you know that the firm is indeed looking into these benefits, you also know that, ultimately, your boss will provide far less lavish benefits than he wants you to intimate.

THE DILEMMA

When you questioned the ethics—and even the legality—of these tactics, your boss responded by saying, "Look, all's fair in love and war, and this is war." He went on to explain that he was seriously concerned that a union victory might actually shut down the company's domestic operations altogether, forcing it to move all of its production capacities to lower-cost foreign plants. He concluded by saying that he was really looking out for the employees, even if he had to play hard ball to help them. You easily see through his hypocrisy, but you also realize that there is some potential truth in his warning: If the union wins, jobs may actually be lost.

QUESTIONS FOR DISCUSSION

1. What are the ethical issues in this situation?
2. What are the basic arguments for and against extreme measures to fight unionization efforts?
3. What do you think most managers would do in this situation? What would you do?

BUILDING YOUR BUSINESS SKILLS

A Little Collective Brainstorming

This exercise enhances the following SCANS workplace competencies: demonstrating basic skills, demonstrating thinking skills, exhibiting interpersonal skills, and working with information.

GOAL

To encourage students to understand why some companies unionize and others do not.

THE SITUATION

You've been working for the same nonunion company for five years. Although there are problems in the company, you like your job and have confidence in your ability to get ahead. Recently, you've heard rumblings that a large group of workers wants to call for a union election. You're not sure how you feel about this because none of your friends or family are union members.

METHOD

Step 1

Come together with three other "coworkers" who have the same questions as you do. Each person should target four companies to learn their union status. Avoid small businesses—choose large corporations such as General Motors, Intel, and Sears. As you investigate, answer the following questions:

- Is the company unionized?
- Is every worker in the company unionized or just selected groups of workers? Describe the groups.
- If a company is unionized, what is the union's history in that company?
- If a company is unionized, what are the main labor–management issues?
- If a company is unionized, how would you describe the current status of labor–management relations? For example, is it cordial or strained?
- If a company is not unionized, what factors are responsible for its nonunion status?

To learn the answers to these questions, contact the company, read corporate annual reports, search the company's Web site, contact union representatives, or do research on a computerized database.

Step 2

Go to the Web site of the AFL-CIO <www.aflcio.org/> to learn more about the current status of the union movement. Then with your coworkers write a short report about the advantages of union membership.

Step 3

Research the disadvantages of unionization. A key issue to address is whether unions make it harder for companies to compete in the global marketplace.

FOLLOW-UP QUESTIONS

1. Based on everything you learned, are you sympathetic to the union movement? Would you want to be a union member?

2. Are the union members you spoke with satisfied or dissatisfied with their union's efforts to achieve better working conditions, higher wages, and improved benefits?
3. What is the union's role when layoffs occur?
4. Based on what you learned, do you think the union movement will stumble or thrive in the years ahead?

CRAFTING YOUR BUSINESS PLAN

Taking the Occasion to Deal with Labor

THE PURPOSE OF THE ASSIGNMENT

1. To familiarize students with the labor and management relations issues faced by a start-up as it develops its business plan, using the planning framework of *Business PlanPro (BPP)* (Version 4.0).
2. To stimulate students' thinking about the application of textbook information on labor and management relations to the preparation of a *BPP* business plan.

FOLLOW-UP ASSIGNMENT

After reading Chapter 9 in the textbook, open the BPP *software and look around for information about labor and management relations as it applies to a sample firm:* Occasions *(Occasions, The Event Planning Specialists). Then respond to the following questions*:

1. Explore the business plan for this company, paying special attention to its product line and the types of clients that will be buying its products. Do you suspect that there will be union members among the employees of some Occasions customers? [Sites to see in *BPP* for this item: In the Plan Outline screen, click on each of the following, in turn: **1.0 Executive Summary, 1.1 Objectives,** and **1.2 Mission.** After returning to the Plan Outline screen, examine each of the following: **Table: Startup** (beneath **2.2 Startup Summary**), **3.0 Products and Services, 3.1 Competitive Comparison,** and **4.1 Market Segmentation.**]
2. Considering Occasion's growth projections, do you foresee increasing likelihood for unionization of its employees? Why or why not? What should Occasions do to accommodate clients' unions? [Sites to see in *BPP* for this item: In the Plan Outline screen, click on **1.1 Objectives.** Also look at each of **2.0 Company Summary** and **6.1 Organization Structure.**]
3. Explain why some experience with labor laws and management–union contract issues would be valuable for Occasions' salespeople in their dealings with clients. [Sites to see in *BPP* for this item: In the Plan Outline screen, click on each of the following, in turn: **1.0 Executive Summary, 3.0 Products and Services,** and **4.1 Market Segmentation.** After returning to the Plan Outline screen, examine each of the following: **4.2 Target Market Segment Strategy** and **4.3 Industry Analysis.** After returning once again to the Plan Outline screen, click on **1.3 Keys to Success.**]

VIDEO EXERCISE

Channeling Human Resources: Showtime

LEARNING OBJECTIVES

The purpose of this video is to help you:

1. Identify the many ways in which HR managers can actively develop human resources.
2. Appreciate the role of mentoring in employee development.
3. Understand how a performance appraisal system can be designed and administered.

BACKGROUND INFORMATION

Showtime Networks Inc. (SNI) <www.showtime.com> is a wholly owned subsidiary of Viacom Inc. <www.viacom.com>, a giant media conglomerate, and operates the premium television networks Showtime, The Movie Channel (TMC), Flix, and Showtime Event Television. It also operates the premium network Sundance Channel <www.sundancechannel.com>, a joint venture with Robert Redford and PolyGram Filmed Entertainment. One of the biggest challenges at SNI is attracting, retaining, and motivating a committed workforce. Demographic changes, work and family issues, and increasing diversities of age, race, and lifestyle tax the creativity of the company's HR staff.

THE VIDEO

This segment introduces various SNI executives who discuss the company's HR policies and challenges. The firm is a leader in creating a broad training and career-development program that serves a wide range of employee needs. It also uses a performance appraisal system that employees helped design and sponsors a formal program for encouraging mentoring.

QUESTIONS FOR DISCUSSION

1. Among the organizational changes recently made at SNI are the combining of the legal and the human resource departments and the

appointment of an HR manager to each SNI division. What are the pros and cons of these changes?

2. How good a job do you think SNI is doing to offer employees a chance to develop and improve their skills? Can you suggest additional programs that the company could undertake to achieve this goal?
3. Do you think the performance appraisal system at SNI is effective? Why or why not?

FOLLOW-UP ASSIGNMENT

Consider a small business such as a restaurant or consulting firm. What particular human resource challenges does this firm face in acknowledging diversity and in planning career-development programs? Sketch a plan for overcoming common obstacles, making your recommendations as specific as you can. Include any benefits that the business will enjoy from diversity and career development.

FOR FURTHER EXPLORATION

Visit the Web site of the Occupational Safety and Health Administration <www.osha.gov> and use the "News Room" or the search function to research the current status of OSHA initiatives on any of the following: indoor air pollution, asbestos removal, workplace violence. Where does OSHA stand on the issue, and what future action, if any, is it planning to take?

Understanding Principles of Marketing

Part IV

CHAPTER 10

Understanding Marketing Processes and Consumer Behavior

After reading this chapter, you should be able to:

1. Define *marketing.*
2. Describe the five forces that constitute the *external marketing environment.*
3. Explain market *segmentation* and show how it is used in *target marketing.*
4. Describe the key factors that influence the *consumer buying process.*
5. Discuss the three categories of *organizational markets.*
6. Identify a *product* and distinguish between *consumer* and *industrial products.*
7. Explain the importance of *branding* and *packaging.*

Xbox Spots the Market

Once the domain of teenage boys, interactive games are now luring a much broader audience, including younger kids and adults. It's easy to become addicted: With cinematically realistic graphics, games involve split-second timing, fast decisions, and rapid-fire movements to navigate challenging action sequences. In addition, today's communications technology allows real-time interaction among gaming enthusiasts, either in side-by-side competition or among opponents in different locations nearly anywhere in the world.

Consider one such enthusiast, Josh Bell, a Grammy Award–winning violinist and one of *People* magazine's "50 Most Beautiful People" for 2001. Bell often spends 20 hours a week gaming, sometimes at the expense of violin practice. He uses a wireless keyboard hooked into a 50-inch plasma wall TV. Six speakers provide surround sound for total immersion in such virtual games as "Quake III" and "Defense," an Internet game. To justify time away from violin practice, admits Bell, "I used to tell my mother it would improve my hand–eye coordination." At age 32, Bell is at the older end of the gaming-enthusiast spectrum. The mainstream includes mid-20s, late and early teens, and, at the youngest end of the demographic, 10-year-olds.

Enthusiasm such as Bell's explains the rapid increase in market size: Computer- and video-game sales have grown 15 percent a year for the past four years. By 2001, they had caught up with the sales of DVDs and videotapes. Sales of game hardware and software in the three biggest markets—the United States, Europe, and Japan—reached $16.5 billion in 2001 and will top $20 billion by 2003. It comes as no surprise that the prospect of such a vast market has attracted the attention of software giant Microsoft.

Before its launch date in November 2001, Xbox—Microsoft's entry into console gaming—was one of the

"I used to tell my mother it would improve my hand–eye coordination."

—Violinist and electronic gamer Josh Bell

industry's most anticipated products. Its $500 million marketing budget included the prelaunch Web site <www.Xbox.com>, which offered volumes of product information to tantalize players and game developers with the wonders of fourth-generation gaming consoles. The green-and-black Xbox boasts the most advanced hardware and claims to deliver the hottest graphics in the industry. Just as importantly, Microsoft intends the Xbox Web site to become *the* gathering place for the "community" of games players and to promote enthusiasm and interaction among gamers everywhere. Thus far, Xbox.com has succeeded both in establishing relationships among gamers and in forming new bonds between gamers and the Xbox brand. Microsoft hopes these relationships will go beyond the initial purchase of the Xbox: The company wants gamers to become loyal, long-term members of the Xbox community.

But industry experts know that it takes more than relationship building and powerful hardware to be successful in this market. Success depends on a steady supply of exciting and customer-grabbing software—games that capture players' imaginations. Says Phaedra Boinodiris, head of Womengamers.com: "The hardware [for Xbox] far outweighs the competition for speed and memory, but there's a serious problem with the lineup [of games] so far." The initial launch of Xbox calls for 12 to 20 games, most of which are action and sports oriented. Only one adventure game, "Munch's Oddysee," caters to gamers who want adventure and strategy games.

Brand loyalty will also play a role in the outcome of the "gaming wars." Nintendo <www.nintendocenter.com> and Sony <www.playstation.com> have established their own hard-core groups of followers. Dan Rescigno, a Long Island high schooler, is a solid Sony supporter. On Microsoft's lineup of games, Rescigno says that "Xbox may have these outstanding graphics, but if it has no selection of games to buy, then why bother? I have to stick with PlayStation."

Nevertheless, Microsoft's start-up marketing has already had an impact. By early 2001—more than six months before the planned release date for Xbox—the head of game buying at Gamestock (the Barnes & Noble division that includes Babbages, Software Etc., and Funco Land Stores) had already stopped accepting advance orders for Xbox at 50,000 units.

Our opening story continues on page 273

WHAT IS MARKETING?

What comes to mind when you think of *marketing*? Most people usually think of advertising for products such as detergent or soft drinks, but marketing encompasses a much wider range of activities. The American Marketing Association <www.ama.org> has formally defined **marketing** as "the process of planning and executing the conception, pricing, promotion, and distribution of ideas, goods, and services to create exchanges that satisfy individual and organizational goals."[1] In this section, we discuss the multifaceted activity of marketing by exploring this definition. We then explore the marketing environment. Finally, we focus on the four activities—developing, pricing, promoting, and placing products—that comprise the *marketing mix*.

marketing
The process of planning and executing the conception, pricing, promotion, and distribution of ideas, goods, and services to create exchanges that satisfy individual and organizational objectives

Marketing: Goods, Services, and Ideas

The marketing of tangible goods is obvious in everyday life. You walk into a department store and a woman with a clipboard asks if you would like to try a new cologne. A pharmaceutical company proclaims the virtues of its new cold medicine. Your local auto dealer offers an economy car at an economy price. These products—the cologne, the cold medicine, and the car—are all **consumer goods**: products that you, the consumer, may buy for personal use. Firms that sell products to consumers for personal consumption are engaged in *consumer marketing*.

consumer goods
Products purchased by consumers for personal use

industrial goods
Products purchased by companies to produce other products

services
Intangible products, such as time, expertise, or an activity that can be purchased

Marketing also applies to **industrial goods**: products used by companies to produce other products. Conveyors, surgical instruments, and earthmovers are industrial goods, as are components and raw materials such as transistors, integrated circuits, coal, steel, and unformed plastic. Firms that sell their products to other manufacturers are engaged in *industrial marketing*.

Marketing techniques can also be applied to **services**: intangible products such as time, expertise, or an activity that can be purchased. *Service marketing* has become a major area of growth in the United States. Insurance companies, airlines, investment counselors, health clinics, and public accountants all engage in service marketing, either to individuals or to other companies.

Marketing is relevant to the promotion of ideas. For example, television advertising and other promotional activities proclaim that teaching is an honorable profession and that teachers are "heroes." Other advertisements stress the importance of driving only when sober and the advantages of not smoking.

Relationship Marketing Although marketing often focuses on single transactions for products, services, or ideas, a longer-term perspective has become equally important for successful marketing. Rather than emphasizing a single transaction, **relationship marketing** emphasizes lasting relationships with customers and suppliers. Stronger relationships—including stronger economic and social ties—can result in greater long-term satisfaction and retention of customers.[2]

relationship marketing
Marketing strategy that emphasizes lasting relationships with customers and suppliers

Commercial banks, for example, feature "loyalty banking" programs that offer *economic* incentives to encourage longer-lasting relationships. Customers who purchase more of the bank's products (for example, checking accounts, savings accounts, and loans) accumulate credits toward free or reduced-price services, such as free traveler's checks or lower interest rates. Harley-Davidson <www.harley-davidson.com> offers social incentives through the Harley Owners Group (H.O.G.)—the largest motorcycle club in the world, with 500,000 members and approximately 900 dealer-sponsored chapters worldwide. H.O.G., explain Harley marketers, "is dedicated to building customers for life. H.O.G. fosters long-term commitments to the sport of motorcycling by providing opportunities for our customers to bond with other riders and develop long-term friendships."

The Marketing Environment

Marketing plans, decisions, and strategies are not determined unilaterally by any business, not even by marketers as experienced and influential as Coca-Cola <www.coke.com> and Procter & Gamble <www.pg.com>. Rather, they are strongly

WEB Connection

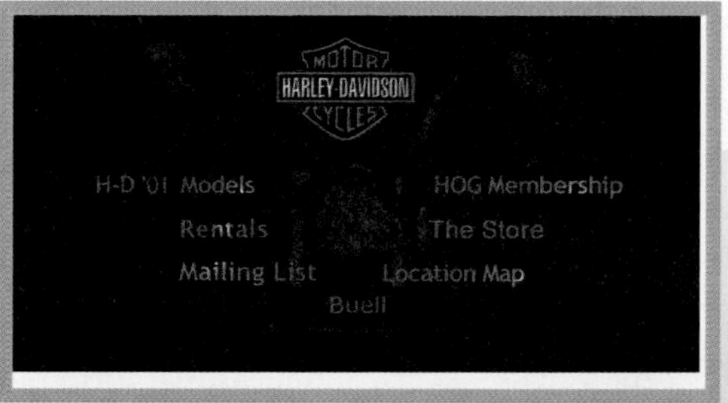

The 500,000-member Harley Owners Group (H.O.G) is a club of Harley-Davidson motorcycle enthusiasts. You can examine the latest Harley models and related merchandise, check out upcoming motorcycle events, and, of course, join H.O.G. at the consumer group's Web site.

www.harleydavidsonofdallas.com

influenced by powerful outside forces. As you can see in Figure 10.1, any marketing program must recognize the outside factors that comprise a company's **external environment**. In this section, we describe five of these environmental factors: the *political-legal, social-cultural, technological, economic*, and *competitive environments*.

external environment Outside factors that influence marketing programs by posing opportunities or threats

Political and Legal Environment Political activities, both foreign and domestic, have profound effects on business. For example, congressional hearings on tobacco, legislation on the use of cell phones in cars, and enactment of the Clean Air Act have substantially determined the destinies of entire industries. E-commerce activities are changing because of expected increases in federal and state taxes for sales on the Internet.

To help shape their companies' futures, marketing managers try to maintain favorable political-legal environments in several ways. For example, to gain public support for their products and activities, marketing uses advertising campaigns for public awareness on issues of local, regional, or national import. They also contribute to

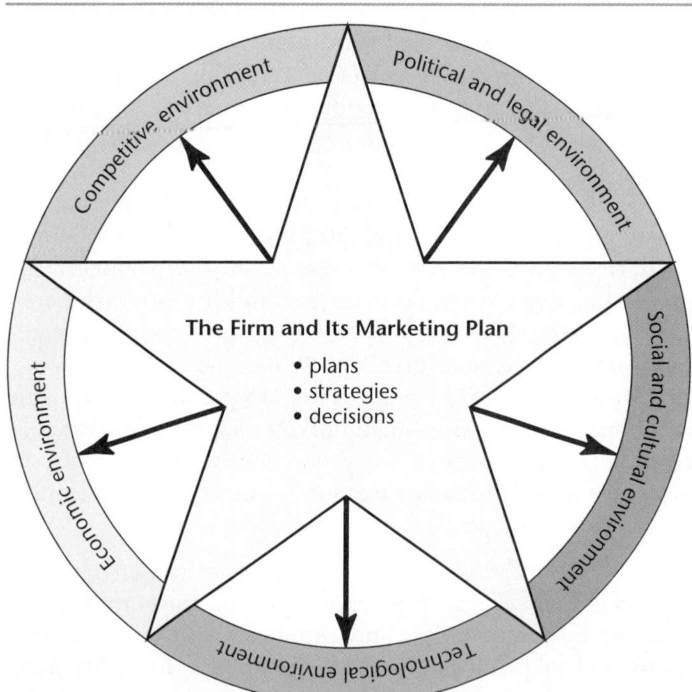

Figure 10.1
The External Marketing Environment

political candidates (although there are legal restrictions on how much they can contribute). Frequently, they support the activities of political action committees (PACs) maintained by their respective industries. Such activities sometimes result in favorable laws and regulations and may even open up new international business opportunities.

Social and Cultural Environment More people are working in home offices, the number of single-parent families is increasing, food preferences and physical activities reflect the growing concern for healthful lifestyles, violent crimes are on the decrease, and the growing recognition of cultural diversity continues. These and other issues reflect the values, beliefs, and ideas that form the fabric of U.S. society today.

The need to recognize social values stimulates marketers to take fresh looks at the ways they conduct their business by developing and promoting new products for both consumers and industrial customers. For example, there are now more than 8 million female golfers spending nearly $250 million on equipment, most of which, in earlier years, had been modeled after men's gear. Responding to the growth in the number of female golfers, Spalding <www.spalding.com> now offers a line of golf gear designed specifically for women. Marketing such equipment has entailed new methods for advertising, promoting, and distributing products to meet the emerging preferences of women golfers.

Technological Environment New technologies affect marketing in several ways. They create new goods (the satellite dish) and services (home television shopping). New products make some existing products obsolete (compact disks are replacing audiotapes), and many of them change our values and lifestyles. In turn, they often stimulate new goods and services not directly related to the new technology itself. Cellular phones, for example, not only facilitate business communication but free up time for recreation and leisure. New communications technologies, which we discuss in Chapter 12, have blazed entirely new paths for marketers to travel. Internet accessibility, for example, provides a new medium for selling, buying, and even distributing products from your own home to customers around the world.

Economic Environment Economic conditions determine spending patterns by consumers, businesses, and governments. Thus, they influence every marketer's plans for product offerings, pricing, and promotional strategies. Among the more significant economic variables, marketers are concerned with inflation, interest rates, recession, and recovery. In other words, they must monitor the general business cycle, which typically features a pattern of transition from periods of prosperity to recession to recovery (return to prosperity). Not surprisingly, consumer spending increases as consumer confidence in economic conditions grows during periods of prosperity. Spending decreases during low-growth periods, when unemployment rises and purchasing power declines.

Traditionally, analysis of economic conditions focused on the national economy and the government's policies for controlling or moderating it. Increasingly, however, as nations form more and more economic connections, the "global economy" is becoming more prominent in the thinking of marketers everywhere.[3] At Wal-Mart <www.walmartstores.com>, for example, about 11 percent of sales revenues come from its international division. At the same time, however, although overall international sales were up 51 percent for 1999, sales in Latin America stalled. Why? Because economic conditions in such markets as Argentina, Brazil, and Mexico are entirely different than in European and Asian countries. Certainly, marketers must now consider a variety of unpredictable economic variables in developing both domestic and foreign marketing strategies.

Competitive Environment In a competitive environment, marketers must convince buyers that they should purchase their products rather than those of some other seller. Because both consumers and commercial buyers have limited resources, every dollar spent on one product is no longer available for other purchases. Each marketing pro-

The euro, *the common currency of the European Union, has certain advantages for member-nation companies doing international business. It eliminates* exchange-rate risk—*the risk that changes in exchange rates might adversely affect a firm conducting international transactions. The exchange rate is an economic variable. Thus multinationals and banks in England—a non-euro nation—want to adopt the euro. Protestors like this one fear that in order to keep the British economy in line with those of other members, the government would have to enact labor and other regulations like those that are common in other EU countries.*

gram, therefore, seeks to make its product the most attractive. Theoretically, a failed program loses the buyer's dollar forever (or at least until it is time for the next purchase decision).

By studying the competition, marketers determine how best to position their own products for three specific types of competition:

- **Substitute products** are dissimilar from those of competitors but can fulfill the same need. For example, your cholesterol level may be controlled with either a physical fitness program or a drug regimen. The fitness program and the drugs compete as substitute products.
- **Brand competition** occurs between similar products, such as the auditing services provided by the large accounting firms of Ernst & Young <www.ey.com> and KPMG Peat Marwick <www.kpmg.com>. The competition is based on buyers' perceptions of the benefits of products offered by particular companies.
- **International competition** matches the products of domestic marketers against those of foreign competitors—a flight on Swissair <www.swissair.com> versus Delta Airlines <www.delta-air.com>. The intensity of international competition has, of course, been heightened by the formation of alliances such as the European Community and NAFTA.

substitute product
Product that is dissimilar to those of competitors but that can fulfill the same need

brand competition
Competitive marketing that appeals to consumer perceptions of similar products

international competition
Competitive marketing of domestic products against foreign products

The Marketing Mix

In planning and implementing strategies, marketing managers rely on four basic components. These elements, often called the "Four P's" of marketing, constitute the **marketing mix.** In this section, we describe each of the following activities:

- Product
- Pricing
- Promotion
- Place

Product Marketing begins with a **product**—a good, a service, or an idea designed to fill a consumer need. Conceiving and developing new products is a constant challenge for marketers, who must always consider the factor of change. Marketers, for example,

marketing mix
The combination of product, pricing, promotion, and distribution strategies used to market products

product
Good, service, or idea that is marketed to fill consumer needs and wants

Mobile phone penetration in Finland is 60 percent, compared with only 28 percent in the United States. Why the big difference? For one thing, Finland is home to Nokia, marketer of the world's most successful brand of cellular phone, with a 27-percent global market share. Nokia <www.nokiausa.com> *created Europe's first digital phone network in 1982 and is now focusing on the technology to provide cell phones with affordable Web content. Internet penetration in Finland is also greater than in the United States—24.5 percent to 20.3 percent.*

must consider changing technology, changing consumer wants and needs, and changing economic conditions. Meeting consumer needs, then, often means changing existing products to keep pace with emerging markets and competitors.

product differentiation
Creation of a product or product image that differs enough from existing products to attract consumers

Product Differentiation Often producers promote particular features or characteristics of their products for the sake of distinguishing them on the marketplace. **Product differentiation** is the creation of a product feature or product image that differs enough from competing products to attract consumers. For example, Volvo automobiles <www.volvo.com> provide newer, better safety features to set them apart from competitors. Services can also be differentiated. Customers of E*Trade™, <www.etrade.com> the online investment service, gain value from after-hours trading that is unavailable from conventional investment-service firms. People differentiation, too, can provide value to customers: Southwest Airlines <www.southwest.com> employees are known for their sense of humor, friendliness, and company spirit. Says CEO Herb Kelleher, who often touts the importance of Southwest's people: "We like mavericks—people who have a sense of humor. We've always done it differently."[4]

Combinations of physical goods and services can also be sources of differentiation. For example, Weyerhaeuser Co. <www.weyerhaeuser.com> developed a computer system that allows customers at retail home centers and lumberyards to custom-design decks and shelving. As a result, the company has differentiated its commodity two-by-fours by turning them into premium products.

Marketing, then, faces continual challenges in offering products that attract new customers. We discuss these product decisions more fully later in this chapter.

Pricing *Pricing* a product—selecting the most appropriate price at which to sell it—is often a balancing act. On the one hand, prices must support a variety of costs—the organization's operating, administrative, and research costs as well as marketing costs such as advertising and sales salaries. On the other hand, prices cannot be so high that consumers turn to competitors. Successful pricing means finding a profitable middle ground between these two requirements. An appliance retailer, for instance, sells refrigerators and washing machines at prices that are both profitable and attractive to customers. The same products, however, are priced lower when customers buy sets of kitchen or laundry appliances to furnish new homes. The retailers' lower transaction costs enable them to reduce their selling prices.

Whereas some firms succeed by offering lower prices than competitors, others price successfully on the high side. Both low- and high-price strategies can be effective in different situations. Low prices, for example, generally lead to larger sales volumes. High prices usually limit market size but increase profits per unit. High prices may also attract customers by implying that a product is of especially high quality. We discuss pricing in more detail in Chapter 11.

Promotion The most highly visible component of the marketing mix is no doubt promotion, which refers to techniques for communicating information about products. We describe promotional activities more fully in Chapter 11. Here we briefly describe the most important promotional tools.

Advertising Advertising is any form of paid nonpersonal communication used by an identified sponsor to persuade or inform potential buyers about a product. For example, The MonyGroup <www.mony.com>, a financial adviser that provides investment and securities products, reaches its customer audience by advertising its services in *Fortune* magazine.

Personal Selling Many products (for example, insurance, clothing, and real estate) are best promoted through personal selling, or person-to-person sales. Industrial goods receive the bulk of personal selling. When companies buy from other companies, purchasing agents and others who need technical and detailed information are usually referred to the selling company's sales representatives.

Sales Promotions Relatively inexpensive items are often marketed through sales promotions, which involve one-time direct inducements to buyers. Premiums (usually free gifts), coupons, and package inserts are all sales promotions meant to tempt consumers to buy products.

Public Relations Public relations includes all communication efforts directed at building goodwill. It seeks to build favorable attitudes toward the organization and its products. Ronald McDonald Houses <www.rmhc.com> are a famous example of public relations. Publicity also refers to a firm's efforts to communicate to the public, usually through mass media. Publicity, however, is not paid for by the firm, nor does the firm control its content. Publicity, therefore, can sometimes hurt a business. In 2000, for example, Firestone suffered a severe downturn in sales after the widely publicized tire failures on Ford Explorer SUVs.

Place (Distribution) In the marketing mix, *place* refers to **distribution**. Placing a product in the proper outlet—say, a retail store—requires decisions about several distribution activities, all of which are concerned with getting the product from the producer to the consumer. For example, transportation options include railroad, truck, air freight, and pipelines. Decisions about warehousing and inventory control are also distribution decisions.

distribution
Part of the marketing mix concerned with getting products from producers to consumers

Firms must also make decisions about the channels through which they distribute their products. Many manufacturers, for instance, sell to other companies that, in turn, distribute the goods to retailers. Del Monte Foods <www.delmonte.com>, for example, produces canned foods that it sells to Nash Finch Co. <www.nashfinch.com> and other distributors, which then sell the food to grocery stores. Other companies sell directly to major retailers such as Sears, Wal-Mart, Kmart, and Safeway. Still others sell directly to final consumers. We explain distribution decisions further in Chapter 11.

TARGET MARKETING AND MARKET SEGMENTATION

Marketers recognized long ago that products and services cannot be "all things to all people." Buyers have different tastes, interests, goals, lifestyles, and so on. Among other things, the emergence of the marketing concept and the recognition of consumer needs and wants led marketers to think in terms of *target marketing*. **Target markets** are groups of people with similar wants and needs. For most companies, selecting target markets is the first step in the marketing strategy.

target market
Group of people that has similar wants and needs and that can be expected to show interest in the same products

market segmentation
Process of dividing a market into categories of customer types

Target marketing clearly requires **market segmentation**—dividing a market into categories of customer types or "segments." Once they have identified market segments, companies may adopt a variety of strategies. Some firms try to market products to more than one segment of the population. For example, General Motors <www.gm.com> offers compact cars, vans, trucks, luxury cars, and sports cars with various features and at various price levels. GM's strategy is to provide an automobile for nearly every segment of the market.

In contrast, some businesses take a narrower approach by offering fewer products, each aimed toward a specific market segment. Note that segmentation is a strategy for analyzing consumers, not products. In marketing, the process of fixing, adapting, and communicating the nature of the product itself is called *product positioning*.

Identifying Market Segments

By definition, the members of a *market segment* must share some common traits that will affect their purchasing decisions. In identifying market segments, researchers look at several different influences on consumer behavior. Three of the most important are *geographic, demographic*, and *psychographic variables*.[5]

geographic variables
Geographical units that may be considered in developing a segmentation strategy

Geographic Variables In many cases, buying decisions are affected by the places that people call home. The heavy rainfall in Washington State, for instance, means that inhabitants purchase more umbrellas than people living in the Sun Belt. Urban residents have little need for agricultural equipment, and sailboats sell better along the coasts than in the Great Plains. **Geographic variables** are the geographical units, from countries to neighborhoods, that may be considered in developing a segmentation strategy.

These patterns affect decisions about the marketing mix for a huge range of products. For example, consider a project to market down-filled parkas in rural Minnesota. Demand will be high and price competition intense. Local newspaper advertising may be very effective, and the best retail location may be one that is easily reached from several small towns. Marketing the same parkas in downtown Honolulu would be considerably more challenging.

Although the marketability of some products is geographically sensitive, others benefit from nearly universal acceptance. Coca-Cola, for example, derives more than 70 percent of its cola sales from international markets. Coke is the market leader in Great Britain, China, Germany, Japan, Brazil, and Spain. Pepsi's international sales equal only about 15 percent of Coke's. In fact, Coke's chief competitor in most countries is some local soft drink, not Pepsi, which earns 78 percent of its income at home.

demographic variables
Characteristics of populations that may be considered in developing a segmentation strategy

Demographic Variables **Demographic variables** describe populations by identifying such traits as age, income, gender, ethnic background, marital status, race, religion, and social class. Table 10.1 lists some possible demographic breakdowns. Depending on the marketer's purpose, a segment could be a single classification (*aged 20–34*) or a combination of categories (*aged 20–34, married with children, earning $25,000–$34,999*). Foreign competitors, for example, are gaining market share in U.S. auto sales by appealing to young buyers (under age 30) with limited incomes (under $30,000). While companies such as Hyundai <www.hyundai.net>, Kia <www.kia.com>, and Daewoo <www.daewoous.com> are winning entry-level customers with high quality and generous warranties, Volkswagen <www.vw.com> has succeeded in targeting under-35 buyers with its entertainment-styled VW Jetta.[6]

Naturally, demographics affect marketing decisions. For example, several general consumption characteristics can be attributed to certain age groups (*18–25, 26–35, 36–45*, and so on). Marketers can thus divide markets into age groups as they develop specific marketing plans.

Age	Under 5, 5–11, 12–19, 20–34, 35–49, 50–64, 65+
Education	Grade school or less, some high school, graduated high school, some college, college degree, advanced degree
Family life cycle	Young single, young married without children, young married with children, older married with children under 18, older married without children under 18, older single, other
Family size	1, 2–3, 4–5, 6+
Income	Under $9,000, $9,000–14,999, $15,000–24,999, $25,000–34,999, $35,000–45,000, over $45,000
Nationality	Including African, American, Asian, British, Eastern European, French, German, Irish, Italian, Latin American, Middle Eastern, and Scandinavian
Race	Including American Indian, Asian, Black, and White
Religion	Including Buddhist, Catholic, Hindu, Jewish, Muslim, and Protestant
Sex	Male, female

Table 10.1
Demographic Variables

In addition, marketers can use demographics to identify trends that might shape future spending patterns. Nursing care and funeral service companies, for example, are expanding offerings in response to projected changes in the U.S. population in the years 1995 to 2005. Those changes are shown in Figure 10.2. As you can see, the number of people between ages 60 and 89—and even the number of those in their 90s—is expected to rise. So-called death care companies, such as Stewart Enterprises and Service Corp. International <www.sci-corp.com>, are preparing for the upturn by acquiring additional cemetery and funeral homes that give customers one-stop shopping.

The "Wired World" box in this chapter shows the computerized collection of demographic data is being used to cut costs in the health care industry.

psychographic variables
Consumer characteristics, such as lifestyles, opinions, interests, and attitudes, that may be considered in developing a segmentation strategy

Psychographic Variables Members of a market can also be segmented according to such **psychographic variables** as lifestyles, opinions, interests, and attitudes. One company that is using psychographic variables to revive its brand is Burberry, whose plaid-lined gabardine raincoats have been a symbol of British tradition since 1856. With a recent downturn in sales, Burberry is repositioning itself as a global luxury brand, like

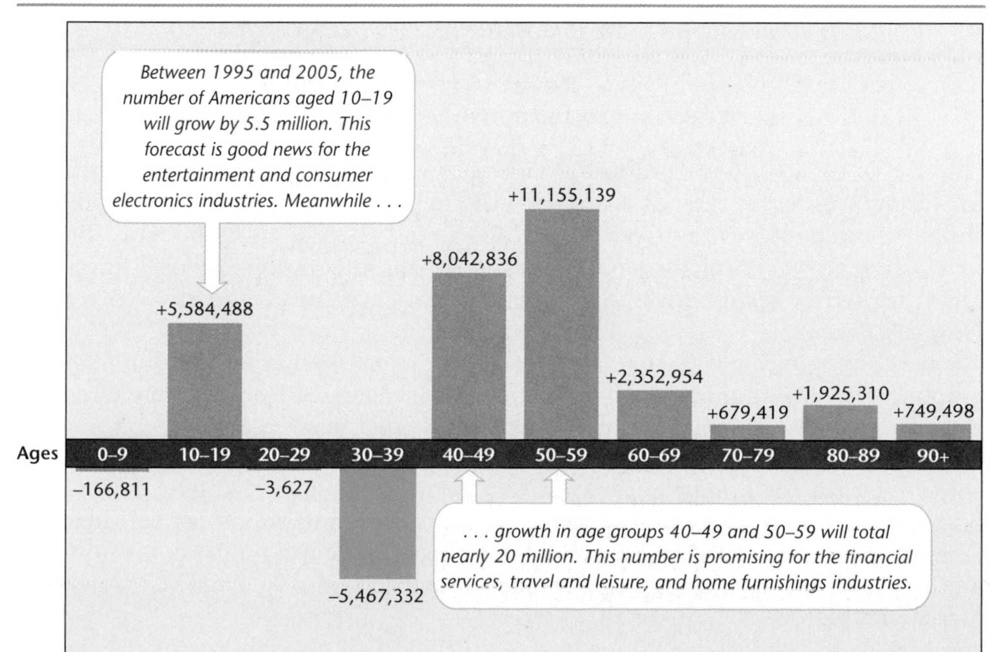

Figure 10.2
Changes in the U.S. Population

IT'S A WIRED WORLD

Better Health Through Cyberspace Demographics

As we have seen, demographic, geographic, and lifestyle variables are useful in identifying market segments for effective target marketing. In an era of heightened concern for costly health care, many insurers are converting demographic and lifestyle information into personal health assessments for employees of their client companies. One way to gather personal information is by paper and pencil, but with online access, the process is fast, convenient, and secure for confidentiality. The approach was developed by Network Health Systems™ (NHS). First, the employee fills out a personal questionnaire with items on physical characteristics, lifestyle practices, dietary patterns, work environment, emotional feelings, medical status, and health history. This information forms the individual's personal demographics package. Online subscribers at Network's Web site <www.nhsinfo.com> can conveniently access the questionnaire, answer the questions, receive instantaneous feedback in the form of a personal report, and pay for the service.

The NHS system evaluates the individual's data using statistical models that determine the chances for experiencing various diseases or ailments. A personalized report is created instantaneously. Based on the individual's response demographics and lifestyle practices, it shows which of some 52 possible conditions and diseases—such as nerve disorders, benign tumors, pregnancy complications, and suicide—are expected. The report offers comments and suggestions about the individual's future health, including recommendations for specific lifestyle changes that can be taken for improvement.

The assessment system is based on a vast database of mortality and hospitalization data for 52 diseases and 24 age, sex, and race categories. Data are updated using medical research and national statistics from such sources as the Centers for Disease Control and the National Center for Health Statistics. The database also incorporates information from a panel of health professionals whose clinical judgments indicate correlations among demographics and various health problems. When an individual's demographics and lifestyle items are entered online, they are assessed against the database by the statistical model. Results are presented instantaneously. Processing reports via the Internet saves time and money for NHS, and it is faster in getting the results to clients.

In addition to individuals, business marketers for various health products benefit from the NHS system. Suppose, for example, a marketer for an insulin product wants to target specific geographic areas with high sales potential. Using demographic data, NHS will search its database to locate concentrations of population, by zip code, that are predisposed to diabetes. Perhaps results will show that while 40 percent of the population is predisposed in one region, just 10 percent is predisposed in another. NHS can report this information to health care providers—hospitals, physicians, HMOs—that can, in turn, use it to deliver services to areas most in need of it.

Gucci <www.gucci.com> and Louis Vuitton <www.vuitton.com>. The strategy calls for luring a different type of customer—the top-of-the-line fashion conscious—who shop at such stores as Neiman Marcus and Bergdorf Goodman. Burberry <www.burberry.com> pictures today's luxury-product shopper as a world traveler who identifies with prestige fashion brands and watches social and fashion trends in *Harper's Bazaar*.[7]

Psychographics are particularly important to marketers because, unlike demographics and geographics, they can sometimes be changed by marketing efforts. For example, many companies in Poland have succeeded in overcoming consumer resistance by promoting the safety and desirability of using credit rather than depending solely on cash for family purchases. One product of such changing attitudes is a booming economy and the emergence of a growing and robust middle class. The increasing number of Polish households owning televisions, appliances, automobiles, and houses is fueling the status of Poland's middle class as the most stable in the former Soviet bloc.[8]

The French cosmetics giant L'Oréal <www.lorealparisusa.com> is working to reposition the 96-year-old Helena Rubenstein brand by appealing to a new psychographic segment. Through trendy spas like this one in New York (L'Oréal's first-ever retailing venture), the parent company is targeting the skin care and cosmetic brand at 20- to 30-year-old women in such urban centers as New York, Paris, London, and Tokyo.

UNDERSTANDING CONSUMER BEHAVIOR

Although marketing managers can tell us what qualities people want in a new VCR, they cannot tell us *why* people buy a particular VCR. What desire are they fulfilling? Is there a psychological or sociological explanation for why consumers purchase one product and not another? These questions and many others are addressed in the area of marketing known as **consumer behavior**—the study of the decision process by which customers come to purchase and consume products.

consumer behavior
Various facets of the decision process by which customers come to purchase and consume products

Influences on Consumer Behavior

According to the title of one classic study, we are "social animals." To understand consumer behavior, marketers draw heavily on the fields of psychology and sociology. The result is a focus on four major influences on consumer behavior: psychological, personal, social, and cultural. By identifying the four influences that are most active, marketers try to explain consumer choices and predict future purchasing behavior:

1. *Psychological influences* include an individual's motivations, perceptions, ability to learn, and attitudes.[9]
2. *Personal influences* include lifestyle, personality, and economic status.
3. *Social influences* include family, opinion leaders (people whose opinions are sought by others), and such reference groups as friends, coworkers, and professional associates.[10]
4. *Cultural influences* include culture (the "way of living" that distinguishes one large group from another), subculture (smaller groups, such as ethnic groups, with shared values), and social class (the cultural ranking of groups according to such criteria as background, occupation, and income).[11]

Although these factors can have a strong impact on consumers' choices, their impact on the actual purchase of some products is either very weak or negligible. Some consumers, for example, exhibit high **brand loyalty**, which means they regularly purchase products because they are satisfied with their performance. Such people (for example, users of Maytag appliances) are generally less subject to typical influences

brand loyalty
Pattern of regular consumer purchasing based on satisfaction with a product

and stick with preferred brands. Closer to home, however, the clothes you wear and the food you eat often reflect social and psychological influences on your consuming behavior.

The Consumer Buying Process

Students of consumer behavior have constructed various models to help marketers understand how consumers come to purchase products. Figure 10.3 presents one such model. At the core of this and similar models is an awareness of the psychosocial influences that lead to consumption. Ultimately, marketers use this information to develop marketing plans.[12]

Problem/Need Recognition The buying process begins when the consumer recognizes a problem or need. After strenuous exercise, for example, you may realize that you are thirsty. After the birth of twins, you may find your one-bedroom apartment too small for comfort.

Need recognition also occurs when you have a chance to change your purchasing habits. For example, when you obtain your first job after graduation, your new income may let you purchase items that were once too expensive for you. You may also discover a need for professional clothing, apartment furnishings, and a car. American Express and Sears recognize this shift in typical needs when they market credit cards to college seniors.

Information Seeking Once they have recognized a need, consumers often seek information. This search is not always extensive. If you are thirsty, for instance, you may simply ask someone to point you to a soft-drink machine. At other times, you may simply rely on your memory for information.

Before making major purchases, however, most people seek information from personal sources, marketing sources, public sources, and experience. For example, if you move to a new town, you will want to identify the best dentist, physician, hair stylist, butcher, or pizza maker in your area. To get this information, you may check with personal sources, such as acquaintances, coworkers, and relatives. Before buying an exercise bike, you may go to the library and read about bikes in *Consumer Reports* <www.consumerreports.org>. You may also question market sources such as salesclerks or rely on direct experience by test-riding several bikes before you buy.

Evaluation of Alternatives If you are in the market for a set of skis, you probably have some idea of who makes skis and how they differ. You may have accumulated some of this knowledge during the information-seeking stage and combined it with

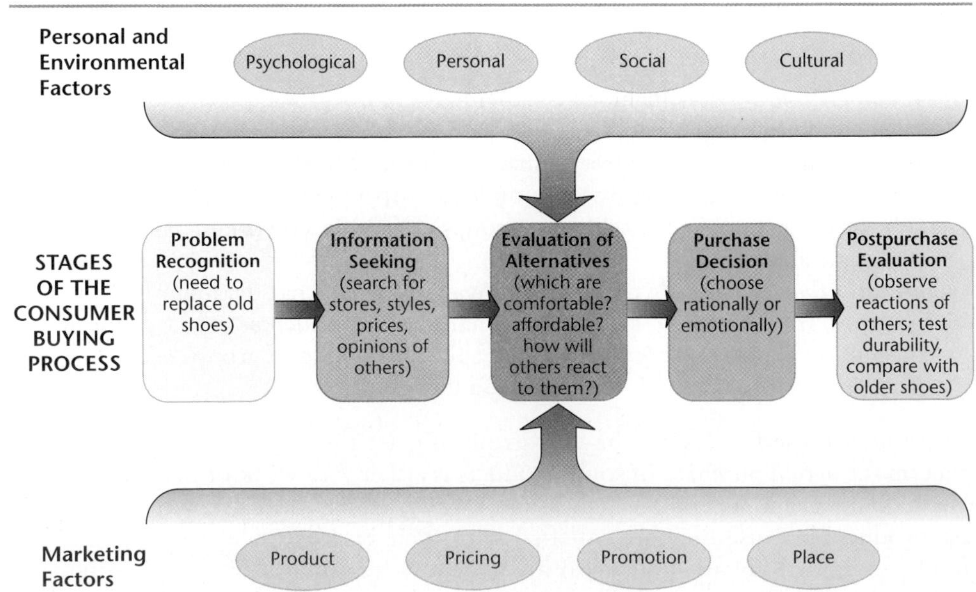

Figure 10.3
Consumer Buying Process

what you knew previously. By analyzing the product attributes that apply to a given product (color, taste, price, prestige, quality, service record) you will consider your choices and compare products before deciding which product best meets your needs.

Purchase Decision Ultimately, consumers must make purchase decisions. They may decide to defer a purchase until a later time or they may decide to buy now. "Buy" decisions are based on rational motives, emotional motives, or both.[13] **Rational motives** involve the logical evaluation of product attributes: cost, quality, and usefulness. **Emotional motives** involve nonobjective factors and lead to irrational decisions. Although not all irrational decisions are sudden, many spur-of-the-moment decisions are emotionally driven. Emotional motives include sociability, imitation of others, and aesthetics—motives that are common. For example, you might buy the same brand of jeans as your friends to feel comfortable among that group, not because your friends happen to have the good sense to prefer durable, comfortably priced jeans.

rational motives
Reasons for purchasing a product that are based on a logical evaluation of product attributes

emotional motives
Reasons for purchasing a product that are based on nonobjective factors

Irrational, therefore, does not mean wrong. It merely refers to a decision based on nonobjective factors. Such decisions can be either satisfying or, largely because they were not based on objective criteria, ill considered. We have all purchased items, taken them home, and then wondered, "Why in the world did I spend good money on this thing?"

Postpurchase Evaluations Marketing does not stop with the sale of a product. It includes the process of consumption. What happens *after* the sale is important. Marketers want consumers to be happy after the consumption of products so that they are more likely to buy them again. Because consumers do not want to go through a complex decision process for every purchase, they often repurchase products they have used and liked.

Not all consumers are satisfied with their purchases, of course. Dissatisfied consumers may complain to sellers, criticize products publicly, or even file lawsuits. Dissatisfied consumers are not likely to purchase the same products again. Moreover, dissatisfied customers are much more likely to broadcast their experiences than are satisfied customers.

ORGANIZATIONAL MARKETING AND BUYING BEHAVIOR

Buying behavior is observable daily in the consumer market, where marketing activities, including buying and selling transactions, are visible to the public. Equally important, however, but far less visible, are *organizational* (or *commercial*) *markets*. Some 23 million organizations in the United States buy goods and services to be used in creating and delivering consumer products. As we will see in the following sections, marketing to these buyers must deal with different kinds of organizational markets and with buying behaviors that are different from those found in consumer markets.

Organizational Markets

Organizational or commercial markets fall into three categories—*industrial*, *reseller*, and *government/institutional markets*. Taken together, these three markets in the United States do about $8 trillion in business annually, approximately three times the business done in the consumer market.

Industrial Market The **industrial market** includes businesses that buy goods to be converted into other products and goods that are used up during production. This market includes farmers, manufacturers, and some retailers. For example, Seth Thomas <www.seththomas.com> purchases electronics, metal components, and glass to make clocks for the consumer market. The company also buys office supplies, tools, and factory equipment—items never seen by clock buyers—to be used during production.

industrial market
Organizational market consisting of firms that buy goods that are either converted into products or used during production

Baskin-Robbins <www.baskinrobbins.com> buys not only ingredients for ice cream but also paper bags and wrappers to package products for customers and freezer cabinets for storage.

reseller market
Organizational market consisting of intermediaries who buy and resell finished goods

Reseller Market Before products reach consumers, they pass through a **reseller market** consisting of intermediaries, including wholesalers and retailers, that buy the finished goods and resell them (wholesalers and retailers are discussed in detail in Chapter 11). The Coast Distribution System, for example, is a leading distributor of parts and accessories for the pleasure boat market. It buys items such as lights, steering wheels, and propellers and resells them to marinas and boat repair shops. On the products resold to their customers, 750,000 U.S. wholesalers have annual sales of $2.4 trillion. Some 2.5 million U.S. retailers purchase merchandise that, when resold to consumers, is valued at $2.6 trillion per year. Retailers also buy such services as maintenance, housekeeping, and communications.[14]

Government and Institutional Market In addition to federal and state governments, more than 87,000 local governments (municipalities, counties, townships, and school districts) are in the United States. State and local governments alone make annual purchases of $1.3 trillion for durable goods, nondurables, purchased services, and construction. Note that, after a 10-year reduction, spending for military procurement is down 46 percent—from $82 billion to $44 billion—since 1989.[15]

institutional market
Organizational market consisting of such nongovernmental buyers of goods and services as hospitals, churches, museums, and charitable organizations

The **institutional market** consists of nongovernment organizations, such as hospitals, churches, museums, and charitable organizations, that also comprise a substantial market for goods and services. Like organizations in other commercial markets, these institutions use supplies and equipment, as well as legal, accounting, and transportation services.[16]

Organizational Buying Behavior

In some respects, organizational buying behavior bears little resemblance to consumer buying practices. Two of these differences include the buyers' purchasing skills and an emphasis on buyer–seller relationships.

Differences in Buyers Unlike most consumers, organizational buyers are professional, specialized, and expert (or at least well informed):

1. As *professionals*, organizational buyers are trained in arranging buyer–seller relationships and in methods for negotiating purchase terms. Once buyer–seller agreements have been reached, industrial buyers also arrange for formal contracts.
2. As a rule, industrial buyers are company *specialists* in a line of items. As one of several buyers for a large bakery, for example, you may specialize in food ingredients such as flour, yeast, butter, and so on. Another buyer may specialize in baking equipment (industrial ovens and mixers), whereas a third may purchase office equipment and supplies.
3. Industrial buyers are often *experts* about the products they are buying. On a regular basis, organizational buyers learn about competing products and alternative suppliers by attending trade shows, reading trade magazines, and conducting technical discussions with sellers' representatives.

Differences in the Buyer–Seller Relationship Consumer–seller relationships are often impersonal and fleeting; they are often short-lived, one-time interactions. In contrast, industrial situations often involve frequent, enduring buyer–seller relationships. The development of a long-term relationship is beneficial to both parties. It provides each with access to the technical strengths of the other as well as the security that comes from knowing what future business each can expect. Thus, a buyer and supplier may jointly form a design team to create products that will benefit both parties. Accordingly, industrial sellers emphasize personal selling by trained representatives who can better understand the needs of each customer.

WHAT IS A PRODUCT?

In developing the marketing mix for any products, whether ideas, goods, or services, marketers must consider what consumers really buy when they purchase products. Only then can they plan their strategies effectively. We begin this section where product strategy begins: with an understanding of product *features* and *benefits*. Next, we describe the major *classifications of products*, both consumer and industrial. Finally, we discuss the most important component in the offerings of any business: its *product mix*.

Features and Benefits

Customers do not buy products simply because they like the products themselves: They buy products because they like what the products can do for them, either physically or emotionally. To succeed, a product must include the right features and offer the right benefits. Product **features** are the qualities, tangible and intangible, that a company builds into its products, such as a 12-horsepower motor on a lawn mower. To be salable, a product's features also must provide *benefits*: The mower must provide an attractive lawn.

feature
Tangible quality that a company builds into a product

Features and benefits play extremely important roles in the attractiveness of products. If you look carefully at the Diners Club ad in Figure 10.4, you will realize that products are much more than visible features and benefits. In buying a product, customers are also buying an image and a reputation. The marketers of the charge card advertised here <www.dinersclub.com> are well aware that brand name, labeling, and after-purchase satisfaction are indispensable facets of their product. The ad is designed to remind customers—especially business customers—that such features as extended billing periods, hands-on service, bonus air miles, and widespread acceptance go hand in hand with the familiar plastic card.

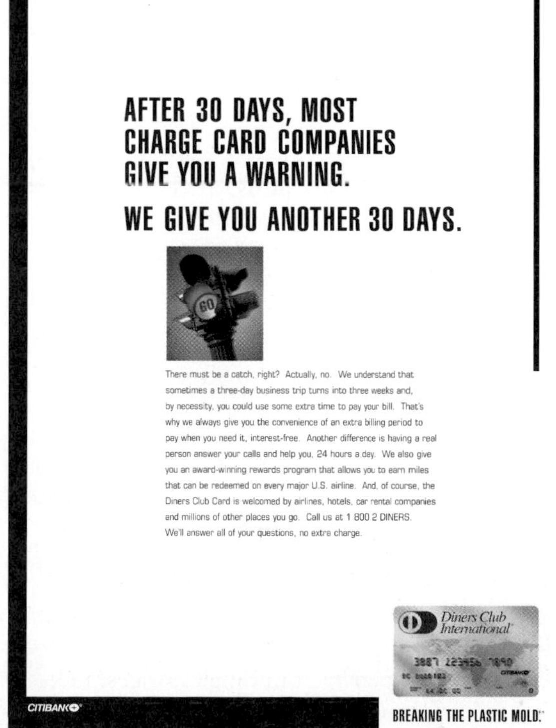

Figure 10.4
The Product: Features and Benefits

"And notice, gentlemen, this year's model has twenty percent more trunk space."

Classifying Goods and Services

One way to classify a product is according to expected buyers. Buyers fall into two groups: buyers of *consumer products* and buyers of *industrial products*.[17] As we saw earlier in this chapter, the consumer and industrial buying processes differ significantly. Not surprisingly, marketing products to consumers is vastly different from marketing them to other companies.

Classifying Consumer Products Consumer products are commonly divided into three categories that reflect buyer behavior:

convenience good/service
Inexpensive product purchased and consumed rapidly and regularly

shopping good/service
Moderately expensive, infrequently purchased product

specialty good/service
Expensive, rarely purchased product

- **Convenience goods** (such as milk and newspapers) and **convenience services** (such as those offered by fast-food restaurants) are consumed rapidly and regularly. They are inexpensive and are purchased often and with little expenditure of time and effort.
- **Shopping goods** (such as stereos and tires) and **shopping services** (such as insurance) are more expensive and are purchased less often than convenience products. Consumers often compare brands, sometimes in different stores. They may also evaluate alternatives in terms of style, performance, color, price, and other criteria.
- **Specialty goods** (such as wedding gowns) and **specialty services** (such as catering for wedding receptions) are extremely important and expensive purchases. Consumers usually decide on precisely what they want and will accept no substitutes. They will often go from store to store, sometimes spending a great deal of money and time to get a specific product.

Classifying Industrial Products Depending on how much they cost and how they will be used, industrial products can be divided into two categories: *expense* and *capital items.*

expense item
Industrial product purchased and consumed rapidly and regularly for daily operations

capital item
Expensive, long-lasting, infrequently purchased industrial product such as a building

Expense Items **Expense items** are any materials and services that are consumed within a year by firms producing other goods or supplying other services. The most obvious expense items are industrial goods used directly in the production process (for example, bulkloads of tea processed into tea bags).

Capital Items **Capital items** are permanent (expensive and long-lasting) goods and services. All these items have expected lives of more than a year and typically up to several years. Expensive buildings (offices, factories), fixed equipment (water towers, baking ovens), and accessory equipment (computers, airplanes) are *capital goods. Capital services* are those for which long-term commitments are made. These may include purchases for employee food services, building and equipment maintenance, or legal services. Because capital items are expensive and purchased infrequently, they often involve decisions by high-level managers.

The Product Mix

The group of products that a company makes available for sale, whether consumer, industrial, or both, is its **product mix**.[18] Black & Decker <www.blackanddecker.com>, for example, makes toasters, vacuum cleaners, electric drills, and a variety of other appliances and tools. 3M Corp. <www.3m.com> makes everything from Post-it notes to laser optics.

product mix
Group of products that a firm makes available for sale

Product Lines Many companies begin with a single product. Over time they find that their initial products fail to suit all the consumers shopping for the product type. To meet market demand, they often introduce similar products designed to reach other consumers. ServiceMaster <www.servicemaster.com> was among the first successful home services, offering mothproofing and carpet cleaning. Then the company expanded into lawn care (TruGreen, ChemLawn), pest control (Terminix), cleaning (Merry Maids), and home warranty services (American Home Shield) for various residential services applications. A group of similar products intended for similar but not identical buyers who will use them in similar ways is a product line.

Companies may extend their horizons and identify opportunities outside existing product lines. The result—*multiple* (or *diversified*) *product lines*—is evident at firms such as ServiceMaster. After years of serving residential customers, ServiceMaster has added Business and Industry Services (landscaping and janitorial), Education Services (management of schools and institutions, including physical facilities and financial and personnel resources), and Healthcare Services (management of support services—plant operations, asset management, laundry/linen, clinical equipment maintenance—for long-term care facilities). Multiple product lines allow a company to grow rapidly and can help to offset the consequences of slow sales in any one product line.

DEVELOPING NEW PRODUCTS

To expand or diversify product lines—just to survive—firms must develop and successfully introduce streams of new products. Faced with competition and shifting consumer preferences, no firm can count on a single successful product to carry it forever. Even basic products that have been widely purchased for decades require constant renewal. Consider one of America's most popular brands—Levi's <www.levistrauss.com>. Its riveted denim styles were once market leaders, but ultimately the company failed to keep pace with changing tastes, falling behind new products from competitors and losing market share among 14- to 19-year-old males during the 1990s. By 1999, at least one industry analyst was forced to report that Levi's "hasn't had a successful new product in years."[19]

In this section, we focus on the process by which companies develop the new goods and services that allow them to survive.

The New Product Development Process

The demand for food and beverage ingredients has grown more than 6 percent per year, reaching $5 billion in the year 2000. Flavors and flavor enhancers are the biggest part of that growth, especially artificial sweeteners. However, companies that develop and sell these products face a big problem: It costs between $30 million and $50 million and can take as long as 8 to 10 years to get a new product through the approval process at the Food and Drug Administration <www.fda.gov>. Testing, both for FDA approval and for marketing, can be the most time-consuming stage of development. For example, acesulfame K beverage sweetener, which is made by Hoechst Celanese Corp. <www.hoechst.com>, has been through more than 90 safety studies and 1,000 technical studies to see how it performs in various kinds of beverages. After testing, additional stages include advertising and demonstration to food producers at the right time (when they are ready to reformulate their products with new ingredients). Cashing in on the growth of the food- and beverage-ingredients market requires an immense amount of time, patience, and money.

Like Hoechst Celanese, many firms maintain research and development departments or divisions for exploring new product possibilities. Why do they devote so many resources to thinking about products and exploring their possibilities, rejecting many seemingly good ideas along the way? How do they conduct these early explorations into new product possibilities?

We address these questions in this section. We see that the high mortality rate for new ideas means that only a few new products eventually reach the market. For many companies, speed to market with a product is often as important as care in developing it. Product development is a long, complex, and expensive process. Companies do not dream up new products one day and ship them to retailers the next. In fact, new products usually involve carefully planned and sometimes risky commitments of time and resources.

Product Mortality Rates It is estimated that it takes 50 new product ideas to generate one product that finally reaches the market. Even then, only a few of those survivors become successful products. Many seemingly great ideas have failed as products. Indeed, creating a successful new product has become increasingly more difficult, even for the most experienced marketers. The number of new products hitting the market each year has increased dramatically. More than 25,000 new household, grocery, and drugstore items are introduced annually. Each year, the beverage industry alone launches up to 3,400 new products. At any given time, however, the average supermarket carries a total of only 20,000 to 25,000 different items. Because of lack of space and customer demand, about 9 out of 10 new products will fail. Products with the best chances for success are the ones that are innovative and deliver unique benefits.

Speed to Market The more rapidly a product moves from the laboratory to the marketplace, the more likely it is to survive. By introducing new products ahead of competitors, companies quickly establish market leadership. They become entrenched in the market before being challenged by late-arriving competitors. How important is **speed to market**—that is, a firm's success in responding to customer demand or market changes? One study has estimated that any product that is only three months late to market (three months behind the leader) sacrifices 12 percent of its lifetime profit potential. A product that is six months late will lose 33 percent.[20]

speed to market
Strategy of introducing new products to respond quickly to customer or market changes

IDENTIFYING PRODUCTS

As we noted earlier, developing a product's features is only part of a marketer's job. Marketers must also encourage consumers to identify products. Two important tools for accomplishing this task are *branding* and *packaging*.

Branding Products

Coca-Cola <www.coca-cola.com> is the best-known brand in the world. The name is so valuable that its executives like to say that if all of the company's other assets were obliterated, they could walk over to the bank and borrow $100 billion for rebuilding, just on the strength of the brand name. Brand names such as Coca-Cola and McDonald's are symbols for characterizing products and distinguishing them from one another. They were originally introduced to simplify the process when consumers are faced with a wealth of purchase decisions. **Branding** is a process of using symbols to communicate the qualities of a particular product made by a particular producer. Brands are designed to signal uniform quality: Customers who try and like a product can return to it by remembering its name.

branding
Process of using symbols to communicate the qualities of a product made by a particular producer

E-Business Branding It takes a long time to establish national or global brand recognition.[21] The expensive, sometimes fierce struggle for brand recognition is perhaps nowhere more evident than in the current branding battles among the dot-com firms. Paying up to $1.3 million for 30-second ads, dot-com companies dominated the advertising spots for Super Bowl XXXIV in January 2000. Why so much expensive promotional activity? Says Priceline.com vice chairman Jay S. Walker: "A lot of companies are saying, 'We have to make it big, fast, or we're not going to make it at all.' " Collectively, the top Internet brands—America Online, Yahoo!, and Amazon.com—spent more than $2 billion in 2000 even though they are just beginning to crack the ranks of the top-60 global brands. Even so, advertising alone is not enough: If a dot-com brand identity is going to emerge, it will be through an accumulation of customer contacts and experiences with products and brands. As the cost of building brand identity increases, it seems increasingly likely that many would-be e-businesses will not make it.[22]

"A lot of companies are saying, 'We have to make it big, fast, or we're not going to make it at all."

—Jay S. Walker, Priceline.com vice chairman

Types of Brand Names Virtually every product has a brand name. Generally, the different types of brand names—national, licensed, and private brands—increase buyers' awareness of the nature and quality of products that must compete with any number of other products. When the consumer is satisfied with the quality of a recognizable product, marketers work to achieve brand loyalty among the largest possible segment of repeat buyers.

National Brands **National brands** are produced by, widely distributed by, and carry the name of the manufacturer. These brands (for example, Scotch tape or Scope mouthwash) are often widely recognized by consumers because of national advertising campaigns. The costs of developing a positive image for a national brand are high. Some companies, therefore, use a national brand on several related products. Procter & Gamble <www.pg.com> now markets Ivory shampoo, capitalizing on the widely recognized name of its bar soap and dishwashing liquid.

national brand
Brand-name product produced by, widely distributed by, and carrying the name of a manufacturer

Many national brand names are valuable assets that signal product recognition. Millions of dollars have been spent developing names such as Noxzema, Prudential, and Minute Maid. Millions more have been spent in getting consumers to attach meaning to these names.

Licensed Brands It has become increasingly common for nationally recognized companies (and even personalities) to sell the rights to place their names on products. These **licensed brands** are very big business today. Ferrari <www.ferrari.com> found that selling its name can be more profitable than selling its famous cars. According to Michele Scannavini, manager of sales and marketing, "Ferrari is as much style as substance . . . as much a legend as it is a car company." Marketers reconceived the company name as a brand to extend and exploit it. The famous stallion logo now appears on luxury goods, sportswear, toys, and school supplies. Brands like Dilbert <www.dilbert.com>, the NFL <www.nfl.com>, and *South Park* <www.southpark.com> will all make millions on licensed-product sales this year. The free advertising that accompanies some licensing—such as T-shirts and other clothing—is an added bonus.

licensed brand
Brand-name product for whose name the seller has purchased the right from an organization or individual

Private Brands When a wholesaler or retailer develops a brand name and has the manufacturer place that name on the product, the resulting product name is a **private brand** (or **private label**). One of the best-known sellers of private brands is Sears, which carries such lines as Craftsman tools <www.craftsman.com>, Canyon River Blues denim clothing, and Kenmore appliances <www.kenmore.com>.

private brand (or private label)
Brand-name product that a wholesaler or retailer has commissioned from a manufacturer

packaging
Physical container in which a product is sold, advertised, or protected

Packaging Products

With a few exceptions (such as fresh fruits and vegetables and structural steel), products need some form of **packaging** in which to be sold. A package also serves as an in-store advertisement that makes the product attractive, displays the brand name, and identifies features and benefits. It also reduces the risk of damage, breakage, or spoilage and increases the difficulty of stealing small products. Recent advances in product usage and the materials available for packaging have created additional roles for packaging. A paper-based material that can be used as a cooking container has made Budget Gourmet <www.budgetgourmet.com> dinners a low-cost entry in the dinner-entrée market. No-drip-spout bottles have enhanced sales and brand loyalty for Clorox bleach <www.clorox.com>.

THE INTERNATIONAL MARKETING MIX

Marketing products internationally means mounting a strategy to support global business operations, which is no easy task. Foreign customers, for example, differ from domestic buyers in language, customs, business practices, and consumer behavior. When they decide to go global, marketers must thus reconsider each element of the marketing mix—product, pricing, promotion, and place.

International Products Some products can be sold abroad with virtually no changes. Budweiser, Coca-Cola, and Marlboros are exactly the same in Peoria and Paris. In other cases, U.S. firms have been obliged to create products with built-in flexibility, for instance, electric shavers that adapt to either 115- or 230-volt outlets.

Sometimes only a redesigned or completely different product will meet the needs of foreign buyers. To sell the Macintosh in Japan, for example, Apple had to develop a Japanese-language operating system. Nevertheless, more companies are designing products for universal application. Whether designed for unique or universal markets, the branding and labeling of products are especially important for communicating global messages about them. For example, KFC (formerly Kentucky Fried Chicken) boxes and Pepsi-Cola cans display universal logos that are instantly recognizable in many nations.

International Pricing When pricing for international markets, marketers must handle all the considerations of domestic pricing while also considering the higher costs of transporting and selling products abroad. Bass Pro Shops <www.basspro.com>, for example,

This Range Rover in Paris represents an upsurge in the sale of American-made sports utility vehicles (SUVs) throughout Europe. The product, however, has required some modification. Because European roads are smaller, the European SUV is essentially a miniature version of the American SUV (some models are nearly 30 inches shorter than American counterparts). Likewise, since gas prices are higher, many European SUVs come with diesel engines, and most feature four-cylinder rather than V6 or V8 engines.

sells outdoor sports equipment to customers in Europe at higher prices that cover the added costs of delivery. In contrast, major products such as jet airplanes are priced the same worldwide because delivery costs are incidental—huge development and production costs are the major considerations regardless of customer location. Meanwhile, because of the higher costs of buildings, rent, equipment, and imported meat, a McDonald's Big Mac that sells for $2.43 in the United States has a price tag of $3.58 in Denmark.

International Promotion Occasionally, a good advertising campaign here is a good advertising campaign just about everywhere else—it can be transported to another country virtually intact. Quite often, however, standard U.S. promotional devices do not succeed in other countries. In fact, many Europeans believe that a product must be inherently shoddy if a company resorts to any advertising, particularly the American hard-sell variety.

International marketers must also be aware that cultural differences can cause negative reactions to products that are advertised improperly. Some Europeans, for example, are offended by television commercials that show weapons or violence. Advertising practices are regulated accordingly. Consequently, Dutch commercials for toys do not feature the guns and combat scenes that are commonplace on Saturday morning U.S. television. Meanwhile, liquor and cigarette commercials that are banned from U.S. television are thriving in many Asian and European markets. Product promotions must be carefully matched to the customs and cultural values of each country.

International Distribution International distribution presents several problems. In some industries, delays in starting new distribution networks can be costly. Therefore, companies with existing distribution systems often enjoy an advantage over new businesses. Similarly, several companies have gained advantages in time-based competition by buying existing businesses. Procter & Gamble, for example, saved three years of start-up time by buying Revlon's Max Factor and Betrix cosmetics, both of which are well established in foreign markets. P&G can thus immediately use these companies' distribution and marketing networks for selling its own U.S. brands in the United Kingdom, Germany, and Japan.

Given the need to adjust the marketing mix, success in international markets is hard won. Even experienced firms can err in marketing to other countries. International success requires flexibility and a willingness to adapt to the nuances of other cultures. Whether a firm markets in domestic or international markets, however, the basic principles of marketing still apply. It is only the implementation of those principles that changes.

SMALL BUSINESS AND THE MARKETING MIX

As noted in Chapter 4, far more small businesses fail than succeed. Yet many of today's largest firms were yesterday's small businesses. McDonald's began with one restaurant, a concept, and one individual (Ray Kroc) who had foresight. Behind the success of many small firms lies a skillful application of the marketing concept and careful consideration of each element in the marketing mix.[23]

Small-Business Products Some new products and firms are doomed at the start simply because few consumers want or need what they have to offer. Too often, enthusiastic entrepreneurs introduce products that they and their friends like but fail to estimate realistic market potential. Other small businesses offer new products before they have clear pictures of their target segments and how to reach them. They try to be everything to everyone, and they end up serving no one well.

In contrast, a thorough understanding of what customers want has paid off for many small firms. A small Boston brewery, for example, learned from experience that customers use two key decision points in stores that sell beer: at the cooler in the back of the store and at the front register. Now, this brewer prefers to display its beer in the aisle closest to the register and in a space just outside the nearby cooler. Little Earth Productions Inc. <www.littlearth.com>, a company that makes fashion accessories, found a new consideration in designing its handbags: Formerly, the company merely considered how the consumer would use the handbag. But after examining customers' shopping habits, Little Earth decided to redesign for better store display: Because stores can give handbags better visibility by hanging them instead of placing them on the floor or on low countertops, Little Earth added little handles designed specifically for that purpose.[24]

Small-Business Pricing Haphazard pricing that is often little more than guesswork can sink even a firm with a good product. Most often, small-business pricing errors result from a failure to project operating expenses accurately. Owners of failing businesses have often been heard to say, "I didn't realize how much it costs to run the business!" and "If I price the product high enough to cover my expenses, no one will buy it!" But when small businesses set prices by carefully assessing costs, many earn very satisfactory profits—sometimes enough to expand or diversify.

Small-Business Promotion Many small businesses are also ignorant when it comes to the methods and costs of promotion. To save expenses, for example, they may avoid advertising and rely instead on personal selling. As a result, too many potential customers remain unaware of their products.

Successful small businesses plan for promotional expenses as part of start-up costs. Some hold down costs by taking advantage of less expensive promotional methods. Local newspapers, for example, are sources of publicity when they publish articles about new or unique businesses. Other small businesses have succeeded by identifying themselves and their products with associated groups, organizations, and events. Thus, a custom crafts gallery might join with a local art league and local artists to organize public showings of their combined products.

Small-Business Distribution Problems in arranging distribution can also make or break small businesses. Perhaps the most critical aspect of distribution is facility location, especially for new service businesses. The ability of many small businesses (retailers, veterinary clinics, and gourmet coffee shops) to attract and retain customers depends partly on the choice of location.

In distribution, as in other aspects of the marketing mix, smaller companies may have advantages over larger competitors, even in highly complex industries. They may be quicker in applying service technologies. Everex Systems Inc. of Fremont, California <www.everex.com>, sells personal computers to wholesalers and dealers through a system the company calls zero response time: Because the company is small and flexible, phone orders can be reviewed every two hours and factory assembly adjusted to match demand.

WEB Connection

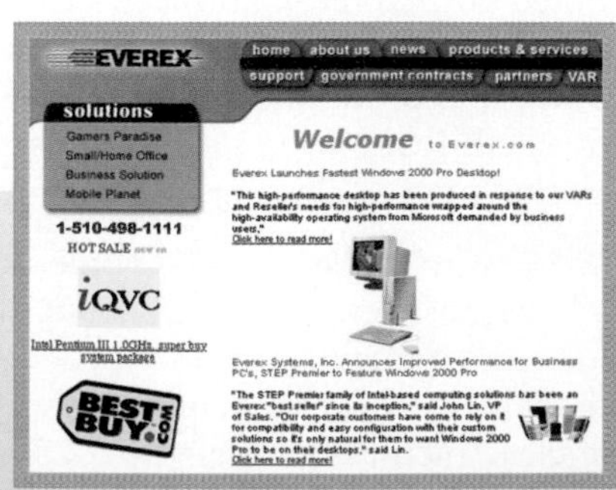

Everex designs, manufactures, and services a complete line of computer products. To examine its online distribution outlet for products and services, including technical support systems and downloadable software to remedy problems with servers, workstations, and PCs, contact the company on its Web site.

www.everex.com

Continued from page 251

Microsoft's Great Xpectations

Although games are not a new business to Microsoft, Xbox is its first venture into game consoles. Xbox's $500 million global marketing budget includes payouts over 12 to 18 months for media buys, interactive displays, Web site content, and retailer incentives. The Web content is especially important for positioning the brand among the millions of game players in the interactive entertainment sector. The Web site and other promotional media are designed to position Xbox as the brand that "enables the realization of creative vision" for gamers. Advertising and promotional activities emphasize the passion and the sense of exhilaration that Xbox brings to the interactive entertainment experience.

The Xbox marketing strategy differs from that of its competitors, especially Nintendo. Whereas Nintendo has generally targeted the younger end of the market, Xbox, says product-team leader Robbie Rash, targets a different audience: "Let's face it," he says, "Nintendo's system is for kids. We're for sophisticated gamers. I don't know any 30-year-olds who want a GameCube [by Nintendo]." Both Xbox and PlayStation 2 (by Sony) are aimed at the 16- to 26-year-old audience. Nintendo, however, wants to shed its "kids only" image and attract more players in the 20s age group, too. Both Xbox and GameCube would like to oust Sony's PlayStation 2 from the top spot in the console market.

With its $299 selling price, the income from each Xbox doesn't begin to cover the costs to make it. That's right. Experts estimate that Microsoft will lose about $125 on every box it sells. Because the consoles cost so much to make, the profits for console makers—Sony and Nintendo, as well as Microsoft—depend on software sales. Thus, the console maker that fails to offer a constant supply of new titles is doomed. Such was the fate of Sega, whose popular Dreamcast console was launched in 1999 but failed when independent software providers refused to write new games for the Dreamcast platform. Although Sega's sales subsequently dwindled and the firm quit making consoles, Sega will be publishing games for the Xbox. Indeed, reports indicate that Microsoft has signed up some 150 game developers, including Activision, Havas Interactive, and Konami, and has a goal of 100 game titles for Xbox by the end of the first year. For international appeal, Sega's participation is also giving Xbox an important boost: Many avid Japanese gamers were unconvinced of Xbox's credibility until they learned of Microsoft's alliance with Sega's respected game publishers.

In addition to differences in its marketing strategy, the Xbox product itself is different from competing products. Sony's PS2 plays music CDs and DVD movies right out of the box. Xbox can also play music and movies—in fact, it delivers theater-quality 3D sound—but if you want DVD, you need a separate remote controller. Nintendo plays games only—no movies or CDs. Xbox also offers broadband multiplayer gaming and allows players to take advantage of high-speed networks by playing online. By uniting gamers on the Internet via the Xbox, Microsoft is laying the groundwork for sales of future home-networking products that will use its Xbox console as the controlling hub. In addition to everything else, then, the Xbox is the centerpiece of Microsoft's home-networking strategy for the future.

Questions for Discussion

1. What social and technological factors have influenced the growth of the interactive entertainment market?
2. What demographics would you use to define the Xbox target market? How about the target market for Nintendo's GameCube?
3. Do you agree or disagree with Microsoft's strategy of featuring hardware, sound, and graphics rather than immediately offering lots of game titles?
4. Suppose you were asked to define the Xbox product. Identify its features and benefits.
5. Which is more important to Xbox's success—the product itself or Microsoft's marketing program for it? Explain your reasoning.

SUMMARY OF LEARNING OBJECTIVES

1 **Define *marketing*.** According to the American Marketing Association, *marketing* is the process of planning and executing the conception, pricing, promotion, and distribution of ideas, goods, and services to create exchanges that satisfy individual and organizational objectives.

2 **Describe the five forces that constitute the *external marketing environment*.** The *external environment* consists of the outside forces that influence marketing strategy and decision making. The *political-legal environment* includes laws and regulations, both domestic and foreign, that may define or constrain business activities. The *social-cultural environment* is the context within which people's values, beliefs, and ideas affect marketing decisions. The *technological environment* includes the technological developments that affect existing and new products. The *economic environment* consists of the conditions, such as inflation, recession, and interest rates, that influence both consumer and organizational spending patterns. Finally, the *competitive environment* is the environment in which marketers must persuade buyers to purchase their products rather than their competitors'.

3 **Explain *market segmentation* and show how it is used in *target marketing*.** *Market segmentation* is the process of dividing markets into categories of customers. Businesses have learned that marketing is more successful when it is aimed toward specific *target markets*: groups of consumers with similar wants and needs. Markets may be segmented by *geographic, demographic,* or *psychographic variables*.

4 **Describe the key factors that influence the *consumer buying process*.** A number of personal and psychological considerations, along with various social and cultural influences, affect consumer behavior. When making buying decisions, consumers first determine or respond to a problem or need and then collect as much information as they think necessary before making a purchase. *Postpurchase evaluations* are also important to marketers because they influence future buying patterns.

5 **Discuss the three categories of *organizational markets*.** The *industrial market* includes firms that buy goods falling into one of two categories: goods to be converted into other products and goods that are used up during production. Farmers and manufacturers are members of the industrial market. Members of the *reseller market* (mostly wholesalers) are intermediaries who buy and resell finished goods. Besides governments and agencies at all levels, the *government and institutional market* includes such nongovernment organizations as hospitals, museums, and charities.

6 **Identify a *product* and distinguish between *consumer* and *industrial products*.** Products are a firm's reason for being. Product *features*—the tangible and intangible qualities that a company builds into its products—offer benefits to buyers, whose purchases are the main source of most companies' profits. In developing products, firms must decide whether to produce *consumer goods* for direct sale to individual consumers or *industrial goods* for sale to other firms. Marketers must recognize that buyers will pay less for common, rapidly consumed *convenience goods* than for less frequently purchased *shopping* and *specialty goods*. In industrial markets, *expense items* are generally less expensive and more rapidly consumed than such *capital items* as buildings and equipment.

7 **Explain the importance of *branding* and *packaging*.** Each product is given an identity by its brand and the way it is packaged and labeled. The goal in developing *brands*—symbols to distinguish products and signal their uniform quality—is to increase *brand loyalty* (the preference that consumers have for a product with a particular brand name). *National brands* are products that are produced and widely distributed by the same manufacturer. *Licensed brands* are items for whose names sellers have bought the rights from organizations or individuals. *Private brands* (or *private labels*) are developed by wholesalers or retailers and commissioned from manufacturers.

QUESTIONS AND EXERCISES

Questions for Review

1. What are the key similarities and differences between consumer buying behavior and organizational buying behavior?
2. Why and how is market segmentation used in target marketing?
3. How do the needs of organizations differ according to the various organizational markets of which they are members?
4. What are the various classifications of consumer and industrial products? Give an example of a good and a service for each category other than those discussed in the text.

Questions for Analysis

5. Select an everyday product (books, CDs, skateboards, dog food, or shoes, for example). Show

how different versions of your chosen product are aimed toward different market segments. Explain how the marketing mix differs for each segment.

6. Select a second everyday product and describe the consumer buying process that typically goes into its purchase.
7. How would you expect the branding and packaging of convenience, shopping, and specialty goods to differ? Why? Give examples to illustrate your answers.
8. If you were starting your own small business (say, marketing a consumer good that you already know something about), which of the forces in the external marketing environment would you believe to have the greatest potential impact on your success?

Application Exercises

9. Interview the marketing manager of a local business. Identify the degree to which this person's job is oriented toward each element in the marketing mix.
10. Select a product made by a foreign company and sold in the United States. Compare it with a similar domestically made product in terms of product features, price, promotion, and distribution. Which of the two products do you believe is more successful with U.S. buyers? Why?

Extra Exercise

11. Break the class into small groups and assign each group a specific industry. Have each group discuss the marketing strategies that they believe are important to the effective marketing of products in that industry.

EXPLORING THE WEB

Dealing in Segments and Variables (I)

To find out about some of the marketing methods used by a world-class company, log on to the Marriott Hotels Web site at:

<www.marriott.com>

In the left column of the Marriott home page, click on **Marriott Hotels, Resorts & Suites**. Next, return to the home page. From here, explore the Web site and read the general description of the company's lodging business. Finally, return to the home page and go to the category **Our Hotels**. One at a time, look into each of Marriott's various hotel brands. Consider the following issues, all of which pertain to the company's marketing processes:

1. Identify a Marriott product that seems oriented toward the consumer market and one that is directed more at the commercial market. What are some specific services that you found that are different for the two product markets?
2. Consider the way in which Marriott has identified market segments for five brands:
   - Marriott Hotels, Resorts, and Suites
   - Courtyard by Marriott
   - Residence Inn
   - Fairfield Inn
   - Renaissance Hotels and Resorts

   Can you find an example of segmentation by geographic variables? By demographic variables? By psychographic variables?
3. Cite examples of incentives that Marriott uses and services that it offers to build relationships with its clients.

EXERCISING YOUR ETHICS

Driving a Legitimate Bargain

THE SITUATION

A firm's marketing methods are sometimes at odds with the consumer's buying process. This exercise involves a retailing situation for an expensive specialty good. It illustrates how ethical considerations can become entwined with personal selling activities, product pricing, and customer relations.

THE DILEMMA

In buying his first-ever new car, Matthew visited showrooms and Web sites for every make of SUV. After weeks of reading and test-driving, he settled on a well-known Japanese-made vehicle with a manufacturer's suggested retail price of $34,500 for the 2001 model. The price included accessories and options that Matthew considered essential. Because he planned to own the car for at least five years, he was willing to wait for just the right package rather than accept a lesser-equipped car already on the lot. Negotiations with Gary, the sales representative, continued for two weeks and, finally, a sales contract was signed for $30,600, with delivery no more than two or three months later (if the vehicle had to be special-ordered from the factory), earlier if the exact car could be found when Gary searched other dealers around the country. On April 30, to close the deal, Matt had to write a check for $1,000.

Matt received a call on June 14 from Angela, Gary's sales manager: "We cannot get your car before October, so it will have to be a 2002 model. You will have to pay the 2002 price." Matt responded with disappointment that the agreement called for a stated price and delivery deadline for 2001, pointing out that money had exchanged hands for the contract. When asked what the 2002 price would be, Angela responded that it had not yet been announced. Angrily, Matt replied that he would be foolish to agree now on some unknown future price. Moreover, he didn't like the way the dealership was jerking him around. He told Angela to send back to him everything he had signed; the deal was off.

QUESTIONS FOR DISCUSSION

1. Given the factors involved in the consumer buying process, how would you characterize the particular ethical issues in this situation?
2. From an ethical standpoint, what are the obligations of the sales representative and the sales manager regarding the pricing of the product in this situation?
3. If you were responsible for maintaining good customer relations, what actions would you take for handling this matter?

BUILDING YOUR BUSINESS SKILLS

Dealing in Segments and Variables (II)

This exercise enhances the following SCANS workplace competencies: demonstrating basic skills, demonstrating thinking skills, exhibiting interpersonal skills, and working with information.

GOAL

To encourage students to analyze the ways in which various market segmentation variables affect business success.

THE SITUATION

You and four partners are thinking of purchasing a heating and air-conditioning (H/AC) dealership that specializes in residential applications priced between \$2,000 and \$40,000. You are now in the process of deciding where that dealership should be. You are considering four locations: Miami, Florida; Westport, Connecticut; Dallas, Texas; and Spokane, Washington.

METHOD

STEP 1

Working with four classmates (your partnership group), do library research to learn how H/AC makers market their residential products. Check for articles in the *Wall Street Journal*, *Business Week*, *Fortune*, and other business publications.

STEP 2

Continue your research. This time focus on the specific marketing variables that define each prospective location. Check Census Bureau and Department of Labor data at your library and on the Internet and contact local chambers of commerce (by phone and via the Internet) to learn about the following factors for each location:

1. Geography
2. Demography (especially age, income, gender, family status, and social class)
3. Psychographic factors (lifestyles, interests, and attitudes)

STEP 3

Come together with group members to analyze which location holds the greatest promise as a dealership site. Base your decision on your analysis of market segment variables and their effects on H/AC sales.

FOLLOW-UP QUESTIONS

1. Which location did you choose? Describe the market segmentation factors that influenced your decision.
2. Identify the two most important variables that you believe will have the greatest impact on the dealership's success. Why are these factors so important?
3. Which factors were least important in your decision? Why?
4. When equipment manufacturers advertise residential H/AC products, they often show them in different climate situations (in winter, summer, or high-humidity conditions). Which market segments are these ads targeting? Describe these segments in terms of demographic and psychographic characteristics.

CRAFTING YOUR BUSINESS PLAN

Picking and Packaging the Right Products

THE PURPOSE OF THE ASSIGNMENT

1. To familiarize students with various marketing issues that a sample firm faces in developing its business plan in the framework of *Business PlanPro (BPP)* (Version 4.0).
2. To demonstrate how four chapter topics—the definition of marketing, relationship marketing, market segmentation, and product differentiation—can be integrated as components in the *BPP* planning environment.

FOLLOW-UP ASSIGNMENT

After reading Chapter 10 in the textbook, open the BPP *software and look around for information about the marketing plans for a sample firm*: Elsewares Products *(Elsewares Promotional Products & Packaging). Then respond to the following items:*

1. Is Elsewares involved in consumer marketing or organizational marketing? [Sites to see in *BPP* for this item: In the Plan Outline screen, click on **1.0 Executive Summary**. Then click on and read each of **1.1 Objectives**, **1.2 Mission**, and **1.3 Keys to Success**.]
2. Identify Elsewares' strategy and methods for building relationships with its customers. [Sites to see in *BPP*: In the Plan Outline screen, click on **5.0 Strategy and Implementation**. Also visit **5.1.4 Service and Support**. Then again read **1.0 Executive Summary** and **1.3 Keys to Success**.]

3. What basis—demographic, psychographic, or geographic—does Elsewares plan to use for its market segmentation strategy? [Sites to see in *BPP*: In the Plan Outline screen, click on **4.0 Market Analysis Summary**; then click on **4.1 Market Segmentation**.]
4. Describe Elsewares' plans for differentiating its product. Do you believe that the plan is clear enough on this matter? Why or why not? [Sites to see in *BPP*: In the Plan Outline screen, click on **4.0 Market Analysis Summary**. Also visit **4.2 Industry Analysis** and explore throughout that section.]

VIDEO EXERCISE

Niche Noshing: Terra Chips

LEARNING OBJECTIVES

The purpose of this video exercise is to help you:

1. Understand marketing research methods.
2. Understand how a niche market can be identified.
3. Appreciate the importance of appropriate pricing, packaging, and distribution in creating a successful new product.

BACKGROUND INFORMATION

In the early 1990s, Dana Sinkler and Alex Dzieduszycki gave up a successful New York catering business to start a new venture called Terra Chips. The company's product was a new kind of snack. Terra Chips are made not from potatoes but from root and vegetable chips: taro, ruby taro, sweet potato, batata, parsnip, yucca, lotus root, blue potato, celeriac root, and Jerusalem artichokes.

By 1993, production was up to 150 cases a day, and orders were pouring in from over 20 states. Dedicated to expanding its presence from gourmet markets to natural food stores, specialty food shops, and supermarkets, Terra Chips adopted distinctive silver and black packaging and widened its distribution. The strategy worked. Today the firm, now a division of the Hain Food Group <www.albafoods.com>, continues to focus on new-product development and market growth.

THE VIDEO

Dana Sinkler discusses Terra Chips' early days, beginning with the owners' recognition of a market niche they could fill, and explains how some of their initial marketing decisions were made. He recalls their focus on a high-quality, affordable luxury item and explains how the packaging and distribution of the product were carefully chosen to match that image—and to assure buyers that the product was worth its premium price. Photos of newspaper and magazine articles about the new chips indicate some of the early publicity that the company was able to garner.

QUESTIONS FOR DISCUSSION

1. Of the research methods discussed in the chapter, which describes best Sinkler and Dzieduszycki's original approach? Which method do you think is most appropriate to the business now, as it seeks to expand its product line and market?
2. Terra Chips has considered going international, although the ingredients of its chip products are not as unusual abroad as they are in the United States. How much do you think novelty contributes to the success of the product, and how well do you think it would fare abroad? What elements of the marketing mix might need to be adjusted for international consumers?
3. How well do you think Terra Chips could succeed if, instead of marketing abroad, it decided to increase market share in the United States by selling to ordinary grocery stores, convenience stores, or cafeterias and vending outlets? What kind of challenges would it face in doing so?

FOLLOW-UP ASSIGNMENT

Find out as much as you can about the range of products made by national snack brands such as Frito-Lay <www.fritolay.com>, Nabisco <www.nabisco.com>, and Newman's Own <www.newmansown.com>. Do you think the product-line breadth of these firms boosts the sales of their individual products? Why or why not? What does a small firm have to do in order to compete with these giant firms?

FOR FURTHER EXPLORATION

Visit Terra Chips' Web site at <www.terrachips.com> and examine the "New Products" page. How well do you think its current new products fit the company's original marketing mix? Do you think the possibilities for new products are limited for this firm? What other new products do you think Terra Chips could research, such as flavored popcorns or whole-wheat pretzels? How should the company go about investigating the market potential for such products?

Pricing, Promoting, and Distributing Products

After reading this chapter, you should be able to:

1. Identify the various *pricing objectives* that govern pricing decisions, describe the *price-setting tools* used in making these decisions, and discuss *pricing strategies* and *tactics* for both existing and new products.
2. Identify the important objectives of *promotion*, discuss the considerations entailed in selecting a *promotional mix*, and describe the key *advertising media*.
3. Outline the tasks involved in *personal selling* and describe the various types of *sales promotions*.
4. Identify the different *channels of distribution* and explain the differences between *merchant wholesalers* and *agents/brokers*.
5. Identify the different types of *retailing* and *retail stores*.
6. Describe the major activities in the *physical distribution process*.

Strike Up the Bandwidth

How about that latest Jennifer Lopez album? Prefer the Metabolics? What about Violent Femmes or maybe Elvis Costello? How about for free? The Internet is changing the way we get our musical entertainment—everything from when we buy, to whom we get it from, to what we pay, to how it gets from sellers to consumers. Consider some of the latest trends. Just five years ago, the record shop was the standard site for finding CDs and tapes in malls, shopping centers, and discount stores. You could save some money by going store to store and comparing prices. In fact, browsing display stands for artists and labels was a way of life for many music buyers.

Then came Internet stores, many of them with discount prices. For example, you can go to a Web site like <www.cdhitlist.com>, which offers more than 55,000 titles among CDs, cassettes, and VHS/DVD movies. You can search every list, place orders electronically or over the phone, and then get your music or movie by mail. You can still browse, of course—electronically, at home—and compare prices without burning gasoline or wearing out shoe leather. Web sites such as <www.evenbetter.com> will even do your comparison shopping for you, listing prices from low to high for any product offered by as many as 50 different e-stores. Then—at least for a while—came the online music service called Napster. When you registered at <www.napster.com>, you got access to "the

> *"The music business as we know it today is hosed. If I were a music-biz exec, I'd be singing the blues."*
>
> —Stewart Alsop, Journalist and venture capitalist

world's largest online music community." Once you were in, you could exchange music by sending your albums to other people on the Internet and getting back albums in return. For free. Napster was accessible 24 hours a day, and there was no waiting for the mail because albums were transmitted digitally and downloaded onto your computer in just a few minutes.

A 19-year-old music lover named Shawn Fanning invented the software that got Napster rolling in 1999. By February 2000, officials at Indiana University had noticed that 60 percent of the institution's Internet bandwidth (system capacity) was consumed by students using Napster to trade online music. The university's servers were so clogged that filters had to be installed to block Napster. The same thing happened on other campuses. By February 2001, Napster boasted a roster of more than 80 million registered users. The business of distributing music would never be the same. "I love Napster," says one 15-year-old fan. "I'm never buying a CD again."

How could billions of recordings be delivered so fast? The music itself was not actually traded on the Napster Web site. Instead, you went to the site to get Napster software, which you could download for free onto your computer. The software would find albums that you'd stored on your hard disk and—along with millions of other users—posted on the Napster site. Then, using an MP3 format (digital file), you could start trading with anyone else who was live on the Net at the same time. You got what you wanted from their hard drives and they got what they wanted from yours. "Napster," boasted the company's site, "is music at Internet speed."

What did all this mean for the music industry—for album producers, distributors, and retail stores? The initial reaction was one of surprise, then fear, and even anger. According to Stewart Alsop, a partner with the venture capital firm New Enterprise Associates, the advent of Napster meant that "the music business as we know it today is hosed. . . . If I were a music-biz exec . . . I'd be singing the blues."

Our opening story continues on page 299

DETERMINING PRICES

As we saw in Chapter 10, product development managers decide what products a company will offer to its customers. In **pricing**, the second major component of the marketing mix, managers decide what the company will receive in exchange for its products. In this section, we first discuss the objectives that influence a firm's pricing decisions. Then we describe the major tools that companies use to meet those objectives.

pricing
Process of determining what a company will receive in exchange for its products

pricing objectives
Goals that producers hope to attain in pricing products for sale

Pricing to Meet Business Objectives

Companies often price products to maximize profits, but they often hope to satisfy other **pricing objectives** as well. Some firms are more interested in dominating the market or securing high market share than in making the highest possible profits. Pricing decisions are also influenced by the need to survive in competitive marketplaces, by social and ethical concerns, and even by corporate image.

Profit-Maximizing Objectives Pricing to maximize profits is tricky. If prices are set too low, the company will probably sell many units of its product but may miss the opportunity to make additional profit on each unit (and may even lose money on each exchange). If prices are set too high, the company will make a large profit on each item but will sell fewer units. Again, the firm loses money. In addition, it may be left with excess inventory and may have to reduce or even close production operations. To avoid these problems, companies try to set prices to sell the number of units that will generate the highest possible total profits.

In calculating profits, managers weigh sales revenues against costs for materials and labor. However, they also consider the capital resources (plant and equipment) that the company must tie up to generate a given level of profit. The costs of marketing (such as maintaining a large sales staff) can also be substantial. Concern over the efficient use of these resources has led many firms to set prices so as to achieve a targeted level of return on sales or capital investment.

Pricing for E-Business Objectives Marketers pricing for sales on the Internet must consider different kinds of costs and different forms of consumer awareness than those pricing products to be sold conventionally. Many e-businesses are lowering both costs and prices because of the Web's unique marketing capabilities. Because the Web typically provides a more direct link between producer and ultimate consumer, buyers avoid the costs entailed by wholesalers and retailers. Another factor in lower Internet prices is the ease of comparison shopping: Obviously, point-and-click shopping is much more efficient than driving from store to store in search of the best price. In addition, both consumers and businesses can force lower prices by joining together in the interest of greater purchasing power. Numerous small businesses, for example, are joining forces on the Web to negotiate lower prices for the health care services offered by employee benefits plans.[1]

Market Share Objectives In the long run, a business must make a profit to survive. Nevertheless, many companies initially set low prices for new products. They are willing to accept minimal profits, even losses, to get buyers to try products. They use pricing to establish **market share**—a company's percentage of the total market sales for a specific product type. Even with established products, market share may outweigh profits as a pricing objective. For a product such as Philadelphia Brand Cream Cheese, dominating a market means that consumers are more likely to buy it because they are familiar with a well-known, highly visible product. Market domination means the continuous sales of more units and thus higher profits even at a lower unit price.

market share
As a percentage, total of market sales for a specific company or product

Price-Setting Tools

Whatever a company's objectives, managers must measure the potential impact before deciding on final prices. Two basic tools are often used for this purpose: *cost-oriented pricing* and *breakeven analysis*. These tools are combined to identify prices that will allow the company to reach its objectives.

Cost-Oriented Pricing Cost-oriented pricing considers the firm's desire to make a profit and takes into account the need to cover production costs. A music store manager would begin to price CDs by calculating the cost of making them available to shoppers. Included in this figure would be store rent, employee wages, utilities, product displays, insurance, and, of course, the cost of buying CDs from the manufacturer.

Let's assume that the cost from the manufacturer is $8 per CD. If the store sells CDs for this price, it will not make any profit. Nor will it make a profit if it sells CDs for $8.50 each or even $10 or $11. The manager must account for product and other costs and stipulate a figure for profit. Together, these figures constitute **markup**. In this case, a reasonable markup of $7 over costs would result in a $15 selling price. Markup is usually stated as a percentage of selling price. Markup percentage is thus calculated as follows:

markup
Amount added to an item's cost to sell it at a profit

$$\text{Markup percentage} = \frac{\text{Markup}}{\text{Sales price}}$$

In the case of our CD retailer, the markup percentage is 46.7:

$$\text{Markup percentage} = \frac{\$7}{\$15} = 46.7\%$$

Out of every dollar taken in, $.467 will be gross profit for the store. From this profit the store must still pay rent, utilities, insurance, and all other costs. Markup can also be expressed as a percentage of cost: The $7 markup is 87.5 percent of the $8 cost of a CD ($7/$8).

Breakeven Analysis: Cost-Volume-Profit Relationships Using cost-oriented pricing, a firm will cover its **variable costs**: costs that change with the number of goods or services produced or sold. It will also make some money toward paying its **fixed costs**: costs that are unaffected by the number of goods or services produced or sold. But how many units must the company sell before all its fixed costs are covered and it begins to make a profit? To determine this figure, it needs a **breakeven analysis**.

variable cost
Cost that changes with the quantity of a product produced or sold

fixed cost
Cost unaffected by the quantity of a product produced or sold

breakeven analysis
Assessment of the quantity of a product that must be sold before the seller makes a profit

breakeven point
Quantity of a product that must be sold before the seller covers variable and fixed costs and makes a profit

To continue our music store example, suppose that the variable cost for each CD (in this case, the cost of buying the CD from the producer) is $8. This means that the store's annual variable costs depend on how many CDs are sold—the number of CDs sold times $8 cost for each CD. Say that fixed costs for keeping the store open for one year are $100,000. These costs are unaffected by the number of CDs sold; costs for lighting, rent, insurance, and salaries are steady whether the store sells any CDs. Therefore, how many CDs must be sold to cover both fixed and variable costs and to generate some profit? The answer is the **breakeven point**, which is 14,286 CDs. We arrive at this number through the following equation:

$$\text{Breakeven point (in units)} = \frac{\text{Total fixed costs}}{\text{Price} - \text{Variable cost}} = \frac{\$100{,}000}{\$15 - \$8} = 14{,}286 \text{ CDs}$$

Figure 11.1 shows the breakeven point graphically. If the store sells fewer than 14,286 CDs, it loses money for the year. If sales exceed 14,286 CDs, profits grow by $7 for each CD sold. If the store sells exactly 14,286 CDs, it will cover all its costs but will earn zero profit.

Zero profitability at the breakeven point can also be seen by using the profit equation:

$$\begin{aligned}\text{Profit} &= \text{Total revenue} - (\text{Total fixed cost} + \text{Total variable cost})\\ &= (14{,}286 \text{ CDs} \times \$15) - (\$100{,}000 \text{ Fixed cost} + [14{,}286 \text{ CDs} \times \$8 \text{ Variable cost}])\\ \$0 &= (\$214{,}290) - (\$100{,}000 + \$114{,}288)(\text{rounded to the nearest whole CD})\end{aligned}$$

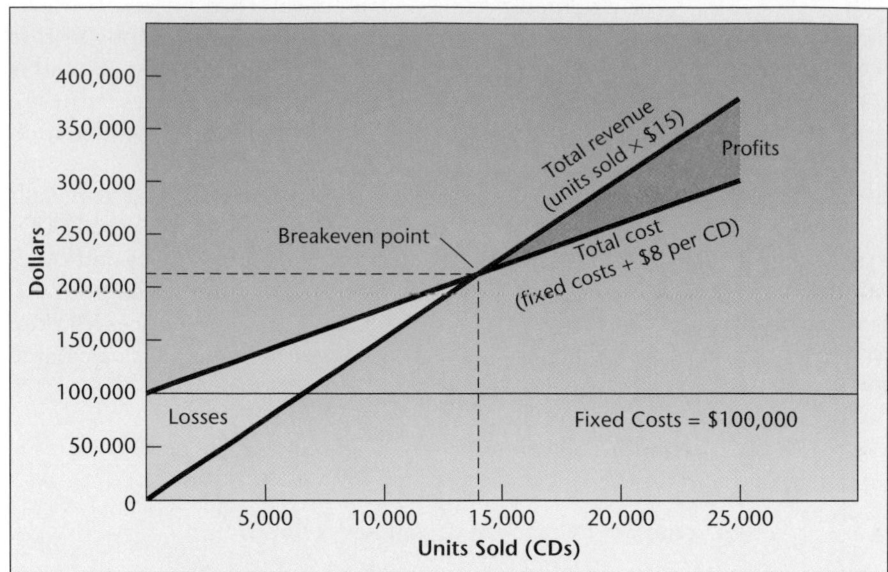

Figure 11.1
Breakeven Analysis

PRICING STRATEGIES AND TACTICS

The pricing tools discussed in the previous section are valuable in helping managers set prices on specific goods; however, they do not help in setting pricing philosophies. In this section, we discuss pricing strategy—pricing as a planning activity. We then describe some basic pricing tactics: ways in which managers implement a firm's pricing strategies.

Pricing Strategies

How important is pricing as an element in the marketing mix? Because pricing has a direct and visible impact on revenues, it is extremely important to overall marketing plans. Moreover, it is a very flexible tool: It is certainly easier to change prices than to change products or distribution channels. In this section, we focus on the ways in which pricing strategies for both new and existing products can result in widely differing prices for very similar products.

Pricing Existing Products A firm has three options for pricing existing products:

- Pricing above prevailing market prices for similar products
- Pricing below market prices
- Pricing at or near market prices

Pricing above the market plays on the common assumption that higher price means higher quality. In contrast, pricing below prevailing market price can succeed if a firm can offer a product of acceptable quality while keeping costs below those of higher-priced competitors.

price skimming
Setting an initial high price to cover new product costs and generate a profit

Pricing New Products Companies introducing new products must often choose between two pricing policy options, selecting either very high prices or very low ones. **Price skimming**—setting an initially high price to cover costs and generate a profit—may allow a firm to earn a large profit on each item sold. The cash income is often needed to cover development and introduction costs. Skimming works only if marketers can convince consumers that a product is truly different from those already on the market. In contrast, **penetration pricing**—setting an initially low price to establish a new product in the market—seeks to generate consumer interest and stimulate trial purchase of new products.[2]

penetration pricing
Setting an initial low price to establish a new product in the market

Fixed Versus Dynamic Pricing for E-Business The electronic marketplace has introduced a highly variable pricing system as an alternative to more conventional—and more stable—pricing structures for both consumer and business-to-business products. So-called dynamic pricing is feasible because the flow of information on the Web notifies millions of buyers around the world of instantaneous changes in product availability. In order to attract sales that might be lost under traditional fixed-price structures, sellers can alter prices privately, on a one-to-one, customer-to-customer basis.[3]

At present, fixed pricing remains the most widely available option for cybershoppers. E-tail giant Amazon.com has maintained the practice as the pricing strategy for its 16 million retail items. That situation, however, is beginning to change as dynamic-price challengers, such as eBay—the online person-to-person auction Web site—and Priceline.com—the online clearinghouse for person-to-business price negotiation, grow in popularity.

An even more novel approach is taken by NexTag.com Inc., whose dynamic-price strategy differs from both online auctions and the Priceline.com model. Instead of requiring buyers to bid up prices against each other, NexTag asks prospective customers to state the price that they are willing to pay for a product. Merchants then compete for the sale. Unlike Priceline customers, NexTag customers do not commit in advance to sale prices: They wait to see how low the price goes. NexTag gathers the offers from the merchants, each of whom decides how low to price a product. The customer can then choose the lowest price. According to Patti Maes of the Massachusetts Institute of Technology's Media Lab, NexTag's dynamic pricing moves a step further from fixed pricing and may indicate the trend of the future. "Fixed prices," she points out, "are only a 100-year-old phenomenon. I think they will disappear online, simply because it is possible—cheap and easy—to vary prices online."[4]

Since the end of the compact-disk boom in about 1994, the ranks of U.S. record store chains have been decimated by a long-running price war. It was started by Best Buy <www.bestbuy.com>—which is an electronics store, not a record store. In the early 1990s, Best Buy tried to attract electronics customers by selling compact disks at discount prices—$2 to $3 less than what record store chains were charging. Circuit City <www.circuitcity.com>—another electronics retailer—followed suit, and soon both chains were featuring discount-CD sections boasting 60,000 titles. Record stores could not match the selection or prices, and in 1995-1996, many—including the nation's largest chains—were forced to declare bankruptcy.

IT'S A WIRED WORLD
The World of Cyberprice Bidding

Sometimes a company getting into e-business is better off outsourcing some e-activities rather than doing them all itself. Consider the experience of United Technologies Corp. (UTC) <www.utc.com>. The Connecticut-based conglomerate needed to renew contracts for the printed circuit boards it was buying from eight suppliers to be used in UTC elevators, air conditioners, and other products. What prices would various suppliers charge? Before accepting estimates from suppliers, UTC hoped to reduce overall prices by 4 percent and, based on the going rate, expected to pay out $74 million. At that point UTC decided to outsource the entire bidding process to FreeMarkets, Inc. <www.freemarkets.com>, an Internet auction company. The results were stunning. FreeMarkets received bids from 29 circuit-board companies in the United States, Europe, and Asia. The winning suppliers signed contracts for $42 million—some 43 percent below UTC's projections.

The Net has created an auction marketplace for industrial goods that makes price setting an art and a gamble for industrial buyers and sellers, just as it did earlier with auction sites for consumer items (such as CyberBuyer.com). The existence of such a marketplace changes the entire method for price setting by firms selling to industrial customers. The conventional price-setting method generally follows established patterns:

- Incumbent suppliers have the inside edge for the new contracts.
- Closed bids prohibit suppliers from knowing competitors' prices.
- Only a few suppliers are invited to submit bids.
- If a firm's bid is not accepted, it has no opportunity to revise it.

FreeMarkets is changing all of that, and in so doing, it saves client companies an average of 15 percent on the costs of their purchases. The savings potential in the $5 trillion industrial-parts market is obvious. That's why FreeMarkets is attracting customers such as Raytheon, Quaker Oats, Emerson Electric, and Owens Corning.

To get suppliers to participate, FreeMarkets does not charge them fees for bidding. Instead, industrial buyers (large companies) pay fixed subscription fees of up to $4 million a year. The auction infrastructure includes not only the software and computer technology necessary to conduct the bidding but also the standardizing of relevant technical requirements: Delivery quantities and schedules, inventory quantities, and quality standards are all clarified before bidding starts. In a recent auction for a parts contract, the client set the most recent price, $745,000, as the starting point. The 25 suppliers at remote locations instantly saw each bid as it was received and posted at FreeMarkets' communications headquarters. With an official 20-minute total time deadline for submitting a better price, the low bid dropped to $612,000 after 10 minutes and then to $585,000 with 30 seconds left. When a bid is received in the last minute of regulation time, the auction kicks into a 60-second overtime period. After 13 minutes of overtime bidding, the final price landed at $518,000—which was 31 percent below the client's expectations. In this environment, the fixed-price approach to selling industrial goods is quickly becoming a thing of the past.

The "Wired World" box in this chapter discusses in detail the methods of online pricing used by FreeMarkets, an Internet auction firm.

Pricing Tactics

price lining
Setting a limited number of prices for certain categories of products

psychological pricing
Pricing tactic that takes advantage of the fact that consumers do not always respond rationally to stated prices

Regardless of its pricing strategy, a company may adopt one or more pricing tactics. Companies selling multiple items in a product category often use **price lining**—offering all items in certain categories at a limited number of prices. With price lining, a store predetermines three or four *price points* at which a particular product will be sold. For men's suits, the price points might be $175, $250, and $400; all men's suits in the store will be priced at one of these three points.

Psychological pricing takes advantage of the fact that customers are not completely rational when making buying decisions. One type of psychological pricing,

odd-even pricing, is based on the theory that customers prefer prices that are not stated in even dollar amounts. Thus, customers see prices of $1,000, $100, $50, and $10 as significantly higher than $999.95, $99.95, $49.95, and $9.95, respectively. Finally, sellers must often offer price reductions—**discounts**—to stimulate sales. Hyatt Hotels <www.hyatt.com>, for example, offer discount room prices to stimulate demand during off-peak seasons.

odd-even pricing
Psychological pricing tactic based on the premise that customers prefer prices not stated in even dollar amounts

discount
Price reduction offered as an incentive to purchase

promotion
Aspect of the marketing mix concerned with the most effective techniques for selling a product

THE IMPORTANCE OF PROMOTION

As we noted in Chapter 10, **promotion**—the third element in the marketing mix—is any technique designed to sell a product. It is part of the communication mix: the total message any company sends to consumers about its product. Promotional techniques, especially advertising, must communicate the uses, features, and benefits of products. Sales promotions also include various programs that add value beyond the benefits inherent in the product. For example, it is nice to get a high-quality product at a reasonable price but even better when the seller offers a rebate or a bonus pack with "20 percent more free." In promoting products, then, marketers have an array of tools at their disposal.

Promotional Objectives

The ultimate objective of any promotion is to increase sales. In addition, marketers may use promotion to *communicate information, position products, add value*, and *control sales volume*. Promotion is effective in communicating information from one person or organization to another. Consumers cannot buy products unless they have been informed about them. Information may thus advise customers that a product exists or educate them about its features.

As we noted in Chapter 10, **positioning** is the process of establishing an easily identifiable product image in the minds of consumers. First, a company must identify which segments are likely to purchase its product and who its competitors are. Only then can it focus its strategy on differentiating its product from the competition's while still appealing to its target audience.[5]

positioning
Process of establishing an identifiable product image in the minds of consumers

Customers gain benefits when the promotional mix is shifted so that it communicates value-added benefits in its products. Thus, Burger King <www.burgerking.com> recently shifted its promotional mix by cutting back on advertising dollars and using those funds for customer discounts: Receiving the same food at a lower price is "value-added" for Burger King's customers. Finally, by increasing promotional activities in slow periods, firms that experience seasonal sales patterns (say, greeting-card companies) can achieve more stable sales volume throughout the year. They can keep production and distribution systems running evenly.

THE PROMOTIONAL MIX

In Chapter 10, we identified four types of promotional tools: *advertising, personal selling, sales promotions*, and *publicity* and *public relations*. The best combination of these tools—that is, the best **promotional mix**—depends on many factors, the most important of which is the target audience.

promotional mix
Combination of tools used to promote a product

The Target Audience: Promotion and the Buyer Decision Process A noteworthy consideration in establishing the promotional mix is matching the promotional tool with the relevant stage in the buyer decision process. As we noted in Chapter 10, this process can be broken down into five steps:

1. Buyers must first recognize the need to make a purchase. At this stage, marketers must make sure the buyer is aware that their products exist. Advertising and publicity, which can reach a large number of people very quickly, are very important.
2. Buyers also want to learn more about available products. Advertising and personal selling are important in this stage because both can be used to educate the customer.

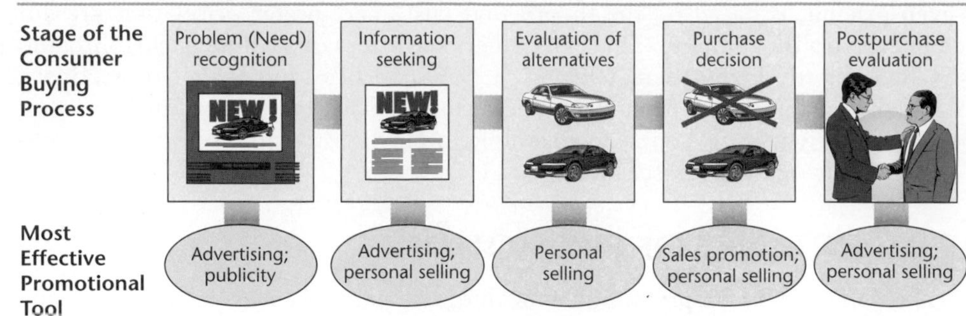

Figure 11.2
The Consumer Buying Process and the Promotional Mix

3. Buyers evaluate and compare competing products. Personal selling can be vital at this point: Sales representatives can demonstrate their product's quality and performance in direct relation to competitors' products.
4. Buyers decide on specific products and purchase them. Sales promotion is effective at this stage because it can give consumers an incentive to buy. Personal selling can also help by bringing products to convenient purchase locations.
5. Buyers evaluate products after purchasing them. Advertising, or even personal selling, is sometimes used after the sale to remind consumers that they made a prudent purchase.[6]

Figure 11.2 summarizes the effective promotional tools for each stage of the consumer buying process.

Advertising Promotions

advertising
Promotional tool consisting of paid, nonpersonal communication used by an identified sponsor to inform an audience about a product

Advertising is paid, nonpersonal communication used by an identified sponsor to inform an audience about a product. In 1999, U.S. firms spent $215 billion on advertising, with nearly $74 billion of this amount being spent by just 100 companies.[7] In this section, we will describe each of the different types of advertising media, noting some of the advantages and limitations of each.

advertising media
Variety of communication devices for carrying a seller's message to potential customers

Advertising Media Bombarded with thousands of advertisements, consumers tend to ignore the bulk of the ads they see or hear. Marketers must find out who their customers are, which media they attend to, what message will appeal to them, and how to get their attention. Marketers thus use several different **advertising media**—that is, specific communication devices for carrying a seller's message to potential customers.[8]

Newspapers, for example, account for about 25 percent of all advertising expenditures. Each day they reach more than 113 million U.S. adults. The main advantage of newspaper advertising is flexible, rapid coverage: Ads can easily be changed from day to day. However, newspapers are generally thrown out after one day, and because their readership is so broad, they do not usually allow advertisers to target audiences very well.

Television accounts for about 22 percent of all advertising outlays. Figure 11.3 shows network TV advertising expenditures for some U.S. firms.[9] In addition to the major networks, cable television has become an important advertising medium. Cable network ad revenues increased from $3.4 billion in 1995 to nearly $9 billion in 1999.[10] Information on viewer demographics for a particular program allows advertisers to aim at target audiences, and television reaches more people than any other medium.

direct mail
Advertising medium in which messages are mailed directly to consumers' homes or places of business

Direct mail, which involves fliers or other types of printed advertisements mailed directly to consumers' homes or places of business, accounts for 18 percent of all advertising outlays. Advertisers can predict in advance how many recipients will take a mailing seriously. These people have a stronger-than-average interest in the product advertised and are more likely than most to buy the promoted product.

About 7 percent of all advertising outlays are for radio advertising. Radio ads are quite inexpensive, and stations are usually segmented into categories such as rock and

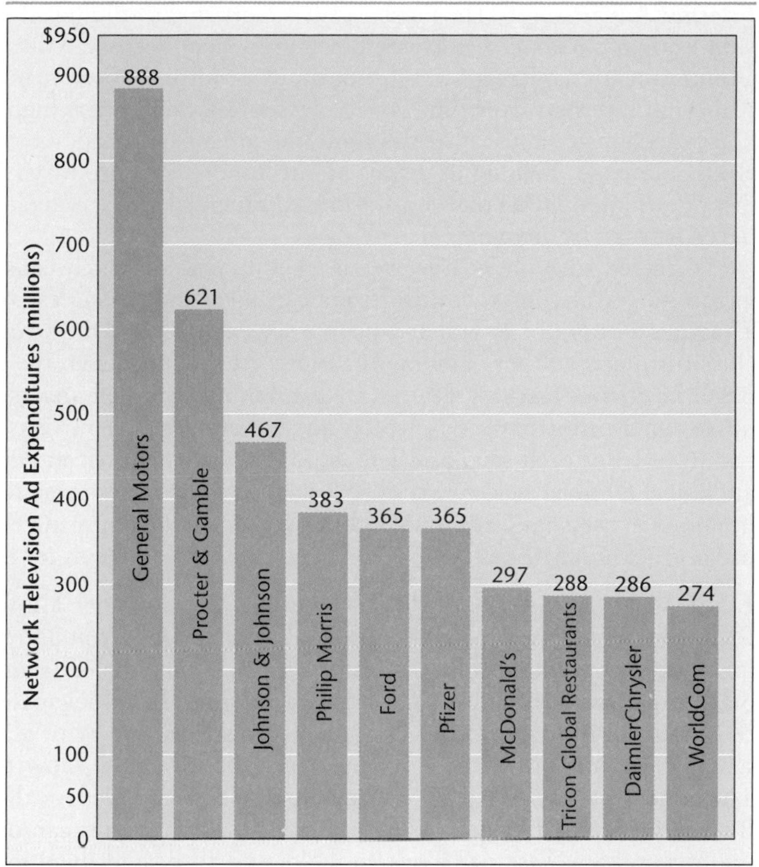

Figure 11.3
Top 10 Network TV Advertisers

roll, country and western, jazz, talk shows, news, and religious programming; their audiences are largely segmented. The huge variety of magazines provides a high level of ready market segmentation, and magazine ads account for roughly 5 percent of all advertising. Outdoor advertising—billboards, signs, and advertisements on buses, street furniture, taxis, stadiums, and subways—makes up about 1 percent of all advertising, but at 10 percent per year, it's growing faster than newspapers, magazines, and television. These ads are inexpensive, face little competition for customers' attention, and are subject to high repeat exposure.

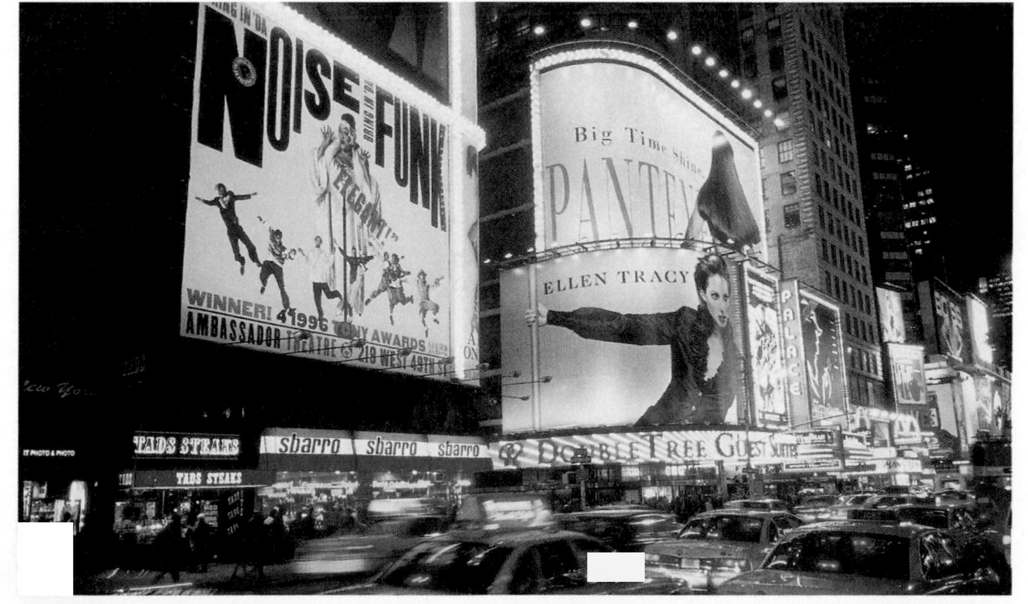

Speed and creativity have given billboards like these in New York's Times Square a new prominence in the world of advertising media. Instead of relying on highly skilled human artists, outdoor ad sellers can now commission digital creations that not only turn heads but still cost less than most other media. Whereas it used to take a month to launch a billboard-based campaign, it now takes just days.

Internet Advertising The most recent advertising medium is the Internet, where such well-known names as 3M Corp., Burlington Coat Factory, Miller Genuine Draft, MCI Communications, Reebok, and thousands of lesser-known firms have all placed ads. Although Internet advertising is still in its infancy and offers high potential, many marketers recognize that it also has limitations: Consumers don't want to wade through electronic pages looking at details about hundreds of products. One expert offers the disappointing opinion that most of the commercial advertisements on the Internet may never be read by anyone.[11]

Targeted advertising, however, is meeting with success because, unlike print or television ad buyers, Internet advertisers can measure the success of each ad they place: They get a count of how many people see each ad and they can track the number of click-throughs by users looking for more information from the advertiser's own Web page. Electronic tracking devices are available for market analysis that relay to e-businesses such information as which ads generate more purchases, the sales margins resulting from each sale, and which ads attract the most attention from each target audience. DoubleClick <www.doubleclick.net> was one of the first companies to help other advertisers take advantage of the Web's unique opportunities for linking up with users, tracking their behavior online, and tailoring ad messages to them.

data mining
Process of searching, sifting, and reorganizing vast pools of data on purchases to reveal patterns of buyer behavior

data warehousing
Collection and storage of data in electronic files to be used in data analysis

Data Mining and Data Warehousing The Internet allows efficient targeting because volumes of data can be gathered electronically from Internet users. The behavior patterns of millions of users, for example, can be traced by analyzing files of information gathered over time. Called **data mining**, this efficient searching, sifting, and reorganizing of vast pools of data on user purchase behavior reveals who has bought which products, how many, when, over what Web site, how they paid, and so on. The collection and storage of these data in electronic files is called **data warehousing**. By analyzing what customers actually do, the e-marketer can determine what subsequent purchases they are likely to make and then send them tailor-made ads.[12] "All we're doing," says Howard Draft, chairman of Draft Worldwide in Chicago <www.draftworldwide.com>, "is using information we have on our customers, with overlays of demographic or psychographic information, to enhance our knowledge of them and market back to them." Instead of using one advertisement to blanket all consumers, data mining makes it feasible to use niche advertising that is targeted one-on-one to individual consumers.[13]

"All we're doing is using information we have on our customers to enhance our knowledge of them and market back to them."

—Howard Draft, Draft Worldwide Marketing Agency

A combination of many additional media, including catalogs, sidewalk handouts, Yellow Pages, skywriting, telephone calls, special events, and door-to-door communication, make up the remaining 22 percent of all U.S. advertising.

WEB Connection

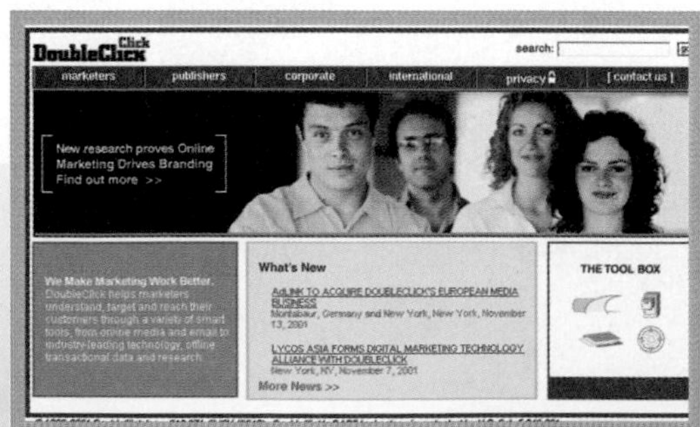

DoubleClick Inc. is a global Internet advertising-solutions company that makes advertising work for Web marketers and publishers. Using DART (Dynamic Advertising Reporting and Targeting) ad serving technology, DoubleClick provides sites and advertisers with high-level targeting and extensive feedback on the performance of their ad campaigns. DoubleClick has global headquarters in New York City and maintains over 40 offices around the world.

www.doubleclick.net

Personal Selling

In **personal selling**, a salesperson communicates one-to-one with potential customers to identify their needs and to line them up with the seller's products. The oldest form of selling, it provides the personal link between seller and buyer and adds to a firm's credibility because it allows buyers to interact with and ask questions of the seller.[14]

personal selling
Promotional tool in which a salesperson communicates one-on-one with potential customers

telemarketing
Tactic of using telephone solicitations to perform the personal selling process

Telemarketing The high costs of traditional personal selling methods have prompted many companies to turn to **telemarketing:** using telephone solicitations to perform the personal selling process. Telemarketing can be used to handle any stage of the personal selling process or to set up appointments for outside salespeople. For example, it saves the cost of personal sales visits to industrial customers. Each industrial buyer requires an average of nearly four visits to complete a sale; thus, some companies have realized savings in sales visits of $1,000 or more. Such savings are stimulating the remarkable growth of telemarketing, which sold over $585 billion in goods and services in 2000, from some 19 billion phone calls each month in the United States.[15]

Personal Selling Tasks

One important aspect of sales force management is overseeing salespeople as they perform three basic tasks generally associated with personal selling. In *order processing*, a salesperson receives an order and sees to its handling and delivery. Route salespeople, who call on regular customers to check their supplies, are often order processors. When the benefits of a product are not entirely clear, *creative selling* can help to persuade buyers. Creative selling is crucial for high-priced consumer products, such as homes and cars, for which buyers comparison shop.

Finally, a company may use *missionary selling* when its purpose is to promote itself and its products rather than simply to close a sale. Drug company representatives promote drugs to doctors who, in turn, prescribe them to patients. The sale, then, is actually made at the drugstore. Depending on the product and company, sales jobs usually require individuals to perform all three tasks to some degree.

sales promotion
Short-term promotional activity designed to stimulate consumer buying or cooperation from distributors and sales agents

coupon
Sales promotion technique in which a certificate is issued entitling the buyer to a reduced price

point-of-purchase (POP) display
Sales promotion technique in which product displays are located in certain areas to stimulate purchase

premium
Sales promotion technique in which offers of free or reduced-price items are used to stimulate purchases

trade show
Sales promotion technique in which various members of an industry gather to display, demonstrate, and sell products

Sales Promotions

Sales promotions are short-term promotional activities designed to stimulate consumer buying or cooperation from distributors, sales agents, or other members of the trade. They are important because they increase the likelihood that buyers will try products. They also enhance product recognition and can increase purchase size and amount.[16] Soap is sometimes bound in packages of four with the promotion "buy three and get one free."

Types of Sales Promotions Most consumers have taken part in a variety of sales promotions. For example, when you use a certificate that entitles you to a stated savings off a regular price, you are participating in a **coupon** promotion. Coupons may be used to encourage customers to try new products, to attract customers away from competitors, or to induce current customers to buy more of a product.

To grab customers' attention as they walk through stores, some companies use **point-of-purchase (POP) displays.** Located at the ends of aisles or near checkout counters, POP displays make it easier for customers to find products and easier for sellers to eliminate competitors from consideration. *Purchasing incentives* include free samples, which allow customers to try products without risk, and **premiums**, which are gifts, such as pens, pencils, calendars, and coffee mugs that are given away to consumers in return for buying a specified product. **Trade shows** allow companies to rent booths to display and demonstrate products to customers who have a special interest in them or who are ready to buy. In *contests*, consumers may be asked to

Organizers of such events as the New Orleans Jazz and Heritage Festival <www.nojazzfest.com> *rely increasingly on money from corporate sponsors such as Ray-Ban* <www.rayban.com> *to pay for entertainment, keep ticket prices down, and finance promotional appeals to broader audiences. Sponsors are trying to foster good public relations, and in the last 15 years, the number of events with corporate sponsors has risen from 25 percent to 85 percent. Corporations now spend nearly $700 million a year on festivals, fairs, and other events.*

enter their cats in the Purina Cat Chow calendar contest by submitting entry blanks from the backs of cat food packages.

publicity
Promotional tool in which information about a company or product is transmitted by general mass media

public relations
Company-influenced publicity directed at building goodwill between an organization and potential customers

distribution mix
Combination of distribution channels by which a firm gets its products to end users

intermediary
Individual or firm that helps to distribute a product

wholesaler
Intermediary that sells products to other businesses for resale to final consumers

retailer
Intermediary that sells products directly to consumers

Publicity and Public Relations

Much to the delight of marketing managers with tight budgets, **publicity** is free. Because it is presented in a news format, consumers often see publicity as objective and highly believable. It is a very important part of the promotional mix.[17] However, marketers often have little control over publicity. **Public relations** is company-influenced publicity that seeks to build good relations with the public and to deal with the effects of unfavorable events. It attempts to establish goodwill with customers (and potential customers) by performing and publicizing a company's public service activities.

THE DISTRIBUTION MIX

It is not enough just to create, price, and promote products. Commercial success depends also on the fourth element in the marketing mix—distribution (place)—so that products reach the customer. Because distribution takes many forms, companies give serious thought in choosing a **distribution mix**: the combination of distribution channels that a firm selects to get a product to end users. In this section, we will consider some of the many factors that enter into the distribution mix. First, we will look at the role of the target audience and explain the need for intermediaries. We will then discuss the basic distribution strategies.

Intermediaries and Distribution Channels

Once called *middlemen*, **intermediaries** are the individuals and firms who help to distribute a producer's goods by either moving the goods or by providing information that stimulates the movement of goods to customers. They are generally classified as wholesalers or retailers. **Wholesalers** sell products to other businesses, which resell them to final consumers. **Retailers** sell products directly to consumers. Some firms rely on independent intermediaries, and others employ their own distribution networks and sales forces.[18]

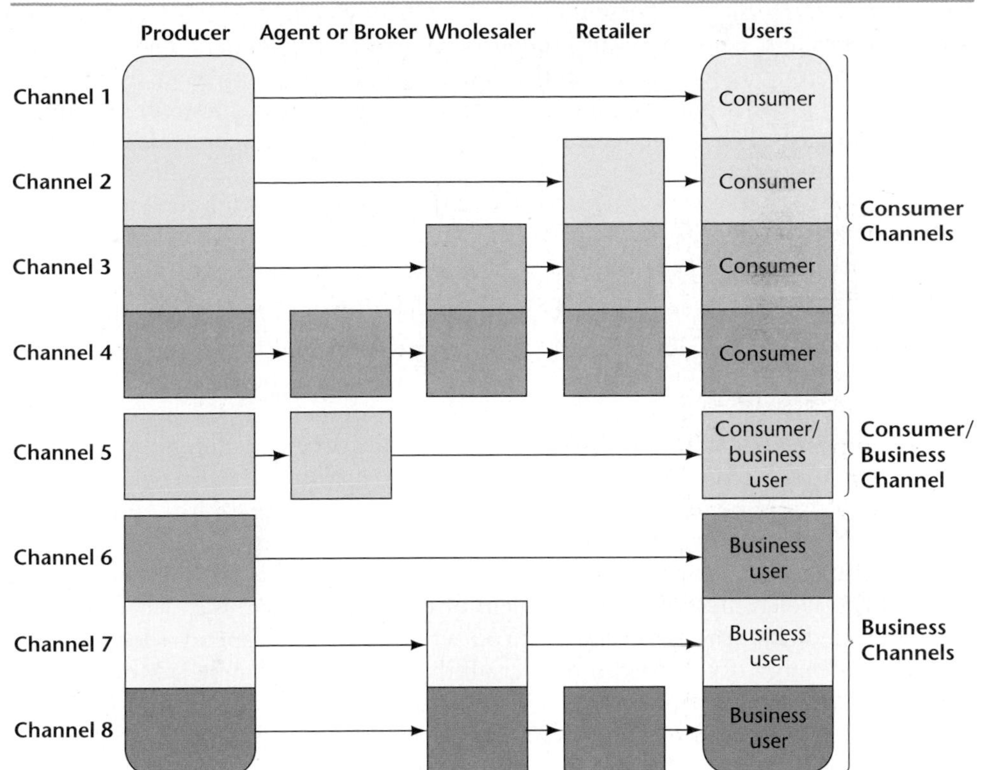

Figure 11.4
Channels of Distribution

distribution channel
Network of interdependent companies through which a product passes from producer to end user

direct channel
Distribution channel in which a product travels from producer to consumer without intermediaries

Distribution of Consumer Products A **distribution channel** is the path that a product follows from producer to end user. Figure 11.4 shows how the eight primary distribution channels can be identified according to the kinds of channel members who participate in getting products to their ultimate destinations. As we move through this discussion, note first that all channels begin with a producer and end either with a consumer or an industrial (business) user. Channels 1 through 4 are most often used for the distribution of consumer goods and services.

Channel 1: Direct Distribution of Consumer Products In a **direct channel**, the product travels from the producer to the consumer without intermediaries. Using their own sales forces, companies such as Avon, Fuller Brush, and Tupperware use this channel. This direct channel is also prominent on the Internet for thousands of products ranging from books and automobiles to insurance and vacation packages sold directly by producers to consumers.

Channel 2: Retail Distribution of Consumer Products In Channel 2, producers distribute products through retailers. Goodyear, for example, maintains its own system of retail outlets. Levi's has its own outlets but also produces jeans for other retailers such as Gap. Many retailers offer Internet sales.

Channel 3: Wholesale Distribution of Consumer Products Until the mid-1960s, Channel 2 was the most widely used method of nondirect distribution. It requires a large amount of floor space, however, both for storing merchandise and for displaying it in retail stores. Faced with the rising cost of retail space, many retailers found that they could not afford both retail and storage space. Thus, wholesalers entered the distribution network to take over more and more of the storage service. An example of Channel 3 is combination convenience stores/gas stations. Approximately 90 percent of the space in these stores is used for merchandise displays while only about 10 percent is left for storage and office facilities. Merchandise in the store is stocked frequently by wholesalers.

Channel 4: Distribution Through Sales Agents or Brokers Channel 4 uses **sales agents,** or **brokers,** who represent producers and sell to wholesalers, retailers, or both. They receive commissions based on the price of goods they sell. Agents generally deal in the related product lines of a few producers, serving as their sales representatives on a long-term basis. For example, travel agents represent airlines, car rental companies, and hotels. In contrast, brokers are hired to assist in buying and selling temporarily, matching sellers and buyers as needed. This channel is often used in the food and clothing industries. The real estate industry also relies on brokers for matching buyers and sellers of property.

sales agent/broker
Independent intermediary that usually represents many manufacturers and sells to wholesalers or retailers

The Pros and Cons of Nondirect Distribution Ultimately, each link in the distribution chain makes a profit by charging a markup or commission. Nondirect distribution channels mean higher prices for end users: The more members in the channel—the more intermediaries—the higher the final price.

At the same time, however, intermediaries can save consumers both time and money. In doing so they provide added value for customers. Moreover, this value-adding activity continues and accumulates at each stage of the supply chain. Intermediaries add value by providing time-saving information and by making the right quantities of products available where and when consumers need them. Consider Figure 11.5, which illustrates the problem of making chili without benefit of a common intermediary—the supermarket. You would obviously spend a lot more time, money, and energy if you tried to gather all the ingredients yourself. Moreover, if we eliminated intermediaries, we would not eliminate either their functions or the costs entailed by what they do. Intermediaries exist because they perform necessary functions in cost-efficient ways.

Distribution by Agents to Consumers and Businesses Channel 5 differs from the previous channels in two ways: (1) It includes an agent as the sole intermediary and (2) it distributes to both consumers and business customers. Consider Vancouver-based Uniglobe Travel International, a travel agent that represents airlines, car rental companies, and hotels. Uniglobe books flight reservations and provides arrangements for complete packages of recreational travel services for consumers. The company also provides services to companies whose employees need lodging and transportation for businesses travel.

Distribution of Business Products

Industrial channels are important because every company is itself a customer that buys other companies' products. **Industrial** (business) **distribution**, therefore, is the network of channel members involved in the flow of manufactured goods to business customers. Unlike consumer products, business products are traditionally distributed through Channels 6, 7, and 8 as shown in Figure 11.4.

industrial distribution
Network of channel members involved in the flow of manufactured goods to industrial customers

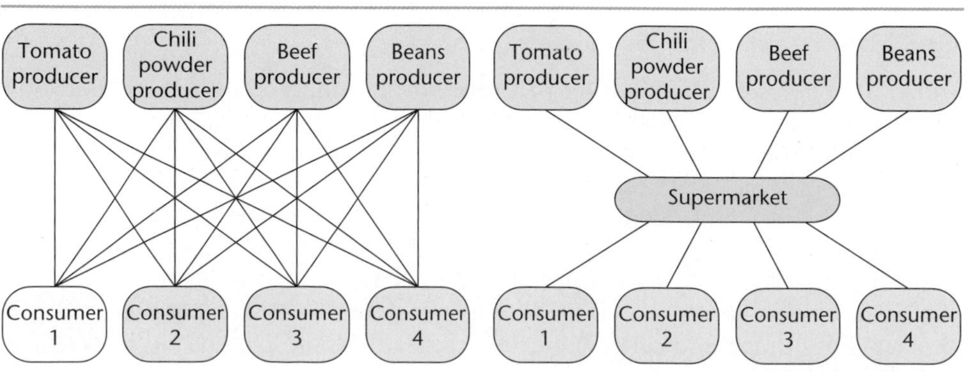

Figure 11.5
The Value-Adding Intermediary

Dell Computer Corp., one of the world's most successful direct distributors of business products, faces competition in China from such entrenched local firms as Legend. Legend and other domestic manufacturers dominate two key markets: retail buyers and state-owned enterprises. The former market accounts for only 10 percent of Dell's Chinese sales, but by relying on speed, convenience, and service, Dell Asia-Pacific <www.dell.com/ap> *has managed to get a foot in the door at many of the country's massive state-owned companies.*

Channel 6: Direct Distribution of Business Products Most business goods are sold directly by the manufacturer to the industrial buyer. As contact points with their customers, manufacturers maintain **sales offices**. These offices provide all services for the company's customers and serve as headquarters for its salespeople.

sales office
Office maintained by a manufacturer as a contact point with its customers

E-commerce technologies have intensified the use of Channel 6. Dell Computer Corp. <www.dell.com>, a pioneer in direct Internet sales, now gets about two-thirds of its $25 billion in sales from other businesses, governments, and schools. Armed with the ever-expanding reach of the Internet, Dell is trying to establish a foothold in the massive Chinese market, where it faces entrenched local market leaders, such as Legend, which, to make matters worse, have no compunctions about copying Dell's direct producer-to-buyer model.

Channel 7: Wholesale Distribution of Industrial Products Channel 7 is most often used for accessory equipment (computers, fax machines, and other office equipment) and supplies (floppy disks, pencils, copier paper). Whereas manufacturers produce these items in large quantities, companies buy them in small quantities. For example, few companies order truckloads of paper clips. As with consumer goods, then, intermediaries help end users by representing manufacturers or by breaking down large quantities into smaller sales units. The traditional office supply store, then, is a wholesaler that sells a variety of goods to other businesses.

Channel 8: Wholesale Distribution to Business Retailers For some industries, the roles of channel members are changing. In the office-products industry, Channel 7 is being displaced by the emergence of a newer channel that looks very much like Channel 3 for consumer products: Instead of buying office supplies from wholesalers (Channel 7), many buyers are now shopping at office discount stores such as Staples, Office Depot, and Office Max. Before selling to large companies, these warehouse-like superstores originally targeted retail consumers and small and mid-size businesses that bought supplies at retail stores (and retail prices). Today, however, small business buyers stroll down the aisles of discount stores for industrial users, selecting from 7,000 items at prices 20 to 75 percent lower than manufacturers' suggested retail.

WHOLESALING

Now that you know something about distribution channels, we can consider the role played by intermediaries in more detail. Wholesalers provide a variety of services to customers who are buying products for resale or business use. In addition to storing and providing an assortment of products, wholesalers offer delivery, credit, and product information.[19]

Merchant Wholesalers

merchant wholesaler Independent wholesaler that takes legal possession of goods produced by a variety of manufacturers and then resells them to other businesses

Of course, not all wholesalers perform all these functions. Services offered depend on the type of intermediary involved. Most wholesalers are independent operations that sell various consumer or business goods produced by a variety of manufacturers. **Merchant wholesalers**, the largest single group of wholesalers, play dual roles, buying products from manufacturers and selling them to other businesses. Merchant wholesalers purchase and own the goods that they resell.

Agents and brokers, including e-agents on the Internet, serve as sales forces for various producers. They are independent representatives of many companies' products. They work on commissions, usually about 4 to 5 percent of net sales. They often provide a wide range of services, including shelf and display merchandising and advertising layout. Many supermarket products are handled through brokers.

The Advent of the E-Intermediary

e-intermediary Internet distribution channel member that assists in moving products through to customers or that collects information about various sellers to be presented in convenient format for Internet customers

syndicated selling E-commerce practice whereby a Web site offers other Web sites commissions for referring customers

The ability of e-commerce to bring together millions of widely dispersed consumers and businesses continues to change the types and roles of intermediaries in distribution channels. **E-intermediaries** are Internet-based distribution channel members who perform one or both of two functions: (1) They collect information about sellers and present it in convenient form to consumers or (2) they help deliver Internet products to consumers.[20] We will examine three types of emerging e-intermediaries: *syndicated sellers, shopping agents*, and *business-to-business brokers*.

Syndicated Sellers One of marketing's new developments, called **syndicated selling**, occurs when a Web site offers other Web sites a commission for referring customers. One such company is Expedia.com, which, with 7.5 million users, was the most-visited Web site for travel services in 1999. Expedia has given Uniglobe.com <www.uniglobe.com>, the travel agent that we described earlier, a special cruise section on its Web page. Here's how syndicated selling works. When Expedia customers click on the Uniglobe banner ad, they are transferred from the Expedia to the Uniglobe Web site. Uniglobe pays a fee to Expedia for each booking that comes through this channel. Although the new intermediary increases the cost of Uniglobe's supply chain, it adds value for customers: Travelers avoid endless searches in cyberspace and are efficiently guided to experts specializing in recreational cruises.[21]

shopping agent (e-agent) E-intermediary (middleman) in the Internet distribution channel that assists users in finding products and prices but that does not take possession of products

Shopping Agents Another new intermediary is the **shopping agent** (or **e-agent**). Shopping agents help Internet consumers by gathering and sorting information they need for making purchases. They do not take possession of any products. The e-agent knows which Web sites and stores to visit, shows accurate comparison prices, identifies product features, and helps consumers complete transactions by pulling information from worldwide sites, sorting it, and presenting it in a usable format, in a matter of seconds. PriceScan <www.pricescan.com> is a well-known shopping agent for computer products. For CDs and tapes, evenbetter.com will search for vendors, do price comparisons (including shipping costs), list the prices from low to high, and then transfer you to the Web sites of up to 50 different e-stores.

WEB Connection

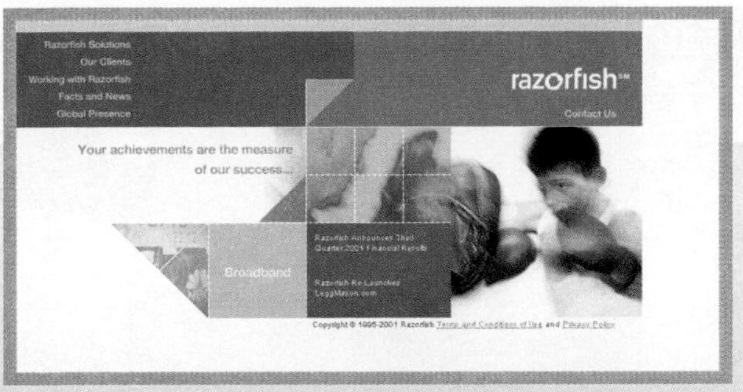

Boasting a client list that includes Time Warner, Charles Schwab, and the Smithsonian, Razorfish is a consulting firm for companies that conduct or want to conduct e-commerce. To find out how the company promotes digital technology in the building of new business models, including new channels and new value chains, log on to its Web site.

www.razorfish.com

Business-to-Business Brokers E-commerce intermediaries have also emerged for business customers. Consider the start-up Internet company Efdex (which stands for *electronic food and drink exchange*). The concept is a massive food exchange to buy and sell foodstuffs among food manufacturers, restaurants, grocers, and farmers. Established first in the United Kingdom in early 2000, Efdex plans to be operating soon in the United States and Europe. Like a stock exchange, the Web site <www.efdex.com> provides up-to-date market information and price and product data from both suppliers and buyers—all listed by type and size of business. Efdex enables businesses to buy and sell from one another and confirm transactions electronically. As a broker, Efdex does not take possession of products. Rather, it functions to bring together timely information and business-to-business exchange linkages.[22]

RETAILING

There are more than 1.6 million retail establishments in the United States. Most of them are small operations, often consisting of owners and part-time help. Indeed, over one-half of the nation's retailers account for less than 10 percent of all retail sales. Retailers also include huge operations such as Wal-Mart, the largest employer in the United States, and Sears. Although there are large retailers in many other countries—Kaufhof <www.kaufhof.de> in Germany, Carrefour in France <www.carrefour.com>, and Daiei in Japan <www.cybercitykobe.com/daiei/index.htm>—more of the world's largest retailers are based in the United States than in any other country.

Types of Retail Outlets

U.S. retail operations vary as widely by type as they do by size. They can be classified in various ways: by pricing strategies, location, range of services, or range of product lines. Choosing the right types of retail outlets is a crucial aspect of every seller's distribution strategy. In this section, we describe U.S. retail stores by using two classifications: *product line retailers* and *bargain retailers*.[23]

Product Line Retailers Retailers featuring broad product lines include **department stores**, which are organized into specialized departments: shoes, furniture, women's

department store
Large product line retailer characterized by organization into specialized departments

In 1993, top management at Costco warehouse clubs <www.costco.com> began to worry that their American market had become saturated. That particular concern turned out to be unwarranted, but it prompted Costco to expand into other countries. The company now operates 20 warehouse stores in Great Britain, Taiwan, South Korea, and Japan. The Costco concept—low prices on high-quality merchandise available to members only—travels well: This store in the London suburb of Watford, England, is one of the chain's most successful outlets anywhere.

petite sizes, and so on. Department stores are usually large and handle a wide range of goods. In addition, they usually offer a variety of services, such as generous return policies, credit plans, and delivery. Similarly, **supermarkets** are divided into departments of related products: food products, household products, and so forth. The emphasis is on low prices, self-service, and wide selection.

In contrast, **specialty stores** are small stores that carry one line of related products. They serve clearly defined market segments by offering full product lines in narrow product fields and often feature knowledgeable sales personnel. Sunglass Hut International <www.sunglasshut.com>, for instance, has 1,600 outlets carrying a deep selection of sunglasses at competitive prices.

supermarket
Large product line retailer offering a variety of food and food-related items in specialized departments

specialty store
Small retail store carrying one product line or category of related products

bargain retailer
Retailer carrying a wide range of products at bargain prices

discount house
Bargain retailer that generates large sales volume by offering goods at substantial price reductions

catalog showroom
Bargain retailer in which customers place orders for catalog items to be picked up at on-premises warehouses

factory outlet
Bargain retailer owned by the manufacturer whose products it sells

Bargain Retailers **Bargain retailers** carry wide ranges of products and come in many forms. After World War II, for example, some U.S. retailers began offering discounts to certain customers. These first **discount houses** sold large numbers of items such as televisions and other appliances by featuring substantial price reductions. As name-brand items became more plentiful in the early 1950s, discounters offered even better product assortments while still embracing a philosophy of cash-only sales conducted in low-rent facilities. As they became firmly entrenched, they began moving to better locations, improving decor, and selling better-quality merchandise at higher prices. They also began offering a few department store services, such as credit plans and noncash sales.

Another form of bargain store that has grown dramatically in recent years is the **catalog showroom**. These firms mail out catalogs to attract customers into showrooms where they can view display samples, place orders, and wait briefly while clerks retrieve orders from attached warehouses. **Factory outlets** are manufacturer-owned stores that avoid wholesalers and retailers by selling merchandise directly from the factory to consumers. The **warehouse club (or wholesale club)** offers large discounts on brand-name clothing, groceries, appliances, automotive supplies, and other merchandise. Unlike customers at discount houses and factory outlets, club customers pay annual membership fees. Finally, neighborhood food retailers such as 7-Eleven and Circle K stores are successful **convenience store** chains, which offer ease of purchase: They stress easily accessible locations with parking, extended store hours (in many

ALEXANDER GRAHAM BELL
INVENTS THE
UNSOLICITED PHONE PITCH

"Mr. Watson, have you ever thought what would happen to your loved ones if you died tomorrow?"

cases 24 hours), and speedy service. They differ from most bargain retailers in that they do not feature low prices. Like bargain retailers they control prices by keeping in-store service levels to a minimum.

Nonstore and Electronic Retailing

Not all goods and services are sold in stores. Some of the nation's largest retailers sell all or most of their products without brick-and-mortar stores. Certain types of consumer goods—soft drinks, candy, and cigarettes—lend themselves to distribution in vending machines. Even at $107 billion per year, vending machine sales still represent less than 4 percent of all U.S. retail sales. And in e-retailing, sales are projected to reach $36 billion by 2002, as some 30 million households with personal computers continue online shopping.[24]

The more important forms of nonstore retailing include **direct-response retailing**, in which firms make direct contact with customers both to inform them about products and to receive sales orders. **Mail order** (or **catalog marketing**), such as that practiced by Spiegel <www.spiegel.com> and its Eddie Bauer <www.eddiebauer.com> subsidiary, is a form of direct-response retailing. So is **telemarketing**—the use of the telephone to sell directly to consumers. Currently, telemarketing is experiencing exceptional growth in the United States, Canada, and Great Britain. Industry analysts estimate that telemarketing sales in the United States alone could grow to more than $800 billion in the year 2004.[25] Finally, **direct selling** is still used by more than 600 U.S. companies that sell door-to-door or through home-selling parties. Avon Products has 465,000 independent U.S. sales representatives.

The Boom in Electronic Retailing **Electronic retailing** is made possible by communications networks that allow sellers to connect to consumers' computers with digital information about products. With over 1.5 million subscribers, for example, Prodigy Communications Corp. <www.prodigy.com>, which was formed as a joint venture of IBM and Sears, is among the largest home networks.

Businesses added more than 2 million new Web sites during 2000 to better interact with customers. Internet sales by businesses in the United States are expected to climb to $3.5 trillion by 2004, while worldwide sales are projected to reach $6.8 trillion.[26] A

warehouse club (or wholesale club)
Bargain retailer offering large discounts on brand-name merchandise to customers who have paid annual membership fees

convenience store
Retail store offering easy accessibility, extended hours, and fast service

direct-response retailing
Nonstore retailing by direct interaction with customers to inform them of products and to receive sales orders

mail order (or catalog marketing)
Form of nonstore retailing in which customers place orders for catalog merchandise received through the mail

telemarketing
Nonstore retailing in which the telephone is used to sell directly to consumers

direct selling
Form of nonstore retailing typified by door-to-door sales

electronic retailing
Nonstore retailing in which information about the sellers' products is connected to consumers' computers, allowing consumers to receive the information and purchase the products in the home

seller's Web site is an **electronic storefront** in which consumers collect information about products and buying opportunities, place sales orders, and pay for their purchases. Search engines like Yahoo! <www.yahoo.com> serve as cybermalls: collections of virtual storefronts representing diverse products. **E-catalogs** use the Internet to display products and services for both retail shoppers and business customers.[27] Finally, video marketing, a long-established form of **interactive marketing**, lets viewers shop at home from television screens.

electronic storefront
Commercial Web site in which customers gather information about products, buying opportunities, placing orders, and paying for purchases

e-catalog
Nonstore retailing in which the Internet is used to display products

interactive marketing
Nonstore retailing that uses a Web site to provide real-time sales and customer service

physical distribution
Activities needed to move a product efficiently from manufacturer to consumer

warehousing
Physical distribution operation concerned with the storage of goods

private warehouse
Warehouse owned by and providing storage for a single company

public warehouse
Independently owned and operated warehouse that stores goods for many firms

PHYSICAL DISTRIBUTION

Physical distribution refers to the activities needed to move products efficiently from manufacturer to consumer. The goals of physical distribution are to make goods available when and where consumers want them, to keep costs low, and to provide services that keep customers satisfied. Thus, physical distribution includes *warehousing* and *transportation operations*, as well as *distribution for e-customers*.

Warehousing Operations

Storing, or **warehousing**, is a major part of distribution management. In selecting a strategy, managers must keep in mind both the different characteristics and costs of warehousing operations. **Private warehouses** are owned and used by a single manufacturer, wholesaler, or retailer. Most are operated by large firms that deal in mass quantities and need storage on a regular basis. JCPenney eases the movement of products to retail stores by maintaining its own warehouses.

Public warehouses are independently owned and operated. Companies rent only the space they need. Public warehouses are popular with firms that need storage only during peak periods. They are also used by manufacturers needing multiple storage locations to get products to numerous markets.

Transportation Operations

The highest cost faced by many companies is the cost of physically moving a product. Thus, cost is a major factor in choosing a transportation method. But firms must also consider several other factors: the nature of the product, the distance it must travel, the speed with which it must be received, and customer wants and needs.

Transportation Modes The major transportation modes include trucks, railroads, planes, water carriers, and pipelines. Differences in cost are most directly related to delivery speed. Air, for instance, is the fastest available mode of transportation, and other advantages include much lower costs in handling, packing, and unpacking compared with other modes. Air freight, however, is the most expensive form of transportation. Water is the least expensive mode but, unfortunately, also the slowest.

Physical Distribution and E-Customer Satisfaction New e-commerce companies often focus on Internet sales, only to discover that after-sale distribution delays cause customer dissatisfaction and discourage repeat sales. Any delay in physical distribution is a breakdown in fulfillment and an obstacle to growth. To improve on-time deliveries, many businesses, such as Amazon.com, maintain their own distribution centers and ship themselves from their own warehouses near major shipping hubs. Other e-tailers, however, entrust their order-filling services to distribution specialists such as Fingerhut Business Services Inc. <www.fingerhut.com> and Keystone Fulfillment, Inc. <www.kfulfillment.com>.[28]

Distribution as a Marketing Strategy

Distribution is an increasingly important way of competing for sales. Instead of just offering advantages in product features and quality, price, and promotion, many firms have turned to distribution as a cornerstone of their business strategies. This approach means assessing and improving the entire stream of activities (wholesaling, warehousing, and transportation) involved in getting products to customers.

Its importance is illustrated at Molex <www.molex.com>, a large manufacturer of electronic connectors and switches. The firm's 100,000 products are used by manufacturers of cars, computers, and consumer products that not only want fast, just-in-time delivery but that are also becoming more and more globalized. To meet its customers' needs, Molex became the first connector manufacturer to sign distribution agreements on a global basis. Its relationships with Arrow Electronics <www.arrow.com> and Avnet <www.avnet.com>, the world's largest distributors of electronic components, allow Molex to better service customers who want a single worldwide source for their products.

Continued from page 279

Why RIAA Got Riled

The Napster phenomenon underscores three features of contemporary commerce that, when taken together, go a long way toward explaining why battle lines are shifting in the music industry:

1. As long as they can be converted into digital format, products can be transmitted on the Internet rather than by mail. This in itself is nothing new. Java has been delivering software products for years on the Internet.
2. Napster demonstrated that users could get the service for free. The availability of such a large menu of free products is in fact revolutionary.
3. The enormous number of participants is significant. Little wonder, then, that music industry businesses—members of the traditional distribution channel—are up in arms.

Entertainment artists, of course, earn their livings from royalties on the sales of their albums. Revenues from those royalties were denied them each time a Napster user got a free album instead of buying it from a legitimate vendor, such as a record store. Without revenues, how can the costs of production be recovered? And at a market price of $0 for an album, how can record stores hope to stay in business when, obviously, they cannot lower their costs to zero? It comes as no surprise, therefore, that an industry trade organization, the Recording Industry Association of America (RIAA) <www.riaa.org>, filed suit claiming that Napster's main function was to violate copyright regulations. Napster, claimed RIAA, was "operating a haven for music piracy on an unprecedented scale." Napster proclaimed its innocence, arguing that it did nothing more than supply software. It neither took possession of albums nor did it buy or sell them. The trading of albums occurred solely among individuals on the open market.

As the battle continued, both the legal and financial stakes grew higher. RIAA claimed the industry has lost more than $1 billion in sales. After a series of court rulings and appeals, in March 2001 a Federal Court judge ordered Napster to remove copyrighted songs from its system. The music-for-free revolution had been put down.

But the forces that Napster unleashed are still alive and are revolutionizing the ways for distributing music. Music companies cannot avoid the latest industrywide trend—the move away from CDs to online music. By 2004, online sales in the United States should hit $1.5 billion. The major recording companies see the Internet as the new distribution alternative. And music lovers are still demanding that they be able to share major-label records online. The questions are how to price the service, how to collect fees from system users, and how to ensure copyright protection.

While the initial battle did not go well for Napster, a turnaround appears to be underway in its new deal with MusicNet—a joint venture with AOL Time Warner, RealNetworks, Bertelsmann, and EMI. In this attractive if-you-can't-beat-'em-join-'em deal, Napster joins forces with three of the world's major record labels (AOL Time Warner, Bertelsmann, and EMI) as the prime distributor in the new Internet music subscription service scheduled for launch in the summer of 2001. The service will allow music lovers to listen to songs over the Internet for a fee (price is yet to be determined). It will also rely on technology to protect the ownership of songs and ensure royalty payments to artists and labels.

In working with Napster, Bertelsmann has far-reaching ambitions: The German firm not only wants to turn Napster into a legitimate generator of royalties for properties copyrighted by companies like itself but it also wants to build a model for downloading a whole spectrum of media products—such as Bertelsmann's own books, magazines, newspapers, music recordings, television programming, and Internet products.

Questions for Discussion

1. What do you think of Napster as an approach for distributing music?
2. Consider the more traditional channels of distribution for music albums. Which channel elements are most affected by the presence of Napster-like services? Explain how those elements are affected.
3. What other products, besides music albums, are the most likely candidates for distribution on the Internet now and in the future?
4. Why is the music industry so concerned about Internet distribution? In addition to threats, do you see any opportunities for the industry in Internet distribution?
5. What kind of pricing method would you recommend for the Napster-MusicNet joint venture? Should users pay a fee per recording or, instead, should they pay a fixed monthly subscription fee? Explain why.
6. Aside from legal arguments, does Napster's emergence raise any ethical issues or social responsibility concerns?

SUMMARY OF LEARNING OBJECTIVES

1 Identify the various *pricing objectives* that govern pricing decisions, describe the *price-setting tools* used in making these decisions, and discuss *pricing strategies* and *tactics* for both existing and new products. A firm's *pricing decisions* reflect the *pricing objectives* set by its management. Although these objectives vary, they all reflect the goals that a seller hopes to reach in selling a product. They include *profit maximizing* (pricing to sell the number of units that will generate the highest possible total profits) and *meeting market share goals* (ensuring continuous sales by maintaining a strong percentage of the total sales for a specific product type). Other considerations include the need to survive in a competitive marketplace, social and ethical concerns, and even a firm's image.

Price-setting tools are chosen to meet a seller's pricing objectives. *Cost-oriented pricing* recognizes the need to cover the *variable costs* of producing a product (costs that change with the number of units produced or sold). A price is chosen so that it covers variable costs and provides some additional funds to cover fixed costs (costs, such as facilities and salaries, that are unaffected by the number of items produced or sold). A second approach—*breakeven analysis*—determines a price level by considering the expected sales volume (number of units that will be sold). For a proposed or planned sales volume, breakeven analysis chooses the price at which all costs, both variable and fixed, will be recovered from sales revenues. If sales exceed the planned volume, then profits will be generated.

Either a *price-skimming strategy* (pricing very high) or a *penetration-pricing strategy* (pricing very low) may be effective for new products. Depending on the other elements in the marketing mix, existing products may be priced at, above, or below prevailing prices for similar products. Guided by a firm's pricing strategies, managers set prices using tactics such as *price lining* (offering items in certain categories at a set number of prices), *psychological pricing* (appealing to buyers' perceptions of relative prices), and *discounting* (reducing prices to stimulate sales).

The electronic marketplace has introduced two competing pricing systems—dynamic versus fixed. *Dynamic pricing* is feasible because the flow of information on the Web notifies millions of buyers around the world of instantaneous changes in product availability. Sellers can also alter prices privately, on a customer-to-customer basis, to attract sales that might be lost under traditional fixed-price structures.

2 **Identify the important objectives of *promotion*, discuss the considerations entailed in selecting a *promotional mix*, and describe the key *advertising media*.** Although the ultimate goal of a *promotion* is to increase sales, other goals include *communicating information, positioning a product, adding value*, and *controlling sales volume*. In deciding on the appropriate *promotional mix*, marketers must consider the good or service being offered, characteristics of the target audience and the buyer's decision process, and the promotional mix budget.

Advertising media include the Internet, newspapers, television, direct mail, radio, magazines, and outdoor advertising, as well as other channels such as *Yellow Pages*, special events, and door-to-door selling. The combination of media that a company chooses is called its *media mix*.

3 **Outline the tasks involved in *personal selling* and describe the various types of *sales promotions*.** *Personal selling* tasks include *order processing, creative selling* (activities that help persuade buyers), and *missionary selling* (activities that *promote firms and products rather than simply close sales)*.

Sales promotions include *coupons*, which provide savings off the regular price of a product. *Point-of-purchase (POP) displays* are intended to grab attention and help customers find products in stores. Purchasing incentives include samples (which let customers try products without buying them) and *premiums* (rewards for buying products). At *trade shows*, sellers rent booths to display products to customers who already have an interest in buying. *Contests* are intended to increase sales by stimulating buyers' interest in products.

4 **Identify the different *channels of distribution* and explain the differences between *merchant wholesalers* and *agents/brokers*.** In selecting a *distribution mix*, a firm may use all or any of eight *distribution channels*. The first four are aimed at getting products to consumers, the fifth is for consumers or business customers, and the last three are aimed at getting products to business customers. Channel 1 involves direct sales to consumers. Channel 2 includes a *retailer*. Channel 3 involves both a retailer and a *wholesaler*, and Channel 4 includes an *agent* or *broker* who enters the system before the wholesaler and retailer. Channel 5 includes only an agent between the producer and the customer. Channel 6, which is used extensively for e-commerce, involves a direct sale to an industrial user. Channel 7, which is used infrequently, entails selling to business users through wholesalers. Channel 8 includes retail superstores that get products from producers or wholesalers (or both) for reselling to business customers.

Wholesalers act as distribution *intermediaries*. They may extend credit as well as store, repackage, and deliver products to other members of the channel. *Merchant wholesalers* buy products from manufacturers and resell them to other businesses. Unlike merchant wholesalers, *agents* and *brokers* never take legal possession of products. Rather, they function as sales and merchandising arms of manufacturers who do not have their own sales forces. They may also provide such services as advertising and display merchandising. In e-commerce, *e-agents* assist Internet users in finding products and best prices.

5 **Identify the different types of *retailing* and *retail stores*.** *Retailers* can be described according to two classifications: *product line retailers* and *bargain retailers*. Product line retailers include *department stores, supermarkets, hypermarkets*, and *specialty stores*. Bargain retailers include *discount houses, catalog showrooms, factory outlets, warehouse clubs*, and *convenience stores*. These retailers differ in terms of size, goods and services offered, and pricing. Some retailing also takes place without stores.

Nonstore retailing may use *mail-order (catalog) marketing, telemarketing, electronic retailing*, and *direct selling*. Internet retail shopping includes *electronic storefronts* where customers can examine a store's products, receive information about sellers and their products, place orders, and make payments electronically. Customers can also visit *cybermalls*—a collection of virtual storefronts representing a variety of product lines on the Internet.

6 **Describe the major activities in the *physical distribution process*.** *Physical distribution* includes all the activities needed to move products from manufacturers to consumers, including *customer service, warehousing*, and *transportation* of products. Warehouses provide storage for products and may be either *public* or *private*.

Transportation operations physically move products from suppliers to customers. Trucks, railroads, planes, water carriers (boats and barges), and pipelines are the major *transportation modes* used in the distribution process. They differ in cost, availability, reliability, speed, and number of points served. Air is the fastest but most expensive mode; water carriers are the slowest but least expensive.

One of the newest transportation modes is the Internet: Products that are storable in digital form, such as music, books, and movies, can be transmitted digitally and downloaded onto the customer's computer for nearly instantaneous delivery.

QUESTIONS AND EXERCISES

Questions for Review

1. How do cost-oriented pricing and breakeven analysis help managers measure the potential impact of prices?
2. What is the overall goal of price skimming? Of penetration pricing?
3. Compare the advantages and disadvantages of different advertising media.
4. Identify the eight channels of distribution. In what key ways do the four channels used only for consumer products differ from the channels used only for industrial products?
5. Explain how the activities of e-agents (Internet shopping agents) or brokers differ from those of traditional agents/brokers.

Questions for Analysis

6. Suppose that a small publisher selling to book distributors has fixed operating costs of $600,000 each year and variable costs of $3.00 per book. How many books must the firm sell to break even if the selling price is $6.00? If the company decides on a 40-percent markup (40 percent of variable costs), what will the selling price be?
7. Take a look at some of the advertising conducted by locally based businesses in your area. Choose two campaigns: one that you think effective and one that you think ineffective. What differences in the campaigns make one better than the other?
8. Consider the various kinds of nonstore retailing. Give examples of two products that typify the products sold to at-home shoppers through each form of nonstore retailing. Explain why different products are best suited to each form of nonstore retailing.

Application Exercises

9. Select a product with which you are familiar and analyze various possible pricing objectives for it. What information would you want to have if you were to adopt a profit-maximizing objective? A market share objective? An image objective?
10. Select a product that is sold nationally. Identify as many media used in its promotion as you can. Which medium is used most? On the whole, do you think the campaign is effective? Why or why not?

EXPLORING THE WEB

Need Help for E-Mail Marketing?

To find out about the kinds of expertise available to help companies that want to do e-mail marketing, log on to the following Web site:

<www.digitalimpact.com>

Read through the posted material, including the following pages: "About Us," "Clients," and "Solutions." Then respond to the following questions:

1. What line of business is Digital Impact in? What does the company sell and to whom?
2. Who are some of Digital's Internet clients? List some of the client companies that are familiar to you. Were you previously aware that they were involved in e-marketing?
3. Examine the site category titled "Press Room" (then see "Press Releases"). In the press releases Digital Impact refers to "measurable results" that it generates for its clients. What measurements does Digital use to indicate "results"? Can you suggest potentially better measurements?
4. Look at the Web category titled "Press Room" (then see "Press Releases") and read any of the recent articles about Digital's success in helping a client company with marketing efforts. List the types of promotional methods that Digital used and the media, if any, that it chose. Explain why those methods and media were selected for the target audience.
5. Why do you suppose companies hire Digital Impact rather than conducting their own marketing promotions? Can you find anything in the Web site that indicates why a company would choose Digital rather than conducting its own e-mail promotions?

EXERCISING YOUR ETHICS

The Chain of Responsibility

THE SITUATION

Because several stages are involved when distribution chains move products from supply sources to end consumers, the process offers ample opportunity for ethical issues to arise. This exercise encourages you to examine some of the ethical issues that can arise during the transactions that take place among suppliers and customers.

THE DILEMMA

A customer bought an expensive wedding gift at a local store and asked that it be shipped to the bride in another state. Several weeks after the wedding, the customer contacted the bride because she had sent no word that the gift had ever been received. In fact, it hadn't. The customer then requested a refund from the store because the merchandise had not been delivered. Investigation by the store manager revealed the following facts:

- All shipments from the store are handled by a well-known national delivery firm.
- The delivery firm verified that the package had been delivered to the designated address two days after sale of the merchandise.
- As a normal practice, the delivery firm does not obtain recipient signatures upon delivery; deliveries are made to the address of record, regardless of the name on the package.

The customer who had bought the gift argued that even though the package had been delivered to the designated address, it had not been delivered to the named recipient. It turns out that, unbeknownst to the gift giver, the bride had moved to another address. It stood to reason, then, that the gift was in the hands of the new occupant of the bride's former address. The store manager informed the gift giver that the store had fulfilled its obligation. The cause of the problem, she explained, was the incorrect address given by the customer. She refused to refund the customer's money and suggested that the customer might want to recover the gift by contacting the stranger who received it at the bride's old address.

QUESTIONS FOR DISCUSSION

1. What are the responsibilities of each party—the customer, the store, the delivery firm—in this situation?
2. From an ethical standpoint, in what ways is the store manager's action right? In what ways is it wrong?
3. If you were appointed to settle this matter, what actions would you take?

BUILDING YOUR BUSINESS SKILLS

Are You Sold on the Net?

This exercise enhances the following SCANS workplace competencies: demonstrating basic skills, demonstrating thinking skills, exhibiting interpersonal skills, and working with information.

GOAL

To encourage students to consider the value of online retailing as an element in a company's distribution system.

THE SITUATION

As the distribution manager of a privately owned clothing manufacturer, specializing in camping gear and outdoor clothing, you are convinced that your product line is perfect for online distribution. But the owner of the company is reluctant to expand distribution from a successful network of retail stores and a catalog operation. Your challenge is to convince the boss that retailing via the Internet can boost sales.

METHOD

STEP 1

Join together with four or five classmates to research the advantages and disadvantages of an online distribution system for your company. Among the factors to consider are the following:

- The likelihood that target consumers are Internet shoppers. Camping gear is generally purchased by young, affluent consumers who are comfortable with the Web.
- The industry trend to online distribution. Are similar companies doing it? Have they been successful?
- The opportunity to expand inventory without increasing the cost of retail space or catalog production and mailing charges.
- The opportunity to have a store that never closes.
- The lack of trust many people have about doing business on the Web. Many consumers are reluctant to provide credit card data on the Web.
- The difficulty that electronic shoppers have in finding a Web site when they do not know the store's name.

- The frustration and waiting time involved in Web searches.
- The certainty that the site will not reach consumers who do not use computers or who are uncomfortable with the Web.

STEP 2
Based on your findings, write a persuasive memo to the company's owner stating your position about expanding to an online distribution system. Include information that will counter expected objections.

FOLLOW-UP QUESTIONS

1. What place does online distribution have in the distribution network of this company?
2. In your view, is online distribution the wave of the future? Is it likely to increase in importance as a distribution system for apparel companies? Why or why not?

CRAFTING YOUR BUSINESS PLAN

Getting the Caffeine into Your Cup

THE PURPOSE OF THE ASSIGNMENT

1. To acquaint students with product distribution issues that a sample firm addresses in developing its business plan, in the framework of *Business PlanPro* (*BPP*) (Version 4.0).
2. To demonstrate how channels of distribution, supply chains, and warehousing can be integrated as components in the *BPP* planning environment.

FOLLOW-UP ASSIGNMENT

After reading Chapter 11 in the textbook, open the BPP *software and look around for information about plans for supply chains and channels of distribution as they apply to a sample firm:* Silvera & Sons *(Sivera & Sons Ltd.). Then respond to the following items:*

1. Describe Silvera's products and customers. Then identify the steps in the supply chain beginning from raw materials through to the final consumer. [Sites to see in *BPP* for this item: In the Plan Outline screen, click on **1.0 Executive Summary.** Then click on each of the following, in turn: **1.1 Objectives, 2.0 Company Summary, 2.2 Company History,** and **3.0 Products.**]
2. Where is Silvera's main warehouse located? What are its activities? [Sites to see in *BPP*: In the Plan Outline screen, click on **2.3 Company Locations and Facilities.** After returning to the Plan Outline screen, click on **3.0 Products.**]
3. Describe the equipment and activities Silvera's uses in the warehouse to prepare coffee beans for shipment. [Sites to see in *BPP*: From the Plan Outline screen, click on each of the following, in turn: **3.1 Competitive Comparison** and **3.4 Technology.**]
4. What steps are involved in getting the product from Silvera's plant in Ouro Fino to Miami? Who is responsible for paying the distribution charges? [Sites to see in *BPP*: In the Plan Outline screen, click on **4.2.2 Distribution Patterns.** After returning to the Plan Outline screen, click on **5.3.4 Distribution Strategy.**]

VIDEO EXERCISE

Promoting White Moustaches: The "Got Milk?" Campaign

LEARNING OBJECTIVES

The purpose of this video is to help you:

1. Understand the purpose of promotional objectives.
2. Identify different ways in which commodities can be promoted.
3. Recognize the link between advertising and promotion.

BACKGROUND INFORMATION

Everyone knows that milk is good for you. Just about everyone keeps milk in the refrigerator. Yet per capita sales of milk were slipping in the mid-1990s, from 29 gallons in 1980 to 23 gallons by 1993. The California Milk Processor Board decided to do something to spark milk consumption—hence, the "Got Milk?" campaign.

THE VIDEO

The segment introduces Jeff Manning, executive director of the California Milk Processor Board <www.gotmilk.com>, and the two ad executives who created the "Got Milk?" campaign, Jeffrey Goodby and Jon Steel. Each contributes his perspective on the problem of milk's reputation, the research and brainstorming that went into addressing it, and the advertisers' solution, which began with an innovative (and award-winning) series of television ads and continues today with the famous milk-moustache campaign.

QUESTIONS FOR DISCUSSION

1. What are some of the difficulties that marketers face in promoting a commodity like milk? What other commodities can you think of that would present similar challenges?

2. Why do you think the "Got Milk?" campaign was first launched on television instead of in another medium?
3. Why do you think it was important for the milk campaign to be somewhat irreverent?

FOLLOW-UP ASSIGNMENT

What brand of bottled water do you prefer? Why? How did the marketer of your brand convince you that this particular water, which is a commodity like milk, is better than others? Make a list of the attributes that your brand's advertising claims for its product. Do you think they are really unique? If so, why?

FOR FURTHER EXPLORATION

Check out the latest entries in the milk moustache campaign and other promotional activities at <www.whymilk.com>. How successfully do you think the campaign is continuing in these other avenues? Now that "Got Milk?" has become a familiar phrase, do you think the promotion should be revitalized with something different? If so, what would you suggest?

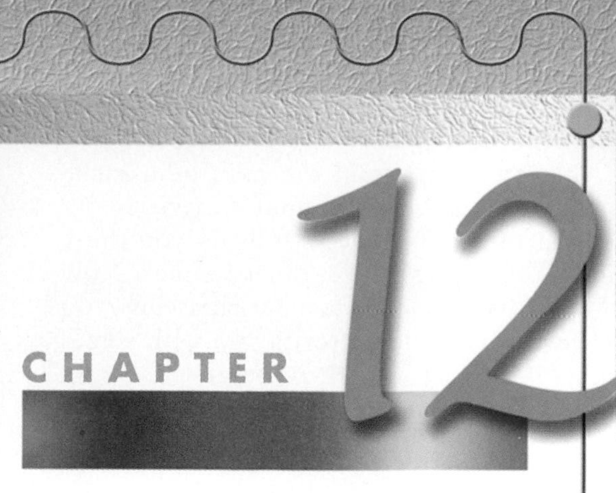

Managing Information Systems and Electronic Commerce

After Reading This Chapter, You Should Be Able To:

1. Explain why businesses must manage *information* and show how computer systems and communication technologies have revolutionized *information management.*
2. Identify and briefly describe three elements of *data communication networks*—the Internet, the World Wide Web, and intranets.
3. Describe five *new options for organizational design* that have emerged from the rapid growth of information technologies.
4. Discuss different information-system *application programs* that are available for users at various organizational levels.
5. Briefly describe the content and role of a *database* and the purpose of *database software* for information systems.

"Life, the Universe, and Everything"

Why does a boss want information on such varied topics as the anatomy of dragonflies, juvenile crime, and Japanese irises instead of just standard reports on department budgets and sales figures? And if gathering these eclectic tidbits is high on the agenda, how does a firm use its "knowledge workers" to build a networked information system for getting it? Consider the information system at Highsmith, Inc. <www.highsmith.com> of Fort Atkinson, Wisconsin. With more than 25,000 products, Highsmith is the country's largest mail-order supplier of equipment (book displays, audio-visual equipment), furniture, and supplies (educational software) for libraries and schools. Because its mission focuses on libraries and learning, it may come as no surprise that a central resource in Highsmith's information system is its corporate library.

President and CEO Duncan Highsmith believes that external events—even some that seem remote and unrelated to the business—can create threats and opportunities for companies. He believes that if employees are focused only on internal operations, they won't see the bigger picture, so he encourages a more eclectic approach of information gathering from a broad range of sources. New cultural trends and political forces eventually change the way a society thinks and lives, and Highsmith doesn't want to get caught short when they do: He wants to foresee changes that can reshape the social environment, and he wants to be prepared in advance rather than forced to react after the fact. Clues might emerge from unexpected and seemingly unrelated sources ranging from

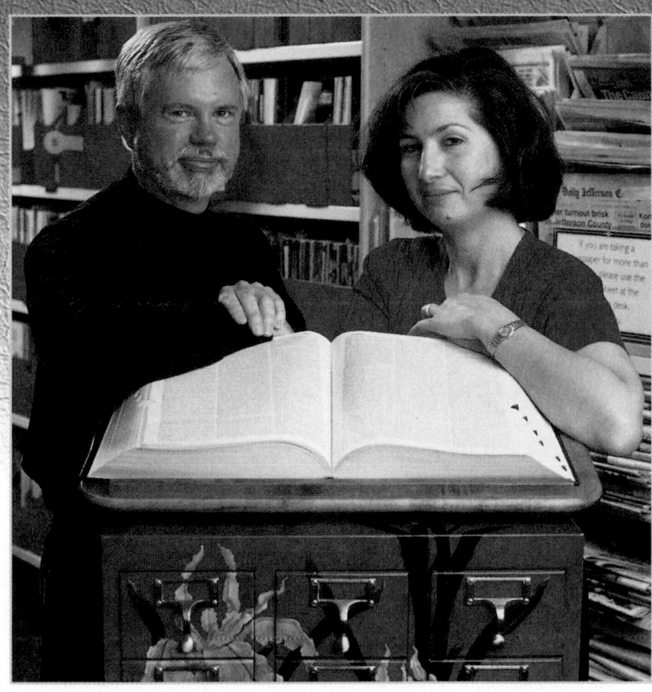

"We tend to behave as though the future will be like the present. Only bigger and faster."

—Duncan Highsmith, CEO of Highsmith Inc.

Popular Mechanics to *South Park* to a UN health report. The job of his company's library is to fuel information brainstorming.

Highsmith is also convinced that if the right data are assembled in the right way, information gleaned from a variety of sources—from seemingly eclectic sources—is the only way to get a clear picture of things to come. He believes that, with access to the right information, his people cannot only anticipate changes but can turn them to the company's advantage. However, he does not believe that focusing on the future comes naturally to most people. "We tend to behave as though the future will be like the present," he says. "Only bigger and faster." That approach, he contends, doesn't work when you need to make strategic-level decisions.

To promote greater linkages with events in the external world, Highsmith launched an information–stimulation program called "Life, the Universe, and Everything"—a weekly closed-door, free-association session in which he and company librarian Lisa Guedea Carreño scan every available information source, from radio to software to newspapers to the Web. They're looking for trends. They search the world for clues to events that might reshape the world around them. Why Guedea Carreño? "The right information," says Highsmith, "can help create strategic choices for a business." An information system, therefore, has to provide more than just sales reports, internally generated cost-control documents, and spreadsheets. For external information gathering, Guedea Carreño is a premier knowledge worker with a knack for gleaning nonquantitative information and collating it with seemingly unrelated resources in different formats. Somehow, she can detect the trends and relationships that emerge as she collates seemingly unrelated information.

As for Guedea Carreño, she believes that being in a small company is an advantage for a professional information provider: She can be more effective in providing value for coworkers if she knows their needs, what they do, and the kinds of problems they deal with. Highsmith sees enormous value in his information–stimulation project, but he also believes that it should go beyond the top-management level. He wants to broaden participation to include other employees. He wants to generate an interest in the long-term development of the business instead of merely its routine operations.

Our opening story continues on page 326

As the Highsmith experience illustrates, information systems and communication networks can have a dramatic effect on the firm's culture and its performance. As an asset that managers rely on for decision making and problem solving, the information system requires a commitment of resources to establish, maintain, and upgrade as new technologies emerge. In addition to human resources, including knowledge workers such as librarian Lisa Guedea Carreño, information networks rely on electronic technologies for retrieving and assimilating information from sources inside the company and from external sources around the world. Computer systems, electronic devices, supporting software, and access to the Internet are all integrated in networked information systems.

INFORMATION MANAGEMENT: AN OVERVIEW

Today's businesses rely on information management in ways that we could not foresee as recently as just a decade ago. Managers now turn to digital technology as an integral part of organizational resources and as a means of conducting everyday business. Every major firm's business activities—designing services, ensuring product delivery and cash flow, evaluating personnel, and creating advertising—are linked to information systems. Thus, the management of information systems is a core business activity that can no longer be delegated to technical personnel.

In addition, most businesses regard their information as a private resource—an asset that they plan, develop, and protect. It is not surprising that companies have **information managers**, just as they have production, marketing, and finance managers. **Information management** is an internal operation that arranges the firm's information resources to support business performance and outcomes. Consider, for example, Chaparral Steel <www.chaparralsteel.com>—a high-performance steel mill that produces structural products from recycled steel. Chaparral's performance—customer service, delivery times, sales, profits, and customer loyalty—has been boosted by an information system that gives customers electronic access to the steel products that are currently available in Chaparral's inventories. The technology that allows customers to shop electronically through its storage yards gives Chaparral greater agility, and because it can respond more rapidly than its competitors, it gets more sales. Modern communications permit businesses to receive up-to-the-minute information from remote plants, branches, and sales offices.

information manager
Manager responsible for designing and implementing systems to gather, organize, and distribute information

information management
Internal operations for arranging a firm's information resources to support business performance and outcomes

To find the information that they need to make critical decisions, managers must often sift through a virtual avalanche of reports, memos, magazines, and phone calls. Thus, the question that faces so many businesses today: How can they get useful information to the right people at the right time? In this section, we will explore the ways in which companies manage information with computers and related information technologies.

Information Systems

One response to the challenge of managing information has been the growth of the **information system (IS)**: a system for transforming data into information and transmitting it for use in decision making. **Data** are raw facts and figures that, by themselves, may not have much meaning. **Information** is the useful interpretation of data. Those charged with running a company's IS must first determine what information will be needed. Then they must gather the data and provide the technology to convert data into desired information. They must also control the flow of information so that it goes only to people who need it.[1]

information system (IS)
System for transforming raw data into information that can be used in decision making

data
Raw facts and figures

information
Meaningful, useful interpretation of data

Information supplied to employees and managers varies according to such factors as the functional areas in which they work (for example, accounting or marketing) and the levels of management they occupy. The quality of the information transmitted to all levels depends increasingly on an organization's technological resources and on the people who manage it. In this section, we discuss the evolution of the technology that processes information and then describe the information requirements in today's organization.

NEW BUSINESS TECHNOLOGIES IN THE INFORMATION AGE

Employees at every level in the organization, ranging from operational specialists to the top executive, use information systems to improve performance. Information systems assist in scheduling day-to-day vehicle trips, evaluating prospective employees, and formulating the firm's business strategy. The widening role of IS results from rapid developments in electronic technologies that allow faster and broader flows of information and communications. As we shall see, however, the networked enterprise is more than a firm equipped with the latest technology. Technology has inspired new organizational designs, innovative relationships with other organizations, and new management processes for improved competitiveness.

The Expanding Scope of Information Systems

The relationship between information systems and organizations is among the fastest-changing aspects of business today. At one time, IS applications were narrow in scope and technically focused—processing payroll data, simulating new engineering designs, compiling advertising expenditures. But, as you can see in Figure 12.1, managers soon began using IS systems not merely to solve technical problems but also to analyze management problems, especially for control purposes—applying quality-control standards to production, comparing costs against budgeted amounts, keeping records on employee absences and turnover.

Today, information systems are also crucial in planning. Managers routinely use the IS to decide on a firm's products and markets for the next 5 to 10 years. The same database that helps marketing analyze demographics for millions of customers is also used for such higher-level applications as financial planning, managing materials flows, and setting up electronic funds transfers with suppliers and customers around the globe.

Another basic change in organizations is an increased interdependence between a company's business strategy and its IS. Today, the choice of a business strategy—to be the low-cost provider or the most flexible provider or the high-quality provider—requires an information system that can support that strategy. Consider a strategy that calls for the rapid receipt of customer orders and fast order fulfillment. Unless the system is specifically designed to handle these tasks, the best-laid plans are probably doomed to failure.

Electronic Business and Communications Technologies

The pressures to maintain better communications and information systems are increasing as competition intensifies and as organizations expand into global and e-business operations. Firms like Ralston Purina Co. <www.ralston.com> need instantaneous communications among managers in those countries in which they either sell products

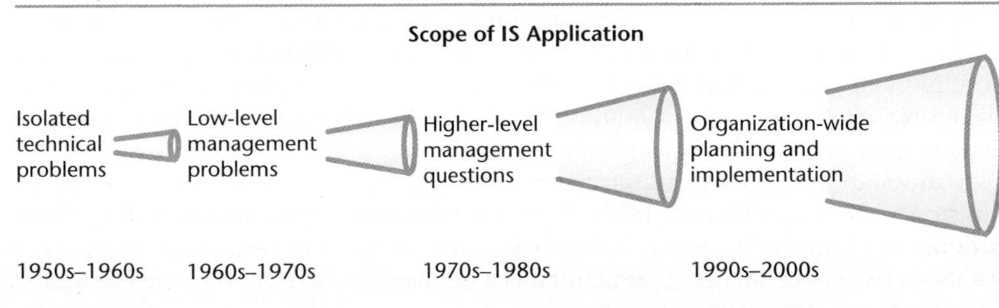

Figure 12.1
Evolution of IS Scope

or buy raw materials, including China, Colombia, Canada, and Brazil. The needs of such companies are being met by new electronic information technologies and more advanced data communication networks.

electronic information technologies (EIT) Information-systems applications, based on telecommunications technologies, that use networks of appliances or devices to communicate information by electronic means

electronic conferencing Computer-based system that allows people to communicate simultaneously from different locations via software or telephone

Electronic Information Technologies **Electronic information technologies (EIT)** are IS applications based on telecommunications technologies. EITs use networks of appliances or devices (such as computers and satellites) to communicate information by electronic means. EITs enhance the performance and productivity of general business activities by performing two functions:

1. Providing coordination and communication within the firm
2. Speeding up transactions with other firms

In this section, we will survey two of the most widely used innovations in today's digital business systems: *electronic conferencing* and *groupware*.

Electronic Conferencing **Electronic conferencing** is popular because it eliminates travel and thus saves money. Teleconferencing allows groups of people to communicate simultaneously from various locations via electronic mail or via telephone. One form of electronic conferencing, *dataconferencing*, allows people in remote locations to work simultaneously on the same document. Working as a team, they can modify part of a database, revise a marketing plan, or draft a press release. Another form of electronic conferencing, *videoconferencing*, allows participants to see one another on a video screen while the teleconference is in progress.[2]

groupware Software that connects members of a group for shared e-mail distribution, electronic meetings, appointments, and group writing

Groupware Collaborative work by teams and other groups is facilitated by **groupware**: software that connects members of the group for e-mail distribution, electronic meetings, message storing, appointments and schedules, and group writing. Linked by groupware, they can work together on their own desktop computers even if they are remotely located. Groupware is especially useful when members work together regularly and rely on intensive information sharing. Groupware products include Lotus Development Corp.'s Lotus Notes <www.lotus.com/home.nsf/welcome/lotusnotes>, and Netscape Communicator <home.netscape.com/communicator/v4.5/index.html>.[3]

data communication network Global network (such as the Internet) that permits users to send electronic messages and information quickly and economically

Internet Global data communication network serving millions of computers with information on a wide array of topics and providing communication flows among certain private networks

Internet service provider (ISP) Commercial firm that maintains a permanent connection to the Net and sells temporary connections to subscribers

Data Communication Networks Popular on both home and business information systems are public and private **data communication networks**: global networks that carry streams of digital data (electronic messages, documents, and other forms of video and sound) back and forth quickly and economically on telecommunication systems. The most prominent network, the Internet, and its companion system, the World Wide Web, have emerged as powerful communication technologies. Let's look a little more closely at each of these networks.

The Internet The **Internet** (or "the Net," for short)—the largest public data communications network—is a gigantic system of networks serving millions of computers offering information on business, science, and government and providing communication flows among more than 170,000 separate networks around the world.[4] Originally commissioned by the Pentagon <www.defenselink.mil> as a communication tool for use during war, the Internet allows personal computers in virtually any location to be linked together. Because it can transmit information fast and at low cost—lower than long-distance phone service, postal delivery, and overnight delivery—the Net has also become the most important e-mail system in the world. For thousands of businesses, therefore, the Net has joined—and is even replacing—the telephone, fax machine, and express mail as a standard means of communication.

Although individuals cannot connect directly to the Internet, for small monthly usage fees they can subscribe to the Net via an **Internet service provider (ISP)**, such as Prodigy <www.prodigy.com>, America Online, or Earthlink <www.earthlink.com>. An ISP is a commercial firm that maintains a permanent connection to the Net and sells temporary connections to subscribers.

In 2000, more than 302 million Net users were active on links connecting more than 180 countries. In the United States, alone, more than 50 million users were on the Net every day. Its power to change the way business is conducted has been amply demonstrated in both large and small firms. Digital Equipment Corp. <www.compaq.com/enterprise> is a heavy Internet user: With more than 31,000 computers connected to the network, DEC's monthly e-mail volume has passed the one-million message mark. DEC also linked its Alpha AXP high-speed business computer to the Internet so that potential buyers and software developers could spend time using and evaluating it. Almost instantly, 2,500 computer users in 27 countries used the Net to explore the Alpha AXP.

The World Wide Web Thanks to the **World Wide Web** (WWW, or simply "the Web"), the Internet is easy to use and allows users around the world to communicate electronically with little effort. The World Wide Web is a system with universally accepted standards for storing, retrieving, formatting, and displaying information.[5] It provides the "common language" that enables us to "surf" the Net and makes the Internet available to a general audience, rather than merely to technical users, such as computer programmers. To access a Web site, for example, the user must specify the *Uniform Resource Locator* (*URL*) that points to the resource's unique address on the Web. Thus, TWA's URL is <www.twa.com>—a designation that specifies the storage location of TWA's Web pages.

World Wide Web
Subsystem of computers providing access to the Internet and offering multimedia and linking capabilities

Servers and Browsers Each Web site opens with a *home page*—a screen display that welcomes the visitor with a greeting that may include graphics, sound, and visual enhancements introducing the user to the site. Additional *pages* give details on the sponsor's products and explain how to contact help in using the site. Often, they furnish URLs for related Web sites that the user can link into by simply pointing and clicking. The person who is responsible for maintaining an organization's Web site is usually called a *Webmaster*. Large Web sites use dedicated workstations—large computers—known as **Web servers** that are customized for managing, maintaining, and supporting Web sites.

With hundreds of thousands of new Web pages appearing each day, cyberspace is now serving up billions of pages of publicly accessible information. Sorting through this maze would be frustrating and inefficient without access to a Web **browser**—the software that enables the user to access information on the Web. A browser runs on the user's PC and supports the graphics and linking capabilities needed to navigate the Web. Netscape Navigator <home.netscape.com/browsers/index.html> has enjoyed as much as an 80 percent market share, although its dominance is now being challenged by other browsers, including its own Netscape Communicator and Microsoft Corp.'s Internet Explorer <www.microsoft.com/windows/ie>.

Web server
Dedicated workstation customized for managing, maintaining, and supporting Web sites

browser
Software supporting the graphics and linking capabilities necessary to navigate the World Wide Web

WEB Connection

The name pretty much tells the story: CandyCommerce.com is the B2B marketplace of the confection industry. Among other pages, the Web site includes an "Auction House" at which sellers can list products for sale and a "Product Showcase" that allows members to shop the organization's listing of online confectionery-supplier catalogs. You can visit the National Confectioners Association Web site for more information.

www.candycommerce.com

Directories and Search Engines The Web browser offers additional tools—Web site directories and search engines—for navigating on the Web. Among the most successful cyberspace enterprises are companies, such as Yahoo! <www.yahoo.com>, that maintain free-to-use *directories* of Web content. When Yahoo! is notified about new Web sites, it classifies them in its directory. The user enters one or two keywords (for example, "compact disk") and the directory responds by retrieving from the directory a list of Web sites with titles containing those words.

search engine
Tool that searches Web pages containing the user's search terms and then displays pages that match

In contrast to a directory, a **search engine** will search cyberspace's millions of Web pages without preclassifying them into a directory. It searches for Web pages that contain the same words as the user's search terms. Then it displays addresses for those that come closest to matching, then the next closest, and so on. A search engine, such as AltaVista <www.altavista.com> or Lycos <www.lycos.com>, may respond to more than 10 million inquiries per day. It is, thus, no surprise that both directories and search engines are packed with paid ads.[6]

intranet
Private network of internal Web sites and other sources of information available to a company's employees

firewall
Software and hardware system that prevents outsiders from accessing a company's internal network

extranet
Internet allowing outsiders access to a firm's internal information system

Intranets The success of the Internet has led some companies to extend the Net's technology internally, for browsing internal Web sites containing information throughout the firm.[7] These private networks, or **intranets**, are accessible only to employees via entry through electronic **firewalls**—hardware and software security systems that are not accessible to outsiders.[8] At Compaq Computer Corp. <www.compaq.com>, the intranet allows employees to shuffle their retirement savings among various investment funds. The Ford Motor Co. <www.ford.com> intranet connects 120,000 workstations in Asia, Europe, and the United States to thousands of Ford Web sites containing private information on Ford activities in production, engineering, distribution, and marketing. Sharing such information has helped reduce the lead time for getting models into production from 36 to 24 months. It also provides shorter delivery times to customers. The savings to Ford will be billions of dollars in inventory and fixed costs.[9]

Extranets Sometimes firms allow outsiders access to their intranets. These so-called **extranets** allow outsiders limited access to a firm's internal information system. The most common application allows buyers to enter the seller's system to see which products are available for sale and delivery, thus providing product-availability information quickly to outside buyers. Industrial suppliers, too, are often linked into their customers' intranets so that they can see planned production schedules and ready supplies as needed for customers' upcoming operations.

New Options for Organizational Design: The Networked Enterprise

The rapid growth of information technologies has changed the very structure of business organizations. We begin this section with a discussion of changes wrought by technology in the workforce and organizational structures of many organizations. We then examine ways in which electronic networks are contributing to greater flexibility in dealing with customers. After discussing the growing importance of collaboration in the workplace, we look at the ways in which information networks can help make the workplace independent of a company's physical location. Finally, we describe new management processes inspired by the availability of electronic networks.

Leaner Organizations Information networks are leading to leaner companies with fewer employees and simpler organizational structures. Because today's networked firm can maintain information linkages among both employees and customers, more work can be accomplished with fewer people. As a bank customer, for example, you can dial into a 24-hour information system and find out your current balance from a digital voice. You no longer need tellers or phone operators. In the industrial sector, assembly workers at an IBM plant used to receive instructions from supervisors or special staff. Now instructions are delivered electronically to their workstations.

Widespread reductions in middle-management positions and the shrinkage of layers in organizational structure are possible because information networks now provide direct communications between the top managers and workers at lower levels. The

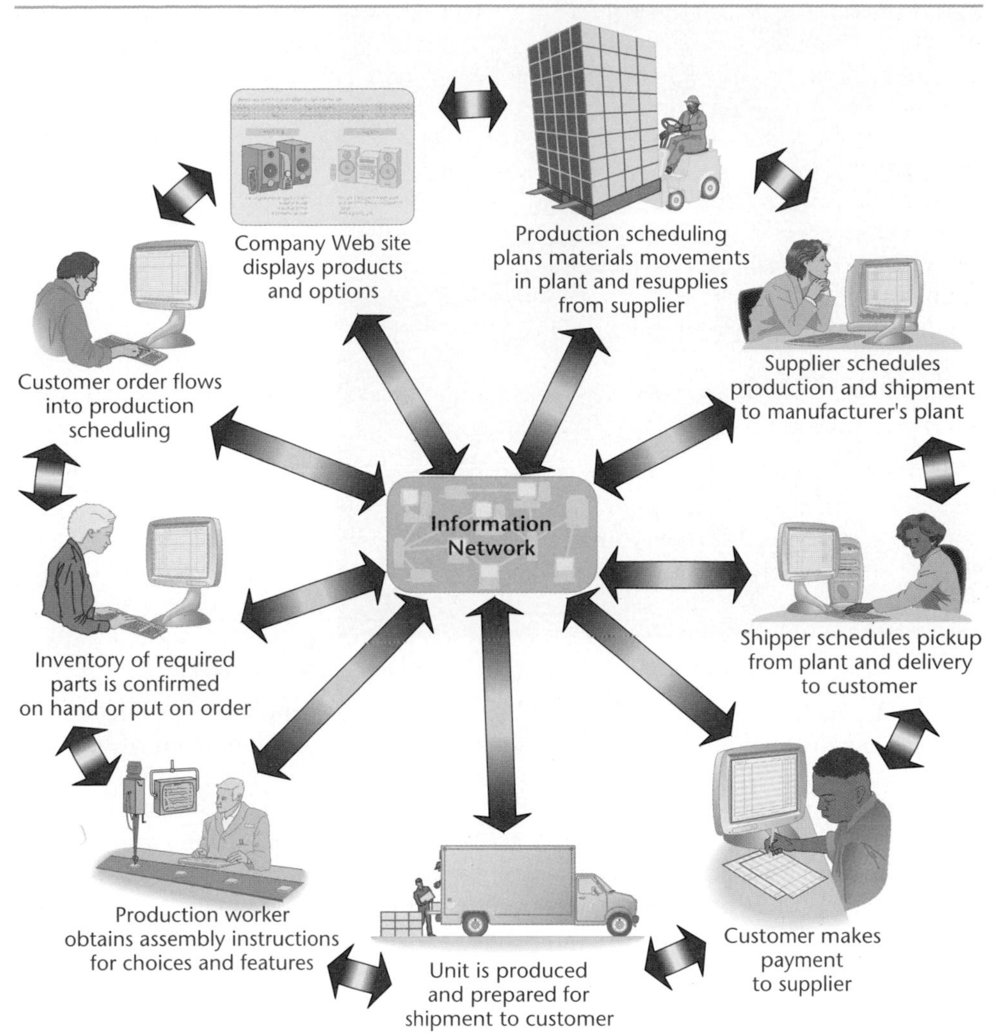

Figure 12.2
Networking for Mass-Customization

operating managers who formerly communicated company policies, procedures, or work instructions to lower-level employees are being replaced by electronic information networks.

More Flexible Operations Electronic networks allow businesses to offer customers greater variety and faster delivery cycles.[10] Recovery after heart surgery is expedited by custom-tailored rehabilitation programs designed with integrated information systems: Each personalized program integrates the patient's history with information from physicians and rehabilitation specialists and then matches the patient with an electronically monitored exercise regimen. Products such as cellular phones, PCs, and audio systems can be custom-ordered, too, with a choice of features and options and next-day delivery. The principle is called **mass-customization:** Although companies produce in large volumes, each unit features the unique variations and options that the customer prefers.[11] As you can see in Figure 12.2, flexible production and fast delivery depend on an integrated network to coordinate all the transactions, activities, and process flows necessary to make quick adjustments in the production process. The ability to organize and store massive volumes of information is crucial, as are the electronic linkages between customers, manufacturer, materials suppliers, and shippers.

mass-customization
Flexible production process that generates customized products in high volumes at low cost

Increased Collaboration Collaboration, not only among internal units but with outside firms as well, is on the rise because networked systems make it cheaper and easier to contact everyone, whether other employees or outside organizations. Aided by intranets, more companies are learning that complex problems can be solved better by

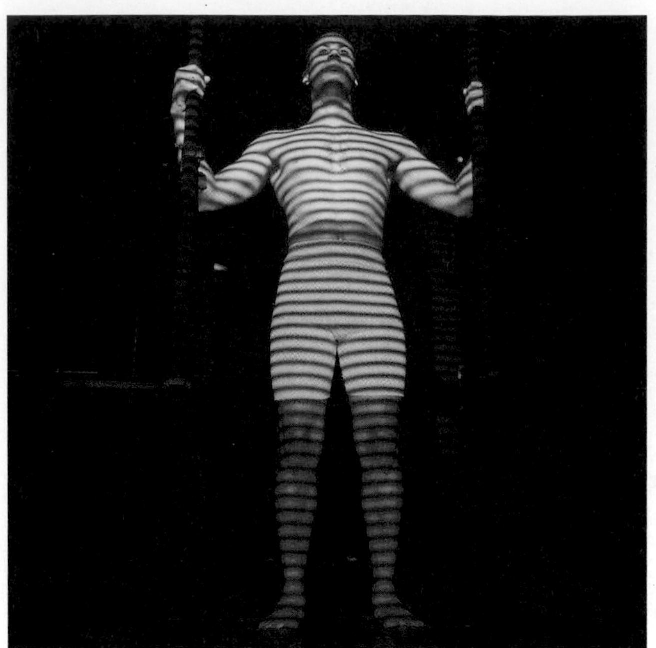

Thanks to networking technology, customers can give manufacturers information that manufacturers can feed into production systems at relatively little cost. The result is so-called mass customization. *At Levi Strauss & Co.* <www.levistrauss.com>, *new technologies can take an apparel buyer's body measurements and transfer the information, via the Web, to a manufacturing plant. There, the data is fed into equally advanced machines designed to handle one-of-a-kind items on an assembly line.*

means of collaboration, either in formal teams or through spontaneous interaction. In the new networked organization, decisions that were once the domain of individuals are now shared among people and departments. The design of new products, for example, was once an engineering responsibility. Now, in contrast, it can be a shared responsibility because so much information is accessible for evaluation from various perspectives: Marketing, finance, production, engineering, and purchasing can share their different stores of information and determine a best overall design.[12]

Networked systems are also helpful in furthering collaboration between companies: the so-called *virtual company* has become possible through networking. As we saw in Chapter 6, a virtual company can be a temporary team assembled by a single organization. But a virtual company can also be created when several firms join forces.[13] Each contributes different skills and resources that collectively result in a competitive business that would not be feasible for any of the collaborators acting alone. A company with marketing and promotional skills, for example, may team up with firms that are experts in warehousing and distribution, engineering, and produc-

WEB Connection

Because "a one-size-fits-all vitamin can't supply you with optimal nutrition," Acumins will customize the precise blend of vitamins, minerals, and herbs that each customer wants. To find out how the process works—and how the Net is essential to businesses in the world of mass-customization—log on to the Acumins Web site.

www.acumins.com

tion. Networking allows collaborators to exchange ideas, plan daily activities, share customer information, and otherwise coordinate their efforts, even if their respective facilities are far apart.

Greater Independence of Company and Workplace Geographic separation of the workplace from the company headquarters is more common than ever because of networked organizations. Employees no longer work only at the office or the factory, nor are all of a company's operations performed at one location. The sales manager for an advertising agency may visit the company office in New York only once every two weeks, preferring instead to work over the firm's electronic network from a home office in Florida. A medical researcher for the Cleveland Clinic may work at a home office networked into the clinic's system.

A company's activities may also be geographically scattered but highly coordinated thanks to a networked system. Many e-businesses, for example, conduct no activities at one centralized location. When you order products from an Internet storefront—say, a chair, a sofa, a table, and two lamps—the chair may come from a cooperating warehouse in Philadelphia and the lamps from a manufacturer in California, while the sofa and table may be direct-shipped from two manufacturers in North Carolina. All these activities are launched instantaneously by the customer's order and coordinated through the network, just as if all of them were being processed at one location.

Improved Management Processes Networked systems have changed the very nature of the management process. The activities, methods, and procedures of today's manager differ significantly from those that were common just a few years ago. At one time, upper-level managers did not concern themselves with all the detailed information that filtered upward in the workplace. Why? Because it was expensive to gather and slow in coming and quickly became out of date. Workplace management was delegated to middle and first-line managers.

With networked systems, however, instantaneous information is accessible in a convenient, usable format. Consequently, more upper managers use it routinely for planning, leading, directing, and controlling operations. Today, a top manager can find out the current status of any customer order, inspect productivity statistics for each workstation, and analyze the delivery performance of any driver and vehicle. More importantly, managers can better coordinate companywide performance. They can identify departments that are working well together and those that are creating bottlenecks.

enterprise resource planning (ERP)
Large information system for integrating all the activities of a company's business units

One of the popular categories of networked systems is **enterprise resource planning (ERP)**—a large information system for integrating the activities of all the company's business units.[14] The system is supported by one large, shared database so that everyone in the system shares the same updated information when each transaction occurs. The biggest supplier of commercial ERP packages is Germany's SAP AG <www.sap.com> followed by Oracle <www.oracle.com>. The network at Hershey Foods <www.hersheys.com>, for example, uses the SAP system. It identifies the current status of any order and traces its progress from order entry on through customer delivery and receipt of payment. Progress and delays at intermediate stages—materials ordering, inventory availability, production scheduling, packaging, warehousing, distribution—can be checked continuously to determine which operations should be more closely coordinated with others to improve overall performance.

TYPES OF INFORMATION SYSTEMS

In a sense, the term *information system* may be a misnomer: It suggests that there is one system when, in fact, a firm's employees will have different interests, job responsibilities, and decision-making requirements. One information system cannot accommodate such a variety of information requirements. Instead, the *information system* is a complex of several information systems that share information while serving different levels of the organization, different departments, or different operations.

User Groups and System Requirements

knowledge worker
Employee who uses information and knowledge as raw materials and who relies on information technology to design new products or business systems

Four user groups, each with different system requirements, are identified in Figure 12.3, which also indicates the kinds of systems best suited to each user level. Among users we include the **knowledge worker**—the employee whose job involves the use of information and knowledge as the raw materials of his or her work. Knowledge workers are specialists, usually professionally trained and certified—engineers, scientists, information technology specialists, psychologists—who rely on information technology to design new products or create new business processes.

Managers at Different Levels Because they work on different kinds of problems, top managers, middle managers, knowledge workers, and first-line managers have different information needs. First-line (or operational) managers need information to oversee the day-to-day details of their departments or projects. Knowledge workers need special information for conducting technical projects. Meanwhile, middle managers need summaries and analyses for setting intermediate and long-range goals for the departments or projects under their supervision. Finally, top management analyzes broader trends in the economy, the business environment, and overall company performance in order to conduct long-range planning for the entire organization.

Consider the various information needs for a flooring manufacturer. Sales managers (first-level managers) supervise salespeople, assign territories to the sales force, and handle customer service and delivery problems. They need current information on the sales and delivery of products: lists of incoming customer orders and daily delivery schedules to customers in their territories. Regional managers (middle managers) set sales quotas for each sales manager, prepare budgets, and plan staffing needs for the upcoming year. They need information on monthly sales by product and region. Knowledge workers developing new flooring materials need information on the chemical properties of adhesives and compression strengths for

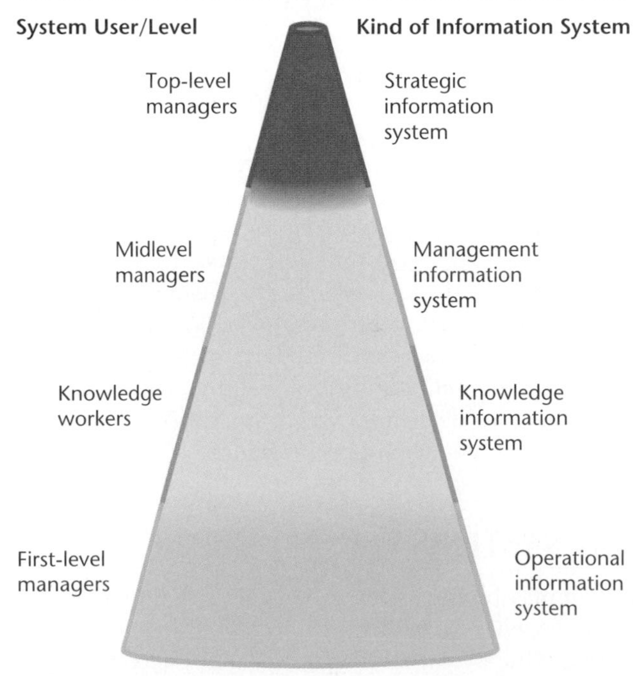

Figure 12.3
Matching Information Users and Systems

floor structures. Finally, top managers need both external and internal information. Internally, they use sales data summarized by product, customer type, and geographic region, along with comparisons to previous years. Equally important is external information on consumer behavior patterns, the competition's performance, and economic forecasts.

Functional Areas and Business Processes Each business *function*—marketing, human resources, accounting, production, finance—has its own information requirements. In addition, as we saw in Chapter 6, many businesses are organized according to various business processes, and these process groups also need special information. Each of these user groups and departments is represented by an information system. When we add to these systems the four systems needed by the four levels of users that we just discussed, we see that the total number of information systems and applications increases significantly.

Each cell in Figure 12.4 describes a potential information system associated with a particular user group. Top-level finance managers, for example, are concerned with long-range planning for capital expenditures for future facilities and equipment and with determining sources of capital funds. In contrast, the arrows on the right side of Figure 12.4 indicate that a business-process group will include users, both managers and employees, drawn from all organizational levels. The supply-chain management group, for instance, may be in the process of trimming down the number of suppliers. The information system supporting this project would contain information ranging across different organization functions and management levels: The group will need information and expert knowledge on marketing, warehousing and distribution, production, communications technology, purchasing, suppliers, and finance. It will also need different perspectives on operational, technical, and managerial issues: determining technical requirements for new suppliers, specifying task responsibilities for participating firms, and determining future financial requirements.

Major Systems by Level

In this section, we discuss different kinds of systems that provide applications at some organizational levels but not at others. For any routine, repetitive transactions, such as

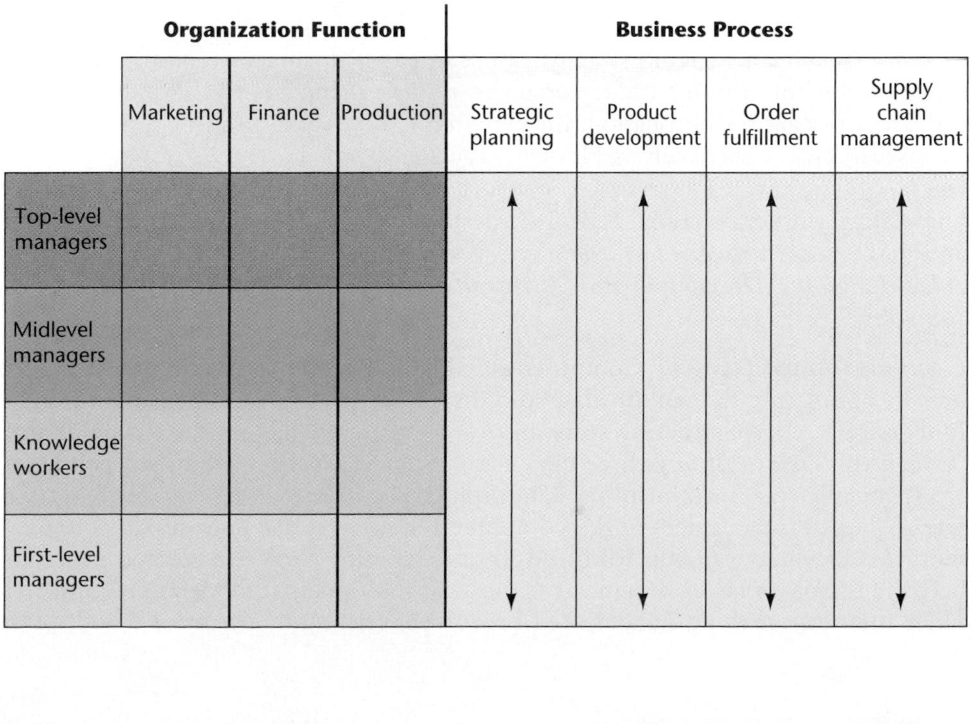

	Organization Function			**Business Process**			
	Marketing	Finance	Production	Strategic planning	Product development	Order fulfillment	Supply chain management
Top-level managers				↕	↕	↕	↕
Midlevel managers							
Knowledge workers							
First-level managers							

Figure 12.4

Matching User Levels with Functional Areas and Business Processes day-to-day order taking by online retailers, a specialized application will suffice. In contrast, system requirements for knowledge workers will probably vary because knowledge workers often face a variety of specialized problems. Applications of information systems for middle- or top-level management decisions must also be flexible, though for different reasons: In particular, they will use a broader range of information collected from a variety of sources, both external and internal.

Systems for Knowledge Workers and Office Applications Systems for knowledge workers and office applications support the activities of both knowledge workers and employees in clerical positions. They provide assistance for data processing and other office activities, including the creation of communications documents. Like other departments, the IS department includes both *knowledge workers* and *data workers*.

IS Knowledge Workers IS knowledge workers include both systems analysts and application or systems programmers:

- *Systems analysts* deal with the entire computer system. They represent the IS group in working with users to learn users' requirements and to design systems that meet them. Generally, they decide on the types and sizes of computers and on how to set up linkages among computers to form a network of users.
- Using various language programs, *programmers* write the software instructions that tell computers what to do. Application programmers, for example, write instructions to address particular problems. Systems programmers ensure that a system can handle the requests made by various application programs.

system operations personnel
Information-systems employees who run a company's computer equipment

Operations Personnel (Data Workers) People who run the company's computer equipment are called **system operations personnel**. They make sure that the right programs are run in the correct sequence and monitor equipment to ensure that it is operating properly. Many organizations also have personnel for entering data into the system for processing.

Knowledge-Level and Office Systems The explosion of new support systems—word processing, document imaging, desktop publishing, computer-aided design, simulation modeling—has increased the productivity of both office and knowledge workers. We will discuss word processing—systems for formatting, editing, and storing documents—later in this chapter. Desktop publishing, also discussed later, combines graphics and word-processing text to publish professional-quality print and Web documents. Document imaging systems can scan paper documents and images, convert them into digital form for storage on disks, retrieve them, and transmit them electronically to workstations throughout the network.

World-class firms such as Harley-Davidson <www.harley-davidson.com>, John Deere <www.deere.com>, and GE <www.ge.com> are using system applications for knowledge workers to reduce product-design times, reduce production-cycle times, and make faster deliveries to customers. Knowledge-level systems include *computer-aided design* (CAD), *computer-aided manufacturing* (CAM), and *computer operation control*.[15]

computer-aided design (CAD)
Computer-based electronic technology that assists in designing products by simulating a real product and displaying it in three-dimensional graphics

Computer-Aided Design **Computer-aided design (CAD)** assists in designing products by simulating the real product and displaying it in three-dimensional graphics. Immersion's MicroScribe-3D software <www.immersion.com> uses a penlike tool to scan the surface of any three-dimensional object, such as a football helmet, and electronically transform it into a 3D graphic. The helmet designer can then try different shapes and surfaces in the computer and analyze the new designs on a video monitor. Products ranging from cell phones to auto parts are created using CAD because it creates faster designs at lower cost than manual modeling methods. The older method—making handcrafted prototypes (trial models) from wood, plastic, or clay—is replaced with *rapid prototyping* (*RP*): The CAD system electronically transfers instructions to a computer-controlled machine that automatically builds the prototype.

Computer-Aided Manufacturing **Computer-aided manufacturing** (CAM) is used to design the manufacturing equipment, facilities, and plant layouts for better product flows and productivity. *Computer operations control* refers to any system for managing the day-to-day production activities for either goods or service production. Hospitals use computer-based scheduling for preparing patients' meals, just as manufacturers do for making cars, clocks, and paper products.

computer-aided manufacturing (CAM)
Computer system used to design and control equipment needed in the manufacturing process

management information system (MIS)
System used for transforming data into information for use in decision making

Management Information Systems **Management information systems** (MIS) support an organization's managers by providing daily reports, schedules, plans, and budgets. Each manager's information activities vary according to the individual's functional area (for example, accounting or marketing) and management level. Whereas midlevel managers focus mostly on internal activities and information, higher-level managers are also engaged in external activities. Middle managers, the largest MIS user group, need networked information to plan such upcoming activities as personnel training, materials movements, and cash flows. They also need to know the current status of the jobs and projects being carried out in their departments: What stage is it at now? When will it be finished? Is there an opening so we can start the next job? Many of a firm's management information systems—cash flow, sales, production scheduling, shipping—are indispensable for helping managers find answers to such questions.[16]

Decision Support Systems Middle- and top-level managers receive decision-making assistance from a **decision support system (DSS)**: an interactive system that locates and presents information needed to support the decision-making process. Whereas some DSSs are devoted to specific problems, others serve more general purposes, allowing managers to analyze different types of problems. Thus, a firm that often faces decisions on plant capacity, for example, may have a *capacity DSS*: The manager inputs data on anticipated levels of sales, working capital, and customer-delivery requirements. Then the DSS's built-in transaction processors manipulate the data and make recommendations on the best levels of plant capacity for each future time period.

decision support system (DSS)
Interactive computer-based system that locates and presents information needed to support decision making

Executive Support Systems An **executive support system** (ESS) is a quick-reference, easy-access application of information systems specially designed for instant access by upper-level managers. ESSs are designed to assist with executive-level decisions and problems, ranging from "What lines of business should we be in five years from now?" to "Based on forecasted developments in electronic technologies, to what extent should our firm be globalized in five years? In 10 years?" The ESS also uses a wide range of both internal information and external sources, such as industry reports, global economic forecasts, and reports on competitors' capabilities.

executive support system (ESS)
Quick-reference information-system application designed specially for instant access by upper-level managers

Artificial Intelligence and Expert Systems **Artificial intelligence** (AI) can be defined as the construction of computer systems, both hardware and software, to imitate human behavior—in other words, systems that perform physical tasks, use thought processes, and learn. In developing AI systems, knowledge workers—business specialists, modelers, information-technology experts—try to design computer-based systems capable of reasoning so that computers, instead of people, can perform certain business activities. One example is a credit-evaluation system that decides which loan applicants are creditworthy, which ones are too risky, and then composes acceptance and rejection letters accordingly.[17]

Robotics—the combination of computers with industrial robots—is a category of AI. With certain "reasoning" capabilities, robots can "learn" repetitive tasks such as painting, assembling components, and inserting screws. They also avoid repeating

artificial intelligence (AI)
Computer-system application that imitates human behavior by performing physical tasks, using thought processes, sensing, and learning

robotics
Combination of computers and industrial robots for use in manufacturing operations

mistakes by "remembering" the causes of past mistakes and, when those causes reappear, adjusting or stopping until adjustments are made.

There are also designed AI systems that possess sensory capabilities, such as lasers that "see," "hear," and "feel." In addition, as machines become more sophisticated in processing natural languages, humans can give instructions and ask questions merely by speaking to a computer.

expert system Form of artificial intelligence that attempts to imitate the behavior of human experts in a particular field

Expert Systems A special form of AI program, the **expert system**, is designed to imitate the thought processes of human experts in a particular field. Expert systems incorporate the rules that an expert applies to specific types of problems, such as the judgments that a physician makes for diagnosing illnesses. In effect, expert systems supply everyday users with "instant expertise."

DATABASES AND SOFTWARE FOR THE INFORMATION SYSTEM

computer network All the computer and information technology devices that, by working together, drive the flow of digital information throughout a system

hardware Physical components of a computer system

We now know that an *information system* is a group of interconnected devices at several different locations that can exchange information. We also know that *networking*—connecting these devices—allows otherwise decentralized computers to exchange data quickly and easily. A key component of the information system is its **computer network:** all the computer and information technology devices that, working together, drive the flow of digital information throughout the system. This includes all the **hardware**—the physical components (equipment) of a computer network—such as keyboards, video monitors, and printers.

Although the hardware is essential, it is only one part of the information system. Data must be organized so they are conveniently accessible to users throughout the network. Likewise, programs (software) must be available to process the data. In this section we will describe the kinds of databases and software that enable the networked information system to function effectively. We will reserve our discussion of telecommunications for the next section.

"Smaller, more powerful chips allow me to have a smaller head."

Databases and Program Software

As we have noted, all computer processing is the processing of data. This processing is carried out by programs—instructions that tell the system to perform specified functions. In this section we begin by briefly describing the nature of computer data and databases. We then discuss a few of the specialized application programs designed for business use.

Data and Databases Computers convert data into information by organizing the data in some meaningful manner. Within a computer system, chunks of data—numbers, words, and sentences—are stored in a series of related collections called *fields, records*, and *files*. Taken together, all these data files constitute a **database**: a centralized, organized collection of related data.[18]

database
Centralized, organized collection of related data

System Programs As we have just seen, hardware needs programs—**software**—to function. There are basically two types of software programs: *system* and *application*. **System programs** tell the computer what resources to use and how to use them. For example, an operating system program tells the computer how and when to transfer data from various storage locations in the system and to return information to the user. You have probably heard of DOS, the disk operating system. It is called DOS because a disk is used to store the operating system software.[19]

software
Programs that instruct a computer in what to do

system program
Software that tells the computer what resources to use and how to use them

Application Programs Most computer users do not write programs but rather use **application programs**: software packages written by others. Each different type of application (such as financial analysis, word processing, or Web browsing) uses a program that meets that need. Programs are available for a huge variety of business-related tasks. Some of these programs address such common, long-standing needs as accounting, payroll, and inventory control. Others have been developed for application to an endless variety of specialized needs. Most business application programs fall into one of four categories—*word processing, spreadsheets, database management*, and *graphics*. Of all PC software applications, 70 percent are designed for the first three types of programs.[20]

application program
Software (such as Word for Windows) that processes data according to a user's special needs

Word Processing Popular **word-processing programs**, such as Microsoft Word for Windows <www.microsoft.com/windows>, Corel WordPerfect, <www.corel.com/products/wordperfect>, and Lotus Development Corporation's Word Pro <www.lotus.com/home/nsf/welcome/smartsuite>, allow computer users to store, edit, display, and print documents. Sentences or paragraphs can be added or deleted without retyping or restructuring an entire document, and mistakes are easily corrected.

word-processing program
Applications program that allows computers to store, edit, and print letters and numbers for documents created by users

Spreadsheets **Electronic spreadsheets** spread data across and down the page in rows and columns. Users enter data, including formulas, at row and column intersections, and the computer automatically performs the necessary calculations. Payroll records, sales projections, and a host of other financial reports can be prepared in this manner.

Spreadsheets are useful planning tools because they allow managers to see how making a change in one item will affect related items. For example, a manager can insert various operating cost percentages, tax rates, or sales revenues into the spreadsheet. The computer will automatically recalculate all the other figures and determine net profit. Three popular spreadsheet packages are Lotus 1-2-3, Quattro Pro, <www.corel/products/wordperfect/cqp>, and Microsoft Excel for Windows.[21]

electronic spreadsheet
Applications program with a row-and-column format that allows users to store, manipulate, and compare numeric data

Database Management In addition to word processing and spreadsheets, another popular type of personal productivity software is a **database management program**. Such programs as Microsoft Access for Windows, and, from Borland <www.borland.com>, InterBase are popular for desktop applications. Oracle9i <www.oracle.com> is a popular database for Internet computing. These systems can store, sort, and search through data and integrate a single piece of data into several different files.

database management program
Applications program for creating, storing, searching, and manipulating an organized collection of data

Graphics **Computer graphics programs** convert numeric and character data into pictorial information such as charts, graphs, and cartoon characters. These programs make computerized information easier to use and understand in two ways. First, graphs and charts summarize data and allow managers to detect problems, opportunities, and relationships more easily. Second, graphics are valuable in creating clearer and more persuasive reports and presentations.

Presentation graphics software, such as CorelDRAW, Microsoft PowerPoint for Windows, and Microsoft Visio 2002 offer choices for assembling graphics for visual displays, slides, video, and even sound splices for professional presentations. The ability to vary color and size, and to use pictures and charts with three-dimensional effects, shadows, and shading with animation and sound is more visually interesting than static presentations.

Computer graphics capabilities extend beyond mere data presentation. They also include stand-alone programs for artists, designers, and special effects designers. Everything from simple drawings to fine art, television commercials, and motion picture special effects are now created by computer graphics software. The realism of the sinking ship in *Titanic* and the physical appearance of the space creatures in the latest *Star Wars* movie, *Episode One: The Phantom Menace*, and *Jurassic Park III* are examples of special effects created with computer graphics.

Some software allows firms to publish their own sales brochures, in-house magazines, or annual reports. The latest of these **desktop publishing** packages combines word-processing and graphics capability to produce typeset-quality text with stimulating visual effects from personal computers. QuarkXPress <www.quark.com> is able to manipulate text, tables of numbers, graphics, and full-color photographs. Desktop publishing eliminates costly printing services for reports and proposals, and Quark is also used by ad agencies such as J. Walter Thompson, whose computer-generated designs offer greater control over color and format. Other desktop publishing packages include Microsoft Publisher and Adobe Systems PageMaker <www.adobe.com/products/ pagemaker/main.html>.

computer graphics program Applications program that converts numeric and character data into pictorial information such as graphs and charts

presentation graphics software Applications that enable users to create visual presentations that can include animation and sound

desktop publishing Process of combining word-processing and graphics capability to produce virtually typeset-quality text from personal computers

graphical user interface (GUI) Software that provides a visual display to help users select applications

Graphical User Interface One of the most helpful software developments is the **graphical user interface** (GUI): the user-friendly visual display that helps users select from among the many possible applications on the computer. Typically, the screen displays numerous icons (small images) representing such choices as word processing, graphics, DOS, fax, printing, CD, or games. The user tells the computer what to do by moving a pointing device (usually an arrow) around the screen to activate the desired icon. Printed text presents simple instructions for using activated features. Today, Microsoft Windows is the most popular GUI because it simplifies computer use while actually making it fun.

Star Wars: Episode I: The Phantom Menace *was recorded on traditional film. Then, nearly all of the film's 2,200 separate shots were digitally scanned into a computer for editing. At director George Lucas's film effects company, Industrial Light and Magic* <www.ilm.com>*, plans for a* Star Wars II *call for shooting the entire film with a digital-videotape system developed in partnership by Sony* <www.sony.com> *and Panavision* <www.panavision. com>*. Videotaped images will be transferred to the hard drives of special computers for editing and special effects. Newly developed laser printers will then expose the footage onto photographic paper.*

TELECOMMUNICATIONS AND NETWORKS

Although communications systems are constantly evolving, some of the fundamental elements are well established: computers, communications devices, and networking. The most powerful vehicle for using these elements to their full potential is the marriage of computers and communication technologies.

A network is a means of organizing telecommunications components into an effective system. When a company decides how to organize its equipment and facilities, it also determines how its information resources will be shared, controlled, and applied by users in its network. In this section, we will first discuss *multimedia communications technologies* and the devices found in today's systems. We will then describe different ways for organizing information resources into effective systems.

Multimedia Communication Systems

Today's information systems include not only computers but also **multimedia communication systems**. These systems are connected networks of communication appliances such as faxes, televisions, sound equipment, cell phones, printers, and photocopiers that may also be linked by satellite with other remote networks. Not surprisingly, the integration of these elements is changing the way we live our lives and manage our businesses. A good example is the modern grocery store. The checkout scanner reads the bar code on the product you buy. Data are then transmitted to the store's inventory-control system, which updates the number of available units. If inventory falls below a given level, more product is ordered electronically. Meanwhile, the correct price is added to your bill and checkout coupons are printed automatically according to the specific product you bought. Your debit card transfers funds, sales reports are generated for the store's management, and all the while, satellite transmissions are dispatching a remote truck to begin loading replacement supplies for the store.

multimedia communication system
Connected network of communication appliances (such as faxes or TVs) that may be linked to forms of mass media (such as print publications or TV programming)

Communication Devices The explosion in personal communications devices now permits people to conduct business across large distances and from territories where communications were not before available. *Global positioning systems (GPSs)*, for example, use satellite transmissions to track and identify the geographic location of a target, such as a boat or even a person. When you're linked into a GPS network, your firm can know your whereabouts at all times. *Personal digital assistants (PDAs)* are tiny handheld computers with wireless telecommunications capabilities. Several of these palm-size devices are capable of accessing the Internet, including receiving and sending e-mail messages from the most primitive locations. *Paging systems* and *cellular telephones* provide instant fingertip connections within one or more communications networks.

Communication Channels Communication channels are the media that make all these transmissions possible.[22] These include wired and wireless transmission. Microwave systems, for example, transmit straight-line radio (wireless) signals through the air between transmission stations. Another system—satellite communications—has also gained popularity in the growing demand for wireless transmission. GE's Technical Response Center, for example, demonstrates the value of satellites for improving aircraft engine maintenance and safety. Relying on wireless systems instead of underground cables, laser beams and radio waves transmit signals from satellite to satellite.

Accessible through satellite networks under development by McCaw <www.mccaw.com>, Hughes <www.hns.com>, Motorola <www.gi.com>, AT&T <www.attws.com>, and Loral <www.loral.com>, the Net is available in remote areas where underground cable is not feasible. All the world is within the instant reach of the Internet. Most of us use communication channels when we use some type of telephone

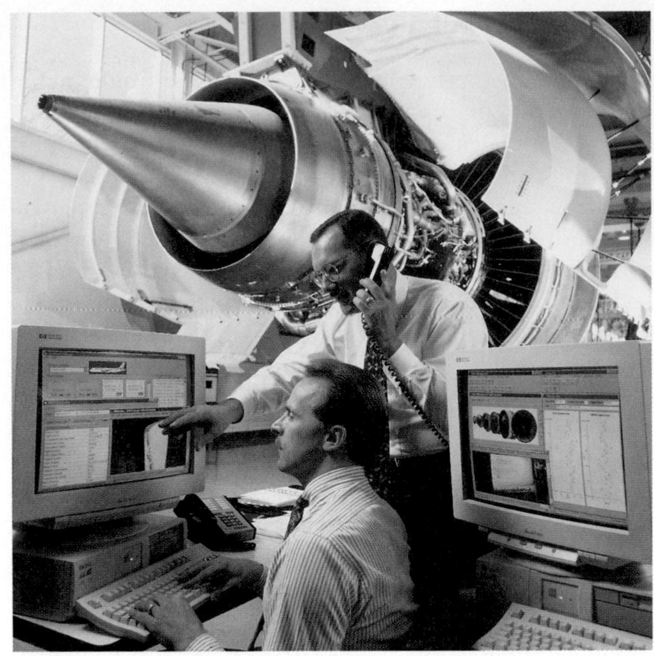

Demonstrating how computers have changed communications, these engineers at GE's corporate research and development center <www.ge.com> can monitor engines in flight from the ground via satellite. The new system can diagnose potential engine problems, plan for maintenance or overhaul, and resolve problems more quickly than ever.

system. Even today, however, the bulk of telephone transmissions are data, not conversations. Fax data account for 90 percent of all telephone signals between the United States and Japan.

System Architecture

There are several ways to organize the components in computer and communications networks. As we see in the next section, one way to classify networks is according to *geographic scope*.[23]

Local and Wide Area Networks Networked systems classified according to geographic scope may be either local or wide area networks. Computers may be linked statewide or even nationwide through telephone lines, microwave, or satellite communications, as in a **wide area network** (**WAN**). Firms can lease lines from communications vendors or maintain private WANs. Wal-Mart, for example, depends heavily on a private satellite network that links more than 2,000 retail stores to its Bentonville, Arkansas, headquarters.

wide area network (WAN)
Network of computers and workstations located far from one another and linked by telephone wires or by satellite

local area network (LAN)
Network of computers and workstations, usually within a company, that are linked together by cable

modem
Device that provides a computer-to-computer link over telephone wires

fiber optic cable
Glass-fiber cables that carry data in the form of light pulses

Internal networks covering limited distances may link all of a firm's nearby computers, as in a **local area network** (**LAN**). Computers within a building, for example, can be linked by cabling (fiber optic, coaxial, or twisted wire) or by wireless technology. Internally networked computers share processing duties, software, storage areas, and data. On cable TV's *Home Shopping Network* <www.hsn.com>, hundreds of operators seated at monitors in a large room are united by a LAN for entering call-in orders from customers. This arrangement allows the use of a single computer system with one database and software system.

Connecting the Hardware Combination systems using local and wide area networks are also possible. Separate plants or offices might handle orders locally while electronically transmitting sales summaries to a corporate office. Using a personal computer with a **modem**—a computer-to-computer link over telephone wires—users can conduct searches in a remote database and exchange messages.

The materials used for making local and wide area networks are changing rapidly. **Fiber optic cable** is made from thousands of strands of ultrathin glass fibers that not only carry data faster but also are lighter and less expensive than older copper media, such as *coaxial cable* (as used in cable television) and *twisted-wire cable* (as in tele-

IT'S A WIRED WORLD

"These Two Companies Are a Natural Fit"

Even a high-tech giant can't be an expert in every new development in the digital world. Consider, for example, America Online <www.aol.com> (including its CompuServ service <www.compuserve.com>—America's largest online Internet service provider) with 22 million subscribers. AOL's customers have Internet access through traditional phone lines. But AOL is thinking about ways to give them even faster Internet service by means of high-speed cable lines. Traditional phone lines are slower than cables in connecting to the Net. They're also slower in downloading information and slower in reading graphics files.

AOL already knows that if it's going to stay competitive in the home Internet market, it will need to offer customers faster Internet connections. On one level, the problem is fairly simple: How do you get from phone lines to cables? One approach—replacing all those phone lines with cables—is more than prohibitively expensive: It simply can't be done. Because AOL doesn't own the lines it uses (the phone company does), it can't replace them. A more feasible approach involves cable service providers. They already have the capability, but they haven't yet exploited their cable technology in the Internet market.

Now consider the situation at Time Warner Inc. <www.timewarner.com/corp>—a cable service provider that also happens to be the world's top media and entertainment company. Time Warner Inc. wants to harness the power of the Internet, which it sees as the future avenue for distributing its entertainment products. Unfortunately, Time Warner can't deliver magazines like *Time, People,* and *Sports Illustrated* without Internet technology. Nor can Time Warner deliver movies and music for downloading. Time Warner's problem, then, was how to get digital when it wasn't skilled at the technology. Ultimately, doing things internally turned out to be too costly: When Time Warner tried to reinvent its own Internet capabilities, it spent some $500 million (in 1999 alone) in a less than successful effort to rework its online approach.

In early 2000, AOL and Time Warner announced a permanent partnering conceived to give each company a much needed lift in overcoming its respective problem: Internet giant AOL would join with media behemoth Time Warner in a corporate merger valued at $166 billion—the largest ever. The new firm, AOL Time Warner Inc., gains the advantages of each partner's technological expertise and resources. AOL, of course, has Internet expertise. It also has 22 million customers who can purchase and download Time Warner's entertainment products from the Internet. Meanwhile, Time Warner brings not only 13 million cable TV subscribers to the merger but also expertise in the high-speed cable lines that AOL needs for faster Internet services. This large base of cable-ready households will be a big boost for AOL because only 6 percent of Web users currently have the high-speed (cable-modem) access that can be up to 100 times faster than modems on traditional phone lines (which are used by some 94 percent of Web users). Thus, two giants, each wanting to grow but hindered by technology shortcomings, believe that, as one firm, they'll grow much faster than each could have grown separately. By early 2001, the newly merged firm had subscription relationships with a whopping 130 million customers. "These two companies," announced former Time Warner chairman Gerald Levin, "are a natural fit."

phone wires). Whereas copper wire cables carry data as electrical signals, fiber optic cable carries data as laser-generated light beams.[24] Wire cables throughout the world are being replaced daily with fiber optic cable, but the change will require many years. Tele Danmark <www.teledanmark.dk/english>, Denmark's leading telecom company, is leading the way. In 1996, it installed the 250-mile BALTICA submarine cable between Poland, Denmark, and Sweden and a 450-mile underwater cable in Brazil.

Wireless Networks Wireless technologies use airborne transmission of electronic signals, instead of wires, for linking the appliances in a network. In addition to popular mobile phones, other consumer applications include wireless laptops, wireless handheld computers, and new applications in cars (including wireless access to the Internet, wireless music players, cameras, map terminals, and game machines). But businesses, too, gain advantages by avoiding layers of wires throughout buildings by using wireless interactions among mobile and fixed devices. Ford, for example, uses an innovative industrial information system—WhereNet—for locating and tracking inventory using identification tags that transmit tracking information on radio waves. Antennas mounted on the factory ceiling receive the tag transmissions and then deliver information to a central computer that identifies the exact location of the tags in the plant. The wireless system saves time and money by coordinating the delivery of hundreds of parts to assembly lines in a timely manner.[25]

client-server network
Information-technology system consisting of clients (users) that are electronically linked to share network resources provided by a server, such as a host computer

Client-Server Systems An obvious advantage of networks is the sharing of resources—and thus the avoidance of costly and unnecessary duplication. In a **client-server network**, clients are the users of services. They are the points of entry, usually laptop computers, workstations, or desktop computers. The server provides the services shared by network users. The powerful minicomputer at the network hub, for example, which is larger and more sophisticated than your PC, or microcomputer, may be the server for the surrounding client PCs in an office network.

More specifically, the server may act as a file server, a print server, and a fax server. As a *file server*, the mini has a large-capacity disk for storing the programs and data shared by all the PCs in the network. It contains customer files plus the database, word-processing, graphics, and spreadsheet programs that may be used by clients. As a *print server*, the mini controls the printer, stores printing requests from client PCs, and routes jobs to the printer as it becomes available. As the *fax server*, it receives, sends, and otherwise controls the system's fax activities. Only one disk drive, one printer, and one fax, therefore, are needed for an entire system of users. Internet computing uses the client-server arrangement.

Continued from page 307

Researching with a Purpose

On Duncan Highsmith's organizational chart, the library is listed on the same level as the firm's other important functions, including marketing, human resources, and accounting. As part of the information system, it adds the power of the Internet to human judgment. It also directs information toward the people who can use it and get results with it, and it's readily available and affordable.

The strength of the system is its knowledge-management tool: Lisa Guedea Carreño. Although Guedea Carreño relies on the Internet, she also realizes that as an information source it isn't necessarily all that it's cracked up to be. It's full of hype and promises, and it's unfamiliar territory to new users. Web-search services—Internet search directories, Web browsers, and search engines—often provide spotty information, ranging from full-disclosure sites to sites that offer the truth but not the whole truth. Some Web services report information only for sites that pay to be listed and ignore others. Even among those that report on a huge number of companies, some may give preferential treatment—that is, more favorable reports—to business partners.

To help internal Highsmith users, Guedea Carreño has thus devised her own rules of thumb for navigating the Net efficiently, sorting through Web sites to discard the bad and retain the useful. Through experience, she's compiled a checklist and some questions. Here's a sample:

- *Quality control.* A quick rule is watch for typos. If it's typed sloppily, the site's content is also probably of questionable quality.
- *Timeliness.* Is the information current? Does the site tell you when it was updated? If not, chances are it's old information (and thus not information at all).
- *Purpose.* What's the site's purpose? If it's ambiguous or not readily apparent, you, too, will probably end up wandering around without purpose.

- *Linkages*. Does the site contain links to other sites? Are the others relevant, accessible, and current? If it links you to unreliable sites, you will be misdirected and lose precious time.
- *Scope of information*. Is the range of information sufficiently rich to meet all your needs at this one site? Obviously, information-rich sites save time and help you get results.
- *Site ownership*. Who owns the site? Who is the author, and what is the agenda? If you know the sponsor or owner, you can get a better idea of what the site's content is likely to be.
- *Bias*. Bias can be good or bad, but it helps if the bias is apparent because it saves time and tells you in advance that you're likely to get just one side of a story.

Questions for Discussion

1. If you were designing a company's information system, how would you go about determining the kinds of external information to include?
2. Discuss the problems that might be encountered in selecting qualitative information consisting of subjective, nonquantifiable content for a communication network. How can such information be organized in electronic files for the database?
3. Do you think that every Highsmith employee would benefit from participating in "Life, the Universe, and Everything"? Identify the advantages and drawbacks to full employee participation.
4. What kind of training would you propose for a new employee who wants to develop the type of knowledge-worker skills that Guedea Carreño has?
5. Draw a diagram to display the components in Highsmith's information system. Describe how each element affects the company's performance.
6. Do you think that an expert system could be developed to capture Guedea Carreño's method for sorting out good and mediocre Web sites? Explain why or why not.

SUMMARY OF LEARNING OBJECTIVES

1 **Explain why businesses must manage *information* and show how computer systems and communication technologies have revolutionized *information management*.** Because businesses are faced with an overwhelming amount of *data* and *information* about customers, competitors, and their own operations, the ability to manage this input can mean the difference between success and failure. The management of its information system is a core activity because all of a firm's business activities are linked to it. New digital technologies have taken an integral place among an organization's resources for conducting everyday business.

2 **Identify and briefly describe three elements of *data communication networks*—the Internet, the World Wide Web, and intranets.** *Data communication networks*, both public and private, carry streams of digital data (electronic messages) back and forth quickly and economically via *telecommunication systems*. The largest public communications network, the *Internet*, is a gigantic system of networks linking millions of computers offering information on business around the world. The Net is the most important e-mail system in the world. Individuals can subscribe to the Net via an *Internet service provider* (*ISP*). The *World Wide Web* is a system with universally accepted standards for storing, formatting, retrieving, and displaying information. It provides the common language that enables users around the world to "surf" the Net using a common format. *Intranets* are private networks that any company can develop to extend Net technology internally—that is, for transmitting information throughout the firm. Intranets are accessible only to employees, with access to outsiders prevented by hardware and software security systems called *firewalls*.

3 **Describe five *new options for organizational design* that have emerged from the rapid growth of information technologies.** Information networks are leading to *leaner* organizations—businesses with fewer employees and simpler organizational structures—because networked firms can maintain electronic, rather than human, information linkages among employees and customers. Operations are *more flexible* because electronic networks allow businesses to offer greater product variety and faster

delivery cycles. Aided by intranets and the Internet, *greater collaboration* is possible, both among internal units and with outside firms. *Geographic separation* of the workplace and company headquarters is more common because electronic linkages are replacing the need for physical proximity between the company and its workstations. *Improved management processes* are feasible because managers have rapid access to more information about the current status of company activities and easier access to electronic tools for planning and decision making.

4 **Discuss different information-system *application programs* that are available for users at various organizational levels.** *Application programs* for *knowledge workers* and *office applications* include personal productivity tools such as *word processing, document imaging, desktop publishing, computer-aided design*, and *simulation modeling. Management information systems (MISs)* support an organization's managers by providing daily reports, schedules, plans, and budgets. Middle managers, the largest MIS user group, need networked information to plan upcoming activities and to track current activities. *Decision support systems (DSSs)* are interactive applications that assist the decision-making processes of middle- and top-level managers. *Executive support systems (ESSs)* are quick-reference, easy-access programs to assist upper-level managers. *Artificial intelligence (AI)* and *expert systems* are designed to imitate human behavior and provide computer-based assistance in performing certain business activities.

5 **Briefly describe the content and role of a *database* and the purpose of *database software* for information systems.** The *database* is a centralized, organized collection of related data, in digital form, within a computer system. The *database* is the storehouse of all the system data that are classified into fields, records, and files having numerical storage locations. The purpose of the *database* and *database software* is to make the data accessible on demand for system users. *Database management programs* are software applications that enable data to be conveniently stored, retrieved, sorted, and searched. This software allows system users to integrate a single piece of data into several different files within the system so that useful information is created.

QUESTIONS AND EXERCISES

Questions for Review

1. Why does a business need to manage information as a resource?
2. How can an electronic conferencing system increase a company's productivity and efficiency?
3. Why do the four levels of user groups in an organization need different kinds of information from the information system?
4. In what ways are local area networks (LANs) different from or similar to wide area networks (WANs)?
5. What are the main types of electronic information technologies being applied in business information systems?

Questions for Analysis

6. Give two examples (other than those in this chapter) for each of the major types of application programs used in business.
7. Describe three or four activities in which you regularly engage that might be made easier by multimedia technology.
8. Give three examples (other than those in this chapter) of how a company can become leaner by adopting a networked information system.

Application Exercises

9. Describe the information system at your college or university. Identify its components and architecture. Identify the features that either promote or inhibit collaboration among system users.
10. Visit a small business in your community to investigate the ways it is using communication technologies and the ways it plans to use them in the future. Prepare a report for presentation in class.

EXPLORING THE WEB

On the Cutting Edge with Experts

Most firms rely on expert assistance to get started on network development and buy the technology they need for their Internet systems. Cisco Systems Inc. is the worldwide leader in Internet networking, providing most of the systems that make the Internet work. By looking at Cisco's products, including hardware, software, and services, we can get an idea about both the needs of Internet users and some of the leading-edge solutions that are available. To learn about Cisco, its products, and its customers, visit its Web site at:

<www.cisco.com/>

Spend some time navigating through the home page. To get an idea of the variety of Cisco's products and services, enter each of the subject gates (point the mouse to the title and click) located up, down, and across the page. Scroll down the page and select "Services" and "Solutions" titles that seem interesting to you. Be sure to note the different kinds of customers at whom each product is directed. After getting acquainted with the site, consider the following items:

1. Under "Solutions for Your Network," look at Cisco's "Internet Communications Software." From the description, identify the company's software products, the purpose of those products, the ways they work, and the benefits from using them.
2. For Cisco's "Internet Business Solutions," look for "Cisco Customers" and their "Success Stories." Then select two categories, such as "E-Commerce" and "Supply Chain Management." Explain how Cisco's "solutions" for these two categories differ from one another.
3. On the Cisco home page, find the title "Solutions for Your Network," then select the "Small/Medium Business" option. What Internet tools does Cisco offer? Explain the ways in which those tools could improve productivity and identify the kinds of organizational conditions under which they would be most appropriate.
4. Suppose you have questions about which products are best suited for your firm's Internet requirements and how certain products would apply to your situation. Where, in the Cisco Web site, would you turn for help?

EXERCISING YOUR ETHICS

Supplying the Right Answers

THE SITUATION

Networked systems facilitate the sharing of information among companies and often include sensitive customer data. This exercise challenges you to think about ethical considerations that arise in developing information technologies and using them in a networked system.

THE DILEMMA

Home Sweet Home-e (HSH-e) was an e-business start-up that sold virtually everything imaginable in home furnishings—from linens and towels to cleaning supplies and furniture. Using computers at home, HSH-e members could shop in virtual storefronts, chat online with other home shoppers, talk live with virtual store clerks, and pay electronically in a one-stop Web site. In reality, HSH-e was a *virtual store*: a network of numerous suppliers located around the country, each specializing in a particular line of goods. The network was electronically connected via a centrally controlled information technology that HSH-e developed, owned, and operated. Once the customer's order was placed, network suppliers received information instantaneously on what to ship, destination, and billing.

HSH-e carefully chose only those suppliers that promised to make fast, reliable deliveries to HSH-e customers and that promised to supply HSH-e exclusively. The linen supplier, for example, could not supply linens for other home-furnishings e-businesses. In return, the supplier was assured of receiving all HSH-e orders for products in its line of business. As HSH-e grew in popularity, suppliers stood to gain more business and prosper with greater sales in an expanding e-tail industry. As it turns out, while some prospective suppliers refused to join the network, others in the network were discontinued by HSH-e for not enlarging their operations fast enough to keep up with customer demand.

QUESTIONS FOR DISCUSSION

1. For a potential HSH-e supplier of a specialized product line, what are the ethical issues in this situation?
2. Consider past suppliers that have been discontinued or have withdrawn from the HSH-e network. Do they face any ethical issues involving HSH-e customers? Involving HSH-e operations? Involving other HSH-e suppliers?
3. Suppose you work at HSH-e and you notice a new supplier that is more attractive than one of the company's existing suppliers. What ethical considerations do you face in deciding whether or not to replace the existing supplier?

BUILDING YOUR BUSINESS SKILLS

The Art and Science of Point-and-Click Research

This exercise enhances the following SCANS workplace competencies: demonstrating basic skills, demonstrating thinking skills, exhibiting interpersonal skills, working with information, applying system knowledge, and using technology.

GOAL

To introduce students to World Wide Web search sites.

BACKGROUND

In a recent survey of nearly 2,000 Web users, two-thirds stated that they used the Web to obtain work-related information. With an estimated 320 million pages of information on the Web, the challenge for business users is fairly obvious: how to find what they're looking for.

METHOD

You'll need a computer and access to the World Wide Web to complete this exercise.

STEP 1

Get together with three other classmates and decide on a business-related research topic. Choose a topic that interests you, for example, "Business Implications of the Year 2000 Census," "Labor Disputes in Professional Sports," or "Marketing Music Lessons and Instruments to Parents of Young Children."

STEP 2

Search the following sites for information on your topic. Divide the sites among group members to speed the process:

- Yahoo! <www.yahoo.com>
- Hotbot <www.hotbot.com>
- Alta Vista <www.altavista.net>
- Excite <www.excite.com>
- Infoseek <www.infoseek.com>
- Lycos <www.lycos.com>
- Metacrawler <www.metacrawler.com>
- Dogpile <www.dogpile.com>
- Ask Jeeves <www.askjeeves.com>
- Northern Light <www.nlsearch.com>
- Internet Sleuth <www.isleuth.com>

Take notes as you search so that you can explain your findings to other group members.

STEP 3

Working as a group, answer the following questions about your collective search:

1. Which sites were the easiest to use?
2. Which sites offered the most helpful results? What specific factors made these sites better than the others?
3. Which sites offered the least helpful results? What were the problems?
4. Why is it important to learn the special code words or symbols, called operators, that target a search? (Operators are words like AND, OR, and NOT that narrow search queries. For example, using AND in a search tells the system that all words must appear in the results—American AND Management AND Association.)

FOLLOW-UP QUESTIONS

1. Research the differences between search *engines* and search *directories*. Then place the sites listed in step 2 in the appropriate category. Did you find search engines or directories more helpful in this exercise?
2. Why is it important to learn to use the search-site "Help" function?
3. Based on your personal career goals, how do you think that mastering Web research techniques might help you in the future?
4. How has the World Wide Web changed the nature of business research?

CRAFTING YOUR BUSINESS PLAN

Getting Wired into Better Information

THE PURPOSE OF THE ASSIGNMENT

1. To familiarize students with issues involving information systems that a sample firm faces in developing its business plan, in the framework of *Business PlanPro (BPP)* (Version 4.0).
2. To demonstrate how communications technologies, the Internet, and database considerations can be integrated as components in the *BPP* planning environment.

FOLLOW-UP ASSIGNMENT

After reading Chapter 12 in the textbook, open the BPP *software and look around for information about plans for computer and communications technologies as they apply to a sample firm:* Travel Agency *(Adventure Travel International). Begin first by looking at ATI's Plan Outline, 1.0 Executive Summary, to get acquainted with the firm. Then respond to the following questions:*

1. How have the Internet and related communications technologies changed the travel agency industry? [Sites to see in *BPP* (for this question): In the Plan Outline screen, click in turn on each of the following: **3.2 Competitive Comparison** and **4.3.1 Industry Participants.**]
2. How might databases be used to advantage at ATI? [Sites to see in *BPP*: In the Plan Outline screen, click in turn on each of the following: **3.3 Sales Literature, 3.5 Technology, 4.1 Market Segmentation, 5.0 Strategy and Implementation Summary,** and **5.3.5 Marketing Programs.**]
3. What are the advantages in ATI's Computerized Reservation System? [Sites to see in *BPP*: From the Plan Outline screen, click in turn on each of the following: **3.5 Technology** and **4.3.2 Distribution Patterns.**]

4. How can ATI's distribution system benefit from using the World Wide Web? After exploring in ATI's Plan Outline, what suggestions would you give them about using the Web? [Sites to see in *BPP*: In the Plan Outline screen, click on **5.3.4 Distribution Strategy** and **5.5 Strategic Alliances**.]

VIDEO EXERCISE

Space Age IT at Boeing

LEARNING OBJECTIVES

The purpose of this video exercise is to help you:

1. Understand why businesses must manage information
2. Understand the role of information systems within an organization
3. Recognize the ways in which information systems contribute to efficiency and productivity

BACKGROUND INFORMATION

The world's leading manufacturer of commercial communications satellites, Boeing Satellite Systems <www.boeing.com/satellite> is a wholly owned subsidiary of The Boeing Co. <www.boeing.com> with customers in 14 countries. It has sent more than 180 spacecraft into orbit and employees more than 8,000 people, each of whom works with a personal computer or laptop. The company's information system (IS) integrates data from all departments, including sales, finance, engineering, manufacturing, legal, human resources, and so on.

THE VIDEO

Vice President and Chief Information Officer (CIO) K. S. Radhakrishnan discusses not only the role of information systems in the organization, but also some of the specific ways in which data and information are generated and collected. He identifies the three major goals of the information management plan, lists some specific ways in which information technology (IT) improves productivity and efficiency at Boeing, and looks at the future, in which integration between the company and its suppliers and customers will be ever tighter thanks to e-commerce and new applications of IT.

QUESTIONS FOR DISCUSSION

1. What role does information systems play in the Boeing Satellite Systems division?
2. What do you think are some of the advantages of automatic data entry and integration? List as many as you can think of.
3. What are some ways in which IT affects productivity and efficiency? List as many as you can.

FOLLOW-UP ASSIGNMENT

The only competitor with Boeing's the aircraft division is Airbus <www.airbus.com>. Log on to the career opportunities section of the Airbus Website and try to locate open positions in information management, information systems, or information technology. What are the requirements for these jobs? The responsibilities? What specific tasks will employees need to perform in these positions?

FOR FURTHER EXPLORATION

Visit The Boeing Co. home page at <www.boeing.com> and use the Internet to explore a divisions other than Boeing Satellite Systems. What appear to be the information needs of this division? What IT applications might be useful to its managers? Its employees? Do you think that this division's IS might need to connect with that of any other Boeing divisions? Which ones, and why?

Understanding Principles of Accounting

After reading this chapter, you should be able to:

1. Explain the role of accountants and distinguish between the kinds of work done by *public* and *private accountants.*
2. Discuss the *CPA Vision Project* and explain how the CPA profession is changing.
3. Explain how the following concepts are used in accounting: the *accounting equation* and *double-entry accounting.*
4. Describe the three basic *financial statements* and show how they reflect the activity and financial condition of a business.
5. Explain how computing key *financial ratios* can help in analyzing the financial strengths of a business.
6. Explain some of the special issues facing accountants at firms that do international business.

Why Banks Have to Clean Up Their Transactions

If you're a bank and you think some of your customers aren't coming clean with you, you can't just turn your back. You have to turn them in. Or else. And the "or else" can result in a serious downturn in your business. That's what Charles Schwab Corp.'s U.S. Trust unit found out in 2001 when the company was fined $10 million—one of the largest fines ever levied against a U.S. bank—for not complying with anti–money-laundering regulations. Regarded in the industry as a rock-solid, blue-blood money management firm, U.S. Trust <www.ustrust.com> neither admitted nor denied any wrongdoing as it paid $5 million in fines to both the New York State Banking Department and the Federal Reserve. Regulators also ordered U.S. Trust to improve compliance procedures and develop a better transaction-reporting system for monitoring and reporting currency transactions of more than $10,000, a federal requirement intended to quash money laundering by U.S. bank clients.

Laundering refers to the movement of illegal money. If, for example, you rob a bank of $100,000, you have $100,000 in "dirty" money. If you take the money and buy a $100,000 house, you have an equally valuable asset that isn't tainted by the crime you committed. Big-time laundering usually involves banking transactions, and it can be done by a number of methods, including cash deposits that are later withdrawn worldwide with debit cards. Even simpler is using wire transfers or converting money into easily movable assets (such as gems, stocks, or bonds). You can even launder your money by trading it at inflated

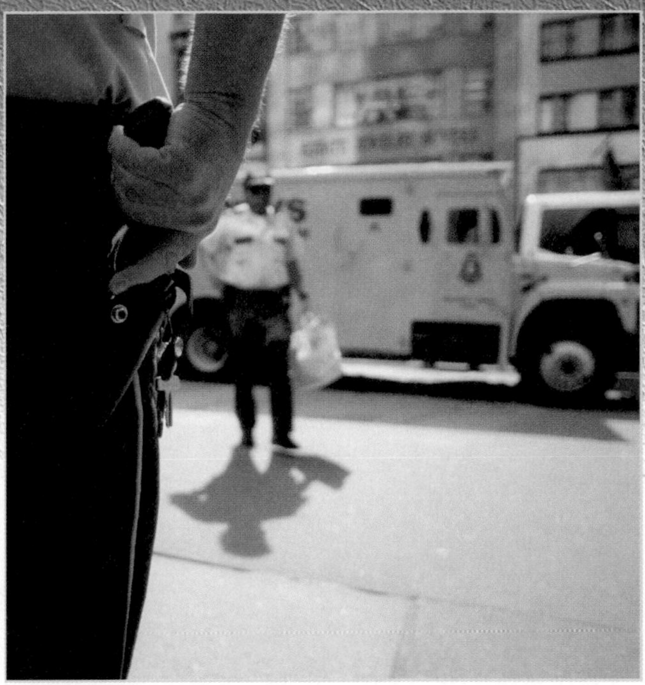

> *"It's a huge math problem."*
>
> —John Day, president of Americas Software, on accounting for criminal bank customers

prices. It is estimated that up to $1.5 trillion gets laundered each year.

Regulators argue that it's not enough for banks like U.S. Trust to enforce the letter of the law. Rather, they must also take steps to detect activities in which customers might be sidestepping the law with deposits or withdrawals of just under the reporting threshold of $10,000. Reports indicate that U.S. Trust allowed numerous customers to make transactions of $9,999 without reporting them to federal authorities. Allegedly, customers also skirted reporting requirements by making a series of smaller withdrawals over a short period instead of a single larger withdrawal that would trigger a report. In fact, regulators want banks to report any suspicious pattern of activities outside the customer's normal pattern of transactions.

So how does U.S. Trust make amends for its violations (besides paying $10 million)? Regulators have ordered the bank to improve its compliance system. That means setting up sure-fire methods for recording and reporting not only currency transactions of more than $10,000 but also any other "potential suspicious or unusual activities" by its customers.

Here are some of the potentially suspicious activities that antilaundering auditors want bankers to watch for:

- Unusual bank account activities such as frequent deposits and withdrawals of funds.
- Large lump-sum payments from abroad.
- Sudden or irregular high volumes of sales and cash deposits by small businesses.
- Purchases of goods and currency at prices significantly above or below market.
- Frequent systematic deposits followed by immediate withdrawals.
- Unexpected check-cashing activity.
- The purchase of large cash value investments, soon followed by heavy borrowing against them.
- Large numbers of $100 bills in cash deposits.
- Sudden high volumes of cash deposits.
- Unusually large transactions—via cash, checks, or money orders—made during a short period of time.

Laundering, however, isn't easy to detect, and effective antilaundering systems can be expensive. Only one in every 2,000 wire transfers involves money laundering. So how can a bank distinguish a criminal transaction from a legitimate one? "It's a huge math problem," says John Day, president of Americas Software in Miami, Florida. "You've got hundreds of thousands, even millions of transactions going through your bank, and you're trying to figure out which ones are the problems." Thus, there is a need for professional help. Forensic accountants—CPAs—scour a financial firm's records for signs of laundering, accumulate evidence to help prosecute offenders, and maintain detection systems to prevent further offenses.

Our opening story continues on page 356

This chapter will introduce you to the work performed by accountants and to the basic financial reports of economic activity that are the primary reason for accounting. As you will see in this chapter, accounting goes hand in hand with information management. In today's complex business environment, the need to manage information efficiently and quickly is crucial. Information can take many forms—information about expenses and assets, information about customers' locations and order patterns, information about supplies and finished goods on hand, information about workers' pay and productivity, information about products in development, and information about competitors and customers.

WHAT IS ACCOUNTING AND WHO USES ACCOUNTING INFORMATION?

Accounting is a comprehensive system for collecting, analyzing, and communicating financial information. It is a system for measuring business performance and translating those measures into information for management decisions. Accounting also uses performance measures to prepare performance reports for owners, the public, and regulatory agencies. To meet these objectives, accountants keep records of such transactions as taxes paid, income received, and expenses incurred. They also analyze the effects of these transactions on particular business activities. By sorting, analyzing, and recording thousands of transactions, accountants can determine how well a business is being managed and how financially strong it is. [1]

accounting
Comprehensive system for collecting, analyzing, and communicating financial information

Bookkeeping, which is sometimes confused with accounting, is just one phase of accounting—the recording of accounting transactions. Accounting is much more comprehensive than bookkeeping because accounting involves more than just the recording of information.

bookkeeping
Recording of accounting transactions

Because businesses engage in many thousands of transactions, ensuring consistent, dependable financial information is mandatory. This is the job of the **accounting system**: an organized procedure for identifying, measuring, recording, and retaining financial information so that it can be used in accounting statements and management reports. The system includes all the people, reports, computers, procedures, and resources for compiling financial transactions. [2]

accounting system
Organized means by which financial information is identified, measured, recorded, and retained for use in accounting statements and management reports

There are numerous users of accounting information:

- *Business managers* use accounting information to set goals, develop plans, set budgets, and evaluate future prospects.
- *Employees and unions* use accounting information to get paid and to plan for and receive such benefits as health care, insurance, vacation time, and retirement pay.
- *Investors and creditors* use accounting information to estimate returns to stockholders, determine a company's growth prospects, and determine whether it is a good credit risk before investing or lending.
- *Tax authorities* use accounting information to plan for tax inflows, determine the tax liabilities of individuals and businesses, and ensure that correct amounts are paid on time.
- *Government regulatory agencies* rely on accounting information to fulfill their duties. The Toronto Stock Exchange in Canada and the Securities and Exchange Commission in the United States require firms to file financial disclosures so that potential investors have valid information about a company's financial status.

WHO ARE ACCOUNTANTS AND WHAT DO THEY DO?

At the head of the accounting system is the **controller**, who manages all the firm's accounting activities. As chief accounting officer, the controller ensures that the accounting system provides the reports and statements needed for planning, controlling, and decision-making activities. This broad range of activities requires different

controller
Person who manages all of a firm's accounting activities (chief accounting officer)

types of accounting specialists. In this section, we begin by distinguishing between the two main fields of accounting: *financial* and *managerial*. Then we discuss the different functions and activities of *certified public accountants* and *private accountants*.

Financial Versus Managerial Accounting

In any company, two fields of accounting (financial and managerial) can be distinguished by the different users they serve. As we have just seen, it is both convenient and accurate to classify users of accounting information as users outside the company and users inside the company. This same distinction allows us to categorize accounting systems as either *financial* or *managerial*. [3]

financial accounting system
Field of accounting concerned with external users of a company's financial information

managerial (or management) accounting system
Field of accounting that serves internal users of a company's financial information

Financial Accounting A firm's **financial accounting system** is concerned with external users of information: consumer groups, unions, stockholders, and government agencies. It prepares and publishes income statements and balance sheets at regular intervals, as well as other financial reports that are published for shareholders and the general public. All of these documents focus on the activities of the company as a whole rather than on individual departments or divisions. [4]

Managerial Accounting In contrast, **managerial** (or **management**) **accounting** serves internal users. Managers at all levels need information to make decisions for their departments, to monitor current projects, and to plan for future activities. Other employees also need accounting information. Engineers, for instance, want to know the costs for materials and production so that they can make product or operations improvements. To set performance goals, salespeople need data on past sales by geographic region. Purchasing agents use information on materials costs to negotiate terms with suppliers.

Certified Public Accountants

certified public accountant (CPA)
Accountant licensed by the state and offering services to the public

Certified public accountants (CPAs) offer accounting services to the public. CPAs are licensed at the state level after passing a three-day written exam prepared by the American Institute of Certified Public Accountants (AICPA), which is the national professional organization of CPAs. The AICPA <www.aicpa.org> also provides technical support to members and discipline in matters of professional ethics.

Professional Practice and the Big 5 Whereas some CPAs work as individual practitioners, many join with other CPAs in partnerships or professional corporations. More than 40,000 CPA firms practice in the United States. However, nearly one-half of

WEB Connection

The AICPA is a national professional association for CPAs with 330,000 members. The organization issues the *AICPA Code of Professional Conduct,* which sets down standards in such areas as "Responsibilities to Clients" and "Independence, Integrity, and Objectivity."

www.aicpa.org

accounting's total revenues in the United States are received by the so-called Big 5 accounting firms: Arthur Andersen <www.arthurandersen.com>, Deloitte & Touche <www.deloitte.com>, Ernst & Young <www.ey.com>, KPMG LLP <www.kpmg.com>, and Price Waterhouse Coopers <www.pwcglobal.com>. In addition to their prominence in the United States, international growth into worldwide accounting operations is a major expansion area for Big 5 firms.

CPA Services Virtually all CPA firms, whether consisting of 10,000 employees in 100 nationwide offices or just one person in a small private facility, provide auditing, tax, and management services. Larger firms earn up to 60 percent of their revenue from auditing services. Consulting services constitute a growth area for larger firms. Smaller firms typically earn most of their income from tax and management services.

Auditing An **audit** examines a company's accounting system to determine whether its financial reports reliably represent its operations. Organizations must normally provide audit reports when applying for loans, selling stock, or when a major restructuring is undertaken. In 2000, for example, an audit report by the accounting firm of Deloitte & Touche revealed a $1 million deficit for the Ann Arbor (Michigan) District Library. The financial losses had accumulated during the three years after the library had separated itself from the local school system. It was caused by the district's faulty automated accounting system, the library's expansion into expensive programs and activities, delays in receiving audit reports, and the failure of library personnel to pay attention to rising costs. Until the audit was completed, the library's true financial condition was unknown. [5]

audit
Systematic examination of a company's accounting system to determine whether its financial reports fairly represent its operations

The auditor must also ensure that the client's accounting system follows **generally accepted accounting principles (GAAP)**: rules and procedures governing the content and form of financial reports. GAAPs are formulated by the Financial Accounting Standards Board (FASB) of the AICPA. [6] By using GAAP, the audit should determine whether a firm has controls to prevent errors and fraud. Ultimately, the auditor will certify whether the client's financial reports comply with GAAP.

generally accepted accounting principles (GAAP)
Accepted rules and procedures governing the content and form of financial reports

Tax Services Tax laws are immensely complex. Tax services thus include assistance not only with tax return preparation but also with tax planning. A CPA's advice can help a business structure (or restructure) operations and investments and perhaps save millions of dollars in taxes. In order to best serve their clients, accountants must stay abreast of changes in tax laws. This is no simple matter: Legislators made more than 70 pages of technical corrections to the 1986 Tax Reform Act before it even became law.

Management Advisory Services When hired as consultants, accounting firms provide **management advisory services** ranging from personal financial planning to planning corporate mergers. Other services include plant layout and design, production scheduling, computer feasibility studies, and accounting system design. Some CPA firms even assist in executive recruitment. On staff at the largest firms are engineers, architects, mathematicians, and psychologists.

management advisory services
Specialized accounting services to help managers resolve a variety of business problems

Noncertified Public Accountants Many accountants choose not to take the CPA exam; others work in the field while preparing to take it or while fulfilling requirements for state certification. Many small businesses, individuals, and even larger firms rely on these noncertified public accountants for income tax preparation, payroll accounting, and financial planning services.

Private Accountants

To ensure integrity in reporting, CPAs are always independent of the firms they audit. As employees of accounting firms, they provide services for many clients. However, many businesses also hire their own salaried employees—**private accountants**—to carry out day-to-day activities.

private accountant
Salaried accountant hired by a business to carry out its day-to-day financial activities

"It's the old story. I was in the middle of a successful acting career when I was bitten by the accounting bug."

Private accountants perform a variety of jobs. An internal auditor at Phillips Petroleum might fly to the North Sea to confirm the accuracy of oil flow meters on offshore drilling platforms. Meanwhile, a supervisor responsible for $2 billion in monthly accounts payable to vendors and employees may travel no farther than the executive suite. Large businesses employ specialized accountants in such areas as budgets, financial planning, internal auditing, payroll, and taxation. In small businesses, a single person may handle all accounting tasks. Most private accountants are management accountants who provide services to support company managers in a variety of activities (marketing, production, engineering, and so forth).

The CPA Vision Project

The CPA Vision Project <www.cpavision.org> is an ambitious, professionwide assessment to see what the future of the accounting profession will be like. [7] A prime reason for the project is a disturbing decline in the number of young people who entered the profession during the 1990s. The growing shortage of talent has forced the profession to rethink its culture and lifestyle. [8] With grassroots participation from practicing CPAs, educators, and industry leaders, the AICPA has undertaken this comprehensive multiyear project to define the role of the accountant in the world economy of the twenty-first century. In recognizing the rapidly changing business world, the project focuses on certain desired results for the profession and identifies the changes that will be needed to accomplish those long-term goals.

Identifying Issues for the Future To begin, the Vision Project has identified key forces, both domestic and global, affecting the profession. Why are fewer students choosing to become CPAs? Technology is replacing many traditional CPA skills, the new borderless business world requires that accountants (like just about everybody else) expand to offer new skills and services, and the perceived value of some traditional accounting services, including auditing, tax preparation, and accounting itself, is declining. In addition, an increasing number of non-CPA competitors are not bound by the accounting profession's code of standards. In considering these forces, the Vision Project has identified the following as the most important issues in the profession's future:

- CPA success will depend on public perceptions of the CPA's abilities and roles.
- CPAs must respond to market needs rather than relying on regulation to keep them in business.
- The market demands more high-value consulting and fewer auditing and accounting services.
- Specialization will be vital.
- CPAs must be conversant in global strategies and global business practices.

IT'S A WIRED WORLD

A Roundabout Look at Conflicting Interests

With all the new dot-com companies popping up, things are looking up for accounting firms. Because all those e-businesses need accounting services—setting up accounting systems, preparing taxes and financial reports, conducting audits—prospects are good for an upsurge of new clients. Or are they? Two factors are getting in the way, one having to do with the lean purses of the dot-coms, and the other with the structure of today's large accounting firms. As a result, accounting firms are running into roadblocks in trying to pursue dot-com clients.

Many dot-coms are short on cash, most of them operating in the red even though prospects may be bright for future earnings. Some of today's financially strapped dot-coms will prosper and become tomorrow's e-commerce giants. Naturally, public accounting firms would like them to become giant clients in need of accounting services for years to come. Price Waterhouse Coopers expects that about half of its consulting revenues will eventually come from e-businesses. Unfortunately, would-be e-giants need accounting services now, including management advisory services to help formulate focused strategies, target desirable markets, and improve operations now, while they're getting started, not later. But they can't pay now.

The answer? Increasingly, accounting firms are accepting equity positions instead of cash payment: In return for its services, the accounting firm becomes part owner of the dot-com. Generally speaking, it's a good arrangement: While the accounting firm gets a new client (and stands to gain future revenues from its ownership position), the dot-com gets timely professional management help without laying out badly needed cash.

But there's a problem: What the accounting firm gains in a present consulting client it may lose in a future auditing client. Public accounting firms are not allowed to make the kind of ownership–investment arrangement described earlier and also provide auditing (or some other financial accounting) services for the same client company. Both the accounting profession and federal regulations frown on the potential conflict of interest. Rules require that auditors have no investment stake in companies they audit. And in fact, it stands to reason that allowing a CPA firm to audit a company in which it has an ownership is an invitation to financial mischief. It would be like asking a bank to audit itself rather than hiring an independent auditor.

Nor do the problems stop here. As part owner, a CPA firm must also steer away from other part owners in the company. Let's say, for example, that a number of other firms, such as a shipping company, an investment firm, a wholesaler, and a computer supplier, also have ownership interests in the same dot-com. The accounting firm must also decline to audit those firms. Again, there is conflict of interest: The accounting firm could make the dot-com's financial position look good in order to burnish its fellow part owners' financial positions.

Therefore, it looks as if the dot-com explosion that seems like such a terrific opportunity for CPA firms may turn out to be much more limited. Currently, the accountant is forced to make a choice: To take on the dot-com as a client for auditing services or as a client for management advisory services? Accountants can't have it both ways. And whatever choice it makes, the accounting firm also has to make sure that its auditors and management consultants know what the others are doing.

Global Forces as Drivers of Change The Vision Project explains how the six categories of global forces shown in Figure 13.1 are driving the profession's reorientation. The wide range of these forces touches on nearly all aspects of the CPA's life—everything from working hours to knowledge requirements to cultural relationships to lifestyle requirements.

Recommendations for Change According to surveys identifying the pertinent issues and forces for change, what needs to be done? The Vision Project indicates that CPAs working in the industry, accounting educators, and accounting professionals must make changes in the ways in which the profession functions. Among the top recommendations for change are the following:

- The profession will be enhanced by adopting a broader focus beyond "numbers" that includes "strategic thinking."

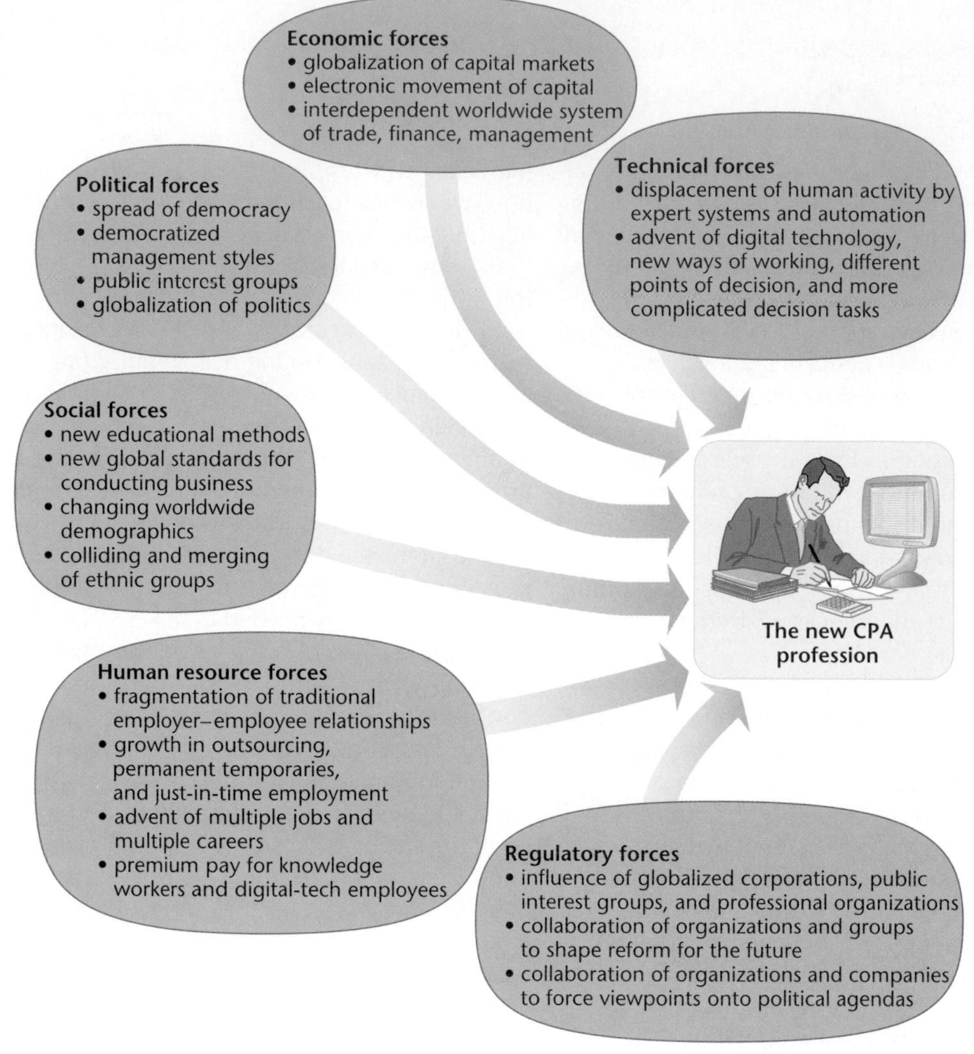
Economic forces
• globalization of capital markets
• electronic movement of capital
• interdependent worldwide system of trade, finance, management
Political forces
• spread of democracy
• democratized management styles
• public interest groups
• globalization of politics
Technical forces
• displacement of human activity by expert systems and automation
• advent of digital technology, new ways of working, different points of decision, and more complicated decision tasks
Social forces
• new educational methods
• new global standards for conducting business
• changing worldwide demographics
• colliding and merging of ethnic groups
The new CPA profession
Human resource forces
• fragmentation of traditional employer–employee relationships
• growth in outsourcing, permanent temporaries, and just-in-time employment
• advent of multiple jobs and multiple careers
• premium pay for knowledge workers and digital-tech employees
Regulatory forces
• influence of globalized corporations, public interest groups, and professional organizations
• collaboration of organizations and groups to shape reform for the future
• collaboration of organizations and companies to force viewpoints onto political agendas

Figure 13.1
Global Forces in the Changing CPA Profession

- The profession will provide more value to society by expanding knowledge, education, and experience.
- CPA education must be revitalized to meet the demands of the future.
- To attract qualified members, the professional culture must increase opportunities for advancement, rewards, and lifestyle preferences.

A New Direction Responses from the many participants in the Vision Project reveal the profession's views of its own future. They are summarized in two categories—*Core Services* and *Core Competencies*—that are designed to shape and guide the CPA profession in the twenty-first century.

Core Services *Core services* refer to the work that the CPA performs. The Vision Project reports a stark departure from the traditional range of accounting activities and strongly recommends a broader perspective that moves into areas that have traditionally remained outside the accounting realm. As you can see in Table 13.1, CPAs will seek to expand their activities with new skills in a variety of business activities that must be integrated for better business performance. Financial planning arguably falls in the realm of financial management and beyond accounting's traditional role of reporting on historical financial performance. The distinction has largely been one of perspective—that is, futuristic outlook (financial planning) versus the historical (financial performance reporting). Most companies, however, agree that they could get a

- *Assurance and Information Integrity*
  A variety of services that improve and assure the quality of information for business activities.
- *Technology*
  Services that utilize technology—new business applications in knowledge management, system security, and new-business practices—to improve business activities.
- *Management Consulting and Performance Management*
  Broad business knowledge and judgment to supply advice on an organization's strategic, operational, and financial performance.
- *Financial Planning*
  Various services—in tax planning, financial transactions, investment portfolio structuring, financial statement analysis—that help clients better understand, interpret, and utilize the full range of financial information.
- *International Business*
  Services that enhance performance in global operations and facilitate global commerce.

Table 13.1
Core Services in Accounting

clearer picture of their competitive health if the two areas were integrated. The accounting profession's movement in this direction will require major commitments of personal and organizational time and resources.

Core Competencies The Vision Project identifies a unique combination of skills, technology, and knowledge—called *core competencies*—that will be necessary for the future CPA. As Table 13.2 shows, those skills go far beyond the ability to "crunch numbers." Rather, they include certain behavioral skills, along with skills in critical thinking and leadership. Indeed, the Vision Project foresees CPAs who combine specialty skills with a broad-based orientation that permit them to communicate more effectively with people in a broad range of business activities.

TOOLS OF THE ACCOUNTING TRADE

All accountants rely on record keeping, either manual or electronic, to enter and track business transactions. Underlying all record-keeping procedures are the two key concepts of accounting: the *accounting equation* and *double-entry accounting*.

- *Strategic and Critical Thinking Skills*
  The accountant can provide competent advice for strategic action by combining data, knowledge, and insight.
- *Communications and Leadership Skills*
  The accountant can exchange information meaningfully in a variety of business situations with effective delivery and interpersonal skills.
- *Focus on the Customer, Client, and Market*
  The accountant can meet the changing needs of clients, customers, and employers better than the competition and can anticipate those needs better than competitors.
- *Skills in Interpreting Converging Information*
  The accountant can interpret new meaning by combining financial and nonfinancial information into a broader understanding that adds more business value.
- *Technology Skills*
  The accountant can use technology to add value to activities performed for employers, customers, and clients.

Table 13.2
Core Competencies in Accounting

The inventory at this Boston-area Volkswagen dealership is among the company's assets: The cars constitute an economic resource because the firm will benefit financially as it sells them. When (and if) they are sold, at the end of the company's accounting period the dealership will convert the cost of the cars as expenses and show them as costs of goods sold.

The Accounting Equation

At various points in the year, accountants use the following equation to balance the data pertaining to financial transactions:

$$\text{Assets} = \text{Liabilities} + \text{Owners' equity}$$

To understand the importance of this equation, we must first understand the terms *assets, liabilities*, and *owners' equity.* [9]

asset
Any economic resource expected to benefit a firm or an individual who owns it

liability
Debt owed by a firm to an outside organization or individual

owners' equity
Amount of money that owners would receive if they sold all of a firm's assets and paid all of its liabilities

Assets and Liabilities

Charm and intelligence are often said to be assets, and a non-swimmer is no doubt a liability on a canoeing trip. Accountants apply these same terms to items with quantifiable value. Thus, an **asset** is any economic resource that is expected to benefit a firm or an individual who owns it. Assets include land, buildings, equipment, inventory, and payments due the company (accounts receivable). A **liability** is a debt that the firm owes to an outside organization or individual.

Owners' Equity

You may also have heard of the "equity" that a homeowner has in a home—that is, the amount of money that could be made by selling the house and paying off the mortgage. Similarly, **owners' equity** is the amount of money that owners would receive if they sold all of a company's assets and paid all of its liabilities. We can rewrite the accounting equation to show this definition:

$$\text{Assets} - \text{Liabilities} = \text{Owners' equity}$$

If a company's assets exceed its liabilities, owners' equity is *positive*: If the company goes out of business, the owners will receive some cash (a gain) after selling assets and paying off liabilities. If liabilities outweigh assets, however, owners' equity is *negative*: Assets are insufficient to pay off all debts. If the company goes out of business, the owners will get no cash and some creditors will not be paid. Owners' equity is a meaningful number to both investors and lenders. For example, before lending money to owners, lenders want to know the amount of owners' equity existing in a business. Owners' equity consists of two sources of capital:

1. The amount that the owners originally invested
2. Profits earned by and reinvested in the company

When a company operates profitably, its assets increase faster than its liabilities. Owners' equity, therefore, will increase if profits are retained in the business instead of paid out as dividends to stockholders. Owners' equity can also increase if owners invest more of their own money to increase assets. However, owners' equity can shrink if the company operates at a loss or if the owners withdraw assets.

Double-Entry Accounting

If your business purchases inventory with cash, you decrease your cash and increase your inventory. Similarly, if you purchase supplies on credit, you increase your supplies and increase your accounts payable. If you invest more money in your business, you increase the company's cash and increase your owners' equity. In other words, *every transaction affects two accounts*. Accountants thus use a **double-entry accounting system** to record the dual effects of financial transactions. [10]

Recording dual effects ensures that the accounting equation always balances. As the term implies, the double-entry system requires at least two bookkeeping entries for each transaction. This practice keeps the accounting equation in balance.

double-entry accounting system
Bookkeeping system that balances the accounting equation by recording the dual effects of every financial transaction

FINANCIAL STATEMENTS

As we noted earlier, the primary purposes of accounting are to summarize the results of a firm's transactions and to issue reports to help managers make informed decisions. Among the most important reports are **financial statements**, which fall into three broad categories—*balance sheets, income statements*, and *statements of cash flows*. [11] We will discuss these three types of financial statements, as well as the function of the budget as an internal financial statement. We will conclude by explaining the most important reporting practices and standards that guide accountants in drawing up financial statements.

financial statement
Any of several types of reports summarizing a company's financial status to aid in managerial decision making

Balance Sheets

Balance sheets supply detailed information about the accounting equation factors: assets, liabilities, and owners' equity. Because they also show a firm's financial condition at one point in time, balance sheets are sometimes called *statements of financial position*. Figure 13.2 shows the balance sheet for a hypothetical wholesaler called Perfect Posters.

balance sheet
Financial statement detailing a firm's assets, liabilities, and owners' equity

Assets As we have seen, an asset is any economic resource that a company owns and from which it can expect to derive some future benefit. From an accounting standpoint, most companies have three types of assets: *current, fixed*, and *intangible*.

Current Assets The **current assets** include cash and assets that can be converted into cash within the following year. They are normally listed in order of **liquidity**: the ease with which they can be converted into cash. Business debts, for example, can usually be satisfied only through payments of cash. A company that needs but cannot generate cash—in other words, a company that is not liquid—may thus be forced to sell assets at sacrifice prices or even go out of business.

By definition, cash is completely liquid. *Marketable securities* purchased as short-term investments are slightly less liquid but can be sold quickly if necessary. Marketable securities include stocks or bonds of other companies, government securities, and money market certificates. There are three other important nonliquid assets held by many companies: *accounts receivable, merchandise inventory*, and *prepaid expenses*.

current asset
Asset that can or will be converted into cash within the following year

liquidity
Ease with which an asset can be converted into cash

Accounts Receivable The **accounts receivable** are amounts due from customers who have purchased goods on credit. Most businesses expect to receive payment

account receivable
Amount due from a customer who has purchased goods on credit

Perfect Posters, INC.
555 RIVERVIEW, CHICAGO, IL 60606

Perfect Posters, Inc.
Balance Sheet
As of December 31, 2001

Assets		
Current Assets:		
Cash		$7,050
Marketable securities		2,300
Accounts receivable	$26,210	
Less: Allowance for doubtful accounts	(650)	25,560
Merchandise inventory		21,250
Prepaid expenses		1,050
Total current assets		**$ 57,210**
Fixed assets:		
Land		18,000
Building	65,000	
Less: Accumulated depreciation	(22,500)	42,500
Equipment	72,195	
Less: Accumulated depreciation	(24,815)	47,380
Total fixed assets		**107,880**
Intangible assets:		
Patents	7,100	
Trademarks	900	
Total intangible assets		**8,000**
Total assets		**$173,090**

Liabilities and Owners' Equity		
Current liabilities:		
Accounts payable	$16,315	
Wages payable	3,700	
Taxes payable	1,920	
Total current liabilities		**$ 21,935**
Long-term liabilities:		
Notes payable, 8% due 2002	10,000	
Bonds payable, 9% due 2004	30,000	
Total long-term liabilities		**40,000**
Total liabilities		**$ 61,935**
Owners' Equity:		
Common stock, $5 par	40,000	
Additional paid-in capital	15,000	
Retained earnings	56,155	
Total owners' equity		**111,155**
Total liabilities and owners' equity		**$173,090**

Perfect Posters' balance sheet as of December 31, 2001. Perfect Posters' balance sheet shows clearly that the firm's total assets equal its total liabilities and owners' equity.

Figure 13.2
Perfect Posters' Balance Sheet

within 30 days of a sale. In our hypothetical example, the entry labeled *Less: Allowance for doubtful accounts* in Figure 13.2 indicates $650 in receivables that Perfect Posters does not expect to collect. Total accounts receivable assets are decreased accordingly.

merchandise inventory
Cost of merchandise that has been acquired for sale to customers and is still on hand

prepaid expense
Expense, such as prepaid rent, that is paid before the upcoming period in which it is due

fixed asset
Asset with long-term use or value, such as land, buildings, and equipment

depreciation
Process of distributing the cost of an asset over its life

Merchandise Inventory Following accounts receivable on the Perfect Posters' balance sheet is **merchandise inventory**—the cost of merchandise that has been acquired for sale to customers and is still on hand. [12] Accounting for the value of inventories on the balance sheet is difficult because inventories are flowing in and out throughout the year. Therefore, assumptions must be made about which ones were sold and which ones remain in storage.

Prepaid Expenses The **prepaid expenses** include supplies on hand and rent paid for the period to come. They are assets because they have been paid for and are available to the company. In all, Perfect Posters' current assets as of December 31, 2001, totaled $57,210.

Fixed Assets The next major classification on the balance sheet is usually **fixed assets.** Items in this category have long-term use or value (for example, land, buildings, and equipment). As buildings and equipment wear out or become obsolete, their value decreases. To reflect decreasing value, accountants use **depreciation** to spread the cost of an asset over the years of its useful life. Depreciation means calculating an asset's useful life in years, dividing its worth by that many years, and sub-

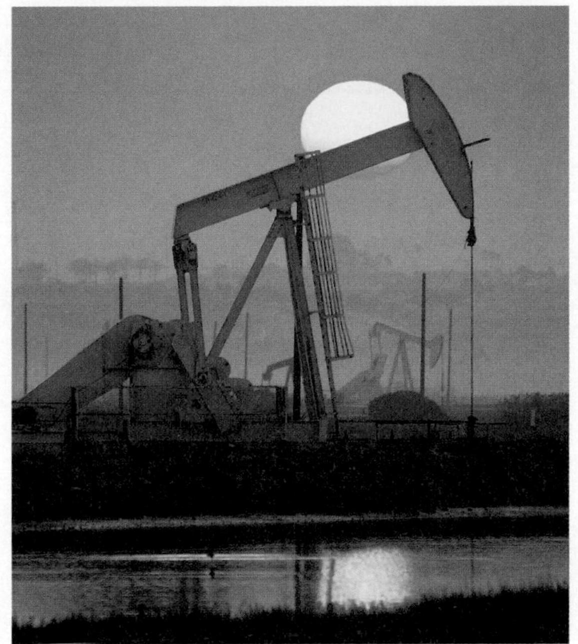

Because equipment such as this oil rig is useful or valuable for a fairly long period of time, it constitutes a fixed asset. Over time, however, it will decrease in efficiency or even become obsolete. In other words, it will depreciate *because it will no longer fill the company's needs as fully as it did originally. Its owners will be allowed to calculate the rig's value over the span of its useful life and convert its per-year cost into a depreciation expense.*

tracting the resulting amount each year. Each year, therefore, the asset's remaining value decreases on the books. In Figure 13.2, Perfect Posters shows fixed assets of $107,880 after depreciation.

Intangible Assets Although their worth is hard to set, **intangible assets** have monetary value. Intangible assets usually include the cost of obtaining rights or privileges such as patents, trademarks, copyrights, and franchise fees. **Goodwill** is the amount paid for an existing business beyond the value of its other assets. A purchased firm, for example, may have a particularly good reputation or location. [13]

Perfect Posters has no goodwill assets; however, it does own trademarks and patents for specialized storage equipment. These are intangible assets worth $8,000. Larger companies, of course, have intangible assets that are worth much more.

Liabilities Like assets, liabilities are often separated into different categories. **Current liabilities** are debts that must be paid within one year. These include **accounts payable**: unpaid bills to suppliers for materials as well as wages and taxes that must be paid in the coming year. Perfect Posters has current liabilities of $21,935.

Long-term liabilities are debts that are not due for at least a year. These normally represent borrowed funds on which the company must pay interest. Perfect Posters' long-term liabilities are $40,000.

Owners' Equity The final section of the balance sheet in Figure 13.2 shows owners' equity broken down into *common stock, paid-in capital*, and *retained earnings*. When Perfect Posters was formed, the declared legal value of its common stock was $5 per share. By law, this $40,000 ($5 × 8,000 shares) cannot be distributed as dividends. **Paid-in capital** is additional money invested in the firm by its owners. Perfect Posters has $15,000 in paid-in capital.

Retained earnings are net profits minus dividend payments to stockholders. Retained earnings accumulate when profits, which could have been distributed to stockholders, are kept instead for use by the company. At the close of 2001, Perfect Posters had retained earnings of $56,155. [14]

intangible asset
Nonphysical asset, such as a patent or trademark, that has economic value in the form of expected benefit

goodwill
Amount paid for an existing business above the value of its other assets

current liability
Debt that must be paid within the year

accounts payable
Current liabilities consisting of bills owed to suppliers, plus wages and taxes due within the upcoming year

long-term liability
Debt that is not due for more than one year

paid-in capital
Additional money, above proceeds from stock sale, paid directly to a firm by its owners

retained earnings
Earnings retained by a firm for its use rather than paid as dividends

Perfect Posters, INC.
555 RIVERVIEW, CHICAGO, IL 60606

Perfect Posters, Inc.
Income Statement
Year Ended December 31, 2001

Revenues (gross sales)			$256,425
Cost of goods sold:			
Merchandise inventory, January 1, 2001	$22,380		
Merchandise purchases during year	103,635		
Goods available for sale		$126,015	
Less: Merchandise inventory December 31, 2000	21, 250		
Cost of goods sold			104,765
Gross profit			151,660
Operating expenses:			
Selling and repackaging expenses:			
Salaries and wages	49,750		
Advertising	6,380		
Depreciation—warehouse and repackaging equipment	3,350		
Total selling and repackaging expenses		59,480	
Administrative expenses:			
Salaries and wages	55,100		
Supplies	4,150		
Utilities	3,800		
Depreciation—office equipment	3,420		
Interest expense	2,900		
Miscellaneous expenses	1,835		
Total administrative expenses		71,205	
Total operating expenses			130,685
Operating income (income before taxes)			20,975
Income taxes			8,390
Net income			$12,585

Figure 13.3
Perfect Posters' Income Statement

Perfect Posters' income statement for year ended December 31, 2001. The final entry on the income statement, the bottom line, reports the firm's profit or loss.

income statement (or profit-and-loss statement)
Financial statement listing a firm's annual revenues and expenses so that a bottom line shows annual profit or loss

revenues
Funds that flow into a business from the sale of goods or services

cost of goods sold
Total cost of obtaining materials for making the products sold by a firm during the year

gross profit (or gross margin)
Revenues obtained from goods sold minus cost of goods sold

Income Statements

The **income statement** is sometimes called a **profit-and-loss statement** because its description of revenues and expenses results in a figure showing the firm's annual profit or loss. In other words,

Revenues – Expenses = Profit (or Loss)

Popularly known as "the bottom line," profit or loss is probably the most important figure in any business enterprise. Figure 13.3 shows the 2001 income statement for Perfect Posters, whose bottom line that year was $12,585. Like the balance sheet, the income statement is divided into three major categories: *revenues, cost of goods sold,* and *operating expenses.*

Revenues When a law firm receives $250 for preparing a will or when a supermarket collects $65 from a customer buying groceries, both are receiving **revenues:** the funds that flow into a business from the sale of goods or services. In 2001, Perfect Posters reported revenues of $256,425 from the sale of art prints and other posters.

Cost of Goods Sold In Perfect Posters' income statement, the **cost of goods sold** category shows the costs of obtaining materials to make the products sold during the year. Perfect Posters began 2001 with posters valued at $22,380. Over the year, it spent another $103,635 to purchase posters. During 2001, then, the company had $126,015 worth of merchandise available to sell. By the end of the year, it had sold all but $21,250 of those posters, which remained as merchandise inventory. The cost of obtaining the goods sold by the firm was, thus, $104,765.

Gross Profit (or Gross Margin) To calculate **gross profit** (or **gross margin**), subtract cost of goods sold from revenues. Perfect Posters' gross profit in 2001 was $151,660

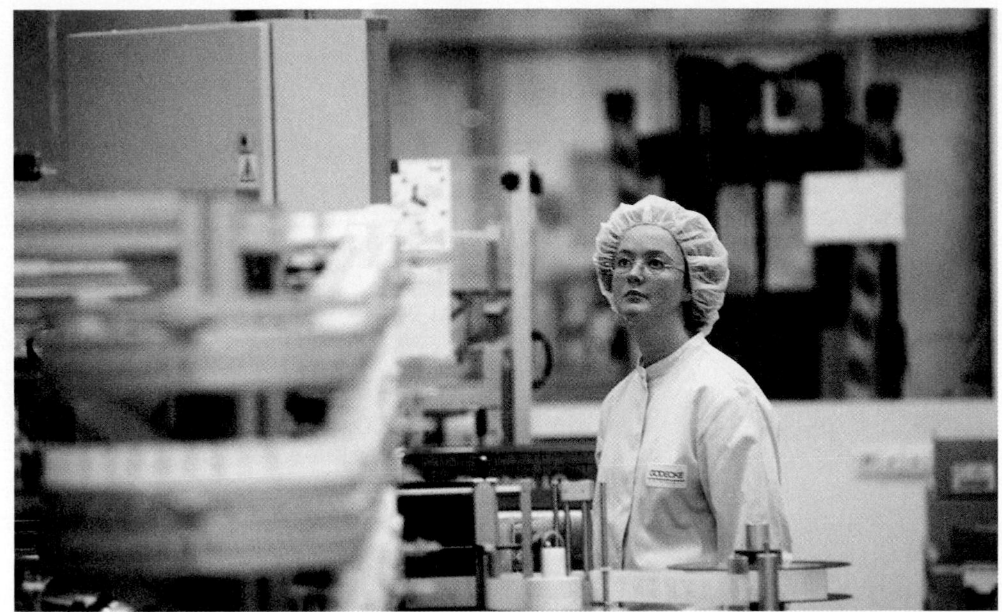

At the end of its accounting period, this pharmaceuticals company will subtract the cost of making the goods that it sold from the revenues it received from the buyers of those goods. The difference will be its gross profit (or gross margin). Note that cost of goods sold does not include the firm's operating expenses, including such selling expenses as advertising and sales commissions. In part, profit margins in the pharmaceuticals industry are high because they do not account for high selling expenses.

($256,425 – $104,765). Expressed as a percentage of sales, gross profit is 59.1 percent ($151,660 / $256,425).

Gross profit percentages vary widely across industries. In retailing, Home Depot <www.homedepot.com> reports a gross profit percentage of 30 percent. In manufacturing, Harley-Davidson <www.harley-davidson.com> reports 34 percent, and in the pharmaceutical industry, American Home Products <www.ahp.com> reports 75 percent. For companies with low gross margins, product costs are a big expense. If a company has a high gross margin, it probably has low cost of goods sold but high selling and administrative expenses.

Operating Expenses In addition to costs directly related to acquiring goods, every company has general expenses ranging from erasers to the president's salary. Like cost of goods sold, **operating expenses** are resources that must flow out of a company for it to earn revenues. As you can see from Figure 13.3, Perfect Posters had 2001 operating expenses of $130,685. This figure consists of $59,480 in selling and repackaging expenses and $71,205 in administrative expenses.

operating expenses
Costs, other than the cost of goods sold, incurred in producing a good or service

Selling expenses result from activities related to selling the firm's goods or services. These may include salaries for the sales force, delivery costs, and advertising expenses. General and administrative expenses, such as management salaries, insurance expenses, and maintenance costs, are expenses related to the general management of the company.

Operating and Net Income Sometimes managers must determine **operating income**, which compares the gross profit from business operations against operating expenses. This calculation for Perfect Posters ($151,660 – $130,685) reveals an operating income, or income before taxes, of $20,975. Subtracting income taxes from operating income ($20,975 – $8,390) reveals **net income** (also called **net profit** or **net earnings**). In 2001, Perfect Posters' net income was $12,585.

operating income
Gross profit minus operating expenses

net income (or **net profit** or **net earnings**)
Gross profit minus operating expenses and income taxes

Statements of Cash Flows

Some companies prepare only balance sheets and income statements. However, the Securities and Exchange Commission <www.sec.gov> also requires all firms whose stock is publicly traded to issue a third report: a **statement of cash flows**.[15] This statement describes a company's yearly cash receipts and cash payments. It shows the effects on cash of three business activities:

statement of cash flows
Financial statement describing a firm's yearly cash receipts and cash payments

- *Cash flows from operations.* This part of the statement is concerned with the firm's main operating activities: the cash transactions involved in buying and selling goods and services. It reveals how much of the year's profits result from the firm's main line of business (for example, Jaguar's sales of automobiles) rather than from secondary activities (for example, licensing fees a clothing firm paid to Jaguar for using the Jaguar logo on shirts).
- *Cash flows from investing.* This section reports net cash used in or provided by investing. It includes cash receipts and payments from buying and selling stocks, bonds, property, equipment, and other productive assets.
- *Cash flows from financing.* The final section reports net cash from all financing activities. It includes cash inflows from borrowing or issuing stock as well as outflows for payment of dividends and repayment of borrowed money.

The overall change in cash from these three sources provides information to lenders and investors. When creditors and stockholders know how firms obtained and used their funds during the course of a year, it is easier for them to interpret the year-to-year changes in the firm's balance sheet and income statement.

The Budget: An Internal Financial Statement

In addition to financial statements, managers need other types of accounting information to aid in internal planning, controlling, and decision making. Probably the most crucial internal financial statement is the **budget**.[16] A budget is a detailed statement of estimated receipts and expenditures for a period of time in the future. Although that period is usually one year, some companies also prepare budgets for three- or five-year periods, especially when considering major capital expenditures.

budget
Detailed statement of estimated receipts and expenditures for a period of time in the future

Budgets are also useful for keeping track of weekly or monthly performance. Procter & Gamble evaluates all of its business units monthly by comparing actual financial results with monthly budgeted amounts. Discrepancies in actual versus budget totals signal potential problems and initiate action to get financial performance back on track.

Although the accounting staff coordinates the budget process, it requires input from many people in the company regarding proposed activities, needed resources, and input sources. Figure 13.4 is a sample sales budget. In preparing such a budget, the accounting department must obtain from the sales group both its projections for units

This concession stand at Dodger Stadium is operated by the Los Angeles Dodgers Inc. <www.dodgers.com> and sells products manufactured largely by members of the Sporting Goods Manufacturers Association (SGMA) <www.sportlink.com>, who make sports apparel, athletic footwear, and sporting equipment. Much of the merchandise on sale here is licensed from Major League Baseball Properties Inc. <www.mlb.com>, which distributes licensing revenues to the sport's 30 franchises. The MLB and World Series logos are assets of MLB Properties, while team logos and uniform designs are assets of the respective teams. In either case, sales of licensed products are treated as cash flows from operations.

Perfect Posters, INC.
555 RIVERVIEW, CHICAGO, IL 60606

Perfect Posters, Inc.
Sales Budget
First Quarter, 2002

	January	February	March	Quarter
Budgeted sales (units)	7,500	6,000	6,500	20,000
Budgeted selling price per unit	$3.50	$3.50	$3.50	$3.50
Budgeted sales revenue	$ 26,250	$ 21,000	$ 22,750	$ 70,000
Expected cash receipts:				
From December sales	$26,210[a]			$26,210
From January sales	17,500[b]	$8,750		26,250
From February sales		14,000	$7,000	21,000
From March sales			15,200	15,200
Total cash receipts:	$ 43,710	$ 22,750	$ 22,200	$ 88,660

[a]This cash from December sales represents a collection of the accounts receivable appearing on the December 31, 2001, balance sheet.
[b]The company estimates that two-thirds of each month's sales revenues will result in cash receipts during the same month. The remaining one-third is collected during the following month.

Figure 13.4
Perfect Posters' Sales Budget

to be sold and expected expenses for each quarter of the coming year. Accountants then draw up the final budget, and throughout the year, the accounting department compares the budget to actual expenditures and revenues in the sales group.

Reporting Standards and Practices

Accountants follow numerous standard reporting practices and principles when they prepare external reports, including financial statements. The common language dictated by standard practices is designed to give external users confidence in the accuracy and meaning of the information in any financial statement. Spelled out in great detail in GAAP, these principles cover a wide range of issues, such as when to recognize revenues from operations, the so-called *matching* of revenues and expenses, and full public disclosure of financial information to the public. Without agreed-upon practices in these and many other accounting categories, users of financial statements would be unable to compare financial information from different companies and thus misunderstand—or be led to misconstrue—a given company's true financial status.

Revenue Recognition As we noted earlier, revenues are funds that flow into a business as a result of its operating activities during the accounting period. *Revenue recognition* is the formal recording and reporting of revenues in the financial statements.[17] Although any firm earns revenues continuously as it makes sales, earnings are not reported until the earnings cycle is completed. This cycle is complete under two conditions:

1. The sale is complete and the product has been delivered.
2. The sale price to the customer has been collected or is collectable (accounts receivable).

The completion of the earning cycle determines the timing for revenue recognition in the firm's financial statements. Revenues are recorded for the accounting period in which sales are completed and collectable (or collected). This practice assures the reader that the statement gives a fair comparison of what was gained for the resources that were given up.

Matching Net income is calculated by subtracting expenses from revenues. The matching principle states that expenses will be matched with revenues to determine net income for an accounting period.[18] Why is this principle important? It permits the user of the statement to see how much net gain resulted from the assets that had to be given up in order to generate revenues during the period covered in the statement. Consequently, when we match revenue recognition with expense recognition, we get net income for the period.

Consider the hypothetical case of Little Red Wagon Co. Let's see what happens when the books are kept in two different ways:

1. Revenue recognition is matched with expense recognition to determine net income when the earnings cycle is *completed* (the correct method).
2. Revenue recognition occurs *before* the earnings cycle is completed (an incorrect method).

Suppose that 500 red wagons are produced and delivered to customers at a sales price of $20 each during the year 2000. In the next year, 600 red wagons are produced and delivered. In part (A) of Table 13.3, the correct matching method has been used: Revenues are recorded for the accounting period in which sales are completed and collectable from customers, as are the expenses of producing and delivering them. The revenues from sales are matched against the expenses of completing them. By using the matching principle, we see clearly how much better off the company is at the end of each accounting period as a result of that period's operations: It earned $2,000 net income for the first year and did even better in 2001.

In part (B) of the table, revenue recognition and the matching principle have been violated. Certain activities of the two accounting periods are disguised and mixed together rather than being separated for each period. The result is a distorted performance report that incorrectly shows that 2000 was a better year than 2001. Here's what Red Wagon's accountants did wrong: The sales department sold 200 red wagons (with revenues of $4,000) to a customer late in year 2000. Those *revenues* are included in the $14,000 for year 2000. But because the 200 wagons were produced and delivered to the customer in year 2001, the *expenses* are recorded, as in (A), for year 2001. The result is a distorted picture of operations: It looks as if expenses for 2001 are out of line for such a low sales level, and it looks as if expenses (as compared to revenues) were kept under better control during 2000. The firm's accountants violated the matching principle by ignoring *the period during which the earnings cycle was completed.* Although $4,000 in sales of wagons occurred in 2000, the earnings cycle for

Table 13.3

Revenue Recognition and the Matching Principle

(A) THE CORRECT METHOD REVEALS EACH ACCOUNTING PERIOD'S ACTIVITIES AND RESULTS

	Year Ended December 31, 2000	Year Ended December 31, 2001
Revenues	$10,000	$12,000
Expenses	8,000	9,000
Net income	2,000	3,000

(B) THE INCORRECT METHOD DISGUISES EACH ACCOUNTING PERIOD'S ACTIVITIES AND RESULTS

	Year Ended December 31, 2000	Year Ended December 31, 2001
Revenue	$14,000	$8,000
Expenses	8,000	9,000
Net income	6,000	(1,000)

those wagons is not completed until they were produced and delivered, which occurred in 2001. Accordingly, both the revenues and expenses for those 200 wagons should have been reported in the same period—namely, in 2001, as was reported in part (A). There we can see clearly what was gained and what was lost on activities that were completed in an *accounting period*. By requiring this practice, the matching principle provides consistency in reporting and avoids financial distortions.

Full Disclosure Full disclosure means that financial statements should include not just numbers but also interpretations and explanations by management so that external users can better understand information contained in the statements. Because they know more about inside events than outsiders, management prepares additional useful information that explains certain events or transactions or discloses the circumstances underlying certain financial results.

ANALYZING FINANCIAL STATEMENTS

Financial statements present a great deal of information, but what does it all mean? How, for example, can statements help investors decide what stock to buy or help managers decide whether to extend credit? Statements provide data, which can in turn be applied to various ratios (comparative numbers). These ratios can then be used to analyze the financial health of one or more companies. They can also be used to check a firm's progress by comparing current with past statements. [19]

Ratios are normally grouped into three major classifications:

- **Solvency ratios**, both short- and long-term, estimate risk.
- **Profitability ratios** measure potential earnings.
- **Activity ratios** reflect management's use of assets.

Depending on the decisions to be made, a user may apply none, some, or all the ratios in a particular classification.

solvency ratio
Financial ratio, either short- or long-term, for estimating the risk in investing in a firm

profitability ratio
Financial ratio for measuring a firm's potential earnings

activity ratio
Financial ratio for evaluating management's use of a firm's assets

Short-Term Solvency Ratios

In the short run, a company's survival depends on its ability to pay its immediate debts. Such payments require cash. Short-term solvency ratios measure a company's relative liquidity and thus its ability to pay immediate debts. The higher a firm's **liquidity ratios**, then, the lower the risk involved for investors. The most commonly used liquidity ratio is the current ratio.

liquidity ratio
Solvency ratio measuring a firm's ability to pay its immediate debts

Current Ratio The most commonly used liquidity ratio is the current ratio, which has been called the "banker's ratio" because it concerns a firm's creditworthiness. The **current ratio** measures a company's ability to meet current obligations out of current assets. It thus reflects a firm's ability to generate cash to meet obligations through the normal, orderly process of selling inventories and collecting accounts receivable. It is calculated by dividing current assets by current liabilities.

current ratio
Solvency ratio that determines a firm's creditworthiness by measuring its ability to pay current liabilities

As a rule, a current ratio is satisfactory if it is 2:1 or higher—that is, if current assets more than double current liabilities. A smaller ratio may indicate that a company will have difficulty paying its bills. Note, however, that a larger ratio may imply that assets are not being used productively and should be invested elsewhere.

How does Perfect Posters measure up? Look again at the balance sheet in Figure 13.2. Judging from its current assets and current liabilities at the end of 2001, we see that

$$\frac{\text{Current assets}}{\text{Current liabilities}} = \frac{\$57,210}{\$21,935} = 2.61$$

How does Perfect Posters' ratio compare with those of other companies? Not bad: It's lower than O'Reilly Automotive <www.oreillyauto.com> (2.94) and higher than those of Gillette <www.gillette.com> (1.56), Cisco Systems <www.cisco.com> (2.14), and Starwood Hotels & Resorts Worldwide <www.sheraton.com> (0.23). Although Perfect Posters may be holding too much uninvested cash, it looks like a good credit risk.

Working Capital A related measure is **working capital**: the difference between the firm's current assets and its current liabilities. Working capital indicates the firm's ability to pay off short-term debts (liabilities) that it owes to outsiders. At the end of 2001, Perfect Posters' working capital was \$35,275 (that is, \$57,210 − \$21,935). Because current liabilities must be paid off within one year, current assets are more than enough to meet current obligations.

working capital
Difference between a firm's current assets and current liabilities

Long-Term Solvency Ratios

To survive in the long run, a company must be able to meet both its short-term (current) debts and its long-term liabilities. These latter debts usually involve interest payments. A firm that cannot meet them is in danger of collapse or takeover—a risk that makes creditors and investors quite cautious. The 1998 Asian financial crisis was fueled by a loss of confidence by investors in large firms in Japan and Korea that could not meet their long-term cash obligations.

debt ratio
Solvency ratio measuring a firm's ability to meet its long-term debts

debt-to-owners' equity ratio (or debt-to-equity ratio)
Solvency ratio describing the extent to which a firm is financed through borrowing

debt
A firm's total liabilities

leverage
Ability to finance an investment through borrowed funds

Debt-to-Owners' Equity Ratio To measure the risk that a company may encounter this problem, we use the long-term solvency ratios called **debt ratios**. The most commonly used debt ratio is the **debt-to-owners' equity ratio** (or **debt-to-equity ratio**), which describes the extent to which a firm is financed through borrowed money. It is calculated by dividing **debt**—total liabilities—by owners' equity.

This ratio is commonly used to compare a given company's status with industry averages. For example, companies with debt-to-equity ratios above 1 are probably relying too much on debt. Such firms may find themselves owing so much debt that they lack the income needed to meet interest payments or to repay borrowed money.

In the case of Perfect Posters, we can see from the balance sheet in Figure 13.2 that the debt-to-equity ratio works out as follows:

$$\frac{\text{Debt}}{\text{Owners' equity}} = \frac{\$61,935}{\$111,155} = 0.56$$

Leverage Note that a fairly high debt-to-equity ratio may sometimes be not only acceptable but also desirable. Borrowing funds provides **leverage**: the ability to make otherwise unaffordable purchases. In *leveraged buyouts* (*LBOs*), firms have willingly taken on sometimes huge debt in order to buy out other companies. When the purchased company allows the buying company to earn profits above the cost of the borrowed funds, leveraging makes sound financial sense, even if it raises the buyer's debt-to-equity ratio. Unfortunately, many buyouts have fallen into financial trouble when actual profits dropped short of anticipated levels or when rising rates increased interest payments on the debt acquired by the buyer.

Profitability Ratios

Although it is important to know that a company is solvent in both the long and the short term, safety or risk alone is not an adequate basis for investment decisions. Investors also want some measure of the returns they can expect. *Return on equity* and *earnings per share* are two commonly used profitability ratios.

return on equity
Profitability ratio measuring income earned for each dollar invested

Return on Equity Owners are interested in the net income earned by a business for each dollar invested. **Return on equity** measures this performance by dividing net income (recorded in the income statement, Figure13.3) by total owners' equity (recorded in the balance sheet, Figure13.2). [20] For Perfect Posters, the return-on-equity ratio in 2001 can be calculated as follows:

$$\frac{\text{Net income}}{\text{Total owners' equity}} = \frac{\$12,585}{\$111,155} = 11.3\%$$

Is this figure good or bad? There is no set answer. If Perfect Posters' ratio for 2001 is higher than in previous years, owners and investors should be encouraged. But if 11.3 percent is lower than the ratios of other companies in the same industry, they should be concerned.

This Wards store in Chicago was one of 250 nationwide that closed its doors after Montgomery Wards filed for bankruptcy in December 2000. Ward executives cited falling revenue in a weak retailing economy, as sales increased by 2 percent for the year instead of the company's projected 9 percent. Analysts were quick to point to stiff competition from larger, more efficient retailers, such as Wal-Mart and Target. In fact, on the basis of a 9.5-percent increase for the same year, Minneapolis-based Target Corp. <www.target.com> *quickly announced plans to leverage a $700 million purchase and conversion of 35 closed Wards stores across the country.*

Earnings per Share Defined as net income divided by the number of shares of common stock outstanding, **earnings per share** determines the size of the dividend that a company can pay its shareholders. Investors use this ratio to decide whether to buy or sell a company's stock. As the ratio gets higher, the stock value increases, because investors know that the firm can better afford to pay dividends. Naturally, stock will lose market value if the latest financial statements report a decline in earnings per share. For Perfect Posters, we can use the net income total from the income statement in Figure 13.3 to calculate earnings per share as follows:

earnings per share
Profitability ratio measuring the size of the dividend that a firm can pay shareholders

$$\frac{\text{Net income}}{\text{Number of common shares outstanding}} = \frac{\$12{,}585}{8{,}000} = \$1.57 \text{ per share}$$

As a baseline for comparison, note that Gucci's <www.gucci.com> recent earnings were $3.31 per share. The Phillips Petroleum Company <www.phillips66.com> earned $7.26.

Activity Ratios

The efficiency with which a firm uses resources is linked to profitability. As a potential investor, then, you want to know which company gets more mileage from its resources. Activity ratios measure this efficiency. For example, say that two firms use the same amount of resources or assets. If Firm A generates greater profits or sales, it is more efficient and, thus, has a better activity ratio.

Inventory Turnover Ratio Certain specific measures can be used to explain how one firm earns greater profits than another. One of the most important is the **inventory turnover ratio**, which measures the average number of times that inventory is sold and restocked during the year—that is, how quickly it is produced and sold.[21] First, you need to know your *average inventory*: the typical amount of inventory on hand during the year. You can calculate average inventory by adding end-of-year inventory to beginning-of-year inventory and dividing by 2. You can now find your inventory turnover ratio, which is expressed as the cost of goods sold divided by average inventory:

inventory turnover ratio
Activity ratio measuring the average number of times that inventory is sold and restocked during the year

$$\frac{\text{Cost of goods sold}}{\text{Average inventory}} = \frac{\text{Cost of goods sold}}{(\text{Beginning inventory} + \text{Ending inventory})/2}$$

A high inventory turnover ratio means efficient operations: Because a smaller amount of investment is tied up in inventory, the company's funds can be put to work elsewhere to earn greater returns. However, inventory turnover must be compared with both prior years and industry averages. An inventory turnover rate of 5, for example, might be excellent for an auto supply store, but it would be disastrous for a supermarket, where a rate of about 15 is common. Rates can also vary within a company that markets a variety of products. To calculate Perfect Posters' inventory turnover ratio for 2001, we take the merchandise inventory figures for the income statement in Figure13.3. The ratio can be expressed as follows:

$$\frac{\$104{,}765}{(\$22{,}380 + \$21{,}250)/2} = 4.8 \text{ times}$$

In other words, new merchandise replaces old merchandise every 76 days (365 days/4.8). The 4.8 ratio is below the average of 7.0 for comparable wholesaling operations, indicating that the business is slightly inefficient.

INTERNATIONAL ACCOUNTING

More U.S. companies are buying and selling goods and services in other countries. Coca-Cola and Boeing receive large portions of their operating revenues from sales in many countries around the globe. Conversely, firms such as Toastmaster Inc. buy components for electric appliances from suppliers in Asia. Retailers such as Sears and Kmart buy merchandise from other countries for merchandising in the United States. In addition, more and more companies own subsidiaries in other countries. Obviously, accounting for foreign transactions involves some special procedures. One of the most basic is translating the values of the currencies of different countries.

Foreign Currency Exchange

foreign currency exchange rate
Value of a nation's currency as determined by market forces

A unique consideration in international accounting is the value of currencies and their exchange rates. [22] As we saw in Chapter 2, the value of any country's currency is subject to occasional change. Political and economic conditions, for instance, affect the stability of a nation's currency and its value relative to the currencies of other countries. Whereas the Swiss franc has a long history of stability, the Brazilian real has a history of instability.

As it is traded each day around the world, any currency's value is determined by market forces: what buyers are willing to pay for it. The resulting values are called **foreign currency exchange rates.** How volatile are such rates? Table 13.4 shows the changes in exchange rates for some foreign currencies during a one-year period. Each table entry shows the U.S. dollar value of a unit of that nation's currency. For example, one French franc was worth 0.173 U.S. dollars in January 2000. When a nation's cur-

Its inventory turnover ratio measures the average number of times that a store sells and restocks its inventory in one year. Obviously, the higher the ratio, the more products that are sold and the more company funds that are free to be invested as needed. Supermarkets—even upscale outlets like this Whole Foods Market <www.wholefoodsmarket.com> in New York City—must have a much higher turnover ratio than, say, auto-supply or toy stores. In almost all retail stores, however, inventory turnover must be considered when managers assign shelf space: Products with the highest ratios get the spaces that generate the most customer traffic and sales.

Country	Monetary Unit	Dollar Value January 31, 1999	Dollar Value January 31, 2000	% Change in Value
Canada	dollar	0.6900	0.6600	−4.3
China	yuan	0.1200	0.1200	0.0
France	franc	0.1480	0.1730	+16.9
Japan	yen	0.0093	0.0086	−7.5
Switzerland	franc	0.6000	0.7100	+18.3

Table 13.4
Foreign Currency Exchange Rates

rency becomes unstable—that is, when its value changes frequently—it is regarded as a *weak currency*. The value of the Brazilian real fluctuated between 0.40 and 0.93—a variation range of 132 percent in U.S. dollars—during the period from 1997 to 2001. On the other hand, the Swiss franc is said to be a *strong currency* because its value historically rises or holds steady in comparison to the U.S. dollar. As exchange rate changes occur, they must be considered by accountants when recording a firm's international transactions. They will have an impact, perhaps profound, on the amount that a firm pays for foreign purchases and the amount it gains from sales to foreign buyers.

International Transactions

International purchases, sales on credit, and accounting for foreign subsidiaries all involve accounting transactions that include currency exchange rates. When a U.S. company called Village Wine and Cheese Shops imports Bordeau wine from a French company called Pierre Bourgeois, its accountant must be sure that Village's books reflect its true costs. The amount owed to Pierre Bourgeois changes daily along with the exchange rate between francs and dollars. Thus, our accountant must identify the actual rate on the day that payment in francs is made so that the correct U.S. dollar cost of the purchased wine is recorded.

International Accounting Standards

Professional accounting groups of about 80 countries are members of the International Accounting Standards Board (IASB) <www.iasb.org.uk>, which is trying to eliminate differences in financial reporting across countries. [23] Bankers, investors, and managers would like to see financial reporting that is comparable from country to country and across all firms regardless of home nation. Standardization is occurring in some areas but is far from universal. The financial statements required by the IASB, for example, include an income statement, a balance sheet, and statement of cash flows similar to those issued by U.S. accountants. International standards, however, do not require a uniform format, and variety abounds.

WEB Connection

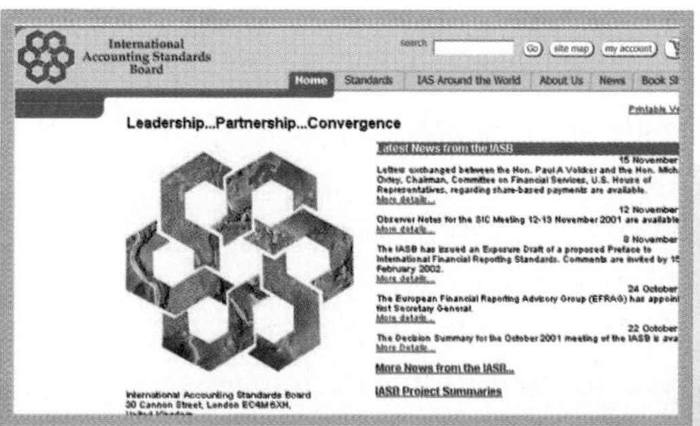

The IASB was founded in 1973, and its current membership consists of more than 140 professional accounting organizations from more than 100 nations. Its Web site publishes its body of standards and interpretations, as well as a wealth of information about accounting on an international scale. To find out why the IASB has undertaken its various projects, log on to its Web site.

www.iasb.org.uk

Continued from page 334

Securing Exchanges

Money laundering is a growth industry, and it's being fueled on an international scale by technology. It generally harms society by hiding and helping financial crime, resulting in higher costs for insurance, higher tax payments, higher interest rates on bank loans, and lower interest payments on savings accounts. Thus, the 1996 Gramm-Leach-Bliley Act requires depository institutions (including banks, broker-dealer subsidiaries, and mutual funds) to file Suspicious Activity Reports—or SARs—whenever criminal activity (including money laundering) is suspected.

In May 2001, the Securities and Exchange Commission's Office of Compliance Inspections and Examinations reported that the agency is focusing more intensely on money-laundering compliance, revamping industrywide compliance efforts to ensure that prevention programs are effective. The FBI and the U.S. Justice Department have joined the fight with new electronic armaments, such as the Internet Fraud Complaint Center <www.ifccfbi.gov>, that seek to uncover and prosecute money laundering and other fraudulent white-collar practices. Accounting firms, too, have joined the antilaundering battle. Deloitte & Touche's Forensic and Investigative Services unit <www.deloitte.co.uk> helps other firms develop systems for prevention and reporting and publishes news updates on fraud-fighting techniques.

Internal auditing teams and CPAs from the Big 5 firms are also among the forces being marshaled as banks establish antilaundering procedures. Some banks are buying electronic technologies—plug-in "Sentinels" and "filtering software"—from outside suppliers such as Americas Software, Prime Associates, and SearchSpace. Others are developing their own systems. When Republic Bank of New York, for example, launched its own in-house anti–money-laundering system, investigators discovered unusual activity flowing through its accounts from the Bank of New York and several Russian banks. Shortly thereafter, they uncovered a large, previously undetected international laundering scheme.

As enforcement experience accumulates, officials have learned that the accounting professionals most likely to encounter signs of possible money laundering include the following:

- Forensic accountants
- Internal financial systems consultants
- Tax accountants
- Public accountants who provide regulatory examination services for client companies
- Public accountants who provide operational audits for client companies

It comes as no surprise, then, that these specialists are vital participants in developing and implementing antilaundering detection systems.

As for U.S. Trust, what caused the problem there? According to chief executive Jeffrey Maurer, the company's rapid expansion in the past five years "stretched our compliance infrastructure. . . . What had been adequate procedures regarding compliance were no longer state of the industry." He also notes that the firm is well along in improving the firm's compliance systems, having committed $20 million on technology improvements for compliance. Regulators have ordered the firm to establish procedures for monitoring each day's cash transactions. The bank must now report all currency transactions of more than $10,000 and any "potential suspicious or unusual activities" on the part of its customers. U.S. Trust also hired KPMG, a Big 5 accounting firm, to review its internal controls and procedures.

Questions for Discussion

1. Do you think customers would object if they knew that their bank was monitoring their financial transactions? Why or why not?
2. What do you believe should be the role of a firm's accounting staff when accountants detect money laundering or other fraudulent practices?

3. Suppose you work for a bank that asks you to set up a system to ensure antilaundering compliance by internal accountants. Do you think a system can work solely with human monitoring, or must electronic technology also be used? Explain the reasons for your answer.
4. When establishing a system to protect against laundering, a bank can either set up its own system using internal personnel and equipment or hire outsiders, such as a major accounting firm, to head up the effort. Under what circumstances would you recommend using internal versus external resources?
5. Consider the U.S. Trust situation and the conditions under which it occurred. Do you think the $10 million penalty was too heavy, too light, or about right? What should U.S. Trust have done to avoid the charges brought against it?

SUMMARY OF LEARNING OBJECTIVES

1 **Explain the role of accountants and distinguish between the kinds of work done by *public* and *private accountants*.** By collecting, analyzing, and communicating financial information, accountants provide business managers and investors with an accurate picture of the firm's financial health. *Certified public accountants (CPAs)* are licensed professionals who provide auditing, tax, and management advisory services for other firms and individuals. *Public accountants* who have not yet been certified perform similar tasks. *Private accountants* provide diverse specialized services for the specific firms that employ them.

2 **Discuss the *CPA Vision Project* and explain how the CPA profession is changing.** The Vision Project is a professionwide assessment to see what the future of the accounting profession will be like. It was initiated because of the declining number of students entering the accounting profession and because of rapid changes in the business world. Practicing CPAs and other industry leaders have participated in identifying key forces that are affecting the profession. Then they developed recommendations for change, including a set of *core services* that the profession should offer clients and a set of *core competencies* that CPAs should possess. Over all, the new vision reflects changes in the CPA's culture and professional lifestyle.

3 **Explain how the following concepts are used in record keeping: the *accounting equation* and *double-entry accounting*.** The *accounting equation* (assets = liabilities + owners' equity) is used to balance the data in accounting documents. *Double-entry accounting* acknowledges the dual effects of financial transactions and ensures that the accounting equation always balances. These tools enable accountants not only to enter but to track transactions. They also serve as double checks for accounting errors.

4 **Describe the three basic *financial statements* and show how they reflect the activity and financial condition of a business.** The *balance sheet* summarizes a company's assets, liabilities, and owners' equity at a given point in time. The *income statement* details revenues and expenses for a given period of time and identifies any profit or loss. The *statement of cash flows* reports cash receipts and payments from operating, investing, and financing activities.

5 **Explain how computing key *financial ratios* can help in analyzing the financial strengths of a business.** Drawing on data from financial statements, ratios can help creditors, investors, and managers assess a firm's finances. The *liquidity ratios—current* and *debt-to-equity*—measure *solvency* (a firm's ability to pay its debt) in both the short and the long run. *Return on equity* and *earnings per share* measure *profitability*. *Inventory turnover ratios* show how efficiently a firm is using its funds.

6 **Explain some of the special issues facing accountants at firms that do international business.** Accounting for foreign transactions involves some special procedures. First, accountants must consider the fact that the *exchange rates* of national currencies change. Accordingly, the value of a foreign currency at any given time, its foreign currency exchange rate, is what buyers are willing to pay for it.

Exchange rates affect the amount of money that a firm pays for foreign purchases and the amount that it gains from foreign sales. U.S. accountants, therefore, must always translate foreign currencies into the value of the U.S. dollar.

QUESTIONS AND EXERCISES

Questions for Review

1. Identify the three types of services performed by CPAs.
2. How does the double-entry system reduce the chances of mistakes or fraud in accounting?
3. What are the three basic financial statements and what major information does each contain?
4. Identify the three major classifications of financial statement ratios and give an example of one ratio in each category.
5. Explain how financial ratios allow managers to monitor their own efficiency and effectiveness.

Questions for Analysis

6. If you were planning to invest in a company, which of the three types of financial statements would you most want to see? Why?
7. Dasar Co. reports the following data in its September 30, 2001, financial statements:

Gross sales	$225,000
Current assets	40,000
Long-term assets	100,000
Current liabilities	16,000
Long-term liabilities	44,000
Owners' equity	80,000
Net income	7,200

Compute the following ratios: current ratio, debt-to-equity ratio, and return on owners' equity.

Application Exercises

8. Interview an accountant at a local manufacturing firm. Trace the process by which budgets are developed in that company. How does the firm use budgets? How does budgeting help managers plan business activities? How does budgeting help them control business activities? Give examples.
9. Interview the manager of a local retail or wholesale business about taking inventory. What is the firm's primary purpose in taking inventory? How often is it done?

EXPLORING THE WEB

A Field Trip to the AICPA

Most business practitioners belong to professional associations that provide services for members. The American Institute of Certified Public Accountants (AICPA) is one of accounting's best-known associations. To learn about the purpose of the AICPA and the activities that it offers, visit its Web site at:

<www.aicpa.org/>

Spend some time navigating through the home page. To get an idea of the variety of topics covered and services offered for AICPA members, enter each of the subject gates (point the mouse to the title and click) ranged up and down the page. Next, scroll down the page into the Site Directory and select **Students**. After reviewing the **Students** area, consider the following questions:

1. Examine the section entitled *The Profession and You*. Notice the variety of topics and information categories—such as "CPA Profiles"—at the bottom of the page. Are any of the topics of interest to you? Do you think that anyone other than accountants might get some value from exploring this Web site? Explain.
2. While still in the section *The Profession and You*, go to the bottom of the screen and click on "Work/Life Balance." As you scan down the list of work/life issues, select two that are most interesting to you. Explain why the two you selected are important considerations for you.
3. After returning to the Site Directory for *Students*, explore the "Landing a Job" section. From a career standpoint, which of the items (the aspects of accounting career opportunities) are appealing to you and which are not? Return to the Students page and scan down to *Becoming a CPA*. Now go to the "150-Hour requirement." What is your opinion about the "150-hour education program"? What are its pros and cons?

EXERCISING YOUR ETHICS

Confidentially Yours

THE SITUATION

Accountants are typically entrusted with private, often sensitive information that should be used confidentially. In this exercise, you are encouraged to think about ethical considerations that might arise when an accountant's career choices come up against his or her professional obligation to maintain confidentiality.

THE DILEMMA

Assume that you are the head accountant in a large electronics firm. Your responsibilities include preparation of the company's income statements and balance sheets for financial reporting to stockholders. In addition, you regularly prepare confidential financial budgets for internal use by managers responsible for planning each department's activities, including future investments for new assets. You have also worked with auditors and supplied sensitive information to consultants from a

CPA firm that assesses financial problems and suggests solutions for your company.

Let's suppose that you are approached by another company—one of the electronics industry's most successful firms—and the firm offers you a higher-level position. If you accept, your new executive position includes responsibility for developing the company's financial plans, as well as serving on its strategic planning committee. You would be involved, then, in evaluating the competition and developing the company's strategy for the future and will probably be called upon to use your knowledge of your previous firm's competitive strengths and weaknesses. You realize that your insider knowledge could be useful in your new position if you decide to accept it.

QUESTIONS FOR DISCUSSION

1. What are roles of financial accounting, managerial accounting, and accounting services in this scenario?
2. What are the main ethical issues in this situation?
3. As the central figure in this scenario, how would you handle this situation?

BUILDING YOUR BUSINESS SKILLS

Putting the Buzz in Billing

This exercise enhances the following SCANS workplace competencies: demonstrating basic skills, demonstrating thinking skills, exhibiting interpersonal skills, working with information, and applying system knowledge.

GOAL

To encourage students to think about the advantages and disadvantages of using an electronic system for handling accounts receivable and accounts payable.

METHOD

STEP 1

Study Figure 13.5 on the following page. The outside circle depicts the seven steps involved in the issuing of paper bills to customers, the payment of these bills by customers, and the handling by banks of debits and credits for the two accounts. The inside circle shows the same bill issuance and payment process handled electronically.

STEP 2

As the chief financial officer of a midwestern utility company, you are analyzing the feasibility of switching from a paper to an electronic system of billing and bill payment. You decide to discuss the ramifications of the choice with three business associates (choose three classmates to take on these roles). Your discussion requires that you research electronic payment systems now being developed. Specifically, using online and library research, you must find out as much as you can about the electronic bill-paying systems being developed by Visa International, Intuit, IBM, and the Checkfree Corp. After you have researched this information, brainstorm the advantages and disadvantages of using an electronic bill-paying system in your company.

FOLLOW-UP QUESTIONS

1. What cost savings are inherent in the electronic system for both your company and its customers? In your answer, consider such costs as handling, postage, and paper.
2. What consequences would your decision to adopt an electronic system have on others with whom you do business, including manufacturers of check-sorting equipment, the U.S. Postal Service, and banks?
3. Switching to an electronic bill-paying system would require a large capital expenditure for new computers and computer software. How could analyzing the company's income statement help you justify this expenditure?
4. How are consumers likely to respond to paying bills electronically? Are you likely to get a different response from individuals than you get from business customers?

CRAFTING YOUR BUSINESS PLAN

The Profitability of Planning

THE PURPOSE OF THE ASSIGNMENT

1. To familiarize students with issues involving accounting that a sample firm faces in developing its business plan, in the framework of *Business PlanPro (BPP)* (Version 4.0).
2. To demonstrate how three chapter topics—accounting skills, financial data reports, and the profit-and-loss statement—can be integrated as components in the *BPP* planning environment.

FOLLOW-UP ASSIGNMENT

After reading Chapter 13 in the textbook, open the BPP *software and search for information about plans for accounting as it applies to a sample firm:* AMT Computer Store *(American Management Technology). Then respond to the following items:*

1. What is your assessment of the accounting skills in AMT's management team? What do you recommend? [Sites to see in *BPP* for this item: In the Plan Outline screen, click on each of the following, in turn: **6.1 Organizational Structure, 6.2 Management Team,** and **6.3 Management Team Gaps.**]

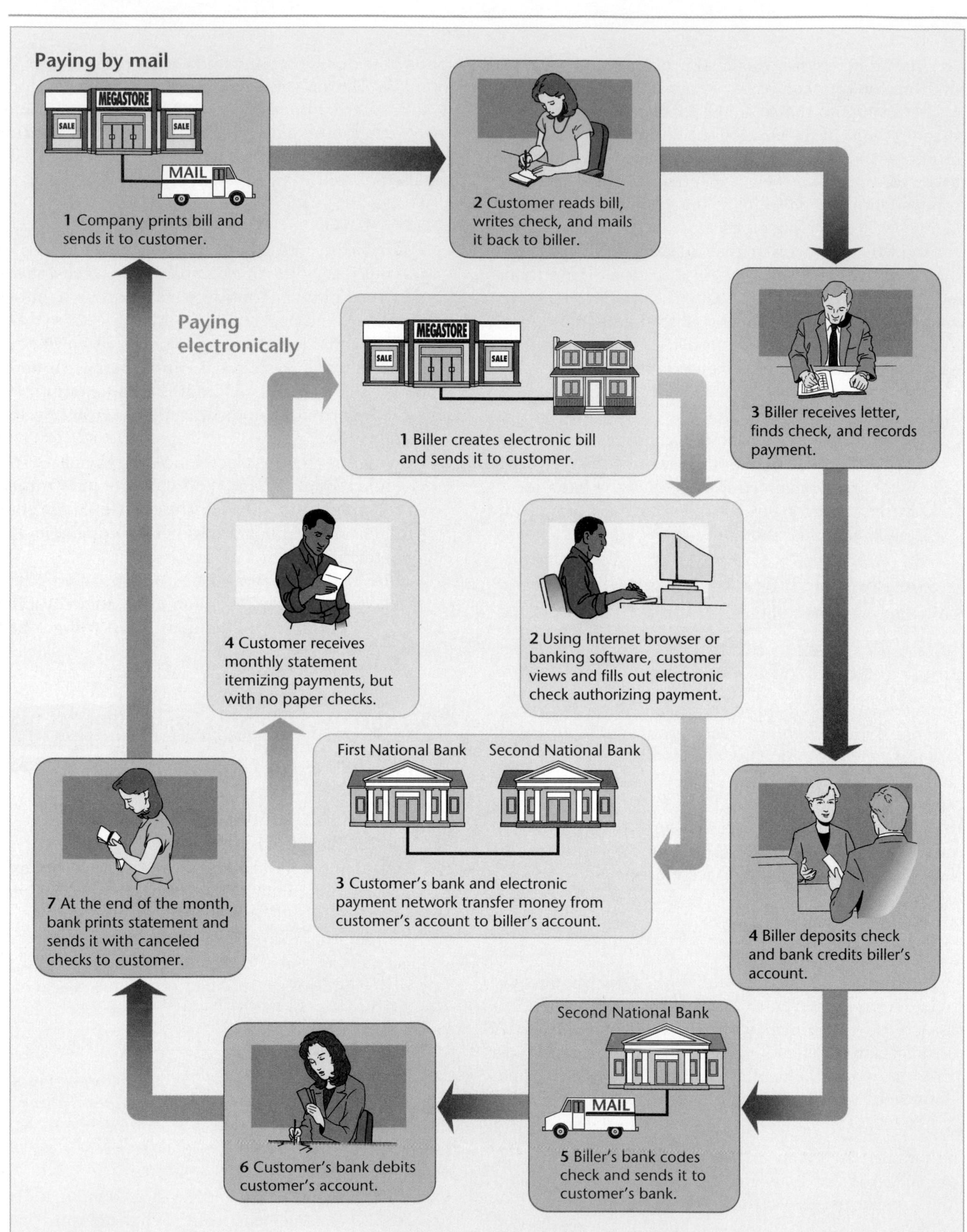

Paying by mail
MEGASTORE
SALE
SALE
MAIL
1 Company prints bill and sends it to customer.
2 Customer reads bill, writes check, and mails it back to biller.
3 Biller receives letter, finds check, and records payment.
4 Biller deposits check and bank credits biller's account.
Second National Bank
MAIL
5 Biller's bank codes check and sends it to customer's bank.
6 Customer's bank debits customer's account.
7 At the end of the month, bank prints statement and sends it with canceled checks to customer.
Paying electronically
MEGASTORE
SALE
SALE
1 Biller creates electronic bill and sends it to customer.
2 Using Internet browser or banking software, customer views and fills out electronic check authorizing payment.
First National Bank
Second National Bank
3 Customer's bank and electronic payment network transfer money from customer's account to biller's account.
4 Customer receives monthly statement itemizing payments, but with no paper checks.

Figure 13.5

2. Use *BPP*'s computer graphics to explore AMT's financial data reports. Describe the kinds of accounting information you find in the charts. [Sites to see in *BPP*: Begin in the Plan Outline screen: Go to the outline section entitled **7.2 Key Financial Indicators**, and beneath it click on **Chart: Benchmarks** (located beneath **7.2 Key Financial Indicators**). Then, in the bottom toolbar, click on **Next** (to advance to the next chart) and continue through the various charts until you return again to **Benchmarks**.]
3. At the time of this plan, AMT Computer Store was expecting large changes in annual net profits in the coming three years. Based on the company's planned profit-and-loss statement, identify the key factors—changes in the revenues and expenses categories—that account for changes in planned net profits from year to year. [Sites to see in *BPP*: From the Plan Outline screen, click on **Table: Profit and Loss** (located beneath **7.4 Projected Profit and Loss**).]

VIDEO EXERCISE

Accounting for a Few Billion Sold: McDonald's

LEARNING OBJECTIVES

The purpose of this video exercise is to help you

1. Understand the value of generally accepted accounting principles (GAAP).
2. Recognize some of the accounting challenges facing multinational firms.
3. Appreciate the impact of foreign exchange rates on the accounting process for multinational firms.

BACKGROUND INFORMATION

From modest beginnings as a simple Illinois hamburger chain in 1954, McDonald's has grown to 25,000 restaurants around the world. Almost 1,800 new stores were added in 1999, about 90 percent of them outside the United States. The company has already opened its 1,000th restaurants in both Germany and the United Kingdom and its 3,000th in Japan. McDonald's not only accounts for nearly half of all globally branded fast-food restaurants outside the United States but also achieves about two-thirds of total fast-food sales outside this country. Management attributes this huge market share to the power of the McDonald's brand.

There are only occasional clouds in the company's bright profit picture. Revenues in Latin America were adversely affected by the recent currency devaluation in Brazil and by difficult economic conditions in several markets whose severity McDonald's had underestimated.

THE VIDEO

Vice President and Assistant Corporate Controller Dave Pojman discusses the evolution of McDonald's financial reporting methods from an originally highly manual process of collating worldwide data to the current, largely computerized method of capturing and analyzing data that are entered to a special Web site, automatically sorted, and transformed into a wide variety of reports in both English and other languages. Information about monthly sales is aggregated from individual store, to country, to country grouping, and finally to international headquarters, where it is incorporated into annual reports and required SEC filings.

QUESTIONS FOR DISCUSSION

1. What are the special accounting problems faced by an international firm like McDonald's when it operates abroad?
2. How does McDonald's deal with some of these accounting challenges?
3. How does a company like McDonald's benefit from having operations in so many different parts of the world?

FOLLOW-UP ASSIGNMENT

Select a country in which McDonald's does business and research some of that country's business practices and social and religious customs. Make a list of as many specific factors as you can find that can affect McDonald's ability to operate in that country, its chance of success there, and its ability to gather accurate financial information.

FOR FURTHER EXPLORATION

Visit the "Investor Relations" pages on the Web sites of some other multinationals, such as Coca-Cola <www.coca-cola.com>, Colgate-Palmolive <www. colgate.com>, and the Disney Co. <www.disney.go.com>, to find out what proportion of the company's earnings is created overseas. What challenges do you think each of these firms faces in reporting earnings accurately?

CHAPTER 14 Understanding Money and Banking

After reading this chapter, you should be able to:

1. Define *money* and identify the different forms that it takes in the nation's money supply.
2. Describe the different kinds of *financial institutions* that comprise the U.S. financial system and explain the services they offer.
3. Explain how banks create money and describe the means by which they are regulated.
4. Discuss the functions of the *Federal Reserve System* and describe the tools that it uses to control the money supply.
5. Identify three important ways in which the financial industry is changing.
6. Understand some of the key activities in *international banking and finance.*

Europe Cashes In

An Italian worker can get a week's pay in cash—about 800,000 lira, which is the equivalent of about U.S.$400. If it's paid in paper currency, this sum can consist of many—even hundreds—of 1-, 50-, and 100-lira bills in a huge wad that easily fills any suit pocket, bag, or purse. Italians are accustomed to thinking in big numbers when it comes to money matters: 2,000 lira for a loaf of bread, 900,000 lira for rent, 30 million lira for a new car. Personal savings accounts run to perhaps 20 million lira.

Now imagine what happens when an Italian worker wakes up one day to find that bread costs only 1 (instead of 2,000), rent just 450 (rather than 900,000), and a new car a meager 15,000 (down from 30 million)? Good news? Not really. At the same time, our worker's weekly salary has fallen to 400 (instead of 800,000) and his or her savings account has dwindled from a lusty 20 million to a paltry 10,000. Unless the general public is prepared in advance, such differences in an individual's vital financial statistics could come as quite a jolt. Financial transactions, even the simplest routine exchanges of money, could suddenly become a matter for concern and calculation.

This scenario isn't a movie script about apocalyptic inflation. It's about the beginning of Europe's changeover to a new monetary unit—the euro. It's the world's first major new currency in more than a century. For more than two years now, officials have been hard at work preparing for January 1, 2002, when the euro replaces the national currencies of 12 European Monetary Union (EMU) countries: Austria, Belgium, Finland, France, Germany, Greece, Ireland, Italy, Luxembourg, the Netherlands, Portugal, and Spain.

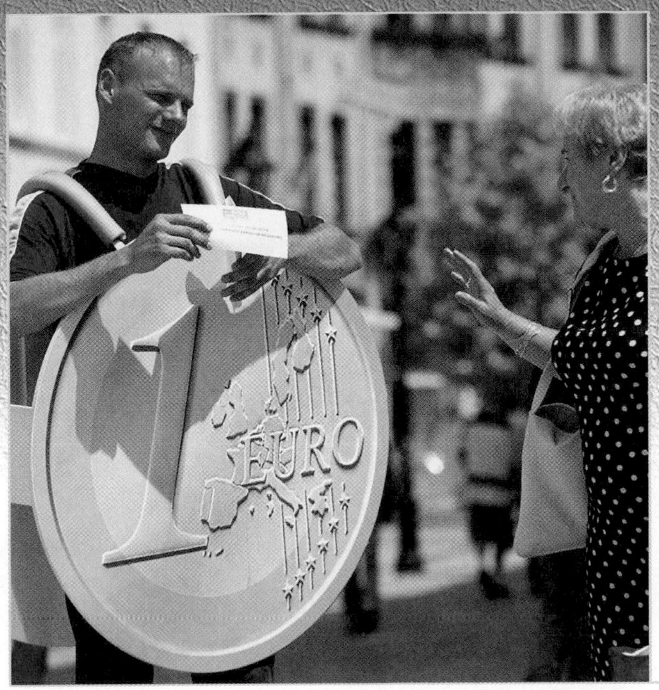

"Consider the psychological effects of confusion, irritation, and suspicion among customers, and uncertainty and unfamiliarity of staff with the new currency."

—Patrick O'Beirne, consultant with Systems Modeling Ltd.

The transition is taking place in a series of steps that has already begun. On January 1, 1999, EMU officials agreed on exchange rates between each country's national currency and the euro. Each country, therefore, knows how many euros its national currency is worth. One euro, for example, is worth 1,936 Italian lira and 1.96 German deutsche marks. Secure in the knowledge that these rates are fixed, citizens of each EMU country can plan their financial activities. They also know that the new currency will be portable—that is, it will be the accepted currency of choice—whenever they travel in other EMU countries.

Step 2 of the changeover involved conditioning the EMU public to think in terms of the new monetary unit. After all, observes Patrick O'Beirne, a consultant with Ireland-based Systems Modeling Ltd., "Consider the psychological effects of confusion, irritation, and suspicion among customers, and uncertainty and unfamiliarity of staff with the new currency." To overcome such fears, for over a year consumers in Italy and other EMU countries have been getting cash register receipts showing purchase prices in two currencies—the national currency and the euro—for everyday goods and services. In this and other ways, EMU citizens are getting accustomed to seeing euro prices and to comparing them with more familiar currencies.

The third step will occur on the first day of 2002, when all EMU transactions must be made in euros. For the first time, euro coins and notes will become legal tender in all EMU countries. In step 4—the dual circulation phase—the real changeover takes place. During a time period ranging up to two months, both the national currency and the euro will be legal tender in each EMU country. At the end of this period, only the euro will be in use by the general public, and only banks will exchange the old national currencies.

Our opening story continues on page 381

Whether it caters to the community of European countries or to a single nation such as the United States, a complex system of financial institutions, especially banks, is needed to meet the money requirements of individuals and businesses. By focusing on the learning objectives of this chapter, you will better understand the environment for banking in the United States and the different kinds of institutions that conduct business in it.

WHAT IS MONEY?

When someone asks you how much money you have, do you count the dollar bills and coins in your pockets? Do you include your checking and savings accounts? What about stocks and bonds? Do you count your car? Taken together, the value of all these things is your "personal wealth." Not all of it, however, is "money." In this section, we consider more precisely what *money* is and does.

The Characteristics of Money

Modern money often takes the form of stamped metal or printed paper—U.S. dollars, British pounds, French francs, Japanese yen—issued by governments. Theoretically, however, just about any object can serve as **money** if it is *portable, divisible, durable*, and *stable*. To appreciate these qualities, imagine using something that lacks them—say, a 70-pound salmon:

money
Any object that is portable, divisible, durable, and stable and serves as a medium of exchange, a store of value, and a unit of account

- *Portability.* Try lugging 70 pounds of fish from shop to shop. In contrast, modern currency is light and easy to handle.
- *Divisibility.* Suppose that you want to buy a hat, a book, and some milk from three different stores. How would you divide your fish-money? Is a pound of its head worth as much as, say, two gills? Modern currency is easily divisible into smaller parts, each with a fixed value. A dollar, for example, can be exchanged for four quarters. More important, units of money can be easily matched with the value of all goods.
- *Durability.* Regardless of whether you "spend" it, your salmon will lose value every day (in fact, it will eventually be too smelly to be worth anything). Modern currency, however, neither dies nor spoils, and if it wears out, it can be replaced. It is also hard to counterfeit—certainly harder than catching more salmon.
- *Stability.* If salmon were in short supply, you might be able to make quite a deal for yourself. In the middle of a salmon run, however, the market would be flooded with fish. Sellers of goods would soon have enough fish and would refuse to produce anything for which they could get only salmon. Goods would become scarcer, but the salmon would continue (or cease) running, regardless of the plenitude or scarcity of buyable goods. The value of our paper money also fluctuates, but it is considerably more stable than salmon. Its value is related to what we can buy with it.

The Functions of Money

Imagine a successful fisherman who needs a new sail for his boat. In a barter economy—one in which goods are exchanged directly for one another—he would have to find someone who not only needs fish but who is also willing to exchange a sail for it. If no sailmaker wants fish, the fisherman must find someone else—say, a shoemaker—who wants fish. Then the fisherman must hope that the sailmaker will trade for his new shoes. Clearly, barter is inefficient in comparison with money. In a money economy, the fisherman would sell his catch, receive money, and exchange the money for such goods as a new sail.

Money serves three functions:[1]

- *Medium of exchange.* Like the fisherman "trading" money for a new sail, we use money as a way of buying and selling things. Without money, we would be bogged down in a system of barter.

The once prosperous economy of Thailand is having trouble generating capital—money created by business activity that can be used to finance further business activity. The value of the country's currency has declined by about 50 percent, and 44 percent of its bank loans are uncollectible. The International Monetary Fund is reluctant to provide funds because it is unhappy with the plans of the current government for achieving stability. The country is thus turning to sources of less "liquid" capital, asking citizens to donate personal wealth in the form of gold necklaces and jewelry.

- *Store of value.* Pity the fisherman who catches a fish on Monday and wants to buy a few bars of candy on, say, the following Saturday, by which time the fish would have spoiled and lost its value. In the form of currency, however, money can be used for future purchases and so "stores" value.
- *Unit of account.* Money lets us measure the relative values of goods and services. It acts as a unit of account because all products can be valued and accounted for in terms of money. For example, the concepts of "$1,000 worth of clothes" or "$500 in labor costs" have universal meaning because everyone deals with money every day.

The Spendable Money Supply: M-1

For money to serve its basic functions, both buyers and sellers must agree on its value. That value depends in part on its *supply*—on how much money is in circulation. When the money supply is high, the value of money drops. When it is low, that value increases.

Unfortunately, it is not easy to measure the supply of money. One of the most commonly used measures, known widely as **M-1**, counts only the most liquid, or spendable, forms of money: currency, demand deposits, and other checkable deposits. These are all non-interest-bearing or low-interest-bearing forms of money. As of June 2001, M-1 totaled $1.12 trillion.[2]

Paper money and metal coins are **currency** issued by the government. Currency is widely used for small exchanges, and the law requires creditors to accept it in payment of debts. As of June 2001, currency in circulation in the United States amounted to $549 billion, or about 49 percent of M-1.[3]

A **check** is essentially an order instructing a bank to pay a given sum to a "payee." Although not all sellers accept them as payment, many do. Checks are usually acceptable in place of cash because they are valuable only to specified payees and can be exchanged for cash. Checking accounts, which are known as **demand deposits**, are counted in M-1 because funds may be withdrawn at any time—"on demand." In June 2001, demand deposits in the United States totaled $311 billion (27 percent of M-1).[4]

M-1
Measure of the money supply that includes only the most liquid (spendable) forms of money

currency
Government-issued paper money and metal coins

check
Demand deposit order instructing a bank to pay a given sum to a specified payee

demand deposit
Bank account funds that may be withdrawn at any time

M-2
Measure of the money supply that includes all the components of M-1 plus the forms of money that can be easily converted into spendable form

M-1 Plus the Convertible Money Supply: M-2

M-2 includes everything in M-1 plus items that cannot be spent directly but are easily converted to spendable forms. The major components of M-2 are M-1, *time deposits, money market mutual funds*, and *savings deposits*. Totaling over $5.2 trillion in June

time deposit
Bank funds that cannot be withdrawn without notice or transferred by check

money market mutual fund
Fund of short-term, low-risk financial securities purchased with the assets of investor-owners pooled by a nonbank institution

2001, M-2 accounts for nearly all of the nation's money supply.[5] Thus, it measures the store of monetary value available for financial transactions. As this overall level of money increases, more is available for consumer purchases and business investment. When the supply is tightened, less money is available, and financial transactions, spending, and business activity, thus, slow down.

Unlike demand deposits, **time deposits**, such as certificates of deposit (CDs) and savings certificates, require prior notice of withdrawal and cannot be transferred by check. However, time deposits pay higher interest rates. Time deposits in M-2 include only accounts of less than $100,000 that can be redeemed on demand with small penalties.

Operated by investment companies that bring together pools of assets from many investors, **money market mutual funds** buy a collection of short-term, low-risk financial securities. Ownership of and profits (or losses) from the sale of these securities are shared among the fund's investors. In mid-2001, these funds held $9.7 billion in assets.[6] In the wake of new, more attractive investments, traditional savings deposits, such as passbook savings accounts, have declined in popularity. Totaling a little over $2 trillion, savings deposits represented 38 percent of M-2 in June 2001.[7]

Figure 14.1 shows how the two measures of money, M-1 and M-2, have grown since 1959. For many years, M-1 was the traditional measure of liquid money. Because it was closely related to gross domestic product, it served as a reliable predictor of the nation's economic health. As you can see, however, this situation changed in the early 1980s, with the introduction of new types of investments and easier transfer of money among investment funds to gain higher interest returns. As a result, M-2 today is a more reliable measure than M-1 and is often used by economists for economic planning.

Credit Cards

Citicorp <www.citicorp.com> is the world's largest credit card issuer, with more than 49 million accounts worldwide. It is estimated that more than 157 million U.S. cardholders carry 1.5 billion cards. Spending with general-purpose credit cards in the United States is estimated at $1.4 trillion—almost half of all transactions—for the year 2000.[8] Indeed, the use of cards such as Visa <www.visa.com>, MasterCard

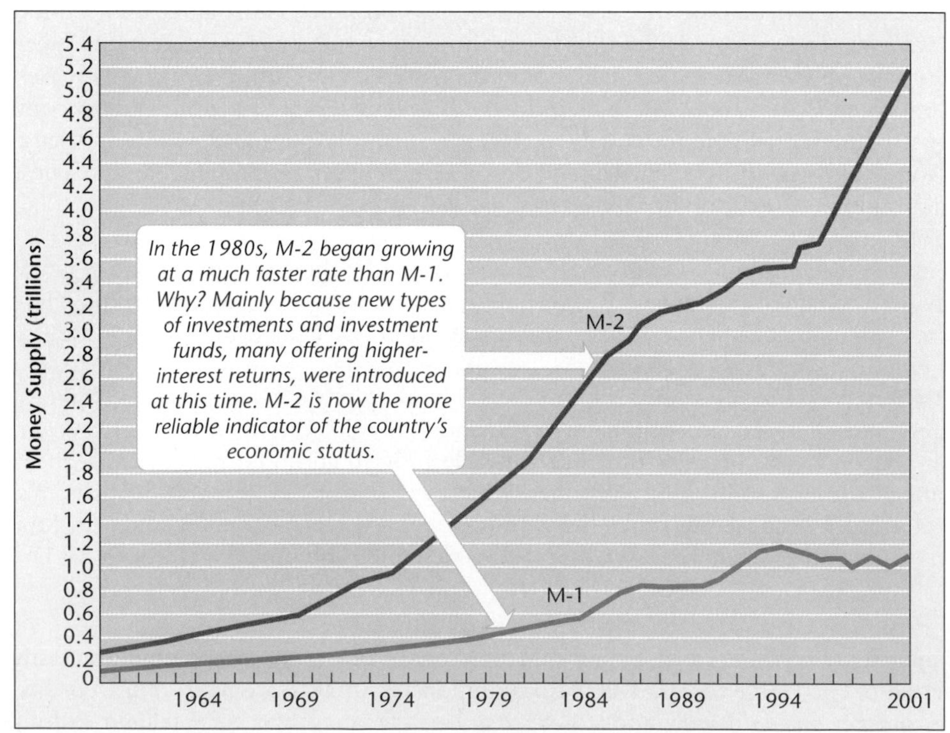

Figure 14.1
Money-Supply Growth

<www.mastercard.com>, American Express <www.americanexpress.com>, Discover <www.discover.com>, and Diners Club <www.dinersclub.com> has become so widespread that many people refer to them as "plastic money."

Credit cards are big business for two basic reasons. First, they are convenient. Second, they are extremely profitable for issuing companies. Profits derive from two sources:

1. Some cards charge annual fees to holders. All charge interest on unpaid balances. Depending on the issuer, and on certain state regulations, cardholders pay interest rates ranging from 11 to 20 percent.
2. Merchants who accept credit cards pay fees to card issuers. Depending on the merchant's agreement with the issuer, 2 to 5 percent of total credit sales dollars goes to card issuers.

THE U.S. FINANCIAL SYSTEM

Many forms of money, especially demand deposits and time deposits, depend on the existence of financial institutions to provide a broad spectrum of services to both individuals and businesses. Just how important are reliable financial institutions to both businesses and individuals? Try asking financial consumers in a country in which commercial banking can be an adventure.

In Russia there is almost no banking regulation and no way to distinguish qualified from unscrupulous bankers in the thousands of different financial institutions, large and small, that exist. Businesses need stable financial institutions to underwrite modernization and expansion, and individuals need them to handle currency. The Moscow City Bank <www.mcbank.ru> has no deposit insurance and only recently added a customer service desk, loan officers, and a cash machine. Imagine, then, just before these new steps at modernization, the disappointment of Vladimir Shcherbakov, who needed to withdraw $500 from his account to buy a car but was turned away by a sign announcing that no withdrawals would be allowed for 10 days. "I'm resigned to losing my money," sighed Shcherbakov. "But if I do get it back, I'll change my rubles into dollars and hold on to it myself."

> *"I'm resigned to losing my money. But if I do get it back, I'll change my rubles into dollars and hold onto it myself."*
>
> —Vladimir Shcherbakov, Moscow City Bank customer

In the sections that follow, we describe the major types of financial institutions, explain how they work when they work as they are supposed to, and survey some of the special services that they offer. We also explain their role as creators of money and discuss the regulation of the U.S. banking system.

Financial Institutions

The main function of financial institutions is to ease the flow of money from sectors with surpluses to those with deficits. They do this by issuing claims against themselves and using the proceeds to buy the assets of—and thus invest in—other organizations. A bank, for instance, can issue financial claims against itself by making available funds for checking and savings accounts. In turn, its assets will be mostly loans invested in individuals and businesses and perhaps government securities. In this section, we discuss each of the major types of financial institutions: *commercial banks, savings and loan associations, mutual savings banks, credit unions*, and various organizations known as *nondeposit institutions*.

Commercial Banks The United States today boasts nearly 10,000 **commercial banks**—companies that accept deposits that they use to make loans and earn profits. Commercial banks range from the very largest institutions in New York, such as Bank of America and Chase Manhattan, to tiny banks dotting the rural landscape. Bank liabilities include checking accounts and savings accounts. Assets consist of a wide variety of loans to individuals, businesses, and governments.

commercial bank
Federal- or state-chartered financial institution accepting deposits that it uses to make loans and earn profits

Diversification and Mergers Many observers today believe that traditional banking has become a "mature" industry, one whose basic operations have expanded as broadly as they can. For instance, 1993 marked the first year in which the money invested in mutual funds—almost $2 trillion—equaled the amount deposited in U.S. banks. Thus, financial industry competitors in areas such as mutual funds are growing, sometimes rapidly.

As consumers continue to look for alternatives to traditional banking services, commercial banks and savings and loan associations find themselves with a dwindling share of market. The investment bank Merrill Lynch <www.ml.com> has originated billions of dollars in commercial loans, formerly the province of commercial banks. Savers, too, have been putting their savings into the money market funds, stocks, and bonds offered by companies such as Charles Schwab <www.schwab.com> instead of into the traditional savings accounts offered by banks. Many observers contend that to compete, banks, too, must diversify their offerings. The only way that they can compete, says banking analyst Thomas Brown, "is to transform themselves into successful retailers of financial services, which involves dramatic, not incremental change."

"The only way banks can compete is to transform themselves into successful retailers of financial services, which involves dramatic, not incremental change."

—Thomas Brown, banking analyst

A related option seems to be to get bigger. In efforts to regain competitiveness, banks were merging at a record-setting pace in the 1990s. When commercial banks merge with investment banks, the resulting companies hold larger shares of the financial market, and the lines become blurred between traditional banking and nonbank financial institutions. Citigroup Inc. <www.citigroup.com>, the result of a 1998 merger between Citicorp (a commercial bank) and Travelers Group (which includes investment bank Salomon Smith Barney <www.smithbarney.com>) is the world's second-largest bank with nearly $700 billion in assets in 1999. Citigroup offers one-stop shopping on a global scale for both consumers and businesses, including private banking, credit card services, mortgages, mutual funds, stock brokerage services, insurance, and loans.

Mergers are the trend, and fewer but larger banks are offering a wide range of financial products. The strategy streamlines operations to reduce costs and focuses on providing products that will win back customers from nonbank competitors.

Commercial Interest Rates Every bank receives a major portion of its income from interest paid on loans by borrowers. As long as terms and conditions are clearly revealed to borrowers, banks are allowed to set their own interest rates. Traditionally, the lowest rates were made available to the bank's most creditworthy commercial customers. That rate is called the **prime rate**. Most commercial loans are set at markups over prime. However, the prime rate is no longer a strong force in setting loan rates. Borrowers can now get funds less expensively from other sources, including foreign banks that set lower interest rates. To remain competitive, U.S. banks now offer some commercial loans at rates below prime.[9] Figure 14.2 shows the changes in the prime rate since 1992.[10]

prime rate
Interest rate available to a bank's most creditworthy customers

savings and loan association (S&L)
Financial institution accepting deposits and making loans primarily for home mortgages

Savings and Loan Associations Like commercial banks, **savings and loan associations (S&Ls)** accept deposits and make loans. They lend money primarily for home mortgages. Most S&Ls were created to provide financing for homes. Many of

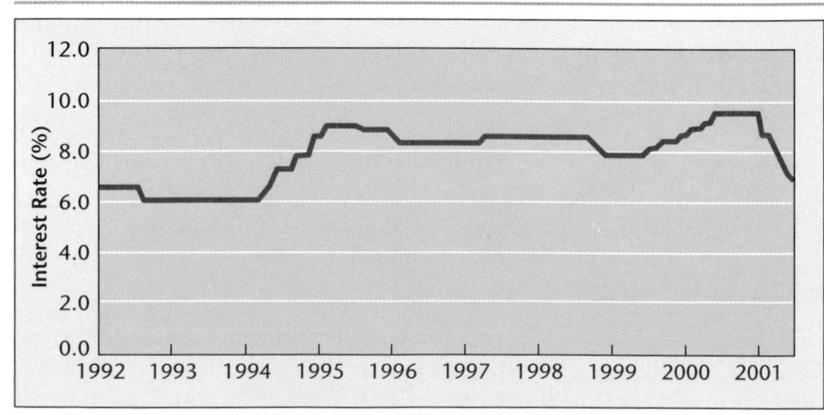

Figure 14.2
The Prime Rate

them, however, have ventured into other investments, with varying degrees of success. S&Ls in the United States now hold $1.1 trillion in assets and deposits of $707 billion.[11]

Mutual Savings Banks and Credit Unions In **mutual savings banks**, all depositors are considered owners of the bank. All profits, therefore, are divided proportionately among depositors, who receive dividends. Like S&Ls, mutual savings banks attract most of their funds in the form of savings deposits, and funds are loaned out in the form of mortgages.

In **credit unions**, deposits are accepted only from members who meet specific qualifications, usually working for a particular employer. Most universities run credit unions, as do the U.S. Navy <www.navy.mil> and the Pentagon <www.defenselink.mil>. Credit unions make loans for automobiles and home mortgages, as well as other types of personal loans. Currently, U.S. credit unions hold $411 billion in assets.[12]

Nondeposit Institutions A variety of other organizations take in money, provide interest or other services, and make loans. Four of the most important are *pension funds, insurance companies, finance companies*, and *securities dealers*.

A **pension fund** is essentially a pool of funds managed to provide retirement income for its members. *Public pension funds* include Social Security <www.ssa.gov> and $1 trillion in retirement programs for state and local government employees. *Private pension funds*, operated by employers, unions, and other private groups, cover about 80 million people and have total assets of $4.9 trillion.[13]

Insurance companies collect large pools of funds from the premiums charged for coverage. Funds are invested in stocks, real estate, and other assets. Earnings pay for insured losses, such as death benefits, automobile damage, and health care expenses.

Finance companies specialize in making loans to businesses and individuals. Commercial finance companies lend to businesses needing capital or long-term funds. They may, for instance, lend to a manufacturer that needs new assembly-line equipment. *Consumer finance companies* devote most of their resources to small noncommercial loans to individuals.

Securities investment dealers (brokers) , such as Merrill Lynch and A.G. Edwards & Sons <www.agedwards.com>, buy and sell stocks and bonds on the New York and other stock exchanges for client investors. They also invest in securities—they buy stocks and bonds for their own accounts in hopes of reselling them later at a profit. These companies hold large sums of money for transfer between buyers and sellers. (We discuss the activities of brokers and investment bankers more fully in Chapter 15.)

mutual savings bank
Financial institution whose depositors are owners sharing in its profits

credit union
Financial institution that accepts deposits from, and makes loans to, only its members, usually employees of a particular organization

pension fund
Nondeposit pool of funds managed to provide retirement income for its members

insurance company
Nondeposit institution that invests funds collected as premiums charged for insurance coverage

finance company
Nondeposit institution that specializes in making loans to businesses and consumers

securities investment dealer (broker)
Nondeposit institution that buys and sells stocks and bonds both for investors and for its own accounts

WEB Connection

Do you want to know the top five minority- and women-owned financial institutions in the country? Try the Financial Data Finder. Do you need a quick definition of *financial leverage?* Try the International Financial Encyclopaedia. Looking for job opportunities in finance? Try the "Finance Student Information" page. Information such as this can be found on the OSU Virtual Finance Library maintained by the Ohio State University Department of Finance.

fisher.osu/edu/fin/cerns.htm

This Manhattan outlet looks like a branch bank, but there are no ATMs at Chase Checks-To-Cash Clubs. At this location, tellers simply exchange cash for payroll checks (for a fee, of course). Institutions such as Chase <www.chase.com> *have entered the check-cashing business, which now processes $60 billion worth of payroll and government checks every year. In industry lingo, customers are ALICs: people who are "asset limited, income constrained."*

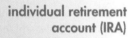

Special Financial Services

The finance business today is a highly competitive industry. No longer is it enough for commercial banks to accept deposits and make loans. Most, for example, now offer bank-issued credit cards and safe-deposit boxes. In addition, many offer pension, trust, international, and brokerage services and financial advice. Most offer ATMs and electronic money transfer.

individual retirement account (IRA)
Tax-deferred pension fund with which wage earners supplement other retirement funds

trust services
Bank management of an individual's investments, payments, or estate

letter of credit
Bank promise, issued for a buyer, to pay a designated firm a certain amount of money if specified conditions are met

banker's acceptance
Bank promise, issued for a buyer, to pay a designated firm a specified amount at a future date

Pension and Trust Services Most banks help customers establish savings plans for retirement. **Individual retirement accounts (IRAs)** are pension funds that wage earners and their spouses can set up to supplement other retirement funds. All wage earners can invest up to $2,000 of earned income annually in an IRA. They offer a significant tax benefit: Under many circumstances, taxes on principal and earnings are deferred until funds are withdrawn upon retirement. Under the 1997 tax changes, some IRAs are entirely tax-free. Banks serve as financial intermediaries by receiving funds and investing them as directed by customers. They also provide customers with information on investment vehicles available for IRAs (deposit accounts, mutual funds, stocks, and so forth).[14]

Many commercial banks offer **trust services**—the management of funds left "in the bank's trust." In return for a fee, the trust department will perform such tasks as making your monthly bill payments and managing your investment portfolio. Trust departments also manage the estates of deceased persons.

International Services The three main international services offered by banks are *currency exchange, letters of credit*, and *banker's acceptances*. Suppose a U.S. company wants to buy a product from a French supplier. For a fee, it can use one or more of three services offered by its bank:

1. It can exchange U.S. dollars for French francs at a U.S. bank and then pay the French supplier in francs.
2. It can pay its bank to issue a **letter of credit**—a promise by the bank to pay the French firm a certain amount if specified conditions are met.
3. It can pay its bank to draw up a **banker's acceptance**, which promises that the bank will pay some specified amount at a future date.

A banker's acceptance requires payment by a particular date. Letters of credit are payable only after certain conditions are met. The French supplier, for example, may not be paid until shipping documents prove that the merchandise has been shipped from France.

Citibank <www.citibank.com/hungary> now has consumer banking outlets in 41 countries, where it strives to make its once specialized products universal. At this ATM machine in Budapest, Hungary, for example, Americans can access their U.S. accounts in English. Then, says Victor Meneszes, head of Citibank's U.S./Europe consumer banking operations, "they can withdraw cash and go across the street to McDonald's. They feel completely at home."

Financial Advice and Brokerage Services Many banks, both large and small, help their customers manage their money. Depending on the customer's situation, the bank may recommend different investment opportunities. The recommended mix might include CDs, mutual funds, stocks, and bonds. Many banks also serve as securities intermediaries, using their own stockbrokers to buy and sell securities and their own facilities to hold them. Bank advertisements often stress the role of banks as financial advisers.

Automated Teller Machines Electronic **automated teller machines (ATMs)** allow customers to withdraw money and make deposits 24 hours a day, 7 days a week. They also allow transfers of funds between accounts and provide information on account status. Some banks offer cards that can be used in affiliated nationwide systems. About 273,000 machines are now located at bank buildings, grocery stores, airports, shopping malls, and other locations. Bank of America, with 14,000 units, is this country's leading owner of ATMs. U.S. bank customers conduct more than 13 billion ATM transactions a year, withdrawing an average of $60 per transaction.[15]

automated teller machine (ATM)
Electronic machine that allows customers to conduct account-related activities 24 hours a day, 7 days a week

Increasingly, ATMs are also becoming global fixtures. In fact, among the world's 708,000 ATMs, 68 percent are located outside the United States. Asia, with 32 percent of the world's total, is the leading region for ATMs, followed by North America (31 percent), Western Europe (25 percent), and Latin America (8 percent). Many U.S. banks now offer international ATM services. Citicorp installed Shanghai's first 24-hour ATM and is the first foreign bank to receive approval from the People's Bank of China to issue local currency through ATMs. Elsewhere, Citibank machines feature touch screens that take instructions in any of 10 languages.

Electronic Funds Transfer ATMs are the most popular form of **electronic funds transfer (EFT)**. These systems transfer many kinds of financial information via electrical impulses over wire, cable, or microwave. In addition to ATMs, EFT systems include automatic payroll deposit, bill payment, and automatic funds transfer. Such systems can help a businessperson close an important business deal by transferring money from San Francisco to Miami within a few hours.[16]

electronic funds transfer (EFT)
Communication of fund-transfer information over wire, cable, or microwave

Banks as Creators of Money

In the course of their activities, financial institutions provide a special service to the economy—they create money. This is not to say that they mint bills and coins. Rather, by taking in deposits and making loans, they *expand the money supply.*[17]

IT'S A WIRED WORLD
To E-Bank or Not to E-Bank

Is banking ready for e-business? It depends on whom you talk to, but based on results to date, bankers have a long way to go before they're completely wired. This centuries-old industry isn't yet set up for Internet retail-customer transactions. Commenting on the relatively poor success of Internet banks, one Dutch banker notes: "We underestimate the value of the trust we have built up. It is one of the highest barriers to entry to our business." In other words, consumers are skeptical about trusting personal financial matters to impersonal Internet acquaintances. They're accustomed to dealing with a particular bank, usually at a local facility. Think of the typical services you use—checking, loans, trusts, investments. Think about face-to-face transactions in a familiar environment. Now contrast that image with an image of Internet transactions with your bank. What if it's a remote bank? What if your contact with your bank is a cyberspace third party?

E-banking raises a basic question that bankers have not encountered before: Should the bank be the party to whom the customer entrusts all of the customer's financial activities? Or, from a strictly financial point of view, would a third party be a better choice? This choice has emerged because the Internet, although introducing a third party into the relationship, offers global access to financial products and services beyond the reach of any single bank. As a nonbank third party, OnMoney.com <www.onmoney.com> allows you to see and manage all your accounts at one Web location. Banks can't match this service. You can receive and pay bills, prepare and file taxes, check out financial news, and get good deals on financial products from leading vendors (some tailored to your particular needs), all by storing your financial data with—and putting your trust in—a single Web destination. The third party also provides interactive financial management and access to services but does not sell financial products, such as car or mortgage loans or stocks and bonds. As a traditional banker, you may like the idea that your customers are linked to a third party that can provide them with a better range of consolidated services. Unfortunately, your customer also gains access to better deals from competing banks and financial services providers.

The alternative is to sell customers on the idea of a centralized bank, but that approach can make customers worry about a bank's objectivity in promoting its own financial products. The customer is likely to ask: If I buy all my products from this bank, how good a deal am I getting on any one of them? The strategic question for the bank, therefore, is how to position itself to win the customer relationship. Bankers disagree on the best approach. The e-Citi unit of Citigroup is hedging its Web strategy by offering a mixture of both Citibank and non-Citibank products for both kinds of customers—those who want one bank to supply all their needs and those who may prefer more diverse offerings. Meanwhile, other banks, especially smaller ones, are leaning toward the option of serving as an adviser who puts customers in touch with outside (third-party) experts for financial advice. Its choice in this matter will undoubtedly have a huge impact on a bank's Web services and customer relationships for the future.

Many bankers are convinced that banks are still dependent on traditional financial products with bank customers who want access to branch locations and human interaction via phone, video, or e-mail. The first generation of Web banks still needs human support and must furnish access to a physical infrastructure (bricks and mortar). Many industry analysts fear that too much technology may push customers into the hands of competitors who still offer face-to-face service.

As Figure 14.3 shows, the money supply expands because banks are allowed to loan out most (although not all) of the money they take in from deposits. Suppose that you deposit \$100 in your bank. If banks are allowed to loan out 90 percent of all their deposits, then your bank will hold \$10 in reserve and loan \$90 of your money to borrowers. (You, of course, still have \$100 on deposit.) Meanwhile, borrowers—or the people they pay—will deposit the \$90 loan in their own banks. Together, the borrowers' banks will then have \$81 (90 percent of \$90) available for new loans. Banks, therefore, have turned your original \$100 into \$271 (\$100 + \$90 + \$81). The chain continues, with borrowings from one bank becoming deposits in the next.

Deposit	Money Held in Reserve by Bank	Money to Lend	Total Supply
$100.00	$10.00	$90.00	$190.00
90.00	9.00	81.00	271.00
81.00	8.10	72.90	343.90
72.90	7.29	65.61	409.51
65.61	6.56	59.05	468.56

Figure 14.3
How Banks Create Money

Regulation of Commercial Banking

Because commercial banks are critical to the creation of money, the government regulates them to ensure a sound and competitive financial system. Later in this chapter, we will see how the Federal Reserve System regulates many aspects of U.S. banking. Other federal and state agencies also regulate banks to ensure that the failure of some banks as a result of competition will not cause the public to lose faith in the banking system itself.

Federal Deposit Insurance Corporation The **Federal Deposit Insurance Corporation (FDIC)** insures deposits in member banks. More than 99 percent of the nation's commercial banks pay fees for membership in the FDIC <www.fdic.gov>. In return, the FDIC guarantees, through its Bank Insurance Fund (BIF), the safety of all deposits up to the current maximum of $100,000. If a bank collapses, the FDIC promises to pay its depositors—through the BIF—for losses up to $100,000 per person. (A handful of the nation's 10,000 commercial banks are insured by states rather than by the BIF.)

Federal Deposit Insurance Corporation (FDIC)
Federal agency that guarantees the safety of all deposits up to $100,000 in the financial institutions that it insures

To insure against multiple bank failures, the FDIC maintains the right to examine the activities and accounts of all member banks. Such regulation was effective from 1941 through 1980, when fewer than 10 banks failed per year. At the beginning of the 1980s, however, banks were deregulated, and between 1981 and 1990, losses from nearly 1,100 bank failures depleted the FDIC's reserve fund. In recent years, the FDIC has thus raised the premiums charged to member banks to keep up with losses incurred by failed banks.

THE FEDERAL RESERVE SYSTEM

Perched atop the U.S. financial system and regulating many aspects of its operation is the Federal Reserve System. Established by Congress in 1913, the **Federal Reserve System** (or the **Fed**) <www.federalreserve.gov> is the nation's central bank. In this section, we describe the structure of the Fed, its functions, and the tools that it uses to control the nation's money supply.

Federal Reserve System (the Fed)
Central bank of the United States, which acts as the government's bank, serves member commercial banks, and controls the nation's money supply

The Structure of the Fed

The Federal Reserve System consists of a board of governors, a group of reserve banks, and member banks. As originally established by the Federal Reserve Act of 1913, the system consisted of 12 relatively autonomous banks and a seven-member committee whose powers were limited to coordinating their activities. By the 1930s, however, both the structure and function of the Fed had changed dramatically.

The Board of Governors The Fed's board of governors consists of seven members appointed by the president for overlapping terms of 14 years. The chair of the board serves on major economic advisory committees and works actively with the administration to formulate economic policy. The board plays a large role in controlling the

WEB Connection

Besides explaining the functions and operations of the Fed, the official site includes such pages as "Monetary Performance" (where you can access semiannual reports on monetary policy and economic performance) and "Research and Data" (which publishes staff studies on a wide range of economic and financial subjects).

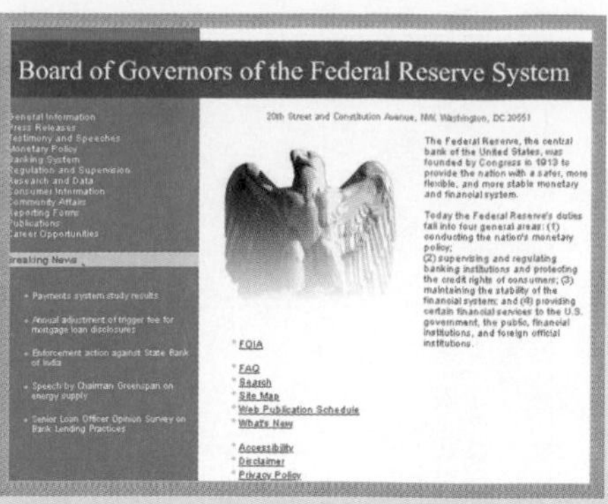

www.federalreserve.gov

money supply. It alone determines the reserve requirements, within statutory limits, for depository institutions. It also works with other members of the Federal Reserve System to set discount rates and handle the Fed's sale and purchase of government securities.

Reserve Banks The Federal Reserve System consists of 12 administrative areas and 12 banks. Each Federal Reserve bank holds reserve deposits from and sets the discount rate for commercial banks in its region. Reserve banks also play a major role in the nation's check-clearing process.

Member Banks All nationally chartered commercial banks are members of the Federal Reserve System, as are some state-chartered banks. The accounts of all member bank depositors are automatically covered by the FDIC/BIF. Although many state-chartered banks do not belong to the Federal Reserve System, most pay deposit insurance premiums and are covered by the FDIC.

The Functions of the Fed

In addition to chartering national banks, the Fed serves as the federal government's bank and the "bankers' bank," regulating a number of banking activities. Most importantly, it controls the money supply. In this section, we describe these functions in some detail.

The Government's Bank Two of the Fed's activities are producing the nation's paper currency and lending money to the government. The Fed decides how many bills to produce and how many to destroy. To lend funds to the government, the Fed buys bonds issued by the Treasury Department <www.ustreas.gov>. The borrowed money is then used to help finance the national deficit.

The Bankers' Bank Individual banks that need money can borrow from the Federal Reserve and pay interest on the loans. In addition, the Fed provides storage for commercial banks, which are required to keep funds on reserve at a Federal Reserve bank.

Check Clearing The Fed also clears checks, some 65 billion of them each year, for commercial banks. To understand the check-clearing process, imagine that you are a photographer living in New Orleans. To participate in a workshop in Detroit, you must send a check for $50 to the Detroit studio. Figure 14.4 traces your check through the clearing process:

1. You send your check to the Detroit studio, which deposits it in its Detroit bank.
2. The Detroit bank deposits the check in its own account at the Federal Reserve Bank of Chicago.

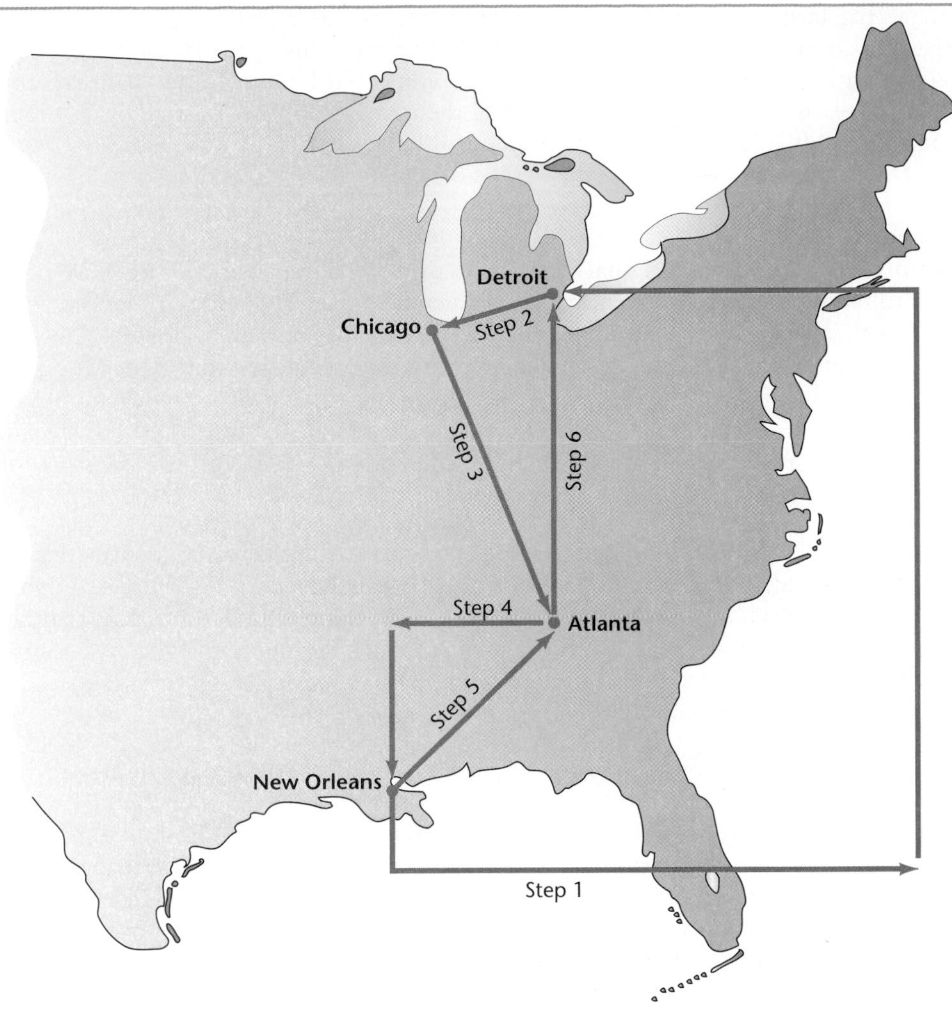

Figure 14.4
Clearing a Check

3. The check is sent from Chicago to the Atlanta Federal Reserve Bank for collection because you, the check writer, live in the Atlanta district.
4. Your New Orleans bank receives the check from Atlanta and deducts the $50 from your personal account.
5. Your bank then has $50 deducted from its deposit account at the Atlanta Federal Reserve Bank.
6. The $50 is shifted from Atlanta to the Chicago Federal Reserve Bank. The studio's Detroit bank gets credited, whereupon the studio's account is then credited $50. Your bank mails the canceled check back to you.

Depending on the number of banks and the distances between them, a check will clear in two to six days. Until the process is completed, the studio's Detroit bank cannot spend the $50 deposited there. Meanwhile, your bank's records will continue to show $50 in your account. Each day, approximately $1 billion in checks is processed by the system. The term **float** refers to all the checks in the process at any one time.

Controlling the Money Supply The Federal Reserve System is responsible for the conduct of U.S. **monetary policy**—the management of the nation's economic growth by managing money supply and interest rates. By controlling these two factors, the Fed influences the ability and willingness of banks throughout the country to loan money.

Inflation Management As we defined it in Chapter 1, *inflation* is a period of widespread price increases throughout an economic system. It occurs if the money supply

float
Total amount of checks written but not yet cleared through the Federal Reserve

monetary policy
Policies by which the Federal Reserve manages the nation's money supply and interest rates

grows too large. Demand for goods and services increases, and the prices of everything rise. (In contrast, too little money means that an economy will lack the funds to maintain high levels of employment.) Because commercial banks are the main creators of money, much of the Fed's management of the money supply takes the form of regulating the supply of money through commercial banks.

The Tools of the Fed

According to the Fed's original charter, its primary duties were to supervise banking and to manage both the currency and commercial paper. The duties of the Fed evolved, however, along with a predominant philosophy of monetary policy. That policy includes an emphasis on the broad economic goals as discussed in Chapter 1, especially growth and stability. The Fed's role in controlling the nation's money supply stems from its role in setting policies to help reach these goals. To control the money supply, the Fed uses four primary tools: *reserve requirements, discount rate controls, open-market operations*, and *selective credit controls*.[18]

reserve requirement
Percentage of its deposits that a bank must hold in cash or on deposit with the Federal Reserve

Reserve Requirements The **reserve requirement** is the percentage of its deposits a bank must hold, in cash or on deposit, with a Federal Reserve bank. High requirements mean that banks have less money to lend. Thus, a high reserve requirement reduces the money supply. Conversely, low requirements permit the supply to expand. Because the Fed sets requirements for all depository institutions, it can adjust them to make changes in the overall supply of money to the economy.

discount rate
Interest rate at which member banks can borrow money from the Federal Reserve

Discount Rate Controls As the "bankers' bank," the Fed loans money to banks. The interest rate on these loans is known as the **discount rate**. If the Fed wants to reduce the money supply, it increases the discount rate, making it more expensive for banks to borrow money and less attractive for them to loan it. Conversely, low rates encourage borrowing and lending and expand the money supply. The Fed used a series of discount rate decreases—from 6.0 percent beginning in May 2000 down to 3.75 percent in July 2001—to speed up the sagging U.S. economy.[19]

open-market operations
The Federal Reserve's sales and purchases of securities in the open market

Open-Market Operations The third instrument for monetary control is probably the Fed's most important tool. **Open-market operations** refer to the Fed's sale and purchase of securities (usually U.S. Treasury notes and bonds) in the open market. Open-market operations are particularly effective because they act quickly and predictably on the money supply. How so? The Fed buys securities from dealers. Because the dealer's bank account is credited for the transaction, its bank has more money to lend, and so expands the money supply. The opposite happens when the Fed sells securities.[20]

selective credit controls
Federal Reserve authority to set both margin requirements for consumer stock purchases and credit rules for other consumer purchases

Selective Credit Controls The Federal Reserve can exert considerable influence on business activity by exercising **selective credit controls**. The Fed may set special requirements for consumer stock purchases and credit rules for other consumer purchases.

As we will see in Chapter 15, investors can set up credit accounts with stockbrokers to buy stocks and bonds. A margin requirement set by the Fed stipulates the amount of credit that the broker can extend to the customer. For example, a 60 percent margin rate means that approved customers can purchase stocks having $100,000 market value with $60,000 in cash (60 percent of $100,000) and $40,000 in loans from the dealer. If the Fed wants to increase securities transactions, it can lower the margin requirement. Customers can then borrow greater percentages of their purchase costs from dealers, thus increasing their purchasing power and the amount of securities that they can buy.

Within stipulated limits, the Fed is also permitted to specify the conditions of certain credit purchases. This authority extends to such conditions as allowable down payment percentages for appliance purchases and repayment periods on automobile loans. The Fed has chosen to not use these powers in recent years.

THE CHANGING MONEY AND BANKING SYSTEM

The U.S. money and banking systems have changed in recent years and continue to change today. Deregulation and interstate banking, for example, have increased competition not only among banks but also between banks and other financial institutions. Electronic technologies affect how you obtain money and how much interest you pay for it.

Deregulation

The Depository Institutions Deregulation and Monetary Control Act (DIDMCA) of 1980 brought many changes to the banking industry. Before its passage, there were clear distinctions between the types of services offered by different institutions. Although all institutions could offer savings accounts, only commercial banks could offer checking accounts, and S&Ls and mutual savings banks generally could not make consumer loans. The DIDMCA and subsequent laws sought to promote competition by eliminating many such restrictions.

Under deregulation, many banks were unable to survive in the new competitive environment. In the 1980s, more than 1,000 banks—more than 7 percent of the total—failed, as did 835 savings and loans. Many economists, however, regard some bank closings as a beneficial weeding out of inefficient competitors.

Interstate Banking

Although interstate banking is commonplace, it is a relatively new development. The Interstate Banking Efficiency Act was passed into law in September 1994, thus allowing banks to enter (gradually) into interstate banking—the operation of banks or branches across state lines. It also mandates regulation by government agencies to ensure proper operation and competition. The key provisions in this act include the following:

- Limited nationwide banking is permitted, beginning in 1995. Bank holding companies can acquire subsidiaries in any state.
- The ultimate *size* of any company is limited. No one company can control more than 10 percent of nationwide insured deposits. No bank can control more than 30 percent of a state's deposits (each state is empowered to set its own limit).
- Beginning in 1995, banks can provide limited transactions for affiliated banks in other states. They can thus accept deposits, close loans, and accept loan payments on behalf of other affiliated banks. (They cannot, however, originate loans or open deposit accounts for affiliates.)
- Beginning in June 1997, banks can convert affiliates into full-fledged interstate branches.

Interstate banking offers certain efficiencies. For example, it allows banks to consolidate services and eliminate duplicated activities. Opponents, however, remain concerned that some banks will gain undue influence, dominate other banks, and hinder competition.

The Impact of Electronic Technologies

Like so many other businesses, banks are increasingly investing in technology as a way to improve efficiency and customer service levels. Many banks offer ATMs and EFT systems. Some offer TV banking, in which customers use television sets and terminals—or home computers—to make transactions. The age of electronic money has arrived. Digital money is replacing cash in stores, taxi cabs, subway systems, and vending machines. Each business day, more than $2 trillion exists in and among banks and other financial institutions in purely electronic form. Each year, the Fed transfers electronically more than $250 trillion in transactions.

Debit Cards One of the electronic offerings from the financial industry that has gained popularity is the debit card. Unlike credit cards, **debit cards** allow only the transfer of money between accounts. They do not increase the funds at an individual's disposal. They can, however, be used to make retail purchases. The number of cards in use doubled from 173 million in 1990 to 353 million in 2000, with $368 billion in transactions.

debit card
Plastic card that allows an individual to transfer money between accounts

In stores with **point-of-sale (POS) terminals**, customers insert cards that transmit to terminals information relevant to their purchases. The terminal relays the information directly to the bank's computer system. The bank automatically transfers funds from the customer's account to the store's account.

point-of-sale (POS) terminal Electronic device that allows customers to pay for retail purchases with debit cards

smart card Credit-card-size computer programmed with electronic money

Smart Cards The so-called **smart card** is a credit-card-size computer that can be programmed with "electronic money." Also known as "electronic purses" or "stored-value cards," smart cards have existed for more than a decade. Phone callers and shoppers in Europe and Asia are the most avid users, holding the majority of the nearly 1.5 billion cards in circulation in 1999. Analysts expect 4 billion cards to be in use by the year 2002.[21]

Why are smart cards increasing in popularity today? For one thing, the cost of producing them has fallen dramatically, from as much as $10 to as little as $1. Convenience is equally important, notes Donald J. Gleason, president of Smart Card Enterprise, a division of Electronic Payment Services <www.eps.com.hk>. "What consumers want," Gleason contends, "is convenience, and if you look at cash, it's really quite inconvenient."

"What customers want is convenience, and if you look at cash, it's really quite inconvenient."

—Donald J. Gleason, president, Smart Card Enterprise Division, Electronic Payment Services

Smart cards can be loaded with money at ATM machines or, with special telephone hookups, even at home. After using your card to purchase an item, you can then check an electronic display to see how much money your card has left. Analysts predict that in the near future, smart cards will function as much more than electronic purses. For example, travel industry experts predict that people will soon book travel plans at home on personal computers and then transfer their reservations onto their smart cards. The cards will then serve as airline tickets and boarding passes. As an added benefit, they will allow travelers to avoid waiting in lines at car rental agencies and hotel front desks.

e-cash Electronic money that moves between consumers and businesses via digital electronic transmissions

E-Cash A new, revolutionary world of electronic money has begun to emerge with the rapid growth of the Internet. Electronic money, known as **e-cash**, is money that moves along multiple channels of consumers and businesses via digital electronic transmissions. E-cash moves outside the established network of banks, checks, and paper currency overseen by the Federal Reserve. Companies as varied as new start-up Mondex <www.mondex.com> and giant Citicorp are developing their own forms of electronic money that allow consumers and businesses to spend money more conveniently, quickly, and cheaply than they can through the banking system. In fact, some observers predict that by the year 2005, as much as 20 percent of all household expenditures will take place on the Internet. "Banking," comments one investment banker, "is essential to the modern economy, but banks are not."

Commuters in metropolitan New York are getting accustomed to paying bridge and tunnel tolls with the E-Z Pass <www.drpa. org/ezintro>, a debit device that the driver attaches to the front windshield. A scanner electronically records trips through participating bridge and tunnel toll booths and debits an account established with the customer's credit card.

How does e-cash work? Traditional currency is used to buy electronic funds, which are downloaded over phone lines into a PC or a portable "electronic wallet" that can store and transmit e-cash. E-cash is purchased from any company that issues (sells) it, including companies such as Mondex, Citicorp, and banks. When shopping online—for example, to purchase jewelry—a shopper sends digital money to the merchant instead of using traditional cash, checks, or credit cards. Businesses can purchase supplies and services electronically from any merchant that accepts e-cash. It flows from the buyer's into the seller's e-cash funds, which are instantaneously updated and stored on a microchip. One system, operated by CyberCash <www.cybercash.com>, tallies all e-cash transactions in the customer's account and, at the end of the day, converts the e-cash balance back into dollars in the customer's conventional banking account.

Although e-cash transactions are cheaper than handling checks and the paper records involved with conventional money, there are some potential problems.[22] Hackers, for example, may break into e-cash systems and drain them instantaneously. Moreover, if the issuer's computer system crashes, it is conceivable that money "banked" in memory may be lost forever. Finally, regulation and control of e-cash systems remain largely nonexistent; there is virtually none of the protection that covers government-controlled money systems.

INTERNATIONAL BANKING AND FINANCE

Along with international banking networks, electronic technologies now permit nearly instantaneous financial transactions around the globe. The economic importance of international finance is evident from both the presence of foreign banks in the U.S. market and the sizes of certain banks around the world. In addition, each nation tries to influence its currency exchange rates for economic advantage in international trade. The subsequent country-to-country transactions result in an *international payments process* that moves money between buyers and sellers on different continents.

The International Payments Process

Now we know why a nation tries to control its balance of payments and what it can do about an unfavorable balance. When transactions are made between buyers and sellers in different countries, exactly how are payments made? Payments are simplified through the services provided by their banks.[23] For example, payments from buyers flow through a local bank that converts them from the local currency into the foreign currency of the seller. The local bank receives and converts incoming money from the banks of foreign buyers. The payment process is shown in Figure 14.5.

- *Step 1.* A U.S. olive importer withdraws $1,000 from its checking account to buy olives from a Greek exporter. The local U.S. bank converts those dollars into Greek drachmas at the current exchange rate (230 drachmas per dollar).
- *Step 2.* The U.S. bank sends a check for 230,000 drachmas (230 × 1,000) to the exporter in Greece.
- *Steps 3 and 4.* The exporter sends olives to its U.S. customer and deposits the check in its local Greek bank. The exporter now has drachmas that can be spent in Greece, and the importer has olives to sell in the United States.

At the same time, a separate transaction is being made between a U.S. machine exporter and a Greek olive oil producer. This time, importer/exporter roles are reversed between the two countries: The Greek firm needs to import a $1,000 olive oil press from the United States.

- *Steps 5 and 6.* Drachmas (230,000) withdrawn from a local Greek bank account are converted into U.S.$1,000 and sent via check to the U.S. exporter.
- *Steps 7 and 8.* The olive oil press is sent to the Greek importer, and the importer's check is deposited in the U.S. exporter's local bank account.

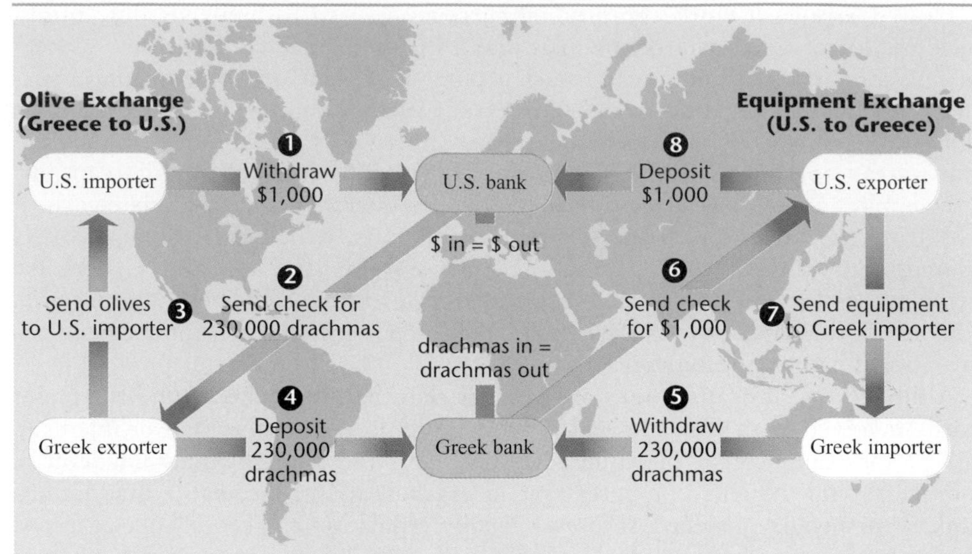

Figure 14.5
International Payments Process

In this example, trade between the two countries is in balance. Money inflows and outflows are equal for both countries. When such a balance occurs, *money does not actually have to flow between the two countries*. Within each bank, the dollars spent by local importers offset the dollars received by local exporters. In effect, therefore, the dollars have simply flowed from U.S. importers to U.S. exporters. Similarly, the drachmas have moved from Greek exporters to Greek importers.

International Bank Structure

There is no worldwide banking system that is comparable, in terms of policy making and regulatory power, to the system of any industrialized nation. Rather, worldwide banking stability relies on a loose structure of agreements among individual countries or groups of countries.

World Bank
United Nations agency that provides a limited scope of financial services, such as funding national improvements in undeveloped countries

The World Bank and the IMF Two United Nations agencies, the World Bank and the International Monetary Fund, help to finance international trade.[24] Unlike true banks, the **World Bank** (technically the International Bank for Reconstruction and Development) <www.worldbank.org> provides only a very limited scope of services. For instance, it funds national improvements by making loans to build roads, schools, power plants, and hospitals. The resulting improvements eventually enable borrowing countries to increase productive capacity and international trade.

"His mood is pegged to the dollar."

The **International Monetary Fund (IMF)** <www.imf.org> is a group of some 150 nations that have combined resources for the following purposes:

- To promote the stability of exchange rates
- To provide temporary, short-term loans to member countries
- To encourage members to cooperate on international monetary issues
- To encourage development of a system for international payments

International Monetary Fund (IMF)
United Nations agency consisting of about 150 nations that have combined resources to promote stable exchange rates, provide temporary short-term loans, and serve other purposes

The IMF makes loans to nations suffering from temporary negative trade balances. By making it possible for these countries to continue buying products from other countries, the IMF facilitates international trade. However, some nations have declined IMF funds rather than accept the economic changes that the IMF demands. For example, some developing countries reject the IMF's requirement that they cut back social programs and spending in order to bring inflation under control.

Continued from page 363

Gentlemen, Start Your Euros!

Changing over to the euro presents a number of advantages and challenges, including some risky problems for banks. First of all, banks will have to handle huge amounts of new currency—funds that will be disbursed—along with the collecting of old currency from businesses and individuals, all within defined time limits. They will have to store both old and new currencies and establish procedures for collecting and distributing funds. Cash-transit trucks will be carrying old and new cash between retailers (and other businesses) and banks, and arrangements must be contracted with transit companies. Security, storage, and insurance procedures for this abundance of on-hand cash must be set up to reduce risks from potential accidents and criminal intrusions. In addition, nearly 200,000 ATMs must be modified to issue euro notes by January 1, 2002. By that same deadline, some 14 billion euro notes and 50 billion coins must be minted and placed into circulation. Says David Wood, a leading underwriter for Lloyd's of London, "This is the biggest logistical issue that cash-in-transit companies probably will ever face."

Aside from banks, virtually all other EMU businesses, both large and small, will be affected. Retail employees, for instance, must be trained to help skeptical and confused customers. More importantly, in order to make change in either currency, retailers will need a considerable amount of extra cash on hand—double the usual amount—during the changeover. Even if Company A is prepared for a normal level of activity, what happens when an unprepared Company B shuts down and sends its customers rushing to Company A in search of transactions? Will Company A be able to handle a sudden upsurge in demand? And what about downturns? "There is the business risk," warns Paul Taylor, deputy president of the Federation of European Risk Management Associations, "that customers may not continue to spend at the normal rate, and there may be a pause in spending because of concerns over exchange rates." Finally, accounting requirements for all businesses will change because transactions and records in two currencies must be reconciled to reflect every firm's financial activities during the transition.

If the euro threatens so many problems, what's the upside? The answer is that the EMU countries expect more business growth and an accompanying economic boost. Medium and small firms that were once reluctant to trade across borders are now more likely to take the step, as are those that hesitated to expand by locating branches or factories in other countries. Moreover, the new single monetary unit eliminates the inherent risks that have always plagued the currency exchange rates among national currencies. Rates varied from day to day, often unpredictably. With the new currency, whose value will be the same in Italy as in Finland, France, and the Netherlands, bankers and other businesspeople can more easily predict selling prices and operating costs. In short, it is expected that the euro, once in place, will provide more monetary stability and portability than existed among the several individual currencies before January 1, 2002.

Questions for Discussion

1. Assume for a moment that you're a consumer of retail goods in an EMU country. Can you identify any problems you might expect to encounter during your country's transition to the euro?
2. Suppose you are manager of an Italian retail store. What preparations would you make to ensure that your business is ready for the transition from lire to euros?
3. Identify the advantages to be gained—for both individuals and companies—from switching to one currency, such as the euro, instead of having individual national currencies. What are the disadvantages?
4. Some countries, including Britain and Switzerland, have refused to join the EMU community. Why do you suppose these countries are retaining their own currencies rather than switching to euros along with their 12 neighbors?
5. Consider the often discussed concept of creating one worldwide currency. Do you believe such an arrangement is feasible? What factors tend to make a one-world currency attractive? What factors might prevent it from becoming a reality?

SUMMARY OF LEARNING OBJECTIVES

1 **Define *money* and identify the different forms it takes in the nation's money supply.** Any item that is portable, divisible, durable, and stable satisfies the four basic characteristics of *money*. Money also serves three functions: It is a medium of exchange, a store of value, and a unit of account. The nation's money supply is often determined by two measures. *M-1* includes liquid (or spendable) forms of money: currency (bills and coins), demand deposits, and other checkable deposits (such as ATM account balances and NOW accounts). *M-2* includes M-1 plus items that cannot be directly spent but can be converted easily to spendable forms: time deposits, money market funds, and savings deposits. *Credit* must also be considered as a factor in the money supply.

2 **Describe the different kinds of *financial institutions* that make up the U.S. financial system and explain the services they offer.** The U.S. financial system includes federal- and state-chartered *commercial banks, savings and loan associations, mutual savings banks, credit unions*, and *nondeposit institutions* such as pension funds and insurance companies. These institutions offer a variety of services, including pension, trust, and international services, financial advice and brokerage services, and electronic funds transfer (EFT), including automated teller machines.

3 **Explain how banks create money and describe the means by which they are regulated.** By taking in deposits and making loans, banks create money or, more accurately, *expand the money supply*. The overall supply of money is governed by the Federal Reserve System, which is the primary agency responsible for ensuring a sound, competitive financial system. The Federal Deposit Insurance Corporation (FDIC) insures deposits in the nation's commercial banks.

4 **Discuss the functions of the *Federal Reserve System* and describe the tools it uses to control the money supply.** The *Federal Reserve System* (or *the Fed*) is the nation's central bank. As the government's bank, the Fed produces currency and lends money to the government. As the bankers' bank, it lends money (at interest) to member banks, stores required *reserve funds* for banks, and clears checks for them. The Fed is empowered to audit member banks and sets U.S. *monetary policy* by controlling the country's money supply. To control the money supply, the Fed specifies *reserve requirements* (the percentage of its deposits that a bank must hold with the Fed). It sets the *discount rate* at which it lends money to banks and conducts *open-market operations* to buy and sell securities. It also exerts influence through *selective*

credit controls (such as margin requirements governing the credit granted to buyers by securities brokers).

5 **Identify three important ways in which the financial industry is changing.** Many changes have affected the financial system in recent years. *Deregulation*, especially of interest rates, and the rise of *interstate banking* have increased competition. *Electronic technologies* offer a variety of new financial conveniences to customers. *Debit cards* are plastic cards that permit users to transfer money between bank accounts. *Smart cards* are credit-card-size computers that can be loaded with electronic money at ATMs or over special telephone hookups. *E-cash* is money that can be moved among consumers and businesses via digital electronic transmissions.

6 **Understand some of the key activities in international banking and finance.** Electronic technologies now permit speedy global financial transactions to support the growing importance of international finance. Country-to-country transactions are conducted according to an *international payments process* that moves money among buyers and sellers in different nations. The payment process recognizes the current *exchange rates* of currencies for all countries involved in international exchange.

QUESTIONS AND EXERCISES

Questions for Review

1. What are the components of M-1? Of M-2?
2. Explain the roles of commercial banks, savings and loan associations, and nondeposit institutions in the U.S. financial system.
3. Explain the types of pension services that commercial banks provide for their customers.
4. Describe the structure of the Federal Reserve System.
5. Show how the Fed uses the discount rate to manage inflation in the U.S. economy.

Questions for Analysis

6. Do you think credit cards should be counted in the money supply? Why or why not? Support your argument by using the definition of money.
7. Should commercial banks be regulated, or should market forces be allowed to determine the money supply? Why?
8. Identify a purchase made by you or a family member in which payment was made by check. Draw a diagram to trace the steps in the clearing process followed by that check.

Application Exercises

9. Start with a $1,000 deposit and assume a reserve requirement of 15 percent. Now trace the amount of money created by the banking system after five lending cycles.
10. Interview the manager of a local commercial bank. Identify several ways in which the Fed either helps the bank or restricts its operations.

EXPLORING THE WEB

Banking on the Fed

The Federal Reserve Board, as the central controlling figure in the U.S. banking system, actively rules on a variety of banking issues. To find out about some of the Fed's recent activities, log on to its Web site at:

<www.federalreserve.gov>

Working from the left column of the home page, you are asked to explore two areas—"Domestic and Foreign Banking Cases" and "Enforcement Actions"—as described here.

- Scroll down to Press Releases; then click on **Domestic and Foreign Banking Cases.** Scan the summaries of the 20 most recent cases and then consider the following questions:
  1. Describe the various *types of actions* taken by the Fed.
  2. How many of the cases involve *bank mergers*?
  3. Select a case that interests you, click on the date, and read the detailed press release. Then prepare a brief report for class that identifies the main banking issue, the business firms involved, the action taken by the Fed, and the economic significance of the case.
- Scroll down to Press Releases; then click on **Enforcement Actions.** Scan the summaries of any 10 recent cases. Describe the types of actions taken by the Fed in these cases.
- Next, select a case that interests you, click on the date, and read the detailed press release. Then prepare a report on the following:
  1. Describe the *banking issue* involved in the case.
  2. Who are the *contestants* in the case?
  3. Explain the *enforcement actions* taken by the Federal Reserve Board in this case.

EXERCISING YOUR ETHICS

Telling the Ethical from the Strictly Legal

THE SITUATION

When upgrading services for convenience to customers, commercial banks are concerned with setting prices that cover all costs so that, ultimately, they make a profit. This exercise challenges you to evaluate one banking service—ATM transactions—to determine if there are also ethical issues that should be considered in a bank's pricing decisions.

THE DILEMMA

A regional commercial bank in the western United States has more than 300 ATMs serving the nearly 400,000 checking and savings accounts of its customers. Customers are not charged a fee for their 30 million ATM transactions each year, so long as they use their bank's ATMs. For issuing cash to noncustomers, however, the bank charges a $2 ATM fee. The bank's officers are reexamining their policies on ATM surcharges because of public protests against other banks in Santa Monica, New York, and Chicago. Iowa has gone even further, becoming the first state to pass legislation that bans national banks from charging ATM fees for noncustomers. To date, the courts have ruled that the access fees are legal, but some organizations—such as the U.S. Public Interest Research Group (PIRG)—continue to fight publicly against them.

In considering its current policies, our western bank's vice president for community relations is concerned with more than mere legalities. She wants to ensure that her company is "being a good citizen and doing the right thing." Any decision on ATM fees will ultimately affect the bank's customers, its image in the community and industry, and its profitability for its owners.

QUESTIONS FOR DISCUSSION

1. From the standpoint of a commercial bank, can you find any economic justification for ATM access fees?
2. Based on the scenario described for our bank, do you find any ethical issues in this situation? Or do you find the main issues legal and economic rather than ethical?
3. As an officer for this bank, how would you handle this situation?

BUILDING YOUR BUSINESS SKILLS

Four Economists in a Room

This exercise enhances the following SCANS workplace competencies: demonstrating basic skills, demonstrating thinking skills, exhibiting interpersonal skills, working with information, and applying system knowledge.

GOAL

To encourage students to understand the economic factors considered by the Federal Reserve Board in determining current interest rates.

BACKGROUND

One of the Federal Reserve's most important tools in setting monetary policy is the adjustment of the interest rates it charges member banks to borrow money. To determine interest rate policy, the Fed analyzes current economic conditions from its 12 districts. Its findings are published eight times a year in a report commonly known as the *Beige Book*.

METHOD

STEP 1

Working with three other students, access the Federal Reserve Web site at <www.federalreserve.gov>. Look for the heading "Monetary Policy" and then look for "Federal Open Market Committee." Next, click on the subheading "Beige Book". When you reach that page, click on **Summary of the Current Report**.

STEP 2

Working with group members, study each of the major summary sections:

- Consumer spending
- Manufacturing
- Construction and real estate
- Banking and finance
- Nonfinancial services
- Labor market, wages, and pricing
- Agriculture and natural resources

Working with team members, discuss ways in which you think that key information contained in the summary might affect the Fed's decision to raise, lower, or maintain interest rates.

STEP 3

At your library find back issues of *Barron's* <www.barrons.com>, the highly respected weekly financial publication. Look for the issue published immediately following the appearance of the most recent *Beige Book*. Search for articles analyzing the report. Discuss with group members what the articles say about current economic conditions and interest rates.

STEP 4

Based on your research and analysis, what factors do you think the Fed will take into account to control inflation? Working with group members, explain your answer in writing.

STEP 5

Working with group members, research what the Federal Reserve chairperson says next about interest rates. Do the chairperson's reasons for raising, lowering, or maintaining rates agree with your group's analysis?

FOLLOW-UP QUESTIONS

1. What are the most important factors in the Fed's interest rate decision?
2. Consider the old joke about economists that goes like this: *When there are four economists in a room analyzing current economic conditions, there are at least eight different opinions.* Based on your research and analysis, why do you think economists have such varying opinions?

CRAFTING YOUR BUSINESS PLAN

How to Bank on Your Money

THE PURPOSE OF THE ASSIGNMENT

1. To familiarize students with banking issues that a sample firm faces in developing its business plan, in the framework of *Business PlanPro* (*BPP*) (Version 4.0).
2. To demonstrate how two chapter topics—bank services and interest rates—can be integrated as components in the *BPP* planning environment.

FOLLOW-UP ASSIGNMENT

After reading Chapter 14 in the textbook, open the BPP *software* and search for information about the financial plans of a sample firm:* Flower Importer *(Fantastic Florals, Inc., FFI). Then respond to the following items:*

1. Consider interest rates that are assumed in the business plan. Are the short-term and long-term rates reasonable in today's economy? Explain. [Sites to see in *BPP* for this item: In the Plan Outline screen, click on **Table: General Assumptions** (located beneath **7.1 Important Assumptions**). Also, read the Instructions section near the top of the screen.]
2. Identify some international banking services that would benefit FFI in its daily operations. [Sites to see in *BPP*: In the Plan Outline screen, click on **1.0 Executive Summary**. Return to the Plan Outline screen and click, in turn, on each of **3.4 Sourcing** and **3.6 Future Products**.]
3. From FFI's financial plan, can you see any need for bank credit? When, during the planning horizon, might the firm need a line of credit and how much? [Sites to see in *BPP*: From the Plan Outline screen, click on each of **7.0 Financial Plan** and **Table: Cash Flow** (located beneath **7.5 Projected Cash Flow**).]
4. Does FFI plan to have excess cash that can be deposited in the bank to earn interest? When, during the planning horizon, might the firm accumulate excess cash and how much? [Sites to see in *BPP*: In the Plan Outline screen, click on **Table: Sales Forecast** (located beneath **5.2.1 Sales Forecast**). Return to the Plan Outline screen, then click on **Table: Cash Flow** (located beneath **7.5 Projected Cash Flow**). Observe the cash balance at the bottom of the table.]

VIDEO EXERCISE

The World's Lenders: The World Bank and the IMF

LEARNING OBJECTIVES

The purpose of this video is to help you

1. Understand the role of the World Bank.
2. Understand the role of the International Monetary Fund.

BACKGROUND INFORMATION

The World Bank <www.worldbank.org> is an international agency established in 1944, the same year as the International Monetary Fund (IMF) <www.imf.org>. It provides loans for development to countries in need and, together with the IMF, is a major player in today's international monetary system.

THE VIDEO

This segment discusses the roles and purposes of the World Bank and International Monetary Fund and describes their origin in the Bretton Woods agreement.

QUESTIONS FOR DISCUSSION

1. What is the role of the World Bank in global financial markets?
2. What was the significance of the 1944 Bretton Woods Agreement?
3. What is the role of the IMF in the contemporary world economy?

FOLLOW-UP ASSIGNMENT

Research some recent articles about the World Bank and the IMF. What are some of the criticisms of the actions being taken by these two organizations around the world? What are some of the positive effects being reported? Do you think the World Bank and the IMF are positive or negative forces in developing nations? Explain your answer and give examples.

FOR FURTHER EXPLORATION

Explore the World Bank's Web site at <www.worldbank.org> and look specifically at the "About Us" page. What are the five different units that make up the World Bank? What is the function of each?

CHAPTER 15 Understanding Securities and Investments

After reading this chapter, you should be able to:

1. Explain the difference between *primary* and *secondary securities markets*.
2. Discuss the value to shareholders of *common* and *preferred stock*, and describe the secondary market for each type of security.
3. Distinguish among various types of *bonds* in terms of their issuers, safety, and retirement.
4. Describe the investment opportunities offered by *mutual funds* and *commodities*.
5. Explain the process by which securities are bought and sold.
6. Explain how securities markets are regulated.

Is Volatility Here to Stay?

Like the space-age roller coaster rides at Disney World and Coney Island, today's stock market promises a little nerve-shattering volatility for everyone with the guts to hop a ride. The best advice for the timid—or those prone to motion sickness—is stay away, especially if the swings that characterized the market in recent years are here to stay.

Why are today's market swings so violent? Why did traders sell off $74 billion in stocks in just one day—55 percent more than in the previous day and 43 percent more than the next trading day—on the New York Stock Exchange in April 2000? Why did the Dow Jones Industrial Average <averages.dowjones.com> surge upward 17 percent between October 1999 and January 2000, only to lose those gains during the next two months while U.S. unemployment remained at record-low levels? Similarly, the Dow shot up nearly 300 points in a single half hour in October 1998 after the Federal Reserve Board <www.federalreserve.gov> announced that it would cut interest rates by a quarter of a percentage point. Only a month earlier, the Dow had surged nearly 400 points on a single day, only to give it all back on the following two days. Market volatility can be traced to several factors, including new Internet stocks, large pools of available cash, new technologies to speed up trading, and global financial deals.

Technology stocks have also added to the market volatility. An abundance of cash-starved e-businesses and high-tech stocks are capturing investor interest and attracting investment dollars as never before, even though many of these firms have yet to turn a profit. High-risk investors, looking beyond today's red ink, are betting on future performance. Thus, it's no surprise when economic conditions, political events, or just plain fright stimulate wild ups and downs in the stock market. The technology-heavy Nasdaq Composite Index,

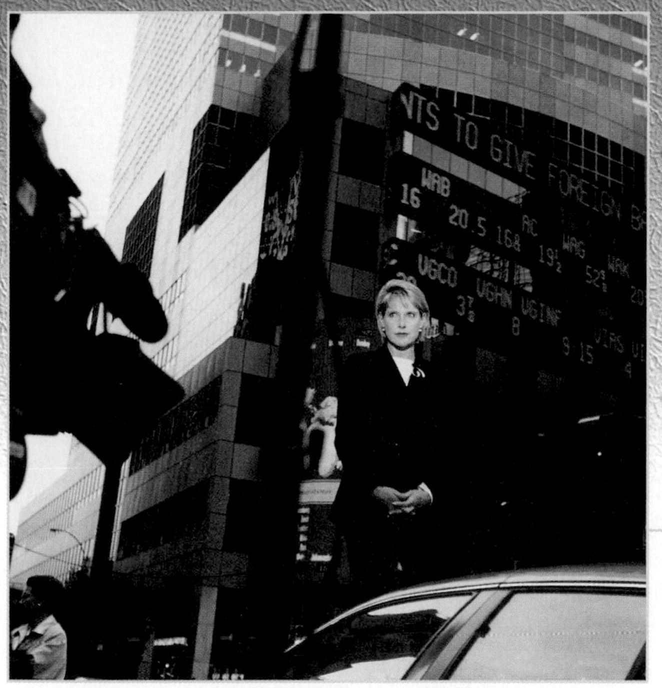

"The speed of transactions is increasing geometrically. Volatility is here to stay."

—Mike Holland, chairman, Holland & Co.

sitting at 2,500 in August 1999, suddenly shot up to a record-setting 5,100 in March 2000—a gain of more than 100 percent in just seven months—for no clear reason. Then, in a stark turnaround, it fell to 3,100 for a near 40 percent loss during the next two months, as the Fed raised interest rates to slow the economy.

On Black Monday—the day in 1987 when the stock market dropped 554 points—684 million shares were traded on the New York Stock Exchange. Thirteen years later, that volume is nothing special. In fact, during 1999 there were 20 days with trading volumes higher than 1 billion shares. For the first five months of 2000, there were 62 days with 1 billion shares traded, with a record-setting 1.5 billion traded on April 4. On a busy day in 2000, the Nasdaq market volume of 2.9 billion shares is nearly five times the 0.6 billion traded on the exchange's busiest day just five years earlier. The New York Stock Exchange, which is now preparing to handle 5 billion trades a day, traded a daily average of 1 billion shares in the first five months of 2000. "The speed of transactions," says Mike Holland, chairman of Holland & Company, a private investment company, "is increasing geometrically as information and technology allow it. That volatility is here to stay," he adds, especially with the proliferation of online brokers.

James B. Lee, vice chairman of Chase Manhattan Bank, agrees: "Today," he notes, "everything happens at a faster rate than it did 10 years ago. What took a year to happen in 1990 . . . occurred [in Fall 1998] in 90 days. It may be the speed and breadth of information was that much slower, that much narrower, then, so it took a year to filter through the system. Now it takes less time." Meanwhile, the ups and downs of stock prices—as much as 5 percent a day—remain a fact of life.

Our opening story continues on page 406

SECURITIES MARKETS

Stocks and bonds are known as **securities** because they represent *secured*, or *asset-based*, claims on the part of investors. In other words, holders of stocks and bonds have a stake in the business that issued them. As we saw in Chapter 4, stockholders have claims on some of a corporation's assets (and a say in how the company is run) because each share of stock represents part ownership.

securities
Stocks and bonds representing secured, or asset-based, claims by investors against issuers

primary securities market
Market in which new stocks and bonds are bought and sold

In contrast, *bonds* represent strictly financial claims for money owed to holders by a company. Companies sell bonds to raise long-term funds. The markets in which stocks and bonds are sold are called *securities markets*.[1]

Primary and Secondary Securities Markets

In **primary securities markets**, new stocks and bonds are bought and sold by firms and governments. Sometimes new securities are sold to single buyers or small groups of buyers. These so-called *private placements* are desirable because they allow issuers to keep their plans confidential.[2]

Each year, more than $100 billion in new private placements are purchased in the United States by large pension funds and other institutions that privately negotiate prices with sellers.[3] Because private placements cannot be resold in the open market, buyers generally demand higher returns from the issuers.

Securities and Exchange Commission (SEC)
Federal agency that administers U.S. securities laws to protect the investing public and maintain smoothly functioning markets

investment bank
Financial institution engaged in issuing and reselling new securities

secondary securities market
Market in which stocks and bonds are traded

Investment Banking Most new stocks and some bonds are sold on the wider public market. To bring a new security to market, the issuing firm must get approval from the **Securities and Exchange Commission** (SEC) <www.sec.gov>—the government agency that regulates securities markets. It also needs the services of an **investment bank**—a financial institution that specializes in issuing and reselling new securities. Such investment banking firms as Merrill Lynch <www.ml.com> and Morgan Stanley <www.msdw.com> provide three important services:

1. They advise companies on the timing and financial terms of new issues.
2. By *underwriting*—that is, buying—new securities, they bear some of the risks of issuing them.
3. They create the distribution networks for moving new securities through groups of other banks and brokers into the hands of individual investors.

In 2000, U.S. investment bankers brought to the market $135 billion in new corporate stocks and $807 billion in new corporate bonds.[4] New securities, however, represent only a minute portion of traded securities. Existing stocks and bonds are sold in the **secondary securities market**, which is handled by such familiar bodies as the New York Stock Exchange. We consider the activities of these markets later in this chapter.

STOCKS

Each year, financial managers, with millions of individual investors, buy and sell the stocks of thousands of companies. This widespread ownership has become possible because of the availability of different types of stocks and because markets have been established for conveniently buying and selling them. In this section, we focus on the value of *common* and *preferred stock* as securities. We also describe the *stock exchanges* on which they are bought and sold.[5]

Common Stocks

Individuals and other companies purchase a firm's common stock in the hope that it will increase in value, provide dividend income, or both. But how is the value of a common stock determined? Stock values are expressed in three different ways—as par, market, and book value.

WEB Connection

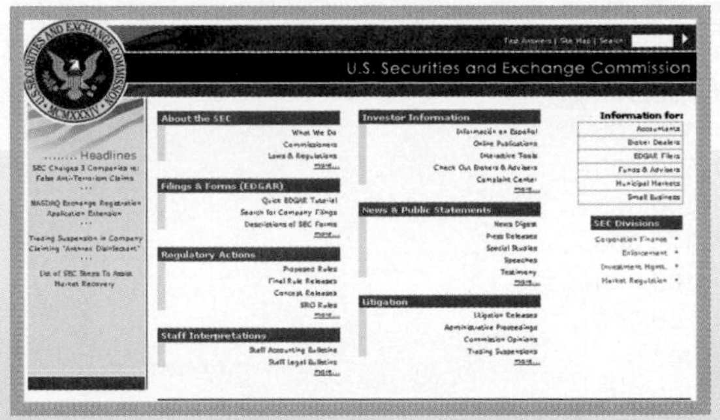

The SEC administers laws regulating the issuance of securities in the United States. Principally, it supplies the information that investors need to make fair decisions about securities, and it also monitors the activities of insiders—directors, officers, major stockholders—that concern the securities of their own firms. To get a much closer look at how the SEC performs such duties, check out its EDGAR (Electronic Data Gathering, Analysis, and Retrieval) Database by logging on to the agency's Web site.

www.sec.gov

- The face value of a share of stock at the time it is originally issued is the **par value.** To receive their corporate charters, all companies must declare par values for their stocks. Each company must preserve the par value money in its retained earnings, and it cannot be distributed as dividends.
- A stock's real value is its **market value**—the current price of a share in the stock market. Market value reflects buyers' willingness to invest in a company.
- Recall from Chapter 13 our definition of *stockholders' equity*—the sum of a company's common stock par value, retained earnings, and additional paid-in capital. The **book value** of common stock represents *stockholders' equity* (see Chapter 13) divided by the number of shares. Book value is used as a comparison indicator because, for successful companies, the market value is usually greater than its book value. Thus, when market price falls to near book value, some investors buy the stock on the principle that it is underpriced and will increase in the future.

par value
Face value of a share of stock, set by the issuing company's board of directors

market value
Current price of a share of stock in the stock market

book value
Value of a common stock expressed as total shareholders' equity divided by the number of shares of stock

Investment Traits of Common Stock Common stocks are among the riskiest of all securities. Uncertainties about the stock market itself, for instance, can quickly change a given stock's value. Furthermore, when companies have unprofitable years, they often cannot pay dividends. Shareholder income, therefore—and perhaps share price—drops. At the same time, however, common stocks offer high growth potential. Naturally the prospects for growth in various industries change from time to time, but the **blue-chip stocks** of well-established, financially sound firms such as Ralston Purina <www.ralston.com> and ExxonMobil <www.exxon.mobil.com> have historically provided investors steady income through consistent dividend payouts.

blue-chip stock
Common stock issued by a well-established company with a sound financial history and a stable pattern of dividend payouts

The "Old" Economy versus the "New": What's a "Blue Chip" Now? Because the very nature of the stock market is continually changing, the future performance of any stock is often unpredictable. With the proliferation of Internet and start-up dot.coms, experts are beginning to realize that many of the old rules for judging the market prospects of stocks are changing. Conventional methods don't seem to apply to the surprising surges in "new economy" stock prices. Old performance yardsticks—a company's history of dividend payouts, steady growth in earnings per share, and a low price-earnings ratio (current stock price divided by annual earnings per share)—do not seem to measure the value of "new economy" stocks. In some cases, market prices are soaring for start-ups that have yet to earn a profit.

While some of the newcomers—America Online, Amazon, eBay, Yahoo!—are regarded by many on Wall Street as "Internet Blue Chips," their financial performance is quite different from that of traditional blue-chip stocks.[6] Let's compare Yahoo! and Wal-Mart. If you had invested $10,000 in Wal-Mart stock in July 1996, the market

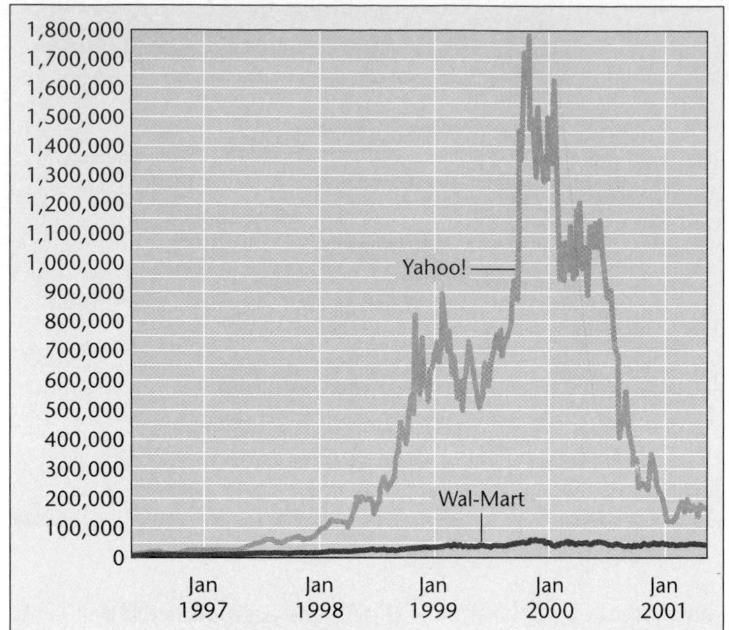

Figure 15.1
Market Value Growth: Wal-Mart versus Yahoo!

value of this blue chip would have increased to more than $48,000 in just five years (see Figure 15.1). The same investment in Yahoo! would have grown to nearly $150,000. At peak value during the five-year period, the Yahoo! investment surged to more than $1.7 million versus Wal-Mart's $60,000.

Could this gigantic difference be predicted from indicators traditionally used by market experts? Hardly. The initial public offering (IPO) of Yahoo! stock in 1996 was priced at $13 per share. It quickly jumped to $43, then settled down to close the day at $33 even though the company had not yet turned a profit. Because Yahoo! was the leading Internet portal brand name, investors were betting that it would become a profitable business in the future—a bet that many traditionalists would view as extremely risky.

Consider the fact that Wal-Mart's book value is more than double that of Yahoo!. Even more glaring is the fact that Wal-Mart's recent net income is nearly 80 times higher than Yahoo!'s. Moreover, Wal-Mart's net earnings have grown steadily during the previous 10 years. The comparison is similar for dividends: Whereas Wal-Mart has a steady history of payouts to stockholders, Yahoo! has never paid a cash dividend. Over all, then, the traditional performance yardsticks favor Wal-Mart heavily. Nevertheless, investors are betting the future on Yahoo!: In July 2000, the original $10,000 investment had accumulated in four years to a market value more than 20 times that of the same investment in Wal-Mart.[7]

Preferred Stock

Preferred stock is usually issued with a stated par value, and dividends are typically expressed as a percentage of par value. If a preferred stock with a $100 par value pays a 6 percent dividend, holders will receive an annual dividend of $6 per share.

Some preferred stock is *callable*. The issuing firm can call in shares by requiring preferred stockholders to surrender them in exchange for cash payments. The amount of this payment—the *call price*—is specified in the purchase agreement between the firm and its preferred stockholders.

cumulative preferred stock
Preferred stock on which dividends not paid in the past must be paid to stockholders before dividends can be paid to common stockholders

Investment Traits of Preferred Stock Because preferred stock has first rights to dividends, income is less risky than income from the same firm's common stock. Most preferred stock is **cumulative preferred stock**, which means that any missed dividend payments must be paid as soon as the firm is able to do so. In addition, the firm cannot pay any dividends to common stockholders until it has made up all late payments to preferred stockholders. Let's take the example of a firm with preferred stock having a $100 par value and paying a 6 percent dividend. If the firm fails to pay that dividend for two years, it must make up arrears of $12 per share to preferred stockholders before it can pay dividends to common stockholders.

Stock Exchanges

Most of the secondary market for stocks is handled by organized stock exchanges. In addition, a dealer or the over-the-counter market handles the exchange of some stocks. A **stock exchange** is an organization of individuals formed to provide an institutional setting in which stock can be bought and sold. The exchange enforces certain rules to govern its members' trading activities. Most exchanges are nonprofit corporations established to serve their members.

stock exchange
Organization of individuals formed to provide an institutional setting in which stock can be traded

To become a member, an individual must purchase one of a limited number of memberships, called *seats*, on the exchange. Only members (or their representatives) are allowed to trade on the exchange. In this sense, because all orders to buy or sell must flow through members, members of the exchange have a legal monopoly. Memberships can be bought and sold like other assets.

The Trading Floor Each exchange regulates the places and times at which trading may occur. Trading is allowed only at an actual physical location called the trading floor. The floor is equipped with a vast array of electronic communications equipment for conveying buy-and-sell orders or confirming completed trades. A variety of news services furnish up-to-the-minute information about world events and business developments. Any change in these factors, then, may be swiftly reflected in share prices.

Brokers Some of the people on the trading floor are employed by the exchange. Others are trading stocks for themselves. Many, however, are **brokers**, who receive and execute buy-and-sell orders from nonexchange members. Although they match buyers with sellers, brokers do not own the securities. They earn commissions from the individuals and organizations for whom they place orders.[8]

broker
Individual or organization who receives and executes buy-and-sell orders on behalf of other people in return for commissions

Discount Brokers Like many products, brokerage assistance can be purchased at either discount or at full-service prices. Buying 200 shares of a $20 stock in 2001 cost the investor $8 at Ameritrade <www.ameritrade.com>, $14.95 at E*Trade <www.etrade.com>, $29.95 at Charles Schwab <www.schwab.com>, and more than

These servers are operated by Island ECN <www.islandecn.com> one block away from the New York Stock Exchange. To some people, however, they are a world away: They represent the forces—technology and entrepreneurship—that are pulling the securities industry off of the traditional trading floor and into the electronic marketplace. ECNs—electronic communications networks—make fast electronic connections between buyers and specific orders. ECNs started by catering to day-traders and now handle about 20 percent of all shares traded on Nasdaq.

$100 at a full-service brokerage firm. Price differences are obvious even among the discount brokers—Ameritrade, E*Trade, and Schwab—but the highest discount price is well below the price of the full-service broker.[9]

Discount brokers offer well-informed individual investors a fast, low-cost way to participate in the market. Charles Schwab's customers are "do-it-yourself" investors: They know what they want to buy or sell, and they usually make trades by using personal computers or Schwab's automated telephone order system without talking with a broker. Why are discount brokerage services low cost? For one thing, sales personnel receive fees or salaries, not commissions. Unlike many full-service brokers, they do not offer investment advice or person-to-person sales consultations. They do, however, offer automated online services, such as stock research, industry analysis, and screening for specific types of stocks.

"The Internet is fundamentally changing the story of investing."

—Gideon Sasson, head of electronic brokerage, Charles Schwab & Company

Online Trading The popularity of online trading stems from convenient access to the Internet, fast no-nonsense transactions, and the opportunity for self-directed investors to manage their own portfolios while paying low fees for trading. Although only 14 percent of all equity trades were executed online in 1998, that number was growing rapidly until the market slowdown in 2000–2001. So popular is online investing that it has become the Internet's second most popular activity, topped only by surfing pornography. The Internet, says Gideon Sasson, head of Schwab's electronic brokerage unit, "is fundamentally changing the story of investing."[10] As you can see in Figure 15.2, the volume of online trading is increasing as competition among brokers drives prices further downward.

Full-Service Brokers Despite the growth in online investing, there remains an important market for full-service brokerages, both for new, uninformed investors and for experienced investors who don't have time to keep up with all the latest developments. When you deal with busy people who want to invest successfully, says Joseph Grano of PaineWebber <www.painewebber.com>, "you can't do it through a telephone response system. In a world that's growing more and more complicated, the advice and counsel of a broker will be more important, not less important."

With full lines of financial services, firms such as Merrill Lynch can offer clients consulting advice in personal financial planning, estate planning, and tax strategies, along with a wider range of investment products. Initial public offerings (IPOs) of

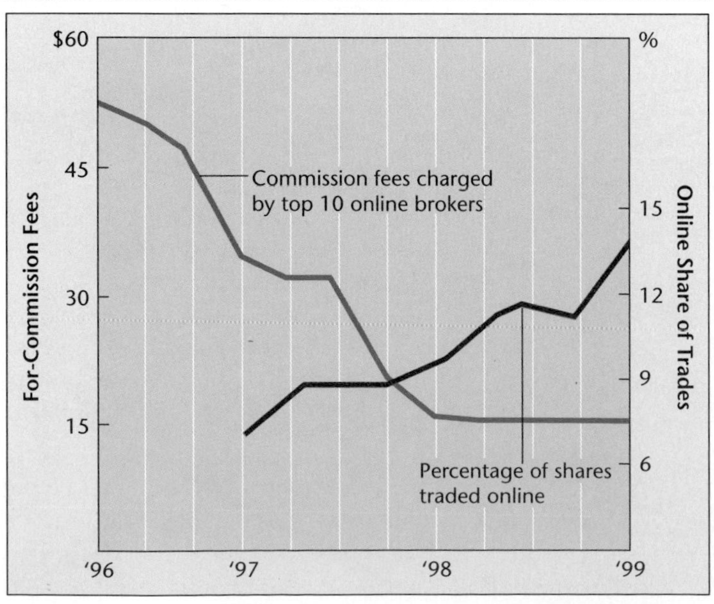

Figure 15.2
Growth of Online Trading

stock, for example, are generally not available to the public through online retail brokers. Rather, a full-service broker—who is also the investment banker that sells the IPO shares—can sell IPO shares to their clients. Financial advisers also do more than deliver information: They offer interpretations of and suggestions on investments that clients might overlook when trying to sift through an avalanche of online financial data.

The Major Exchanges and the OTC Market The two major stock exchanges that operate on trading floors in the United States are the New York and American Stock Exchanges. The New York Stock Exchange, for many years the largest exchange in the United States, has recently begun to face stiff competition from both the electronic market in the United States and large foreign exchanges, especially in London and Tokyo.

The most important differences between exchanges and the electronic market are (1) the activity of *dealers* and (2) the geographic location of the market. On the trading floor of an exchange, one dealer, called a *specialist*, is appointed by the exchange to control trading for each stock. The specialist not only buys and sells that stock for his or her own inventory but acts as exclusive auctioneer for it.[11] The electronic market, on the other hand, conducts trades electronically among thousands of dealers in remote locations around the world.

The New York Stock Exchange For many people, "the stock market" means the New York Stock Exchange (NYSE) <www.nyse.com>. Founded in 1792 and located at the corner of Wall and Broad Streets in New York City, the largest of all U.S. exchanges is the model for exchanges worldwide. An average of 1.2 million shares valued at $37 billion change hands each day. About 40 percent of all shares traded on U.S. exchanges are traded here. Only firms meeting certain minimum requirements—earning power, total value of outstanding stock, and number of shareholders—are eligible for listing on the NYSE.[12]

The American Stock Exchange The second-largest floor-based U.S. exchange, the American Stock Exchange (AMEX) <www.amex.com>, is also located in New York. It accounts for about 3 percent of all shares traded on U.S. exchanges and, like the NYSE, has minimum requirements for listings. They are, however, less stringent. The minimum number of publicly held shares, for example, is 500,000 versus 1.1 million for the NYSE.

Regional Stock Exchanges Established long before the advent of modern communications, the seven regional stock exchanges were organized to serve investors in places other than New York. The largest regional exchanges are the Chicago (formerly the Midwest) Stock Exchange and the Pacific Stock Exchange in Los Angeles and San Francisco. Other exchanges are located in Philadelphia, Boston, Cincinnati, and Spokane. Many corporations list their stocks both regionally and on either the NYSE or the AMEX.

Foreign Stock Exchanges As recently as 1980, the U.S. market accounted for more than half the value of the world market in traded stocks. Indeed, as late as 1975, the equity of IBM alone <www.ibm.com> was greater than the national market equities of all but four countries. Market activities, however, have shifted as the value of shares listed on foreign exchanges continues to grow. The annual dollar value of trades on exchanges in London, Tokyo, and other cities is in the trillions. In fact, the London exchange exceeds even the NYSE in number of stocks listed. In market value, however, transactions on U.S. exchanges remain larger than those on exchanges in other countries. Relatively new exchanges are also flourishing in cities from Shanghai to Warsaw.

Over-the-Counter Market The **over-the-counter (OTC) market** is so called because its original traders were somewhat like retailers. They kept supplies of shares on hand and, as opportunities arose, sold them over the office counter to interested buyers. Even today, the OTC market has no trading floor. Rather, it consists of many people in different locations who hold an inventory of securities that are not listed on any of the

over-the-counter (OTC) market
Organization of securities dealers formed to trade stock outside the formal institutional setting of the organized stock exchanges

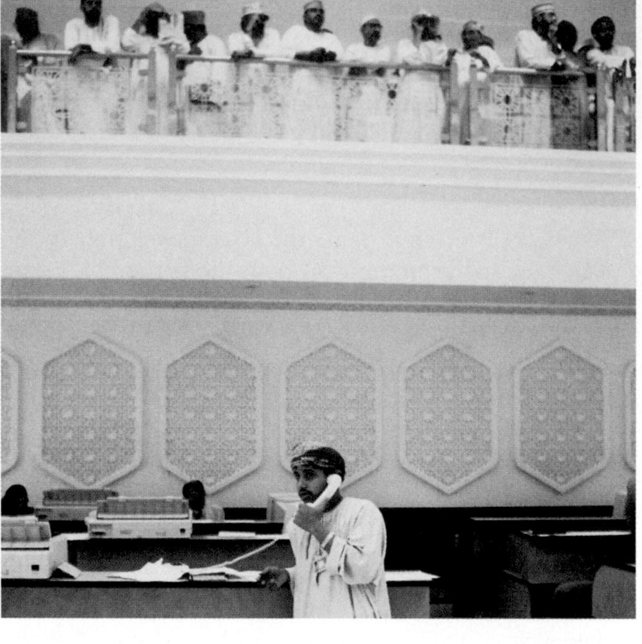

In Muscat, the capital of Oman, a tiny sultanate on the Arabian peninsula, the tax laws have been changed to encourage more foreign investment. One immediate result has been a 62-percent increase in activity on the Muscat Securities Market, where "high-tech" accoutrements still consist of telephones and (for interested local parties stationed in the gallery) binoculars. There is, of course, a Web site: <www.msm-oman.com>.

national U.S. securities exchanges. The OTC consists of independent dealers who own the securities that they buy and sell at their own risk. Although OTC activities are of interest from an historical perspective, trading volume is small in comparison to other markets.[13]

National Association of Securities Dealers Automated Quotation (NASDAQ) system
Organization of over-the-counter dealers who own, buy, and sell their own securities over a network of electronic communications

Nasdaq and NASD In the 1960s, an SEC study reported that the OTC, on which the shares of thousands of companies were traded, was unduly fragmented. One proposal recommended automation of the OTC, calling for a new system be to implemented by the **National Association of Securities Dealers Inc. (NASD)**.The resulting automated OTC system, launched in 1971, is known as the National Association of Securities Dealers Automated Quotation—or Nasdaq—system, the world's first electronic stock market.[14]

With more than 5,500 member firms, NASD <www.nasd.com> is the largest securities-regulation organization in the United States. Every broker/dealer in the United States who conducts securities business with the public is required by law to be a member of the NASD.[15] NASD includes dealers (not just brokers) who must pass qualification exams and meet certain standards for financial soundness. The privilege of trading in the market is granted by federal regulators and by NASD.

The organization's telecommunications system includes the Nasdaq system, which operates the Nasdaq Stock Market by broadcasting trading information on an intranet to over 350,000 terminals worldwide. Whereas orders at the NYSE are paired on the trading floor, Nasdaq orders are paired and executed on a computer network. Currently, the NASD is working with officials in an increasing number of countries who want to replace the trading floors of traditional exchanges with electronic networks like Nasdaq.

The stocks of some 4,800 companies are traded by Nasdaq. Newer firms are often listed here when their stocks first become available in the secondary market. Current listings include such well-known technology stocks as Intel <www.intel.com>, Dell Computer <www.dell.com>, Oracle Technology <www.oracle.com>, and Microsoft <www.microsoft.com>.

In early 2001, Nasdaq, the fastest-growing U.S. stock market, set a record volume of over 3 billion shares traded in one day. Its 1999 volume of 270 billion shares traded was the industry leader, and it is the leading U.S. market for non-U.S. listings, with a total of 429 non-U.S. companies. Although the volume of shares traded surpasses that of the New York Stock Exchange, the total market value of Nasdaq's U.S. stocks is only about one-half of that of the NYSE.

In the battle for premier companies, both the New York Stock Exchange <www.nyse.com> and Nasdaq <www.nasd.com> have taken to marketing themselves much more aggressively. Each, for example, has expanded operations at its broadcast center and permitted more and more TV stations to air real-time stock prices. A virtual high-tech market site, the Nasdaq center features 100 video monitors and provides a showplace to impress new or prospective companies.

The Steps to a Global Stock Market With its electronic telecommunication system, Nasdaq possesses an infrastructure that could eventually lead to a truly global stock market—one that would allow buyers and sellers to interact from any point in the world. Currently, Nasdaq provides equal access to both the market and market information via simultaneous broadcasts of quotes from more than 1,000 participating firms. Nasdaq communication networks enter customer orders and then display new quotes reflecting those orders.

In laying the groundwork for a system that would connect listed companies and investors for worldwide 24-hour-a-day trading, Nasdaq is taking the following steps:

- The Nasdaq Japan Market was launched in 2000, in partnership with the Osaka Securities Exchange <www.ose.or.jp/e>. This electronic securities market uses a technology that can eventually link Europe and the United States as well.
- Plans are underway for expanding Nasdaq-Europe, an Internet-accessible stock market patterned after Nasdaq. It would offer European traders access to the stocks of listed U.S. and Asian companies.
- It has agreed to a deal with the government of Quebec to launch Nasdaq Canada.

WEB Connection

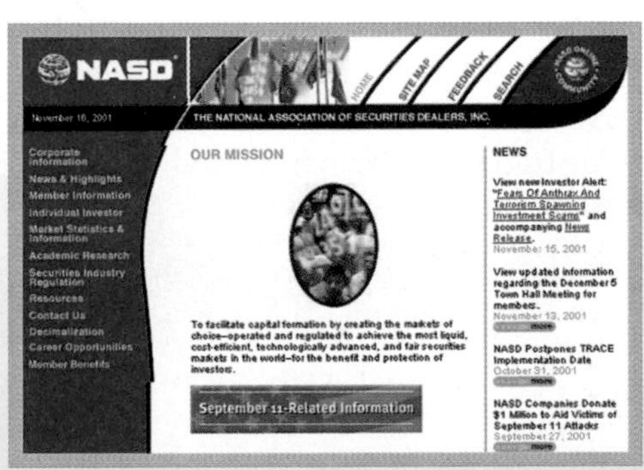

The National Association of Securities Dealers (NASD) is authorized by the Securities and Exchange Commission to set standards of conduct for about 500,000 brokers and dealers who issue and sell securities to the public. In this capacity, the NASD monitors the trading of shares in the thousands of companies in the over-the-counter market. To find out more about the Nasdaq Stock Market or the NASD's merger with the American Stock Exchange, log on to the organization's Web site.

www.nasd.com

IT'S A WIRED WORLD
Opening the Portals to Cross-Border Trading

In addition to being prominent European cities, what do London, Amsterdam, Frankfurt, Paris, and Stockholm have in common? In the world of business and investments, they are among the many cities with their own stock markets. Some, like Frankfurt, are just one of several stock exchanges in a given country, where trading on any one market is independent of the others. Lately, Europe's traditional exchanges have gotten bogged down; they're too cumbersome for today's business world. There are so many stock exchanges that the system isn't user friendly for European investors who want a system that makes trades across national boundaries more easily and cheaply.

As often happens in the business world, some upstart companies have recognized the gap and are responding to customers' needs: Internet-based newcomers are opening their portals all over Europe. Nasdaq-Europe, for example, was launched in November 1999 and targets traders who want to deal in the stocks of technology and start-up firms. Similarly, Jiway, which opened in autumn 2000, is luring retail brokers who want to trade across European borders. Two new Internet-based exchanges—Tradepoint <www.tradepoint.co.uk> and EASDAQ <www.easdaq.be>—are just getting started by connecting brokers to a system built for cross-border trading. Easdaq allows transactions in euros, pounds sterling, or U.S. dollars. Two other Web sites, Posit <www.itginc.com> and E-Crossnet <www.escrossnet.com>, bypass stock exchanges altogether and match up buyers and sellers directly, allowing them to complete their trades independently.

In addition to technology's influence, some organizational changes are also forcing European exchanges to rethink their traditional roles. In March 2000, three exchanges—the French, Dutch, and Belgian—announced that they were merging into a new exchange called Euronext, thus putting additional pressure on competitors to become more Pan-European. As a result, merger negotiations are underway between two of Europe's giant exchanges—London and Frankfurt. For years the London Stock Exchange (LSE) <www.londonstockexchange.com> has held the premier spot among Europe's equities markets, the value of shares listed there being double that of any other European exchange. The Frankfurt exchange <www.exchange.de> has not only worked its way up to the number-two position among Europe's financial centers but is also twice as profitable as the LSE. Now, as the LSE and Frankfurt negotiate a merger, they watch while newer competitors, especially Internet exchanges, encroach on their traditional markets. Just how long negotiations will continue is anybody's guess. Meanwhile, however, reports indicate that other European exchanges—Milan, Madrid, Ireland, Austria—have approached Frankfurt with a view to joining the newly merged exchange.

- An agreement with the Hong Kong Stock Exchange allows some of Nasdaq's shares to trade in Hong Kong and some of Hong Kong's shares to trade in the United States.
- News reports indicate that Nasdaq has established relationships with Sydney, Australia's stock market and that negotiations are underway with South Korea's stock market.[16]

Although these initiatives are promising, it will take several years to resolve differences in market regulation and trading practices that currently separate various countries.

BONDS

bond
Security through which an issuer promises to pay the buyer a certain amount of money by a specified future date

A **bond** is an IOU—a promise by the issuer to pay the buyer a certain amount of money by a specified future date, usually with interest paid at regular intervals. The U.S. bond market is supplied by three major sources—the U.S. government, municipalities, and corporations. Bonds differ in terms of maturity dates, tax status, and level of risk versus potential yield.[17]

To aid bond investors in making purchase decisions, several services rate the quality of bonds. Table 15.1, for example, shows the systems of two well-known services,

	High Grades	Medium Grades (Investment Grades)	Speculative	Poor Grades
Moody's	Aaa, Aa	A, Baa	Ba, B	Caa to C
Standard & Poor's	AAA, AA	A, BBB	BB, B	CCC to D

Table 15.1
Bond Rating Systems

Moody's <www.moodys.com> and Standard & Poor's <www.standardpoors.com>. Ratings measure default risk—the chance that one or more promised payments will be deferred or missed altogether. The highest grades are *AAA* and *Aaa*, the lowest *C* and *D*. Low-grade bonds are usually called *junk bonds*.

U.S. Government Bonds

The U.S. government is the world's largest debtor. New federal borrowing from the public actually decreased by $222 billion in 2000. In other words, the federal government's repayments of loans exceeded the funds it raised in new loans. Nevertheless, the total U.S. debt hovered near $3.4 trillion.[18] To finance its debt, the federal government issues a variety of government bonds. The U.S. Treasury issues Treasury bills (T-bills), Treasury notes, and Treasury bonds (including U.S. savings bonds). Many government agencies (for example, the Federal Housing Administration) also issue bonds.

government bond
Bond issued by the federal government

Government bonds are among the safest investments available. Securities with longer maturities are somewhat riskier than short-term issues because their longer lives expose them to more political, social, and economic changes. All federal bonds, however, are backed by the U.S. government. Government securities are sold in large blocks to institutional investors who buy them to ensure desired levels of safety in their portfolios. As investors' needs change, they may buy or sell government securities to other investors.

Municipal Bonds

municipal bond
Bond issued by a state or local government

State and local governments issue **municipal bonds** to finance school and transportation systems and a variety of other projects. In 2000, new municipal bonds were issued at a value of more than $180 billion.

Some bonds, called *obligation bonds*, are backed by the issuer's taxing power. A local school district, for example, may issue $50 million in obligation bonds to fund new elementary and high schools. The issuer intends to retire the bonds from future tax revenues. In contrast, revenue bonds are backed only by the revenue generated by a specific project.

The most attractive feature of municipal bonds is the fact that investors do not pay taxes on interest received. Commercial banks invest in bonds nearing maturity because they are relatively safe, liquid investments. Pension funds, insurance companies, and even private citizens also make longer-term investments in municipals.

Corporate Bonds

corporate bond
Bond issued by a company as a source of long-term funding

Although the U.S. government and municipalities are heavy borrowers, corporate long-term borrowing is even greater. **Corporate bonds** issued by U.S. companies are a large source of financing, involving more money than government and municipal bonds combined.[19] U.S. companies raised nearly $807 billion from new bond issues in 2000. Bonds have traditionally been issued with maturities ranging from 20 to 30 years. In the 1980s, 10-year maturities came into wider use.

Like municipal bonds, longer-term corporate bonds are somewhat riskier than shorter-term bonds. To help investors evaluate risk, Standard & Poor's and Moody's rate both new and proposed issues on a weekly basis. Remember, however, that negative ratings do not necessarily keep issues from being successful. Rather, they raise the interest rates that issuers must offer. Corporate bonds may be categorized in terms of the method of interest payment or in terms of whether they are *secured* or *unsecured*.

registered bond
Bond bearing the name of the holder and registered with the issuing company

bearer (or coupon) bond
Bond requiring the holder to clip and submit a coupon to receive an interest payment

secured bond
Bond backed by pledges of assets to the bondholders

debenture
Unsecured bond for which no specific property is pledged as security

Interest Payment: Registered and Bearer Bonds **Registered bonds** register the names of holders with the company, which simply mails out checks. Certificates are of value only to registered holders. **Bearer** (or **coupon**) **bonds** require bondholders to clip coupons from certificates and send them to the issuer to receive payment. Coupons can be redeemed by anyone, regardless of ownership.

Secured Bonds With **secured bonds**, issuers can reduce the risk to holders by pledging assets in case of default. Bonds can be backed by first mortgages, other mortgages, or other specific assets. In 1994, Union Pacific Railroad Co. <www.uprr.com> issued $76 million in bonds to finance the purchase and renovation of equipment. Rated *Aaa* (prime) by Moody's and maturing in 2012, the bonds are secured by the newly purchased and rehabilitated equipment itself—80 diesel locomotives, 1,300 hopper cars, and 450 auto-rack cars.

Debentures Unsecured bonds are called **debentures.** No specific property is pledged as security. Rather, holders generally have claims against property not otherwise pledged in the company's other bonds. Thus, debentures are said to have "inferior claims" on a corporation's assets. Financially strong firms often use debentures. An example is the $175 million debenture issued by Boeing <www.boeing.com> in 1993, with maturity on April 15, 2043. Similar issues by weaker companies often receive low ratings and may have trouble attracting investors.

Secondary Markets for Bonds Nearly all secondary trading in bonds occurs in the OTC market rather than on organized exchanges. Thus, precise statistics about annual trading volumes are not recorded. As with stocks, however, market values and prices change daily. The direction of bond prices moves *opposite* to interest rate changes. As interest rates move up, bond prices tend to go down. The prices of riskier bonds fluctuate more widely than those of higher-grade bonds.

MUTUAL FUNDS

mutual fund
Company that pools investments from individuals and organizations to purchase a portfolio of stocks, bonds, and other securities

no-load fund
Mutual fund in which investors pay no sales commissions when they buy in or sell out

load fund
Mutual fund in which investors are charged sales commissions when they buy in or sell out

Companies called **mutual funds** pool investments from individuals and organizations to purchase a portfolio of stocks, bonds, and other securities. Investors are thus part owners of the portfolio.[20] If you invest $1,000 in a mutual fund with a portfolio worth $100,000, you own 1 percent of that portfolio. Investors in **no-load funds** are not charged sales commissions when they buy into or sell out of funds. Investors in **load funds** generally pay commissions of 2 to 8 percent.

Reasons for Investing The total assets invested in U.S. mutual funds have grown significantly every year since 1991, to a total of $7 trillion in more than 10,000 different funds in 2000.[21] Why do investors find them so attractive? Remember first of all that mutual funds vary in their investment goals. Naturally, different funds are designed to appeal to the different motives and goals of investors. Funds stressing safety often include money market mutual funds and other safe issues offering immediate income. Investors seeking higher current income must generally sacrifice some safety. Typically, these people look to long-term municipal bond, corporate bond, and income mutual funds that invest in common stocks with good dividend-paying records.

Mutual funds that stress growth include *balanced mutual funds*—portfolios of bonds and preferred and common stocks, especially the common stocks of established firms. Aggressive growth funds seek maximum capital appreciation. They sacrifice current income and safety and invest in stocks of new (and even troubled) companies and other high-risk securities.

WEB Connection

A subsidiary of Mellon Bank, Dreyfus manages $120 billion in 150 mutual fund portfolios. You can find out more about Dreyfus's various funds, such as the Dreyfus S&P 500 Index Fund, as well as the rationale for arranging them on a spectrum running from "aggressive" to "conservative" to meet the differing needs of individual investors, by logging on to the company's Mutual Fund Center.

www.dreyfus.com

BUYING AND SELLING SECURITIES

The process of buying and selling securities is complex. First, you need to find out about possible investments and match them to your investment objectives. Then you must select a broker and open an account. Only then can you place orders and make different types of transactions.

Financial Information Services

Have you ever looked at the financial section of your daily newspaper and wondered what all those tables and numbers mean? It is a good idea to know how to read stock, bond, and mutual fund quotations if you want to invest in issues. Fortunately, this skill is easily mastered.

Stock Quotations Daily transactions for NYSE and Nasdaq common stocks are reported in most city newspapers. Figure 15.3 shows part of a listing from the *Wall Street Journal*, with columns numbered 1 through 11. Let us analyze the listing for the company at the top, Gap Inc. <www.gap.com>:

- The first column ("YTD % CHG") shows the stock price percentage change for the calendar year to date. Gap's common stock price has increased 4.9 percent for 2001.
- The next two columns ("High" and "Low") show the highest and lowest prices paid for one share of Gap stock *during the past year*. Note that stock prices throughout are expressed in dollars per share. In the past 52 weeks, then, Gap's stock ranged in value from $38.63 to $18.50 per share. This range reveals a fairly volatile stock price.
- The fourth column ("Stock") is the abbreviated company name.
- The NYSE *symbol* for the stock is listed in column 5 ("Sym").
- The sixth column ("Div") indicates that Gap pays an annual *cash dividend* of $0.09 per share. This amount can be compared with payouts by other companies.
- Column 7 ("Yld %") is the *dividend yield* expressed as a percentage of the stock's current price (shown in column 10). Gap's dividend yield is 0.3 percent (0.09/26.76, rounded). Potential buyers can compare this yield with returns they might get from alternative investments.
- Column 8 ("PE") shows the **price-earnings ratio**—the current price of the stock divided by the firm's current annual earnings per share. On this day, Gap's PE is 31, meaning that investors are willing to pay $31 for each dollar of reported profits to own Gap stock. This figure can be compared with PE ratios of other stocks to decide which is the best investment.

price-earnings ratio
Current price of a stock divided by the firm's current annual earnings per share

- The last three columns detail the day's trading. Column 9 ("Vol 100s") shows the *number of shares* (in hundreds) that were traded—in this case, 78,092. Some

Figure 15.3
Reading a Stock Quotation

1	2	3	4	5	6	7	8	9	10	11
Yld % Chg	52 Weeks High	Low	Stock	Sym	Div	Yld %	PE	Vol 100s	Last	Net Chg
+ 4.9	38.63	18.50	Gap Inc	GPS	.09	.3	31	78092	26.76	−1.23
+50.7	14.75	5.65	Gartner	IT		...	...	1052	10.40	−0.04
+52.2	13.06	4.95	Gartner B	ITB		...	...	101	9.65	−0.05
−46.2	69.88	9.45	Gateway	GTW		...	...	14757	9.67	−0.07
+31.7	29.15	19.31	GaylEnt	GET		...	...	181	27.50	+0.67
+35.6	14.25	6.81	GenCorp	GY	.12	.9	12	537	13.05	+0.08
−49.6	97.25	37.99	Genentech	DNA s		...	...	27178	41.10	+0.18
− 8.7	60.50	36.42	GenElec	GE	.64	1.5	32	235700	43.75	−0.05
▼−36.7	18.04	10.56	GenMaritime	GMR n		...	...	476	10.60	+0.03
−57.0	17.75	4.42	GenTek	GK	.20	2.8	4	75	7.10	+0.05
+31.8	35	13.44	Genesco	GCO		...	24	1708	32.20	+0.79

investors interpret increases in trading volume as an indicator of forthcoming price changes in a stock.

- Column 10 ("Close") shows that Gap's *last sale of the day* was for $26.76.
- The final column ("Net Chg") shows the *difference between the previous day's close and the close on the day being reported*. The closing price of Gap stock is $1.23 lower than it was on the previous business day. Day-to-day changes are indicators of recent price stability or volatility.

The listings also report unusual conditions of importance to investors. Note, the *s* next to the stock symbol for Genentech Inc. (DNA). This symbol indicates either a *stock split* (a division of stock that gives stockholders a greater number of shares but that does not change each individual's proportionate share of ownership) or an *extra stock dividend* paid by the company during the past 52 weeks. The *n* accompanying the General Maritime Corp. (GMR) indicates that this stock was *newly issued* during the past 52 weeks. Finally, look back at the far-left column, which has no heading. The downward-pointing symbol (▼) indicates a new 52-week low in the price of General Maritime (GMR).

Reports on daily transactions for preferred stocks use a similar format to that for common stocks.

"The market closed down forty-three points, Mr. Murray, but the wind chill factor makes it feel like a hundred points."

Bond Quotations Daily quotations on corporate bonds from the NYSE are also widely published. Bond quotations contain essentially the same type of information as stock quotations. One difference is that the year in which it is going to mature is listed beside each bond.

Mutual Funds Quotations Selling prices for mutual funds are reported daily in most city newspapers. Additional investor information is also available in the financial press. Figure 15.4 shows how to read a typical weekly mutual funds quotation.

- Column 1 is the *net asset value* (NAV), or the value of a single share as calculated by the fund.
- Column 2 shows the *net asset value change*, the gain or loss based on the previous day's NAV.
- Column 3 lists the *fund family* at the top and the individual fund names beneath the family name.
- Column 4 reports *each fund's objective*. The "IB" code stands for an intermediate-term bond fund; "GR" indicates a growth stock fund. This allows readers to compare the performance of funds with similar objectives.
- The next five columns report *each fund's recent and long-term performance* and rank the funds within each investment objective. These numbers reflect the percentage change in NAV plus accumulated income for each period, assuming that all distributions are reinvested in the fund. These five columns show the return of the fund for the year to date, the last 4 weeks, 12 months, 3 years, and 5 years.

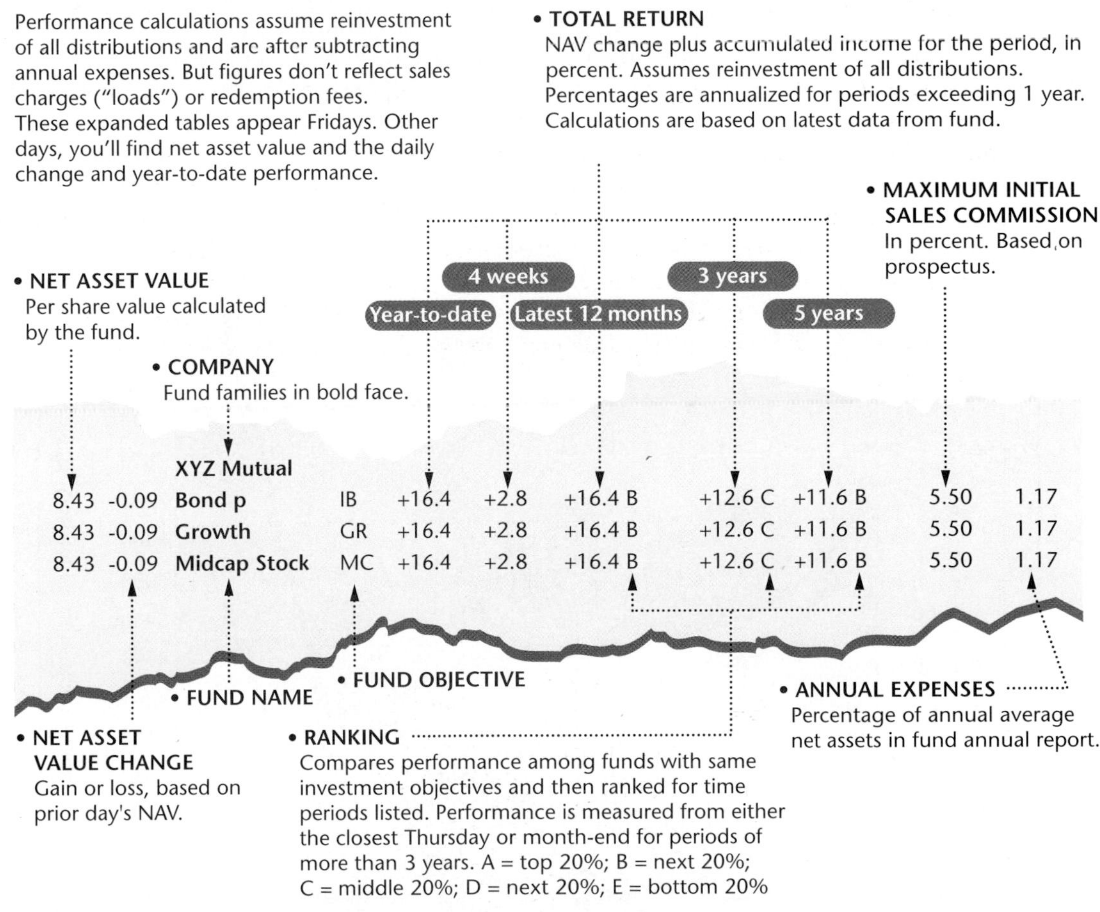

Performance calculations assume reinvestment of all distributions and are after subtracting annual expenses. But figures don't reflect sales charges ("loads") or redemption fees.
These expanded tables appear Fridays. Other days, you'll find net asset value and the daily change and year-to-date performance.
• TOTAL RETURN
NAV change plus accumulated income for the period, in percent. Assumes reinvestment of all distributions. Percentages are annualized for periods exceeding 1 year. Calculations are based on latest data from fund.
• MAXIMUM INITIAL SALES COMMISSION
In percent. Based on prospectus.
• NET ASSET VALUE
Per share value calculated by the fund.
4 weeks
3 years
Year-to-date
Latest 12 months
5 years
• COMPANY
Fund families in bold face.
XYZ Mutual
8.43 -0.09 Bond p IB +16.4 +2.8 +16.4 B +12.6 C +11.6 B 5.50 1.17
8.43 -0.09 Growth GR +16.4 +2.8 +16.4 B +12.6 C +11.6 B 5.50 1.17
8.43 -0.09 Midcap Stock MC +16.4 +2.8 +16.4 B +12.6 C +11.6 B 5.50 1.17
• FUND OBJECTIVE
• FUND NAME
• ANNUAL EXPENSES
Percentage of annual average net assets in fund annual report.
• NET ASSET VALUE CHANGE
Gain or loss, based on prior day's NAV.
• RANKING
Compares performance among funds with same investment objectives and then ranked for time periods listed. Performance is measured from either the closest Thursday or month-end for periods of more than 3 years. A = top 20%; B = next 20%; C = middle 20%; D = next 20%; E = bottom 20%

Figure 15.4
Reading a Mutual Fund Quotation

The numbers for periods exceeding a year show an average annual return for the period and are followed by letters indicating the fund's performance relative to other funds with the same objective. "A" means the fund was among the top 20 percent of funds in that category; "B" indicates the second 20 percent, and so on.

- The next column reports the *maximum initial sales commission*, expressed in percent, which the investor would have to pay to purchase shares in the fund.
- The last column shows the fund's *average annual expenses*, as a percentage of the fund's assets, paid annually by investors in the fund.

market index
Summary of price trends in a specific industry and/or the stock market as a whole

bull market
Period of rising stock prices

bear market
Period of falling stock prices

Dow Jones Industrial Average (DJIA)
Market index based on the prices of 30 of the largest industrial firms listed on the NYSE

Market Indexes Although they do not indicate the status of particular securities, **market indexes** provide useful summaries of trends, both in specific industries and in the stock market as a whole. Market indexes, for example, reveal bull and bear market trends. **Bull markets** are periods of rising stock prices. Periods of falling stock prices are called **bear markets.**

As Figure 15.5 shows, the years 1981 to 2000 boasted a strong bull market, the longest in history. Inflation was under control as business flourished in a healthy economy. In contrast, the period 1972 to 1974 was characterized by a bear market. The Mideast oil embargo caused a business slowdown, and inflation was beginning to dampen economic growth. A more recent bear market emerged in 2000. As you can see, the data that characterize such periods are drawn from three leading market indexes—the Dow Jones, Standard & Poor's, and the Nasdaq Composite.

The Dow The **Dow Jones Industrial Average (DJIA)** is the most widely cited American index. The "Dow" measures the performance of U.S. financial markets by focusing on 30 blue-chip companies as reflectors of economic health. The Dow is an average of the stock prices for these 30 large firms and, by tradition, traders and investors use it as a barometer of the market's overall movement. Because it includes

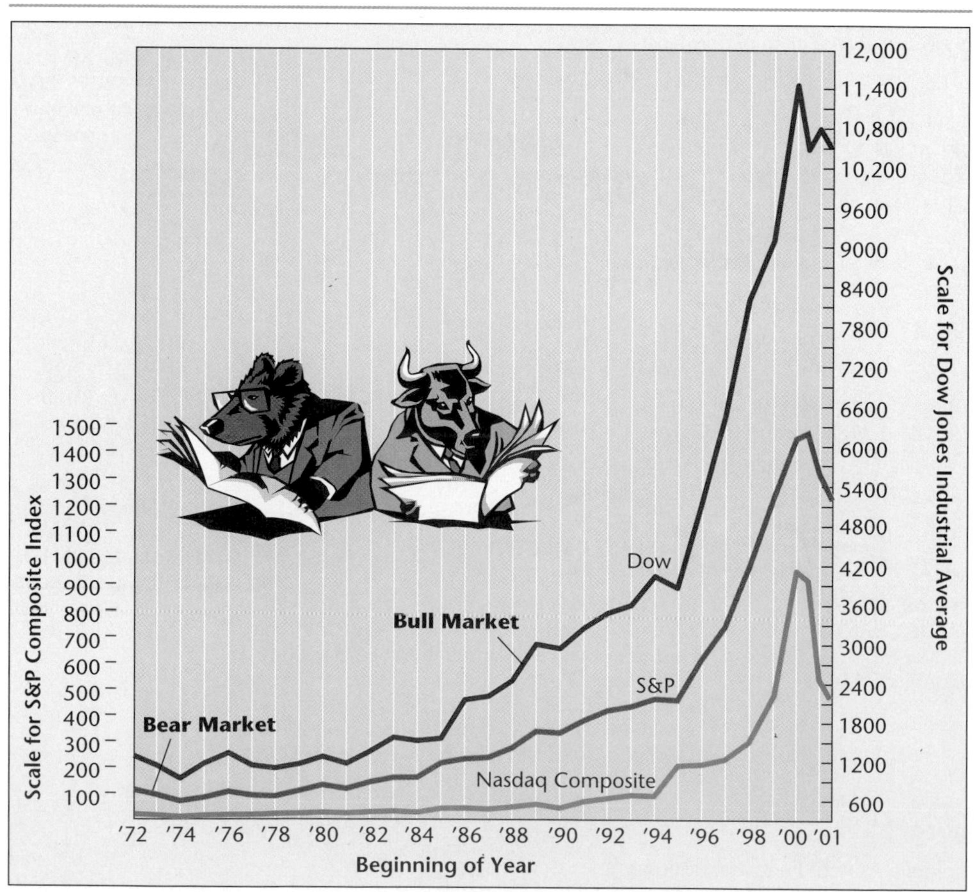

Figure 15.5
Bull and Bear Markets, 1972–2000

only 30 of the thousands of companies on the market, the Dow is only an approximation of the overall market's price movements.

Over the decades, the Dow has been revised and updated to reflect the changing composition of U.S. companies and industries. The most recent modification occurred in November 1999, when four companies were added—Home Depot <www.homedepot.com>, Intel, Microsoft, and SBC Communications <www.sbc.com>—replacing Chevron <www.chevron.com>, Goodyear <www.goodyear.com>, Sears <www.sears.com>, and Union Carbide <www.unioncarbide.com>. These changes not only reflect the increasing importance of technology stocks, but also include for the first time two stocks from the Nasdaq market rather than including only companies listed on the NYSE.

The Dow average is computed as the sum of the current prices of the 30 stocks divided not by 30 (as might be expected) but rather by a number that compensates for stock splits and each stock's available number of shares. On May 1, 2001, the value of that divisor was 0.1537. Each day, the divisor's value is printed in the *Wall Street Journal*, as is the DJIA.

The S&P 500 Because it considers very few firms, the Dow is a limited gauge of the overall U.S. stock market. **Standard & Poor's Composite Index** is a broader report. It consists of 500 stocks, including 400 industrial firms, 40 utilities, 40 financial institutions, and 20 transportation companies. Because the index average is weighted according to the total market values of each stock, the more highly valued companies exercise a greater influence on the index.

Standard & Poor's Composite Index
Market index based on the performance of 400 industrial firms, 40 utilities, 40 financial institutions, and 20 transportation companies

The Nasdaq Composite Because it considers more stocks, some Wall Street observers regard the **Nasdaq Composite Index** as the most important of all market indexes. Unlike the Dow and the S&P 500, all Nasdaq-listed companies, not just a selected few, are included in the index, for a total of over 5,000 firms (both U.S. and non-U.S.)—more than most other indexes.

Nasdaq Composite Index
Value-weighted market index that includes all Nasdaq-listed companies, both domestic and foreign

The popularity of the Nasdaq Index goes hand in hand with investors' growing interest in technology and small-company stocks. Compared with other markets, the Nasdaq market has enjoyed a remarkable level of activity. By 1995, so many shares were being traded on Nasdaq that its share-of-market surpassed that of the NYSE. Figure 15.6 shows steady growth in the dollar volume of Nasdaq trades, which continue to capture market share. In a further display of Nasdaq's emerging role in the stock market, it has also overtaken the NYSE in terms of investor awareness. NYSE's

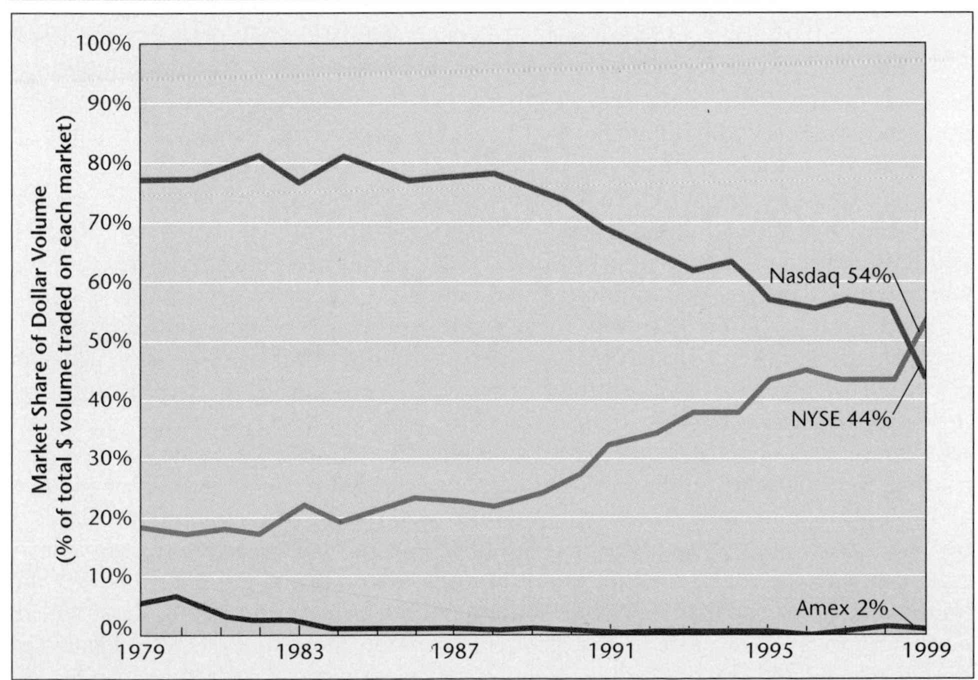

Figure 15.6
The Stock Markets: Comparative Dollar Volume of Trades

historical dominance as the market's flagship brand is being challenged by the newer Nasdaq, which, according to one study, even enjoys greater name recognition among U.S. investors.

Placing Orders

After doing your own research and getting recommendations from your broker, you can choose to place several different types of orders:[22]

market order
Order to buy or sell a security at the market price prevailing at the time the order is placed

limit order
Order authorizing the purchase of a stock only if its price is equal to or less than a specified amount

stop order
Order authorizing the sale of a stock if its price falls to or below a specified level

round lot
Purchase or sale of stock in units of 100 shares

odd lot
Purchase or sale of stock in fractions of round lots

- A **market order** requests that a broker buy or sell a certain security at the prevailing market price at the time of the order. For example, look again at Figure 15.3. On that day, your broker would have sold your Gap stock at a price near $26.76.
  Note that when you gave your order to sell, you did not know exactly what the market price would be. This situation can be avoided with limit and stop orders, which allow for buying and selling only if certain price conditions are met.
- A **limit order** authorizes the purchase of a stock only if its price is less than or equal to a specified limit. For example, an order to buy at $30 a share means that the broker is to buy if and only if the stock becomes available for a price of $30 or less. A **stop order** instructs the broker to sell if a stock price falls to a certain level. For example, an order of $25 on a particular stock means that the broker is to sell that stock if and only if its price falls to $25 or below.
- Orders also differ by size. An order for a **round lot** requests 100 shares of a particular stock or some multiple thereof. Fractions of round lots are called **odd lots**. Because an intermediary—an *odd-lot broker*—is often involved, odd-lot trading is usually more expensive than round-lot trading.

Financing Purchases

When you place a buy order of any kind, you must tell your broker how you will pay for the purchase. For example, you might maintain a cash account with your broker. Then, as you buy and sell stocks, your broker adds proceeds to your account while deducting commissions and purchase costs. Like almost every product in today's economy, securities can also be purchased on credit.

Margin Trading Like futures contracts, stocks can be bought *on margin*—that is, the buyer can put down a portion of the stock's price. The rest is borrowed from the buyer's broker, who secures special-rate bank loans with stock. Controlled by the Federal Reserve Board, the margin requirement has remained fixed at 50 percent since 1974.

Margin trading offers several advantages. Suppose you purchased $100,000 worth of stock in Intel Corp. Let's also say that you paid $50,000 of your own money and borrowed the other $50,000 from your broker at 10 percent interest. Valued at its market price, your stock serves as your collateral. If shares have risen in value to $115,000 after one year, you can sell them and pay your broker $55,000 ($50,000 principal plus $5,000 interest). You will have $60,000 left over. Your original investment of $50,000 will have earned a 20 percent profit of $10,000. If you had paid the entire price out of your own pocket, you would have earned only a 15-percent return.

Although investors often recognize possible profits to be made in margin trading, they sometimes fail to consider that losses, too, can be amplified. The rising use of margin credit by investors had become a growing concern during the recent bull market. Investors seem focused on the upside benefits with confidence that the market trend would continue upward, and they were less sensitive to the downside risks of margin trading. Especially at online brokerages, inexperienced traders were borrowing at an alarming rate, and some were using the borrowed funds for risky and speculative day trading. Day traders visited Web sites online to buy and sell a stock in the same day (so-called intraday trades), seeking quick in-and-out fractional gains on large volumes (many shares) of each stock. While some day traders were successful, most ended up financial losers. With more investors buying on debt, more of them were headed for a serious accelerated crash. Bradley Skolnick, president of the North American Securities

Administrators Association, voices the opinion held by many investment experts: "A lot of people are purchasing rather speculative, high-risk stocks with borrowed money, and that's a source of concern for me. In a volatile market, trading on margin can find you in a whole lot of hurt very quickly."[23]

"In a volatile market, trading on margin can find you in a whole lot of hurt very quickly."

—Bradley Skolnick, president, North American Securities Administrators Association

Short Sales In addition to lending money, brokerages also lend securities. A **short sale** begins when you borrow a security from your broker and sell it (one of the few times that it is legal to sell something that you do not own). At a given point in the future, you must restore an equal number of shares of that issue to the brokerage, along with a fee.

We now return to our Gap example. Suppose that in January you believe the price of Gap stock will soon fall. You therefore order your broker to "sell short" 100 shares at the market price of $26.76 per share. Your broker will make the sale and credit $2,676 to your account. If Gap's price falls to $20 per share in July, you can buy 100 shares for $2,000 and use them to repay your broker. You will have made a $676 profit (before commissions). Your risk, of course, is that Gap's price will not fall. If it holds steady or rises, you will take a loss.

short sale
Stock sale in which an investor borrows securities from a broker to be sold and then replaced at a specified future date

SECURITIES MARKET REGULATION

In addition to regulation by government agencies, both the NASD and the NYSE exercise self-regulation to maintain the public trust and to assure professionalism in the financial industry. A visible example is the NYSE's actions in establishing so-called *circuit breakers*—trading rules for reducing excessive market volatility and promoting investor confidence—that suspend trading for a preset length of time. Adopted first in October 1988, with approval of the SEC, the rules suspend trading on the NYSE whenever the market begins spiraling out of control during a single day. The 1988 rules stipulated that trading would halt for one hour on any day when the Dow Jones Industrial Average dropped 250 points and would close for two hours with any 400-point decline. The interruption provides a "cooling off" period that slows trading activity, allows investors to reconsider their trading positions, and allows computer programs to be revised or shut down.[24]

Because circuit-breaker thresholds are updated periodically to keep up with the Dow's growth, as of April 2000 the following single-day declines will halt trading market wide:

- A 1,050-point drop in the DJIA before 2 P.M. halts trading for one hour.
- A 2,100-point drop before 1 P.M. halts trading for two hours.
- A 3,150-point drop at any time halts trading for the day.

Although circuit breaker rules were initiated in response to severe market plunges in October 1987 and October 1988, they have been triggered only once, on October 27, 1997, when the DJIA fell 350 points at 2:35 P.M. and 550 points at 3:30 P.M., for an overall 7-percent plunge that shut down trading for the day.

One oft-cited cause of sudden market fluctuations is **program trading**—the portfolio trading strategy involving the sale or purchase of a group of stocks valued at $1 million or more, often triggered by computerized trading programs that can be launched without human supervision or control. It works in the following way. As market values change and economic events transpire during the course of a day, computer programs are busy recalculating the future values of stocks. Once a calculated value reaches a critical point, the program automatically signals a buy or sell order. Because electronic trading could cause the market to spiral out of control, it has contributed to the setting up of circuit breakers.

program trading
Large purchase or sale of a group of stocks, often triggered by computerized trading programs that can be launched without human supervision or control

The Securities and Exchange Commission

To protect the investing public and to maintain smoothly functioning markets, the Securities and Exchange Commission (SEC) oversees many phases in the process through which securities are issued. The SEC regulates the public offering of new securities by requiring that all companies file prospectuses before proposed offerings commence. To protect investors from fraudulent issues, a **prospectus** contains pertinent information about both the offered security and the issuing company. False statements are subject to criminal penalties.

prospectus
Registration statement filed with the SEC before the issuance of a new security

insider trading
Illegal practice of using special knowledge about a firm for profit or gain

Insider Trading The SEC also enforces laws against **insider trading**—the use of special knowledge about a firm for profit or gain. In June 2000, for example, the SEC filed suit in U.S. District Court for Northern California against 12 people on charges of using insider information and tips to gain at least $680,000 in illegal profits. The suit alleges that in 1995, one of the defendants, while working for Bay Networks Inc. <www.baynetworks.com>, learned of Bay's agreement to buy Xylogics Inc. <www.nortelnetworks.com>, before any public announcement. The defendant then allegedly purchased 6,215 shares of Xylogics during the two trading days before the public announcement. He subsequently made $105,000 in profits from the trades. He also contacted several friends who, in turn, contacted others who also grabbed up Xylogics stock and allegedly profited from trading in violation of the Securities Exchange Act of 1934.[25]

The SEC also offers a bounty to any person who provides information leading to a civil penalty for illegal insider trading. The courts can render such a penalty of up to three times the illegal profit that was gained, and the bounty can, at most, be 10 percent of that penalty.

Along with the SEC's enforcement efforts, the stock exchanges cooperate in detecting and stopping insider action. In any given year, NASD may refer more than 100 cases to the SEC for charges of possible insider trading. In addition, NASD's self-regulation results in actions ranging from fining member firms and officers to barring or suspending them.

blue-sky laws
Laws requiring securities dealers to be licensed and registered with the states in which they do business

Blue-Sky Laws State governments also regulate the sale of securities. For example, commenting that some promoters would sell stock "to the blue sky itself," one legislator's speech led to the phrase **blue-sky laws** and the passage of statutes requiring securities to be registered with state officials. In addition, securities dealers must be registered and licensed by the states in which they do business. Finally, states may prosecute the sale of fraudulent securities.

Continued from page 387

The Stuff that Rumors and Inflated Expectations are Made Of

Never before have investors had such immediate access to financial market information and analysis. From such sources as Reuters financial news services <www.reuters.com>, we can access our home PCs for real-time securities quotes and financial news from any market in the world. We can plug into hundreds of Internet-based online brokers for both analysis and full-color graphic explanations. We can watch CNBC's 24-hour cable operation <www.cnbc.com> or listen to the Bloomberg financial radio network <www.bloomberg.com/wbbr> for news and trends. We can get a copy of Fed chairman Alan Greenspan's latest speech by clicking on the Fed's Web site. The media give us not only instant information, but an instant "feedback loop" through which our reactions to facts, expectations, and rumors have the power to influence market swings.

Media analysts who feel compelled to give their spin on market changes also affect volatility. Without analysis, the business report would be little more than a recitation of numbers that would sell very few newspapers or hold the attention of very few viewers. "It's impossible to know why the stock market rose or fell," admits Associated Press <www.ap.org> business editor Rick Gladstone, "when there's no . . . obvious news. It may have nothing to do with the news or with anything. But reporters are obliged to say what might've been at work." This penchant for public speculation is the stuff that rumors, inflated expectations, and volatility are made of.

Immediate media access has turned many avid investors into 24-hour-a-day tradaholics. Securities are traded among investors in New York, Tokyo, London, and Buenos Aires any time, day or night. When investors wake up in the morning, they can check the latest dollar–yen relationship or Standard & Poor's futures prices. The pace is exhausting and so is the volatility.

Questions for Discussion

1. How do you think stock market volatility will affect today's investors in both the short term and in the long term?
2. What is the relationship between the growth of privately managed retirement accounts, in the form of Individual Retirement Accounts, Roth IRAs, and 401(K) pension plans, and stock market volatility?
3. In a volatile stock market, why is it important for investors to assess their reaction to financial risk and to put together short-term and long-term financial plans?
4. Is increasingly more sophisticated computer technology necessarily a good thing for the market? Explain your answer.
5. Computer programs now use mathematical formulas to make buy-and-sell decisions for large institutions without benefit of human intervention. Is this progress? Explain your answer.
6. What do you think about the media's role in stock market volatility?

SUMMARY OF LEARNING OBJECTIVES

1 **Explain the difference between *primary* and *secondary* securities markets.** *Primary securities markets* involve the buying and selling of new securities, either in public offerings or through private placements (sales to single buyers or small groups of buyers). *Investment bankers* specialize in issuing securities in primary markets. *Secondary markets* involve the trading of stocks and bonds through such familiar bodies as the New York and American Stock Exchanges.

2 **Discuss the value to shareholders of *common* and *preferred stock* and describe the secondary market for each type of security.** *Common stock* affords investors the prospect of capital gains and/or dividend income. Common stock values are expressed in three ways: as *par value* (the face value of a share when it is issued), *market value* (the current market price of a share), and *book value* (the value of shareholders' equity divided by the number of shares). Market value is most important to investors. *Preferred stock* is less risky. Cumulative preferred stock entitles holders to missed dividends as soon as the company is financially capable of paying. It also offers the prospect of steadier income. Shareholders of preferred stock must be paid dividends before shareholders of common stock.

Both common and preferred stock are traded on *stock exchanges* (institutions formed to conduct the trading of existing securities) including floor-based exchanges, electronic markets, and in *over-the-counter (OTC) markets* (dealer organizations formed to trade securities outside stock exchange settings). "Members" who hold seats on exchanges act as brokers—agents who execute buy-and-sell orders—for nonmembers. Floor-based exchanges include the New York, American, and regional and foreign exchanges. Nasdaq is a leading electronic market.

3 **Distinguish among various types of *bonds* in terms of their issuers, safety, and retirement.** The issuer of a *bond* promises to pay the buyer a certain amount of money by a specified future date, usually with interest paid at regular intervals. U.S. *government bonds* are backed by government institutions and agencies such as the Treasury Department or the Federal Housing Administration. *Municipal bonds*, which are offered by state and local governments to finance a variety of projects, are also usually safe, and the interest is ordinarily tax exempt. *Corporate bonds* are issued by companies to gain long-term funding. They may be secured (backed by pledges of the issuer's assets) or unsecured, and offer varying degrees of safety. The

safety of bonds issued by various borrowers is rated by Moody's and Standard & Poor's.

4 **Describe the investment opportunities offered by *mutual funds* and *commodities*.** Like stocks and bonds, *mutual funds*—companies that pool investments to purchase portfolios of financial instruments—offer investors different levels of risk and growth potential. *Load funds* require investors to pay commissions of 2 to 8 percent. *No-load funds* do not charge commissions when investors buy in or out. *Futures contracts*—agreements to buy specified amounts of commodities at given prices on preset dates—are traded in the *commodities market*. Commodities traders often buy on margins—percentages of total sales prices that must be put up to order futures contracts.

5 **Explain the process by which securities are bought and sold.** Investors generally use such *financial information services* as newspaper and online stock, bond, and OTC quotations to learn about possible investments. *Market indexes* such as the Dow Jones Industrial Average, the Standard & Poor's Composite Index, and the Nasdaq Composite provide useful summaries of trends, both in specific industries and in the market as a whole. Investors can then place different types of orders. *Market orders* are orders to buy or sell at current prevailing prices. Because investors do not know exactly what prices will be when market orders are executed, they may issue *limit* or *stop orders* that are to be executed only if prices rise to or fall below specified levels. *Round lots* are purchased in multiples of 100 shares. *Odd lots* are purchased in fractions of round lots. Securities can be bought on margin or as part of *short sales*—sales in which investors sell securities that are borrowed from brokers and returned at a later date.

6 **Explain how securities markets are regulated.** To protect investors, the *Securities and Exchange Commission (SEC)* regulates the public offering of new securities and enforces laws against such practices as *insider trading* (using special knowledge about a firm for profit or gain). To guard against fraudulent stock issues, the SEC lays down guidelines for *prospectuses*—statements of information about stocks and their issuers. Many state governments also prosecute the sale of fraudulent securities as well as enforce *blue-sky laws*, which require dealers to be licensed and registered where they conduct business. The securities industry also regulates itself through the National Association of Securities Dealers (NASD), which sets standards for membership and oversees enforcement of NASD rules.

QUESTIONS AND EXERCISES

Questions for Review

1. What are the purposes of the primary and secondary markets for securities?
2. Which of the three measures of common stock value is most important? Why?
3. How do government, municipal, and corporate bonds differ from one another?
4. How might an investor lose money in a commodities trade?
5. How does the Securities and Exchange Commission regulate securities markets?
6. Which U.S. stock market has the largest volume of trade?

Questions for Analysis

7. Suppose you decide to invest in common stocks as a personal investment. Which kind of broker—full service or online discount—would you use for buying and selling? Why?
8. Which type of mutual fund would be most appropriate for your investment purposes at this time? Why?
9. Using a newspaper, select an example of a recent day's transactions for each of the following: a stock on the NYSE, a stock on the AMEX, a Nasdaq stock, a bond on the NYSE, and a mutual fund. Explain the meaning of each element in the listing.

Application Exercises

10. Interview the financial manager of a local business or your school. What are the investment goals of this person's organization? What securities does it use? What advantages and disadvantages do you see in its portfolio?
11. Either in person or through a toll-free number, contact a broker and request information about setting up a personal account for trading securities. Prepare a report on the broker's policies regarding the following: buy/sell orders, credit terms, cash account requirements, services available to investors, and commissions/fees schedules.

EXPLORING THE WEB

What to Do during Trading Hours

Because stock market action can be fast and furious, up-to-date information is a must for most investors. Current regulations allow information about sales to become publicly available only minutes after transactions have been made on the stock markets. To get an idea of the types of information available on the Internet, access the Web site maintained by Nasdaq at:

<www.nasdaq.com>

To observe the process and results of trading activity, both current and past, explore the diverse information that this Web site provides to potential investors. Accessing it during actual daytime trading hours enables you to see minute-to-minute changes. On the Nasdaq home screen, for example, examine "Market Activity" option for an overview of Nasdaq market information. Explore the **Stock Quotes** dialogue box, including its **Symbol Look-Up** option. Then click on the **Market Indices** option and use information from it as you consider the following questions:

1. What is the Nasdaq Composite Index? How many and what types of companies are included in it? Compare it with the Dow Jones Industrial Average Index. Which of the indexes is more representative of overall market activity? Why?
2. Select any two stocks (from the newspaper or other source). Using the **Symbol Look-Up** option on the initial screen, examine the volatility of the stocks' values during the past six months. Which stock was most volatile? What was the percentage change (from high to low) during the six months? [To get there, first look up the stock's symbol, then click on **InfoQuotes** and enter the stock symbol. Then click on **Chart These Securities** and set the selector on **6 months.**]
3. Select any two mutual funds (from the newspaper or other source). Using the **Symbol Look-Up** option on the initial screen, examine the volatility of the funds' values during the past six months. Which of the funds was most volatile? What was the percentage change (from high to low) during the six months?
4. Select the **News** option (at the top of the screen) and explore some current news releases. How recently were these news items published? Why do you think Nasdaq displays these news releases at its Web site?
5. Using the **News** option, can you find a news release that might influence investors to buy or sell the stock of a particular company? An item that might influence investors to trade the stocks of companies in a particular industry?

EXERCISING YOUR ETHICS

Are You Endowed with Good Judgment?

THE SITUATION

Every organization faces decisions about whether to make conservative or risky investments. Let's assume that you have been asked to evaluate the advantages and drawbacks of conservative versus risky investments, including all relevant ethical considerations, by Youth Dreams Charities (YDC), a local organization that assists low-income families in gaining access to educational opportunities. YDC is a not-for-profit firm that employs a full-time professional manager to run daily operations. Overall governance and policy making reside with a board of directors—10 part-time community-minded volunteers who are entrusted with carrying out YDC's mission.

For the current year, 23 students receive tuition totaling $92,000 paid by YDC. Tuition comes from annual fund-raising activities (a white-tie dance and a seafood carnival) and from financial returns from YDC's $2.1 million endowment. The endowment has been amassed from charitable donations during the past 12 years and this year has yielded some $84,000 for tuitions. The board's goal is to increase the endowment to $4 million in five years in order to provide $200,000 in tuition annually.

THE DILEMMA

Based on the Finance Committee's suggestions, the board is considering a change in YDC's investment policies. The current, rather conservative approach invests the endowment in CDs and other low-risk instruments that have consistently yielded a 6-percent annual return. This practice has allowed the endowment to grow modestly (at about 2 percent per year). The remaining investment proceeds (4 percent) flow out for tuitions. The proposed plan would invest one-half of the endowment in conservative instruments and the other half in blue-chip stocks. Finance Committee members believe that, with market growth, the endowment has a good chance of reaching the $4 million goal within five years. While some board members like the prospects of faster growth, others think the proposal is too risky. What happens if, instead of increasing, the stock market collapses and the endowment shrinks? What will happen to YDC's programs? Your opinion has been asked on the following issues:

1. Why might a conservative versus risky choice be different at a not-for-profit organization than at a for-profit organization?
2. What are the main ethical issues in this situation?
3. What action should the board take?

BUILDING YOUR BUSINESS SKILLS

Market Ups and Downs

This exercise enhances the following SCANS workplace competencies: demonstrating basic skills, demonstrating thinking skills, exhibiting interpersonal skills, and working with information.

GOAL
To encourage students to understand the forces that affect fluctuations in stock price.

BACKGROUND
Investing in stocks requires an understanding of the various factors that affect stock price. These factors may be intrinsic to the company itself or part of the external environment.

- Internal factors relate to the company itself, such as an announcement of poor or favorable earnings, earnings that are more or less than expected, major layoffs, labor problems, management issues, and mergers.
- External factors relate to world or national events, such as a threatened war in the Persian Gulf, the Asian currency crisis, weather conditions that affect sales, the Federal Reserve Board's adjustment of interest rates, and employment figures that were higher or lower than expected.

By analyzing these factors, you will often learn a lot about why a stock did well or why it did poorly. Being aware of these influences will help you anticipate future stock movements.

METHOD

STEP 1
Working alone, choose a common stock that has experienced considerable price fluctuations in the past few years. Here are several examples, but there are many others: IBM, J.P. Morgan, AT&T, Amazon.com, Oxford Health Care, and Apple Computer. Find the symbol for the stock (for example, J.P. Morgan is JPM) and the exchange on which it is traded (JPM is traded on the New York Stock Exchange).

STEP 2
At your library, find the *Daily Stock Price Record*, a publication that provides a historical picture of daily stock closings. There are separate copies for the New York Stock Exchange, the American Stock Exchange, and the Nasdaq markets. Find your stock and study its trading pattern.

STEP 3
Find four or five days over a period of several months or even a year when there have been major price fluctuations in the stock. (A two- or three-point price change from one day to the next is considered major.) Then research what happened on that day that might have contributed to the fluctuation. The best place to begin is with the *Wall Street Journal* or on the business pages of a national newspaper, such as the *New York Times* or the *Washington Post*.

STEP 4
Write a short analysis that links changes in stock price to internal and external factors. As you analyze the data, be aware that sometimes it is difficult to know why a stock price fluctuates.

STEP 5
Get together with three other students who studied different stocks. As a group, discuss your findings, looking for fluctuation patterns.

FOLLOW-UP QUESTIONS

1. Do you see any similarities in the movement of the various stocks during the same period? For example, did the stocks move up or down at about the same time? If so, do you think the stocks were affected by the same factors? Explain your thinking.
2. Based on your analysis, did internal or external factors have the greater impact on stock price? Which factors had the more long-lasting effect? Which factors had the shorter effect?
3. Why do you think it is so hard to predict changes in stock price on a day-to-day basis?

CRAFTING YOUR BUSINESS PLAN

A Capital Idea

PURPOSE OF THE ASSIGNMENT

1. To familiarize students with securities and investments issues that a sample firm may face in developing its business plan, in the framework of *Business PlanPro* (*BPP*) (Version 4.0).
2. To demonstrate how three chapter topics—issuing stock, issuing bonds, and making securities-market transactions—can be integrated as components in the BPP planning environment.

FOLLOW-UP ASSIGNMENT
After reading Chapter 15 in the textbook, open the BPP *software* and search for information about financial plans, equity financing (stocks), and debt financing via bonds as they apply to a sample firm:* Sample Software Company *(Sample Software, Inc.). Then respond to the following questions:*

1. Evaluate Sample Software's plans for financing its operations. Does the company have any outstanding stock? Does it plan to issue stock or bonds in the future? [Sites to see in *BPP* for this question: In the Plan Outline screen, click on **7.0 Financial Plan.**]
2. What sources of capital have been used to meet Sample Software's financial requirements? What equity (stock) sources are available for meeting the

firm's financial needs? What debt sources are available? [Sites to see in *BPP*: In the Plan Outline screen, click on **1.0 Executive Summary**. Return to the Plan Outline screen and click, in turn, on each of **2.1 Company Ownership, 2.2 Company History, 7.1 Important Assumptions**, and then **Table: General Assumptions.**]

3. Based on the company's "net profit" projections, at what points in time will Sample Software be able to pay dividends or repay its debt obligations? How much financing will be needed according to this plan, and at what points in time? [Sites to see in *BPP*: From the Plan Outline screen, click on each of **7.4 Projected Profit and Loss** and **Table: Profit and Loss.**]

VIDEO EXERCISE

Information Pays Off: Anatomy of a Stock Trade

LEARNING OBJECTIVES

The purpose of this video is to help you:

1. Identify the basic characteristics of stocks and bonds.
2. Understand the nature of other marketable securities, such as mutual funds.
3. Describe the process by which securities are bought and sold.

BACKGROUND INFORMATION

Today's news is sprinkled liberally with stories of instant millionaires whose shares of Internet start-up companies appear to have mushroomed into enormous fortunes overnight. In reality, investing in the stock market—or any other market for securities—is a complex process that entails a certain amount of risk. Investors should be prepared to research the firms in which they are interested, but even before taking this step, they should know what kinds of securities are available and what regulations govern their sale. They should also have a very good idea of what constitutes an acceptable risk for them.

THE VIDEO

Experts in the fields of finance and investing answer questions about the types of securities and the differences between them, the kinds of securities markets in which they are traded, and the regulations that govern them. They also present an anatomy of an actual stock trade.

QUESTIONS FOR DISCUSSION

1. What are securities and why do they exist?
2. What role do you think the Internet may play in the future of securities trading? What kind of regulation do you think will be necessary?
3. What are some reliable sources of information about securities?

FOLLOW-UP ASSIGNMENT

Select a publicly traded company in which you have some personal interest; perhaps you use its products, would like to work there, or know someone who works there. Follow the firm's stock price for a week or 10 days until you see a change in price, whether positive or negative. What is your best guess as to the reason for the change? Did the company take some important action or make a major announcement? Or is its stock price simply following a general market trend (all prices are rising or falling)? If the latter, what do you think is the reason for the general trend?

FOR FURTHER EXPLORATION

Mutual funds that seek out environmentally and socially conscious firms in which to invest are becoming more popular, offering investors a way to earn returns that don't offend their principles. Investigate two or three of the following and find out what types of firms they avoid and what type they invest in:

- <www.socialinvest.org>
- <www.coopamerica.org>
- <socialfunds.com>
- <goodmoney.com>
- <greenmoney.com>

If you were to invest in a mutual fund, would you choose one of these? Why or why not?

Appendix I

Understanding Financial Risk and Risk Management

THE ROLE OF THE FINANCIAL MANAGER

The business activity known as **finance** (or **corporate finance**) typically entails four responsibilities:

- Determining a firm's long-term investments
- Obtaining funds to pay for those investments
- Conducting the firm's everyday financial activities
- Helping to manage the risks that the firm takes

As we saw in Chapter 7, production managers plan and control the output of goods and services. In Chapter 10, we saw that marketing managers plan and control the development and marketing of products. Similarly, **financial managers** plan and control the acquisition and dispersal of a firm's financial resources. In this section, we will see in some detail how those activities are channeled into specific plans for protecting—and enhancing—a firm's financial well-being.

finance (or corporate finance)
Activities concerned with determining a firm's long-term investments, obtaining the funds to pay for them, conducting the firm's everyday, financial activities, and managing the firm's risks

financial manager
Manager responsible for planning and controlling the acquisition and dispersal of a firm's financial resources

Responsibilities of the Financial Manager

Financial managers collect funds, pay debts, establish trade credit, obtain loans, control cash balances, and plan for future financial needs. But a financial manager's overall objective is to increase a firm's value—and thus stockholders' wealth. Whereas accountants create data to reflect a firm's financial status, financial managers make decisions for improving that status. Financial managers, then, must ensure that a company's earnings exceed its costs—in other words, that it earns a profit. In sole proprietorships and partnerships, profits translate directly into increases in owners' wealth. In corporations, profits translate into an increase in the value of common stock.

The various responsibilities of the financial manager in increasing a firm's wealth fall into two general categories: *cash-flow management* and *financial planning*.

Cash-Flow Management To increase a firm's value, financial managers must ensure that it always has enough funds on hand to purchase the materials and human resources that it needs to produce goods and services. At the same time, of course, there may be funds that are not needed immediately. These must be invested to earn more money for the firm. This activity—**cash-flow management**—requires careful planning. If excess cash balances are allowed to sit idle instead of being invested, a firm loses the cash returns that it could have earned.

How important to a business is the management of its idle cash? One study has revealed that companies averaging $2 million in annual sales typically hold $40,000 in non-interest-bearing accounts. Larger companies hold even larger sums. More and more companies, however, are learning that these idle funds can become working funds. By locating idle cash and putting it to work, for instance, they can avoid borrowing from outside sources. The savings on interest payments can be substantial.

cash-flow management
Management of cash inflows and outflows to ensure adequate funds for purchases and the productive use of excess funds

Financial Planning The cornerstone of effective financial management is the development of a financial plan. A **financial plan** describes a firm's strategies for reaching some

financial plan
A firm's strategies for reaching some future financial position

future financial position. In constructing the plan, a financial manager must ask several questions:

- What amount of funds does the company need to meet immediate needs?
- When will it need more funds?
- Where can it get the funds to meet both its short- and long-term needs?

To answer these questions, a financial manager must develop a clear picture of why a firm needs funds. Managers must also assess the relative costs and benefits of potential funding sources. In the sections that follow, we will examine the main reasons for which companies generate funds and describe the main sources of business funding, both for the short term and the long term.

WHY DO BUSINESSES NEED FUNDS?

Every company must spend money to survive: According to the simplest formula, funds that are spent on materials, wages, and buildings eventually lead to the creation of products, revenues, and profits. In planning for funding requirements, financial managers must distinguish between two different kinds of expenditures: *short-term (operating)* and *long-term (capital) expenditures.*

Short-Term (Operating) Expenditures

Short-term expenditures are incurred regularly in a firm's everyday business activities. To manage these outlays, managers must pay special attention to *accounts payable, accounts receivable*, and *inventories*. We will also describe the measures used by some firms in managing the funds known as working capital.

Accounts Payable In Chapter 13, we defined *accounts payable* as unpaid bills owed to suppliers plus wages and taxes due within the upcoming year. For most companies, this is the largest single category of short-term debt. To plan for funding flows, financial managers want to know *in advance* the amounts of new accounts payable as well as when they must be repaid. For information about such obligations and needs—say, the quantity of supplies required by a certain department in an upcoming period—financial managers must rely on other managers.

Accounts Receivable As we also saw in Chapter 13, *accounts receivable* consist of funds due from customers who have bought on credit. A sound financial plan requires financial managers to project accurately both how much and when buyers will make payments on these accounts. For example, managers at Kraft Foods must know how many dollars' worth of cheddar cheese Kroger's supermarkets will order each month; they must also know Kroger's payment schedule. Because they represent an investment in products for which a firm has not yet received payment, accounts receivable temporarily tie up its funds. Clearly, the seller wants to receive payment as quickly as possible.

inventory
Materials and goods that are held by a company but that will be sold within the year

Inventories Between the time a firm buys raw materials and the time it sells finished products, it ties up funds in **inventory**—materials and goods that it will sell within the year.

Failure to manage inventory can have grave financial consequences. Too little inventory of any kind can cost a firm sales. Too much inventory means tied-up funds that cannot be used elsewhere. In extreme cases, a company may have to sell excess inventory at low profits simply to raise cash.

working capital
Liquid current assets out of which a firm can pay current debts

Working Capital Basically, **working capital** consists of a firm's current assets on hand. It is a liquid asset out of which current debts can be paid. A company calculates its working capital by adding up the following:

- Inventories—that is, raw materials, work-in-process, and finished goods on hand
- Accounts receivable (minus accounts payable)

How much money is tied up in working capital? *Fortune* 500 companies typically devote 20 cents of every sales dollar—about $800 billion total—to working capital. What are the benefits of reducing these sums? There are two very important pluses:

1. Every dollar that is not tied up in working capital becomes a dollar of more useful cash flow.
2. Reduction of working capital raises earnings permanently.

The second advantage results from the fact that money costs money (in interest payments and the like). Reducing working capital, therefore, means saving money.

Long-Term (Capital) Expenditures

In addition to needing funds for operating expenditures, companies need funds to cover long-term expenditures on fixed assets. As we saw in Chapter 13, *fixed assets* are items with long-term use or value, such as land, buildings, and machinery.

Long-term expenditures are usually more carefully planned than short-term outlays because they pose special problems. They differ from short-term outlays in the following ways, all of which influence the ways that long-term outlays are funded:

- Unlike inventories and other short-term assets, they are not normally sold or converted into cash.
- Their acquisition requires a very large investment.
- They represent a binding commitment of company funds that continues long into the future.

SOURCES OF SHORT-TERM FUNDS

Firms can call on many sources for the funds they need to finance day-to-day operations and to implement short-term plans. These sources include *trade credit* and *secured* and *unsecured loans*.

Trade Credit

Accounts payable are not merely expenditures. They also constitute a source of funds for the buying company. Until it pays its bill, the buyer has the use of *both* the purchased product and the price of the product. This situation results when the seller grants **trade credit**, which is effectively a short-term loan from one firm to another. The most common form of trade credit, **open-book credit**, is essentially a "gentlemen's agreement." Buyers receive merchandise along with invoices stating credit terms. Sellers ship products on faith that payment will be forthcoming.

trade credit
Granting of credit by one firm to another

open-book credit
Form of trade credit in which sellers ship merchandise on faith that payment will be forthcoming

Secured Short-Term Loans

For most firms, bank loans are a very important source of short-term funding. Such loans almost always involve promissory notes in which the borrower promises to repay the loan plus interest. In **secured loans**, banks also require **collateral**: a legal interest in certain assets that can be seized if payments are not made as promised.

Secured loans allow borrowers to get funds when they might not qualify for unsecured credit. Moreover, they generally carry lower interest rates than unsecured loans. Collateral may be in the form of inventories or accounts receivable, and most businesses have other types of assets that can be pledged. Some, for instance, own marketable securities, such as stocks or bonds of other companies (see Chapter 15). Many more own fixed assets, such as land, buildings, or equipment. Fixed assets, however, are generally used to secure long-term rather than short-term loans. Most short-term business borrowing is secured by inventories and accounts receivable.

secured loan
Loan for which the borrower must provide collateral

collateral
Borrower-pledged legal asset that may be seized by lenders in case of nonpayment

When a loan is made with inventory as a collateral asset, the lender loans the borrower some portion of the stated value of the inventory. When accounts receivable are used as collateral, the process is called **pledging accounts receivable**. In the event of nonpayment, the lender may seize the receivables—that is, funds owed the borrower by its customers.

pledging accounts receivable
Using accounts receivable as loan collateral

Unsecured Short-Term Loans

unsecured loan
Loan for which collateral is not required

With an **unsecured loan**, the borrower does not have to put up collateral. In many cases, however, the bank requires the borrower to maintain a *compensating balance*: the borrower must keep a portion of the loan amount on deposit with the bank in a non-interest-bearing account.

The terms of the loan—amount, duration, interest rate, and payment schedule—are negotiated between the bank and the borrower. To receive an unsecured loan, then, a firm must ordinarily have a good banking relationship with the lender. Once an agreement is made, a promissory note will be executed and the funds transferred to the borrower. Although some unsecured loans are one-time-only arrangements, many take the form of *lines of credit, revolving credit agreements*, or *commercial paper*.

line of credit
Standing arrangement in which a lender agrees to make available a specified amount of funds upon the borrower's request

revolving credit agreement
Arrangement in which a lender agrees to make funds available on demand and on a continuing basis

commercial paper
Short-term securities, or notes, containing a borrower's promise to pay

A **line of credit** is a standing agreement between a bank and a business in which the bank promises to lend the firm a specified amount of funds on request. **Revolving credit agreements** are similar to consumer bank cards. A lender agrees to make some amount of funds available on demand and on a continuing basis. The lending institution guarantees that these funds will be available when sought by the borrower. In return for this guarantee, the bank charges the borrower a *commitment fee* for holding the line of credit open. This fee is payable even if the customer does not borrow any funds. It is often expressed as a percentage of the loan amount (usually 0.5 to 1 percent of the committed amount).

Finally, some firms can raise short-term funds by issuing **commercial paper**—short-term securities, or notes, containing the borrower's promise to pay. Because it is backed solely by the issuing firm's promise to pay, commercial paper is an option for only the largest and most creditworthy firms.

How does commercial paper work? Corporations issue commercial paper with a certain face value. Buying companies pay less than that value. At the end of a specified period (usually 30 to 90 days, but legally up to 270 days), the issuing company buys back the paper—*at face value*. The difference between the price paid and the face value is the buyer's profit. For the issuing company, the cost is usually lower than prevailing interest rates on short-term loans.

SOURCES OF LONG-TERM FUNDS

Firms need long-term funding to finance expenditures on fixed assets: the buildings and equipment necessary for conducting their business. They may seek long-term funds through *debt financing* (that is, from outside the firm) or through *equity financing* (by drawing on internal sources). We will discuss both options in this section, as well as a middle ground called hybrid financing. We will also analyze some of the options that enter into decisions about long-term financing, as well as the role of the *risk-return relationship* in attracting investors to a firm.

Debt Financing

debt financing
Long-term borrowing from sources outside a company

Long-term borrowing from sources outside the company—**debt financing**—is a major component of most firms' long-term financial planning. Long-term debts are obligations that are payable more than one year after they were originally issued. The two primary sources of such funding are *long-term loans* and the sale of *corporate bonds*.

Long-Term Loans Most corporations get long-term loans from commercial banks, usually those with which they have developed long-standing relationships. Credit companies (such as Household Finance Corp.), insurance companies, and pension funds also grant long-term business loans.

Long-term loans are attractive to borrowers for several reasons:

- Because the number of parties involved is limited, loans can often be arranged very quickly.
- The firm need not make public disclosure of its business plans or the purpose for which it is acquiring the loan. (In contrast, the issuance of corporate bonds requires such disclosure.)
- The duration of the loan can easily be matched to the borrower's needs.
- If the firm's needs change, loans usually contain clauses making it possible to change terms.

Long-term loans also have some disadvantages. Borrowers, for instance, may have trouble finding lenders to supply large sums. Long-term borrowers may also face restrictions as conditions of the loan. For example, they may have to pledge long-term assets as collateral or agree to take on no more debt until the loan is paid.

Corporate Bonds As we saw in Chapter 15, a *corporate bond*, like commercial paper, is a contract—a promise by the issuer to pay the holder a certain amount of money on a specified date. Unlike issuers of commercial paper, however, bond issuers do not pay off quickly. In many cases, bonds may not be redeemable for 30 years. Also, unlike commercial paper, most bonds pay bondholders a stipulated sum of annual or semiannual interest. If the company fails to make a bond payment, it is said to be *in default*.

Bonds are the major source of long-term debt financing for most corporations. They are attractive when firms need large amounts for long periods of time. The issuing company also gains access to large numbers of lenders through nationwide bond markets and stock exchanges. On the other hand, bonds entail high administrative and selling costs. They may also require stiff interest payments, especially if the issuing company has a poor credit rating.

Equity Financing

Although debt financing often has strong appeal, looking inside the company for long-term funding is sometimes preferable. In small companies, for example, founders may increase personal investments in their own firms. In most cases, **equity financing** means issuing common stock or retaining the firm's earnings. Both options involve putting the owners' capital to work.

equity financing
Use of common stock and/or retained earnings to raise long-term funding

Common Stock People who purchase common stock seek profits in two forms—dividends and appreciation. Over all, shareholders hope for an increase in the market value of their stock (appreciation) because the firm has profited and grown. By issuing shares of stock, the company gets the funds it needs for buying land, buildings, and equipment.

Consider, for example, a hypothetical company called Sunshine Tanning. Suppose the company's founders invested $10,000 by buying the original 500 shares of common stock (at $20 per share) in 1995. The company used these funds to buy equipment, and it succeeded financially. By 2001, then, it needed funds for expansion. A pattern of profitable operations and regularly paid dividends now allows Sunshine to raise $50,000 by selling 500 new shares of stock at $100 per share. This $50,000 would constitute *paid-in capital*—additional money, above the par value of its original stock sale, paid directly to a firm by its owners. As Table AI.1 shows, this additional paid-in capital would increase total stockholders' equity to $60,000.

retained earnings
Earnings retained by a firm for its use rather than paid out as dividends

Retained Earnings **Retained earnings** are profits retained for the firm's use rather than paid out in dividends. If a company uses retained earnings as capital, it will not have to borrow money and pay interest. If a firm has a history of reaping profits by

Table AI.1
Stockholders' Equality for Sunshine Tanning

Common Stockholders' Equity, 1995	
Initial common stock (500 shares issued @ $20 per share, 1995)	$10,000
Total stockholders' equity	$10,000
Common Stockholders' Equity, 2001	
Initial common stock (500 shares issued @ $20 per share, 1995)	$10,000
Additional paid-in capital (500 shares issued @ $100 per share, 2001)	50,000
Total stockholders' equity	$60,000

reinvesting retained earnings, it may be very attractive to some investors. Retained earnings, however, mean smaller dividends for shareholders. In this sense, then, the practice may decrease the demand for—and thus the price of—the company's stock.

For example, if Sunshine Tanning had net earnings of $50,000 in 2001, it could pay a $50-per-share dividend on its 1,000 shares of common stock. Let's say, however, that Sunshine plans to remodel at a cost of $30,000, intending to retain $30,000 in earnings to finance the project. Only $20,000—$20 per share—will be available for shareholders.

Hybrid Financing: Preferred Stock

A middle ground between debt financing and equity financing is the use of preferred stock (see Chapter 15). Preferred stock is a "hybrid" because it has some of the features of both corporate bonds and common stocks. As with bonds, for instance, payments on preferred stock are fixed amounts such as $6 per share per year. Unlike bonds, however, preferred stock never matures; like common stock, it can be held indefinitely. In addition, preferred stocks have first rights (over common stock) to dividends.

A major advantage to the issuer is the flexibility of preferred stock. Because preferred stockholders have no voting rights, the stock secures funds for the firm without jeopardizing corporate control of its management. Furthermore, corporations are not obligated to repay the principal and can withhold payment of dividends in lean times.

Choosing Between Debt and Equity Financing

capital structure
Relative mix of a firm's debt and equity financing

Needless to say, an aspect of financial planning is striking a balance between debt and equity financing. Because a firm relies on a mix of debt and equity to raise the cash needed for capital outlays, that mix is called its **capital structure**. Financial plans, thus, contain targets for capital structure; an example would be 40 percent debt and 60 percent equity. But choosing a target is not easy. A wide range of mixes is possible, and strategies range from conservative to risky.

The most conservative strategy is all-equity financing and no debt: A company has no formal obligations to make financial payouts. As we have seen, however, equity is an expensive source of capital. The riskiest strategy is all-debt financing. Although less expensive than equity funding, indebtedness increases the risk that a firm will be unable to meet its obligations (and even go bankrupt). Somewhere between the two extremes, financial planners try to find mixes that will increase stockholders' wealth with a reasonable exposure to risk.

The Risk-Return Relationship

While developing plans for raising capital, financial managers must be aware of the different motivations of individual investors. Why, for example, do some individuals and firms invest in stocks while others invest only in bonds? Investor motivations, of course, determine who is willing to buy a given company's stocks or bonds. Investors give money to firms and, in return, anticipate receiving future cash flows. Thus, everyone who invests money is expressing a personal preference for safety versus risk.

In other words, some cash flows are more certain than others. Investors generally expect to receive higher payments for higher uncertainty. They do not generally expect large returns for secure investments like government-insured bonds. Each type of investment, then, has a **risk-return relationship** reflecting the principle that whereas safer investments tend to offer lower returns, riskier investments tend to offer higher returns.

risk-return relationship
Principle that, whereas safer investments tend to offer lower returns, riskier investments tend to offer higher returns

Risk-return differences are recognized by financial planners, who try to gain access to the greatest funding at the lowest possible cost. By gauging investors' perceptions of their riskiness, a firm's managers can estimate how much they must pay to attract funds to their offerings. Over time, a company can reposition itself on the risk continuum by improving its record on dividends, interest payments, and debt repayment.

FINANCIAL MANAGEMENT FOR SMALL BUSINESS

New business success and failure are often closely related to adequate or inadequate funding. For example, one study of nearly 3,000 new companies revealed a survival rate of 84 percent for new businesses with initial investments of at least $50,000. Unfortunately, those with less funding have a much lower survival rate. Why are so many start-ups underfunded? For one thing, entrepreneurs often underestimate the value of establishing bank credit as a source of funds and use trade credit ineffectively. In addition, they often fail to consider *venture capital* as a source of funding, and they are notorious for not planning *cash-flow needs* properly.

Establishing Bank and Trade Credit Some banks have liberal credit policies and offer financial analysis, cash-flow planning, and suggestions based on experiences with other local firms. Some provide loans to small businesses in bad times and work to keep them going. Some, of course, do not. Obtaining credit, therefore, begins with finding a bank that can—and will—support a small firm's financial needs. Once a line of credit is obtained, the small business can seek more liberal credit policies from other businesses. Sometimes, for instance, suppliers give customers longer credit periods—say, 45 or 60 days rather than 30 days. Liberal trade credit terms with their suppliers let firms increase short-term funds and avoid additional borrowing from banks.

Long-Term Funding Naturally, obtaining long-term loans is more difficult for new businesses than for established companies. With unproven repayment ability, start-up firms can expect to pay higher interest rates than older firms. If a new enterprise displays evidence of sound financial planning, however, the Small Business Administration (see Chapter 2) may support a guaranteed loan.

Venture Capital Many newer businesses—especially those undergoing rapid growth—cannot get the funds they need through borrowing alone. They may, therefore, turn to **venture capital**: outside equity funding provided in return for part ownership of the borrowing firm. *Venture capital firms* actively seek chances to invest in new firms with rapid growth potential. Because failure rates are high, they typically demand high returns, which are now often 20 to 30 percent.

venture capital
Outside equity financing provided in return for part ownership of the borrowing firm

Planning for Cash-Flow Requirements

Although all businesses should plan for their cash flows, this planning is especially important for small businesses. Success or failure may hinge on anticipating those times when either cash will be short or excess cash can be expected.

Figure AI.1 shows possible cash inflows, cash outflows, and net cash position (inflows minus outflows) month by month for Slippery Fish Bait Supply—a highly seasonal business. As you can see, bait stores buy heavily from Slippery during the spring and summer months. Revenues outpace expenses, leaving surplus funds that can be

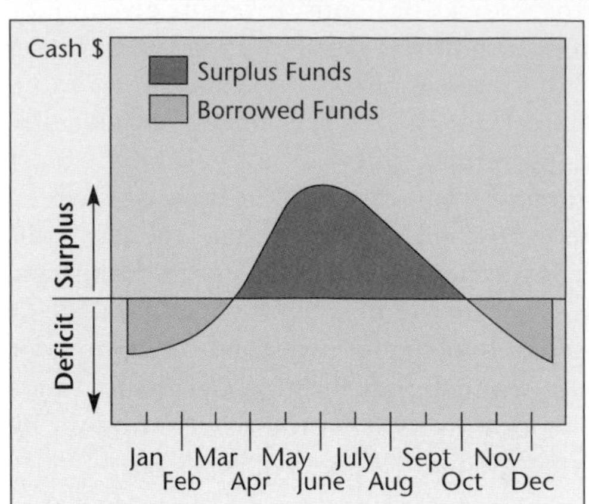

Figure AI.1
Projected Cash Flow for Slippery Fish Bait Supply Co.

invested. During the fall and winter, however, expenses exceed revenues. Slippery must borrow funds to keep going until revenues pick up again in the spring. Comparing predicted cash inflows from sales with outflows for expenses shows the firm's expected monthly cash-flow position.

Such knowledge can be invaluable for the small business manager. By anticipating shortfalls, for example, a financial manager can seek funds in advance and minimize their cost. By anticipating excess cash, a manager can plan to put the funds to work in short-term, interest-earning investments.

RISK MANAGEMENT

Financial risks are not the only risks faced every day by companies (and individuals). In this section, we will describe various other types of risks that businesses face and analyze some of the ways in which they typically manage them.

Coping with Risk

risk
Uncertainty about future events

speculative risk
Risk involving the possibility of gain or loss

pure risk
Risk involving only the possibility of loss or no loss

risk management
Process of conserving the firm's earning power and assets by reducing the threat of losses due to uncontrollable events

Businesses constantly face two basic types of **risk**—that is, uncertainty about future events. **Speculative risks**, such as financial investments, involve the possibility of gain or loss. **Pure risks** involve only the possibility of loss or no loss. Designing and distributing a new product, for example, is a speculative risk. The product may fail, or it may succeed and earn high profits. In contrast, the chance of a warehouse fire is a pure risk.

For a company to survive and prosper, it must manage both types of risk in a cost-effective manner. We can thus define the process of **risk management** as conserving the firm's earning power and assets by reducing the threat of losses due to uncontrollable events. In every company, each manager must be alert for risks to the firm and their impact on profits. The risk-management process usually entails five steps.

Step 1: Identify Risks and Potential Losses Managers analyze a firm's risks to identify potential losses. For example, a firm with a fleet of delivery trucks can expect that one of them will eventually be involved in an accident. The accident may cause bodily injury to the driver or others, may cause physical damage to the truck or other vehicles, or both.

Step 2: Measure the Frequency and Severity of Losses and Their Impact To measure the frequency and severity of losses, managers must consider both past history and current activities. How often can the firm expect the loss to occur? What is the likely size of the loss in dollars? For example, our firm with the fleet of delivery trucks may have had two accidents per year in the past. If it adds trucks, however, it may reasonably expect the frequency of accidents to increase.

Step 3: Evaluate Alternatives and Choose the Techniques That Will Best Handle the Losses Having identified and measured potential losses, managers are in a better position to decide how to handle them. With this third step, they generally have four choices: *risk avoidance, control, retention*, or *transfer*.

Risk Avoidance A firm opts for **risk avoidance** by declining to enter or by ceasing to participate in a risky activity. For example, the firm with the delivery trucks could avoid any risk of physical damage or bodily injury by closing down its delivery service. Similarly, a pharmaceutical maker may withdraw a new drug for fear of liability suits.

risk avoidance
Practice of avoiding risk by declining or ceasing to participate in an activity

Risk Control When avoidance is not practical or desirable, firms can practice **risk control**—say, the use of loss-prevention techniques to minimize the frequency of losses. A delivery service, for instance, can prevent losses by training its drivers in defensive-driving techniques, mapping out safe routes, and conscientiously maintaining its trucks.

risk control
Practice of minimizing the frequency or severity of losses from risky activities

Risk Retention When losses cannot be avoided or controlled, firms must cope with the consequences. When such losses are manageable and predictable, they may decide to cover them out of company funds. The firm is thus said to assume or retain the financial consequences of the loss: hence the practice known as **risk retention**. For example, our firm with the fleet of trucks may find that vehicles suffer vandalism totaling $100 to $500 per year. Depending on its coverage, the company may find it cheaper to pay for repairs out of pocket rather than to submit claims to its insurance company.

risk retention
Practice of covering a firm's losses with its own funds

Risk Transfer When the potential for large risks cannot be avoided or controlled, managers often opt for **risk transfer**. They transfer the risk to another firm—namely, an insurance company. In transferring risk to an insurance company, a firm pays a sum called a premium. In return, the insurance company issues an insurance policy—a formal agreement to pay the policyholder a specified amount in the event of certain losses. In some cases, the insured party must also pay a deductible—an agreed-upon amount of the loss that the insured must absorb prior to reimbursement. Thus, our hypothetical company may buy insurance to protect itself against theft, physical damage to trucks, and bodily injury to drivers and others involved in an accident.

risk transfer
Practice of transferring a firm's risk to another firm

Step 4: Implement the Risk-Management Program The means of implementing risk-management decisions depend on both the technique chosen and the activity being managed. For example, risk avoidance for certain activities can be implemented by purchasing those activities from outside providers—say, hiring delivery services instead of operating delivery vehicles. Risk control might be implemented by training employees and designing new work methods and equipment for on-the-job safety. For situations in which risk retention is preferred, reserve funds can be set aside out of revenues. When risk transfer is needed, implementation means selecting an insurance company and buying the right policies.

Step 5: Monitor Results Because risk management is an ongoing activity, follow-up is always essential. New types of risks, for example, emerge with changes in customers, facilities, employees, and products. Insurance regulations change, and new types of insurance become available. Consequently, managers must continually monitor a company's risks, reevaluate the methods used for handling them, and revise them as necessary.

Insurance as Risk Management

To deal with some risks, both businesses and individuals may choose to purchase one or more of the products offered by insurance companies. Buyers find insurance appealing for a very basic reason: In return for a relatively small sum of money, they are protected against certain losses, some of them potentially devastating. In this sense, buying insurance is a function of risk management. To define it as a management activity dealing with insurance, we can thus expand our definition of *risk management* to say that it is the logical development and implementation of a plan to deal with chance losses.

With insurance, then, individuals and businesses share risks by contributing to a fund out of which those who suffer losses are paid. But why are insurance companies willing to accept these risks for other companies? Insurance companies make profits by taking in more **premiums** than they pay out to cover policyholders' losses. Quite simply, although many policyholders are paying for protection against the same type of loss, by no means all of them will suffer such a loss.

premium
Fee paid by a policyholder for insurance coverage

Insurable versus Uninsurable Risks Like every business, insurance companies must avoid certain risks. Insurers thus divide potential sources of loss into *insurable* and *uninsurable risks*. Obviously, they issue policies only for insurable risks. Although there are some exceptions, an insurable risk must meet the four criteria described in the following sections.

Predictability The insurer must be able to use statistical tools to forecast the likelihood of a loss. For example, an auto insurer needs information about the number of car accidents in the past year to estimate the expected number of accidents for the following year. With this knowledge, the insurer can translate expected numbers and types of accidents into expected dollar losses. The same forecast, of course, also helps insurers determine premiums charged to policyholders.

Casualty A loss must result from an accident, not from an intentional act by the policyholder. Obviously, insurers do not have to cover damages if a policyholder deliberately sets fire to corporate headquarters. To avoid paying in cases of fraud, insurers may refuse to cover losses when they cannot determine whether policyholders' actions contributed to them.

Unconnectedness Potential losses must be random and must occur independently of other losses. No insurer can afford to write insurance when a large percentage of those who are exposed to a particular kind of loss are likely to suffer such a loss. One insurance company, for instance, would not want all the hurricane coverage in Miami or all the earthquake coverage in Los Angeles. By carefully choosing the risks that it will insure, an insurance company can reduce its chances of a large loss or even insolvency.

Verifiability Finally, insured losses must be verifiable as to cause, time, place, and amount. Did an employee develop emphysema because of a chemical to which she was exposed or because she smoked 40 cigarettes a day for 30 years? Did the policyholder pay the renewal premium before the fire destroyed his factory? Were the goods stolen from company offices or from the president's home? What was the insurable value of the destroyed inventory? When all these points have been verified, payment by the insurer goes more smoothly.

The Insurance Product Insurance companies are often distinguished by the types of insurance coverage they offer. Whereas some insurers offer only one area of coverage—life insurance, for example—others offer a broad range. In this section, we describe the four major categories of business insurance: *liability, property, life*, and *health*.

liability insurance
Insurance covering losses resulting from damage to people or property when the insured is judged responsible

workers' compensation coverage
Coverage provided by a firm to employees for medical expenses, loss of wages, and rehabilitation costs resulting from job-related injuries or disease

Liability Insurance As we will see in Appendix II, liability means responsibility for damages in case of accidental or deliberate harm to individuals or property. **Liability insurance** covers losses resulting from damage to people or property when the insured party is judged liable.

Workers' Compensation A business is liable for any injury to an employee when the injury arises from activities related to occupation. When workers are permanently or temporarily disabled by job-related accidents or disease, employers are required by law to provide **workers' compensation coverage** for medical expenses, loss of wages, and rehabilitation services. U.S. employers now pay out approximately $60 billion in workers' compensation premiums each year, much of it to public insurers.

Property Insurance Firms purchase **property insurance** to cover injuries to themselves resulting from physical damage to or loss of real estate or personal property. Property losses may result from fire, lightning, wind, hail, explosion, theft, vandalism, or other destructive forces. Losses from fire alone in the United States come to over $10 billion per year.

property insurance
Insurance covering losses resulting from physical damage to or loss of the insured's real estate or personal property

Business Interruption Insurance In some cases, loss to property is minimal in comparison to loss of income. A manufacturer, for example, may have to close down for an extended time while repairs to fire damage are being completed. During that time, of course, the company is not generating income. Even so, however, certain expenses—such as taxes, insurance premiums, and salaries for key personnel—may continue. To cover such losses, a firm may buy **business interruption insurance.**

business interruption insurance
Insurance covering income lost during times when a company is unable to conduct business

Life Insurance Insurance can also protect a company's human assets. As part of their benefits packages, many businesses purchase **life insurance**for employees. Life insurance companies accept premiums in return for the promise to pay beneficiaries after the death of insured parties. A portion of the premium is used to cover the insurer's own expenses. The remainder is invested in various types of financial instruments such as corporate bonds and stocks.

life insurance
Insurance paying benefits to the policyholder's survivors

Group Life Insurance Most companies buy **group life insurance**, which is underwritten for groups as a whole rather than for each individual member. The insurer's assessment of potential losses and its pricing of premiums are based on the characteristics of the whole group. Johnson & Johnson's benefit plan, for example, includes group life coverage with a standard program of protection and benefits—a master policy purchased by J & J—that applies equally to all employees.

group life insurance
Insurance underwritten for a group as a whole rather than for each individual in it

Health Insurance **Health insurance** covers losses resulting from medical and hospital expenses as well as income lost from injury or disease. It is, of course, no secret that the cost of health insurance has skyrocketed in recent years. In one recent year, for example, companies paid an average of $3,781 per employee on health insurance premiums to both commercial insurers like Prudential, Metropolitan, and Nationwide and special health insurance providers like Blue Cross/Blue Shield and other organizations called *health maintenance organizations* and *preferred provider organizations.*

health insurance
Insurance covering losses resulting from medical and hospital expenses as well as income lost from injury or disease

Disability Income Insurance **Disability income insurance** provides continuous income when disability keeps the insured from gainful employment. Many health insurance policies cover short-term disabilities, sometimes up to two years. Coverage for permanent disability furnishes some stated amount of weekly income—usually 50 to 70 percent of the insured's weekly wages—with payments beginning after a six-month waiting period. Group policies account for over 70 percent of all disability coverage in the United States.

disability income insurance
Insurance providing continuous income when disability keeps the insured from gainful employment

Special Health Care Providers Instead of reimbursement for a health professional's services, Blue Cross/Blue Shield, which is made up of nonprofit health care membership groups, provides specific service benefits to its subscribers. Many other commercial insurers do the same. What is the advantage to the subscriber or policyholder? No matter what the service actually costs, the special health care provider will cover the cost. In contrast, when policies provide reimbursement for services received, the policyholder may pay for a portion of the expense if the policy limit is exceeded. Other important options include *HMO*s and *PPO*s:

- A **health maintenance organization** (HMO) is an organized health care system providing comprehensive medical care to its members for a fixed, prepaid fee. In an HMO, all members agree that, except in emergencies, they will receive their health care through the organization.
- A **preferred provider organization** (PPO) is an arrangement whereby selected hospitals and/or doctors agree to provide services at reduced rates and to accept thorough review of their recommendations for medical services. The objective of the

health maintenance organization (HMO)
Organized health care system providing comprehensive care in return for fixed membership fees

preferred provider organization (PPO)
Arrangement whereby selected professional providers offer services at reduced rates and permit thorough review of their service recommendations

PPO is to help control health care costs by encouraging the use of efficient providers' health care services.

key person insurance
Special form of business insurance designed to offset expenses entailed by the loss of key employees

business continuation agreement
Special form of business insurance whereby owners arrange to buy the interests of deceased associates from their heirs

Special Forms of Business Insurance Many forms of insurance are attractive to both businesses and individuals. For example, homeowners are as concerned about insuring property from fire and theft as are businesses. Businesses, however, have some special insurable concerns. In this section, we will discuss two forms of insurance that apply to the departure or death of key employees or owners.

Key Person Insurance Many businesses choose to protect themselves against loss of the talents and skills of key employees. For example, if a salesperson who annually rings up $2.5 million dies or takes a new job, the firm will suffer loss. It will also incur recruitment costs to find a replacement and training expenses once a replacement is hired. **Key person insurance** is designed to offset both lost income and additional expenses.

Business Continuation Agreements Who takes control of a business when a partner or associate dies? Surviving partners are often faced with the possibility of having to accept an inexperienced heir as a management partner. This contingency can be handled in **business continuation agreements**, whereby owners make plans to buy the ownership interest of a deceased associate from his or her heirs. The value of the ownership interest is determined when the agreement is made. Special policies can also provide survivors with the funds needed to make the purchase.

Appendix II

Understanding the Legal Context of Business

In this appendix, we describe the basic tenets of U.S. law and show how these principles work through the court system. We will also survey a few major areas of business-related law. By focusing on the learning objectives of this appendix, you will see that laws may create opportunities for business activity just as readily as they set limits on them.

THE U.S. LEGAL AND JUDICIAL SYSTEMS

If people could ignore contracts or drive down city streets at any speed, it would be unsafe to do business on Main Street—or even to set foot in public. Without law, people would be free to act "at will," and life and property would constantly be at risk. **Laws** are the codified rules of behavior enforced by a society. In the United States, laws fall into three broad categories according to their origins: *common, statutory*, and *regulatory*. After discussing each of these types of laws, we will briefly describe the three-tier system of courts through which the judicial system administers the law in the United States.

laws
Codified rules of behavior enforced by a society

Types of Law

Law in the United States originates primarily with English common law. Its sources include the U.S. Constitution, state constitutions, federal and state statutes, municipal ordinances, administrative agency rules and regulations, executive orders, and court decisions.

Common Law Court decisions follow *precedents*, or the decisions of earlier cases. Following precedent lends stability to the law by basing judicial decisions on cases anchored in similar facts. This principle is the keystone of **common law**: the body of decisions handed down by courts ruling on individual cases. Although some facets of common law predate the American Revolution (and even hearken back to medieval Europe), common law continues to evolve in the courts today.

common law
Body of decisions handed down by courts ruling on individual cases

Statutory Law Laws created by constitutions or by federal, state, or local legislative acts constitute **statutory law**. For example, Article I of the U.S. Constitution is a statutory law that empowers Congress to pass laws on corporate taxation, the zoning authority of municipalities, and the rights and privileges of businesses operating in the United States.

statutory law
Law created by constitutions or by federal, state, or local legislative acts

State legislatures and city councils also pass statutory laws. Some state laws, for example, prohibit the production or sale of detergents containing phosphates, which are believed to be pollutants. Nearly every town has ordinances specifying sites for certain types of industries or designating areas where cars cannot be parked during certain hours.

Regulatory Law Statutory and common law have long histories. Relatively new is **regulatory** (or **administrative**) **law:** law made by the authority of administrative agencies. By and large, the expansion of U.S. regulatory law has paralleled the nation's economic and technological development. Lacking the technical expertise to develop specialized legislation for specialized business activities, Congress established the first administrative agencies to create and administer the needed laws in the late 1800s. Before the early 1960s, most agencies concerned themselves with the *economic* regulation of specific areas of business—say, transportation or securities. Since then, many agencies have been established to pursue narrower *social* objectives. They focus on issues that cut across different sectors of the economy—clean air, for example, or product testing.

regulatory (or administrative) law
Law made by the authority of administrative agencies

Today a host of agencies, including the Equal Employment Opportunity Commission (EEOC), the Environmental Protection Agency (EPA), the Food and Drug Administration (FDA), the Federal Trade Commission (FTC), and the Occupational Safety and Health Administration (OSHA), regulate U.S. business practices.

In this section, we look briefly at the nature of regulatory agencies and describe some of the key legislation that makes up administrative law in this country. We also discuss an area of increasing importance in the relationship between government and business: regulation—or, more accurately, *deregulation*.

Agencies and Legislation Although Congress retains control over the scope of agency action, once passed, regulations have the force of statutory law. Government regulatory agencies act as a secondary judicial system, determining whether regulations have been violated and imposing penalties. A firm that violates OSHA rules, for example, may receive a citation, a hearing, and perhaps a heavy fine. Much agency activity consists of setting standards for safety or quality and monitoring the compliance of businesses. The FDA, for example, is responsible for ensuring that food, medicines, and even cosmetics are safe and effective.

Regulatory laws have been on the books for nearly a century. As early as 1906, for example, the Pure Food and Drug Act mandated minimum levels of cleanliness and sanitation for food and drug companies. More recently, the Children's Television Act of 1990 requires that broadcasters meet the educational and informational needs of younger viewers and limit the amount of advertising broadcast during children's programs. In 1996, a sweeping new law to increase competition in the communications industry required television makers to install a "V-chip," which allows parents to block undesirable programming. And Congress continues to debate the possibility of regulating the Internet.

Congress has created many new agencies in response to pressure to address social issues. In some cases, agencies were established in response to public concern about corporate behavior. The activities of these agencies have sometimes forced U.S. firms to consider the public interest almost as routinely as they consider their own financial performance.

The Move Toward Deregulation Although government regulation has benefited U.S. business in many ways, it is not without its drawbacks. Businesspeople complain—with some justification—that government regulations require too much paperwork. To comply with just one OSHA regulation for a year, Goodyear once generated 345,000 pages of computer reports weighing 3,200 pounds. It now costs Goodyear $35.5 million each year to comply with the regulations of six government agencies, and it takes 36 employee-years annually (the equivalent of one employee working full time for 36 years) to fill out the required reports.

deregulation
Elimination of rules that restrict business activity

Not surprisingly, many people in both business and government support broader **deregulation**: the elimination of rules that restrict business activity. Advocates of both regulation and deregulation claim that each acts to control business expansion and prices, increase government efficiency, and right wrongs that the marketplace cannot or does not handle itself. Regulations such as those enforced by the EEOC, for example, are supposed to control undesirable business practices in the interest of social equity. In contrast, the court-ordered breakup of AT&T was prompted by a perceived need for greater market efficiency. For these and other reasons, the federal government began deregulating certain industries in the 1970s.

It is important to note that the United States is the only industrialized nation that has deregulated key industries—financial services, transportation, telecommunications, and a host of others. A 1996 law, for instance, allowed the seven "Baby Bells"—regional phone companies created when AT&T was broken up—to compete for long-distance business. It also allowed cable television and telephone companies to enter each other's markets by offering any combination of video, telephone, and high-speed data communications services. Many analysts contend that such deregulation is now and will become an even greater advantage in an era of global competition. Deregulation, they argue, is a primary incentive to innovation.

According to this view, deregulated industries are forced to innovate in order to survive in fiercely competitive industries. Those firms that are already conditioned to compete by being more creative will outperform firms that have been protected by regulatory climates in their home countries. "What's important," says one economist, "is that competition energizes new ways of doing things." The U.S. telecommunications industry, proponents of this view say, is twice as productive as its European counterparts because it is the only such industry forced to come out from under a protective regulatory umbrella.

The U.S. Judicial System

Laws are of little use unless they are enforced. Much of the responsibility for law enforcement falls to the courts. Although few people would claim that the courts are capable of resolving every dispute, there often seem to be more than enough lawyers to handle them all: Indeed, there are 140 lawyers for every 100,000 people in the United States. Litigation is a significant part of contemporary life, and we have given our courts a voice in a wide range of issues, some touching profoundly personal concerns, some ruling on matters of public policy that affect all our lives. In this section, we look at the operations of the U.S. judicial system.

The Court System There are three levels in the U.S. judicial system—*federal, state*, and *local*. These levels reflect the federalist structure of a system in which a central government shares power with state or local governments. Federal courts were created by the U.S. Constitution. They hear cases on questions of constitutional law, disputes relating to maritime laws, and violations of federal statutes. They also rule on regulatory actions and on such issues as bankruptcy, postal law, and copyright or patent violation. Both the federal and most state systems embody a three-tiered system of *trial, appellate*, and *supreme courts*.

Trial Courts At the lowest level of the federal court system are the **trial courts**, general courts that hear cases not specifically assigned to another court. A case involving contract violation would go before a trial court. Every state has at least one federal trial court, called a district court.

trial court
General court that hears cases not specifically assigned to another court

Trial courts also include special courts and administrative agencies. Special courts hear specific types of cases, such as cases involving tax evasion, fraud, international disputes, or claims against the U.S. government. Within their areas of jurisdiction, administrative agencies also make judgments much like those of courts.

Courts in each state system deal with the same issues as their federal counterparts. However, they may rule only in areas governed by state law. For example, a case involving state income tax laws would be heard by a state special court. Local courts in each state system also hear cases on municipal ordinances, local traffic violations, and similar issues.

Appellate Courts A losing party may disagree with a trial court ruling. If that party can show grounds for review, the case may go before a federal or state **appellate court**. These courts consider questions of law, such as possible errors of legal interpretation made by lower courts. They do not examine questions of fact. There are now 13 federal courts of appeal, each with 3 to 15 judges. Cases are normally heard by three-judge panels.

appellate court
Court that reviews case records of trials whose findings have been appealed

Supreme Courts Cases still not resolved at the appellate level can be appealed to the appropriate state supreme courts or to the U.S. Supreme Court. If it believes that an appeal is warranted or that the outcome will set an important precedent, the U.S. Supreme Court also hears cases appealed from state supreme courts. Each year, the U.S. Supreme Court receives about 5,000 appeals but typically agrees to hear fewer than 200.

BUSINESS LAW

Most legal issues confronted by businesses fall into one of six basic areas: *contract, tort, property, agency, commercial*, or *bankruptcy law*. These areas cover a wide range of business activity.

Contract Law

contract
Agreement between two or more parties enforceable in court

A **contract** is any agreement between two or more parties that is enforceable in court. As such, it must meet six conditions. If all these conditions are met, one party can seek legal recourse from another if the other party breaches (that is, violates) the terms of the agreement.

1. *Agreement.* Agreement is the serious, definite, and communicated offer and acceptance of the same terms. Let us say that an auto parts supplier offers in writing to sell rebuilt engines to a repair shop for $500 each. If the repair shop accepts the offer, the two parties have reached an agreement.
2. *Consent.* A contract is not enforceable if any of the parties has been affected by an honest mistake, fraud, or pressure. For example, a restaurant manager orders a painted sign, but the sign company delivers a neon sign instead.
3. *Capacity.* To give real consent, both parties must demonstrate legal **capacity** (competence). A person under legal age (usually 18 or 21) cannot enter into a binding contract.
4. *Consideration.* An agreement is binding only if it exchanges **considerations**, that is, items of value. If your brother offers to paint your room for free, you cannot sue him if he changes his mind. Note that items of value do not necessarily entail money. For example, a tax accountant might agree to prepare a homebuilder's tax return in exchange for a new patio. Both services are items of value. Contracts need not be rational, nor must they provide the best possible bargain for both sides. They need only include legally sufficient consideration. The terms are met if both parties receive what the contract details.
5. *Legality.* A contract must be for a lawful purpose and must comply with federal, state, and local laws and regulations. For example, an agreement between two competitors to engage in price fixing—that is, to set a mutually acceptable price—is not legal.
6. *Proper form.* A contract may be written, oral, or implied from conduct. It must be written, however, if it involves the sale of land or goods worth more than $500. It must be written if the agreement requires more than a year to fulfill—say, a contract for employment as an engineer on a 14-month construction project. All changes to written contracts must also be in writing.

capacity
Competence required of individuals entering into a binding contract

considerations
Any item of value exchanged between parties to create a valid contract

Breach of Contract What can one party do if the other fails to live up to the terms of a valid contract? Contract law offers a variety of remedies designed to protect the reasonable expectations of the parties and, in some cases, to compensate them for actions taken to enforce the agreement.

As the injured party to a breached contract, any of the following actions might occur:

- You might cancel the contract and refuse to live up to your part of the bargain. For example, you might simply cancel a contract for carpet shampooing if the company fails to show up.
- You might sue for damages up to the amount that you lost as a result of the breach. Thus, you might sue the original caterer if you must hire a more expensive caterer for your wedding reception because the original company canceled at the last minute.
- If money cannot repay the damage you suffered, you might demand specific performance—that is, require the other party to fulfill the original contract. For example, you might demand that a dealer in classic cars sell you the antique Stutz Bearcat he agreed to sell you and not a classic Jaguar instead.

Tort Law

tort
Civil injury to people, property, or reputation for which compensation must be paid

Tort law applies to most business relationships *not governed by contracts.* A **tort** is a *civil*—that is, noncriminal—injury to people, property, or reputation for which compensation must be paid. For example, if a person violates zoning laws by opening a convenience store in a residential area, he or she cannot be sent to jail as if the act were a criminal violation. But a variety of other legal measures can be pursued, such as fines or seizure of property. Trespass, fraud, defamation, invasion of privacy, and even assault can be torts, as can interference with contractual relations and wrongful use of trade secrets. In this section, we explain three classifications of torts: *intentional, negligence*, and *product liability*.

intentional tort
Tort resulting from the deliberate actions of a party

Intentional Torts **Intentional torts** result from the deliberate actions of another person or organization—for instance, a manufacturer knowingly fails to install a relatively inexpensive safety device on a product. Similarly, refusing to rectify a product design flaw, as in the case of the space shuttle *Challenger* disaster, can render a firm liable for an intentional tort. The actions of employees on the job may also constitute intentional torts—say, an overzealous security guard who wrongly accuses a customer of shoplifting. To remedy torts, courts will usually impose **compensatory damages**: payments intended to redress an injury actually suffered. They may also impose **punitive damages**: fines that exceed actual losses suffered by plaintiffs and that are intended to punish defendants.

compensatory damages
Monetary payments intended to redress injury actually suffered because of a tort

punitive damages
Fines imposed over and above any actual losses suffered by a plaintiff

negligence
Conduct falling below legal standards for protecting others against unreasonable risk

Negligence Torts Ninety percent of tort suits involve charges of **negligence**, conduct falling below legal standards for protecting others against unreasonable risk. If a company installs a pollution-control system that fails to protect a community's water supply, it may later be sued by an individual who gets sick from drinking the water.

Negligence torts may also result from employee actions. For example, if the captain of a supertanker runs aground and spills 11 million gallons of crude oil into coastal fishing waters, the oil company may be liable for potentially astronomical damages. Thus, in September 1994, a jury in Alaska ordered Exxon Corp. to pay $5 billion in punitive damages to 34,000 fishermen and other plaintiffs as a consequence of the Exxon *Valdez* disaster of 1989. (Plaintiffs had asked for $15 billion.) A month earlier, the jury had awarded plaintiffs $287 million in compensatory damages. In 1993, the firm responsible for pipeline operations at the Valdez, Alaska, terminal (which is partially owned by Exxon) agreed to pay plaintiffs in the same case $98 million in damages. In a separate case, Exxon paid $20 million in damages to villages whose food supply had been destroyed. A separate state jury will consider another $120 million in claims by Alaskan corporations and municipalities. Even before any of these awards were handed down, Exxon had spent $2.1 billion on the cleanup effort and paid $1.3 billion in civil and criminal penalties.

product liability tort
Tort in which a company is responsible for injuries caused by its products

Product Liability Torts In cases of **product liability,** a company may be held responsible for injuries caused by its products. According to a special government panel on product liability, about 33 million people are injured and 28,000 killed by consumer products each year.

strict product liability
Principle that liability can result not from a producer's negligence but from a defect in the product itself

Strict Product Liability Since the early 1960s, businesses have faced a number of legal actions based on the relatively new principle of **strict product liability**: the principle that liability can result not from a producer's negligence but from a defect in the product itself. An injured party need show only that

1. The product was defective.
2. The defect was the cause of injury.
3. The defect caused the product to be unreasonably dangerous.

Many recent cases in strict product liability have focused on injuries or illnesses attributable to toxic wastes or other hazardous substances that were legally disposed of. Because plaintiffs need not demonstrate negligence or fault, these suits frequently succeed. Not surprisingly, the number of such suits promises to increase.

Property Law

property
Anything of value to which a person or business has sole right of ownership

As the name implies, *property law* concerns property rights. But what exactly is "property"? Is it the land under a house? The house itself? A car in the driveway? A dress in the closet? The answer in each case is yes: In the legal sense, **property** is anything of value to which a person or business has sole right of ownership. Indeed, property is technically those rights.

Within this broad general definition, we can divide property into four categories. In this section, we define these categories and then examine more fully the legal protection of a certain kind of property—intellectual property.

tangible real property
Land and anything attached to it

tangible personal property
Any movable item that can be owned, bought, sold, or leased

intangible personal property
Property that cannot be seen but that exists by virtue of written documentation

intellectual property
Property created through a person's creative activities

copyright
Exclusive ownership right belonging to the creator of a book, article, design, illustration, photo, film, or musical work

- **Tangible real property** is land and anything attached to it. A house and a factory are both tangible real property, as are built-in appliances or the machines inside the buildings.
- **Tangible personal property** is any movable item that can be owned, bought, sold, or leased. Examples are automobiles, clothing, stereos, and cameras.
- **Intangible personal property** cannot be seen but exists by virtue of written documentation. Examples are insurance policies, bank accounts, stocks and bonds, and trade secrets.

Intellectual property is created through a person's creative activities. Books, articles, songs, paintings, screenplays, and computer software are all intellectual property.

Protection of Intellectual Rights The U.S. Constitution grants protection to intellectual property by means of copyrights, trademarks, and patents. Copyrights and patents apply to the tangible expressions of an idea—not to the ideas themselves. Thus, you could not copyright the idea of cloning dinosaurs from fossil DNA. Michael Crichton could copyright his novel, *Jurassic Park*, which is a tangible result of that idea, and sell the film rights to producer-director Steven Spielberg. Both creators are entitled to the profits, if any, that may be generated by their tangible creative expressions.

Copyrights **Copyrights** give exclusive ownership rights to the creators of books, articles, designs, illustrations, photos, films, and music. Computer programs and even semiconductor chips are also protected. Copyrights extend to creators for their entire lives and to their estates for 70 years thereafter. All terms are automatically copyrighted from the moment of creation.

trademark
Exclusive legal right to use a brand name or symbol

Trademarks Because the development of products is expensive, companies must prevent other firms from using their brand names. Often they must act to keep competitors from seducing consumers with similar or substitute products. A producer can apply to the U.S. government for a **trademark**—the exclusive legal right to use a brand name.

Trademarks are granted for 20 years and may be renewed indefinitely if a firm continues to protect its brand name. If a firm allows the brand name to lapse into common usage, it may lose protection. Common usage takes effect when a company fails to use the ® symbol to indicate that its brand name is a registered trademark. It also takes effect if a company seeks no action against those who fail to acknowledge its trademark. Recently, for example, the popular brand-name sailboard Windsurfer lost its trademark. Like *trampoline, yo-yo*, and *thermos, windsurfer* has become the common term for the product and can now be used by any sailboard company. In contrast, Formica Corp. successfully spent the better part of a decade in court to protect the name *Formica* as a trademark. The Federal Trade Commission had contended that the word had entered the language as a generic name for any similar laminate material.

patent
Exclusive legal right to use and license a manufactured item or substance, manufacturing process, or object design

Patents **Patents** provide legal monopolies for the use and licensing of manufactured items, manufacturing processes, substances, and designs for objects. A patentable invention must be *novel, useful*, and *nonobvious*. Since June 1995, U.S. patent law has been in harmony with that of most developed nations. For example, patents are now valid for 20 years rather than 17 years. In addition, the term now runs from the date on which the application was *filed*, not the date on which the patent itself was *issued*.

Although the U.S. Patent Office issues about 1,200 patents a week, requirements are stringent, and U.S. patents actually tend to be issued at a slow pace. While Japan and most European countries have installed systems to speed up patent filing and research, the U.S. system can extend the process to years. Other observers argue that American firms trail their foreign counterparts in patents because of the sluggishness with which U.S. companies move products through their own research and development programs.

Restrictions on Property Rights Property rights are not always absolute. For example, rights may be compromised under any of the following circumstances:

- Owners of shorefront property may be required to permit anglers, clam diggers, and other interested parties to walk near the water.
- Utility companies typically have rights called easements, such as the right to run wire over private property or to lay cable or pipe under it.
- Under the principle of **eminent domain**, the government may, upon paying owners fair prices, claim private land to expand roads or erect public buildings.

eminent domain
Principle that the government may claim private land for public use by buying it at a fair price

Agency Law

The transfer of property—whether the deeding of real estate or the transfer of automobile title—often involves agents. An **agent** is a person who acts for, and in the name of, another party, called the **principal**. The most visible agents are those in real estate, sports, and entertainment. Many businesses, however, use agents to secure insurance coverage and handle investments. Every partner in a partnership and every officer and director in a corporation is an agent of that business. Courts have also ruled that both a firm's employees and its outside contractors may be regarded as its agents.

agent
Individual or organization acting for, and in the name of, another party

principal
Individual or organization authorizing an agent to act on its behalf

express authority
Agent's authority, derived from written agreement, to bind a principal to a certain course of action

implied authority
Agent's authority, derived from business custom, to bind a principal to a certain course of action

apparent authority
Agent's authority, based on the principal's compliance, to bind a principal to a certain course of action

Authority of Agents Agents have the authority to bind principals to agreements. They receive that authority, however, from the principals themselves; they cannot create their own authority. An agent's authority to bind a principal can be express, implied, or apparent.

Let's say, for example, that Ellen is a salesperson in Honest Sam's Used Car Lot. Her written employment contract gives her **express authority** to sell cars, to provide information to prospective buyers, and to approve trade-ins up to $2,000. Derived from the custom of used-car dealers, she also has **implied authority** to give reasonable discounts on prices and to make reasonable adjustments to written warranties. Furthermore, Ellen may—in the presence of Honest Sam—promise a customer that she will match the price offered by another local dealer. If Honest Sam assents—perhaps merely nods and smiles—Ellen may be construed to have the **apparent authority** to make this deal.

Responsibilities of Principals Principals have several responsibilities to their agents. They owe agents reasonable compensation, must reimburse them for related business expenses, and should inform them of risks associated with their business activities. Principals are liable for actions performed by agents *within the scope of their employment*. Thus, if agents make untrue claims about products or services, the principal is liable for making amends. Employers are similarly responsible for the actions of employees. In fact, firms are often liable in tort suits because the courts treat employees as agents.

Businesses are increasingly being held accountable for *criminal* acts by employees. Court findings, for example, have argued that firms are expected to be aware of workers' propensities for violence, to check on their employees' pasts, and to train and supervise employees properly. Suppose, for instance, that a delivery service hires a driver with a history of driving while intoxicated. If the driver has an accident with a company vehicle while under the influence of alcohol, the company may be liable for criminal actions.

Commercial Law

Managers must be well acquainted with the most general laws affecting commerce. Specifically, they need to be familiar with the provisions of the *Uniform Commercial Code*, which sets down rules regarding *warranties*.

The Uniform Commercial Code For many years, companies doing business in more than one state faced a special problem: Laws governing commerce varied, sometimes widely, from state to state. In 1952, however, the National Conference of Commissioners on Uniform State Laws and the American Law Institute drew up the **Uniform Commercial Code (UCC)**. Subsequently accepted by every state except Louisiana, the UCC describes the rights of buyers and sellers in transactions.

Uniform Commercial Code (UCC)
Body of standardized laws governing the rights of buyers and sellers in transactions

For example, buyers who believe that they have been wronged in agreements with sellers have several options. They can cancel contracts, refuse deliveries, and demand the return of any deposits. In some cases, they can buy the same products elsewhere and sue the original contractors to recover any losses incurred. Sellers, too, have several options. They can cancel contracts, withhold deliveries, and sell goods to other buyers. If goods have already been delivered, sellers can repossess them or sue the buyers for purchase prices.

Warranties A **warranty** is a seller's promise to stand by its products or services if a problem occurs after the sale. Warranties may be *express* or *implied*. The terms of an **express warranty** are specifically stated by the seller. For example, many stereo systems are expressly warranted for 90 days. If they malfunction within that period, they can be returned for full refunds.

warranty
Seller's promise to stand by its products or services if a problem occurs after the sale

express warranty
Warranty whose terms are specifically stated by the seller

An **implied warranty** is dictated by law. Implied warranties embody the principle that a product should (1) fulfill the promises made by advertisements and (2) serve the purpose for which it was manufactured and sold. If you buy an advertised frost-free refrigerator, the seller implies that the refrigerator will keep your food cold and that you will not have to defrost it. It is important to note, however, that warranties, unlike most contracts, are easily limited, waived, or disclaimed. Consequently, they are the source of more and more tort action, as dissatisfied customers seek redress from producers.

implied warranty
Warranty, dictated by law, based on the principle that products should fulfill advertised promises and serve the purposes for which they are manufactured and sold

Bankruptcy Law

At one time, individuals who could not pay their debts were jailed. Today, however, both organizations and individuals can seek relief by filing for **bankruptcy**—the court-granted permission not to pay some or all debts.

bankruptcy
Permission granted by the courts to individuals and organizations not to pay some or all of their debts

Hundreds of thousands of individuals and tens of thousands of businesses file for bankruptcy each year, and their numbers continue to increase. Why do individuals and businesses file for bankruptcy? Cash-flow problems and drops in farm prices caused many farmers, banks, and small businesses to go bankrupt. In recent years, large enterprises such as Continental Airlines and R. H. Macy have sought the protection of bankruptcy laws as part of strategies to streamline operations, cut costs, and regain profitability.

Three main factors account for the increase in bankruptcy filings:

1. The increased availability of credit
2. The "fresh-start" provisions in current bankruptcy laws
3. The growing acceptance of bankruptcy as a financial tactic

In some cases, creditors force an individual or firm into **involuntary bankruptcy** and press the courts to award them payment of at least part of what they are owed. Far more often, however, a person or business chooses to file for court protection against creditors. In general, individuals and firms whose debts exceed total assets by at least $1,000 may file for **voluntary bankruptcy**.

involuntary bankruptcy
Bankruptcy proceedings initiated by the creditors of an indebted individual or organization

voluntary bankruptcy
Bankruptcy proceedings initiated by an indebted individual or organization

Business Bankruptcy A business bankruptcy may be resolved by one of three plans:

- Under a *liquidation plan*, the business ceases to exist. Its assets are sold and the proceeds used to pay creditors.
- Under a *repayment plan*, the bankrupt company simply works out a new payment schedule to meet its obligations. The time frame is usually extended, and payments are collected and distributed by a court-appointed trustee.

- *Reorganization* is the most complex form of business bankruptcy. The company must explain the sources of its financial difficulties and propose a new plan for remaining in business. Reorganization may include a new slate of managers and a new financial strategy. A judge may also reduce the firm's debts to ensure its survival. Although creditors naturally dislike debt reduction, they may agree to the proposal, since 50 percent of one's due is better than nothing at all.

Legislation passed since 1994 has made some major revisions in bankruptcy laws. For example, it is now easier for individuals with up to $1 million in debt to make payments under installment plans instead of liquidating assets immediately. In contrast, the new law restricts how long a company can protect itself in bankruptcy while continuing to do business. Critics have charged, for instance, that many firms have succeeded in operating for many months under bankruptcy protection. During that time, they were able to cut costs and prices, not only competing with an unfair advantage but dragging down overall industry profits. The new laws place time limits on various steps in the filing process. The intended effect is to speed the process and prevent assets from being lost to legal fees.

THE INTERNATIONAL FRAMEWORK OF BUSINESS LAW

Laws can vary dramatically from country to country, and many businesses today have international markets, suppliers, and competitors. It follows that managers need a basic understanding of the international framework of business law that affects the ways in which they can do business.

National laws are created and enforced by countries. The creation and enforcement of international law is more complicated. For example, if a company shipping merchandise between the United States and Mexico breaks an environmental protection law, to whom is that company accountable? The answer depends on several factors. Which country enacted the law in question? Where did the violation occur? In which country is the alleged violator incorporated?

Issues such as pollution across borders are matters of **international law**: the very general set of cooperative agreements and guidelines established by countries to govern the actions of individuals, businesses, and nations themselves. In this section, we examine the various sources of international law. We then discuss some of the important ways in which international trade is regulated and place some key U.S. trade laws in the international context in which they are designed to work.

international law
Set of cooperative agreements and guidelines established by countries to govern actions of individuals, businesses, and nations

Sources of International Law

International law has several sources. One source is custom and tradition. Among countries that have been trading with each other for centuries, many customs and traditions governing exchanges have gradually evolved into practice. Although some trading practices still follow ancient unwritten agreements, there has been a clear trend in more recent times to approach international trade within a more formal legal framework. Key features of that framework include a variety of formal trade agreements.

Trade Agreements In addition to subscribing to international rules, virtually every nation has formal trade treaties with other nations. A *bilateral agreement* is one involving two countries; a *multilateral agreement* involves several nations.

GATT and the WTO The **General Agreement on Tariffs and Trade** (GATT) was first signed shortly after the end of World War II. Its purpose is to reduce or eliminate trade barriers, such as tariffs and quotas. It does so by encouraging nations to protect domestic industries within internationally agreed-upon limits and to engage in multilateral negotiations.

General Agreement on Tariffs and Trade (GATT)
International trade agreement to encourage the multilateral reduction or elimination of trade barriers

In December 1994, the U.S. Congress ratified a revision of GATT that had been worked out by 124 nations over a 12-year period. Still, many issues remain unresolved—for example, the opening of foreign markets to most financial services. Governments may still provide subsidies to manufacturers of civil aircraft, and no agreement was reached on limiting the distribution of American cultural exports—movies, music, and the like—in Europe. With those agreements that have been reached, however, one international economic group predicts that world commerce will have increased by $270 billion by 2002.

World Trade Organization (WTO)
Organization through which member nations negotiate trading agreements and resolve disputes about trade policies and practices

North Amercian Free Trade Agreement (NAFTA)
Agreement to gradually eliminate tariffs and other trade barriers between the United States, Canada, and Mexico

European Union (EU)
Agreement among major Western European nations to eliminate or make uniform most trade barriers affecting group members

The **World Trade Organization (WTO)** came into being on January 1, 1995, as the result of a complex round of GATT negotiations lasting from 1986 to 1994. The 140 member countries are required to open their markets to international trade, and the WTO is empowered to pursue three goals:

1. Promote trade by encouraging member nations to adopt fair trade policies and practices
2. Reduce trade barriers by promoting multilateral negotiations among member nations
3. Establish fair procedures for resolving disputes among member nations

North American Free Trade Agreement The **North American Free Trade Agreement (NAFTA)** was negotiated to remove tariffs and other trade barriers among the United States, Canada, and Mexico. NAFTA also included agreements to monitor environmental and labor abuses. It took effect on January 1, 1994, and immediately eliminated some tariffs; others will disappear after 5-, 10-, or 15-year intervals.

European Union Originally called the Common Market, the **European Union (EU)** includes the principal Western European nations. These countries have eliminated most quotas and have set uniform tariff levels on products imported and exported within their group. In 1992, virtually all internal trade barriers were eliminated, making the European Union the largest free marketplace in the world.

Notes, Sources, and Credits

Reference Notes

CHAPTER 1

[1] See John D. Daniels and Lee H. Radebaugh, *International Business: Environments and Operations*, 9th ed. (Upper Saddle River, NJ: Prentice Hall, 2001) 125–31.

[2] See Karl E. Case and Ray C. Fair, *Principles of Economics*, 6th ed. (Upper Saddle River, NJ: Prentice Hall, 2002) 47.

[3] See Robert A. Collinge and Ronald M. Ayers, *Economics by Design: Principles and Issues*, 2nd ed. (Upper Saddle River, NJ: Prentice Hall, 2000) 41–42; Michael J. Mandel, "The New Economy," *Business Week*, January 31, 2000, 73–77.

[4] See Rick Kuhn. "Marxism Page" (July 9, 2001) at <www.anu.edu.au/polsci/marx/marx.html>.

[5] See Case and Fair, *Principles of Economics*, 103–05.

[6] Deborah Orr, "The Post Office with a Ticker," *Forbes*, November 29, 1999, 77–78.

[7] See David Frew and Robert W. Sexty, "Nav Canada: Analyzing Government's Privatization Model" (July 9, 2001) at <www.ucs.mun.ca/~rsexty/business8107/navcanB.htm>; and Matthew L. Wald, "Canada's Private Control Towers," *New York Times*, October 23, 1999, C1.

[8] Peter Burrows, "Personal Computers: Are the Glory Days Over?" *Business Week*, February 14, 2000, 50.

[9] See Case and Fair, *Principles of Economics*, 48–67.

[10] See Gabrielle Saveri, "This Is No Fashion Victim," *Business Week*, May 31, 1999, 89; Gina M. Larson, "Bebe Bridges Style Gap" (July 10, 2001) at <www.office.com/global/0,2724,509-10386_1,FF.html>.

[11] *Hoover's Handbook of World Business 2001* (Austin, TX: Hoover's Business Press, 2001) 72–73; "Let's Play Oligopoly!" *Wall Street Journal*, March 8, 1999, B1, B10.

[12] See Henry R. Cheesman, *Business Law: Ethical, International, and E-Commerce Environment*, 4th ed. (Upper Saddle River, NJ: Prentice Hall, 2001) 965–66.

[13] Case and Fair, *Principles of Economics*, 432–33.

[14] Case and Fair, *Principles of Economics*, 15.

[15] Case and Fair, *Principles of Economics*, 15.

[16] Central Intelligence Agency, *The World Factbook 2000* (July 10, 2001) at <www.odci.gov/cia/publications/factbook/geos/us.html>.

[17] See Olivier Blanchard, *Macroeconomics*, 2nd ed. (Upper Saddle River, NJ: Prentice Hall, 2000) 22–23.

[18] See Jay Heizer and Barry Render, *Operations Management*, 6th ed. (Upper Saddle River, NJ: Prentice Hall, 2001) 15–16.

[19] United Auto Workers, *AUW Research Bulletin: Productivity and Growth* (March 9, 2001) at <http://uaw.com/publications/bobs_pay/0700/jpe03.html>.

[20] See Bureau of the Public Debt, "Statutory Debt Limit" (July 10, 2001) at <www.publicdebt.treas.gov/com/comlimit.htm>.

[21] This section follows Collinge and Ayers, *Economics by Design*, 356–58. See also Bureau of Labor Statistics, "Consumer Price Indexes" (July 10, 2001) at <http://stats.bls.gov/cpihome.htm>.

[22] See Collinge and Ayres, *Economics by Design*, 362–65.

[23] See Case and Fair, *Principles of Economics*, 416.

[24] See Howard Gleckman with Lorraine Woellert and Joann Muller, "Tax Cuts: The Coming Battle," *Business Week*, February 26, 2001, 28–31; Gleckman with Lee Walczak and Woellert, "Will We Feel the Tax Cut?" *Business Week*, June 4, 2001, 34–37.

[25] See Rich Miller, "If the Worst Is Over, Why Is the Fed So Tense?" *Business Week*, June 4, 2001, 38.

[26] See Case and Fair, *Principles of Economics*, 729.

[27] Ram Charan and Geoffrey Colvin, "Managing for the Slowdown," *Fortune*, February 5, 2001, 78–88.

[28] See "Rethinking the Internet," *Business Week*, March 26, 2001, 116–136.

[29] See David Fairlamb and Gail Edmondson, "Work in Progress—Signs Abound of a Nascent New Economy," *Business Week*, January 31, 2000, 80–87.

[30] See Brian Bremner and Moon Ihlwan, "Edging toward the Information Age," *Business Week*, January 31, 2000, 90–91.

[31] Charan and Colvin, "Managing for the Slowdown," 78–88.

[32] Bremner and Ihlwan, "Edging toward the Information Age," 91.

[33] Rich Miller et al., "How Prosperity Is Reshaping the American Economy," *Business Week*, February 14, 2000, 100–41.

CHAPTER 2

[1] *Hoover's Handbook of World Business 2001* (Austin, TX: Hoover's Business Press, 2001).

[2] Ricky W. Griffin and Michael W. Pustay, *International Business: A Managerial Perspective*, 3rd ed. (Upper Saddle River, NJ: Prentice Hall, 2002); 27.

[3] Trade Partners UK, "Automotive Industries Market in Mexico" (July 10, 2001) at <www.tradepartners.gov/uk/automotive/mexico/opportunities/opportunities.shtml>; Nafta Works, "Mexico Auto Sector Sees $15 Billion Investment in 5 Years" (July 10, 2001) at <www.naftaworks.org/papers/2000/automex.htm>.

[4] David Fairlamb and Gail Edmondson, "Work in Progress," *Business Week*, January 31, 2000, 80–81+.

[5] See Stephen Baker, "Invasion of the E-Vikings," *Business Week*, July 26, 1999, EB53–EB54+; Rob Norton, "The Luck of the Irish," *Fortune*, October 25, 1999, 194–96+.

[6] See Edmund L. Andrews, "The Metamorphosis of Germany Inc.," *New York Times*, March 12, 2000, sec. 3, 1, 12.

[7] See Mark Landler, "Mapping Out Silicon Valley East," *New York Times*, April 5, 1999, pp. C1, C10; and Bruce Einhorn with Cathy Yang, "Portal Combat," *Business Week*, January 17, 2000, 96–97.

[8] See Griffin and Pustay, *International Business*, 125–27. See also Steven Husted and Michael Melvin, *International Economics*, 5th ed. (Boston: Addison Wesley Longman, 2001) 54–61; and Karl E. Case and Ray C. Fair, *Principles of Economics*, 6th ed. (Upper Saddle River, NJ: Prentice Hall, 2002) 669–77.

[9]This section is based on Michael Porter, *The Competitive Advantage of Nations* (Boston: Harvard Business School Press, 1990), Chs. 3 and 4. See also John J. Wild, Kenneth L. Wild, and Jerry C. Y. Han, *International Business: An Integrated Approach* (Upper Saddle River, NJ: Prentice Hall, 2000) 175–78; Warren J. Keegan and Mark C. Green, *Global Marketing*, 2nd ed. (Upper Saddle River, NJ: Prentice Hall, 2000) 359–66.

[10]*Hoover's Handbook of World Business 2001*, 56.

[11]See Case and Fair, *Principles of Economics*, 675–77; Husted and Melvin, *International Economics*, 306–10.

[12]Robyn Meredith, "Dollar Makes Canada a Land of the Spree," *New York Times*, August 1, 1999, sec. 3, 1, 1. See also Currencies Direct, "Canada—Cautious Optimism" (July 10, 2001) at <www.currenciesdirect.com/mecklai/NTFxCanadaReport.html>.

[13]Jeremy Kahn, "Wal-Mart Goes Shopping in Europe," *Fortune*, June 7, 1999, 105–12; and Wendy Zellner, "Someday, Lee, This May All Be Yours," *Business Week*, November 15, 1999, 84, 88, 92; Michael McCarthy, "Wal-Mart Takes Slow Road in Germany," *USA Today*, May 10, 2000, 3B.

[14]John Tagliabue, "Now Playing Europe: The Invasion of the Multiplex," *New York Times*, January 27, 2000, C1, C23.

[15]*Hoover's Handbook of World Business 2001*.

[16]See Norman M. Scarborough and Thomas W. Zimmerer, *Effective Small Business Management: An Entrepreneurial Approach*, 6th ed. (Upper Saddle River, NJ: Prentice Hall, 2000) 374–98.

[17]Jeremy Kahn, "The Fortune Global 500," *Fortune*, April 16, 2001, 100–03+.

[18]See Wild, Wild, and Han, *International Business*, Ch. 7; Griffin and Pustay, *International Business*, 332–35.

[19]See Robert L. Simison and Scott Miller, "Ford Grabs Big Prize as Steep Losses Force BMW to Sell Rover," *Wall Street Journal*, March 17, 2000, A1, A8; Shelly Branch and Ernest Beck, "For Unilever, It's Sweetness and Light," *Wall Street Journal*, April 13, 2000, B1, B4.

[20]Bureau of Economic Analysis, "Foreign Direct Investment in the U.S." (July 11, 2001) at <www.bea.doc.gov/bea/di/di1fdibal.htm>; Progressive Policy Institute, "Foreign Direct Investment Is on the Rise Around the World" (July 11, 2001) at <www.neweconomyindex.org/section1_page04.html>.

[21]World Trade Organization, "Foreign Direct Investment Seen as Primary Motor of Globalization" (July 11, 2001) at <www.wto.org/english/news_e/pres96_e/_pr042_e.htm>.

[22]See Robert Frank, "In Paddies of Vietnam, Americans Once Again Land in Quagmire," *Wall Street Journal*, April 21, 2000, A1, A6.

[23]Anthony DePalma, "Chiquita Sues Europeans, Citing Banana Quota Losses," *New York Times*, January 26, 2001, C5; Brian Lavery, "Trade Feud on Bananas Not as Clear as It Looks," *New York Times*, February 7, 2001, W1; David E. Sanger, "Miffed at Europe, U.S. Raises Tariffs for Luxury Goods," *New York Times*, March 4, 1999, A1, A5.

[24]See Keegan and Green, *Global Marketing*, 441–45.

[25]David E. Sanger, "U.S. Says Japan, Brazil Dumped Steel," *New York Times*, February 13, 1999, C1, C2.

CHAPTER 3

[1]This section follows the logic of Gerald F. Cavanaugh, *American Business Values with International Perspectives*, 4th ed. (Upper Saddle River, NJ: Prentice Hall, 1998), Chapter 3.

[2]See "Are Your Work Ethics in Line?" *CNN.com* (July 11, 2001) at <www.cnn.com/TECH/computing/9906/22/ethics.ent.idg/>.

[3]Tamara Kaplan, "The Tylenol Crisis: How Effective Public Relations Saved Johnson & Johnson" (July 11, 2001) at <www.personal.psu.edu/users/w/x/wxk116/tylenol/crisis.html>.

[4]William Echikson with Stephen Baker and Dean Foust, "Things Aren't Going Better with Coke," *Businessweek Online* (July 11, 2001) at <www.businessweek.com:/1999/99_26/b3635131.htm>; Andrew Marshall, "Why Some Things Don't Always Go Better with Coke," *The Age* (July 11, 2001) at <www.theage.com.au/daily/990712/news/specials/news2.html>.

[5]See Abagail McWilliams and Donald Siegel, "Corporate Social Responsibility: A Theory of the Firm Perspective," *Academy of Management Review*, 2001, vol. 26, no. 1, 117–27.

[6]Jeffrey S. Harrison and R. Edward Freeman, "Stakeholders, Social Responsibility, and Performance: Empirical Evidence and Theoretical Perspectives," *Academy of Management Journal*, 1999, vol. 42, no. 5, 479–85. See also David P. Baron, *Business and Its Environment*, 3rd ed. (Upper Saddle River, NJ: Prentice Hall, 2000), Chapter 17.

[7]Alex Berenson, "Computer Associates Officials Stand By Their Accounting Methods," *New York Times*, May 1, 2001, C1, C7.

[8]Richard S. Dunham, "Bush's Softer Sell," *Business Week*, June 25, 2001, 34–37; Paul Raeburn, "Global Warming Needs More Than Just Another Study," *Business Week*, June 25, 2001, 36–37.

[9]Andrew C. Revkin, "Who Cares About a Few Degrees?" *New York Times*, December 12, 1997, F1, F4.

[10]See Baron, *Business and Its Environment*, Chapter 12.

[11]Marilyn Adams, "Careless Cargo," *Danatec Educational Services* (July 11, 2001) at <www.danatec.com/freebie9.htm>; Cat Lazaroff, "American Airlines Guilty of Hazmat Storage, Shipment Violations," *Environment News Service* (July 11, 2001) at <http://ens.lycos.com/ens/dec99/1999L-12-17-06.html>.

[12]Susan Warren, "Recycler's Nightmare: Beer in Plastic," *Wall Street Journal*, November 16, 1999, B1, B4.

[13]U.S. Department of Health and Human Services, "Abbott Labs Signs Consent Decree with FDA," *SafetyAgent.com* (July 11, 2001) at <www.safetyagent.com/reports/_P_99_17400.asp>.

[14]Richard B. Schmitt and Robert Langreth, "American Home Products Agrees to Pay Up to $3.75 Billion in Diet-Drug Lawsuits," *WSJ Interactive Edition* (July 11, 2001) at <www.productslaw.com/diet21.html>. See also Nancy Shute, "Pills Don't Come with a Seal of Approval," *U.S. News Online* (July 11, 2001) at <www.usnews.com/usnews/issue/970929/29fen.htm>.

[15]Department of Justice, "F. Hoffmann-La Roche and BASF Agree to Pay Record Criminal Fines for Participating in International Vitamin Cartel" (July 11, 2001) at <www.usdoj.gov/atr/public/press_releases/1999/2450.htm>; Alain L. Sanders, "The 'C' in Vitamin C No Longer Stands for Cartel," *Time.com* (July 11, 2001) at <www.time.com/time/nation/article/0,8599,25068,00.html>.

[16]Michael McCarthy and Lorrie Grant, "Sears Drops Benetton after Controversial Death Row Ads," *USA Today*, February 18, 2000, 2B.

[17]See Baron, *Business and Its Environment*, 704–06; Jerald Greenberg and Robert A. Baron, *Behavior in Organizations: Understanding and Managing the Human Side of Work*, 7th ed. (Upper Saddle River, NJ: Prentice Hall, 2000), 374–75.

[18]Rick Lyman, "A Tobacco Whistle-Blower's Life Is Transformed," *New York Times*, October 15, 1999, A24.

[19]See Henry R. Cheesman, *Business Law: Ethical, International, and E-Commerce Environment*, 4th ed. (Upper Saddle River, NJ: Prentice Hall, 2001), 144–145.

[20]Andy Pasztor and Peter Landers, "Toshiba to Pay $2B Settlement on Laptops," *ZD Net News* (July 12, 2001) at <www.zdnet.com/zdnn/stories/news/0,4586,2385037,00.html>.

[21]See Cheesman, *Business Law*, 809–11.

[22]Tom Lowry, "Merger Mania Revives Insider Trading," *USA Today*, August 11, 1998, A1.

[23]For a recent discussion of these issues, see Amy Hillman and Gerald Keim, "Shareholder Value, Stakeholder Management, and Social Issues: What's the Bottom Line?" *Strategic Management Journal*, 2001, vol. 22, no. 2, 125–39.

[24]Bruce Horovitz, "Employers Back Olympic Hopefuls," *USA Today*, February 7, 2000, 1B.

[25]See Michael E. Porter and Mark R. Kramer, "Philanthropy's New Agenda: Creating Value," *Harvard Business Review*, November–December 1999, 121–30.

[26]See Sandra Waddock and Neil Smith, "Corporate Responsibility Audits: Doing Well by Doing Good," *Sloan Management Review*, Winter 2000, 75–85.

CHAPTER 4

[1]U.S. Department of Commerce, "Statistics about Business Size (Including Small Business) from the U.S. Census Bureau," *Statistical Abstract of the United States* (September 6, 2001) at <www.census.gov/epcd/www/smallbus.html>.

[2]Small Business Administration (SBA), "Learn about SBA" (September 6, 2001) at <www. sba.gov/aboutsba/>.

[3]SBA, "Learn about SBA," at <www.sba.gov/aboutsba/>.

[4]See Henry R. Cheeseman, *Contemporary Business Law* (Upper Saddle River, NJ: Prentice Hall, 2000) 553-55; Norman M. Scarborough and Thomas W. Zimmerer, *Effective Small Business Management: An Entrepreneurial Approach*, 6th ed. (Upper Saddle River, NJ: Prentice Hall, 2000) 73–76.

[5]Department of Commerce, "Statistics about Business Size," *Statistical Abstracts*, at <www.census.gov/epcd/www/smallbus.html>.

[6]See Cheeseman, *Contemporary Business Law*, 554–55.

[7]See Cheeseman, *Contemporary Business Law*, Chapter 24; Scarborough and Zimmerer, *Effective Small Business Management*, 77–84.

[8]Department of Commerce, "Statistics about Business Size," *Statistical Abstracts*, at <www.census.gov/epcd/www/smallbus.html>.

[9]"Fortune Five Hundred Largest Corporations," *Fortune*, April 16, 2001, F1–F20.

[10]See Cheeseman, *Contemporary Business Law*, Chapter 25.

[11]See Cheeseman, *Contemporary Business Law*, 652–54.

[12]See Cheeseman, *Contemporary Business Law*, 672–76.

[13]See Cheeseman, *Contemporary Business Law*, 611–13.

[14]See Cheeseman, *Contemporary Business Law*, Chapter 26.

[15]See Thomas L. Wheelen and J. David Hunger, *Strategic Management and Business Policy*, 7th ed. (Upper Saddle River, NJ: Prentice Hall, 2000) 125–29.

[16]Go to The National Center for Employee Ownership (September 6, 2001) at <http://www.nceo.org/>.

[17]See Thomas W. Zimmerer and Norman M. Scarborough, *Essentials of Entrepreneurship and Small Business*, 3rd ed. (Upper Saddle River, NJ: Prentice Hall, 2002), especially 4–6.

[18]See Efraim Turban et al., *Electronic Commerce: A Managerial Perspective* (Upper Saddle River, NJ: Prentice Hall, 2000) 449–51.

[19]Andy Serwer, "There's Something about Cisco," *Fortune*, May 15, 2000, 114–38.

[20]Go to the U.S. Census Bureau, "Surveys of Minority- and Women-Owned Enterprises," *Statistical Abstract of the United States* (September 6, 2001) at <www.census.gov/csd/mwb>.

[21]Bill Meyers, "Women Increase Standing as Business Owners," *USA Today*, June 29, 1999, 1B.

[22]Noelle Knox, "Women Entrepreneurs Attract New Financing," *New York Times*, July 26, 1998, 10.

[23]Scarborough and Zimmerer, *Effective Small Business Management*, Chapter 12.

[24]See Scarborough and Zimmerer, *Effective Small Business Management*, 412–13.

[25]Jim Hopkins, "Expert Entrepreneur Got Her Show on the Road at an Early Age," *USA Today*, May 24, 2000, 5B.

[26]Thea Singer, "Brandapalooza," *Inc. 500*, 1999, 69–72.

[27]See Scarborough and Zimmerer, *Effective Small Business Management*, Chapter 4.

CHAPTER 5

[1]Louise Lee, "A Savvy Captain for Old Navy," *BusinessWeek Online* (July 17, 2001) at <www.businessweek.com/magazine/channeltop.htm>; "Old Navy's Skipper," *BusinessWeek Online* (July 17, 2001) at <www.businessweek.com/2000/00 02/ b3663014.htm>.

[2]"The Top 25 Managers of the Year," *Business Week*, January 8, 2001, 62; Michael Ryan, "AmEx Charges Ahead," *ZD Net News* (July 17, 2001) at <www.zdnet.com/zdnn/stories/news/0,4586,2688779,00.html>.

[3]David Dorsey, "Andy Pearson Finds Love," *Fast Company*, August 2001, 78–86.

[4]See Thomas L. Wheelan and J. David Hunger, *Strategic Management and Business Policy*, 7th ed. (Upper Saddle River, NJ: Prentice Hall, 2000), 12–14; and Mary K. Coulter, *Strategic Management in Action*, 2nd ed. (Upper Saddle River, NJ: Prentice Hall, 2002) 9–12.

[5]Mike Hofman, "Two Guys and a Start-Up: The True-Life Adventures of First-Time Company Founders," *Inc.*, February 2001, 76–81.

[6]See Wheelan and Hunger, *Strategic Management*, 10–14.

[7]Janet Guyon, "Getting the Bugs Out at VW," *Fortune*, March 29, 1999, 96–102; and Dale Jewett, "Running near the Front," *Automotive Industries* (July 18, 2001) at <www.findarticles.com/m3012/4 180/61892631/p1/article.jhtml>.

[8]Melanie Wells, "Red Baron," *Forbes*, July 3, 2000, 150–60; Andrew Ross Sorkin, "Taking Virgin's Brand into Internet Territory," *New York Times*, February 14, 2000, C1, C17.

[9]"Cruise-Ship Delays Leave Guests High and Dry," *Wall Street Journal*, October 24, 1997, B1, B10; *Hoover's Handbook*

of American Business 2001 (Austin, TX: Hoover's Business Press, 2001) 1512–13.

[10]John Markoff, "A Disruptive Virus Invades Computers around the World," *New York Times*, May 5, 2000, A1, C9; Markoff, "Law Officials Seek Origins of the Virus," *New York Times*, May 6, 2000, C1, C3.

[11]Peter Burrows, "The Radical—Carly Fiorina's Bold Management Experiment at HP," *Business Week*, February 19, 2001, 70–80.

[12]Brian O'Reilly, "The Mechanic Who Fixed Continental," *Fortune*, December 20, 1999, 176–86; David Field, "Fliers Give Continental Sky-High Marks," *USA Today*, May 10, 2000, 3B.

[13]See David A. Whetten and Kim S. Cameron, *Developing Management Skills*, 5th ed. (Upper Saddle River, NJ: Prentice Hall, 2002) Chapter 6.

[14]Frank Rose, "Vivendi's High Wireless Act," *Wired* (July 18, 2001) at <www.wired.com/wired/archive/8.12/vivendi.html>; Mike Trigg, "Vivendi Grabs Houghton Mifflin," *The Motley Fool* (July 18, 2001) at <www.fool.com/news/2001/v010601.htm>.

[15]See also Whetten and Cameron, *Developing Management Skills*, 113–20.

[16]"Rallying the Troops at P&G," *Wall Street Journal*, August 31, 2000, B1, B4.

CHAPTER 6

[1]Robert L. Simison, "Ford Rolls Out New Model of Corporate Culture," *Wall Street Journal*, January 13, 1999, B1, B4; Joann S. Lublin, "Place vs. Product: It's Tough to Choose a Management Model," *Wall Street Journal*, June 27, 2001, A1, A4.

[2]Joann Muller, "Ford: Why It's Worse Than You Think," *Business Week*, June 25, 2001, 80–84+.

[3]See Gregory Moorhead and Ricky W. Griffin, *Organizational Behavior: Managing People and Organizations*, 6th ed. (Boston: Houghton Mifflin, 2001) 420–79.

[4]See Amy Wrzesniewski and Jane Dutton, "Crafting a Job: Revisioning Employees as Active Crafters of Their Work," *Academy of Management Review*, 2001, vol. 26, no. 2, 179–201.

[5]"Lucent to Break Up into Four Divisions," Associated Press news story reported in *Houston Chronicle*, October 27, 1999, B2.

[6]Rachel Konrad, "Lucent's Hits and Misses," *News.com* (July 19, 2001) at <news.cnet.com/news/0-1004-200-6078084.html>; Stephanie N. Mehta, "Lessons from the Lucent Debacle," *Fortune*, February 5, 2001, 142–46+; Mark Lewis, "Lucent's Name in Vain," *Forbes.com* (July 19, 2001) at <www.forbes.com/2001/05/04/0504lucent.html>; Steven Baker and Steve Rosenbush, "Alcatel's U.S. Dream," *Business Week*, June 4, 2001, 54–55.

[7]Bruce Horovitz, "Restoring the Golden-Arch Shine," *USA Today*, June 16, 1999, 3B; "Industry Report: Restaurant Industry," *US Business Reporter* (July 19, 2001) at <www.activemedia-guide.com/print_restaurant.htm>; Michael Arndt, "There's Life in the Old Bird Yet," *Business Week*, May 14, 2001, 77–78.

[8]See David A. Whetten and Kim S. Cameron, *Developing Management Skills*, 5th ed. (Upper Saddle River, NJ: Prentice Hall, 2002) 427–35.

[9]Linda Formichelli, "Letting Go of the Details," *Nation's Business* (November 1997) 501.

[10]See also Gary Yukl, *Leadership in Organizations*, 5th ed. (Upper Saddle River, NJ: Prentice Hall, 2002) 100–02.

[11]Michael E. Raynor and Joseph L. Bower, "Lead From the Center," *Harvard Business Review* (May 2001) 93–102.

[12]Horovitz, "Restoring the Golden-Arch Shine," 3B.

[13]Stephanie Forest, "Can an Outsider Fix J.C. Penney?" *Business Week*, February 12, 2001, 56–58.

[14]Joann Muller, "Thinking Out of the Cereal Box," *Business Week*, January 15, 2001, 54–55.

[15]Donna Fenn, "Redesign Work," *Inc.* (June 1999) 75–83.

[16]See Yukl, *Leadership in Organizations*, 35–36.

[17]Philip Siekman, "Where 'Build to Order' Works Best," *Fortune*, April 26, 1999, 160C–160V; "Multi-Tasking: Cost-Reduction Strategy at Case Corp.," Machinery Systems Inc. (July 20, 2001) at <www.machinerysystems.com/RavingFan/CaseCorp.html>.

[18]See Whetten and Cameron, *Developing Management Skills*, Chapter. 9; Yukl, *Leadership in Organizations*, Chapter 11.

[19]Lublin, "Place vs. Product," A1, A4.

[20]Robert Berner and Kevin Helliker, "Heinz's Worry: 4,000 Products, Only One Star," *Wall Street Journal*, September 17, 1999, B1, B4.

[21]Diane Brady, "Martha Inc.," *Business Week*, January 17, 2000, 62–66.

[22]Mitchell Lee Marks and Philip H. Mirvis, "Creating an Effective Transition Structure," *Organizational Dynamics* (Winter 2000) 35–44. See also Helen Deresky, *International Management: Managing across Borders and Cultures*, 3rd ed. (Upper Saddle River, NJ: Prentice Hall, 2000) Chapter 9.

[23]"Wal-Mart Acquires Interspar," *Management Ventures* (July 20, 2001) at <www.mventures.com/news/Key1998/flash98/wmtinters.asp>; Kerry Capell et al., "Wal-Mart's Not-So-Secret British Weapon," *Business Week Online* (July 20, 2001) at <www.businessweek.com:/2000/00_04/b3665095.htm>.

[24]Gail Edmondson, "Danone Hits Its Stride," *Business Week*, February 1, 1999, 52–53.

[25]Thomas A. Stewart, "See Jack. See Jack Run," *Fortune*, September 27, 1999, 124–271; Geoffrey Colvin, "America's Most Admired Companies," *Fortune*, February 21, 2000, 108–10.

[26]Leslie P. Willcocks and Robert Plant, "Getting from Bricks to Clicks," *Sloan Management Review* (Spring 2001) 50–60.

[27]Ethan Smith, "Business-Driven CUs Take Many Forms," *Corporate University Review* (July 20, 2001) at <www.traininguniversity.com/magazine/mar_apr97/starting.html>.

[28]See, for example, Denise M. Rousseau, "The Idiosyncratic Deal: Flexibility versus Fairness?" *Organizational Dynamics*, 2001, vol. 29, no. 4, 260–73.

[29]See Moorhead and Griffin, *Organizational Behavior*, 248–78.

CHAPTER 7

[1]Jennifer L. Martel and Laura A. Kelter, "The Job Market Remains Strong in 1999," *Monthly Labor Review* (February 2000) 3–23.

[2]Martel and Kelter, "The Job Market Remains Strong in 1999," 3–23; *Employment & Earnings* (Washington, DC: U.S. Dept. of Labor: Bureau of Labor Statistics, June 2001) 70; *Survey of Current Business* (Washington, DC: U.S. Dept. of Commerce, June 2001) D-4.

[3]Richard Tomlinson, "China's Reform: Now Comes the Hard Part," *Fortune*, March 1, 1999, 159.

[4]*GE Annual Report: 1999* (Fairfield, CT: General Electric Co., 2000) 8.

[5]See Christopher Lovelock, *Services Marketing: People, Technology, Strategy*,

4th ed. (Upper Saddle River, NJ: Prentice Hall, 2001) 56–59.

[6]See Lovelock, *Services Marketing*, 8–15.

[7]Eryn Brown, "America's Most Admired Companies," *Fortune*, March 1, 1999, 68, 70–73; *Wal-Mart Annual Report 2001* (Bentonville, AR: Wal-Mart Stores, 2001) 6.

[8]See Lovelock, *Services Marketing*, 37–41.

[9]See Judy Strauss and Raymond Frost, *E-Marketing*, 2nd ed. (Upper Saddle River, NJ: Prentice Hall, 2001) 280–325.

[10]See Lee J. Krajewski and Larry P. Ritzman, *Operations Management: Strategy and Analysis*, 6th ed. (Upper Saddle River, NJ: Prentice Hall, 2002), Chapter 8.

[11]Dawn Kawamoto, "FTC Approves Digital-Intel Deal," *News.com* (August 9, 2001) at <http://news.cnet.com/news/0-1005-200-328663.html?tag=rltdnws>.

[12]See Krajewski and Ritzman, *Operations Management*, Chapter 9.

[13]Barbara McClellan, "Brazilian Revolution," *Ward's Auto World* (September 2000) 69–74.

[14]See Krajewski and Ritzman, *Operations Management*, Chapter 10.

[15]See Krajewski and Ritzman, *Operations Management*, 504–06.

[16]See Krajewski and Ritzman, *Operations Management*, 799–805.

[17]Vince Hanks, "Cruising with Harley-Davidson," *Fool.com* (August 9, 2001) at <www.fool.com/dripport/2000/dripport000727.htm>.

[18]*United Parcel Service 1999 Annual Report* (Atlanta, GA: United Parcel Service Inc., 2000); "Fortune 500," *Fortune*, April 16, 2001, F-57.

[19]Paul C. Judge, "The Inside Story of How Mike Ruettgers Turned EMC into a High Flyer," *Business Week*, March 15, 1999, 72–76+.

[20]See S. Thomas Foster Jr., *Managing Quality: An Integrative Approach* (Upper Saddle River, NJ: Prentice Hall, 2001) 195–203.

[21]See Foster, *Managing Quality*, 99–104.

[22]Joel Kurtzman, "Is Your Company Off Course? Now You Can Find Out Why," *Fortune*, February 17, 1997, 133.

[23]See Foster, *Managing Quality*, 105–07.

[24]See Sunil Chopra and Peter Meindl, *Supply Chain Management: Strategy, Planning, and Operation* (Upper Saddle River, NJ: Prentice Hall, 2001) 3–6; Krajewski and Ritzman, *Operations Management*, Chapter 11.

[25]See Chopra and Meindl, *Supply Chain Management*, Chapter 2.

[26]See Chopra and Meindl, *Supply Chain Management*, 348–49.

CHAPTER 8

[1]Richard B. Chase and Sriram Dasu, "Want to Perfect Your Company's Service? Use Behavioral Science," *Harvard Business Review*, June 2001, 79–88.

[2]Daniel M. Cable and Charles K. Parsons, "Socialization Tactics and Person-Organization Fit," *Personnel Psychology*, Spring 2001, 1–24.

[3]Gregory Moorhead and Ricky W. Griffin, *Organizational Behavior*, 6th ed. (Boston: Houghton Mifflin 2001) 95–99.

[4]Jerry Useem, "Welcome to the New Company Town," *Fortune*, January 10, 2000, 62–70.

[5]See Jerald Greenberg and Robert A. Baron, *Behavior in Organizations: Understanding and Managing the Human Side of Work*, 7th ed. (Upper Saddle River, NJ: Prentice Hall, 2000) 177–79.

[6] "Perks That Work," *Time*, November 9, 1998, 54.

[7]Anne Fisher, "Surviving the Downturn," *Fortune*, April 2, 2001, 98–106.

[8]See Moorhead and Griffin, *Organizational Behavior*, Chapters 5 and 6.

[9]Ralph King, Jr., "Levi's Factory Workers Are Assigned to Teams, and Morale Takes a Hit," *Wall Street Journal*, May 20, 1998, A1, A6; *Hoover's Handbook of American Business 2001* (Austin, TX: Hoover's Business Press, 2001) 860–61.

[10]See Moorhead and Griffin, *Organizational Behavior*, Chapter 7.

[11]See Moorhead and Griffin, *Organizational Behavior*, Chapter 7.

[12]See Moorhead and Griffin, *Organizational Behavior*, Chapter 7.

[13]*Hoover's Handbook of American Business 2001*, 1328–29.

[14]Robert Levering and Milton Moskowitz, "The 100 Best Companies to Work For," *Fortune*, January 8, 2001, 148–66.

[15]See Gary Yukl, *Leadership in Organizations*, 5th ed. (Upper Saddle River, NJ: Prentice Hall, 2002) Chapter 1.

[16] "Insanity, Inc.," *Fast Company*, January 1999, 100–08.

[17]See Francis J. Yammarino, Fred Dansereau, and Christina J. Kennedy, "A Multiple-Level Multidimensional Approach to Leadership," *Organizational Dynamics*, vol. 29, no. 3, 2001, 149–63.

[18]See Yukl, *Leadership in Organizations*, Chapter 8; Jon P. Howell and Dan L. Costley, *Understanding Behaviors for Effective Leadership* (Upper Saddle River, NJ: Prentice Hall, 2001) Chapter 3.

[19]See Moorhead and Griffin, *Organizational Behavior*, Chapters 13, 14.

[20]See Greenberg and Baron, *Behavior in Organizations*, 193–99; Yukl, *Leadership in Organizations*, 418–20.

[21]Frederick F. Reichheld, "Lead for Loyalty," *Harvard Business Review*, July–August 2001, 76–86.

CHAPTER 9

[1]See Angelo S. DeNisi and Ricky W. Griffin, *Human Resource Management* (Boston: Houghton Mifflin, 2001) 34–67.

[2]See Luis R. Gómez-Mejía, David B. Balkin, and Robert L. Cardy, *Managing Human Resources*, 3rd ed. (Upper Saddle River, NJ: Prentice Hall, 2001) 64–71.

[3]See Gary Dessler, *Human Resource Management*, 8th ed. (Upper Saddle River, NJ: Prentice Hall, 2000) 126.

[4]Matthew Boyle, "The Not-So-Fine Art of the Layoff," *Fortune*, March 19, 2001, 209–10.

[5]Associated Press, "Unemployment Steady but Hiring Slows," *WFAA.com* (August 21, 2001) at <http://www.wfaa.com/wfaa/articledisplay/1,1002,18294,00.html>.

[6]See Dessler, *Human Resource Management*, 177.

[7]See Dessler, *Human Resource Management*, Chapter 5.

[8]Kenneth Brown, "Using Computers to Deliver Training: Which Employees Learn and Why?" *Personnel Psychology*, Summer 2001, 271–96.

[9]Abby Ellin, "Training Programs Often Miss the Point on the Job," *New York Times*, March 29, 2000, C12.

[10]See Richard I. Henderson, *Compensation Management in a Knowledge-Based World*, 8th ed. (Upper Saddle River, NJ: Prentice Hall, 2000) 17–18.

[11]See Dessler, *Human Resource Management*, Chapter 12.

[12]See Gómez-Mejía, Balkin, and Cardy, *Managing Human Resources*, 366–69.

[13]See James Bateslos, "Eisner's Stock-Option Profit: $565 Million" (August 21, 2001) at <http://www.onlineathens.com/1997/120597/1205.a3eisnerdisney.html>.

[14]See Gómez-Mejía, Balkin, and Cardy, *Managing Human Resources*, 376–78.

[15]Barbara Carton, "In 24-Hour Workplace, Day Care Is Moving to the Night Shift," *Wall Street Journal*, July 6, 2001, A1, A4.

[16]See Henry R. Cheeseman, *Business Law: Ethical, International, and E-Commerce Environment*, 4th ed. (Upper Saddle River, NJ: Prentice Hall, 2001) Chapter 42.

[17]See Dessler, *Human Resource Management*, 44–46.

[18]See Cheeseman, *Business Law*, 843–47; Dessler, *Human Resource Management*, 40–44.

[19]Jeremy Kahn, "Diversity Trumps the Downturn," *Fortune*, July 9, 2001, 114–28.

[20]See Henderson, *Compensation Management*, 3–6.

[21]Thomas Stewart, "In Search of Elusive Tech Workers," *Fortune*, February 16, 1998, 171–72.

[22]Matt Richtel, "Need for Computer Experts Is Making Recruiters Frantic," *New York Times*, December 18, 1999, C1.

[23]Aaron Bernstein, "When Is a Temp Not a Temp?" *Business Week*, December 7, 1998, 90–92.

[24]See Michael R. Carrell and Christina Heavrin, *Labor Relations and Collective Bargaining: Cases, Practice, and Law*, 6th ed. (Upper Saddle River, NJ: Prentice Hall, 2001) Chapter 1.

[25]David Koenig, "Labor Unions Say Recent Victories Signal a Comeback," Associated Press news release published in *The Bryan-College Station Eagle*, June 11, 2000, E1, E6.

[26]Aaron Bernstein, "Welch's March to the South," *Business Week*, December 6, 1999, 74, 78.

[27]See Carrell and Heavrin, *Labor Relations and Collective Bargaining*, 90–91.

[28]See also Carrell and Heavrin, *Labor Relations and Collective Bargaining*, 189–97.

[29]See Carrell and Heavrin, *Labor Relations and Collective Bargaining*, 197–211.

[30]*New York Times Almanac 2000* (New York: Penguin Reference, 1999), 351.

[31]See Carrell and Heavrin, *Labor Relations and Collective Bargaining*, Chapter 11; Cheeseman, *Business Law*, 38–41.

CHAPTER 10

[1]American Marketing Association, "Marketing Services Guide" (August 23, 2001) at <www.ama.org/about/ama/markdef.asp>.

[2]See Philip Kotler, *Marketing Management*, Millennium ed. (Upper Saddle River, NJ: Prentice Hall, 2000). 50–54.

[3]See Warren J. Keegan and Mark C. Green, *Global Marketing*, 2nd ed. (Upper Saddle River, NJ: Prentice Hall, 2000) 7-15.

[4]Herb Kelleher, "A Brief History of Southwest Airlines" (August 23, 2001) at <www.southwest.com/aboutswa>.

[5]See Leon G. Schiffman and Leslie Lazar Kanuk, *Consumer Behavior*, 7th ed. (Upper Saddle River, NJ: Prentice Hall, 2000) Chapter 3; Kotler, *Marketing Management*, Chapter 9.

[6]Alex Taylor III, "Detroit: Every Silver Lining Has a Cloud," *Fortune*, January 24, 2000, 92–93.

[7]"Burberry Earns Independence," *BBC News* (August 23, 2001) at <http://newsvote.bbc.co.uk/hi/english/business/newsid_1047000/1047772.stm>.

[8]Kitty McKinsey, "Poland: Credit and Debit Cards Take Off," *Radio Free Europe* (August 23, 2001) at <http://www.rferl.org/nca/features/1997/03/ F.RU.970303160756. html>; Jane Perlez, "Joy of Debts: Eastern Europe on Credit Fling," *New York Times*, May 30, 1998, A3.

[9]See Schiffman and Kanuk, *Consumer Behavior*, Chapters 6, 7, 8.

[10]See Schiffman and Kanuk, *Consumer Behavior*, Chapter 11.

[11]See Schiffman and Kanuk, *Consumer Behavior*, Chapter 12.

[12]See also Schiffman and Kanuk, *Consumer Behavior*, pp. 442–51.

[13]See Schiffman and Kanuk, *Consumer Behavior*, pp. 69–70.

[14]U.S. Department of Commerce, *Statistical Abstract of the United States: 1998* (Washington, DC: Bureau of the Census, 1999) 305–09, 547, 768, 776.

[15]*Statistical Abstract of the United States: 1998*, pp. 306, 358.

[16]See Kotler, *Marketing Management*, pp. 208–11.

[17]See Kotler, *Marketing Management*, pp. 396–98.

[18]See Kotler, *Marketing Management*, pp. 398-400.

[19]Nina Munk, "How Levi's Trashed a Great American Brand," *Fortune*, April 12, 1999, 83.

[20]See James C. Anderson and James A. Narus, *Business Market Management: Understanding, Creating, and Delivering Value* (Upper Saddle River, NJ: Prentice Hall, 1999) 203-06.

[21]See Eloise Coupey, *Marketing and the Internet* (Upper Saddle River, NJ: Prentice Hall, 2001) 174-79.

[22]Paul C. Judge et al., "The Name's the Thing," *Business Week*, November 15, 1999, 36–39.

[23]See Norman N. Scarborough and Thomas W. Zimmerer, *Effective Small Business Management: An Entrepreneurial Approach*, 6th ed. (Upper Saddle River, NJ: Prentice Hall, 2000) Chapter 6.

[24]Paco Underhill, "What Shoppers Want," *Inc.*, July 1999, 76, 80.

CHAPTER 11

[1]Robert D. Hof, "The Buyer Always Wins," *Business Week*, March 22, 1999, EB26, EB28. See also Judy Strauss and Raymond Frost, *E-Marketing*, 2nd ed. (Upper Saddle River, NJ: Prentice Hall, 2001) 165–67.

[2]See Roger J. Best, *Market-Based Management: Strategies for Growing Customer Value and Profitability*, 2nd ed. (Upper Saddle River, NJ: Prentice Hall, 2000) 189–91.

[3]Strauss and Frost, *E-Marketing*, 166–67; Eloise Coupey, *Marketing and the Internet* (Upper Saddle River, NJ: Prentice Hall, 2001) 281–83.

[4]Robert D. Hof and Linda Himelstein, "eBay vs. Amazon.com," *Business Week*, May 31, 1999, 128–32+; Hof, "The Buyer Always Wins," EB26, EB28; Janet Rae-Dupree and Diane Brady, "Let the Buyer Be in Control," *Business Week*, November 8, 1999, 100.

[5]See Kenneth E. Clow and Donald Baack, *Integrated Advertising, Promotion, and Marketing Communications* (Upper Saddle River, NJ: Prentice Hall, 2002) 128–32.

[6]See also Clow and Baack, *Integrated Advertising*, Chapter 5.

[7]*Advertising Age*, September 25, 2000, S4.

[8]See Clow and Baack, *Integrated Advertising*, Chapter 8.

[9]*Advertising Age*, September 25, 2000, S54.

[10]*Advertising Age*, September 25, 2000, S4.

[11]See Strauss and Frost, *E-Marketing*, 248–62; Efraim Turban et al., *Electronic Commerce: A Managerial Perspective* (Upper Saddle River, NJ: Prentice Hall, 2000) Chapter 4.

[12]See Strauss and Frost, *E-Marketing*, 115–19.

[13]Stuart Elliott, "You've Got Mail, Indeed," *New York Times*, October 25, 1999, C1, C23.

[14]See Clow and Baack, *Integrated Advertising*, Chapter 13.

[15]Keith Fiotta, "Telemarketing in the Age of Compliance," *Advisor Today*, August 2001, 64.

[16]See Clow and Baack, *Integrated Advertising*, Chapter 12.

[17]See Scott M. Cutlip, Allen H. Center, and Glen M. Broom, *Effective Public Relations*, 8th ed. (Upper Saddle River, NJ: Prentice Hall, 2000) 9–10.

[18]See also Anne T. Coughlan et al., *Marketing Channels*, 6th ed. (Upper Saddle River, NJ: Prentice Hall, 2001) 9–17.

[19]See Coughlan et al., *Marketing Channels*, Chapter 15.

[20]See esp. Coupey, *Marketing and the Internet*, Chapter 11; Coughlin et al., *Marketing Channels*, 447–69.

[21]"Expedia.com" (April 19, 2000) at <www.expedia.com>.

[22]Diane Brady, "From Nabisco to Tropicana to . . . EFDEX?" *Business Week*, September 20, 1999, 100; "Efdex™" (April 19, 2000) at <www.efdex.com>.

[23]See also Barry Berman and Joel R. Evans, *Retail Management: A Strategic Approach*, 8th ed. (Upper Saddle River, NJ: Prentice Hall, 2001) Chapter 5.

[24]Patrick C. O'Connor, "Which Retail Properties Are Getting Market Share?" *The Appraisal Journal*, January 1999, 37–40.

[25]Gene Gray, "The Future of the Teleservices Industry—Are You Aware," *Telemarketing*, January 1999, 90–96.

[26]Daniel W. Guido, "Where's the Wow? Virtual Customer Service," *Builder*, July 2001, 141–48.

[27]See Turban et al., *Electronic Commerce*, 407–08.

[28]See Coughlin et al., *Marketing Channels*, 458–62

CHAPTER 12

[1]See Kenneth C. Laudon and Jane P. Laudon, *Management Information Systems: Managing the Digital Firm*, 7th ed. (Upper Saddle River, NJ: Prentice Hall, 2002) 7–11.

[2]See Laudon and Laudon, *Management Information Systems*, 252–53.

[3]See Larry Long and Nancy Long, *Computers: Information Technology in Perspective*, 9th ed. (Upper Saddle River, NJ: Prentice Hall, 2002) 241–42.

[4]See Long and Long, *Computers*, Chapter 7 and Chapter 8.

[5]See Laudon and Laudon, *Management Information Systems*, 273–83.

[6]Steve Jarvis, "Ain't Nothin' for Free," *Marketing News*, April 23, 2001, 3; Alex Salkever and Sheridan Prasso, "Search Engines: Leading US Astray?" *Business Week (Industry/Technology Edition)*, August 6, 2001, 8.

[7]See Laudon and Laudon, *Management Information Systems*, 122–27, 276–77.

[8]Jennifer Tanaka, "Don't Get Burned," *Newsweek*, August 20, 2001, 52–53.

[9]Mary J. Cronin, "Ford's Intranet Success," *Fortune*, March 30, 1998, 158; Rick Gurin, "Online System to Streamline Ford's Delivery Process," *Frontline Solutions*, April 2000, 1, 8.

[10]See Laudon and Laudon, *Management Information Systems*, 21–22.

[11]See Lee J. Krajewski and Larry P. Ritzman, *Operations Management: Strategy and Analysis*, 6th ed. (Upper Saddle River, NJ: Prentice Hall, 2002) 46–48.

[12]See Gary W. Dickson and Gerardine DeSanctis, *Information Technology and the Future Enterprise: New Models for Managers* (Upper Saddle River, NJ: Prentice Hall, 2001) Chapter 4.

[13]Krajewski and Ritzman, *Operations Management: Strategy and Analysis*, 106.

[14]See Krajewski and Ritzman, *Operations Management: Strategy and Analysis*, 205–10.

[15]See Krajewski and Ritzman, *Operations Management: Strategy and Analysis*, 232–33.

[16]See Laudon and Laudon, *Management Information Systems*, esp. 40–45.

[17]See Laudon and Laudon, *Management Information Systems*, 383–91.

[18]See Long and Long, *Computers*, 24–26, 107–12.

[19]See Long and Long, *Computers*, Chapter 2.

[20]See esp. Long and Long, *Computers*, 52–54.

[21]See Long and Long, *Computers*, 101–06.

[22]See Laudon and Laudon, *Management Information Systems*, 237–44.

[23]See Laudon and Laudon, *Management Information Systems*, 270–71.

[24]See Long and Long, *Computers*, 225–26.

[25]Nathalie Raffray, "Portal Power," *Communications International*, August 2001, 30–35; David Maloney, "The Newest Better Idea at Ford," *Modern Materials Handling*, June 2000, 34–39. See also Laudon and Laudon, *Management Information Systems*, 239–44.

CHAPTER 13

[1]Charles T. Horngren, Walter T. Harrison Jr., and Linda Smith Bamber, *Accounting*, 5th ed. (Upper Saddle River, NJ: Prentice Hall, 2002) 5.

[2]See Kumen H. Jones et al., *Introduction to Accounting: A User Perspective* (Upper Saddle River, NJ: Prentice Hall, 2000) F-231.

[3]See Anthony A. Atkinson et al., *Management Accounting* (Upper Saddle River, NJ: Prentice Hall, 2001) 5–6.

[4]See Walter T. Harrison Jr. and Charles T. Horngren, *Financial Accounting*, 4th ed. (Upper Saddle River, NJ: Prentice Hall, 2000) 6.

[5]Michael Rogers and Norman Oder, "Ann Arbor Audit Reveals Big Deficit," *Library Journal*, March 15, 2000, 13–16.

[6]See Horngren, Harrison, and Bamber, *Accounting*, 9–11.

[7]This section is based on material from the following sources: AICPA, "CPA Vision Project" (July 31, 2001) at <www.aicpa.org>; AICPA, "CPA Vision Project: 2011 and Beyond" (July 31, 2000) at <www.cpavision.org/finalreport/>.

[8]Nanette Byrnes, "Where Have All the Accountants Gone?" *Business Week*, March 27, 1999, 203–04.

[9]See Horngren, Harrison, and Bamber, *Accounting*, 11–12, 39–41.

[10]See Horngren, Harrison, and Bamber, *Accounting*, 41–56.

[11]See Harrison and Horngren, *Financial Accounting*, 17–20.

[12]See Lawrence Revsine, Daniel W. Collins, and W. Bruce Johnson, *Financial Reporting and Analysis*, 2nd ed. (Upper Saddle River, NJ: Prentice Hall, 2002) 387.

[13]See Revsine, Collins, and Johnson; *Financial Reporting and Analysis,* 179–81, 468–70.

[14]See Revsine, Collins, and Johnson; *Financial Reporting and Analysis,* Chapter 15.

[15]See Horngren, Harrison, and Bamber, *Accounting*, Chapter 17.

[16]See Horngren, Harrison, and Bamber, *Accounting*, 927–40.

[17]See Jones et al., *Accounting: A User Perspective*, F-187.

[18]See Horngren, Harrison, and Bamber, *Accounting*, 86.

[19]See Jones et al., *Accounting: A User's Perspective*, F-454–F479.

[20]See Horngren, Harrison, and Bamber, *Accounting*, 728–29; Arthur J. Keown et al., *Foundations of Finance: The Logic and Practice of Financial Management*, 3rd ed. (Upper Saddle River, NJ: Prentice Hall, 2001) 118–20.

[21]See Horngren, Harrison, and Bamber, *Accounting*, 186–88.

[22]See Frederick D. S. Choi, Carol Ann Frost, and Gary K. Meek, *International Accounting*, 3rd ed. (Upper Saddle River: Prentice Hall, 1999), Chapter 6.

[23]See Choi, Frost, and Meek, *International Accounting*, 255–65.

CHAPTER 14

[1]See Arthur O'Sullivan and Steven M. Sheffrin, *Economics: Principles and Tools,* 2nd ed. (Upper Saddle River, NJ: Prentice Hall, 2001) 566–68.

[2]Federal Reserve Board of Governors, "M1 Money Stock Seasonally Adjusted" (July 16, 2001) at <www.federalreserve.gov>.

[3]Federal Reserve Board of Governors, "Currency Component of Money Stock" (July 16, 2001) at <www.federalreserve.gov>.

[4]Federal Reserve Board of Governors, "Demand Deposits at Commercial Banks" (July 16, 2001) at <www.federalreserve.gov>.

[5]Federal Reserve Board of Governors, "M2 Money Stock" (July 16, 2001) at <www.federalreserve.gov>.

[6]"Money Market Mutual Fund Assets Up," *Blackstocks* (July 16, 2001) at <www.blackstocks.com/in_news/9298.c/page2350.htm>.

[7]Federal Reserve Board of Governors, "Total Savings Deposits" (July 16, 2001) at <www.federalreserve.gov>.

[8]Citigroup, "Global Consumer Business" (July 17, 2001) at <www.citigroup.com/citigroup/corporate/gcb_m.htm>.

[9]See James C. Van Horne, *Financial Management and Policy,* 12th ed. (Upper Saddle River, NJ: Prentice Hall, 2002) 494–95.

[10]See "Prime Rate," *Money.café* (July 16, 2001) at <www.nfsn.com/library/prime.htm>.

[11]U.S. Census Bureau, *Statistical Abstract of the United States* (2000) 799, 808, at <www.census.gov/statab/www>.

[12]U.S. Census Bureau, *Statistical Abstract of the United States* (2000) 799, at <www.census.gov/statab/www>.

[13]U.S. Census Bureau, *Statistical Abstract of the United States* (2000) 789, at <www.census.gov/statab/www>.

[14]See Gordon J. Alexander, William F. Sharpe, and Jeffery V. Bailey, *Fundamentals of Investments,* 3rd ed. (Upper Saddle River, NJ: Prentice Hall, 2001) 100–01.

[15]American Bankers Association, "aba.com Press Room" (July 16, 2001) at <www.aba.com/Press+Room/ATMfacts2001.htm>.

[16]See Marshall B. Romney and Paul John Steinbart, *Accounting Information Systems,* 8th ed. (Upper Saddle River, NJ: Prentice Hall, 2000) 218–19.

[17]See Karl E. Case and Ray C. Fair, *Principles of Economics,* 6th ed. (Upper Saddle River, NJ: Prentice Hall, 2002) 483–89.

[18]See O'Sullivan and Sheffrin, *Economics,* 574–76.

[19]See "Fed Archives," *Financial Market Center* (July 16, 2001), at <www.fmcenter.org/fmc_superpage.asp?ID=46>.

[20]See Case and Fair, *Principles of Economics,* 497–99.

[21]Lisa Daigle, "Beyond Expectations," *Credit Card Management* (May 2000) 50–52.

[22]See Michael Froomkin, "The Unintended Consequences of E-Cash" (July 16, 2001) at <www.law.miami.edu/~froomkin/articles/cfp97.htm>.

[23]See Charles T. Horngren, Walter T. Harrison Jr., and Linda Smith Bamber, *Accounting,* 5th ed. (Upper Saddle River, NJ: Prentice Hall, 2002) 636–37.

[24]See Ricky W. Griffin and Michael W. Pustay, *International Business: A Managerial Perspective,* 3rd ed. (Upper Saddle River, NJ: Prentice Hall, 2002) 159–61.

CHAPTER 15

[1]See Gordon J. Alexander, William F. Sharpe, and Jeffery V. Bailey, *Fundamentals of Investments*, 3rd ed. (Upper Saddle River, NJ: Prentice Hall, 2001) 2–7.

[2]See Arthur J. Keown et al., *Foundations of Finance: The Logic and Practice of Financial Management*, 3rd ed. (Upper Saddle River, NJ: Prentice Hall, 2001) 51–52; Alexander, Sharpe, and Bailey, *Fundamentals of Investments*, 261, 478.

[3]*Federal Reserve Bulletin* (Washington, DC: Board of Governors of the Federal Reserve System, July 2001) A31.

[4]*Federal Reserve Bulletin* (July 2001) A31.

[5]See Keown et al., *Foundations of Finance*, 230–38.

[6]Joseph Nocera, "Do You Believe? How Yahoo Became a Blue Chip," *Fortune*, June 7, 1999, 76–81.

[7]See Cory Johnson, "The Internet Blue Chip," *The Industry Standard* (August 7, 2001) at <www.thestandard.com/article/0,1902,4088,00html>; Chris Nerney "Yahoo: Bargain or Big Trouble?" *The Internet Stock Report* (August 7, 2001) at <www.internetstockreport.com/column/print/0,,530021,00.html>.

[8]See Alexander, Sharpe, and Bailey, *Fundamentals of Investments*, 21-22.

[9]Chilik Wollenberg, "How Does Your Broker Measure Up?" *Medical Economics*, May 28, 2001, 98–100; Leah Nathans Spiro and Edward C. Baig, "Who Needs a Broker?" *Business Week*, February 22, 1999, 113–161.

[10]Borzou Daragahi, "E-Finance Forecast," *Money*, March 2001, 129–33; Joseph Kahn, "Schwab Lands Feet First on Net," *New York Times*, February 10, 1999, C1, C5.

[11]See Alexander, Sharpe, and Bailey, *Fundamentals of Investments*, 39.

[12]See Alexander, Sharpe, and Bailey, *Fundamentals of Investments*, 36–39.

[13]See Alexander, Sharpe, and Bailey, *Fundamentals of Investments*, 44–46.

[14]Nasdaq (June 25, 2000) at <www.nasdaq.com/about/ timeline.stm>.

[15]NASD (June 25, 2000) at <www.nasd.com>.

[16]"The World in Its Hands," *The Economist*, May 6, 2000, 77; "The Nasdaq Japan Market Launches First Day of Trading; First Step in Creating Nasdaq Global Platform Is Achieved" (June 19, 2000); at <www.nasdaq.co.uk/ reference>. "Globalization and International Reach" (June 23, 2000) at *Nasdaq Initiatives* at <www.nasdaq.com>.

[17]See Frank J. Fabozzi, *Bond Markets, Analysis and Strategies*, 4th ed. (Upper Saddle River, NJ: Prentice Hall, 2000), Chapter 1; Keown et al., *Financial Management*, Chapter 7.

[18]*Federal Reserve Bulletin* (July 2001), A25, A27, A28, A31, A37, A38, A41.

[19]See Fabozzi, *Bond Markets, Analysis and Strategies*, Chapter 7.

[20]See George W. Tivoli, *Personal Portfolio Management: Fundamentals and Strategies* (Upper Saddle River, NJ: Prentice Hall, 2000), Chapter 5.

[21]*Wiesenberger Mutual Funds Update* (Rockville, MD: CDA Investment Technologies, August 31, 2000) iv–ix.

[22]See Alexander, Sharpe, and Bailey, *Fundamentals of Investments*, 39–43.

[23]Gretchen Morgenson, "Buying on Margin Becomes a Habit," *New York Times*, March 24, 2000, C1, C7; David Barboza, "Wall Street after Dark," *New York Times*, February 13, 2000, BU1, BU14–BU15.

[24]See Alexander, Sharpe, and Bailey, *Fundamentals of Investments*, 37–38.

[25]U.S. Securities and Exchange Commission, *SEC Litigation Release* no. 16591 (June 29, 2000) at <www.sec.gov>.

Source Notes

CHAPTER 1

What's Hot on the Cyberspace Hit List / Sounding Out the Music-Industry Oligopoly Robert La Franco, "Record Companies, Awake!" *Forbes*, November 15, 1999, pp. 76-80; Laura M. Holson, "Conducting Music's Digital Shift," *The New York Times*, August 20, 2001, pp. C1, C10; Courtney, Macavinta, "Launch Media Makes First Foray into Retail," *CNet News.com* (January 31, 2000), at <http://news.cnet.com/news/0-1005-200-1538457.html?tag=rltdnws>; Beth Cox, "Yahoo! Acquiring Launch Media," *InternetNews* (June 28, 2001), at <www.internetnews.com/streaming-news/article/ 0,,8161_793351,00.html>. **It's a Wired World: *Electronic B2B in the Auto Industry*** Keith Bradsher, "Carmakers to Buy Parts on Internet," *The New York Times*, February 26, 2000, pp. A1, C14; "Big Three Car Makers Plan Net Exchange," *The Wall Street Journal*, February 28, 2000, pp. A3, A16; Lee Copeland, "Major Automakers Team Up on Second B2B Venture," *CNN.com* (December 11, 2000), at <www.cnn.com/ 2000/TECH/computing/12/11/automaker. portal.idg/>; David Welch, "Can Covisint Climb Out of a Ditch?" *Business Week*, May 21, 2001, pp. 128B, 128D; Robyn Meredith, "Harder Than the Hype," *Forbes.com* (April 16, 2001), at <www.forbes.com/global/2001/0416/082. html>. **Figure 1.1** Adapted from Karl E. Case and Ray C. Fair, *Principles of Economics*, 6th ed. (Upper Saddle River, NJ: Prentice Hall, 2002), p. 47. **Figure 1.4** United Auto Workers, *AUW Research Bulletin: Productivity and Growth* (March 9, 2001) at <http://uaw.com/publications/ jobs_pay/0700/jpe.html>. Data from Bureau of Economic Analysis, U.S. Dept. of Commerce; Bureau of Labor Statistics, U.S. Dept. of Labor. **Table 1.4** Robert A. Collinge and Ronald M. Ayers, *Economics by Design: Principles and Issues* (Upper Saddle River, NJ: Prentice Hall, 2000), p. 357. Data from *1999 Economic Report of the President*, Table B-60. **Figure 1.5** Michael J. Mandel, "The New Economy," *Business Week*, January 31, 2000, p. 75. Data from *Computer Industry Almanac*. **Figure 1.6** Mandel, "The New Economy," p. 77. Data from International Data Corp. Figure 1.7 Mandel, "The New Economy," p. 75. Data from Standard & Poor's DRI.

CHAPTER 2

The New ETO (European Theater of Operations / It's a Smallworld.com After All William Echikson, Carol Matlack, and David Vannier, "American E-Tailers Take Europe by Storm," *Business Week*, August 7, 2000, pp. 54-55; Matlack, "eBay Steams into Europe," *BusinessWeek Online* (October 16, 2000), at <www.businessweek. com:/2000/00_42/b3703183.htm>; Echikson, "Home Field Disadvantage," *Business Week*, December 13, 1999, pp. EB72-EB74; Nora Macaluso, "Europe's Online Auction War Rages On," *E-Commerce Times* (August 4, 2000), at <www.ecommercetimes.com/ perl/story/3956.html>; George Anders, "First E-Shopping, Now E-Swapping," *Wall Street Journal*, January 17, 2000, pp. B1, B4; Miguel Helft, "Going, Going . . .," *The Industry Standard* (June 26, 2000), at <www.thestandard.com/ article/0,1902,16025,00. html>; "E-Europe: Top 25 Web Sites in Europe," *CNN.com* (September 12, 2001), at <www.cnn.com/SPECIALS/2000/e.europe/ stories/top.25.sites/>. **Table 2.1** *Hoover's Handbook of World Business 2001* (Austin, TX: Hoover's Business Press, 2001), p. 52. Data from: <http://www.ita.doc.gov/td/industry/otea/u stth/tabcon.html>. **It's a Wired World: *Nokia Puts the Finishing Touches on a Communications Giant*** Justin Fox, "Nokia's Secret Code," *Fortune*, May 1, 2000, pp. 160-74; "It Takes a Cell Phone," *The Wall Street Journal*, June 25, 1999, pp. B1, B4; Tish Williams, "Nokia Won't Be Reading from Motorola's Script," *The Street.com* (July 16, 2001), at <www.thestreet.com_cnet/tech/ telecom/1490870.html>; Joris Evers, "Ericsson, Nokia, Motorola Team on Mobile IM," *PCWorld.com* (April 26, 2001), at <www.pcworld.com/news/ article/0,aid, 48570,00.asp>. **Figure 2.4** Michael E. Porter, *The Competitive Advantage of Nations* (New York: Free Press, 1990), p. 72. **Table 2.2** Robyn Meredith, "Dollar Makes Canada a Land of the Spree," *The New York Times*, August 1, 1999, p. C11. **Figure 2.5 & Figure 2.6** *Survey of Current Business*, July 2000 (Washington, DC: U.S. Department of Commerce), pp. 88-89. **Building Your Business Skills: *"I Intend to Be a Global Company"*** Maria Atanasov, "Taking Her Business on the Road," *Fortune*, April 13, 1998, pp. 158-60.

CHAPTER 3

A Tale of Two Companies / Some Ethical Rants and Raves **Hoover's Handbook of American Business 2000** (Austin, TX: Hoover's Business Press, 2000), pp. 750-51; Roger Rosenblatt, "Reaching the Top by Doing the Right Thing," *Time*, October 18, 1999, pp. 89-91; Jacquelyn A. Ottman, "Patagonia: A Deep-Seated Commitment to Environmentalism," *Green Marketing* (February 2001), at <www.greenmarketing.com/ Green_Marketing_Book/Patagonia.html>; Richard Fleming, "Patagonia's Journey to Sustainability," *LOHAS Journal* (January 2001), at <www.lohasjournal.com/ja01/ patagonia.html>; Elliott Blair Smith, "Stench Chokes Nebraska Meatpacking Towns," *USA Today*, February 14, 2000, pp. 1B, 2B; Nikki Tait, "Tyson Agrees to

$32b Deal for IBP," *The Financial Times,* January 2, 2001, p. 13; Greg Winter, "After a Rocky Courtship, Tyson and IBP Will Merge," *The New York Times,* June 28, 2001, p. C6. **Figures 3.1 & 3.2** Based on Gerald S. Cavanaugh, *American Business Values: With International Perspectives,* 4th ed. (Upper Saddle River, NJ: Prentice Hall, 1998), pp. 71 and 84. **It's a Wired World: *When It Comes to Privacy, It's a Small World After All*** Michael Schrage, "If You Passed Notes in School, You'll Love This Idea," *Fortune,* May 1, 2000, p. 340; Michael J. McCarthy, "Your Manager's Policy on Employees' E-Mail May Have a Weak Spot," *The Wall Street Journal,* April 25, 2000, pp. A1, A10; Rich Morin, "Read an E-Mail, Lose Your Privacy," *CNN.com* (January 14, 2000), at <www.cnn.com/2000/TECH/computing/01/14/email.privacy.idg/>; "It's Time for Rules in Wonderland," *Time,* March 20, 2000, pp. 83-96. **Figure 3.3** David P. Baron, *Business and Its Environment,* 3rd ed. (Upper Saddle River, NJ: Prentice Hall, 2000), p. 669. **Figure 3.5** Based on Andrew C. Revkin, "Who Cares about a Few Degrees?" *The New York Times,* December 12, 1997, p. F1. **Table 3.1** The Foundation Center, "Fifty Largest Corporate Foundations by Total Giving" (July 10, 2001), at <fdncenter.org/research/trends_analysis/top50giving.html>.

CHAPTER 4

Planting the Seeds of a Netpreneurial Idea / Tapping Out Edward O. Welles, "The Perfect Internet Business," *Inc.,* August 1999, pp. 70-74+; Penelope Patsuris, "Disaster of the Day: Garden.com," *Forbes.com* (November 15, 2000), at <www.forbes.com/20.../1115disaster.html>; Greg Sandoval, "Garden.com Throwing in the Trowel," *The New York Times on the Web* (November 15, 2000), at <www.nytimes.com/cnet/CNET_0_4_3698475_00.html>; Monica Summers, "Garden.com to Close Retail Operations, Cut Jobs," *BusinessWeek Online* (November 15, 2000), at <www.businessweek.com>. **Figures 4.1, 4.2 & 4.3** Data from U.S. Department of Commerce, "Statistics about Business Size (Including Small Business) from the U.S. Census Bureau," *Statistical Abstract of the United States* (September 6, 2001), at <www.census.gov/epcd/www/smallbus.html>. **Figure 4.4** Based on Nancy A. Kubasek, Bartley A. Brennan, and M. Neil Browne, *The Legal Environment of Business,* 2nd ed. (Upper Saddle River, NJ: Prentice Hall, 1999), p. 346. Reprinted by permission of Prentice Hall Inc., Upper Saddle River, NJ. **Figure 4.5** Norman M. Scarborough and Thomas W. Zimmerer, *Effective Small Business Management: An Entrepreneurial Approach,* 6th ed. (Upper Saddle River, NJ: Prentice Hall, 2000), p. 15. Data from Forrester Research Inc. **It's a Wired World: *A Wealth of Investors for Picky Tech Start-Ups*** Deborah Solomon, "A Wealth of Investors for Picky Tech Start-Ups," *USA Today,* February 8, 2000, p. 1B.

CHAPTER 5

Grounds for the Defense / Down East Showdown Louise Lee, "Now, Starbucks Uses Its Bean," *Business Week,* February 14, 2000, pp. 92-93; Vijay Vishwanath and David Harding, "The Starbucks Effect," *Harvard Business Review,* March-April 2000, pp. 17-18; Joseph Rosenbloom, "Battle Grounds," *Inc.,* July 1999, pp. 53-57; Joel Kotkin, "Helping the Little Guy Fight the Big Guy," *The New York Times,* October 24, 1999, p. 7. **Figure 5.1** Based on Thomas L. Wheelen and J. David Hunger, *Strategic Management and Business Policy,* 7th ed. (Upper Saddle River, NJ: Prentice Hall, 2000), p. 13. **Figure 5.2** Based on Stephen P. Robbins and Mary Coulter, *Management,* 6th ed. (Upper Saddle River, NJ: Prentice Hall, 1999), p. 239. **It's a Wired World: *How to Spot the E-CEO*** Geoffrey Colvin, "How to Be a Great E-CEO," *Fortune,* May 24, 1999, pp. 104-10; Patricia Sellers, "The Big Score," *Fortune,* February 7, 2000, pp. 134-46; David Leonhardt, "At Graduate Schools, a Great Divide Over E-Business Studies," *The New York Times,"* January 16, 2000, p. 7. **Table 5.1** Geoffrey Colvin, "How to Be a Great E-CEO," *Fortune,* May 24, 1999, pp. 107. **Building Your Business Skills: *Speaking with Power*** Information from Justin Martin, "How You Speak Shows Where You Rank," *Fortune,* February 2, 1998, p. 156.

CHAPTER 6

Forging E-Connections / Building on Cybersites Bob Tedeschi, "Construction Heads into the Internet Age," *The New York Times,* February 21, 2000, pp. C1, C9; Melanie Warner, "Bidcom," *Fortune,* July 5, 1999, pp. 100-04; Edward Iwata, "Despite the Hype, B2B Marketplaces Struggle," *USA Today,* May 10, 2000, pp. 1B, 2B; *Hoover's Handbook of American Business 2001* (Austin, TX: Hoover's Business Press, 2001), pp. 232-33, 1412-13. **It's a Wired World: *Hot-Wiring Ford*** David Welch, "At Ford, E-Commerce Is Job 1," *Business Week,* February 28, 2000, pp. 74-78; Ford Motor Co., "Ford to Bring Internet to Millions of Vehicles," *Techmall* (January 9, 2001), at <www8.techmall.com/techdocs/TS000110-3.html>; Chuck Moozakis, "Ford to Conduct Parts Design Online," *Internet Week* (January 3, 2001), at <www.internetwek.com/story/INW20010103S0001>; Gavin McCormick, "Ford: Oculus' Technology without Peer," *Internet.com* (May 27, 2001), at <http://boston.internet.com/news/article/ 0,1928,2001_725141,00.html>; Eryn Brown, "Nine Ways to Win on the Web," *Fortune,* May 24, 1999, pp. 112-25.

CHAPTER 7

"Speed Is Everything" / Got a Problem with Your Peripheral? Ask Dudley Adam Aston, "How Dell Keeps from Stumbling," *Business Week,* May 14, 2001, pp. 38B-38D; Andrew Park and Peter Burrows, "Dell, the Conqueror," *Business Week,* September 24, 2001, pp. 92-93+; John H. Sheridan, "Dell Courts Customers Online," *Industry Week,* April 3, 2000, p. 23; April Jacobs, "Dell Takes Aim at Internet with One-Stop Shopping," *Network World,* April 10, 2000, p. 8; Paul McDougall, "Dell Mounts Internet Push to Diversify Revenue," *Informationweek,* April 10, 2000, p. 32; Judi Patrizi, "Dell Dominates Direct Sales," *Industry Week,* April 17, 2000, p. 60; John H. Sheridan, "Now It's a Job for the CEO," *Industry Week,* March 20, 2000, pp. 22-26; Barbara Schmitz, "Dell Computer Builds a Framework for Success," *CAE: Computer-Aided Engineering,* February 2000, p. 10; Michael Dell, "21st Century Commerce," *Executive Excellence,* December 1999, pp. 3-4. **Figure 7.1** Bureau of Labor Statistics, *Employment & Earnings,* June 2001 (Washington, DC: Dept. of Labor, 2001), p. 70. **Figure 7.2** *Survey of Current Business,* June 2001 (Washington, DC: Dept. of Commerce, 2001), p. D4. **It's a Wired World: *Selling the Idea of Culture Shift*** Philip Siekman, "Mercury Marine: Focusing on the Demand Side," *Fortune [Industrial Management & Technology],* November 8, 1999, pp. 272[N]-272[O]; "Mercury: The Water Calls" (May 22, 2000), at <www.mercurymarine.com/mercuryhome/merchome.cfm>; Lynne M. Almvig, "Robotics Milling Department," *Robotics Today,* First Quarter 2000, pp. 1-4.

CHAPTER 8

A New Deal in the Workplace / What Did You Expect? Jerry Useem, "Welcome to the New Company Town," *Fortune,* January 10, 2000, pp. 62-70; Nicholas Stein, "Winning the War to Keep Top Talent," *Fortune,* May 29, 2000, pp. 132-138; Robert Levering and Milton Moskowitz, "The 100 Best Companies to Work For," *Fortune,* January 10, 2000, pp. 82-110; John J. Clancy, "Is Loyalty Really Dead?" *Across the Board,* June 1999, pp. 15-19. **Figure 8.1** "Corporations That Prize Skills and Hands-On Experience Are Adapting at the Fringes," *Time,* November 9, 1998, p. 21. **Figure 8.2** A.H. Maslow, *Motivation and Personality,* 2nd ed. (Upper Saddle River, NJ: Prentice Hall, 1970). Reprinted by permission of Prentice Hall Inc. **It's a Wired World: *The Future of Compensation?*** "Hire Now, Pay Later?" *Forbes,* August 23, 1999, p. 62; "Net Start-Ups Pull Out of the Garage," *USA Today,* October 1, 1999, pp. 1B, 2B; "From Zip to Zoom: An Internet Success Story," *Female Executives Network* (November 18, 1999), at <www.femaleexecutives.com/nov.18.htm>; Liz Garone, "99% Brains, 1% Sweat for These Tech Bigwigs," *San Mateo County Times* (September 13, 2001), at <www.garone.com/writing/millions.html>.

CHAPTER 9

And All the M&Ms You Can Eat . . . / How Paternal Is Too Paternal? Charles Fishman, "Sanity Inc.," *Fast Company,* January 1999, pp. 84-96; Michelle Conlin and Kathy Moore with Anne States, "Dr. Goodnight's Company Town," *Business Week,* June 19, 2000, pp. 192-96+; "SAS Institute," *ZDNet News* (April 10, 2000), at <www.zdnet. com/zdnn/stories/news/0,4586,2523215-7,00.html>; Robert Levering and Milton Moskowitz, "The 100 Best Companies to Work For," *Fortune,* January 10, 2000, pp. 82-110; "High Tech Snapsots: SAS Institute," *JobCircle* (September 14, 2001), at <www.jobcircle.com/career/profiles/171.html>. **It's a Wired World: *Companies Put Web to Work as Recruiter*** Stephanie Arour, "Companies Put Web to Work as Recruiter," *USA Today,* January 25, 2000, p. 1B. **Figure 9.2** *The Wall Street Journal Almanac 1999,* p. 226. Reprinted by Permission of Dow Jones Inc. via Copyright Clearance Center Inc. © 1999 Dow Jones and Co. Inc. All rights reserved. **Figure 9.3(a)** Adapted from David Whitford, "Labor's Lost Chance," *Fortune,* September 28, 1998, p. 180. **Figure 9.3(b)** Dan Seligman, "Driving the AFL-CIO Crazy," *Forbes,* November 1, 1999, p. 106. Data from Leo Troy and Neil Sheflin, *Union Sourcebook* (1985) and Barry T. Hirsch and David A. MacPherson, *Union Membership and Earnings Data Book* (1999).

CHAPTER 10

Xbox Spots the Market / Microsoft's Great Xpectations Chris Gaither, "Microsoft Explores a New Territory: Fun," *The New York Times,* November 4, 2001, Sec. 3, pp. 1, 7; Leslie P. Norton, "Toy Soldiers," *Barron's,* May 14, 2001, pp. 25-30; Chris Taylor, "The Battle of Seattle," *Time,* May 21, 2001, pp. 58-59; N'Gai Croal, "Game Wars 5.0," *Newsweek,* May 28, 2001, pp. 65+; Tobi Elkin, "The X Factor: Microsoft, Sony Prepare for E3," *Advertising Age,* April 23, 2001, pp. 4+.; Bill Powell, "Gamemakers Aren't Racking Up Bonus Points," *Fortune,* April 16, 2001, p. 58; Danny Bradbury, "Home Free," *Communications International,* February 2001, p. 41; Tobi Elkin, "Gearing Up for Xbox Lunch," *Advertising Age,* November 20, 2000, pp. 16+. **Figure 10.2** Erick Schonfield, "Changes in the U.S. Population: Betting on the Boomers," *Fortune,* December 25, 1995, pp. 78–80. Reprinted from the December 25, 1995 issue of *Fortune* by special permission; copyright 1995, Time Inc. **It's a Wired World: *Better Health through Cyberspace Demographics*** *Costpredict: Organizational Health Cost Analysis* (Columbia, MO: Network Health Systems®, 2000); © *Health & Lifestyle Assessment Handbook* (Columbia, MO: Network Health Systems®, 1999).

CHAPTER 11

Strike Up the Bandwidth / Why RIAA Is Riled Amy Kover, "Who's Afraid of This Kid?" *Fortune,* March 20, 2000, pp. 129-30; Kover, "The Hot Idea of the Year," *Fortune,* June 26, 2000, pp. 128-30+; Stewart Alsop, "Bye-Bye Music Business," *Fortune,* March 20, 2000, p. 72; Devin Leonard, "The Music Men Are Out of Tune," *Fortune,* June 11, 2001, pp. 144-48; Shawn Tully, "Big Man against Big Music," *Fortune,* August 14, 2000, pp. 186-88+; Spencer E. Ante, "Inside Napster," *Business Week,* August 14, 2000, pp. 112-16+; Jack Ewing, "A New Powerhouse," *Business Week,* November 13, 2000, pp. 46-50+; "Swan Song?: Judge Shuts Down Napster," *ABC News Internet Ventures* (July 27, 2000), at <www.abcnews.go.com>; Laura Hodges, "This Is Not Your Founding Fathers' Copyright Law," *TNR Online* (December 8, 2000), at <www.thenewrepublic.com/cyberspace/hodes120800.html>; *"AM&M Records v. Napster:* MP3 File Sharing Disputes Continue in the Aftermath of Recent Court Rulings," *The UCLA Online Institute for Cyberspace Law and Policy* (June 7, 2001), at <www.gseis.ucla/iclp/napster.htm>. Matt Richtel, "A New Suit against Online Music Sites," *The New York Times,* October 4, 2001, p. C4. **It's a Wired World: *The World of Cyberprice Bidding*** Shawn Tully, "The B2B Tool That Really Is Changing the World," *Fortune,* March 20, 2000, pp. 132-34+; Ken Zapinsky, "FreeMarkets Is the Easy Winner in Having the Biggest Stock Price Increase," Post-Gazette.com (April 9, 2000), at <www.post-gazette.com/businessnews/20000409stock.asp>; "American Management Systems and FreeMarkets Form Strategic Alliance to eEmpower Public Sector Purchasing," *AMS News Room* (March 9, 2000), at <www3.amsinc.com/CMC/newsroom.nsf/prMBRY-4HQM3Z>; "FreeMarkets and webPLAN Form Strategic Alliance to Deliver Web-Based B2B eMarketplace and e-Supply Chain Solutions," *TechMall* (May 16, 2000), at <www8.techmall.com/techdocs/TS000516-html>; Shawmut Capital Partners, "Leaseforum and FreeMarkets Partner to Power Equipment Remarketing," Our Portfolio (July 24, 2000), at <www.shawmutcapital.com/leaseforum.html>. **Figure 11.3** *Advertising Age,* September 25, 2000, p. S54.

CHAPTER 12

"Life, the Universe, and Everything" / Researching with a Purpose Leigh Buchanan, "The Smartest Little Company in America," *Inc.,* January 1999, pp. 42-54; Edward C. Baig, "'Shopping Bots' Are Hot to Trot," *USA Today,* December 1, 1999, p. 8D; Mick O'Leary, "Dialog's New Tools for Web-Age Knowledge Workers," *Online,* May/June 2000, pp. 91-92; Baig, "Online Buying Assistants Produce a Mixed Bag," *USA Today,* December 1, 1999, p. 8D; Rick Dove, "The Knowledge Worker," *Production,* June 1998, pp. 26-28; "What's Ahead for 2000?" *Information Today,* January 2000, pp. 1, 62+. **Figure 12.3** Adapted from Kenneth C. Laudon and Jane P. Laudon, *Management Information Systems: Organization and Technology in the Networked Enterprise,*

6th ed. (Upper Saddle River, NJ: Prentice Hall, 2000), p. 37. **It's a Wired World: *"These Two Companies Are a Natural Fit"*** Saul Hansell, "Two Become One, and Then What?" *The New York Times,* December 15, 2000), pp. C1, C7; Larry Dignan, "America Online to Merge," *ZDNet News* (January 10, 2000), at <www.zdnet. com/zdnn/stories/news/0,4586,2419558,00.html>; Dandeep Junnakar and Jim Hu, "AOL Buys Time Warner in Historic Merger," *CNET News.com* (January 10, 2000), at <http://news.cnet.com/news/0-1005-200-1518888.html>; "AOL Time Warner Merger Could Net Consumers More or Less," *CNN.com* (January 11, 2000), at <www7.cnn.com/2001/ TECH/computing/01/11/aol.tw.merger/>; Sally C. Pipes, "AOL's Access Saga," *Chief Executive,* March 2000, p. 18; "FTC Approves AOL/Time Warner Merger with Conditions," *Federal Trade Commission* (December 14, 2000), at <www.ftc.gov/opa/ 2000/12/aol.htm>; Jeffrey Chester, "Will the AOL-Time Merger Flop?" *AlterNet* (October 6, 2000), at <www.alternet.org/print.html?StoryID=9886>.

CHAPTER 13

Why Banks Have to Clean Up Their Transactions / Securing Exchanges Paul Beckett, "U.S. Trust Unit of Schwab Gets $10 Million Fine by Regulators," *Wall Street Journal,* July 16, 2001, pp. C1, C15; Alan S. Abel and James S. Gerson, "The CPA's Role in Fighting Money Laundering," *Journal of Accountancy,* June 2001, pp. 26-31; "Global Fraud: A Growth Industry," *Financial Executive,* May 2001, p. 11; Ivan Schneider, "Some Firms Elude Anti-Money Laundering Rules," *Bank Systems & Technology,* July 2001, p. 8; "SEC to Focus on Money Laundering Efforts by Broker-Dealers," "Treasury Reviewing SAR Rules," "FinCEN Warns of Link between Phone Card Sales and Money Laundering," *ABA Banking Compliance,* June 2001, p. 6; Nigel Morris-Cotterill, "Money Laundering," *Foreign Policy,* May/June 2001, pp. 14-22; Ivan Schneider, "Cleaning House," *Bank Systems & Technology,* May 2001, pp. 24-28. **It's a Wired World: *A Roundabout Look at Conflicting Interests*** David LeonHardt, "Consultants Are Putting a New Price On Advice," *The New York Times,* January 19, 2000, pp. C1, C10; Floyd Norris, "Accounting Firm Is Said to Violate Rules Routinely," *The New York Times,* January 7, 2000, pp. A1, C6; Norris, "Rules That Only an Accountant Could Fail to Understand?" *The New York Times,* January 8, 2000, pp. C1, C14. **Figure 13.1** Adapted from "CPA Vision Project: 2011 and Beyond" (September 18, 2001) at <www.cpavision.org/final report>; **Tables 13.1 & 13.2** Adapted from "CPA Vision Project: 2011 and Beyond" (September 18, 2001) at <www.cpavision.org/ final report>.

CHAPTER 14

Europe Cashes In / Gentlemen, Start Your Euros! David Fairlamb, "Ready, Set, Euros!" *Business Week,* July 2, 2001, pp. 48-50; Fairlamb with Gail Edmondson, "Out from Under the Table," *Business Week,* September 24, 2001, pp. 116-18; Suzanne Daley, "New Currency Feeding Jitters for Europeans," *The New York Times,* August 15, 2001, pp. A1, A6; Keith Nuthall, "Anyone for Euros?" *The Banker,* June 2001, pp. 98-99; Carolyn Aldred, "Euro Transition Mints New Risks," *Business Insurance,* July 9, 2001, p. 17; "Readiness for Euro Is Falling," *Credit Management,* July 2001, p. 8; Jack White and Doug Ramsey, "Editorial Commentary: Making New Money," *Barron's,* April 23, 2001, p. 59; Parveen Bansal, "All in an E-Day's Work," *The Banker,* May 2001, pp. 110-11. **Figure 14.1** Data compiled from Federal Reserve Board of Governors (July 16, 2001) at <www.stls.frb.org/fred/data/ monetary/>. **It's a Wired World: *To E-Bank or not to E-Bank*** Bill Streeter, "Who's In Charge: The Dot-Coms vs. the Banks," *ABA Banking Journal,* February 2000, pp. 43, 45, 46; "You and Your Bank on the Net: The Next Generation and the 'Nyet' Generation," *ABA Banking Journal,* February 2000, pp. S13-S15; Bill Orr, "Easy Money," *ABA Banking Journal,* March 2000, pp. 41, 42, 46, 47; Alex Sheshunoff, "Internet Banking—An Update from the Frontlines," *ABA Banking Journal,* January 2000, pp. 51-55.

CHAPTER 15

Is Volatility Here to Stay? / The Stuff That Rumors and Inflated Expectations Are Made Of E. S. Browning, Greg Ip, and Leslie Scism, "With Dazzling Speed, Market Roars Back to Another New High," *The Wall Street Journal,* November 24, 1998, p. A1; James M. Pethokoukis and Mind Charski, "Lessons Learned: The Volatile Market Is Trying to Tell Us Something," *U.S. News & World Report,* September 21, 1998, pp. 651; Fred Vogelstein and William J. Holstein, "Fasten Your Seat Belts," *U.S. News & World Report,* October 26, 1998, pp. 43–46; "Circuit Breakers and Other Market Volatility Procedures," *Securities and Exchange Commission* (September 18, 2001), at <www.sec.gov/answers/circuit.htm>; Stephen Labaton, "S.E.C. Waives Some Rules to Try to Ease Market Volatility," *The New York Times,* September 15, 2001, pp. C1, C4; Rosemarie Maldonado, "Blame for Volatility Belongs to Street and Media," *Investment News* (May 28, 2001), at <www.investmentnews.com/news/010528-18-002453.shtml>. **Figure 15.1** "Wal-Mart Stores," "Yahoo Inc.," *Quicken.com* (July 31, 2001), at <www.quicken.com/investments/charts/...>. **Figure 15.2** Leah Nathans Spiro and Edward C. Baig, "Who Needs a Broker?" *Business Week,* February 22, 1999, pp. 113-16+. **It's a Wired World: *Opening the Portals to Cross-Border Training*** "Grappling With Change," *The Economist,* April 29, 2000, pp. 71-72; "The World at Its Hands," *The Economist,* May 6, 2000, p. 77. **Figure 15.5** Data from *The Wall Street Journal.* **Figure 15.6** Nasdaq, "Market Performance & Highlights: Section 3," *Nasdaq.com* (June 23, 2000), at <www.nasdaq.com/about/NBW2000Sec3.pdf>.

Cartoon, Photo, and Screen Credits

CHAPTER 1

Page 3/25: Reuters/Fred Prouser/Getty Images Inc.; page 5: The New Yorker Collection 1992 William Hamilton from cartoonbank.com. All Rights Reserved. page 8: Thomas Sandberg. page 14: Used with permission of bebe stores, Inc. © 2001. All Rights Reserved. bebe is a registered trademark of bebe stores, Inc. page 15: Reuters/HO/Getty Images, Inc. page 17: Joao Silva/New York Times Pictures.

CHAPTER 2

Page 31/52: Amazon.co.uk. page 33: Thomas J. Mueller. page 36 (top): Used with permission of www.Letsbuyit.com. page 36 (bottom): Heimo Aga. page 45: © AFP/Corbis. page 46: © 2001 Robert Mankoff from cartoonbank.com. All Rights Reserved. page 47: Bernd Auers. page 49: Used with permission of Al

Ahram Beverages Co. page 51: Claude Paris/AP/Wide World Photos.

CHAPTER 3

Page 59/81: Jean-Marc Giboux/Getty Images, Inc. page 65: AP/Wide World Photos. page 67 (top): Willis Knight/Fort Worth-Star-Telegram/SIPA Press. page 67 (bottom): © 2000 The New Yorker Collection 1997 Leo Cullum from cartoonbank.com. All Rights Reserved. page 71: Ch. Simonpietri/Corbis/Sygma. page 72: Used with permission of Patagonia, Inc. page 73: John G. Mabanglo/Agence France-Presse. page 75: Used with permission of ESOMAR. page 80: Ken Gabrielsen/Kenneth Gabrielsen Photography.

CHAPTER 4

Page 87/108: Bill Bastas/Pearson Education/PH College. page 91: Norman Y. Lono/New York Times Pictures. page 92: © Mark Langello Photography. page 94: Used with permission of Pentagram Design Inc. page 103 (top): Robert King/ Corbis/Sygma. page 103 (bottom): The New Yorker Collection 1993 Ed Fisher from cartoonbank.com. All Rights Reserved. page 106: © Kevin Fleming/ Corbis. page 108: Used with permission of U.S. Small Business Association.

CHAPTER 5

Page 115/134: Tim Gray/Furnald/Gray Photography. page 120: Bastienne Schmidt/Bastienne Schmidt. page 121: Used with permission of www.virgin.com. page 125: Mark Peterson/Corbis/SABA Press Photos, Inc. page 127: R. McHam/ Business Week. page 131: Kistone Photography. page 133: The New Yorker Collection 1994 Mick Stevens from cartoonbank.com. All Rights Reserved. page 134: © Ted Rice 1999.

CHAPTER 6

Page 141/160: Thor Swift/New York Times Pictures. page 145: © Walt Disney Pictures/Photofest. page 146: Mark Richards. page 147: Used with permission of IBM, Inc. page 150: Bill Cawley. page 154: © 2001 W.B. Park from cartoonbank.com. All Rights Reserved. page 157: Bernd Auers.

CHAPTER 7

Page 165/188: Richard Drew/AP/Wide World Photos. page 168: Kenneth Chen/Kenneth Chen. page 171: Used with permission of Lightning Rod Software. page 175: Nancy Seisel/New York Times Pictures. page 180: Joe Traver/Getty Images, Inc. page 181: Used with permission of American Society of Quality. page 182: © The New Yorker Collection 1989 Robert Weber from cartoonbank.com. All Rights Reserved. page 183: Ray Ng Photography, Inc. page 185: Used with permission of Federal Express Corp.

CHAPTER 8

Page 195/215: Robert Wright/Robert Wright Photography. page 197: Bryce Duffy/Corbis/SABA Press Photos, Inc. page 198: Reprinted by permission of The Container Store. page 205: Greg Smith/Corbis/SABA Press Photos, Inc. page 207: Bryce Duffy/Corbis/SABA Press Photos, Inc. page 210: Used with permission of American Management Systems, Inc. page 211 (top): Robert Wright Photography. page 211 (bottom): © The New Yorker Collection 1992 Charles Barsotti from cartoonbank.com. All Rights Reserved. page 213: Reprinted by permission of Growth & Leadership Center (GLC), Mountain View, CA.

CHAPTER 9

Page 221/244: Ann States/Corbis/SABA Press Photos, Inc. page 225: Ann Grillo/New York Times Pictures. page 227: Len Rubenstein Photography. page 228: Used with permission of ManagedOps.com. page 236: John Madere/Corbis/Stock Market. page 239: © The New Yorker Collection 1993 Leo Cullum from cartoonbank.com. All Rights Reserved. page 240: Porter Gifford/Getty Images, Inc. page 242: Reprinted by permission of Labor Project for Working Families, Berkeley, CA. page 243: AP/Wide World Photos.

CHAPTER 10

Page 251/273: Chuck Fishman. page 253: Reprinted by permission of Harley-Davidson. page 255: AP/Wide World Photos. page 256: Decout/REA/Corbis/ SABA Press Photos, Inc. page 261: Nina Berman/SIPA Press. page 266: © The New Yorker Collection 1997 Bernard Schoenbaum from cartoonbank.com. All Rights Reserved. page 271: © 1999 Patrick ARTINIAN/CONTACT Press Images. page 272: Used with permission of Everex Systems, Inc.

CHAPTER 11

Page 279/299: Eric O'Connell Photography. page 283: James Schnepf Photography, Inc. page 287: Alon Reininger/Contact Press Images Inc. page 288: Used with permission by DoubleClick, Inc. page 290: © 1999 Girard Mouton, III. All Rights Reserved. page 293: Greg Girard/Contact Press Images Inc. page 295: Used with permission of razorfish.com. page 296: David Gamble. page 297: © The New Yorker Collection 2000 Lee Lorenz from cartoonbank.com. All Rights Reserved.

CHAPTER 12

Page 307/326: AP/Wide World Photos. page 311: Used with permission of National Confectioners Association. page 314 (top): © 2001 Robert Houser. page 477 (bottom): Reprinted by permission of Acumins, Inc. page 320: © The New Yorker Collection 1997 Peter Steiner from cartoonbank.com. All Rights Reserved. page 322: Photofest. page 324: Brownie Harris/Brownie Harris.

CHAPTER 13

Page 333/356: © Charles OíRear/Corbis. page 336: Reprinted by permission from www.aicpa.org. © 2001 by American Institute of Certified Public Accountants, Inc. page 338: © The New Yorker Collection 1992 Leo Cullum from cartoonbank.com. All Rights Reserved. page 342: AP/Wide World Photos. page 345: Howard Folsom/Photo Network. page 347: Patrick Artinian/Contact Press Images Inc. page 348: Michael Newman/PhotoEdit. page 353: AP/WideWorld Photos. page 354: Jonathan Barth/Liaison/ Getty Images/Planet Earth Pictures Ltd. page 355: Reprinted by permission of International Accounting Standards Board, London, England.

CHAPTER 14

Page 363/381: Sean Gallup/Getty Images/Planet Earth Pictures Ltd. page 365: Getty Images/Planet Earth Pictures Ltd. page 369: From www.cob.ohio-state.edu/dept/fin/overview.htm page. Reprinted by permission. page 370: Greg Miller Photography. Page 371: Peter Korniss. page 374: Used with permission of the U.S. Federal Reserve. page 378: Richard B. Levine; Frances

M. Roberts. page 380: © 2001 Mick Stevens from cartoonbank.com. All Rights Reserved.

CHAPTER 15

Page 387/406: Jonathan Saunders/Jonathan Saunders. page 389: Used with permission of the U.S. Securities and Exchange Commission. page 391: © Raimund Koch. page 394: Dod Miller/Network/Corbis/SABA Press Photos, Inc. page 395 (top): Richard B. Levine/Frances M. Roberts. page 395 (bottom): Reprinted by permission of the National Association of Securities Dealers, Inc. page 399: Used with permission of Dreyfus Service Corp. page 400: © The New Yorker Collection 1994 Mick Stevens from cartoonbank.com. All Rights Reserved.

Glossary

absolute advantage The ability to produce something more efficiently than any other country can [37]

accommodative stance Approach to social responsibility by which a company, if specifically asked to do so, exceeds legal minimums in its commitments to groups and individuals in its social environment [78]

account receivable Amount due from a customer who has purchased goods on credit [343]

accountability Liability of subordinates for accomplishing tasks assigned by managers [148]

accounting Comprehensive system for collecting, analyzing, and communicating financial information [335]

accounting system Organized means by which financial information is identified, measured, recorded, and retained for use in accounting statements and management reports [335]

accounts payable Current liabilities consisting of bills owed to suppliers, plus wages and taxes due within the upcoming year [345]

acquisition The purchase of one company by another [100]

activity ratio Financial ratio for evaluating management's use of a firm's assets [351]

advertising Promotional tool consisting of paid, nonpersonal communication used by an identified sponsor to inform an audience about a product [286]

advertising media Variety of communication devices for carrying a seller's message to potential customers [286]

affirmative action plan Practice of recruiting qualified employees belonging to racial, gender, or ethnic groups who are underrepresented in an organization [232]

agent Individual or organization acting for, and in the name of, another party [AP-19]

aggregate output Total quantity of goods and services produced by an economic system during a given period [15]

analytic process Production process in which resources are broken down into components to create finished products [169]

apparent authority Agent's authority, based on the principal's compliance, to bind a principal to a certain course of action [AP-19]

appellate court Court that reviews case records of trials whose findings have been appealed [AP-15]

application program Software (such as Word for Windows) that processes data according to a user's special needs [321]

artificial intelligence (AI) Computer-system application that imitates human behavior by performing physical tasks, using thought processes, sensing, and learning [319]

assembly line Product layout in which a product moves step-by-step through a plant on conveyor belts or other equipment until it is completed [174]

asset Any economic resource expected to benefit a firm or an individual who owns it [342]

audit Systematic examination of a company's accounting system to determine whether its financial reports fairly represent its operations [337]

authority Power to make the decisions necessary to complete a task [148]

autocratic style Managerial style in which managers generally issue orders and expect them to be obeyed without question [212]

automated teller machine (ATM) Electronic machine that allows customers to conduct account-related activities 24 hours a day, 7 days a week [371]

balance of payments Flow of all money into or out of a country [41]

balance of trade Economic value of all products a country imports minus the economic value of all products it exports [40]

balance sheet Financial statement detailing a firm's assets, liabilities, and owners' equity [343]

banker's acceptance Bank promise, issued for a buyer, to pay a designated firm a specified amount at a future date [370]

bankruptcy Permission granted by the courts to individuals and organizations not to pay some or all of their debts [AP-20]

bargain retailer Retailer carrying a wide range of products at bargain prices [296]

bear market Period of falling stock prices [402]

bearer (or coupon) bond Bond requiring the holder to clip and submit a coupon to receive an interest payment [398]

benefits Compensation other than wages and salaries [231]

bill of materials Production control tool that specifies the necessary ingredients of a product, the order in which they should be combined, and how many of each are needed to make one batch [180]

blue-chip stock Common stock issued by a well-established company with a sound financial history and a stable pattern of dividend payouts [389]

blue-sky laws Laws requiring securities dealers to be licensed and registered with the states in which they do business [406]

board of directors Governing body of a corporation that reports to its shareholders and delegates power to run its day-to-day operations while remaining responsible for sustaining its assets [98]

bond Security through which an issuer promises to pay the buyer a certain amount of money by a specified future date [396]

bonus Individual performance incentive in the form of a special payment made over and above the employee's salary [230]

book value Value of a common stock expressed as total shareholders' equity divided by the number of shares of stock [389]

bookkeeping Recording of accounting transactions [335]

boycott Labor action in which workers refuse to buy the products of a targeted employer [243]

branch office Foreign office set up by an international or multinational firm [48]

brand competition Competitive marketing that appeals to consumer perceptions of similar products [255]

brand loyalty Pattern of regular consumer purchasing based on satisfaction with a product [261]

branding Process of using symbols to communicate the qualities of a product made by a particular producer [269]

breakeven analysis Assessment of the quantity of a product that must be sold before the seller makes a profit [281]

breakeven point Quantity of a product that must be sold before the seller covers variable and fixed costs and makes a profit [281]

broker Individual or organization who receives and executes buy-and-sell orders on behalf of other people in return for commissions [391]

browser Software supporting the graphics and linking capabilities necessary to navigate the World Wide Web [311]

budget Detailed statement of estimated receipts and expenditures for a period of time in the future [348]

bull market Period of rising stock prices [402]

business An organization that provides goods or services to earn profits [5]

business (or **competitive**) **strategy** Strategy, at the business-unit or product-line level, focusing on a firm's competitive position [117]

business continuation agreement Special form of business insurance whereby owners arrange to buy the interests of deceased associates from their heirs [AP-12]

business cycle Pattern of short-term expansions and contractions in an economy [15]

business ethics Ethical or unethical behaviors by a manager or employer of an organization [61]

business interruption insurance Insurance covering income lost during times when a company is unable to conduct business [AP-11]

business practice law Law or regulation governing business practices in given countries [51]

business process reengineering Redesigning of business processes to improve quality, performance, and customer service [185]

cafeteria benefit plan Benefit plan that sets limits on benefits per employee, each of whom may choose from a variety of alternative benefits [231]

capacity In law, competence required of individuals entering into a binding contract [AP-16]

capacity In operations management, amount of a product that a company can produce under normal working conditions [172]

capital The funds needed to create and operate a business enterprise [6]

capital item Expensive, long-lasting, infrequently purchased industrial product such as a building [266]

capital structure Relative mix of a firm's debt and equity financing [AP-6]

capitalism Market economy that provides for private ownership of production and encourages entrepreneurship by offering profits as an incentive [8]

cartel Association of producers whose purpose is to control supply and prices [51]

cash-flow management Management of cash inflows and outflows to ensure adequate funds for purchases and the productive use of excess funds [AP-1]

catalog showroom Bargain retailer in which customers place orders for catalog items to be picked up at on-premises warehouses [296]

cellular layout Spatial arrangement of production facilities designed to move families of products through similar flow paths [174]

centralized organization Organization in which most decision-making authority is held by upper-level management [149]

certified public accountant (CPA) Accountant licensed by the state and offering services to the public [336]

chain of command Reporting relationships within a company [143]

check Demand deposit order instructing a bank to pay a given sum to a specified payee [365]

check kiting Illegal practice of writing checks against money that has not yet been credited at the bank on which the checks are drawn [76]

chief executive officer (CEO) Top manager hired by the board of directors to run a corporation [98]

classical theory of motivation Theory holding that workers are motivated solely by money [199]

client-server network Information-technology system consisting of clients (users) that are electronically linked to share network resources provided by a server, such as a host computer [326]

closely held (or **private**) **corporation** Corporation whose stock is held by only a few people and is not available for sale to the general public [96]

collateral Borrower-pledged legal asset that may be seized by lenders in case of nonpayment [AP-3]

collective bargaining Process by which labor and management negotiate conditions of employment for union-represented workers [237]

collusion Illegal agreement between two or more companies to commit a wrongful act [73]

commercial bank Federal- or state-chartered financial institution accepting deposits that it uses to make loans and earn profits [367]

commercial paper Short-term securities, or notes, containing a borrower's promise to pay [AP-4]

committee and team authority Authority granted to committees or work teams involved in a firm's daily operations [152]

common law Body of decisions handed down by courts ruling on individual cases [AP-13]

common stock Stock that pays dividends and guarantees corporate voting rights but offers last claims over assets [98]

comparative advantage The ability to produce some products more efficiently than others [37]

compensation system Set of rewards that organizations provide to individuals in return for their willingness to perform various jobs and tasks within the organization [230]

compensatory damages Monetary payments intended to redress injury actually suffered because of a tort [AP-17]

competition Vying among businesses for the same resources or customers [12]

compulsory arbitration Method of resolving a labor dispute in which both parties are legally required to accept the judgment of a neutral party [244]

computer graphics program Applications program that converts numeric and character data into pictorial information such as graphs and charts [322]

computer network All the computer and information technology devices that, by working together, drive the flow of digital information throughout a system [320]

computer-aided design (CAD) Computer-based electronic technology that assists in designing products by simulating a real product and displaying it in three-dimensional graphics [318]

computer-aided manufacturing (CAM) Computer system used to design and control equipment needed in the manufacturing process [319]

conceptual skills Abilities to think in the abstract, diagnose and analyze different situations, and see beyond the present situation [129]

considerations Any item of value exchanged between parties to create a valid contract [AP-16]

consumer behavior Various facets of the decision process by which customers come to purchase and consume products [261]

consumer goods Products purchased by consumers for personal use [252]

consumer price index (CPI) Measure of the prices of typical products purchased by consumers living in urban areas [20]

consumerism Form of social activism dedicated to protecting the rights of consumers in their dealings with businesses [73]

contingency approach to managerial style Approach to managerial style holding that the appropriate behavior in any situation is dependent (contingent) on the unique elements of that situation [213]

contingency planning Identifying aspects of a business or its environment that might entail changes in strategy [122]

contingent worker Employee hired on something other than a full-time basis to supplement an organization's permanent workforce [236]

contract Agreement between two or more parties enforceable in court [AP-16]

control chart Process control method that plots test sampling results on a diagram to determine when a process is beginning to depart from normal operating conditions [183]

controller Person who manages all of a firm's accounting activities (chief accounting officer) [335]

controlling Management process of monitoring an organization's performance to ensure that it is meeting its goals [125]

convenience good/service Inexpensive product purchased and consumed rapidly and regularly [266]

convenience store Retail store offering easy accessibility, extended hours, and fast service [297]

copyright Exclusive ownership right belonging to the creator of a book, article, design, illustration, photo, film, or musical work [AP-18]

corporate bond Bond issued by a company as a source of long-term funding [397]

corporate culture The shared experiences, stories, beliefs, and norms that characterize an organization [132]

corporate governance Roles of shareholders, directors, and other managers in corporate decision making [97]

corporate strategy Strategy for determining the firm's overall attitude toward growth and the way it will manage its businesses or product lines [117]

corporation Business that is legally considered an entity separate from its owners and is liable for its own debts; owners' liability extends to the limits of their investments [95]

cost of goods sold Total cost of obtaining materials for making the products sold by a firm during the year [346]

cost-of-living adjustment (COLA) Labor contract clause tying future raises to changes in consumer purchasing power [241]

coupon Sales promotion technique in which a certificate is issued entitling the buyer to a reduced price [289]

credit union Financial institution that accepts deposits from, and makes loans to, only its members, usually employees of a particular organization [369]

crisis management Organization's methods for dealing with emergencies [123]

cumulative preferred stock Preferred stock on which dividends not paid in the past must be paid to stockholders before dividends can be paid to common stockholders [390]

currency Government-issued paper money and metal coins [365]

current asset Asset that can or will be converted into cash within the following year [343]

current liability Debt that must be paid within the year [345]

current ratio Solvency ratio that determines a firm's creditworthiness by measuring its ability to pay current liabilities [351]

customer departmentalization Departmentalization according to types of customers likely to buy a given product [146]

data Raw facts and figures [308]

data communication network Global network (such as the Internet) that permits users to send electronic messages and information quickly and economically [310]

data mining Process of searching, sifting, and reorganizing vast pools of data on purchases to reveal patterns of buyer behavior [288]

data warehousing Collection and storage of data in electronic files to be used in data analysis [288]

database Centralized, organized collection of related data [321]

database management program Applications program for creating, storing, searching, and manipulating an organized collection of data [321]

debenture Unsecured bond for which no specific property is pledged as security [398]

debit card Plastic card that allows an individual to transfer money between accounts [377]

debt A firm's total liabilities [352]

debt financing Long-term borrowing from sources outside a company [AP-4]

debt ratio Solvency ratio measuring a firm's ability to meet its long-term debts [352]

debt-to-owners' equity ratio (or **debt-to-equity ratio**) Solvency ratio describing the extent to which a firm is financed through borrowing [352]

decentralized organization Organization in which a great deal of decision-making authority is delegated to levels of management at points below the top [150]

decision support system (DSS) Interactive computer-based system that locates and presents information needed to support decision making [319]

decision-making skills Skills in defining problems and selecting the best courses of action [129]

defensive stance Approach to social responsibility by which a company meets only minimum legal requirements in its commitments to groups and individuals in its social environment [78]

delegation Assignment of a task, responsibility, or authority by a manager to a subordinate [148]

demand The willingness and ability of buyers to purchase a good or service [10]

demand and supply schedule Assessment of the relationships between different levels of demand and supply at different price levels [10]

demand curve Graph showing how many units of a product will be demanded (bought) at different prices [11]

demand deposit Bank account funds that may be withdrawn at any time [365]

democratic style Managerial style in which managers generally ask for input from subordinates but retain final decision-making power [212]

demographic variables Characteristics of populations that may be considered in developing a segmentation strategy [258]

department store Large product line retailer characterized by organization into specialized departments [295]

departmentalization Process of grouping jobs into logical units [145]

depreciation Process of distributing the cost of an asset over its life [344]

depression Particularly severe and long-lasting recession [21]

deregulation Elimination of rules that restrict business activity [AP-14]

desktop publishing Process of combining word-processing and graphics capability to produce virtually typeset-quality text from personal computers [322]

direct channel Distribution channel in which a product travels from producer to consumer without intermediaries [291]

direct mail Advertising medium in which messages are mailed directly to consumers' homes or places of business [286]

direct selling Form of nonstore retailing typified by door-to-door sales [297]

directing Management process of guiding and motivating employees to meet an organization's objectives [124]

direct-response retailing Nonstore retailing by direct interaction with customers to inform them of products and to receive sales orders [297]

disability income insurance Insurance providing continuous income when disability keeps the insured from gainful employment [AP-11]

discount Price reduction offered as an incentive to purchase [285]

discount house Bargain retailer that generates large sales volume by offering goods at substantial price reductions [296]

discount rate Interest rate at which member banks can borrow money from the Federal Reserve [376]

distribution Part of the marketing mix concerned with getting products from producers to consumers [257]

distribution channel Network of interdependent companies through which a product passes from producer to end user [291]

distribution mix Combination of distribution channels by which a firm gets its products to end users [290]

divestiture Strategy whereby a firm sells one or more of its business units [100]

division Department that resembles a separate business in producing and marketing its own products [153]

divisional organization Organizational structure in which corporate divisions operate as autonomous businesses under the larger corporate umbrella [153]

double taxation Situation in which taxes may be payable both by a corporation on its profits and by shareholders on dividend incomes [96]

double-entry accounting system Bookkeeping system that balances the accounting equation by recording the dual effects of every financial transaction [343]

Dow Jones Industrial Average (DJIA) Market index based on the prices of 30 of the largest industrial firms listed on the NYSE [402]

dumping Practice of selling a product abroad for less than the cost of production [52]

earnings per share Profitability ratio measuring the size of the dividend that a firm can pay shareholders [353]

e-cash Electronic money that moves between consumers and businesses via digital electronic transmissions [378]

e-catalog Nonstore retailing in which the Internet is used to display products [298]

economic strike Strike usually triggered by stalemate over one or more mandatory bargaining items [242]

economic system A nation's system for allocating its resources among its citizens [5]

e-intermediary Internet distribution channel member that assists in moving products through to customers or that collects information about various sellers to be presented in convenient format for Internet customers [294]

electronic conferencing Computer-based system that allows people to communicate simultaneously from different locations via software or telephone [310]

electronic funds transfer (EFT) Communication of fund-transfer information over wire, cable, or microwave [371]

electronic information technologies (EIT) Information-systems applications, based on telecommunications technologies, that use networks of appliances or devices to communicate information by electronic means [310]

electronic retailing Nonstore retailing in which information about the sellers' products is connected to consumers' computers, allowing consumers to receive the information and purchase the products in the home [297]

electronic spreadsheet Applications program with a row-and-column format that allows users to store, manipulate, and compare numeric data [321]

electronic storefront Commercial Web site in which customers gather information about products, buying opportunities, placing orders, and paying for purchases [298]

embargo Government order banning exportation and/or importation of a particular product or all products from a particular country [50]

eminent domain Principle that the government may claim private land for public use by buying it at a fair price [AP-19]

emotional motives Reasons for purchasing a product that are based on nonobjective factors [263]

employee information system (skills inventory) Computerized system containing information on each employee's education, skills, work experiences, and career aspirations [224]

employee stock ownership plan (ESOP) Arrangement in which a corporation holds its own stock in trust for its employees, who gradually receive ownership of the stock and control its voting rights [98]

employment-at-will Principle, increasingly modified by legislation and judicial decision, that organizations should be able to retain or dismiss employees at their discretion [233]

enterprise resource planning (ERP) Large information system for integrating all the activities of a company's business units [315]

entrepreneur Businessperson who accepts both the risks and the opportunities involved in creating and operating a new business venture [100]

environmental analysis Process of scanning the business environment for threats and opportunities [120]

equal employment opportunity Legally mandated nondiscrimination in employment on the basis of race, creed, sex, or national origin [232]

Equal Employment Opportunity Commission (EECO) Federal agency enforcing several discrimination-related laws [232]

equity financing Use of common stock and/or retained earnings to raise long-term funding [AP-5]

equity theory Theory of motivation holding that people evaluate their treatment by employers relative to the treatment of others [203]

ethical behavior Behavior conforming to generally accepted social norms concerning beneficial and harmful actions [61]

ethics Beliefs about what is right and wrong or good and bad in actions that affect others [61]

European Union (EU) Agreement among major Western European nations to eliminate or make uniform most trade barriers affecting group members [AP-22]

exchange rate Rate at which the currency of one nation can be exchanged for the currency of another country [41]

executive support system (ESS) Quick-reference information-system application designed specially for instant access by upper-level managers [319]

expectancy theory Theory of motivation holding that people are motivated to work toward rewards that they want and that they believe they have a reasonable chance of obtaining [201]

expense item Industrial product purchased and consumed rapidly and regularly for daily operations [266]

expert system Form of artificial intelligence that attempts to imitate the behavior of human experts in a particular field [320]

export Product made or grown domestically but shipped and sold abroad [32]

exporter Firm that distributes and sells products to one or more foreign countries [45]

express authority Agent's authority, derived from written agreement, to bind a principal to a certain course of action [AP-19]

express warranty Warranty whose terms are specifically stated by the seller [AP-20]

external environment Outside factors that influence marketing programs by posing opportunities or threats [253]

external failures Reducible costs incurred after defective products have left a plant [184]

external recruiting Attracting persons outside the organization to apply for jobs [226]

extranet Internet allowing outsiders access to a firm's internal information system [312]

factors of production Resources used in the production of goods and services—labor, capital, entrepreneurs, physical resources, and information resources [6]

factory outlet Bargain retailer owned by the manufacturer whose products it sells [296]

feature Tangible quality that a company builds into a product [265]

Federal Deposit Insurance Corporation (FDIC) Federal agency that guarantees the safety of all deposits up to $100,000 in the financial institutions that it insures [373]

Federal Reserve System (the Fed) Central bank of the United States, which acts as the government's bank, serves member commercial banks, and controls the nation's money supply [373]

fiber optic cable Glass-fiber cables that carry data in the form of light pulses [324]

finance company Nondeposit institution that specializes in making loans to businesses and consumers [369]

finance (or **corporate finance**) Activities concerned with determining a firm's long-term investments, obtaining the funds to pay for them, conducting the firm's every-day, financial activities, and managing the firm's risks [AP-1]

financial accounting system Field of accounting concerned with external users of a company's financial information [336]

financial manager Manager responsible for planning and controlling the acquisition and dispersal of a firm's financial resources [AP-1]

financial plan A firm's strategies for reaching some future financial position [AP-1]

financial statement Any of several types of reports summarizing a company's financial status to aid in managerial decision making [343]

firewall Software and hardware system that prevents outsiders from accessing a company's internal network [312]

first-line managers Managers responsible for supervising the work of employees [127]

fiscal policies Government economic policies that determine how the government collects and spends its revenues [22]

fixed asset Asset with long-term use or value, such as land, buildings, and equipment [344]

fixed cost Cost unaffected by the quantity of a product produced or sold [281]

flat organizational structure Characteristic of decentralized companies with relatively few layers of management and relatively wide spans of control [150]

flextime programs Method of increasing job satisfaction by allowing workers to adjust work schedules on a daily or weekly basis [208]

float Total amount of checks written but not yet cleared through the Federal Reserve [375]

follow-up Production control activity for ensuring that production decisions are being implemented [178]

foreign currency exchange rate Value of a nation's currency as determined by market forces [354]

foreign direct investment (FDI) Arrangement in which a firm buys or establishes tangible assets in another country [48]

franchise Arrangement in which a buyer (franchisee) purchases the right to sell the good or service of the seller (franchiser) [107]

free-rein style Managerial style in which managers typically serve as advisers to subordinates who are allowed to make decisions [213]

functional departmentalization Departmentalization according to groups' functions or activities [147]

functional organization Form of business organization in which authority is determined by the relationships between group functions and activities [153]

functional strategy Strategy by which managers in specific areas decide how best to achieve corporate goals through productivity [117]

gainsharing plan Incentive plan that rewards groups for productivity improvements [231]

General Agreement on Tariffs and Trade (GATT) International trade agreement to encourage the multilateral reduction or elimination of trade barriers [AP-21]

general partnership Business with two or more owners who share in both the operation of the firm and the financial responsibility for its debts [93]

generally accepted accounting principles (GAAP) Accepted rules and procedures governing the content and form of financial reports [337]

geographic departmentalization Departmentalization according to areas served by a business [147]

geographic variables Geographical units that may be considered in developing a segmentation strategy [258]

globalization Process by which the world economy is becoming a single interdependent system [32]

goal Objective that a business hopes and plans to achieve [117]

goods production Produces tangible products, such as radios, newspapers, buses, and textbooks [166]

goodwill Amount paid for an existing business above the value of its other assets [345]

government bond Bond issued by the federal government [397]

grapevine Informal communication network that runs through an organization [159]

graphical user interface (GUI) Software that provides a visual display to help users select applications [322]

gross domestic product (GDP) The value of all goods and services produced in a year by a nation's economy through domestic factors of production [16]

gross national product (GNP) The value of all goods and services produced by an economic system in a year regardless of where the factors of production are located [16]

gross profit (or **gross margin**) Revenues obtained from goods sold minus cost of goods sold [346]

group life insurance Insurance underwritten for a group as a whole rather than for each individual in it [AP-11]

groupware Software that connects members of a group for shared e-mail distribution, electronic meetings, appointments, and group writing [310]

hardware Physical components of a computer system [320]

Hawthorne effect Tendency for productivity to increase when workers believe they are receiving special attention from management [199]

health insurance Insurance covering losses resulting from medical and hospital expenses as well as income lost from injury or disease [AP-11]

health maintenance organization (HMO) Organized health care system providing comprehensive care in return for fixed membership fees [AP-11]

hierarchy of human needs model Theory of motivation describing five levels of human needs and arguing that basic needs must be fulfilled before people work to satisfy higher-level needs [200]

high-contact system Level of customer contact in which the customer is part of the system during service delivery [169]

hostile work environment Form of sexual harassment deriving from off-color jokes, lewd comments, and so forth [233]

human relations Interactions between employers and employees and their attitudes toward one another [196]

human relations skills Skills in understanding and getting along with people [128]

human resource management (HRM) Set of organizational activities directed at attracting, developing, and maintaining an effective workforce [223]

implied authority Agent's authority, derived from business custom, to bind a principal to a certain course of action [AP-19]

implied warranty Warranty, dictated by law, based on the principle that products should fulfill advertised promises and serve the purposes for which they are manufactured and sold [AP-20]

import Product made or grown abroad but sold domestically [32]

importer Firm that buys products in foreign markets and then imports them for resale in its home country [45]

incentive program Special compensation program designed to motivate high performance [230]

income statement (or **profit-and-loss statement)** Financial statement listing a firm's annual revenues and expenses so that a bottom line shows annual profit or loss [346]

independent agent Foreign individual or organization that agrees to represent an exporter's interests [47]

individual retirement account (IRA) Tax-deferred pension fund with which wage earners supplement other retirement funds [370]

industrial distribution Network of channel members involved in the flow of manufactured goods to industrial customers [292]

industrial goods Products purchased by companies to produce other products [252]

industrial market Organizational market consisting of firms that buy goods that are either converted into products or used during production [263]

inflation Occurrence of widespread price increases throughout an economic system [19]

informal organization Network, unrelated to the firm's formal authority structure, of everyday social interactions among company employees [158]

information Meaningful, useful interpretation of data [308]

information management Internal operations for arranging a firm's information resources to support business performance and outcomes [308]

information manager Manager responsible for designing and implementing systems to gather, organize, and distribute information [308]

information resources Data and other information used by business [6]

information system (IS) System for transforming raw data into information that can be used in decision making [308]

input market Market in which firms buy resources from supplier households [7]

insider trading Illegal practice of using special knowledge about a firm for profit or gain [406]

institutional investor Large investor, such as a mutual fund or a pension fund, that purchases large blocks of corporate stock [99]

institutional market Organizational market consisting of such nongovernmental buyers of goods and services as hospitals, churches, museums, and charitable organizations [264]

insurance company Nondeposit institution that invests funds collected as premiums charged for insurance coverage [369]

intangible asset Nonphysical asset, such as a patent or trademark, that has economic value in the form of expected benefit [345]

intangible personal property Property that cannot be seen but that exists by virtue of written documentation [AP-18]

intellectual property Property created through a person's creative activities [AP-18]

intentional tort Tort resulting from the deliberate actions of a party [AP-17]

interactive marketing Nonstore retailing that uses a Web site to provide real-time sales and customer service [298]

intermediary Individual or firm that helps to distribute a product [290]

intermediate goals Goals set for a period of one to five years into the future [119]

internal failures Reducible costs incurred during production and before bad products leave a plant [184]

internal recruiting Considering present employees as candidates for openings [225]

international competition Competitive marketing of domestic products against foreign products [255]

international firm Firm that conducts a significant portion of its business in foreign countries [46]

international law Set of cooperative agreements and guidelines established by countries to govern actions of individuals, businesses, and nations [AP-21]

International Monetary Fund (IMF) United Nations agency consisting of about 150 nations that have combined resources to promote stable exchange rates, provide temporary short-term loans, and serve other purposes [381]

international organizational structures Approaches to organizational structure developed in response to the need to manufacture, purchase, and sell in global markets [155]

Internet Global data communication network serving millions of computers with information on a wide array of topics and providing communication flows among certain private networks [310]

Internet service provider (ISP) Commercial firm that maintains a permanent connection to the Net and sells temporary connections to subscribers [310]

intranet Private network of internal Web sites and other sources of information available to a company's employees [312]

intrapreneuring Process of creating and maintaining the innovation and flexibility of a small-business environment within the confines of a large organization [159]

inventory Materials and goods that are held by a company but that will be sold within the year [AP-2]

inventory control In materials management, receiving, storing, handling, and counting of all raw materials, partly finished goods, and finished goods [179]

inventory turnover ratio Activity ratio measuring the average number of times that inventory is sold and restocked during the year [353]

investment bank Financial institution engaged in issuing and reselling new securities [388]

involuntary bankruptcy Bankruptcy proceedings initiated by the creditors of an indebted individual or organization [AP-20]

job analysis Systematic analysis of jobs within an organization [223]

job description Outline of the duties of a job, working conditions, and the tools, materials, and equipment used to perform it [223]

job enrichment Method of increasing job satisfaction by adding one or more motivating factors to job activities [207]

job redesign Method of increasing job satisfaction by designing a more satisfactory fit between workers and their jobs [208]

job satisfaction Degree of enjoyment that people derive from performing their jobs [196]

job specialization The process of identifying the specific jobs that need to be done and designating the people who will perform them [144]

job specification Description of the skills, abilities, and other credentials required by a job [223]

joint venture Strategic alliance in which the collaboration involves joint ownership of the new venture [98]

just-in-time (JIT) production Production method that brings together all materials and parts needed at each production stage at the precise moment they are required [179]

key person insurance Special form of business insurance designed to offset expenses entailed by the loss of key employees [AP-12]

knowledge worker Employee who uses information and knowledge as raw materials and who relies on information technology to design new products or business systems [316]

knowledge workers Employees who are of value because of the knowledge they possess [235]

labor (or **human resources**) The physical and mental capabilities of people as they contribute to economic production [6]

labor relations Process of dealing with employees who are represented by a union [237]

labor union Group of individuals working together to achieve shared job-related goals, such as higher pay, shorter working hours, more job security, greater benefits, or better working conditions [237]

law of demand Principle that buyers will purchase (demand) more of a product as its price drops and less as its price increases [10]

law of supply Principle that producers will offer (supply) more of a product for sale as its price rises and less as its price drops [10]

laws Codified rules of behavior enforced by a society [AP-13]

leadership Process of motivating others to work to meet specific objectives [212]

letter of credit Bank promise, issued for a buyer, to pay a designated firm a certain amount of money if specified conditions are met [370]

leverage Ability to finance an investment through borrowed funds [352]

liability Debt owed by a firm to an outside organization or individual [342]

liability insurance Insurance covering losses resulting from damage to people or property when the insured is judged responsible [AP-10]

licensed brand Brand-name product for whose name the seller has purchased the right from an organization or individual [269]

licensing arrangement Arrangement in which firms choose foreign individuals or organizations to manufacture or market their products in another country [47]

life insurance Insurance paying benefits to the policyholder's survivors [AP-11]

limit order Order authorizing the purchase of a stock only if its price is equal to or less than a specified amount [404]

limited liability Legal principle holding investors liable for a firm's debts only to the limits of their personal investments in it [95]

limited liability corporation, or **LLC** Hybrid of a publicly held corporation and a partnership in which owners are taxed as partners but enjoy the benefits of limited liability [96]

line authority Organizational structure in which authority flows in a direct chain of command from the top of the company to the bottom [152]

line department Department directly linked to the production and sales of a specific product [152]

line of credit Standing arrangement in which a lender agrees to make available a specified amount of funds upon the borrower's request [AP-4]

liquidity Ease with which an asset can be converted into cash [343]

liquidity ratio Solvency ratio measuring a firm's ability to pay its immediate debts [351]

load fund Mutual fund in which investors are charged sales commissions when they buy in or sell out [398]

local area network (LAN) Network of computers and workstations, usually within a company, that are linked together by cable [324]

local content law Law requiring that products sold in a particular country be at least partly made there [51]

lockout Management tactic whereby workers are denied access to the employer's workplace [243]

long-term goals Goals set for an extended time, typically five years or more into the future [119]

long-term liability Debt that is not due for more than one year [345]

low-contact system Level of customer contact in which the customer need not be a part of the system to receive the service [170]

M-1 Measure of the money supply that includes only the most liquid (spendable) forms of money [365]

M-2 Measure of the money supply that includes all the components of M-1 plus the forms of money that can be easily converted into spendable form [365]

mail order (or **catalog marketing**) Form of nonstore retailing in which customers place orders for catalog merchandise received through the mail [297]

management Process of planning, organizing, directing, and controlling an organization's resources to achieve its goals [123]

management advisory services Specialized accounting services to help managers resolve a variety of business problems [337]

management by objectives (MBO) Set of procedures involving both managers and subordinates in setting goals and evaluating progress [205]

management information system (MIS) System used for transforming data into information for use in decision making [319]

managerial (or **management**) **accounting system** Field of accounting that serves internal users of a company's financial information [336]

managerial style Pattern of behavior that a manager exhibits in dealing with subordinates [212]

market Mechanism for exchange between buyers and sellers of a particular good or service [7]

market economy Economy in which individuals control production and allocation decisions through supply and demand [6]

market index Summary of price trends in a specific industry and/or the stock market as a whole [402]

market order Order to buy or sell a security at the market price prevailing at the time the order is placed [404]

market price (or **equilibrium price**) Profit-maximizing price at which the quantity of goods demanded and the quantity of goods supplied are equal [11]

market segmentation Process of dividing a market into categories of customer types [258]

market share As a percentage, total of market sales for a specific company or product [280]

market value Current price of a share of stock in the stock market [389]

marketing The process of planning and executing the conception, pricing, promotion, and distribution of ideas, goods, and services to create exchanges that satisfy individual and organizational objectives [252]

marketing mix The combination of product, pricing, promotion, and distribution strategies used to market products [255]

markup Amount added to an item's cost to sell it at a profit [281]

mass-customization Flexible production process that generates customized products in high volumes at low cost [313]

master production schedule Schedule showing which products will be produced, when production will take place, and what resources will be used [177]

material requirements planning (MRP) Production method in which a bill of materials is used to ensure that the right amounts of materials are delivered to the right place at the right time [180]

materials management Planning, organizing, and controlling the flow of materials from design through distribution of finished goods [178]

matrix structure Organizational structure in which teams are formed and team members report to two or more managers [154]

mediation Method of resolving a labor dispute in which a third party suggests, but does not impose, a settlement [244]

merchandise inventory Cost of merchandise that has been acquired for sale to customers and is still on hand [344]

merchant wholesaler Independent wholesaler that takes legal possession of goods produced by a variety of manufacturers and then resells them to other businesses [294]

merger The union of two corporations to form a new corporation [100]

merit salary system Individual incentive linking compensation to performance in nonsales jobs [230]

middle managers Managers responsible for implementing the strategies, policies, and decisions made by top managers [126]

mission statement Organization's statement of how it will achieve its purpose in the environment in which it conducts its business [118]

mixed market economy Economic system featuring characteristics of both planned and market economies [9]

modem Device that provides a computer-to-computer link over telephone wires [324]

monetary policies Government economic policies that determine the size of a nation's money supply [22]

monetary policy Policies by which the Federal Reserve manages the nation's money supply and interest rates [375]

money Any object that is portable, divisible, durable, and stable and serves as a medium of exchange, a store of value, and a unit of account [364]

money market mutual fund Fund of short-term, low-risk financial securities purchased with the assets of investor-owners pooled by a nonbank institution [366]

monopolistic competition Market or industry characterized by numerous buyers and relatively numerous sellers trying to differentiate their products from those of competitors [13]

monopoly Market or industry in which there is only one producer, which can therefore set the prices of its products [14]

morale Overall attitude that employees have toward their workplace [196]

motivation The set of forces that cause people to behave in certain ways [199]

multimedia communication system Connected network of communication appliances (such as faxes or TVs) that may be linked to forms of mass media (such as print publications or TV programming) [323]

multinational firm Firm that designs, produces, and markets products in many nations [46]

multinational or **transnational corporation** Form of corporation spanning national boundaries [97]

municipal bond Bond issued by a state or local government [397]

mutual fund Company that pools investments from individuals and organizations to purchase a portfolio of stocks, bonds, and other securities [398]

mutual savings bank Financial institution whose depositors are owners sharing in its profits [369]

Nasdaq Composite Index Value-weighted market index that includes all Nasdaq-listed companies, both domestic and foreign [403]

National Association of Securities Dealers Automated Quotation (NASDAQ) system Organization of over-the-counter dealers who own, buy, and sell their own securities over a network of electronic communications [394]

national brand Brand-name product produced by, widely distributed by, and carrying the name of a manufacturer [269]

national competitive advantage International competitive advantage stemming from a combination of factor conditions, demand conditions, related and supporting industries, and firm strategies, structures, and rivalries [38]

national debt Total amount that a nation owes its creditors [19]

natural monopoly Industry in which one company can most efficiently supply all needed goods or services [14]

negligence Conduct falling below legal standards for protecting others against unreasonable risk [AP-17]

net income (or **net profit** or **net earnings**) Gross profit minus operating expenses and income taxes [347]

no-load fund Mutual fund in which investors pay no sales commissions when they buy in or sell out [398]

nominal GDP GDP measured in current dollars or with all components valued at current prices [16]

North American Free Trade Agreement (NAFTA) Agreement to gradually eliminate tariffs and other trade barriers between the United States, Canada, and Mexico [AP-22]

obstructionist stance Approach to social responsibility that involves doing as little as possible and may involve attempts to deny or cover up violations [77]

Occupational Safety and Health Act of 1970 (OSHA) Federal law setting and enforcing guidelines for protecting workers from unsafe conditions and potential health hazards in the workplace [233]

odd lot Purchase or sale of stock in fractions of round lots [404]

odd-even pricing Psychological pricing tactic based on the premise that customers prefer prices not stated in even dollar amounts [285]

off-the-job training Training conducted in a controlled environment away from the work site [228]

oligopoly Market or industry characterized by a handful of (generally large) sellers with the power to influence the prices of their products [14]

on-the-job training Training, sometimes informal, conducted while an employee is at work [228]

open-book credit Form of trade credit in which sellers ship merchandise on faith that payment will be forthcoming [AP-3]

open-market operations The Federal Reserve's sales and purchases of securities in the open market [376]

operating expenses Costs, other than the cost of goods sold, incurred in producing a good or service [347]

operating income Gross profit minus operating expenses [347]

operational plans Plans setting short-term targets for daily, weekly, or monthly performance [122]

operations control Process of monitoring production performance by comparing results with plans [178]

operations (or **production**) **management** Systematic direction and control of the processes that transform resources into finished products [168]

operations (or **production**) **managers** Managers responsible for production, inventory, and quality control [168]

operations process Set of methods used in the production of a good or service [169]

organization chart Diagram depicting a company's structure and showing employees where they fit into its operations [143]

organizational analysis Process of analyzing a firm's strengths and weaknesses [121]

organizational stakeholders Those groups, individuals, and organizations that are directly affected by the practices of an organization and who therefore have a stake in its performance [66]

organizational structure Specification of the jobs to be done within an organization and the ways in which they relate to one another [142]

organizing Management process of determining how best to arrange an organization's resources and activities into a coherent structure [124]

output market Market in which firms supply goods and services in response to demand on the part of households [7]

over-the-counter (OTC) market Organization of securities dealers formed to trade stock outside the formal institutional setting of the organized stock exchanges [393]

owners' equity Amount of money that owners would receive if they sold all of a firm's assets and paid all of its liabilities [342]

packaging Physical container in which a product is sold, advertised, or protected [270]

paid-in capital Additional money, above proceeds from stock sale, paid directly to a firm by its owners [345]

par value Face value of a share of stock, set by the issuing company's board of directors [389]

participative management and empowerment Method of increasing job satisfaction by giving employees a voice in the management of their jobs and the company [206]

patent Exclusive legal right to use and license a manufactured item or substance, manufacturing process, or object design [AP-18]

pay for performance (or **variable pay**) Individual incentive that rewards a manager for especially productive output [231]

pay-for-knowledge plan Incentive plan to encourage employees to learn new skills or become proficient at different jobs [231]

penetration pricing Setting an initial low price to establish a new product in the market [283]

pension fund Nondeposit pool of funds managed to provide retirement income for its members [369]

perfect competition Market or industry characterized by numerous small firms producing an identical product [13]

performance appraisal Evaluation of an employee's job performance in order to determine the degree to which the employee is performing effectively [229]

performance quality The performance features offered by a product [181]

personal selling Promotional tool in which a salesperson communicates one-on-one with potential customers [289]

physical distribution Activities needed to move a product efficiently from manufacturer to consumer [298]

physical resources Tangible things organizations use in the conduct of their business [6]

picketing Labor action in which workers publicize their grievances at the entrance to an employer's facility [243]

planned economy Economy that relies on a centralized government to control all or most factors of production and to make all or most production and allocation decisions [6]

planning Management process of determining what an organization needs to do and how best to get it done [123]

pledging accounts receivable Using accounts receivable as loan collateral [AP-4]

point-of-purchase (POP) display Sales promotion technique in which product displays are located in certain areas to stimulate purchase [289]

point-of-sale (POS) terminal Electronic device that allows customers to pay for retail purchases with debit cards [378]

positioning Process of establishing an identifiable product image in the minds of consumers [285]

preferred provider organization (PPO) Arrangement whereby selected professional providers offer services at reduced rates and permit thorough review of their service recommendations [AP-11]

preferred stock Stock that offers its holders fixed dividends and priority claims over assets but no corporate voting rights [98]

premium In risk management, fee paid by a policyholder for insurance coverage [AP-10]

premium In sales promotion, technique in which offers of free or reduced-price items are used to stimulate purchases [289]

prepaid expense Expense, such as prepaid rent, that is paid before the upcoming period in which it is due [344]

presentation graphics software Applications that enable users to create visual presentations that can include animation and sound [322]

price lining Setting a limited number of prices for certain categories of products [284]

price skimming Setting an initial high price to cover new product costs and generate a profit [282]

price-earnings ratio Current price of a stock divided by the firm's current annual earnings per share [399]

pricing Process of determining what a company will receive in exchange for its products [280]

pricing objectives Goals that producers hope to attain in pricing products for sale [280]

primary securities market Market in which new stocks and bonds are bought and sold [388]

prime rate Interest rate available to a bank's most creditworthy customers [368]

principal Individual or organization authorizing an agent to act on its behalf [AP-19]

private accountant Salaried accountant hired by a business to carry out its day-to-day financial activities [337]

private brand (or **private label**) Brand-name product that a wholesaler or retailer has commissioned from a manufacturer [269]

private enterprise Economic system that allows individuals to pursue their own interests without undue governmental restriction [11]

private warehouse Warehouse owned by and providing storage for a single company [298]

privatization Process of converting government enterprises into privately owned companies [9]

proactive stance Approach to social responsibility by which a company actively seeks opportunities to contribute to the well-being of groups and individuals in its social environment [78]

process departmentalization Departmentalization according to production processes used to create a good or service [146]

process layout Spatial arrangement of production activities that groups equipment and people according to function [174]

product Good, service, or idea that is marketed to fill consumer needs and wants [255]

product departmentalization Departmentalization according to specific products being created [146]

product differentiation Creation of a product or product image that differs enough from existing products to attract consumers [256]

product layout Spatial arrangement of production activities designed to move resources through a smooth, fixed sequence of steps [174]

product liability tort Tort in which a company is responsible for injuries caused by its products [AP-17]

product mix Group of products that a firm makes available for sale [267]

productive facility Workstation or equipment for transforming raw materials [174]

productivity Measure of economic growth that compares how much a system produces with the resources needed to produce it [18]

professional corporation Form of ownership allowing professionals to take advantage of corporate benefits while granting them limited business liability and unlimited professional liability [96]

profit center Separate company unit responsible for its own costs and profits [145]

profitability ratio Financial ratio for measuring a firm's potential earnings [351]

profits The difference between a business's revenues and its expenses [5]

profit-sharing plan Incentive plan for distributing bonuses to employees when company profits rise above a certain level [231]

program trading Large purchase or sale of a group of stocks, often triggered by computerized trading programs that can be launched without human supervision or control [405]

promotion Aspect of the marketing mix concerned with the most effective techniques for selling a product [285]

promotional mix Combination of tools used to promote a product [285]

property Anything of value to which a person or business has sole right of ownership [AP-17]

property insurance Insurance covering losses resulting from physical damage to or loss of the insured's real estate or personal property [AP-11]

prospectus Registration statement filed with the SEC before the issuance of a new security [406]

protected class Set of individuals who by nature of one or more common characteristics are protected under the law from discrimination on the basis of that characteristic [232]

protectionism Practice of protecting domestic business against foreign competition [50]

psychographic variables Consumer characteristics, such as lifestyles, opinions, interests, and attitudes, that may be considered in developing a segmentation strategy [259]

psychological contract Set of expectations held by an employee concerning what he or she will contribute to an organization (referred to as *contributions*) and what the organization will in return provide the employee (referred to as inducements) [196]

psychological pricing Pricing tactic that takes advantage of the fact that consumers do not always respond rationally to stated prices [284]

public relations Company-influenced publicity directed at building goodwill between an organization and potential customers [290]

public warehouse Independently owned and operated warehouse that stores goods for many firms [298]

publicity Promotional tool in which information about a company or product is transmitted by general mass media [290]

publicly held (or **public**) **corporation** Corporation whose stock is widely held and available for sale to the general public [96]

punitive damages Fines imposed over and above any actual losses suffered by a plaintiff [AP-17]

purchasing Acquisition of the raw materials and services that a firm needs to produce its products [179]

purchasing power parity Principle that exchange rates are set so that the prices of similar products in different countries are about the same [17]

pure risk Risk involving only the possibility of loss or no loss [AP-8]

quality control Management of the production process designed to manufacture goods or supply services that meet specific quality standards [180]

quality ownership Principle of total quality management that holds that quality belongs to each person who creates it while performing a job [182]

quality reliability Consistency of a product's quality from unit to unit [181]

quality/cost study Method of improving quality by identifying current costs and areas with the greatest cost-saving potential [184]

quid pro quo harassment Form of sexual harassment in which sexual favors are requested in return for job-related benefits [233]

quota Restriction on the number of products of a certain type that can be imported into a country [50]

rational motives Reasons for purchasing a product that are based on a logical evaluation of product attributes [263]

real GDP GDP calculated to account for changes in currency values and price changes [17]

recession Period during which aggregate output, as measured by real GDP, declines [21]

recruiting Process of attracting qualified persons to apply for jobs an organization is seeking to fill [225]

registered bond Bond bearing the name of the holder and registered with the issuing company [398]

regulatory (or **administrative**) **law** Law made by the authority of administrative agencies [AP-13]

reinforcement Theory that behavior can be encouraged or discouraged by means of rewards or punishments [205]

relationship marketing Marketing strategy that emphasizes lasting relationships with customers and suppliers [252]

replacement chart List of each management position, who occupies it, how long that person will likely stay in the job, and who is qualified as a replacement [224]

reseller market Organizational market consisting of intermediaries who buy and resell finished goods [264]

reserve requirement Percentage of its deposits that a bank must hold in cash or on deposit with the Federal Reserve [376]

responsibility Duty to perform an assigned task [148]

retailer Intermediary that sells products directly to consumers [290]

retained earnings Earnings retained by a firm for its use rather than paid as dividends [345; AP-5]

return on equity Profitability ratio measuring income earned for each dollar invested [352]

revenues Funds that flow into a business from the sale of goods or services [346]

revolving credit agreement Arrangement in which a lender agrees to make funds available on demand and on a continuing basis [AP-4]

risk Uncertainty about future events [AP-8]

risk avoidance Practice of avoiding risk by declining or ceasing to participate in an activity [AP-9]

risk control Practice of minimizing the frequency or severity of losses from risky activities [AP-9]

risk management Process of conserving the firm's earning power and assets by reducing the threat of losses due to uncontrollable events [AP-8]

risk retention Practice of covering a firm's losses with its own funds [AP-9]

risk transfer Practice of transferring a firm's risk to another firm [AP-9]

risk-return relationship Principle that, whereas safer investments tend to offer lower returns, riskier investments tend to offer higher returns [AP-7]

robotics Combination of computers and industrial robots for use in manufacturing operations [319]

round lot Purchase or sale of stock in units of 100 shares [404]

S corporation Hybrid of a closely held corporation and a partnership, organized and operated like a corporation but treated as a partnership for tax purposes [96]

salary Compensation in the form of money paid for discharging the responsibilities of a job [230]

sales agent/broker Independent intermediary that usually represents many manufacturers and sells to wholesalers or retailers [292]

sales office Office maintained by a manufacturer as a contact point with its customers [293]

sales promotion Short-term promotional activity designed to stimulate consumer buying or cooperation from distributors and sales agents [289]

savings and loan association (S&L) Financial institution accepting deposits and making loans primarily for home mortgages [368]

search engine Tool that searches Web pages containing the user's search terms and then displays pages that match [312]

secondary securities market Market in which stocks and bonds are traded [388]

secured bond Bond backed by pledges of assets to the bondholders [398]

secured loan Loan for which the borrower must provide collateral [AP-3]

securities Stocks and bonds representing secured, or asset-based, claims by investors against issuers [388]

Securities and Exchange Commission (SEC) Federal agency that administers U.S. securities laws to protect the investing public and maintain smoothly functioning markets [388]

securities investment dealer (broker) Nondeposit institution that buys and sells stocks and bonds both for investors and for its own accounts [369]

selective credit controls Federal Reserve authority to set both margin requirements for consumer stock purchases and credit rules for other consumer purchases [376]

service operations Produces tangible and intangible services, such as entertainment, transportation, and education [166]

services Intangible products, such as time, expertise, or an activity that can be purchased [252]

sexual harassment Practice or instance of making unwelcome sexual advances in the workplace [233]

shopping agent (e-agent) E-intermediary (middleman) in the Internet distribution channel that assists users in finding products and prices but that does not take possession of products [294]

shopping good/service Moderately expensive, infrequently purchased product [266]

short sale Stock sale in which an investor borrows securities from a broker to be sold and then replaced at a specified future date [405]

shortage Situation in which quantity demanded exceeds quantity supplied [11]

short-term goals Goals set for the very near future, typically less than one year [119]

slowdown Labor action in which workers perform jobs at a slower than normal pace [243]

small business Independently owned and managed business that does not dominate its market [89]

Small Business Administration (SBA) Federal agency charged with assisting small businesses [89]

Small Business Development Center (SBDC) SBA program designed to consolidate information from various disciplines and make it available to small businesses [107]

small-business investment company (SBIC) Government-regulated investment company that borrows money from the SBA to invest in or lend to a small business [106]

smart card Credit-card-size computer programmed with electronic money [378]

social audit Systematic analysis of a firm's success in using funds earmarked for meeting its social responsibility goals [80]

social responsibility The attempt of a business to balance its commitments to groups and individuals in its environment, including customers, other businesses, employees, and investors [66]

socialism Planned economic system in which the government owns and operates only selected major sources of production [9]

software Programs that instruct a computer in what to do [321]

sole proprietorship Business owned and usually operated by one person who is responsible for all of its debts [92]

solvency ratio Financial ratio, either short- or long-term, for estimating the risk in investing in a firm [351]

span of control Number of people supervised by one manager [151]

specialty good/service Expensive, rarely purchased product [266]

specialty store Small retail store carrying one product line or category of related products [296]

speculative risk Risk involving the possibility of gain or loss [AP-8]

speed to market Strategy of introducing new products to respond quickly to customer or market changes [268]

spin-off Strategy of setting up one or more corporate units as new, independent corporations [100]

stability Condition in which the balance between the money available in an economy and the goods produced in it are growing at about the same rate [19]

stabilization policy Government policy, embracing both fiscal and monetary policies, whose goal is to smooth out fluctuations in output and unemployment and to stabilize prices [22]

staff authority Authority based on expertise that usually involves advising line managers [152]

staff members Advisers and counselors who aid line departments in making decisions but do not have the authority to make final decisions [152]

Standard & Poor's Composite Index Market index based on the performance of 400 industrial firms, 40 utilities, 40 financial institutions, and 20 transportation companies [403]

standard of living Total quantity and quality of goods and services that people can purchase with the currency used by their economic system [15]

standardization Use of standard and uniform components in the production process [178]

statement of cash flows Financial statement describing a firm's yearly cash receipts and cash payments [347]

statistical process control (SPC) Methods for gathering data to analyze variations in production activities to see when adjustments are needed [183]

statutory law Law created by constitutions or by federal, state, or local legislative acts [AP-13]

stock Share of ownership in a corporation [97]

stock exchange Organization of individuals formed to provide an institutional setting in which stock can be traded [391]

stockholder (or **shareholder**) Owner of shares of stock in a corporation [97]

stop order Order authorizing the sale of a stock if its price falls to or below a specified level [404]

strategic alliance Strategy in which two or more organizations collaborate on a project for mutual gain [98]

strategic alliance (or **joint venture**) Arrangement in which a company finds a foreign partner to contribute approximately half of the resources needed to establish and operate a new business in the partner's country [48]

strategic goals Long-term goals derived directly from a firm's mission statement [119]

strategic plans Plans reflecting decisions about resource allocations, company priorities, and steps needed to meet strategic goals [122]

strategy Broad set of organizational plans for implementing the decisions made for achieving organizational goals [117]

strategy formulation Creation of a broad program for defining and meeting an organization's goals [119]

strict product liability Principle that liability can result not from a producer's negligence but from a defect in the product itself [AP-17]

strike Labor action in which employees temporarily walk off the job and refuse to work [242]

strikebreaker Worker hired as permanent or temporary replacement for a striking employee [244]

subsidy Government payment to help a domestic business compete with foreign firms [50]

substitute product Product that is dissimilar to those of competitors but that can fulfill the same need [255]

supermarket Large product line retailer offering a variety of food and food-related items in specialized departments [296]

supplier selection Process of finding and selecting suppliers from whom to buy [179]

supply The willingness and ability of producers to offer a good or service for sale [10]

supply chain Flow of information, materials, and services that starts with raw-materials suppliers and continues through other stages in the operations process until the product reaches the end customer [186]

supply chain management (SCM) Principle of looking at the supply chain as a whole in order to improve the overall flow through the system [187]

supply curve Graph showing how many units of a product will be supplied (offered for sale) at different prices [11]

surplus Situation in which quantity supplied exceeds quantity demanded [11]

sympathy strike (or **secondary strike**) Strike in which one union strikes to support action initiated by another [243]

syndicated selling E-commerce practice whereby a Web site offers other Web sites commissions for referring customers [294]

synthetic process Production process in which resources are combined to create finished products [169]

system operations personnel Information-systems employees who run a company's computer equipment [318]

system program Software that tells the computer what resources to use and how to use them [321]

tactical plans Generally short-range plans concerned with implementing specific aspects of a company's strategic plans [122]

tall organizational structure Characteristic of centralized companies with multiple layers of management and relatively narrow spans of control [150]

tangible personal property Any movable item that can be owned, bought, sold, or leased [AP-18]

tangible real property Land and anything attached to it [AP-18]

target market Group of people that has similar wants and needs and that can be expected to show interest in the same products [258]

tariff Tax levied on imported products [50]

technical skills Skills needed to perform specialized tasks [128]

telecommuting Form of flextime that allows people to perform some or all of a job away from standard office settings [209]

telemarketing In nonstore retailing, technique in which the telephone is used to sell directly to consumers [297]

telemarketing In personal selling, tactic of using telephone solicitations [289]

tender offer Offer to buy shares made by a prospective buyer directly to a target corporation's shareholders, who then make individual decisions about whether to sell [95]

Theory X Theory of motivation holding that people are naturally irresponsible and uncooperative [200]

Theory Y Theory of motivation holding that people are naturally responsible, growth oriented, self-motivated, and interested in being productive [200]

time deposit Bank funds that cannot be withdrawn without notice or transferred by check [366]

time management skills Skills associated with the productive use of time [130]

top managers Managers responsible to the board of directors and stockholders for a firm's overall performance and effectiveness [126]

tort Civil injury to people, property, or reputation for which compensation must be paid [AP-16]

total quality management (TQM) (or **quality assurance**) The sum of all activities involved in getting high-quality products into the marketplace [181]

trade credit Granting of credit by one firm to another [AP-3]

trade deficit Situation in which a country's imports exceed its exports, creating a negative balance of trade [40]

trade show Sales promotion technique in which various members of an industry gather to display, demonstrate, and sell products [289]

trade surplus Situation in which a country's exports exceed its imports, creating a positive balance of trade [40]

trademark Exclusive legal right to use a brand name or symbol [AP-18]

trial court General court that hears cases not specifically assigned to another court [AP-15]

trust services Bank management of an individual's investments, payments, or estate [370]

turnover Annual percentage of an organization's workforce who leave and must be replaced [198]

two-factor theory Theory of motivation holding that job satisfaction depends on two types of factors, hygiene and motivation [201]

unemployment Level of joblessness among people actively seeking work [21]

unethical behavior Behavior that does not conform to generally accepted social norms concerning beneficial and harmful actions [61]

Uniform Commercial Code (UCC) Body of standardized laws governing the rights of buyers and sellers in transactions [AP-20]

unlimited liability Legal principle holding owners responsible for paying off all debts of a business [93]

unsecured loan Loan for which collateral is not required [AP-4]

utility A product's ability to satisfy a human want [168]

validation Process of determining the predictive value of a selection technique [227]

variable cost Cost that changes with the quantity of a product produced or sold [281]

venture capital Outside equity financing provided in return for part ownership of the borrowing firm [AP-7]

venture capital company Group of small investors who invest money in companies with rapid growth potential [105]

vestibule training Off-the-job training conducted in a simulated environment [229]

voluntary arbitration Method of resolving a labor dispute in which both parties agree to submit to the judgment of a neutral party [244]

voluntary bankruptcy Bankruptcy proceedings initiated by an indebted individual or organization [AP-20]

wage reopener clause Clause allowing wage rates to be renegotiated during the life of a labor contract [241]

wages Compensation in the form of money paid for time worked [230]

warehouse club (or **wholesale club**) Bargain retailer offering large discounts on brand-name merchandise to customers who have paid annual membership fees [297]

warehousing Physical distribution operation concerned with the storage of goods [298]

warranty Seller's promise to stand by its products or services if a problem occurs after the sale [AP-20]

Web server Dedicated workstation customized for managing, maintaining, and supporting Web sites [311]

whistle-blower Employee who detects and tries to put an end to a company's unethical, illegal, or socially irresponsible actions by publicizing them [75]

wholesaler Intermediary that sells products to other businesses for resale to final consumers [290]

wide area network (WAN) Network of computers and workstations located far from one another and linked by telephone wires or by satellite [324]

wildcat strike Strike that is unauthorized by the strikers' union [243]

word-processing program Applications program that allows computers to store, edit, and print letters and numbers for documents created by users [321]

work sharing (or **job sharing**) Method of increasing job satisfaction by allowing two or more people to share a single full-time job [208]

workers' compensation coverage Coverage provided by a firm to employees for medical expenses, loss of wages, and rehabilitation costs resulting from job-related injuries or disease [AP-10]

workers' compensation insurance Legally required insurance for compensating workers injured on the job [231]

workforce diversity Range of workers' attitudes, values, and behaviors that differ by gender, race, and ethnicity [234]

working capital In accounting, difference between a firm's current assets and current liabilities [352]

working capital In financial management, liquid current assets out of which a firm can pay current debts [AP-2]

World Bank United Nations agency that provides a limited scope of financial services, such as funding national improvements in undeveloped countries [380]

World Trade Organization (WTO) Organization through which member nations negotiate trading agreements and resolve disputes about trade policies and practices [32; AP-22]

World Wide Web Subsystem of computers providing access to the Internet and offering multimedia and linking capabilities [311]

Index

Name, Company, Product Index

Subject Index

Mastering Business Essentials CD Integration

Chapter1
Understanding the U.S. Business System

• *Episode 2* brings up the idea that we live in a world where resources are limited but where people's wants are unlimited. It also talks about the use and availability of resources to organizations. This coincides with the discussion of the factors of production in Chapter 1; however, it brings it one step further. This episode encourages the student to think about scarcity and opportunity costs.

Chapter 2
Understanding the Global Context of Business

• *Episode 9* concentrates heavily on maintaining a competitive advantage. Management must not lose sight of the company's competitive advantage, as this is what separates a firm from other competitors in the same industry. This episode stresses the importance of this. The concept of national competitive advantage is introduced in Chapter 2 of the text.

• *Episode 10* poses questions to students to allow them to think about the challenges of addressing the consumer buying process in international markets.

Chapter 3
Conducting Business Ethically and Socially

• *Episode 3* raises the issue of corporate social responsibility as the CanGo management team discusses the potentially adverse effects of violent online games. A very important concept is introduced. The company is searching for a way to balance the company's reputation and the market's demands. The chapter focuses on the various areas of social responsibility: responsibilities toward the environment, its customers, its employees, and its investors. All of these areas need to be carefully considered when a company is faced with the challenge of coordinating company image and policy with product strategies and personal values.

• *Episode 8* introduces the issue of ethics in the workplace and the difficulty to promote ethical conduct because ethical dilemmas occur frequently in organizational life. It is important to understand that not all individuals have the same ethical standards; therefore, providing employees with a written code of ethics is essential. These issues are discussed in detail in Chapter 3 of the text.

Chapter 5
Managing the Business Enterprise

• *Episode 12* emphasizes the importance of setting goals and formulating strategies as the starting points for effective management as presented in the chapter. The evaluation of these plans are necessary to focus on continuously improving business operations. The students are presented with a common real-world occurrence. In the past, the CanGo Management Team has neglected to formally develop strategic plans.

Chapter 6
Organizing the Business Enterprise

• *Episode 7* describes the formation of a work team assigned to develop an important presentation that is critical to the future existence of CanGo. It discusses some of the characteristics of effective work teams. Chapter 6 introduces the concept of committee and team authority and the idea that organizations may find it beneficial to grant special authority to work teams working on important projects so they may function more effectively.

Chapter 7
Managing Operations and Supply Chain Management

• *Episode 11* compares last year's performance with this year's performance and emphasizes the changes that need to be made to improve the performance. The fit between the organization's overall business strategy and the organization's approach to production is discussed. This is clearly related to the chapter's discussion of the operations planning and operations control. The issues of capacity planning, quality planning, materials management and production process control are indirectly or directly covered in this episode.

Ebert/Griffin